Patterns of
World History

Patterns of World History

Since 1750

Peter von Sivers
University of Utah

Charles A. Desnoyers
La Salle University

George B. Stow
La Salle University

New York   Oxford
OXFORD UNIVERSITY PRESS

Oxford University Press, Inc., publishes works that further Oxford University's objective of excellence in research, scholarship, and education.

Oxford   New York
Auckland   Cape Town   Dar es Salaam   Hong Kong   Karachi
Kuala Lumpur   Madrid   Melbourne   Mexico City   Nairobi
New Delhi   Shanghai   Taipei   Toronto

With offices in
Argentina   Austria   Brazil   Chile   Czech Republic   France   Greece
Guatemala   Hungary   Italy   Japan   Poland   Portugal   Singapore
South Korea   Switzerland   Thailand   Turkey   Ukraine   Vietnam

Copyright © 2012 by Oxford University Press, Inc.

Published by Oxford University Press, Inc.
198 Madison Avenue, New York, New York, 10016
http://www.oup.com

Library of Congress Cataloging-in-Publication Data
Von Sivers, Peter.
  Patterns of world history / Peter von Sivers, Charles A. Desnoyers, George Stow.
    v. cm.
  Includes bibliographical references and index.
  Contents: v. 1. To 1600 — v. 2. Since 1400 — [v. 3.] Since 1750.
    ISBN 978-0-19-533287-2 (combined v.: acid-free paper) — ISBN 978-0-19-533288-9
(v. 1: acid-free paper) — ISBN 978-0-19-985898-9 (v. 2: acid-free paper) — ISBN 978-
0-19-533334-3 (Since 1750: acid-free paper) 1. World history—Textbooks. I. Desnoyers,
Charles, 1952– II. Stow, George B. III. Title.
  D21.V66 2012
  909—dc23

Printing number: 9 8 7 6 5 4 3 2
Printed in the United States of America
on acid-free paper

Coniugi Judithae dilectissimae
        —Peter von Sivers

To all my students over the years, who have taught me at least as much as I've taught them; and most of all to my wife, Jacki, beloved in all things, but especially in her infinite patience and fortitude in seeing me through the writing of this book.

                                                —Charles A. Desnoyers

For Susan and our children, Meredith and Jonathan.

                        —George B. Stow

—I hear and I forget; I see and I remember; I do and I understand
(Chinese proverb) 我听见我忘记；我看见我记住；我做我了解

Brief Contents

Contents

PART FIVE

The Origins of Modernity
1750–1900

Chapter 22
1750–1871

Nation-States and Patterns of Culture in Europe and North America

Features:

Patterns Up Close:
The Guillotine   758

Concept Map:
Patterns of Nation-State Formation in Europe and North America   784

Chapter 23
1750–1914

Industrialization and Its Discontents

Features:

Patterns Up Close:
"The Age of Steam"   791

Concept Map:
Industrialization and Its Impact, 1800–1914   820

Chapter 24
1750–1910

Features:

Patterns Up Close:
Interaction and
Adaptation: "Self-
Strengthening" and
"Western Science and
Eastern Ethics"   834

Concept Map:
Chinese and Japanese
Responses to the
Western Challenge: 856

Chapter 25
1683–1908

Features:

Patterns Up Close:
From Constitutional to
Ethnic Nationalism   870

Concept Map:
Adaptation and
Resistance to the Western
Challenge: The
Ottoman and Russian
Empires   894

Chapter 26
1750–1914

Features:

Patterns Up Close:
Military Transformations
and the New
Imperialism   908

Concept Map:
Patterns of Imperialism
and Colonialism:
Continuity and
Change   932

Chapter 27
1790–1917

Features:

Patterns Up Close:
Slave Rebellions in
Cuba and Brazil   954

Concept Map:
Latin America in the
Nineteenth Century   969

PART SIX

From Three Modernities to One
1914–Present   972

Chapter 28
1900–1945

Chapter 29
1945–1962

Chapter 30
1963–1991

Chapter 31

1991–2011

Features:

Patterns Up Close:

Social Networking   1126

Concept Map:
The Human Impact
on the Planet   1138

Maps

Studying with Maps and Concept Maps

MAPS

World history cannot be fully understood without a clear comprehension of the chronologies and parameters within which different empires, states, and peoples have changed over time. Maps facilitate this understanding by illuminating the significance of time, space, and geography in shaping the patterns of world history.

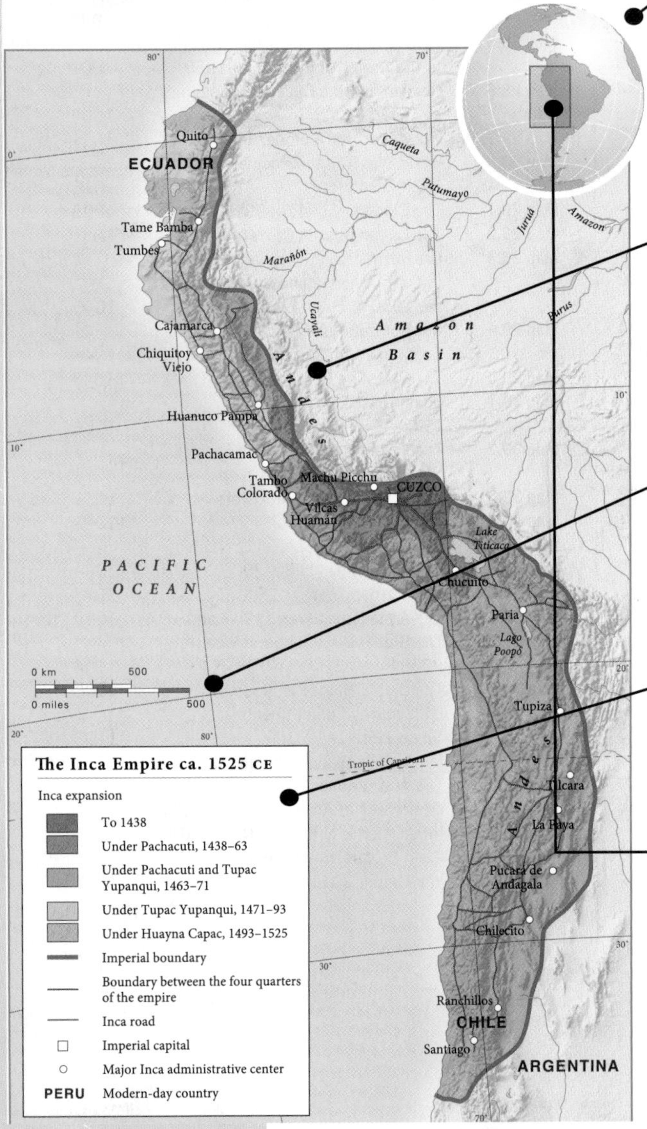

Projection

A map *projection* portrays all or part of the earth, which is spherical, on a flat surface. All maps, therefore, include some distortion. The projections in *Patterns of World History* show the earth at global, continental, regional, and local scales.

Topography

Many maps in *Patterns of World History* show *relief*—the contours of the land. Topography is an important element in studying maps because the physical terrain has played a critical role in shaping human history.

Scale Bar

Every map in *Patterns of World History* includes a *scale* that shows distances in both miles and kilometers and, in some instances, in feet as well.

Map Key

Maps use symbols to show the location of features and to convey information. Each symbol is explained in the map *key*.

Global Locator

Many of the maps in *Patterns of World History* include *global locators* that show the area being depicted in a larger context.

The Inca Empire ca. 1525 CE

Inca expansion

- To 1438
- Under Pachacuti, 1438–63
- Under Pachacuti and Tupac Yupanqui, 1463–71
- Under Tupac Yupanqui, 1471–93
- Under Huayna Capac, 1493–1525
- Imperial boundary
- Boundary between the four quarters of the empire
- Inca road
- ☐ Imperial capital
- ○ Major Inca administrative center
- **PERU** Modern-day country

Map labels: Quito, ECUADOR, Caqueta, Patumayo, Jurua, Amazon, Tame Bamba, Tumbes, Marañón, Usayali, Amazon Basin, Purus, Cajamarca, Chiquitoy Viejo, Andes, Huanuco Pampa, Pachacamac, Tambo Colorado, Machu Picchu, CUZCO, Vilcas Huaman, Lake Titicaca, PACIFIC OCEAN, Chucuito, Paria, Lago Poopó, Tupiza, Tropic of Capricorn, Tilcara, La Paya, Pucará de Andagala, Chilecito, Ranchillos, CHILE, Santiago, ARGENTINA

CONCEPT MAPS

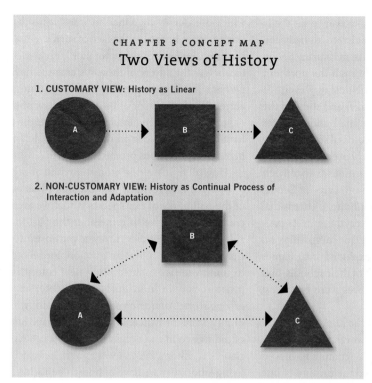

CHAPTER 3 CONCEPT MAP
Two Views of History

1. CUSTOMARY VIEW: History as Linear

A → B → C

2. NON-CUSTOMARY VIEW: History as Continual Process of Interaction and Adaptation

B
A
C

Ideas and concepts are at the center of *Patterns of World History*. Tackling these ideas and concepts—instead of simply memorizing dates and facts—is what makes history interesting. To help "see" core ideas, *concept maps* at the end of each chapter **use clear, simple, yet provocative graphics to synthesize key take-away points.**

Concept maps **employ simple, universal shapes** to symbolize ideas and processes.

Many concept maps, such as this one, use juxtaposition **to compare and contrast different ways of looking at a topic** or, in the example shown here, to **show change over time**

Clean graphics and clear colors **express big ideas simply and without fuss**—in this case, the changing dynamic between Europe, India, and China between 1500 and 1800.

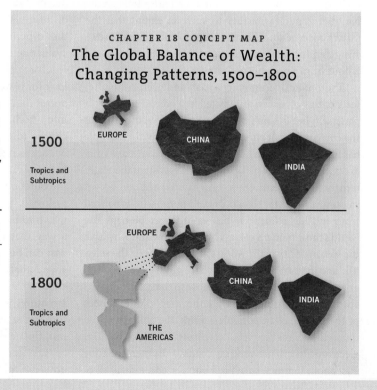

CHAPTER 18 CONCEPT MAP
The Global Balance of Wealth: Changing Patterns, 1500–1800

1500

Tropics and Subtropics

EUROPE   CHINA   INDIA

1800

Tropics and Subtropics

EUROPE   CHINA   INDIA

THE AMERICAS

Preface

It was the most violent earthquake ever to hit the islands in the 150 years during which records had been kept. On March 11, 2011, a quake measuring 8.9 on the 9-point Richter scale ripped through the northern part of the main Japanese island of Honshu. Despite Japan's long experience with earthquakes and some of the most stringent protection measures and building codes on earth, the destruction was on a colossal scale. But the damage itself was almost immediately overshadowed by the destruction wrought by the enormous tsunami generated by the quake, which hit the port city of Sendai and its surrounding vicinity within hours of the initial shocks. A 23-foot wave crushed everything in its path for miles inland and landed even giant cargo ships on the wharves. Oil refinery tanks exploded into flames, children were trapped on the roofs of their schools, and warnings of the tsunami's shockwaves were broadcast around the Pacific Rim.

Amid the vast debris fields and the hundreds of bodies washing up on the beaches, however, the most ominous part of the disaster was only beginning to unfold. The waves in their fury had wrecked the turbine of one nuclear power plant and flooded the entire Fukushima Number 2 nuclear facility to such an extent that the plant had to be shut down—but not before repair crews struggled for weeks to contain the radiation leaks and fallout from a possible meltdown.

The political, economic, social, and even cultural effects of this disaster naturally tell us a great deal about Japan itself; but in some ways they tell us even more about the current state of our modern world. How, for example, has the world come to be globalized to such an extent that an extreme disaster in Japan generates instantaneous international concern? Or, to take things back one historical step, how is it that Japan, once so purposefully isolated from outside influences, has emerged as perhaps the world's most modern society? Indeed, how and why have the vast majority of the world's nations adopted the scientific and industrial systems that have given us the oil refineries and nuclear power plants now so threatened by this epic natural disaster? What are the larger consequences of these systems in possibly altering the balance of life on earth? In another vein, how has the development of electronic "social networking" media—Twitter, YouTube, Facebook, Internet, smart cell phones, and e-mail, all of which are deeply ingrained in our lives—changed the way societies behave in the face of such events? How did human beings cope with natural or human-created disasters before the advent of these systems and devices? And, perhaps the largest question of all, what are the broad currents in human societies over the tens of thousands of years that modern humans have walked the earth that have brought us to our present state in which modernity holds such enormous promise and peril?

How all of these things and a myriad of others came to be is, in a large sense, the theme of this book. One of the hallmarks of our species is that we are historical creatures. We strive to remember the past in innumerable ways for an endless array of purposes: for cultural transmission, for moral instruction, for record keeping, to minimize risk in attempting new enterprises, to improve society or individuals, to tell entertaining or satisfying stories of ourselves. You, your family, your town or city, state, province, or country all have histories, all of them used in an endless variety of ways. As the historian G. R. Elton (1921–1994) put it, history is the only living laboratory we have of human behavior. So how is one to make sense of this bewildering, unending stream of information—especially if, as Elton would have it, the "experiments" in the "laboratory" are running and evaluating themselves?

Our approach in this book is, as the title suggests, to look for patterns in world history. We should say at the outset that we do not mean to select certain categories into which we attempt to stuff the historical events we choose to emphasize; nor do we claim that all world history is reducible to such patterns; nor do we mean to suggest that the nature of the patterns determines the outcome of historical events. We see them instead as broad, flexible, organizational frameworks around which to build the structure of a world history in such a way that the enormous sweep and content of the past can be viewed in a comprehensible narrative, with sound analysis and ample scope for debate and discussion. In this sense, we view them much like the role of armatures in clay sculptures, giving support and structure to the final figure but not necessarily preordaining its ultimate shape.

Take, for example, the role of innovation, in the broadest sense, in world history. The quest for the new and better has always been an animating spirit within the human saga—from the first wheel to the latest smart phone. Certainly, all such innovations, whether they are technological, intellectual, social, political, and so on, are vital to an understanding of human history. Our approach is to highlight the patterns we find in the development of such innovations as a way of taking a step back to make sense of them and the way that they foster change. Take the history of something from our recent past, e-mail, for example: Although electronic technology had advanced to the point in the 1960s where messages could be sent by computer, they could be sent and received only by operators using the same "server," as we would say today. What was needed, therefore, was a new system whereby messages could be sent and received by multiple servers in remote locations. The young engineer Ray Tomlinson (b. 1941), well versed in an early form of computer communication known as "ARPANET," which the American military used to share classified documents, concluded that, given the correct linkage, computers in far-flung locations could "talk" to each other. He worked out the missing piece in the form of the simple "@" sign, which he said "was used to indicate that the user was 'at' some other host rather than being local." Thus, the text message—and the e-mail address format we use today—originated through Tomlinson's interactions with other people and by means of his adapting other technologies available to him; these were then expanded exponentially by millions of others interacting with Tomlinson's breakthrough. This is but one recent example of the unfolding of a pattern of innovation; world history is full of them, and tracing their stories, effects, and implications comprises the heart of this book.

From its origins, human culture grew through interactions and adaptations on all the continents except Antarctica. A voluminous scholarship on all regions of the world has thus been accumulated, which those working in the field have to attempt to master if their explanations and arguments are to sound even remotely persuasive. The sheer volume and complexity of the sources, however, mean that even the knowledge and expertise of the best scholars are going to be incomplete. Moreover, the humility with which all historians must approach their material contains within it the realization that no historical explanation is ever fully satisfactory or final: As a driving force in the historical process, creative human agency moves this process into directions that are never fully predictable.

As we enter the second decade of the twenty-first century, world historians have long since left behind the "West plus the rest" approach that marked the field's early years, together with economic and geographical reductionism, in the search for a new balance between comprehensive cultural and institutional examinations, on the one hand, and those highlighting human agency, on the other. All too often, however, this is reflected in texts that seek broad coverage at the expense of analysis, thus resulting in a kind of "world history-lite." Our aim is therefore to simplify the study of the world—to make it accessible to the student—without making world history itself simplistic.

World History and Patterns of World History

Patterns of World History thus comes to the teaching of world history from the perspective of the relationship between continuity and change. What we advocate in this book is a distinct intellectual framework for this relationship and the role of innovation and historical change through patterns of origins, interactions, and adaptations, or as we like to call it, O-I-A. Each small or large technical or cultural innovation originated in one geographical center or independently in several different centers. As people in the centers interacted with their neighbors, the neighbors adapted to, and in many cases were transformed by, the innovations. By "adaptation" we include the entire spectrum of human responses, ranging from outright rejection to creative borrowing and, at times, forced acceptance.

Small technical innovations often went through the pattern of origin, interaction, and adaptation across the world without arousing much attention, even though they had major consequences. For example, the horse collar, which originated in ninth-century China and allowed for the replacement of oxen with stronger horses, gradually improved the productivity of agriculture in eleventh-century western Europe. More sweeping intellectual–cultural innovations, by contrast, such as the spread of universal religions like Buddhism, Christianity, and Islam and the rise of science, have often had profound consequences—in some cases leading to conflicts lasting centuries—and affect us even today.

Sometimes change was effected by commodities that to us seem rather ordinary. Take sugar, for example:

It originated in southeast Asia and was traded and grown in the Mediterranean, where its cultivation on plantations created the model for expansion into the vast slave system of the Atlantic basin from the fifteenth through the nineteenth centuries, forever altering the histories of four continents. What would our diets look like today without sugar? Its history continues to unfold as we debate its merits and health risks and it supports huge multinational agribusinesses. Or take a more obscure commodity: opium. Opium had been used medicinally for centuries in regions all over the world. But the advent of tobacco traded from the Americas to the Philippines to China created an environment in which the drug would be smoked for the first time. Enterprising rogue British merchants, eager to find a way to crack closed Chinese markets for other goods, began to smuggle it in from India. The market grew, the price went down, addiction spread, and Britain and China ultimately went to war over China's attempts to eliminate the traffic. Here, we have an example of an item generating interactions on a worldwide scale, with impacts on everything from politics to economics, culture, and even the environment. The legacies of the trade still weigh heavily on two of the rising powers of the twenty-first century: China and India. And opium and its derivatives, like morphine and heroin, continue to bring relief and suffering on a colossal scale to hundreds of millions of people.

What, then, do we gain by studying world history through the use of such patterns? First, if we consider innovation to be a driving force of history, it helps to satisfy an intrinsic human curiosity about origins—our own and others. Perhaps more importantly, seeing patterns of various kinds in historical development brings to light connections and linkages among peoples, cultures, and regions—as in the examples—that might not otherwise present themselves.

Second, such patterns can also reveal differences among cultures that other approaches to world history tend to neglect. For example, the differences between the civilizations of the Eastern and Western Hemispheres are generally highlighted in world history texts, but the broad commonalities of human groups creating agriculturally based cities and states in widely separated areas also show deep parallels in their patterns of origins, interactions, and adaptations: Such comparisons are at the center of our approach.

Third, this kind of analysis offers insights into how an individual innovation was subsequently developed and diffused across space and time—that is, the patterns by which the new eventually becomes a necessity in our daily lives. Through all of this we gain a deeper appreciation of the unfolding of global history from its origins in small, isolated areas to the vast networks of global interconnectedness in our present world—that is, how a tsunami in Japan can affect everything from early warning systems in coastal areas of distant countries to fluctuations in international bond and currency markets.

Finally, our use of a broad-based understanding of continuity, change, and innovation allows us to restore culture in all its individual and institutionalized aspects—spiritual, artistic, intellectual, scientific—to its rightful place alongside technology, environment, politics, and socioeconomic conditions. That is, understanding innovation in this way allows this text to help illuminate the full range of human ingenuity over time and space in a comprehensive, evenhanded, and open-ended fashion.

It is widely agreed that world history is more than simply the sum of all national histories. Likewise, *Patterns of World History* is more than an unbroken sequence of dates, battles, rulers, and their activities; and it is more than the study of isolated stories of change over time. Rather, in this textbook we endeavor to present in a clear and engaging way how world history "works." Instead of merely offering a narrative history of the appearance of this or that innovation, we present an analysis of the process by which an innovation in one part of the world is diffused and carried to the rest of the globe. Instead of focusing on the memorization of people, places, and events, we strive to present important facts in context and draw meaningful connections, analyzing whatever patterns we find and drawing conclusions where we can. In short, we seek to examine the interlocking mechanisms and animating forces of world history, without neglecting the human agency behind them.

Patterns of Change and Six Periods of World History

For the convenience of instructors teaching a course over two 15-week semesters, we have limited the book to 31 chapters. For the sake of continuity and to accommodate the many different ways schools divide the midpoint of their world history sequence, Chapters 15–18 overlap in both volumes; in Volume 2, Chapter

15 is given as a "prelude" to Part 4. Those using a trimester system will also find divisions made in convenient places, with Chapter 10 coming at the beginning of Part 3 and Chapter 22 at the beginning of Part 5. Finally, for those schools that offer a modern world history course that begins at approximately 1750, a volume is available that includes only the final two parts of the book.

Similarly, we have attempted to create a text that is adaptable to both chronological and thematic styles of instruction. We divide the history of the world into six major time periods and recognize for each period one or two main patterns of innovation, their spread through interaction, and their adoption by others. Obviously, lesser patterns are identified as well, many of which are of more limited regional interactive and adaptive impact. We wish to stress again that these are broad categories of analysis and that there is nothing reductive or deterministic in our aims or choices. Nevertheless, we believe the patterns we have chosen help to make the historical process more intelligible, providing a series of lenses that can help to focus the otherwise confusing facts and disparate details that comprise world history.

Part 1 (Prehistory–600 BCE): Origins of human civilization—tool making and symbol creating—in Africa as well as the origins of agriculture, urbanism, and state formation in the three agrarian centers of the Middle East, India, and China.

Part 2 (600 BCE–600 CE): Emergence of the axial age thinkers and their visions of a transcendent god or first principle in Eurasia; elevation of these visions to the status of state religions in empires, in the process forming multiethnic and multilinguistic polities.

Part 3 (600–1450): Disintegration of classical empires and formation of religious civilizations in Eurasia, with the emergence of religiously unified regions divided by commonwealths of multiple states.

Part 4 (1450–1750): Rise of new empires; interaction, both hostile and peaceful, among the religious civilizations and new empires across all continents of the world. Origins of the New Science in Europe, based on the use of mathematics for the investigation of nature.

Part 5 (1750–1900): Origins of scientific–industrial "modernity," simultaneous with the emergence of constitutional and ethnic nation-states, in the West (Europe and North America); interaction of the West with Asia and Africa, resulting in complex adaptations, both coerced as well as voluntary, on the part of the latter.

Part 6 (1900–Present): Division of early Western modernity into the three competing visions: communism, fascism, and capitalism. After two horrific world wars and the triumph of nation-state formation across the world, capitalism remains as the last surviving version of modernity. Capitalism is then reinvigorated through the "dot.com revolution," in which increasingly sophisticated software, Internet applications, and electronic communication devices lead to increasing use of social networking media in popularizing both "traditional" religious and cultural ideas and constitutional nationalism in authoritarian states.

Chapter Organization and Structure

Each part of the book addresses the role of change and innovation on a broad scale during a particular time and/or region, and each chapter contains different levels of exploration to examine the principal features of particular cultural or national areas and how each affects, and is affected by, the patterns of origins, interactions, and adaptations:

- *Geography and the Environment*: As we saw in the opening of this preface, the relationship between human beings and the geography and environment of the places they inhabit is among the most basic factors in understanding human societies. In Japan, for example, earthquakes and tsunamis have always been seen as part of the natural condition of things. Indeed, "tsunami" is a Japanese word with the tragically evocative meaning of "harbor wave." In this chapter segment, therefore, the topics under investigation involve the natural environment of a particular region and the general conditions affecting change and innovation. Climatic conditions, earthquakes, tsunamis, volcanic eruptions, outbreaks of disease, and so forth all have obvious effects on how humans react to the challenge of survival. The initial portions of chapters introducing new regions for study therefore include environmental and geographical overviews, which are revisited and expanded in later chapters as necessary. The larger issues of how decisive the impact of geography on the development of human societies is—as in the commonly asked question "Is geography destiny?"—are also examined here.

- *Political Developments*: In this segment, we ponder such questions as how rulers and their supporters wield political and military power. How do different political traditions develop in different areas? How do states expand, and why? How do different political arrangements attempt to strike a balance between the rulers and the ruled? How and why are political innovations transmitted to other societies? Why do societies accept or reject such innovations from the outside? Are there discernable patterns in the development of kingdoms or empires or nation-states?

- *Economic and Social Developments*: The relationship between economics and the structures and workings of societies has long been regarded as crucial by historians and social scientists. But what, if any, patterns emerge in how these relationships develop and function among different cultures? This segment explores such questions as the following: What role does economics play in the dynamics of change and continuity? What, for example, happens in agrarian societies when merchant classes develop? How does the accumulation of wealth lead to social hierarchy? What forms do these hierarchies take? How do societies formally and informally try to regulate wealth and poverty? How are economic conditions reflected in family life and gender relations? Are there patterns that reflect the varying social positions of men and women that are characteristic of certain economic and social institutions? How are these in turn affected by different cultural practices?

- *Intellectual, Religious, and Cultural Aspects*: Finally, we consider it vital to include an examination dealing in some depth with the way people understood their existence and life during each period. Clearly, intellectual innovation—the generation of new ideas—lies at the heart of the changes we have singled out as pivotal in the patterns of origins, interactions, and adaptations that form the heart of this text. Beyond this, those areas concerned with the search for and construction of meaning—particularly religion, the arts, philosophy, and science—not only reflect shifting perspectives but also, in many cases, play a leading role in determining the course of events within each form of society. For example, the shift to the use of mathematics as a foundation of the "scientific revolution" contributed mightily to the rationalism and empiricism of the Enlightenment—and hence to the development of the modernity that we find ourselves in today. All of these facets of intellectual life are, in turn, manifested in new perspectives and representations in the cultural life of a society.

Features

- **Seeing Patterns/Thinking Through Patterns:** Successful history teachers often employ recursive, even reiterative, techniques in the classroom to help students more clearly perceive patterns. In a similar fashion, "Seeing Patterns" and "Thinking Through Patterns" use a question–discussion format in each chapter to pose several broad questions ("Seeing Patterns") as advance organizers for key themes, which are then matched up with short essays at the end ("Thinking Through Patterns") that examine these same questions in a sophisticated yet student-friendly fashion. Designed to foster discussion, instructors who have class-tested *Patterns of World History* report that "Thinking Through Patterns" also serve as excellent models for writing short essays.

- **Patterns Up Close:** Since students frequently better apprehend macro-level patterns when they see their contours brought into sharper relief, "Patterns Up Close" essays in each chapter highlight a particular innovation that demonstrates origins, interactions, and adaptations in action. Spanning technological, social, political, intellectual, economic, and environmental developments, the "Patterns Up Close" essays combine text, visuals, and graphics to consider everything from the pepper trade to the guillotine to rock and roll.

- **Concept Maps/Putting It All Together:** To further reinforce understanding of the central ideas presented in *Patterns of World History*, each chapter concludes with a "Putting It All Together" section that includes compelling yet simple graphics, called "Concept Maps," that synthesize key take-away points. Carefully designed and field-tested with direct input from world history instructors, Concept Maps can be used to prompt classroom discussion and to help students focus on the big picture. They have been widely praised for the opportunities they offer for visual learning and critical thinking.

- **Voices and Vignettes:** In the end, history is made by people, not anonymous social forces; and while we examine large trends throughout the book, we try never to lose sight of how people in all walks of life originated, interacted, and adapted to the circumstances in which they found themselves or, in some cases, created for themselves. Thus, each chapter includes approximately four "voices"—short excerpts from people from all walks of life whose life experiences shed light on the patterns discussed in each chapter. Additionally, many different people—from contemporary figures like the female Yemeni activist Tawakkol Karman (Chapter 31) to Leo Africanus in the sixteenth century (Chapter 16) and the Chinese sage Mencius in the fourth century BCE (Chapter 9)—are featured in opening vignettes and then woven throughout the chapters to further reinforce the concept of human agency within history.
- **Photo Clusters:** In keeping with the patterns approach of the book, each chapter includes at least one and sometimes as many as three "photo clusters"—assemblages of visual sources, each of which pertains to the same topic, and all sharing a common caption.
- **Marginal Glossary:** To avoid the necessity of having to flip pages back and forth, definitions of words that the reader may not know, as well as definitions of key terms, are set directly in the margin at the point where they are first introduced.

Today, more than ever, students and instructors are confronted by a vast welter of information on every conceivable subject. Beyond the ever-expanding print media, the Internet and the Web have opened hitherto unimaginable amounts of data to us. Despite such unprecedented access, however, all of us are too frequently overwhelmed by this undifferentiated—and all too often indigestible—mass. Nowhere is this more true than in world history, by definition the field within the

historical profession with the broadest scope. Therefore, we think that an effort at synthesis—of narrative and analysis structured around a clear, accessible, widely applicable theme—is needed, an effort that seeks to explain critical patterns of the world's past behind the billions of bits of information accessible at the stroke of a key on a computer keyboard. We hope this text, in tracing the lines of transformative ideas and things that left their patterns deeply imprinted into the canvas of world history, will provide such a synthesis.

Additional Learning Resources for *Patterns of World History*

- **Instructor's Resource Manual:** Includes, for each chapter, a detailed chapter outline, suggested lecture topics, learning objectives, map quizzes, geography exercises, classroom activities, "Patterns Up Close" activities, "Seeing Patterns and Making Connections" activities, "Concept Map" exercises, biographical sketches, a correlation guide for the list of assets on the Instructor's Resource DVD, as well as suggested Web resources and digital media files. Also includes, for each chapter, approximately 40 multiple-choice, short-answer, true-or-false, and fill-in-the-blank as well as approximately 10 essay questions.
- **Instructor's Resource DVD:** Includes PowerPoint slides and JPEG and PDF files for all the maps and photos in the text, an additional 400 map files from *The Oxford Atlas of World History*, as well as approximately 250 additional PowerPoint-based slides organized by theme and topic. Also includes approximately 1,500 questions that can be customized by the instructor.
- **Sources in Patterns of World History: Volume 1:** *To 1600:* Includes approximately 200 text and visual sources in world history, organized to match the chapter organization of *Patterns of World History*. Each source is accompanied by a headnote and reading questions.
- **Sources in Patterns of World History: Volume 2:** *Since 1400:* Includes approximately 200 text and visual sources in world history, organized by the chapter organization of *Patterns of World History*.

Each source is accompanied by a headnote and reading questions.

- **Mapping Patterns of World History, Volume 1: To 1600:** Includes approximately 50 full-color maps, each accompanied by a brief headnote, as well as Concept Map exercises.
- **Mapping Patterns of World History, Volume 2: Since 1400:** Includes approximately 50 full-color maps, each accompanied by a brief headnote, as well as Concept Map exercises.
- **Companion Web Site (www.oup.com/us/von sivers):** Includes quizzes, flashcards, map exercises, documents, interactive Concept Map exercises, and links to YouTube videos.
- **ClassMate for Patterns of World History:** Includes approximately 800 quizzes (25–30 per chapter) for low- or mid-stakes testing as well as an online gradebook for instructors.
- **E-book for Patterns of World History, Volumes 1 and 2:** An e-book is available for purchase at www.coursesmart.com.

Bundling Options

Patterns of World History can be bundled at a significant discount with any of the titles in the popular Very Short Introductions or Oxford World's Classics series, as well as other titles from the Higher Education division world history catalog (www.oup.com/us/catalog/he). Please contact your OUP representative for details.

Acknowledgments

Throughout the course of writing, revising, and preparing *Patterns of World History* for publication we have benefited from the guidance and professionalism accorded us by all levels of the staff at Oxford University Press. John Challice, vice president and publisher, had faith in the inherent worth of our project from the outset and provided the initial impetus to move forward. In the early stages of the editorial process, Brian Wheel and Frederick Speers provided helpful critiques and advice, saving us from textual infelicities; Meg Botteon later added a final polish. Lauren Aylward carried out the thankless task of assembling the manuscript and did so with generosity and good cheer. Picture researcher Francelle Carapetyan diligently tracked down every photo request despite the sometimes sketchy sources

we provided, Andrew Pachuta copyedited the manuscript with meticulous attention to detail, and Barbara Mathieu steered us through the intricacies of production with the stoicism of a saint.

Most of all, we owe a special debt of gratitude to Charles Cavaliere, our editor. Charles took on the daunting task of directing the literary enterprise at a critical point in the book's career. He pushed this project to its successful completion, accelerated its schedule, and used a combination of flattery and hard-nosed tactics to make sure we stayed the course. His greatest contribution, however, is in the way he refined our original vision for the book with several important adjustments that clarified its latent possibilities. From the maps to the photos to the special features, Charles's high standards and concern for detail are evident on every page.

Developing a book like *Patterns of World History* is an ambitious project, a collaborative venture in which authors and editors benefit from the feedback provided by a team of outside readers and consultants. We gratefully acknowledge the advice that the many reviewers, focus group participants, and class testers (including their students) shared with us along the way. We tried to implement all of the excellent suggestions. Of course, any errors of fact or interpretation that remain are solely our own.

Reviewers

Stephanie Ballenger, Central Washington University

Alan Baumler, Indiana University of Pennsylvania

Robert Blackey, California State University

Robert Bond, San Diego Mesa College

Mauricio Borrero, St. John's University

Linda Bregstein-Scherr, Mercer County Community College

Scott Breuninger, University of South Dakota

Paul Brians, Washington State University

Gayle K. Brunelle, California State University-Fullerton

James De Lorenzi, City University of New York, John Jay College

Jennifer Kolpacoff Deane, University of Minnesota-Morris

Andrew D. Devenney, Grand Valley State University

Francis A. Dutra, University of California, Santa Barbara

Jeffrey Dym, Sacramento State University

Jennifer C. Edwards, Manhattan College

Lisa M. Edwards, University of Massachusetts-Lowell

Charles T. Evans, Northern Virginia Community College

Christopher Ferguson, Auburn University

Scott Fritz, Western New Mexico State University

Arturo Giraldez, University of the Pacific

Candace Gregory-Abbott, California State University-Sacramento

Derek Heng, Ohio State University

Eric Hetherington, New Jersey Institute of Technology

Laura J. Hilton, Muskingum University

Elizabeth J. Houseman, State University of New York-Brockport

Hung-yok Ip, Oregon State University

Geoffrey Jensen, University of Arkansas

Roger E. Kanet, University of Miami

Kelly Kennington, Auburn University

Amelia M. Kiddle, University of Arizona

Frederic Krome, University of Cincinnati-Clermont College

Mark W. Lentz, University of Louisiana, Lafayette

Heather Lucas, Georgia Perimeter College

Susan Mattern, University of Georgia

Susan A. Maurer, Nassau Community College

Jason McCollom, University of Arkansas

Douglas T. McGetchin, Florida Atlantic University

Stephen Morillo, Wabash College

Carolyn Neel, Arkansas Tech University

Kenneth J. Orosz, Buffalo State College

Alice K. Pate, Columbus State University

Patrick M. Patterson, Honolulu Community College

Daniel Pope, University of Oregon

G. David Price, Santa Fe College

Michael Redman, University of Louisville

Leah Renold, Texas State University

Jeremy Rich, Middle Tennessee State University

Jason Ripper, Everett Community College

Chad Ross, East Carolina University

Nana Yaw B. Sapong, Southern Illinois University-Carbondale

Daniel Sarefield, Fitchburg State College

Claire Schen, State University of New York, Buffalo

Robert C. Schwaller, University of North Carolina-Charlotte

George Sochan, Bowie State University

Ramya Sreenivasan, State University of New York, Buffalo

John Stanley, Kutztown University

Vladimir Steffel, Ohio State University

Anthony J. Steinhoff, University of Tennessee-Chattanooga

Micheal Tarver, Arkansas Tech University

Shane Tomashot, Georgia State University

Kate Transchel, California State University-Chico

Melanie Tubbs, Arkansas Tech University

Andrew Wackerfuss, Georgetown University

Evan R. Ward, Brigham Young University

Joseph K. S. Yick, Texas State University-San Marcos

Focus Group Participants
San Diego, California

Robert Bond, San Diego Mesa College

Lisa Marie Edwards, University of Massachusetts-Lowell

Christine Moore, Palomar College

Elizabeth Ann Pollard, San Diego State University

Charles Romney, Whittier College

Tom Sanders, United States Naval Academy

Sharlene Sayegh-Canada, California State University-Long Beach

Micheal Tarver, Arkansas Tech University

Michael G. Vann, California State University-Sacramento

Russellville, Arkansas

Michael Cox, Rich Mountain Community College

Peter Dykema, Arkansas Tech University

Karen Franks, University of the Ozarks

Jan Jenkins, Arkansas Tech University

Alexander Mirkovic, Arkansas Tech University

Carolyn Neel, Arkansas Tech University

Micheal Tarver, Arkansas Tech University

Melanie Tubbs, Arkansas Tech University

Class Testers

Barbara Allen, La Salle University

Robert Bond, San Diego Mesa College

John A. Dempsey, Westfield State University

Candace Gregory-Abbott, California State University-Sacramento

Jeffrey Hamilton, Baylor University

Padhraig Higgins, Mercer County Community College

Lybeth Hodges, Texas Woman's University

John M. Hunt, University of North Florida

Kara Kaufman, Salem State University

Kelly Kennington, Auburn University

Mark Lentz, University of Louisiana, Lafayette

Margaret Markmann, La Salle University

Douglas T. McGetchin, Florida Atlantic University

J. Kent McGaughy, Houston Community College, Northwest

Carolyn Neel, Arkansas Tech University

Patricia O'Neill, Central Oregon Community College

David Peck, Brigham Young University

Walter D. Penrose, San Diego State University

William Pierce, Northern Virginia Community College

G. David Price, Santa Fe College

Michael Redman, University of Louisville

Jason Ripper, Everett Community College

Chad Ross, East Carolina University

Linda Rupert, University of North Carolina-Greensboro

Cliff Stratton, Washington State University-Pullman

Micheal Tarver, Arkansas Tech University

Evan R. Ward, Brigham Young University

Please let us know your experiences with *Patterns of World History* so that we may improve it in future editions. We welcome your comments and suggestions.

Peter von Sivers
pv4910@xmission.com

Charles A. Desnoyers
desnoyer@lasalle.edu

George B. Stow
gbsgeorge@aol.com

Note on Dates and Spellings

In keeping with widespread practice among world historians, we use "BCE" and "CE" to date events and the phrase "years ago" to describe developments from the remote past.

The transliteration of Middle Eastern words has been adjusted as much as possible to the English alphabet. Therefore, long vowels are not emphasized. The consonants specific to Arabic (alif, dhal, ha, sad, dad, ta, za, ayn, ghayn, and qaf) are either not indicated (except for ayn in the middle of words) or rendered with common English letters. A similar procedure is followed for Farsi. Turkish words follow the alphabet reform of 1929, which adds the following letters to the Western alphabet or modifies their pronunciation: c (pronounced "j"), ç (pronounced "tsh"), ğ (not pronounced, lengthening of preceding vowel), ı ("i" without dot, pronunciation close to short e), i/İ ("i" with dot, including in caps), ö (no English equivalent), ş ("sh"), and ü (no English equivalent). The spelling of common Middle Eastern and Islamic terms follows daily press usage (which, however, is not completely uniform). Examples are "al-Qaeda," "Quran," and "sharia."

The system used in rendering the sounds of Mandarin Chinese—the northern Chinese dialect that has become in effect the national spoken language in China and Taiwan—into English in this book is *hanyu pinyin*, usually given as simply *pinyin*. This is the official Romanization system of the People's Republic of China and has also become the standard outside of Taiwan, Republic of China. Most syllables are pronounced as they would be in English, with the exception of the letter *q*, which is given an aspirated "ch" sound; *ch* itself has a less aspirated "ch" sound. *Zh* carries a hard "j" and *j*, a soft, English-style "j." Some syllables also are pronounced—particularly in the regions around Beijing—with a retroflex *r* so that the syllable *shi*, for example, carries a pronunciation closer to "shir." Finally, the letter *r* in the *pinyin* system has no direct English equivalent, but an approximation may be had by combining the sounds of "r" and "j."

Japanese terms have been Romanized according to a modification of the Hepburn system. The letter *g* is always hard; vowels are handled as they are in Italian—*e*, for example, carries a sound like "ay." We have not, however, included diacritical markings to indicate long vowel sounds in *u* or *o*. Where necessary, these have been indicated in the pronunciation guides.

For Korean terms, we have used a variation of the McCune-Reischauer system, which remains the standard Romanization scheme for Korean words used in English academic writing, but eliminated any diacritical markings. Here again, the vowel sounds are pronounced more or less like those of Italian and the consonants, like those of English.

For Vietnamese words, we have used standard renditions based on the modern Quoc Ngu ("national language") system in use in Vietnam today. The system was developed by Jesuit missionaries and is based on the Portuguese alphabet. Once more, we have avoided diacritical marks, and the reader should follow the pronunciation guides for approximations of Vietnamese terms.

Latin American terms (Spanish, Nahua, or Quechua) generally follow local usage, including accents, except where they are Anglicized, per the *Oxford English Dictionary*. Thus, the Spanish-Quechua word "Tiahuanacu" becomes the Anglicized word "Tiwanaku."

We use the terms "Native American" and "Indian" interchangeably to refer to the peoples of the Americas in the pre-Columbian period and "Amerindian" in our coverage of Latin America since independence.

In keeping with widely recognized practice among paleontologists and other scholars of the deep past, we use the term "hominins" in Chapter 1 to emphasize their greater remoteness from apes and proximity to modern humans.

Phonetic spellings often follow the first appearance of a non-English word whose pronunciation may be unclear to the reader. We have followed the rules for capitalization per *The Chicago Manual of Style*.

About the Authors

Peter von Sivers is associate professor of Middle Eastern history at the University of Utah. He has previously taught at UCLA, Northwestern University, the University of Paris VII (Vincennes), and the University of Munich. He has also served as chair, Joint Committee of the Near and Middle East, Social Science Research Council, New York, 1982–1985; editor, *International Journal of Middle East Studies*, 1985–1989; member, Board of Directors, Middle East Studies Association of North America, 1987–1990; and chair, SAT II World History Test Development Committee of the Educational Testing Service, Princeton, NJ, 1991–1994. His publications include *Caliphate, Kingdom, and Decline: The Political Theory of Ibn Khaldun*, several edited books, and three dozen peer-reviewed chapters and articles on Middle Eastern and North African history, as well as world history. He received his Dr. Phil. from the University of Munich.

Charles A. Desnoyers is associate professor of history and director of Asian studies at La Salle University, Philadelphia. He is also past director of the Greater Philadelphia Asian Studies Consortium and president (2011–2012) of the Mid-East Region Association for Asian Studies. His scholarly publications include *A Journey to the East: Li Gui's "A New Account of a Trip Around the Globe"* (University of Michigan Press, 2004) and former coeditor of the World History Association's *Bulletin*.

George B. Stow is professor of history and director of the graduate program in history at La Salle University, Philadelphia. His teaching experience embraces a variety of undergraduate and graduate courses in ancient Greece and Rome, medieval England, and world history; and for excellence in teaching he has been awarded the Lindback Distinguished Teaching Award. Professor Stow is a member of the Medieval Academy of America and a fellow of the Royal Historical Society. He is the recipient of a National Defense Education Act Title IV Fellowship, a Woodrow Wilson Foundation Fellowship, and research grants from the American Philosophical Society and La Salle University. His publications include a critical edition of a fourteenth-century monastic chronicle, *Historia Vitae et Regni Ricardi Secundi* (University of Pennsylvania Press), as well as numerous articles and reviews in scholarly journals including *Speculum*, *The English Historical Review*, the *Journal of Medieval History*, the *American Historical Review*, and several others. He received his PhD from the University of Illinois.

Patterns of
World History

PART FIVE

The Origins of Modernity

1750–1900

What we have termed "modernity" in this section may be said to have begun roughly around 1800 in western Europe and may be characterized as the product of what historian Eric Hobsbawm (b. 1917) called "the twin revolutions" of the late eighteenth century. One of these was the new political landscape brought into being by the trio of constitutional revolutions in North America, France, and Haiti, which dealt a telling blow to the concept of traditional monarchial rule by divine right and introduced popular sovereignty as the new justification for political power. The other was the Industrial Revolution, which began in England with the introduction of steam-driven, machine-produced textiles and other goods. Scientific–industrial modernity, with its developing constellation of values marked by experimentation, political, social, and technological progress, social mobility, and secularism, was thus set on a path to displace the older agrarian–urban order of religious civilizations that had been characterized by hierarchy, natural order, and divinely ordained law and morality. This transition is, in fact, still ongoing. Although the old agrarian–urban *political* order has been almost universally superseded, its values still contend with those of modernity in many parts of the world today.

The Origins of Modernity

The political and industrial revolutions that define modernity have intellectual roots reaching back to the 1500s. As scholars increasingly recognize, the discovery of the Americas, as well as the Copernican revolution in astronomy, provided powerful incentives for the introduction of new patterns of science and political philosophy. For more than two centuries, however, these ideas remained the province of only a small intellectual elite.

Political and Industrial Revolutions

By the 1700s, however, adherents of the new science and philosophy among urban, educated administrators and professionals in northwestern Europe had grown in numbers and began to become influential in society. In Britain, the *theory* of the social contract entered into the *practice* of constitutionalism following the Glorious Revolution of 1688. Both were vastly expanded by thinkers during the

1765
James Watt Perfects the Steam Engine

1776–1804
American, French, and Haitian Revolutions

1798–1801
Napoleon's Occupation of Egypt

1815
Congress of Vienna

1832
Greece Wins Independence from the Ottomans

1839–1876
Tanzimat Reforms in the Ottoman Empire

1848
Karl Marx and Friedrich Engels Publish *The Communist Manifesto*

1853–1854
Commodore Perry Opens Trade and Diplomatic Relations with Japan

eighteenth-century Enlightenment and helped to inspire the American, French, and Haitian Revolutions. These were narrow revolutions in the sense of ending monarchial–aristocratic rule—courageous revolts during still deeply religious times. Nonetheless, this era set human emancipation from the confining traditions of the past as a goal to be achieved. And in the case of Haiti, the idea that "all men are created equal" emblazoned earlier in the American Declaration of Independence and the French Declaration of the Rights of Man, formed the basis of a successful slave rebellion against revolutionary France itself.

The Industrial Revolution, beginning around 1800 in Great Britain, was a socially transformative and self-sustaining sequence of technical inventions and commercial applications. Britain industrialized during the first half of the 1800s through steam-driven iron foundries, textile factories, overland transportation, and ocean travel. In a second wave, Germany and the United States industrialized, with the introduction of chemicals, electricity, and motorcars into the factory system. The two waves of industrialization created an unequal class system, with a citizenry composed of both landed aristocrats—fading in power as the old agrarian–urban order decayed—and a new, dynamic urban middle class amassing political and economic power. But the equally new phenomenon of the industrial working class, bidding for political, social, and economic equality, added a volatile social factor to the mix as its members sought to make good on the promises of the constitutional revolutions.

Resistance and Adaptation to the Western Challenge

The twin political–industrial revolutions in Europe were a major factor in the mid-nineteenth-century expansion of the existing seaborne European empires in Asia and Africa. Postrevolutionary France renewed its competition with Britain, and both later used "gunboat diplomacy" to establish favorable commercial conditions and trade outposts. From here, these two and other European nations proceeded to compete in imperial conquests for what they now considered to be strategically important territories across the globe.

The traditional agrarian and religious empires and states of Asia and Africa responded to the increasingly superior military power of the European maritime empires and the United States during the 1800s with both resistance and adaptation. Resisting with traditional armies and weapons, however, became more difficult as the 1800s unfolded and the industrial development of the West spawned new and sophisticated weaponry. "Adaptation," as it occurred under the duress of imperialism, was a creative process in which the states under challenge selected generic elements from the constitutional and industrial revolutions that had made the West powerful and attempted to harmonize them with their inherited traditions.

Thinking Like a World Historian

▶ What were the origins of the "twin revolutions" of the late eighteenth century? How did they combine to create what we call "modernity"?

▶ Why were the values of scientific–industrial society opposed to the older agrarian–urban order? Why does this conflict still persist in many parts of the world today?

▶ What patterns of resistance and adaptation characterized the responses of traditional agrarian and religious empires to European military power and expansion?

1857
Sepoy Mutiny, India

1868–1912
Reign of Emperor Meiji, Japan

1878–1885
Independence of Serbia, Montenegro, Rumania, and Bulgaria

1888
End of Slavery, Brazil

1894–1895
Sino-Japanese War

1904–1905
Russo-Japanese War

1861
Emancipation of Serfs in Russian Empire

1869
Opening of Suez Canal

1884
Hiram Maxim Invents the First Fully Automatic Machine Gun

1900
Boxer Rebellion and Anti-Foreign War

1905
Albert Einstein Publishes Theory of Relativity

1908
Young Turks Rise to Power in Ottoman Empire

Chapter 22

1750-1871

Nation-States and Patterns of Culture in Europe and North America

THE NORTH ATLANTIC, 1750-1900

In a diary entry dated June 4, 1785, George Washington, the hero of the American War for Independence and future first president of the United States, noted that "the celebrated Mrs. Macauly [sic] Graham & Mr. Graham her Husband . . . arrived here." Washington seems to have thoroughly enjoyed the visit, for after their departure he wrote to his friend Richard Henry Lee to express his appreciation for his letter of introduction to this distinguished

▶ How did the pattern of constitutional nationalism, emerging from the American and French Revolutions, affect the course of events in the Western world during the first half of the nineteenth century?

▶ In what ways did ethnolinguistic nationalism differ from constitutional nationalism, and what was its influence on the formation of nation-states in the second half of the nineteenth century?

▶ What were the reactions among thinkers and artists to the developing pattern of nation-state formation? How did they define the intellectual–artistic movements of romanticism and realism?

Constitutional Nationalism in Action, London 1831. This colored lithograph, entitled *Staunch Reformers*, captures the way in which many ordinary Europeans and Americans, such as the rag-tag crew depicted here on a London street corner, saw themselves as part of a wider political reform movement. The drawing makes references to many important political developments and symbols of the era—one man holds a placard that reads, "Tom Paine's *Rights of Man*—one penny!' topped by a red liberty cap, symbol of revolutionary France." In the left background, a sign outside a doorway reads "Support The Crown"—a reminder that in Britain at least, political reform went hand in hand with loyalty to the King.

visitor from England, "whose principles are so much, & so justly admired by the friends of liberty and of Mankind."

Who was this "celebrated" woman, and what had she done to earn the abiding respect of George Washington? Biographical dictionaries of her day called Catharine Macaulay Graham (1731–1791) "the patroness of liberty," for her staunch views on constitutional liberties and rights, including women's rights. But British contemporaries also considered her an eccentric for her flamboyant personal lifestyle: After the death of her husband in 1785, she married William Graham, a medical apprentice—she was 47 and he was 21. Her star dimmed somewhat thereafter in Great Britain, but North Americans continued to admire her, as evidenced by the eager invitation to Washington's Mt. Vernon.

She published her political views on British constitutionalism and the American and French Revolutions in a number of widely read essays and books. For example, in a pamphlet of 1775, Graham expressed her support for the North American colonists, who "year by year [have been] stripped of the most valuable of their rights" and who have suffered under "oppressive taxes," particularly the Stamp Act, "by which they were to be taxed in an arbitrary manner." In 1783 she published the eight-volume *History of England*, which reflected many ideals of the Enlightenment, particularly antimonarchical sentiments, and support for the concept of natural rights and the sovereignty of the people. And in 1791, shortly before her death, she wrote a review of Edmund Burke's *Reflections on the Revolution in France* (1790), in which she issued a strongly worded rebuke of Burke's castigation of the French Revolution. Among other things, she observed "[t]hat the people have often abused their power, it must be granted . . . but *no abuse* of their power *can take away their right*, because their rights exists [sic] *in the very constitution of things*."

Graham's writings fell into oblivion during the 1800s and through much of the 1900s when the defense of constitutional nationalism no longer aroused the passions of citizens in many nation-states. Indeed, the very fact that such debate no longer seemed fashionable is testimony to the ultimate success of her cause. But like her more famous contemporary, Mary Wollstonecraft, her early advocacy of feminism and views on education attracted attention again during the second half of the twentieth century; and today she is increasingly recognized as a pioneer of gender equality.

The first half of this chapter focuses on this new pattern of state formation that the American and French Revolutions of 1776–1789 introduced into world history—and that was so passionately espoused by Catharine Graham in its time. The revolutionaries in North America and France, and the many other places that followed in their wake, renounced or overthrew traditional divine-right kingdoms and empires and replaced them with the *constitutional nation-state*, that is, a state where all people were citizens with the same constitutional rights and duties and where the borders of the political state corresponded more or less to territories where people had developed a sense of collective identity: the *nation*. The ideology of constitutional nationalism became a powerful driving force in state formation during the 1800s and 1900s.

The constitutional nation-states that emerged after these initial revolutions, however, fell short of the lofty ideals above; and, in a backlash, monarchical and imperial regimes making minimal concessions to constitutional nationalism survived in Europe. Toward the middle of the 1800s, the new ideology of *ethnolinguistic nationalism* arose: the nation consists of people with strong ethnic ties and often sharing a common language, religion, and historical experience. It followed that such nations should also have their own states.

The movement toward ethnolinguistic nationalism was especially strong in central and eastern Europe, which had not had constitutional movements. It also developed in western Europe, where it grew to rival constitutional nationalism as a force within the pattern of nation-state formation. In some cases it led to the unification of ethnically related peoples who lived in smaller states into one large state, as with Italy and Germany. More frequently, it led people who saw themselves as nations governed by large empires to agitate for autonomy or independence in order to form their own ethnic nation-states—as with the many Balkan peoples under control of the Ottomans (see Chapter 25).

To complicate matters further, many people did not draw sharp distinctions between the two nation-state ideologies, especially in the realm of culture, on which the second half of this chapter concentrates. Indeed, ethnolinguistic nation-states that adopted constitutions embodied both trends, though sometimes rather uncomfortably. Moreover, these new patterns of state formation stimulated competition and disputes over national boundaries, which were now more intense because of the ethnic component. All of this would play a large role in the events leading up to World War I. Thus, the new culture of modernity that emerged in the nation-states during the nineteenth century was a complex and often volatile mixture of these two sometimes competing forms of nationalism. But as these forms evolved in the twentieth century, they became the pattern to which more and more states ultimately adhered. Today, the nation-state is not only the dominant form of polity but virtually the only one.

Origins of the Nation-State, 1750–1815

The subject of our vignette, Catharine Macaulay Graham, wrote many of her essays within the tradition of the rights and liberties obtained through the Glorious Revolution of 1688 in England. She was steeped, therefore, in not only the ideas but also the practices of constitutional nationalism that the Glorious Revolution pioneered. In this revolution, for the first time in Europe, the traditional divine rights of a monarch had been curbed through a set of constitutional rights and duties granted to the subjects of the kingdom. The innovative ideas of *subjects* becoming *citizens* with constitutionally guaranteed rights and duties and of the Parliament representing the nation—the people living in England—also became central in the American Revolution and developed close parallels during the French Revolution. Beyond the Glorious Revolution, however, the American and French Revolutions were more radical in the sense that they ended the British compromise of royal and parliamentary power and resulted in republican, middle-class nation-states without traditional divine-right monarchies.

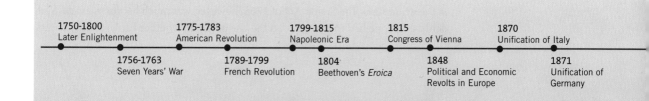

1750-1800 Later Enlightenment	1775-1783 American Revolution	1799-1815 Napoleonic Era	1815 Congress of Vienna	1870 Unification of Italy
1756-1763 Seven Years' War	1789-1799 French Revolution	1804 Beethoven's *Eroica*	1848 Political and Economic Revolts in Europe	1871 Unification of Germany

The American and French Revolutions

The two revolutions were outgrowths of the Seven Years' War, in which Great Britain and France fought for the dominance of their respective seaborne empires in the world. The governments of both kingdoms went deeply into debt to win the war. They owed this debt to their wealthy subjects, many of whom were landowners and administrators forming the ruling class. To pay back the debt, however, the kings had to go to their subjects at large and raise their taxes. The incongruence of monarchs holding the mass of their subjects responsible for their debts to a few wealthy subjects was apparent to a large number of people, who had found the intellectual movement of the Enlightenment congenial and formulated political principles of reform, if not revolution.

Conditions for Revolution in North America   When Britain won the Seven Years' War, it acquired France's trade forts in India as well as French possessions in Canada and the Ohio–Mississippi River valley. France turned Louisiana over to its ally Spain (which had lost Florida to Britain) and retreated entirely from North America. But the British territorial gains came at the price of a huge debt: The payment of the interest alone devoured most of the country's regular annual budget. Taxes had to be raised domestically as well as overseas, and in order to do so the government had to strengthen its administrative hand in an empire that had grown haphazardly and—in North America—without much oversight.

By 1763, the 13 North American colonies had experienced both rapid demographic and powerful economic growth. Opening lands beyond the Appalachian Mountains into the Ohio valley would relieve a growing population pressure on the strip of land along the Atlantic coast that the colonies occupied. Environmental degradation, through overplanting and deforestation, had increased the landless population and contributed to the presence of growing numbers of poor people in the burgeoning cities of Philadelphia, Boston, and New York. The occupation of new land across the Appalachians, on the other hand, increased the administrative challenges for the British. They had to employ large numbers of standing troops to protect not only the settlers from the hostility of the Native Americans but also the native peoples from aggression by settlers. Grain, timber, and tobacco exports from the colonies had made the colonies rich immediately before 1763, but the war boom inevitably gave way to a postwar bust. While new land created new opportunities, the economic slump created hardships (see Map 22.1).

As the government faced the task of strengthening the British administration of the colonies, a young and inexperienced monarch, George III (r. 1760–1820), was determined to increase the influence of the Crown on British politics. Unfortunately, he was not terribly adept at surrounding himself with capable advisors. Furthermore, instead of conceiving a systematic plan for governing the colonies, British politics lurched from one measure to another. The Proclamation of 1763, for example, limited the expansion of settlement to lands east of the Appalachians, to forestall difficulties with England's recent Iroquois allies. In addition to protests from those hoping to open up the new lands acquired from France, it resulted in expanded migrations to the cities and towns.

Settlers could simply ignore the proclamation if they chose to take their chances in the wilderness. The Stamp Act of 1765, however, was much harder to evade. Suddenly, everyone had to pay a tax on the use of paper, whether for legal documents,

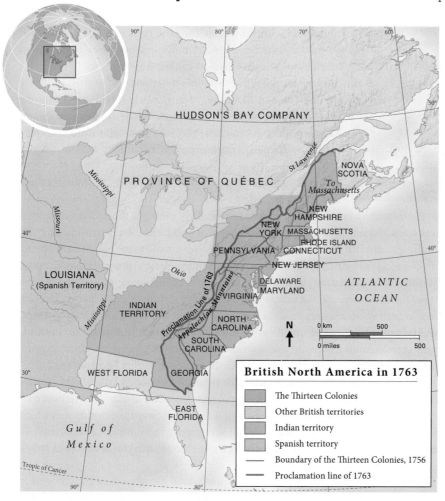

MAP **22.1 British North America in 1763.**

newspapers, or even playing cards. The tax was to be used for the upkeep of the standing troops, many of which were withdrawn from the Ohio valley, ordered to be quartered in the colonies, and intended to be used for the enforcement of increased taxes.

A firestorm of protest against the Stamp Act broke out among the urban lower middle ranks of shopkeepers, small merchants, mechanics, and printers, who organized themselves in groups such as the "Daughters" or "Sons of Liberty." The Daughters declared a highly successful boycott of British goods and promoted the production of homespun textiles. Parliament withdrew the Stamp Act when British exports fell, but the efforts by British troops to suppress the urban riots that continued even after the act's withdrawal only inflamed an increasingly volatile situation. In Boston, one of the flashpoints of unrest, the British administration also managed to offend colonists of the upper urban classes when it dissolved the Massachusetts Assembly.

Two of its members were Samuel Adams and John Hancock, the one a repentant tax collector and son of a brewer-merchant and the other a nephew of a merchant and successful shipping entrepreneur. They became prominent organizers of the opposition to new and less visible indirect taxes, which the British sought to collect in

The Boston Tea Party. This print from the late 1700s is one of dozens of depictions of this famous incident during which a group of Bostonians dumped some 300 chests of tea shipped by the East India Company into the harbor.

place of the direct Stamp Tax. The Parliament in Britain, well aware that the taxes yielded only a fraction of colonial expenditures in North America, canceled all taxes in 1770 except for the tea duty. But since this decision came at the same time as the "Boston Massacre," a particularly incendiary killing by British troops of five Bostonians during a riot, this cancelation turned out to be too little too late: Principles came into play that now hardened the positions of both sides.

Sovereignty versus Independence   Britain retained the tea tax to assert a basic right of sovereignty. This elevation of the tea tax to a matter of principle was particularly galling to the Americans since it was actually a subsidy to keep the near bankrupt East India Company afloat and had nothing to do with America. On the other side, Adams and many others were openly propagating the principle of independence from about 1769 onward: "No Taxation Without Representation" had become one of the main rallying cries of the protestors. The governmental tax subsidy for a private company in India quickly became fodder for a vociferous propaganda campaign against an allegedly arbitrary, corrupt, and tyrannical George III who dared to rule North America from afar. The colonists' propaganda culminated with the symbolic—and rather expensive—dumping of a cargo of tea into Boston Harbor in 1773. In response to this "Boston Tea Party," Britain closed the harbor, demanded restitution, and passed the so-called Coercive Acts (called the "Intolerable Acts" in the colonies), which put Massachusetts into effective bankruptcy. Both sides now moved inexorably toward a showdown in which Thomas Hobbes's principle of indivisible sovereignty and John Locke's principle of equal representation would become locked in a bloody struggle for supremacy.

The War for Independence   Two Continental Congresses of the colonies in 1774–1775 failed to resolve this clash of principles. The colonial assemblies elevated themselves into the Continental Association, which claimed to speak for all the people. But the debate about representation—with one-third of the North American population not sufficiently propertied to have the right to vote for the assemblies—reverberated into the colonial assemblies themselves. Demands for expanded voting rights confronted complaints about "low" people like cobblers, caulkers, blacksmiths, religious dissenters, and non-Christians participating in the debate for independence. As with the French Revolution later on, the leaders needed the masses to support them in their bid for independence but were afraid of the potential violence and momentum of these masses, which might at any time overwhelm them.

While this coalition of leaders and the masses was coming together, Britain seized the initiative. In an effort to isolate the revolutionary hotbed of Massachusetts from the rest of the colonies, British troops ventured out in April 1775 to seize a suspected cache of arms and ammunition in Concord. The silversmith Paul Revere, son of a French Huguenot immigrant, in the midnight ride of later fame, warned Adams and Hancock of the British plans to arrest them and roused a militia of farmers—the famous "Minute Men"—near Concord to arms. War broke out in earnest, and the Second Continental Congress appointed George Washington, a former officer from a wealthy Virginian family of tobacco planters, as commander of the colonists' troops.

Feelings on both sides now ran at a fever pitch, as exemplified by Thomas Paine's widely read pamphlet *Common Sense*. Paine had been a corset maker and tax officer in Britain before emigrating to Pennsylvania in 1774. His plainspoken prose style powerfully appealed to craftspeople and laborers, as did his use of well-known biblical examples and avoidance of high-toned Latin quotes. By contrast, when the Second Continental Congress voted to separate the colonies from Britain on July 4, 1776, the resulting Declaration of Independence was a highly literate document steeped in Enlightenment thought. Its author was Thomas Jefferson, like Washington the son of a Virginian planter with an advanced university education that included the New Sciences. The great majority of the signers were also educated men of means—planters, landowners, merchants, and lawyers. Thus, the American and earlier English Revolutions shared a certain similarity in their leadership.

Although the revolution affirmed the Enlightenment idea that the equality of all "men" was "self-evident," it tacitly excluded the one-fifth of all Americans who were black slaves and the roughly half who were women, not to mention the Native Americans. On the other hand, the signers also excluded Locke's property ownership from what they considered to be the most valuable rights of citizens and rendered these rights as "life, liberty, and the pursuit of happiness." When the colonists eventually won the war of independence in 1783, the founders created a revolutionary federal republic with a Congress that was far more representative of its citizens than the Parliament in Great Britain.

The new republic's initial years, however, were fraught with organizational difficulties. The governing document, the Articles of Confederation, granted so much power to the individual states that the latter operated in effect like separate countries. In 1787 a constitutional convention was called in Philadelphia and a far more effective federal system created. Careful to add checks and balances in the form of a bicameral legislature and separation of powers into legislative, executive, and judicial branches, the new constitution seemed to embody many of the ideals of the Enlightenment—including a set of 10 initial amendments: the Bill of Rights. Though still imperfect—particularly in sidestepping the contentious issue of slavery—it provided a model for nearly all the world's constitutions that followed. A later commentator praised it as "a machine that would go of itself"; another, more critical one called its checks and balances "a harmonious system of mutual frustration." In 1789, under the new system, George Washington was elected the first president of the United States.

Though the new republic fell far short of what we would consider today to be "representative," its abolition of the divine right of monarchial rule and its replacement by the sovereignty of the people was for most people a previously unimaginable reversal of the natural order of things. In this respect, the American and French Revolutions signaled the inauguration of a new pattern of state formation and the advent of modernity.

The French Revolution   King Louis XVI (r. 1774–1792) and the French government had watched the American War for Independence with great sympathy, hoping for an opportunity to avenge the kingdom's defeat in the Seven Years' War. It supplied the Americans with money, arms, and officers and in 1778–1779, in alliance with Spain, declared war on Great Britain. The French–Spanish entry into the war forced Britain into an impossible defense of its entire colonial empire. Although

Redstion de L'Armée Angloises Commandée par Mylord, Comte de Cornwallis aux Armees Combinées des Etats unis de L'Amerique, et de France aux ordres des Generaux Washington et de Rochambeau a Yorck town et Glocester dans la Virginie. le 19 Octobre 1781. Il s'est trouvée dans ces deux postes 6000 hommes de troupes reglées Angloises ou Hesboises et 22 Drapeaux 3800 Matelots 160 Canons de tout Calibre dont 75 de Fonte 8 Mortiers 40 Batimens dont un Vaisseau de 50 Canons qui a eté Brûlé 20 Coulés Bas : Ce jour a jamais memorables pour les Etats unis en ce qui assura definitivement leurs independances

A. Yorck Town   C . Armée Angloise sortant de la place   E. Armée Francoise   G Armée naval de France aux Ordres du Comte de Grace   I. Riviere d'Yorck .
B . Glocester   D . Les Armée des memes posée en Poissance   F Armée Americaine   H Baye de Chesapeack.

The Battle of Yorktown, 1781. This French engraving emphasizes the key role they played in this decisive battle of the war. A large French army assisted in the siege of Yorktown, visible in the background, while the French fleet cut off British attempts to escape, forcing them to surrender.

mounting a creditable military effort, Britain conceded defeat in 1783 in the hope of escaping with minimal territorial losses, apart from the North American colonies. Indeed, in the peace negotiations France and Spain made few territorial gains. The French government furthermore had to begin exorbitant payments—much higher than what Britain faced after the Seven Years' War—on the interest for the loans to carry out the war. Crippling debt, which the French government was ultimately unable to pay, played a large role in establishing the preconditions underlying the outbreak of the French Revolution.

The Crises of the 1780s   As in America, the French population had increased sharply during the 1700s. Food production could barely keep up, and inflation increased. As recent scholarship has shown, the rural economy responded to the rising demand, though with difficulty; and in the region of Paris, production for the market was highly profitable. Furthermore, colonial trade with the Caribbean colonies boomed. Had it not been for the debt, the government would have been well-financed: It collected direct taxes as well as monies from compulsory loans and the sale of titles and offices to a large upper stratum of ordinary people of means—merchants, lawyers, and administrators. These people were deeply invested in the regime, buying themselves into the ranks of the aristocracy and benefiting from administrative offices handling the kingdom's tax revenue. Although claiming to be absolute, the king in reality shared power and wealth with a large ruling class of old and new aristocrats as well as aspiring ordinary urban people of wealth.

In 1781, suspicions arose about the solvency of the regime when the finance minister, who had kept the extent of the subsidies for the American revolutionaries a secret, quit. But the government continued to borrow, even though bad weather leading to two poor harvests in 1786–1787 diminished tax revenues. The hardship caused by these 2 years became crucial for the eventual revolution in 1789: Without reserves in grain and animals, the peasants suffered severe famine and grew increasingly angry when government imports intended to help ended up in the hands of profiteers and hoarders.

By 1788, the government was unable to make payments on short-term loans and had to hand out promissory notes, with bankruptcy looming in the background. As in Britain in the 1760s, a reform of the tax system became unavoidable. At first, the king sought to initiate this reform with the help of a council of appointed notables. When this failed, he held general elections for a popular assembly to meet in Versailles (called the "Estates-General," last convened in 1614). Voters, defined as males over 25 who were French and paid taxes, met in constituent meetings in their districts across France, according to their "estate" as clergy, aristocrats, or commoners. Peasants met in large numbers in the "Third Estate," or commoner meetings; but the deputies they elected to meet in Paris were overwhelmingly administrators, lawyers, doctors, academics, businessmen, and debt holders. At the request of the king, the deputies composed petitions in which they listed their grievances about taxes, waste, luxury at court, and ministerial "despotism" to form the basis for the reform legislation.

The most famous among the petitions was the pamphlet of the priest (*abbé*) Emmanuel-Joseph Sieyès [See-YES], entitled *What Is the Third Estate?* Sieyès was elected as a commoner from Paris and became one of the leading intellectual figures in the revolution. In his pamphlet he put forward the revolutionary idea that the French nation of 25 million *was* the Third Estate, while the other two estates, totaling 200,000 members, were no more than a tiny fraction. The Third Estate, embodying Rousseau's idea of the "general will" of the nation, should alone form the "National Assembly" and translate this general will into a constitution, fiscal reform, and the abolition of aristocratic privileges.

Outbreak of the Revolution   Amid widespread unrest and rioting among peasants in many places in France and workers in Paris, the Third Estate now outmaneuvered the other estates and the king. In June 1789 they seceded from the Estates-General and relocated to a local tennis court where they swore an oath not to disband until they had formed a constitution. Following this Tennis Court Oath, they declared themselves a National Assembly. Louis XVI had initially been favorably inclined toward the Third Estate since the other two estates had rejected the government's reform plans. But he changed his mind after the Third Estate's declaration. Pressured by the pro-aristocracy faction at court, he issued a veiled threat that if it would not support his reforms, "I alone should consider myself their [the people's] representative." The king then reinforced his troops in and around Paris and Versailles and dismissed his popular finance minister, Jacques Necker (1732–1804), who had brought some famine relief in spring. Parisians, afraid of an imminent military occupation of the city, swarmed through the streets on July 14, 1789, and provisioned themselves with arms and gunpowder from arsenals, gunsmith shops, and the Bastille, the royal fortress and prison inside Paris, which they stormed. Thus,

The French Revolution. The French Revolution began with the storming of the Bastille for weapons and gunpowder on July 14, 1789 (top left). It gained momentum when Parisian women marched to Versailles, demanding that the king reside in Paris and end the famine there (top right). The inevitability of a republic became clear when the king and queen were captured after they attempted to flee (bottom left).

by his vacillation—first inclining to accept the role as a constitutional monarch, then switching to a reassertion of absolutism—Louis XVI lost the initiative.

Three Phases of Revolution The French Revolution, unfolding from 1789 to 1799, went through three phases: constitutional monarchy (1789–1792), radical republicanism (1792–1795), and military consolidation (1795–1799). The first phase began with the "great fear" of near anarchy, which reigned during July and August 1789. People in the provinces, mostly peasants, chased their aristocratic and commoner landlords from their estates. Paris, too, remained in an uproar since food supplies, in spite of a good harvest, remained spotty. Agitation climaxed in October when thousands of working women, many with arms, marched from Paris to Versailles, forcing the king to move to Paris and concern himself directly with their plight.

No longer threatened by the king, the National Assembly issued the Declaration of the Rights of Man and of the Citizen (1789), subjected the Catholic Church to French civil law (1790), established a constitutional monarchy (1791), and issued laws ending the unequal taxes of the Old Regime (1792). The principal author of the Declaration of the Rights of Man and of the Citizen was Marie-Joseph Gilbert du Motier, Marquis de Lafayette (1757–1834), descendant of an old French aristocratic family but an early joiner of the Third Estate Assembly. Earlier, Lafayette had made major contributions to the American War for Independence as a military officer, and during the French Revolution he was the commander of the fledgling French National Guard, engaged in efforts to protect what was at this point a constitutional revolution favoring an emerging propertied and urban middle class.

The second phase of the revolution, the period of radical republicanism (1792–1795), began when the revolutionaries found themselves unable to establish a stable constitutional regime. After the king tried unsuccessfully to flee with his unpopular Austrian-born, Habsburg wife Marie-Antoinette from Paris to a monarchist stronghold in eastern France in the summer of 1791, Austria and Prussia threatened to intervene if the king and queen were harmed. The idea of preventive war now gained adherents across the political spectrum as patriotic feelings were invoked: Many aristocratic families had fled to their relatives in Austria and Prussia. In April 1792 the prowar party declared war on its eastern neighbors. Then, in September, republicans seized the government, deposed the king, and held elections for a new assembly to draw up a republican constitution. They separately executed the king and queen in 1793, while the huge *levée en masse*, or conscript army, of the republic regained control of the French borders in 1794 after a lengthy and difficult war against its European neighbors.

In the meantime, a Committee of Public Safety had assumed power and launched the "Reign of Terror," in which perhaps 30,000 citizens were executed. One of its leaders was Maximilien Robespierre (1758–1794), a well-educated lawyer from an old administrative family in northern France who prided himself on his alliance with the laborers and craftspeople of Paris. Because they wore no middle-class silk breeches, they were called *sans-culottes* [san-coo-LOTT] and had become the shock troops of the revolution, particularly in Paris. Robespierre's theory of terror held that France needed to be cleansed of "counter-revolutionaries" and that by surmounting this last difficulty, all the benefits of the revolution would then take effect. Thus, he insisted, "there is only one crime, treason; and one punishment, death." At the same time, the new government was enacting laws designed to remake society along Enlightenment ideology in an astonishingly ambitious fashion. Robespierre, for example, promoted the new state Cult of the Supreme Being, a variation on the idea of deism. The Supreme Being was to be celebrated every tenth day of the new 10-day week in the new "rational" republican calendar that was dated to January 2, 1792. 1792 was now to be Year I of the Republic. The names of months were changed to match the seasons: Germinal for March, Floreal for April, Thermidor for July/August. New systems of measurement that culminated in the metric system were also developed. Egalitarianism in everyday life, such as addressing everyone as "Citizen" or "Citizeness," was pressed; and schemes were even proposed to eliminate private property. But such wholesale changes also alienated increasing numbers of people; and thus, the ranks of "counter-revolutionaries" multiplied as the revolution became more and more radical.

> ### From Declaration of the Rights of Man and of the Citizen
>
> "Article 1. Men are born and remain free and equal in rights. Social distinctions can be based only on public utility.
>
> Article 2. The aim of every political association is the preservation of the natural and imprescriptible rights of man. These rights are liberty, property, security, and resistance to oppression.
>
> Article 3. The source of all sovereignty resides essentially in the nation. No body, no individual can exercise authority that does not explicitly proceed from it."
>
> —Primary Sources of the French Revolution, http://www.thecaveonline.com/APEH/frrevdocuments.html

The Directory   With the foreign wars ended and the danger of a monarchist counterrevolution diminished, many revolutionaries grew fearful of Robespierre's dictatorial powers and use of terror. Plotters arrested him and had him and many supporters guillotined in July 1794. Since this coincided with the new French month of Thermidor, scholars of revolution sometimes refer to such a retreat from radicalism as a "Thermidorean reaction." With a new constitution and bicameral legislature, the revolution entered its third and final phase (1795–1799) under the so-called Directory. But political and financial stability remained elusive, and the Directory increasingly depended on an army that had become professionalized during the defense of the revolution against Austria and Prussia in 1792–1794. Within the army, a brash young brigadier general named Napoleon Bonaparte (1769–1821), of minor aristocratic Corsican descent, was the most promising person to continue the foreign wars successfully. From 1796 to 1798 Napoleon scored major victories against the Austrians in northern Italy and invaded Egypt, which he occupied in

Patterns Up Close | The Guillotine

It is estimated that during the period of the Terror (June 1793–July 1794) the guillotine was responsible for around 1,000 executions in Paris alone and for perhaps as many as 15,000–30,000 throughout France. This iconic symbol of grisly public executions is attended by many myths. Among these is the idea that the guillotine was invented by—and took its name from—one Dr. Guillotin solely for the purpose of speeding up executions of perceived enemies of the republic during the infamous Reign of Terror. Neither of these notions is true however. Indeed, the actual train of events is far more compelling—and ironic.

Far from appearing for the first time during the French Revolution, the first known model of a "decapitation machine" is probably the "Halifax Gibbet," in use in England from around 1300 until 1650. Another model, the "Scottish Maiden," was derived from the Halifax Gibbet and used in 150 executions from 1565 until 1708. It was subsequently turned over to a museum in Edinburgh in 1797 and may have earlier served as a model for the French machine.

The Execution of Marie-Antoinette. During the radical republican period of the French Revolution, the Committee of Public Safety had Queen Marie-Antoinette condemned to death for treason after a sham trial. She was executed on October 16, 1793, 9 months after the execution of her husband, Louis XVI.

When and how did the instrument first appear in France? Ironically, it came as an indirect result of efforts to end the death penalty. During the early days of the revolution the National Assembly pondered the abolition of the death penalty in France altogether. On October 10, 1789, the Assembly was addressed by Dr. Joseph Ignace Guillotin (1738–1814), founder of the French Academy of Medicine and a staunch opponent of capital punishment, who urged the assembly to at the very least find "a machine that beheads painlessly," if they could not ultimately agree to stop executions altogether. Toward this end Guillotin presented sketches of the kind of machine

preparation for an invasion of British India. But thwarted by a pursuing British fleet, he returned to France. There, the Abbé Sieyès, resurgent as a constitutionalist and worried about continued plots against the government, encouraged Napoleon to take over the weak Directory. But Napoleon outfoxed Sieyès and overthrew the Directory altogether in November 1799, thus ending the revolution.

Revival of Empire Napoleon embarked on sweeping domestic reforms that taken together curtailed much of the revolutionary fervor but restored order and stability in France. His crowning achievement was the reform of the French legal system, promulgated in the Civil Code of 1804, which in theory established the equality of all male citizens before the law but in reality imposed restrictions on many revolutionary freedoms. In 1804 Napoleon sealed his power and cloaked he had in mind, but his initial design was rejected, followed by a second rejection on December 1 of the same year. In 1791 the Assembly finally agreed to retain the death penalty, noting that "every person condemned to the death penalty shall have his head severed." But instead of adopting Dr. Guillotin's design, the Assembly accepted a model designed by Dr. Antoine Louis, secretary of the Academy of Surgery; Dr. Louis then turned to a German engineer, Tobias Schmidt, who constructed the first version of the "painless" decapitation machine. It was not until April 25, 1792, that the guillotine, nicknamed "Louisette" after Dr. Louis, claimed its first victim. It is not clear when the name was changed to "Guillotine" (the final "e" was added later), but historians speculate that Dr. Guillotin's early advocacy of quick and painless executions was a major factor. As for Dr. Guillotin himself, the crowning irony was that after fighting a losing battle with the government to change the name of the machine because of embarrassment to his family, he changed his own name and retreated to the obscurity he now craved.

Execution by Guillotine in France, 1929. An Enlightenment innovation, the guillotine was intended to execute humans swiftly and humanely. But the mass executions of the French Revolution turned the guillotine into a symbol of barbarism. It was not until 1977 that France executed its last criminal by guillotine. Today, most countries subscribe to the belief that even criminals have inalienable human rights, the most basic being the right to live.

Questions

- Can the guillotine be viewed as a practical adaptation of Enlightenment ideas? If so, how?

- Why do societies, like France in the late eighteenth century, debate the forms of punishment they use to execute prisoners? What are the criteria by which one type of punishment is considered more humane than others?

himself in legitimacy by crowning himself emperor of the French. Secure in his authority at home, he now struck out on a lengthy campaign of conquest in Europe. Victory followed upon victory from 1805 to 1810, resulting in the French domination of most of continental Europe. The goal was the construction of a European empire, by necessity land-based and in the tradition of the Habsburgs, Ottomans, and Russians. With this empire, he planned to challenge the maritime British Empire that had thwarted the French ambitions in the Seven Years' War. As justification for his empire, ironically, he used the constitutional ideas of the French Revolution, allegedly destined to replace the old absolutist regimes of Europe (see Map 22.2).

The failure of Napoleon's Russian campaign in 1812, however, marked the beginning of the end of Napoleon's grand scheme. Sensing his weakness, Great Britain, Austria, Prussia, and Russia formed an alliance that brought about Napoleon's defeat

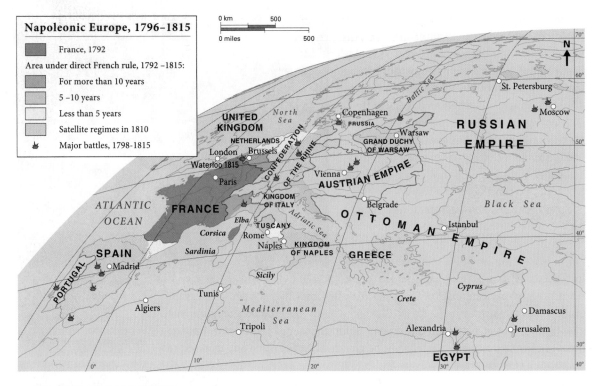

MAP 22.2 Napoleonic Europe, 1796–1815.

at Waterloo in Belgium on June 18, 1815. In exile on the British-controlled island of St. Helena off the west coast of Africa, Napoleon lived until 1821, composing his memoirs. His legacy was equivocal. On the one hand, his revival of traditional imperialism, under the pretense of creating republican nations, only to turn them into vassals of France, discredited constitutionalism. On the other hand, what now could be called a middle class of urban professionals, property owners, and entrepreneurs, liberated by the Napoleonic conquests, was in the process of emerging, which—through the pursuit of constitutional nationalism—began to implement the pattern of modernity that is still with us today.

Enlightenment Culture: Radicalism and Moderation

Enlightenment:
European intellectual movement (1650–1800) growing out of the New Science and based on the ideology of materialism in which matter is considered the basic constituent of reality and mind or reason is a derivative.

The American and French Revolutions flowed out of the culture of the later **Enlightenment** (ca. 1750–1800). This culture both influenced the revolutions and, in turn, was influenced by them. The political heritage of the early Enlightenment (1650–1750), whose twin poles were represented by Thomas Hobbes (1588–1679) and John Locke (1632–1704), had witnessed a new, narrow definition of reality modeled after the New Science (see Chapter 17). The primacy of mathematics as the means to understand nature pioneered by Galileo and the thinkers who championed the New Science had a profound effect on these men—as they did on many of the later Enlightenment *philosophes*. For Hobbes and Locke, reality consisted only of matter detectable by the senses, and mind or reason existed only insofar as it was embodied in matter in the form of consciousness. Hobbes, the more radical thinker and a mathematician himself, viewed consciousness as a kind of bundle in which the passions held reason hostage; Locke, in most ways a more moderate thinker, assumed that reason could dominate the passions. But both radical and moderate strains of these ideas, though undergoing considerable transformation, continued into the later Enlightenment.

Early and Late Enlightenment

The early Enlightenment, of course, embodied modes of thought shared by many other thinkers besides Hobbes and Locke, who are usually categorized as part of a distinct "English Enlightenment." Outstanding figures whose works are still read today include Baruch Spinoza (1632–1677), Gottfried-Wilhelm Leibniz (1646–1716), George Berkeley (1685–1753), and Charles-Louis de Secondat, Baron de Montesquieu (1689–1755), to name just a few. Taken together, the representatives of the early Enlightenment came close to forming a movement in the loose sense of the word: People read each other's works, often corresponded with each other, and sometimes engaged in protracted criticisms of and polemics against each other. What changed in the period after 1750 was not so much the culture; Enlightenment thinkers continued to adhere to the idea of reason or consciousness embedded in the material world as the basic constitution of reality. What

Napoleon. This dazzling portrait of Napoleon by the French painter Jean Ingres (1780–1867) shows the glitzy majesty of the "Little Corporal" who crowned himself emperor in 1804.

gradually grew was the social dimension of the Enlightenment: Thanks to a number of energetic writers popularizing the new ideas, the later eighteenth century saw thousands subscribing to Enlightenment-themed books, pamphlets, and newspapers or attending academies, salons, and lectures. They still were a minority even among the growing middle class of urban administrators, professionals, merchants, and landowners, not to mention the 80 percent of the population engaged in the crafts and in farming. But their voices as radical or moderate "progressives" opposing tradition-bound ministers, aristocrats, or clergy became measurably louder.

It was the late eighteenth-century generation of this vociferous minority that was central to the revolutions in America and France and—a minority within the minority—in the French slave colony Haiti (see Chapter 27). They translated their materialist conception of reality into such "self-evident" ideals as life, liberty, equality, social contract, property, representation, nation, popular sovereignty, and constitution. In the wider, more broadly conceived culture of the Enlightenment, they translated the materialist approach into the creation of new scholarly disciplines and new forms of artistic expression.

Voltaire and Social Criticism   Perhaps the most famous champion of Enlightenment ideas and an accomplished writer, social critic, and *philosophe*, as the French thinkers were known, was François-Marie Arouet, better known by his pen name of Voltaire (1694–1778). He was also the most prolific of the Enlightenment writers, producing more than 2,000 books, articles, and pamphlets during his career. As a young man Voltaire experienced the arbitrary justice of France's absolute monarchy when he was imprisoned in the famous Bastille without trial for insulting a well-connected aristocrat. He managed to have his open-ended sentence commuted to exile in England, where he came away impressed with the balance of the English constitutional monarchy and the findings of the New Science as codified by Isaac Newton. On his return to France he formed a long and fruitful relationship with the Marquise Gabrielle-Emilie du Châtelet (1706–1749), who not only gave him emotional support but was a considerable scholar in her own right. They assembled a library of over 20,000 volumes and produced a formidable array of historical, political, philosophical, and scientific works. Following the death of the marquise, Voltaire accepted an invitation from the "enlightened despot" Frederick the Great of Prussia and moved to his court for a time. His quick temper and outspokenness again landed him in trouble however, and he left Prussia for Geneva and, finally, an estate just inside the French border at Ferney.

The most quotable of the *philosophes*, Voltaire is still remembered today for such sayings as "history is a pack of lies we play on the dead" and "if God did not exist it would be necessary to invent Him." He signed many of the thousands of letters he wrote with the injunction to "crush the infamous thing," by which he meant the Catholic Church. He is also reputed to have come up with the story of Isaac Newton grasping the nature of gravity when an apple fell on his head. But his most famous work was the savagely satirical, picaresque tale *Candide* (1759). As the hero, Candide, lurches from tragic–comic misadventure to misadventure, his experiences lay bare all the venality, corruption, and absurdity of government, religion, and even some Enlightenment ideas themselves. Indeed, Candide's mentor, the thinly disguised figure of Leibniz in the person of Dr. Pangloss, constantly informs anyone who will listen that "all is for the best in this best of all possible worlds"—this while he suffers misfortunes ranging from being hanged to contracting syphilis. Such sunny optimism outraged Voltaire, who wrote the book against the backdrop of the Lisbon earthquake of 1755, which killed perhaps 50,000 people.

Denis Diderot and the *Encyclopédie*

The most visible manifestation of the social broadening of the Enlightenment in 1750–1800 was the differentiation of an autonomous, secular realm of material nature into a multiplicity of self-contained scientific and artistic branches. In the following sections we will look at representative figures in the fields of philosophy, economics, literature, and music. Here, Denis Diderot (1713–1784) will be the focus of attention as a man of many philosophical and literary talents whose most important contribution to the Enlightenment proliferation of secular scholarly and artistic knowledge was the assembly of this knowledge into an encyclopedia.

Diderot was a precocious son of a knife maker in northeast France, who had received his education at a religious school. But he abandoned the study first of theology and then of law in favor of becoming an independent writer, a new occupation in the urban world of later Enlightenment modernity. During his early years he was penniless and came into a modest income only when he sold his library to Empress Catherine the Great of Russia, who also gave him a regular stipend. In the course of a long life, he composed a great variety of works, from philosophy to literature and art criticism. As an ardent materialist, he became an atheist and spent time in prison for his radical views, unable to publish many of his writings.

The *Encyclopédie*, originally conceived as the translation of an earlier (1728) English encyclopedia, began as an independent work when the publisher hired Diderot. Under the editorship of Diderot, the first volume appeared in 1751 as a work that would encompass not only the fields covered by the academic disciplines but all fields of knowledge. Not only that, it was also to have the power "to change men's common way of thinking." For the next quarter of a century, Diderot poured all his energy into writing entries and soliciting contributions from the "republic of letters," as the French Enlightenment thinkers were called. Many entries dealt with delicate subjects, such as science, industry, commerce, freedom of thought, slavery, and religious tolerance, sometimes edited by the cautious publisher without Diderot's knowledge. Publication itself was not easy since the Catholic Church and the French crown banned the project for several years and forced its continuation in secret. But the roughly 4,000 subscribers received their twenty-eighth and last volume in 1772, ready and able to assimilate everything modern, urbane gentlemen and gentlewomen should know.

Philosophy: Rousseau and Kant Diderot and his radical friends contributing to the *Encyclopédie* believed in the primacy of freedom and equality of individuals in their natural state. Political and social institutions, they concluded, should be shaped in such a way that they would guarantee a maximum of freedom and equality for every person. What they brushed aside, however, was the problem that this maximum freedom and its justification could not be inherent in matter; therefore, consciousness would have to come from outside, for example, in the form of morality.

It was this unwillingness of the radicals to admit the necessity of this external or transcendent morality that was the point of departure for the philosopher Jean-Jacques Rousseau (1712–1778). Rousseau, in contrast to his atheist Enlightenment colleagues, was a firm believer in the existing Protestant and Catholic morality. The son of a cultivated and music-loving Geneva watchmaker, Rousseau was a philosophical moderate. To the consternation of the radicals in France, he espoused in his *Social Contract* (1762) the notion that humans had suffered a steady decline from their "natural" state ever since civilization began and imposed its own external authority on them. The radicals held that even though humans had lost their natural state of freedom and equality and had come under arbitrary authority, they were experiencing a steady progress of civilization toward ever improving degrees of freedom and equality. Rousseau did share with his former friends a low opinion of the absolutist French regime, of which he ran afoul just as much as they did. But he had little faith in such concepts as popular sovereignty, elections, and electoral reforms that they propagated. Instead, he believed that people, rallying in a nation, should express their unity directly through a "general will," a sort of direct democracy— more applicable to his native Geneva than a large nation like France.

Immanuel Kant (1724–1804) lived far away from France in Königsberg, East Prussia, which he never left and from which he was an observer of postrevolutionary France. A much more disciplined philosopher than Rousseau, he was nevertheless also a believer in the progress of civilization and history, as expressed in his *Perpetual Peace* (1795). In fact, he quite immodestly thought of himself as having performed a second "Copernican turn" in modernity with his two main books, *Critique of Pure Reason* (1781, second revised edition 1787) and *Critique of Practical Reason* (1787). As a moderate Enlightenment thinker he made the crucial contribution, through a

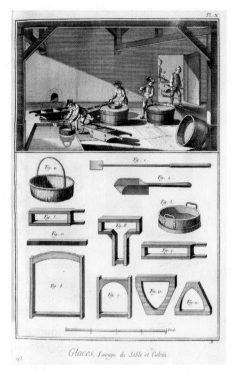

The *Encyclopédie*. Denis Diderot's massive work promoted practical, applied science, such as this illustration showing glass-making.

systematic study of the "antinomies" (internal contradictions) of reason. Pure reason, said Kant, does not reside in material nature and is transcendent; practical reason, which does reside in nature and is immanent, has to be carefully distinguished from pure reason. In contrast to Rousseau, however, with his traditional Christian ethics, Kant sought to build morality on transcendent reason and came to the conclusion that this morality had to be erected on the basis of the *categorical imperative*: Act in such a way that the principle of your action can be a principle for anyone's action. This highly abstract principle entered modern thought as the basis for human rights, with their claim to transcendence or universality, as in the Charter of the United Nations (1945).

Economics   The late Enlightenment saw the birth of the academic discipline of economics. French and British thinkers who were appalled by the inefficient administration of finances, taxes, and trade by the regimes in their countries found the official pursuit of mercantilism wanting. As discussed in previous chapters, mercantilism was the effort to import as little as possible, except from the colonies, and develop domestic crafts so as to export manufactured goods in exchange for the warm-weather commodities of the colonies. Building on the philosophical assumption of the material state of nature, the so-called Physiocrats, most notably François Quesnay (1694–1774) and Anne-Robert-Jacques Turgot (1727–1781), argued that freedom and equality should be the principles of the economy. The state should reduce taxes and other means of control to a minimum so that entrepreneurism in the general population could flourish. It should adopt a policy of *laissez-faire* [les-say-FAIR], that is, "hands-off." The Scottish economist Adam Smith (1723–1790), who spent some time in Paris and was familiar with many of the Physiocrats, developed a British version of laissez-faire economics. In his *Inquiry into the Nature and Causes of the Wealth of Nations* (1776) Smith argued that if the market were largely left to its own devices, without many state regulations and restrictions, it would regulate itself through the forces of supply and demand, appropriate prices, and so forth. It would then move in the direction of increasing efficiency as if guided by "an unseen hand." Like Kant in philosophy, Smith became the founding father of modern economics, whose ideas are still regularly invoked today.

Literature and Music   As in the other fields of modern cultural expression, the Enlightenment also inspired writers, poets, and composers. Noteworthy among the writers and poets were Johann Wolfgang von Goethe (1749–1832) and Friedrich Schiller (1759–1805), sons of a lawyer and a military doctor, respectively. Goethe, a moderate Enlightenment thinker, had a low opinion of his native Lutheranism. He trained as a lawyer but, on the strength of his early writings, found employment under the duke of Weimar in central Germany. Among his numerous poems, novels, plays, and even scientific works (on color), his drama *Faust*, about an ambitious experimenter who sells his soul to the devil to acquire mastery of nature, became a metaphor of modernity—of the technicians and engineers whose dominance of natural forces ran roughshod over environmental concerns.

Schiller, Goethe's younger contemporary, was a trained doctor and later professor of history and philosophy. A moderate Enlightenment thinker, he was greatly disappointed by the violence of the French Revolution. Feeling drawn to Kant's thinking, he strove to harmonize the "sensual passions" and the "formal passions" with which Enlightenment thinkers reflecting on the natural state of humans were wrestling.

Schiller composed major, mostly historical, dramas; and his poem "Ode to Joy" (1785), celebrating the brotherhood and unity of humanity and set to music by Ludwig van Beethoven (1770–1827) in his Ninth Symphony (1824), can be considered the hymn of Enlightenment. As such, it became the anthem of the European Union in 1993.

Wolfgang Amadeus Mozart (1756–1791), son of the music director of the archbishop of Salzburg, was a child prodigy who, as an adult, spent his most productive years at the Habsburg imperial court in Vienna. There, he joined the local lodge of the Freemasons. During the early Enlightenment, Freemasonry had grown from Scottish masonry guilds into one of the many fraternal organizations, friendship circles, salons, and other associations that celebrated sociability. The Freemason slogan was "liberty, fraternity, and equality"— evidently a precursor to the similar slogan of the French Revolution. Toward the end of the 1700s Freemasonry was a substantial organization all across Europe, without, however, being involved in politics. It included many French thinkers, as well as Goethe, the composer Haydn, Benjamin Franklin, and George Washington. Mozart wrote half a dozen pieces for Washington's Masonic lodge, and his opera *The Magic Flute* (1791) is strongly influenced by Masonic concepts and ideas. Together with his older contemporary Franz Joseph Haydn (1732–1809), Mozart was the creator of the classical style, which succeeded the highly complex music of the baroque and was more suited, especially through the new genres of trios and quartets with independent voices, to the cultural sensibilities of the rising urban, educated classes.

Ludwig van Beethoven, from a family of royal court musicians in Cologne, Germany, was likely also a mason during his time in Vienna. (The Austrian emperor ordered the Vienna lodge to be closed down after the restoration of the monarchy, and the records were destroyed.) Beethoven was perhaps the most revolutionary composer of these revolutionary times: Full of admiration for the French Revolution in 1804, he composed his third symphony, the *Eroica* ("Heroic") for Napoleon, a work in which he broke—or departed—from the Classical style. But when Napoleon crowned himself emperor, Beethoven was so deeply disappointed that he is reported to have exploded in anger, ripping the name "Buonaparte" from the title page.

The imperial turn of the French Revolution may be said to have effectively ended the Enlightenment. A few years later, with the fall of Napoleon and the restoration of monarchies, the European kings actively worked on rescinding its effects; and in the face of overwhelming power, the constitutionalists went either silent or underground.

Last Movement of Beethoven's Piano Sonata no. 30 in E Major. Composed in 1820 or 1821, this is one of Beethoven's last piano sonatas.

The Other Enlightenment: The Ideology of Ethnic Nationalism

Most adherents of the Enlightenment in the German-speaking parts of Europe were moderate constitutionalists similar to Rousseau. Like the latter, they sought to combine reason and the "good" passions with tradition. Accordingly, they were constitutionalists but, for the most part, not republicans. In their view, monarchies were part and parcel of a heritage of ethnic, linguistic, and even religious traditions peculiar to a specific nation. They sought to combine the universalism of constitutional nationalism with the ethnic specificity of a people: a *nation*.

Ethnic and Linguistic Traditions

Ethnic and linguistic traditions had existed in Germany for centuries before they became a nationalist ideology. It was not easy to identify these traditions, however, given their great diversity. German thinkers frequently invented traditions and imagined earlier communities, as modern scholars have often charged. But while these charges are often justified, it would be wrong to characterize these traditions as simply fictitious. Aware of the general reality of so many of these traditions, therefore, historians have postulated a "protonationalism," which the German Enlightenment thinkers allegedly turned into an actual **nationalism**. At present, however, both the "imagination" and "protonationalism" interpretations are considered problematic, so historians are again going to the sources in search of more viable interpretations.

In the case of language barriers to unity we can say that when the revolutions of 1776–1789 occurred in America and France, the constitutional nationalists aspired to universal human rights against a background of monarchical states that had existed for centuries within broadly defined borders. The court and administration in the capital had fostered a culture centered on the specific dialect of English or French spoken and written in London or Paris. But the grammatically complex High French which the revolutionary leaders spoke, for example, was manifestly not shared with the rest of the people living within the borders of the French kingdom. Nearly half of the French spoke dialects; the other half, in the northwest and southwest, spoke no French at all. There is evidence that the French revolutionaries expected everyone to learn "good" French, the "male and sublime" language of French culture. But in 1789 it was clear that plurality was a reality, and uniformity was—at best—a dream.

A similar situation existed concerning ethnicity. The constitutional nationalists took it for granted that there had been kings in the past who represented a population that had a common origin, distinguished between themselves and foreigners, had won and lost battles together, shared the same legal tradition, possessed a central administration, sang the same songs and hymns, and so forth. That all this constituted "Frenchness" was quite clear to the revolutionaries, as is evident in many documents; but it formed the background for, not the conscious content of, a revolution that declared universal human rights. In the American colonies, the "Britishness" of the revolution was more complex since, in pursuit of their struggle for independence, the revolutionaries had to pick and choose what they wanted to retain and what to reject. Here, too, the British character of the United States remained largely unexpressed except for what was to be rejected, as enumerated in the Declaration of Independence. Whatever specific ethnolinguistic character appeared in the two revolutions was not overly emphasized.

Germany displayed ethnolinguistic characteristics very similar to those of Britain and France but, of course, was politically fragmented. Even though it had always possessed a central ruling institution, its imperial, rather than royal, constitution made for a much higher degree of decentralization than in the English and French kingdoms. In addition, many Germans in eastern Europe were widely dispersed among peoples with different ethnic–linguistic–religious heritages, such as Czechs, Slovaks, Hungarians, and Poles, to name only the largest ones. In the west, the Alsatians were ethnolinguistically German but under French royal authority. When the

Nationalism: Belief that people who share the same language, history, and sense of identity make up a nation and that every nation has the right to pursue its own destiny.

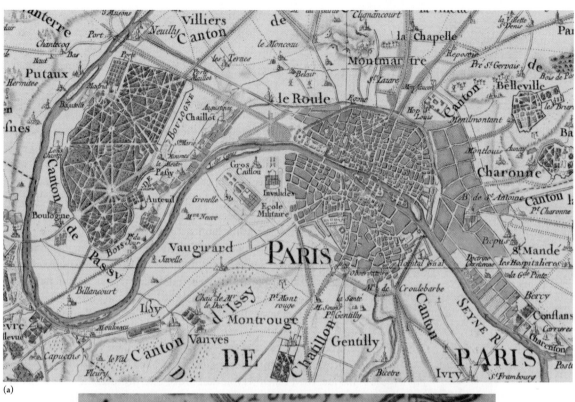

(a)

(b)

Mapping a Nation. Evidence for the emergence of a French national identity can be found by examining two maps that were drawn for the French monarchy at different periods in its history. Commissioned by Louis XIV in 1669, four succeeding generations of the Cassini family produced the first multisheet, topographic map series of an entire country (a). Over 100 years later, in 1789, the Geometric Map of France was finally completed on the eve of the revolution, consisting of 182 sheets that form a 36-foot square when assembled. Shown here is a detail of Paris and its environs. With its recognizable topography and realistic symbols, the map profoundly contributed to the idea of a French nation by articulating a vision of a country whose land was owned by all French citizens. By comparison, a map of France commissioned by King Henry IV in 1594, during a time when France was riven by political and religious strife, shows a completely different spatial geography (b). In contrast to the social patterns of life that can be discerned in the Cassini map, the General Map of France simply concerns itself with depicting the dynastic claims of the monarch. Towns are clearly labeled, but no information is conveyed about the land itself. In the 200 years that separate the two maps, the way the French viewed their land had changed.

In Praise of Language and Heritage

"What a treasure language is when kinship groups grow into tribes and nations! Even the smallest of nations . . . cherishes in and through its language the history, the poetry, and songs about the great deeds of its forefathers. The language is its collective treasure, the source of its social wisdom and communal self-respect. Instruction, games, and dances are connected with it."

—F. M. Barnard, trans. *Johann Gottfried Herder on Social and Political Culture*, p. 165. Cambridge: Cambridge University Press, 1969.

Grimm's Fairy Tales. Perhaps the most famous collection of folktales in the Western tradition, *Children's and Household Stories* (1812) was assembled by Wilhelm and Jakob Grimm as a way to preserve their country's national spirit and to rekindle in their countrymen an appreciation for their Germanic roots. The stories they collected, such as this illustration from *Rapunzel*, were brought together through fieldwork and by peasant women who would visit the brothers and recite stories that awoke "thoughts of the heart."

Enlightenment spread in educated circles, there was clearly an ethnolinguistic background; but in the absence of a central state, the educated urban professionals, administrators, and educators professed a constitutional nationalism tinged with ethnic and linguistic elements.

Herder's Ethnic German Nationalism   A central figure in articulating these ethnolinguistic elements in Germany into what was later to become a German nationalist ideology was Johann Gottfried Herder (1744–1803). Herder's father was an elementary school teacher and Lutheran church warden in eastern Germany. At university, Herder studied with Kant but also with others under whose influence he became familiar with Pietism, a Lutheran version of the medieval Catholic mystical tradition. Employed first as a preacher and then as an administrator at assorted courts in central Germany, he published widely as a literary critic and was on close terms with Goethe and other German Enlightenment figures. Like Locke, he distinguished between negative and positive passions; and like Rousseau, he subverted the exaggerated emphasis on reason by an exploration of aesthetic and emotional "sentiments," as the positive passions were called. When, toward the end of his life, the French Revolution broke out, however, he gave it his full support, to the consternation of the German monarch as well as many of his Enlightenment colleagues who decried the republicanism in the revolution.

In his writings, Herder sought to meld a highly diffuse ethnic heritage into a more or less coherent set of ideas to be preached not only to the educated but to the people in general through school curricula, history, and the arts. His major work, *On the Origin of Language* (1772), contains the core concepts of his new ideology of ethnolinguistic nationalism.

Herder not only focused on the traditions of high culture but also encouraged the collection of folk stories and fairy tales, even though he realized that peasants and laborers were completely outside the nationalism he projected. Similarly, given his interests in mysticism, his extensive references to religion were reflective more of the enlightened but moderate urban, educated population than either the clergy or the Catholic and Lutheran peasants. In principle, however, ethnolinguistic nationalism was open to an incorporation of religion; and thus, this nationalism may be defined as "religio-ethnolinguistic." Finally, while the ethnolinguistic nationalism of Herder's writings centered on "Germanness," it did not exclude pluralism. Far from elevating German culture to the pinnacle of all culture, Herder recognized that other peoples, notably the Slavs, had their own traditions and were therefore entitled to their own nation-states.

Germany's ethnolinguistic version of the Enlightenment received a major boost during the transition from the French Revolution to the Napoleonic wars. The turning point was Napoleon's self-elevation as emperor, as we have already seen in the case of Beethoven. Another influential figure was Johann Gottlieb Fichte

(1762–1814), a student of Kant. In 1806, when the French had defeated Prussia, Fichte turned from his highly abstract Enlightenment thought in the tradition of Kant to flaming patriotic appeals for the liberation from French imperialism.

By this time, a German middle class of urban professionals, administrators, and educators was emerging whose members met at student fraternities, public lectures, salons, musical evenings, and gymnastics clubs. Aroused for the patriotic liberation of their states and political unification into a single Germany, they were deeply disappointed by the restoration of the pre-1789 regional monarchies, which made minimal concessions to constitutionalism. Superior force for the moment cowed them into reluctant acceptance or underground agitation.

The Growth of the Nation-State, 1815–1871

Napoleon's defeat in Russia in 1812 and the Congress in Vienna of 1815 were major turning points in the political development of Europe. Monarchies and aristocracies reappeared throughout the continent, and the restored kings allowed only for the barest minimum of popular representation in parliaments, if at all. In France, where republicans were the most numerous, monarchists and republicans went through several further rounds of revolution before the republican nation-state emerged supreme. The other countries of continental Europe did not go that far; here, constitutional monarchies survived, in spite of a major challenge in 1848. By contrast, in Anglo-America, the supremacy of constitutionalism was unchallenged during the 1800s. Here, the nation-state grew with no disruptions, gradually incorporating more citizens into the constitutional process. The exception in the United States, however, was the Civil War, over the question of slavery and the incorporation of African-Americans into full citizenship. The victory of the Union, however, guaranteed and even strengthened the continuation of the pattern of modern nation-state formation.

Restoration Monarchies, 1815–1848

For a full generation, monarchists in Europe sought to return to the politics of absolutism. This return required repression and elaborate political manipulation to keep the now identifiable middle class of public employees, professionals, schoolteachers, and early factory entrepreneurs away from meaningful political participation. A "Concert of Europe" emerged in which rulers avoided intervention in the domestic politics of fellow monarchs, except in cases of internal unrest when they appealed to their neighbors for support. This was especially the case in Italy, where Austria intervened in several places and at several occasions to suppress nationalist agitation.

The Congress of Vienna   European leaders met in 1815 at Vienna after the fall of Napoleon in an effort to restore order to a war-torn continent. The driving principle at the session was monarchical conservatism, articulated mainly by Prince Klemens von Metternich (1773–1859), Austria's prime minister. An opponent of

> **Germanness**
>
> "Thus was the German nation [*Volk*] placed—sufficiently united within itself by a common language and a common way of thinking, and sharply enough severed from the other peoples—in the middle of Europe, as a wall to divide races not akin.... Only when each people, left to itself, develops and forms itself in accordance with its own peculiar quality ... does the manifestation of divinity appear in its true mirror as it ought to be."
>
> —Johann Gottlieb Fichte. *Thirteenth Address, Addresses to the German Nation.* Edited by George A. Kelly, p. 190. New York: Harper Torch Books, 1968.

Contempt for Constitutionalism

"We see this intermediary class abandon itself with a blind fury and animosity ... to all the means which seem proper to assuage its thirst for power, applying itself to the task of persuading kings that their rights are confined to sitting upon a throne, while those of the people are to govern, and to attack all that centuries have bequeathed as holy and worthy of man's respect."

—"Confession of Faith, Metternich's Secret Memorandum to the Emperor Alexander," in Clemens Wenzel Lothar Metternich (Fürst von), *Memoirs of Prince Metternich, 1773–1829*, ed. Prince Richard Metternich and trans. Mrs. Alexander Napier, vol. 3, p. 468 (New York: Charles Scribner's Sons, 1881).

constitutional nationalism, now called "republicanism," Metternich was determined to resist the aspirations of the still struggling middle classes outside France, whose members, as he saw it, were driven by the "evil" of "presumption." Metternich depicted this presumption as a "moral gangrene."

To accomplish his objective of reinstituting kings and emperors ruling by divine grace, Metternich had the congress hammer out two principles: legitimacy and balance of power. The principle of legitimacy was conceived as a way to both recognize exclusive monarchial rule in Europe and to reestablish the borders of France as they were in 1789. The principle of the balance of power involved a basic policy of preventing any one state from rising to dominance over any other. In the case of internal uprisings, member states promised to come to each other's aid. Members agreed to convene at regular intervals in the future in what they called the "Concert," so as to ensure peace and tranquility in Europe. What is remarkable about this is that with only minor exceptions this policy of the balance of power remained intact down to 1914 (see Map 22.3).

As successful as the implementation of these two principles was, the solution devised for the German territories—now no longer with an overall ruler since the Holy Roman Empire was dissolved in 1806—was less satisfactory. The Congress of Vienna created an unwieldy and weak confederation of 39

MAP **22.3** **Europe After the Congress of Vienna.**

Europe After the Congress of Vienna

—— Border of German Confederation

German states, including the empire of Austria and the kingdoms of Prussia, Denmark, and the Netherlands. Prussia and Austria promptly embarked on a collision course over dominance in the confederation, with Prussia keeping the initiative and creating a customs union in 1834. Prussia's main purpose in this was to find outlets for its rising industrial and commercial interests in the northern German Ruhr region. Constitutionalist and republican Germans disliked the confederation as well since they had no meaningful voice in it. Thus, by resolving the overall issue of coexistence among the German states, but not of their fragmentation, the Congress was only partially successful.

Further Revolutions in France   In keeping with the principle of legitimacy, the Congress restored the French Bourbon monarchy with the coronation of King Louis XVIII (r. 1814–1824), a brother of Louis XVI. Louis, even though determined to restore full absolutist powers, was indecisive as to which republican institutions to abolish first. Playing for time, he tolerated the "White Terror," during which the returning aristocracy and other royalists pursued revenge for their sufferings during the revolution. When Louis died in 1824 the conservatives succeeded in putting Charles X (1824–1830), a second brother of Louis XVI, on the throne. Charles took the extreme course of restoring the property of the aristocracy lost during the revolution and reestablishing the crown's ties to the Catholic Church.

Republican reaction to Charles's restoration policy was swift. In two elections, the republicans won a majority and overthrew the king in the 1830 election. But they stopped short of abolishing the monarchy and elevated Louis-Philippe (1830–1848), son of a pro-republican duke who had been guillotined and had fought in the republican guards during 1789–1792, to the throne. Under this "bourgeois king," as he was sometimes caricatured, however, rising income gaps in the middle class as well as difficult living conditions among the nascent industrial working class led to new tensions. In the ensuing revolution of 1848, in which thousands of workers perished, the adherents of restoration and republicanism attempted another compromise: Louis-Philippe went into exile, and the parliament elected Louis-Napoleon Bonaparte (r. 1848–1852; self-declared emperor 1852–1870), a nephew of the former emperor, as president.

Rebellion. Following the successful revolution of 1848 that ended the monarchy of Louis-Philippe in France, similar uprisings broke out across Europe. This image shows the Berlin Alexander Square barricades of March 1848.

Uprisings Across Europe   After the revolution in Paris, uprisings occurred in the spring of 1848 in cities such as Berlin, Vienna, Prague, Budapest, Palermo, and Milan, as well as in three Irish counties. In Prussia the king seemingly bowed to pressure from revolutionaries and promised constitutional reforms. In Austria, hit by uprisings in multiple cities and by multiple nationalities, both the emperor and Metternich, the driving forces of 1815, resigned. The successor with Russian help slowly regained military control over the Italians, Czechs, and Hungarians, as well as his own Austrians.

In the German Confederation, also hit by uprisings, moderate and republican delegates convened a constitutional assembly in Frankfurt in May 1848. This assembly elaborated the basic law for a new, unified state for German speakers and elected a provisional government. The new hard-line Austrian emperor, however, refused to let go of his non-German subjects. Therefore, the constitution joined only the German Federation and Prussia (also with non-German minorities) into a unitary state, with the provision for a future addition of German-speaking Austria. Against strong resistance by republicans, the delegates offered the Prussian king a new hereditary imperial crown in the name of the German people. But the king, unwilling to accept the principle of popular sovereignty, refused the crown "of clay." This refusal turned the tide against this Frankfurt Assembly. Moderate delegates departed, and radical ones instigated revolts. Prussian troops stepped in and relieved a group of grateful regional monarchs of their insurrectionists. By July 1849, the provisional Frankfurt government had come to an end and Germany's constitutional experiment had ended.

Irish Nationalism   In Ireland, ethnolinguistic nationalism found adherents among groups of urban professionals and educators in the early 1800s. Since they were acutely aware that Ireland did not possess much in terms of a literary-artistic tradition, they sought to position the Catholic tradition as a nationalizing element, around which to center nationalism, while others were more firmly wedded to secularism. In the uprising of 1848 the secularists won out. But the example of Catholicism in Ireland demonstrates that ethnolinguistic nationalism could easily be extended into the religious heritage if desired, foreshadowing trends of the twentieth century.

The events of 1848 had their origins in the Young Irelander opposition movement against the British Union Act of 1800. Through newspapers, lectures, and election campaigns this movement demanded a repeal of the act, frequently invoking Catholic "Irishness." When in 1845 a potato blight broke out on the island (which probably arrived through guano fertilizer imports mined in potato-growing Peru) causing a severe famine, perhaps one-fifth of the population perished. Only mass emigration to the United States alleviated further suffering. The Young Irelanders vehemently (and justifiably) accused the British government of inaction. Groups of Young Irelanders, tenant farmers, and even a few landlords rose in insurrection and battled police forces in three counties. But they were no match for the police, and the revolt quickly collapsed. Ethnolinguistic nationalism with elements of Catholicism had not yet coalesced into a full nationalist ideology.

Ethnolinguistic Nationalism in Italy   Italy was as fragmented politically as Germany, but unlike Germany it was also largely under foreign domination. Austria controlled the north directly and the center indirectly through relatives from the house of Habsburg. The monarchy of Piedmont in the northwest, the Papal States in the center, and the kingdom of Naples and Sicily (the "Two Sicilies") were independent but administratively and financially weak. After the Metternich restoration, the Italian dynasties had made concessions to constitutionalists; but Austria repressed uprisings in 1820–1821 and 1831–1832 without granting liberties. The republican Carbonari inspired both uprisings; they were members of the crafts guild of "charcoal burners" who had formed fraternities similar to the Freemasons during the eighteenth century. After their decisive defeat in 1831, the remnants formed the "Young Italy" movement.

Realistic second-generation politicians of the Restoration recognized that the middle-class ethnolinguistic nationalism coming to the fore in 1848 was a potent force that could be dipped into. By remobilizing this force in the 1860s, they would be able to end state fragmentation and make Italy and Germany serious players in the European Concert. These politicians were more sympathetic toward French-style constitutionalism than the Restoration politicians but still opposed to republicanism. Their pursuit of "Realpolitik"—exploitation of political opportunities—resulted in 1870–1871 in the transformations of the Italian kingdom of Piedmont and the German Empire of Prussia into the nation-states of Italy and Germany.

The Italian politician who did the most to realize Italy's unification was the prime minister of Piedmont-Sardinia, Count Camillo di Cavour (1810–1861). Cavour was the scion of an old aristocratic family in northwestern Italy with training as a military officer. While in the army, he read widely among French and British political philosophers and became a constitutional nationalist. A supporter of Adam Smith's liberal trade economics, he imported guano fertilizer and grew cash crops, like sugar beets, on his estate. As prime minister he was the driving force behind the development of railroads, first in Piedmont and later in Italy. With the backing of his similarly liberal-minded king, Victor Emanuel II (r. 1849–1878), he engineered the unification of most of Italy under decidedly trying circumstances.

Cavour began the unification process in 1858 with lukewarm support from Louis Napoleon of France for Piedmontese military action against Austria. When Cavour was victorious, however, France withdrew its support (fearing a powerful Piedmont) and Austria did not budge from its fortifications in northern Italy. Through adroit maneuvering, Cavour was able to arrange for a favorable plebiscite in north-central Tuscany and Emilia in 1859, gaining these two regions from Austria for Piedmont. A year later Cavour occupied the Papal States and accepted the offer of Giuseppe Garibaldi (1807–1882) to add adjoining Naples and Sicily to a now nearly unified Italy.

Garibaldi, a mariner from Nice in the northwest (present-day France), was a Carbonari and Young Italy republican nationalist with a colorful career as a freedom fighter not only in Italy but also in Brazil and Uruguay. Dressed in his trademark red gaucho shirt with poncho and sombrero, the inspiring Garibaldi attracted large numbers of volunteers wherever he went to fight. Despairing of any republican future for Italy, he threw in his lot with Piedmont and, after invading Naples and Sicily and deposing its monarch in 1860, delivered these two regions to Cavour. Cavour died shortly afterward and, thus, did not live to see Piedmont transform itself into Italy in 1870, when it gained Venice from Austria and Rome from France in the wake of the Prussian–Austrian war of 1870–1871. But he clearly was the power politician who laid the decisive groundwork.

Giuseppe Garibaldi. Garibaldi was an Italian nationalist who, in collaboration with Count Cavour, prime minister of the kingdom of Piedmont, contributed decisively to the unification of Italy. Garibaldi and his "Red Shirts" were able to seize Sicily and Naples from its Bourbon-descended monarch in 1860. He then unified his conquests with the constitutional kingdom of Piedmont to form the nucleus of Italy, which was fully unified a decade later.

Bismarck and Germany　In contrast to Italy, neither King Wilhelm I (r. 1861–1888) nor his chancellor (prime minister) Otto von Bismarck (in office 1862–1890) had deep sympathies for constitutionalism. By combining their antipathies

and forming a coalition of convenience, they succeeded in keeping the constitutionalists in the Prussian parliament in check. But they realized they could dip into the ethnolinguistic nationalism that had poured forth in 1848, using it for power politics: Realpolitik.

Bismarck was a Prussian aristocrat with a legal education rather than a military career. He was multilingual, widely read, and experienced in the diplomacy of the European Concert. He realized that Prussia, a weak player in the Concert, had a chance for greater influence only if the kingdom could absorb the German Federation. For Prussia to do so, Bismarck argued, it had to progress from the talk about unification, as in Frankfurt, to military action, using "blood and iron." From the time of his appointment to 1871, he systematically maneuvered Prussia into an internationally favorable position for the coup that would eventually bring unification: war with France.

First, he exploited a succession crisis in Denmark for a combined Prussian–Austrian campaign to annex Denmark's southern province of Schleswig-Holstein in 1865. Then, when Austria objected to the terms of annexation, he declared war on Austria. After Prussia succeeded in defeating Austria, Bismarck dissolved the German Confederation and annexed several German principalities. In France, Louis-Napoleon Bonaparte was greatly concerned about the rising power of Prussia. He had carried out a coup d'état in 1852, ending the Second Republic and declaring himself emperor—an act that prompted the always quotable Karl Marx to claim that "history always repeats itself, the first time as tragedy, the second time as farce." A distraction on his eastern flank was not at all what Emperor Napoleon III desired.

But he carelessly undermined his precarious strength. First, he prevented a relative of King Wilhelm from succeeding to the throne of Spain when it fell vacant. But when he demanded through his minister, then meeting with Wilhelm at the spa in Bad Ems, additional assurances that Prussia would not put forward candidates

Prussian Victory. After Napoleon III's defeat and surrender in the Franco–Prussian War of 1870–1871, French republican politicians declared the Third Republic and continued the war. But in spite of heroic defensive efforts, Prussian troops occupied Paris in January 1871 (the photo shows the victory parade on the Champs-Elysées) and in Versailles declared the unification of Germany and the foundation of the Second German Empire.

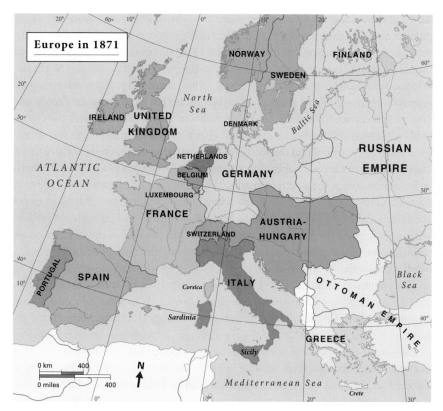

MAP **22.4** **Europe in 1871.**

for any thrones in the future, the canny Bismarck outmaneuvered him. When King Wilhelm politely refused the demand, the chancellor edited the refusal in such a way as to make it insulting to the French. France then declared war on Prussia and was defeated in the crucial battle of Sedan in 1870. Now Bismarck had the upper hand for which he had been diligently working. He used it to annex Alsace-Lorraine from the French, carried out the final unification of Germany, and elevated the new state to the status of an empire in 1871 (see Map 22.4).

Nation-State Building in Anglo-America, 1783–1865

After the independence of the United States in 1783, both the United States and Great Britain were free to pursue their versions of constitutional nation-state development. In the United States, the revolutionaries, as well as subsequent generations, remained faithful to the idea of a republican nation. The restoration of monarchies and ethnolinguistic nationalism that complicated nation-state formation in Europe did not affect the United States and gave rise to a long tradition among American historians of claiming American "exceptionalism." While it is indeed true that the growth of the United States in the 1800s followed its own trajectory, there is also no question that the underlying pattern of modern nation-state formation was very similar to that of Europe. The same conclusion can be drawn concerning Great Britain, which was exceptional in that it became the dominant seaborne world empire but similarly came together as a nation on Atlantic islands subordinating English, Scottish, and Welsh ethnolinguistic traditions to a national constitutionalism.

The United States   During the first half of the nineteenth century the newly independent American states not only prospered but also began a rapid westward expansion. As this process unfolded toward 1850 it became increasingly apparent that sectional differences were developing in the process. Whereas the North developed an industrial and market-driven agricultural economy, the South remained primarily agrarian, relying heavily upon the production of cotton for its economic vitality. Even more, the South relied upon vast numbers of slaves to work the cotton fields of plantations. Cotton was the main fiber for the industrial production of textiles, and it not only defined the wealth of the plantation owners but led them to see chattel slavery as the only viable means to keep the "cotton kingdom" prosperous. In defense of its stance, the South increasingly relied upon the notion of states' rights in opposition to federal control. With the acquisition of new territory extending to the Pacific coast after the war with Mexico from 1846 to 1848 and the constant push of settlement beyond the Mississippi, the vital question of which of the new territories would become "free states" and "slave states" resulted in increasing tensions between North and South.

The result was an attempt by a number of southern states to secede and form a new government, the Confederate States of America. When the new administration of President Abraham Lincoln attempted to suppress this movement, the disastrous American Civil War (1861–1865) began. Resulting in an enormous loss of life—more than 600,000 combatants on both sides were killed—the Civil War finally ended with a northern victory in 1865. There were several major results of the conflict, not least of which was an enhanced unification of the country during the occupation of the southern states by federal troops enforcing the policies of the Reconstruction (1865–1877). First, Lincoln's concept of the primacy of national government over individual assertions of states' rights was now guaranteed. Second, slavery was abolished and slaves were granted full citizenship. Third, rebuilding of the country and opening of the west resulted in a remarkable period of growth, facilitated especially by the expansion of a national network of railroads. By 1900, about 200,000 miles of uniform-gauge track crisscrossed the country and the United States was on its way to becoming the world's predominant industrial power (see Map 22.5). Moreover, there emerged a growing consensus that the American nation had come together after a divisive war, and this was aided by the adoption of signs like the Pledge of Allegiance to the national flag, along with a national anthem, "The Star-Spangled Banner." As a subtle testament to this national unification, historians have noted that before the war people said "the United States *are* . . .; after the war, it became "the United States *is*. . . ."

Despite the new bonds of national unification, the price of reintegrating the old South into the new order was the end of Reconstruction and the reversion over the course of two generations to an imposition of a de facto peonage on its black citizens. Indeed, between 1877 and 1914 state legislatures in the South systematically stripped African Americans of voting rights by means of poll taxes and literacy tests and imposed formal and informal segregation in social and public accommodations. These were enforced by law and all too often by lynchings and other forms of violence. In order to accommodate the sensibilities of white southerners regarding race, most northern policy and opinion makers gradually backed away from the views espoused by the champions of racial equality during Reconstruction and gave tacit acquiescence to southern efforts to retain white hegemony. The drive for full

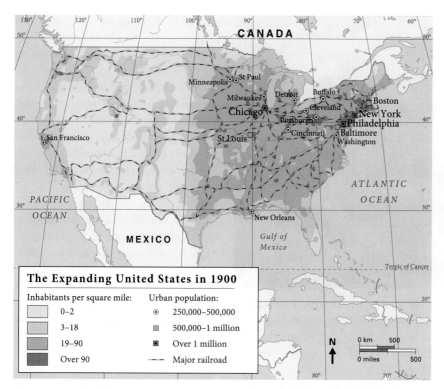

MAP 22.5 **The Expanding United States in 1900.**

civil rights would thus occupy a sizeable share of American domestic policy debates throughout the twentieth century.

Reform Measures   As in other Western nation-states, rapid industrialization produced social and labor unrest, resulting in the reforming initiatives of the Progressive era, which extended from 1890 to 1914. Although the later nineteenth century is referred to as the Gilded Age, epitomized by the staggering wealth of industrial tycoons like Andrew Carnegie (1835–1919) and John D. Rockefeller (1839–1937), all was not well beneath the surface. Big business had grown to such an extent that in the early 1900s a few hundred firms controlled two-fifths of all American manufacturing. The "trust buster" president, Theodore Roosevelt (r. 1901–1909), and Congress ended the monopolies of many firms, Rockefeller's Standard Oil among them, which had to cut itself up into 30 smaller companies. A new Department of Commerce and Labor (1903) and the Pure Food and Drug and Meat Inspection Acts (1906) helped the hard-pressed workers and consumers. With the Federal Reserve Act (1913) and the Federal Trade Commission Act (1914) Congress created an overall framework for the supervision of the financial and business sectors. As many contemporaries realized, a free market prospered only with at least a minimum of regulations.

Great Britain   The pattern of constitutional nation-state construction that Britain pursued in the eighteenth and nineteenth centuries was somewhat steadier. It remained more or less uninterrupted even during the Napoleonic wars, during

Evicted. Demolishing the houses of evicted tenants was ruthlessly practiced by British authorities in Ireland, particularly during the famine years of 1847–50. The wholesale destruction of homes—and livelihoods—horrified many contemporary observers, so much so that when Queen Victoria visited Ireland in 1849 she was publicly rebuked: "Thy royal name must be connected in future history with the astounding record of extermination of our unhappy race." This 1890 painting by Elizabeth Thompson, Lady Butler (1846–1933), one of the most accomplished English women artists of the time, is all the more striking because most of her other works portray the heroism and valor of British soldiers.

which Great Britain was the one enemy Napoleon was unable to harm. As was the Ile de France around Paris during the revolution and throughout the nineteenth century, England remained the core of the nation, to which the other British nationalities had to acculturate culturally if not ethnically. Scotland, traditionally divided between the highlands and lowlands, developed a greater sense of its own identity only slowly. The development began on the level of folklore, with the revival of Scottish dress and music (clan tartans, kilts, and bagpipes). More serious constitutional issues came to the fore in 1853 when the Scots, upset by what they thought was more attention paid by the government to Ireland, founded an association for the vindication of Scottish rights. The Scottish demand for home rule found sympathetic ears in the Liberal Party but not among the Conservatives. In 1885, the government established the position of secretary for Scotland. But home rule would come only after World War I.

The Welsh were even less satisfied with being ruled by London. In part this was due to the relatively early industrialization in Wales and the development of a Welsh working class, which had organized uprisings in the 1830s. Religious issues, mostly related to opposition to the Church of England among nonconformists (e.g., Methodists, Quakers, and Presbyterians), and education issues surrounding the so-called Treachery of the Blue Books added to the unrest. A governmental report of 1847, bound in blue covers, found that education in Wales was substandard: Sunday schools were the only schools offering education in Welsh, while regular schools were based on English for children who spoke only Welsh. Throughout the report ethnic stereotypes proliferated, documenting the fissures in the English-dominated acculturation process. As in Scotland, home rule came only after the Great War.

In Ireland, after the Great Famine of 1845–1849 already discussed in this chapter, rural production and land issues remained the main points of contention around which Irish demands for home rule and independence crystallized. A Protestant Irish landlord class still controlled most of the land in the second half of the nineteenth century. During the worldwide Long Depression of 1873–1896 Irish tenant farmers received low prices for their crops but no reductions in rent. Land reform became a large issue, woven closely into the politics of self-determination. A "land war" ensued between organized tenants and nationalists, on the one hand, and the British Army, on the other. It eventually led in 1898 to local self-rule for the Irish and in 1903–1909 to land reform. Home rule also did not come before World War I.

Apart from the issue of the constitutional nation-state, Britain's Parliament took cognizance of the growing middle class and the need to enact reforms for the working class. A contest between Liberal and Conservative governments ensued over the enactment of increasingly inclusive reforms. For example, the Great Reform Bill of 1832 shifted seats from southern districts to the more industrialized center and north. The result is often called the "victory of the middle classes" because industrial interests now took control of Parliament away from the propertied aristocracy. Further reforms followed: The repeal of the Corn Laws in 1846 liberated imports and made grain cheaper, and the Second Reform Act of 1867 extended the franchise to larger numbers of working-class voters. The end result was not only that Britain escaped the revolutions of 1848 but also that the British electorate was largely united during the Victorian period in its support for British imperialism around the globe.

Romanticism and Realism: Philosophical and Artistic Expression to 1850

The Victorian period, named after the long reign of Queen Victoria of Britain (r. 1837–1901), was a time in which Europeans and Americans alike celebrated the sobriety, frugality, and discipline of the emancipated urban middle class. While the perception of the superficial, extravagant, and dissolute aristocracy had now lost some of its power, the working classes—with their allegedly coarse, violent, and gullible ways—were increasingly seen as a threat to the social stability and moral fiber of the nation. This new "realist" middle class aesthetic at the end of the century was in many ways the opposite of the earlier "romantic" one, which had emerged from the Enlightenment at the beginning of the century. Early on, the liberation from political and artistic absolutism was exhilarating; as time wore on, however, the grim realities of the industrial transformation made this liberty considerably less exciting and more disturbing.

Romanticism: Intellectual and artistic movement that emphasized emotion and imagination over reason and sought the sublime in nature.

Romanticism

As we have seen, Rousseau and Kant had demonstrated the limitations of Enlightenment materialist thought in which *embodied reason*, surrounded by the senses and passions, constituted reality. Kant, therefore, proposed that reason, or mind, is in part independent or transcendent, containing the categories without which any talk about senses and passions would not even be possible. Philosophers, writers, composers, and painters of the period of **romanticism** drew the conclusion that the mind was entirely independent, creating aesthetic categories out of its own powers. Not all romantic thinkers and artists went this far, but for romantics creativity became absolute. Indeed, the stereotype of the creative "genius" heroically attempting to cross imaginative thresholds to grasp at transcendence became firmly implanted in the public imagination during this time.

Dialectic: The investigation of truth by discussion; in the context here, dialectic refers to Hegel's belief that a higher truth is comprehended by a continuous unification of opposites.

Philosophers and Poets The one philosopher who, building on Kant, postulated the complete freedom of mind or spirit was Georg Wilhelm Friedrich Hegel (1770–1831). The most systematic of the so-called idealist philosophers in Germany, Hegel asserted that all thought proceeded dialectically from the "transcendental ego" to its opposite, matter, and from there to the spiritualized synthesis of nature. This **dialectic** permeates his entire "system" of philosophy.

Nature as Teacher

One impulse from a vernal wood
May teach you more of man,
Of moral evil and of good,
Than all the sages can.

"The Tables Turned; An Evening Scene on the Same Subject," (1798). William Wordsworth, *The Complete Poetical Works*, ed. Henry Reed, p. 393 (Philadelphia: Trautmann & Hayes, 1854).

A parallel "ego-"centered creative poetry burst forth, with William Wordsworth (1770–1850), Samuel Taylor Coleridge (1772–1834), and Percy Bysshe Shelley (1792–1822) in Britain. In America, the "transcendentalist" Ralph Waldo Emerson (1803–1882) was the self-declared prophet of the absolute, imaginative self. Under Emerson's influence, the American Emily Dickinson (1830–1886) wrote poetry welling up "from the interior drama" of imagination. An afterglow of this imaginative absolute was still present in the later French symbolist Arthur Rimbaud (1854–1891), who sought ineffable beauty and pure feeling in the mere evocation by words, rather than formal rhyme.

Composers   While the romantics were struggling to express the sublime, ephemeral evocation of beauty with words that were at least in part concrete, the romantic composers had no such problems. The transitional figure of the German Ludwig van Beethoven, already discussed above, and the Frenchman Hector Berlioz (1803–1869) pioneered the new genre of program music, with the *Pastoral Symphony* (Symphony #6) and the *Symphonie phantastique*, respectively, emphasizing passion and emotional intensity and the freedom of the musical spirit over traditional form. From among the emerging middle class, eager to develop their romantic sensibilities and play music at home, a veritable explosion of composers erupted during the first half of the 1800s, such as Nicolò Paganini (1782–1840), Franz Schubert (1797–1828), Felix Mendelssohn (1809–1847), Frédéric Chopin (1810–1849), Robert Schumann (1810–1856), and Johannes Brahms (1833–1897). Often composing at a furious rate, these musicians were also virtuosi on the violin or piano, playing their own new musical forms and traveling on concert circuits all across Europe.

Painters   Similar to music, the medium of painting also lent itself to the expression of romantic feelings of passion and the mind's overflowing imaginative aesthetics. Not surprisingly, the proliferation of romantic painters numbered in the hundreds, and a small handful will have to suffice for discussion here. The common feature of these painters is that they departed from the established academic practices and styles. They either let nature dictate the direction and extent of their absorption into it or expressed their personal impressions forcefully with new, dramatic topics.

A follower of the first direction was Caspar David Friedrich (1774–1840) in Germany, who drew solitary figures absorbed by and absorbing an all-encompassing nature. Similarly, John Constable (1776–1837) was a British painter of superficially conventional landscapes that dramatically expressed the shapes and forces of nature. The French Théodore Géricault [Ge-ree-CO] (1791–1824) and Eugène Delacroix (1798–1863) followed the second direction and depicted dramatic or unusual scenes, as well as revolutionary gestures. Géricault caused a scandal when he exhibited *Raft of the Medusa* (1819), a float packed with sailors but without a captain: The conventions of traditional society demanded an orderly social hierarchy, even if in distress. Delacroix sought to express the drama of the French revolution of 1830 as well as Orientalist themes, for example, in *The Women of Algiers in Their Apartment* (1834), showing three women in languid poses with a black slave girl. While holding still firmly to the Renaissance style of perspective, light, and shadow, the turn to romantic freedom in these painters is unmistakable.

(a)

(b)

Romantic Art. Romantic painters expressed an absorbing, encompassing nature in their art. Note the barely recognizable steam-powered train in this painting (a) by J. M. W. Turner, *Rain, Steam, and Speed: The Great Western Railway* (1844). Romantic painters also depicted dramatic or exotic scenes relating to revolutions or foreign lands, such as the languid, bored harem scene in *The Women of Algiers in Their Apartment* (1834) by Delacroix (b).

Novels and Stories   As in the other art forms, romanticism in literature appears in heroines or heroes and their passions and sentiments. In the still strongly late Enlightenment-informed prose of the British author Jane Austen (1775–1817), witty and educated urbane society shapes the character and sensibilities of young women and prepares them for their reward, that is, love of the proper gentleman and marriage to him. These plots are developed with great intricacy in, for example, *Pride and Prejudice* (1813) and *Emma* (1816). A generation later, also in Britain, the three Brontë sisters, Charlotte (1816–1855), Emily (1818–1848), and Anne (1820–1849), published novels with equally complex plots but much greater emphasis on romantic passion, on the one hand, and character flaws or social ills, on the other. Charlotte's *Jane Eyre* (1847) and Emily's *Wuthering Heights* (1847) are two examples. Anne's *The Tenant of Wildfell Hall* (1848) goes a step further by including taboo topics such as a sensitive and suffering woman leaving her alcoholic and abusive husband with her son to live in hiding as an artist. The novels also contain mysterious, seemingly inexplicable happenings—artistic devices which the American Edgar Allan Poe (1809–1849) used more explicitly in his thematic Gothic stories and tales, such as "The Fall of the House of Usher" (1839).

Realism

Toward the middle of the 1800s, many artists and writers shifted their focus from the romanticism of the self and its aesthetic or moral sentiments to the **realism** of the middle classes, arraning this new group in an industrializing world. In philosophy, thinkers identified stages leading progressively to the rise of middle classes and industrialism. And in literature, the complex and tangled relationships that characterized the plots of the romantics continued, but now in the more prosaic urban world of factories and working classes.

Realism: The belief that material reality exists independently of the people who observe it.

Histories of Philosophy   One of the works in Hegel's system was *Lectures on the Philosophy of History* (1822–1830). In this work, the philosopher sketches the dialectical progression of the spirit to a progressively more differentiated

Realism. The documentary power of photography spurred the new impulses of realism that emerged around 1850. The photograph here shows the execution of hostages in the Commune of Paris in the spring of 1871 shortly before its final defeat by troops of the provisional French national government. One of the executed hostages was Georges Darboy, archbishop of Paris, a critic of the pope and strong patriot who cared for the wounded of the war against Prussia in 1870.

ASSASSINAT DES OTAGES À LA PRISON DE LA ROQUETTE LE 24 MAI 1871
Mr Darboy   Bonjean   Duguerry   Ducoudray   Clerc   Allard.

self-consciousness, until it culminates in his own time with the transcendental ego. The progression was also one from east to west, from India and China via the Middle East to Europe, culminating with the new revolutionary nations of 1776–1789. The French thinker Auguste Comte (1798–1857) composed a six-volume study entitled *The Positive Philosophy* (1830–1842), in which he arranged world history into the three successive stages of the theological, metaphysical, and scientific. In his view, the scientific advances of the sciences had all but phased out the metaphysical stage and had ushered in the last, scientific era. For Comte this was a sign of Europe's progress and a "positive" stage; his philosophy is therefore labeled "positivism." Comte further argued that the only sure way of arriving at truth was based on scientific facts and knowledge of the world acquired through the senses. Since in Comte's view the laws governing human behavior could be ascertained with the same degree of precision as the laws of nature, he became the founder of the science of sociology. Karl Marx (1818–1883), as we will see in more detail in Chapter 23, equally convinced of the scientific character of his philosophy of history, proposed the stages of slavery, feudalism, capitalism, world revolution, and socialism or communism. Today, these Eurocentric assumptions about Western triumphalism are no longer supportable, given that Enlightenment materialism, constitutionalism, nationalism, and industrialization have become the common, generic property of the contemporary world.

Prose Literature   Prose writers, of course, were for the most part unconcerned about the allegedly scientific character of their writings. On the other hand, as writers of fiction, the move away from sentiments to realistic scenes as they were encountered in middle-class society required new aesthetic experimentation so that the ordinary could be a heightened reflection of the new "reality" of life in the industrial age. William Makepeace Thackeray (1811–1863) in England, for example, was a supreme satirist, as displayed in *Vanity Fair*, a book on human foibles and peccadilloes. His compatriot Charles Dickens (1812–1870) had a similar focus but used working- and lower middle-class characters in his many novels. The English-woman George Eliot, born Mary Ann Evans, (1819–1880) was politically oriented, placing small-town social relations into sets of concrete political events in Great Britain, as in *Middlemarch* (1874). Gustave Flaubert (1821–1880) in France experimented with a variety of styles, among which extremely precise and unadorned description of objects and situations is perhaps the most important, for example, in *Madame Bovary* (1857). Henry James (1843–1916), an American living in Britain, in his self-declared masterpiece, *The Ambassadors* (1903), explored the psychological complexities of individuals whose entwined lives crossed both sides of the Atlantic. In the end, realism, with its individuals firmly anchored in the new class society of the 1800s, had moved far from the freedom and equality celebrated by the romantics.

Putting It All Together

Though the pattern of nation-state building in Europe and North America was relatively slow and, in places, painful, it has become the dominant mode of political organization in the world today. As we will see in subsequent chapters, the aftermath of World War I and the decolonization movement following World War II gave a tremendous boost to the process of nation-state formation around the world. Here, the legacy of European colonialism both planted these ideas among the colonized and, by supplying the Enlightenment ideas of revolution and the radical remaking of society, provided the ideological means of achieving their own liberation from foreign rule. In both cases, the aspirations of peoples to "nationhood" followed older European models as the colonies were either granted independence or fought to gain it from declining empires. But, in many respects, their efforts mirrored the difficulties of the first constitutional nationalist states and, more commonly, the initial ethnolinguistic ones.

Take the example of the United States. Though it achieved world economic leadership by 1914, it had faced an early constitutional crisis, endured a prolonged sectional struggle in which slavery marred the constitutional order for almost three-quarters of a century, fought a bloody civil war for national unification that very nearly destroyed it, and remained united in part by acquiescing in practices of overt segregation and discrimination against the 10 percent of its population that was of African descent. Or take the case of France. Its people adopted constitutional nationalism in 1789, but the monarchy it seemingly replaced bounced back three times. Thus, even in the later nineteenth century, Abraham Lincoln's hope that "government of the people, by the people, for the people shall not perish from the earth" was still very much open to question.

Yet another example is the case of Germany, where ethnolinguistic nationalism diluted the straightforward enthusiasm for the constitution and the symbols accompanying it. Historians continue to argue over whether Germany, and by extension other central and eastern European nations, took a special route (*Sonderweg*) to constitutional normality or whether the path was the same except that the pace slowed at critical times. In retrospect, it is impossible to say which of the speed bumps on the way toward the nation-state—slavery/racism, residual monarchism, or the

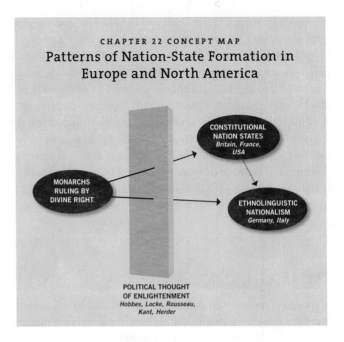

CHAPTER 22 CONCEPT MAP
Patterns of Nation-State Formation in Europe and North America

twentieth-century experiments of communism and supremacist nationalism—were responsible for the longest delay. In Part 6 we will consider all of these developments in more detail (see Concept Map).

Review and Respond

1. What were the origins and outcomes of the American Revolution? Of the French Revolution?

2. Why was there a period of monarchical restoration, in Europe in the first half of the nineteenth century?

3. What motivated the successful/abortive revolutions of 1848? Discuss their spread across Europe.

4. Which factors contributed to the unification of Italy and Germany?

5. Which parts of human nature did the romantics glorify and why? With what results?

6. How did realism differ from romanticism?

For additional resources, including maps, primary sources, visuals, and quizzes, please go to www.oup.com/us/vonsivers. Please see the Further Resources section at the back of the book for additional readings and suggested websites.

Thinking Through Patterns

▶ **How did the pattern of constitutional nationalism, emerging from the American and French Revolutions, affect the course of events in the Western world during the first half of the nineteenth century?**

Constitutional nationalism emerged as a result of the American and French revolutionaries succeeding in overthrowing absolute rule. The constitutional revolutionaries replaced the loyalty of subjects to a monarch with that of free and equal citizens to the national constitution. This form of nationalism called for unity among the citizens regardless of ethnic, linguistic, or religious identity. In the United States, this nationalism had to overcome a conservative adherence to slavery in the South before it gained general recognition after the end of the Civil War. In France, republican nationalists battled conservative monarchists for nearly a century before they were able to finally defeat them in the Third Republic.

Constitutional nationalists emphasized the principles of freedom, equality, constitution, rule of law, elections, and representative assembly regardless of ethnicity, language, or religion. However, nationalists in areas of Europe lacking centralized monarchies sought to first unify what they identified as dispersed members of their nation through ideologies that emphasized common origin, centuries of collective history, and shared literary, artistic, and religious traditions. In these ethnolinguistic (and sometimes religious) ideologies constitutional principles were secondary. Only once unification in a nation-state was achieved, the form of government—monarchist, constitutional-monarchist, republican—would then be chosen.

▶ **In what ways did ethnolinguistic nationalism differ from constitutional nationalism, and what was its influence on the formation of nation-states in the second half of the nineteenth century?**

▶ **What were the reactions among thinkers and artists to the developing pattern of nation-state formation? How did they define the intellectual-artistic movements of romanticism and realism?**

Philosophers and artists in the romantic period put a strong emphasis on individual creativity. They either viewed this creativity as an upwelling of impulses and sentiments pouring forth with little intellectual control or, conversely, considered their creativity as the result of an absolute or transcendent mind working through them as individuals. As middle classes emerged toward the mid-1800s, individual creativity gave way to a greater awareness, called "realism," of the social environment with its class structure and industrial characteristics.

Chapter 23 | Industrialization and Its Discontents

1750–1914

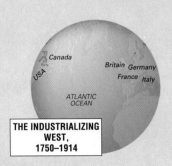

THE INDUSTRIALIZING
WEST,
1750–1914

In the late summer of 1845, Mary Paul, age 15, came to a decision that would alter her life forever. Already at this tender age she had begun to realize just how limited her prospects were in the hardscrabble farm country of rural Vermont, so she decided to head for Massachusetts and stake her future on finding a job in the newly expanding textile industry.

Exactly how that future would unfold can be seen in numerous letters she wrote to her widowed father, Bela, over the coming years. As her correspondence reveals, the primary reason behind her dramatic decision to uproot herself was simply to make steady wages, rather than rely on the uncertainties and drudgery of farm work. On September 13, 1845, Mary

Seeing Patterns

▶ Where and when did the Industrial Revolution originate?

▶ What were some effects of industrialization on Western society? How did social patterns change?

▶ In what ways did industrialization contribute to innovations in technology? How did these technological advances contribute to Western imperialism in the late nineteenth century?

▶ What new directions in science, philosophy, religion, and the arts did industrialism generate? What kind of responses did it provoke?

wrote for her father's consent to leave her nearby domestic job and seek employment in the booming mill town of Lowell, Massachusetts. On November 20, Mary wrote that she had already "found a place in a spinning room and the next morning I went to work." She continued, "I like very well have [sic] 50cts first payment increasing every payment as I get along in work. [I] have a first rate overseer and a very good boarding place." Shortly before Christmas, Mary reported that her wages had increased: "Last Tuesday we were paid. In all I had six dollars and sixty cents paid $4.68 for board. With the rest I got me a pair of rubbers and a pair of 50.cts shoes. Next payment I am to have a dollar a week beside my board." She then went on to offer her father some insights into her daily routine in the mill, one with which millions of workers around the world would soon grow quite familiar: "At 5 o'clock in the morning the bell rings for the folks to get up and get breakfast. At half past six it rings for the girls to get up and at seven they are called into the mill. At half past 12 we have dinner are called back again at one and stay till half past seven." Mary closes by pointing out that "I think that the factory is the best place for me and if any girl wants employment I advise them to come to Lowell."

Child Workers, North Carolina, 1910. The American photojournalist, sociologist, and reformer Lewis Hine (1874–1940) was hired by The National Child Labor Committee in 1908 to document the prevalence of underage boys and girls working in mills and factories throughout the rapidly industrializing United States. The young "spinners" in this North Carolina textile mill smile shyly, even proudly, but they cannot hide their disheveled appearance, visible signs of fatigue, and the psychological stress they endured working long hours for little pay in dangerous conditions.

787

After working for 4 years in the mill at Lowell, Mary moved to Claremont, New Hampshire, to be with her aging father. Two years later, however, she relocated to Brattleboro, Vermont, where she and another woman started a coat-making business. On November 27, 1853, Mary's letter to her father reveals her guilt about a conflict that would become all too familiar to workers in this new age: how to balance the need to earn a living with the obligation to take care of one's family: "It troubles me very much, the thought of your being lame so much and alone too. If there were any way that I could make it expedient I would go back to Claremont myself and I sometimes think I ought to do so but the chance for one there is so *small* [sic]."

Things apparently did not work out in Brattleboro, and 2 years later Mary's search for better employment led her to one of the many experimental communities that had sprung up in the United States during the first half of the nineteenth century. In this case it was the North American Phalanx, a utopian agricultural community in Red Bank, New Jersey, based on the socialist ideas of the Frenchman Charles Fourier. A little over a year later, however, the Phalanx dissolved, forcing Mary to move back to New Hampshire, where she found work as a housekeeper. Finally, at the age of 27, Mary married and moved to Lynn, Massachusetts, where she and her husband settled down to raise a family.

Mary Paul's experiences, reflecting those of thousands of other young, single women in rural farming regions, signaled a momentous change in the patterns of American and world history. Like Great Britain and areas throughout northern Europe, the northeastern United States was now in the initial stages of what we have termed "scientific–industrial society." The agrarian–urban model, which had lasted for millennia on every inhabited continent except Australia, was now slowly giving way to a society based on machine-made goods, large-scale factories, regimented work hours, and wage labor. Moreover, the economies of the industrializing states would increasingly be dominated by the developing practices of capitalism. An ideology of progress, backed by the acceleration of technology and science, along with the legacy of the Enlightenment, would constitute an important step toward creating what we term in this section "the challenge of modernity." That challenge was already being spread throughout the world, backed by the revolutions in transportation, communications, and weaponry produced by this Industrial Revolution.

For Mary Paul and her fellow mill hands, however, their primary concerns were much closer to home. They saw clearly that the rapid growth of textile factories rendered obsolete the home spinning and weaving of cloth and cottage occupations of farming communities. By migrating to industrial centers in New England like Lowell, where textile mills offered employment opportunities, they could attain economic independence by working for cash wages. In many cases, however, they also witnessed epic and sometimes bloody struggles between management and labor as the laws, institutions, and social norms of this new society were being painfully worked out. And amid the countless interactions and adaptations in which Mary and her fellow workers engaged, the modern world we live in today began to take shape.

Origins and Growth of Industrialism, 1750–1914

Like the agricultural revolution of the Neolithic age, which resulted in humankind's transition from foragers to food producers and made possible urbanization, the Industrial Revolution forever altered the lives of tens of millions around the globe. Whether or not this movement was in fact a "revolution," however, is a matter of some debate. It is perhaps more accurate to say that the process of industrialization evolved over time, originating in Britain in the eighteenth century, then spreading to the European continent and North America in the nineteenth century and subsequently around the globe, interacting with and adapting to local circumstances and cultures along the way. But there is no question that the transition from manual labor and natural sources of power to the implementation of mechanical forms of power and machine-driven production resulted in a vast increase in the production of goods and new modes of transportation, as well as new economic policies and business procedures. In the process the lives of untold numbers of people were forever transformed.

Early Industrialism, 1750–1870

The industrialization of western Europe began in Britain. As with all transformative events in history, however, a number of important questions arise. Why did the industrial movement begin in Britain? Why not, say, in China in the Song or Ming period? Why in the eighteenth century? Why in such areas as textiles, iron, mining, and transport? How did these changes become not only self-sustaining but also able to transform so many other manufacturing processes? And was this process "inevitable," as some have claimed, or was it contingent on a myriad of complex interactions that we are still struggling to comprehend?

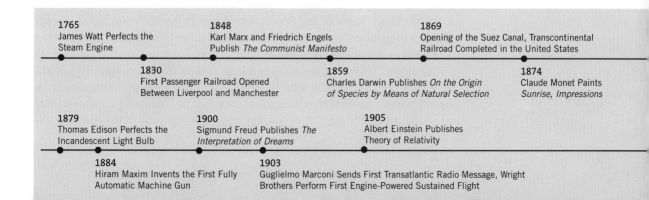

1765
James Watt Perfects the Steam Engine

1848
Karl Marx and Friedrich Engels Publish *The Communist Manifesto*

1869
Opening of the Suez Canal, Transcontinental Railroad Completed in the United States

1830
First Passenger Railroad Opened Between Liverpool and Manchester

1859
Charles Darwin Publishes *On the Origin of Species by Means of Natural Selection*

1874
Claude Monet Paints *Sunrise, Impressions*

1879
Thomas Edison Perfects the Incandescent Light Bulb

1900
Sigmund Freud Publishes *The Interpretation of Dreams*

1905
Albert Einstein Publishes Theory of Relativity

1884
Hiram Maxim Invents the First Fully Automatic Machine Gun

1903
Guglielmo Marconi Sends First Transatlantic Radio Message, Wright Brothers Perform First Engine-Powered Sustained Flight

Preconditions   Although there are no simple answers to these questions, it is possible to cite several conditions enjoyed by the British Isles that rendered them especially suitable for launching the industrial movement. Among other things, Britain benefited from what historians sometimes refer to as the "coal and colonies" theory. Britain has been described as "an island floating on a sea of coal." Large reserves of coal and iron ore, combined with the establishment of overseas colonies and subsequent global trading networks, provided a foundation for commercial expansion, which in turn would help provide capital to fund the new enterprises. In addition, a thriving merchant class, empowered by the Glorious Revolution of 1688, grew in significance in the House of Commons of the British Parliament and supported legislation aimed at economic development. At the same time, Britain developed a flourishing banking system; the Bank of England (1694) provided needed funds to entrepreneurs willing to make risky investments in new ventures.

Thanks to agricultural improvements, due in part to the introduction of new crops from the Americas such as potatoes and new fodder crops for livestock such as clover and turnips, Britain experienced a surge in population. Whereas in 1600 Britain's population amounted to no more than around 5 million, by 1700 it had nearly doubled to around 9 million. At the same time there was a demographic shift, in which displaced tenant farmers migrated to towns and cities, causing a rapid increase in urban growth and creating greater demand for food and consumer goods. In addition, urban dwellers began to crave more exotic consumer products now available from Britain's warm-weather colonies.

One of the first areas in which we see the effects of these changes was the textile industry. Although woolen cloth had long been the staple of the British textile industry, the introduction of new fabrics from Asia, such as silk and cotton, began to gain in popularity among consumers. Cotton's advantages of light weight and ease of cleaning resulted in a growing demand for the domestic production of affordable cotton clothing, or "calicoes." At first, the demand for finished cloth goods was satisfied by weavers working in the older, domestic cottage industries, a system known as "proto-industrialism." Due in large part to concerns for the woolen industry, however, Parliament enacted the protectionist Calico Acts of 1700 and 1720, which prohibited the importation of cotton goods from India. But this legislation had the unintended consequence of increasing domestic demand for English-made cotton textiles, which quickly outstripped available supplies. Given soaring demand, it was apparent that some sort of means was needed to speed up production.

British Resources   The impasse was resolved by a combination of factors peculiar to Britain at this time, which taken together made the use of machines more practical and cost-efficient than it might have been somewhere else. Since wages for workers in rural industries were high, the use of labor-saving machinery was increasingly seen as a means to help firms be profitable. By contrast, wages were relatively low in the Dutch Republic and France, with the result that there was no felt urgency in developing more cost-effective means of production. At the same time, Britain's vast reserves of coal resulted in cheap energy.

Moreover, Britain was singularly fortunate in its social and cultural capital. The composition of British society in the seventeenth and eighteenth centuries was unusually attuned to what historians sometimes call the "Industrial Enlightenment." As discussed in Chapter 17, eighteenth-century Britain was at the center of the

European scientific revolution. From Bacon to Boyle and from Harvey to Newton, the scientific revolution—particularly in its practical and empirical areas—was realized in a more widespread fashion in Britain than elsewhere. Here, too, was a flourishing group of scientific societies—for example, the Lunar Society in Birmingham and the Royal Society, founded in 1660—and the majority of British inventors had interests in and ties to societies aligned with scientific aspects of the Enlightenment. These groups served as centers of discourse and exchange between leading scientists and more down-to-earth men of a practical bent, including inventors, experimenters, and mechanics, who were not only often highly literate but also frequently educated in mathematics.

New Technologies and Sources of Power   These factors produced an explosion of technological innovation in Britain. From 1700 to 1800 over 1,000 inventions were developed, most of which were related to the textile industry. Among the most prominent were the flying shuttle (1733), the spinning jenny (1764), the water frame (1769), and the spinning mule (1779). Each of these devices greatly increased the speed and quality of spinning or weaving; the mule combined both operations into one machine. The power loom (1787) then set the technological stage for full-scale machine production of textiles.

Even these improvements were not enough, however, to supply both domestic and colonial markets with sufficient quantities of textiles. What was needed in order to speed up production was some sort of reliable mechanical power, instead of human, animal, wind, or water to drive the looms. The solution was provided by the development of the steam engine, easily the most important—and iconic—innovation produced during the industrial era.

The Factory System   The growing dependence on large machinery, the necessity of transporting fuel and raw materials to centers of production, and the increased efficiency of housing a multitude of machines under one roof necessitated the construction of large manufacturing buildings. These facilities were initially located near sources of running water in order to provide the necessary power to run mechanical looms. The implementation of steam power to drive machinery allowed entrepreneurs to move mills and production centers away from water sources in rural areas to urban settings, where there were large pools of cheap labor. Another attraction of urban areas was their greater accessibility to roads, canals, and, later, railroads. Once established, these factories in their turn drew larger and larger numbers of workers, contributing to population surges, particularly in the cities of the north and Midlands of England. Manchester, for instance, the leading textile manufacturing center, grew nearly 10-fold from 1750 to 1830. By the 1830s over 1 million people drew wages from textile factories and close to 25 percent of Britain's industrial production came from factories (see Map 23.1).

Railroads   While steam-powered factories provided much of the muscle of the Industrial Revolution, it was the steam railroad that captivated the imagination of the public. The spectacle of great locomotives pulling long trains of cars at previously unheard-of speeds, their pistons panting like the breath of giants, their plaintive whistles haunting the night, all became fixtures of the romance of rail travel. Their origins, like those of the earlier stationary pumping engines, began at the

Patterns Up Close | "The Age of Steam"

More than any other innovation of the industrial age, the advent of practical steam power revolutionized manufacturing, transportation, communications, economics, and even politics and military matters. Indeed, at the height of steam's dominance, many people saw its ability to move freight and people and to run myriad kinds of machines as close to divine. As Frederic A. Bartholdi, builder of the Statue of Liberty, rhapsodized at the American Centennial Exhibition in 1876, the mammoth Corliss steam engine dominating the Machinery Hall there had "the beauty, and almost the grace of human form" in its operation. Even today, one sees a particular kind of avant-garde science fiction based on fanciful nineteenth-century contraptions labeled as "steam-punk."

The origins of the steam age lie in an environmental crisis. A growing shortage of wood for fuel and charcoal making in Britain in the early 1700s forced manufacturers to turn to another fuel source: coal. As we have seen, Britain was blessed with vast amounts of coal, but getting to it was difficult because of a high water table: Mineshafts often flooded after only a few feet and had to be abandoned. Early methods of water extraction featured pumps operated by either human or animal power; but these were inefficient, expensive, and limited in power.

The first steam-driven piston engine based on experimentation with vacuum chambers and condensing steam came from the French Huguenot Denis Papin (1647–ca. 1712), who spent his later career in England. Thomas Savery (ca. 1650–1715), also taking up the idea of condensing steam and vacuum power, built a system of pipes employing the suction produced by this process dubbed the "Miner's Friend" that was able to extract water from shallow shafts but was useless for the deeper mines that were more common in rural Britain.

This drawback was partially addressed by Thomas Newcomen (1663–1729). In 1712 Newcomen took Papin's piston-and-cylinder design and vastly improved its practicality. Newcomen's model featured a large wooden rocking beam, weighted on one end, to operate the pump. When the weighted beam was pulled down by the force of gravity, steam was drawn into a cylinder and then condensed by a spray of cold water. The resulting partial vacuum below the piston, augmented by atmospheric pressure above, pulled it downward, forcing the weighted end of the beam upward. The beam was in turn connected to another piston in the mineshaft, which sucked water in and drew it up a pipe.

Though over 100 Newcomen engines were in place throughout Britain and Europe at the time of Newcomen's death in 1729, a number of flaws still rendered them very slow and energy-inefficient, suitable only for places like coal mines, where abundant fuel was available. It remained for James Watt (1736–1819), a Scottish engineer, to make the final changes needed to create the prototype for fast engines sufficiently efficient and versatile to drive factory machinery. Watt had been engaged in repairing Newcomen engines and quickly realized their limitations. To

Corliss Steam Engine. A tribute to the new power of the steam engine was this huge power plant in the Machinery Hall of the American Centennial Exposition in 1876. The Corliss engine pictured here developed over 1,400 horsepower and drove nearly all the machines in the exhibition hall—with the distinct exception of those in the British display. Along with the arm of the Statue of Liberty, also on exhibition there, it became the most recognized symbol of America's first world's fair.

correct them he developed a separate condensing chamber, which allowed the piston cylinder to remain constantly hot; he also added a valve to eliminate the condensed steam after the piston stroke. The newly refined model, completed in 1765 and patented in 1769, was five times as efficient as Newcomen's engine and used 75 percent less coal.

After making several refinements Watt introduced a further improved model in 1783 that incorporated more advances. First, by injecting steam into both the top and bottom of the piston cylinder, its motion was converted to double action, making it more powerful and efficient. Second, through a system of "planetary gearing"—in which the piston shaft was connected by a circular gear to the hub of a flywheel—the back-and-forth rhythm of the piston was converted to smooth, rotary motion, suitable for driving machines in factories and mills. Watt's steam engines proved so popular that by 1790 they had replaced all of the Newcomen engines and by 1800 nearly 500 Watt engines were in operation in mines and factories.

Within a few decades, adaptations of this design were being used not just for stationary engines to run machinery but also to move vehicles along tracks and turn paddle wheels and screw propellers on boats—the first railroad engines and steamships. Both of these innovations soon provided the muscle and sinew of enhanced commerce and empire building among the newly industrializing nations. They were also among the most attractive as well as troublesome innovations for other countries around the globe to adopt. The Japanese fascination with the railroad can be said to date from its first demonstration by Commodore Perry's men in 1853 (see Chapter 24). Settlement of the United States was enormously accelerated by the advent of the railroad and river steamer. Indeed, by 1914, there was scarcely a place on the globe not accessible by either railroad or steamship. Yet, for societies seeking to protect themselves from outside influence, the railroad and steamer were seen as forces of chaos. The first railroad built in China, for example, was purchased by Qing officials and destroyed lest it upset the local economy and facilitate further foreign penetration of the empire. Nevertheless, as the web of railroad lines grew denser on every inhabited continent and the continents themselves were connected by the tissue of shipping lines, steam may indeed be said to be the power behind the creation of modern global society.

The Tools of Empire. Steam power allowed European colonizers and explorers to penetrate into the heart of hitherto inaccessible regions, such as this paddle steamer, the *Ma Roberts*, chugging up the Lower Zambezi in southern Africa in 1859. The bull elephant in the foreground roars in defiance, and while it appears the shooters on deck have missed their mark, the mood of the painting suggests that time is on their side.

Questions

- How does the innovation of steam power show the culmination of a pattern that began with the rise of the New Science in western Europe in the sixteenth and seventeenth centuries?

- Does Frederic A. Bartholdi's statement in 1876 that the Corliss steam engine "had the beauty and almost the grace of the human form" reflect a romantic outlook? If so, how?

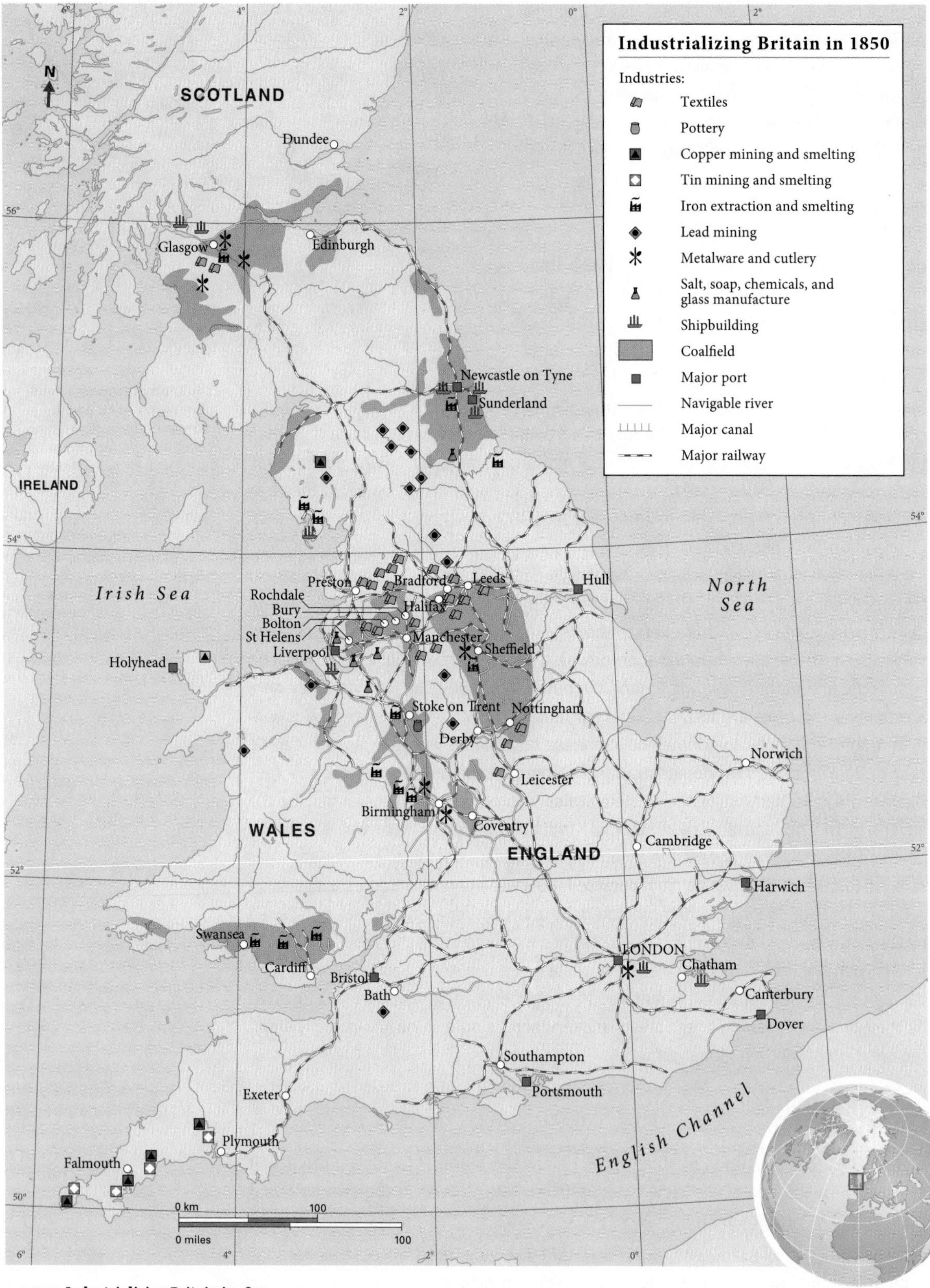

Industrializing Britain in 1850

Industries:
- Textiles
- Pottery
- Copper mining and smelting
- Tin mining and smelting
- Iron extraction and smelting
- Lead mining
- Metalware and cutlery
- Salt, soap, chemicals, and glass manufacture
- Shipbuilding
- Coalfield
- Major port
- Navigable river
- Major canal
- Major railway

MAP 23.1 **Industrializing Britain in 1850.**

mines. For more than a century, miners had used track-mounted cars to pull loads of coal and iron out of mines. By the 1820s experiments were already under way to attach Watt-type engines to moving carriages. In 1825, under the guidance of British engineer and inventor George Stephenson (1781–1848), the first freight line, the Darlington–Stockton, and in 1829–1830 the first passenger line, the Manchester–Liverpool, were opened; and travelers thrilled to the astonishing speeds of 15–20 miles per hour. This newfound speed, efficiency, and capability of moving passengers and freight resulted in a British railroad boom. Whereas in 1840 Great Britain counted only 1,800 miles of rail, by 1870 the figure had jumped nearly ninefold to 15,600 miles. Railroads not only vastly improved the shipping of coal and other bulk commodities but also greatly enhanced the sale and distribution of manufactures of all kinds. The railroad itself developed into a self-sustaining industry, employing thousands in all sorts of related jobs and spurring further investment by wealthy entrepreneurs.

Steamships   Although their impact was realized somewhat later, the application of steam to ships had far-reaching ramifications, especially in the second half of the nineteenth century. Credit for the first practical steam-powered riverboat goes to the American engineer and inventor Robert Fulton (1765–1815). Fulton's *Clermont*, constructed in 1807, plied the Hudson River from New York to Albany. English engineers were quick to copy Fulton's lead; by 1815 there were 10 steamboats busy hauling coal across the Clyde River in Scotland. In 1816 a steamship sailed from Liverpool to Boston in 17 days, cutting the transatlantic journey to one-half the time taken by sailing ships. In 1838 the *Great Western* began regular transatlantic service; its initial crossing from Bristol to New York took only 19 days. During the 1820s and 1830s steamboats were in regular use on Europe's principal rivers: the Rhine, the Danube, the Rhône, the Seine, and others. During the same time they played a vital role in opening up the Great Lakes and the Ohio and Mississippi Rivers to commerce in the United States. The year 1839 saw the inauguration of regular transatlantic steamship service from England to New York; 2 years later the famous Cunard line was founded. Then, during the 1830s and 1840s the British East India Company used iron-hulled steamers to facilitate maritime trade with its markets in India. Military uses soon presented themselves as well: as we will see in Chapter 24, the innovative iron-clad steam gunboat *Nemesis* shocked its opponents with its durability, mobility, and firepower during the Anglo–Chinese Opium War of 1839–1842.

An important innovation in maritime steam navigation was the development of the screw propeller in the late 1830s. Paddle-wheeled oceangoing ships tended to be top-heavy, and their "walking-beam" drive mechanisms and the paddle wheels themselves were vulnerable to damage in bad weather or, in the case of warships, to hits from enemy fire. The fast-turning screw propeller, in line with the ship's keel and rudder below the water line, proved far less troublesome and allowed all the moving parts of the engine and power train to be enclosed and protected. Still, paddle steamers remained in wide use until the latter part of the century and were the preferred system in shallow-draft river steamers.

The Spread of Early Industrialism

By the 1830s, in Belgium, northern France, and the northern German states—all of which had coal reserves—conditions had grown more suitable for industrialization than earlier when wages were low. More settled political conditions after the Napoleonic Wars led to population increases, contributing to higher consumer demand. At the same time, larger urban areas provided greater pools of available workers for factories. Moreover, within these regions improved networks of roads, canals, and now railways facilitated the movement of both raw materials to industrial centers and manufactured goods to markets. For example, in 1840 only 400 miles of rail were in existence in German territories, but that figure soared to 3,500 in 1850 and then to 11,150 in 1870. In addition, governmental involvement greatly enhanced the investment climate; protective tariffs for manufactures and the gradual removal of internal toll restrictions, particularly in the northern German states, opened up the trading industry.

The United States   Industrialism was imported to the United States toward the end of the eighteenth century by Samuel Slater (1768–1835), a British engineer. Known as the "father of the American Industrial Revolution," Slater established the first water-powered textile factory, in Rhode Island in 1793. By 1825 factories in the northeastern section of the country were producing vast quantities of textile goods on mechanically powered looms.

After a brief interruption during the American Civil War—during which the majority of factories on both sides were engaged in producing munitions and war materiel—industrialization in America resumed at a greatly accelerated pace. As production data indicate, by 1870 America was producing far more spindles of cotton than Great Britain, and its production of iron ingots was swiftly catching up to that of British and European producers. By 1914 the United States had become the world's single largest industrial economy.

In addition to manufacturing, trade and commerce across the vast span of the American continent were facilitated by a national network of railroads, which swiftly took over the carrying trade from the canal networks created in the early nineteenth century. Data for US rail construction show this astonishing growth: only 2,800 miles of rail in 1840 but 9,000 in 1850. At the conclusion of the Civil War there were already about 35,000 miles of railroads in the country—more than the rest of the world combined—though many were still of different gauges. By 1869 the first transcontinental single-gauge railroad was joined with a final golden spike at Promontory Point, Utah, resulting in an astonishing total of 53,000 rail miles by 1870.

Later Industrialism, 1871–1914

In many ways the next stage of industrialism, often referred to as "the second Industrial Revolution," grew out of the first phase. Perhaps the best measure of the difference in the two periods, however, is that while the first stage relied upon steam power, the second introduced several high-technology innovations that taken together altered the course not only of the Industrial Revolution but also of world history. Among the most significant of these were three major innovations: steel, electricity, and chemicals (see Map 23.2).

New Materials: Steel   A significant element in the second Industrial Revolution was the increasing use of steel instead of iron. Refined techniques of making steel had existed for many hundreds of years in different parts of the world but were largely the province of highly skilled craftspeople such as swordsmiths. New

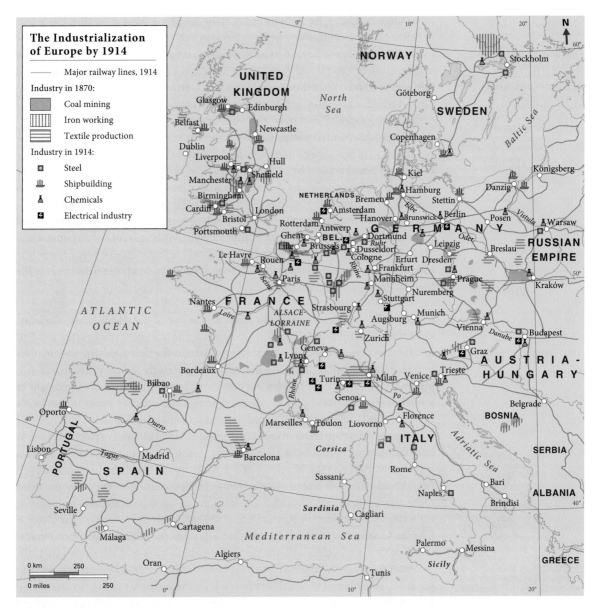

MAP **23.2 The Industrialization of Europe by 1914.**

technical advances, however, now made it possible to produce large quantities of high-grade *cheap* steel. The first of these was made in Britain by Henry Bessemer (1813–1898) in 1856, who devised a way to increase its carbon content in his "Bessemer Converter." Subsequent improvements in production soon followed in the 1860s and 1870s with the advent of the blast furnace and the open-hearth smelting method.

Following the conclusion of the Franco–Prussian war, Germany's annexation of the ore-rich regions of Alsace-Lorraine led to a dramatic increase in industrial production. Starting with almost no measurable steel production in the 1870s, Germany managed to catch up to British annual steel production in 1893 and then went on to surge far ahead: By 1914 its annual tonnage of steel was more than twice that of Britain. One advantage enjoyed by Germany was that it was able to model its new industrial facilities on those of its most modern competitors, saving substantial time and investment capital and resulting in newer and more efficient equipment and business methods. Yet another advantage was Germany's development of sophisticated research capabilities at universities, particularly in the sciences.

The advantages of steel over iron were that it was lighter, harder, and more durable. Thus, it provided better rails for railroads and, increasingly, girders for the construction of high-rise buildings. Indeed, structural steel and steel-reinforced concrete made possible the construction of high-rise "skyscrapers," which by the turn of the century were soaring past the tallest masonry buildings. The switch from iron to steel construction of ships also marked a significant advance in steamship technology during the third quarter of the nineteenth century. Steel ships greatly improved the travel time between far-flung continents. By 1900, 95 percent of all commercial ocean liners were being constructed of steel. Steel made possible stronger, faster, and roomier ships, while steel warships also proved far more durable in battle and set the tone for naval construction to this day.

Chemicals   Advances were also made in the use of chemicals. Here, the most significant developments were initiated by academic scientists, whose work resulted in later advances in the chemical industry. In 1856 the first synthetic dye, mauveine, was created, which initiated the synthetic dyestuffs industry. The result was not only a wider array of textiles but also new chemical compounds important in the refinement of wood pulp products, ranging from cheaper paper in the 1870s to artificial silk, referred to as "rayon." Later discoveries, such as the synthesizing of ammonia and its conversion to nitrates for use in fertilizers and explosives, were to have far-reaching effects during World War I. Associated with advances in chemical experimentation was the invention of dynamite by the Swedish chemist and engineer Alfred Bernhard Nobel (1833–1896). This powerful new explosive provided the means to blast through rock formations, resulting in great tunnels and massive excavation projects like the Panama Canal (1914). In yet another chemical advance, Charles Goodyear (1800-1860) invented a process in 1839 that produced vulcanized rubber; and celluloid—the first synthetic plastic—was developed in 1869. Additional offshoots, ranging from pharmaceuticals and drugs like aspirin to soap products, contributed to healthier lifestyles. By the early part of the twentieth century, these developments had led to a "hygiene revolution" among the industrialized countries.

New Energies: Electricity   Although electricity had been in use during the first period of industrialization, its development and application were greatly advanced after 1850, especially in the generation of electrical power. The first step came with Michael Faraday (1791–1867) patenting the electromagnetic generator in 1861. But large-scale electrical generation would require a number of other innovations before it became a reality. Perhaps the most important devices in this regard were developed by a relatively obscure engineer, Nikola Tesla (1856–1943). Among Tesla's inventions were alternating current (AC), the Tesla Coil (1891) for the more efficient transmission of electricity, and a host of generators, motors, and transformers. In 1888 the introduction of Tesla's "electric induction engine" led to the widespread adoption of electricity-generating power plants throughout industrialized Europe.

The first widespread use of electricity, however, had come earlier, in the realm of communications. Although electric telegraph messages were transmitted as early as the 1840s with the advent of Samuel F. B. Morse's (1791-1872) devices and code, it was only in the 1860s and 1870s that major continental landmasses were linked by submarine transoceanic cables. The first successful link from Britain to India was installed in 1865. The first transatlantic cable from Britain to America was laid as early as 1858, though it was only in 1866 that the cable was deemed operationally successful. By the latter part of the nineteenth century, telegraphic communication was a worldwide phenomenon, which has been likened to the Internet in its impact on human contact. This was vastly augmented with Alexander Graham Bell's (1847–1922) telephone in 1876, which made voice contact possible by wire.

But perhaps most revolutionary of all was the advent of wireless communication. The theoretical groundwork for this had been laid by James Clerk Maxwell (1831–1879), a Scottish physicist researching the theoretical properties of electromagnetism, and Heinrich Rudolf Hertz (1857–1894). In 1885 Hertz—whose name was later given to the units of measurement for radio wave cycles—discovered that electromagnetic radiation actually produces unseen waves that emanate through the universe. In the later 1890s, Guglielmo Marconi (1874–1937) developed a device using these radio waves generated by electric sparks controlled by a telegraph key to send and receive messages over several miles. By 1903 Marconi had enhanced the power and range of the device enough to send the first transatlantic radio message from Cape Cod in the United States to Cornwall in England. The "wireless telegraph" was quickly adopted by ships for reliable communication at sea. Subsequent improvements, such as the development of the vacuum tube amplifier and oscillator, resulted in greater power and reliability and, within a few years, the ability to transmit sound wirelessly.

New Energies: The Internal Combustion Engine

When oil, or liquid petroleum, was commercially developed in the 1860s and 1870s, it was at first refined into kerosene and used for illumination. One of the by-products of this process, gasoline, however, soon revealed its potential as a new fuel source. The first experimental internal combustion engines utilizing the new fuel appeared in the 1860s. Their light weight relative to their power was superior to steam engines of comparable size, and the first practical attempts to use them in powering vehicles came along in the next decade.

Who invented the automobile? Although it is usual to credit two Germans, Gottlieb Daimler (1834-1900) and Karl Benz (1844-1929), with the invention, the first true automobile was invented by an unheralded Austrian mechanic and inventor named Siegfried Marcus (1831–1898). As early as 1864 Marcus harnessed his own experimental internal combustion engine to a cart, which moved under its own power for over 200 yards. Over the next several years Marcus tinkered with several gadgets and devices in order to perfect his self-propelled contraption. Among these were the carburetor, the magneto ignition, various gears, the clutch, a steering mechanism, and a braking system. All of these inventions were incorporated in the first real combustion-engine automobile, which Marcus drove through the streets of Vienna in 1874.

Hiram Maxim. In this photo, taken in 1900, the proud inventor of the machine gun looks on with self-satisfied pride as Albert Edward, prince of Wales (the future King Edward VII), experiences for himself the awesome firepower of Maxim's "little daisy of a gun." In 1885 Maxim put on a similar demonstration for Lord Wolseley, commander-in-chief of the British Army. The British War Office adopted the gun 3 years later. The lethal power of the machine was first put to use in Africa at the Battle of Omdurman in 1898, where 20,000 Sudanese cavalrymen were slaughtered in fruitless charges against a line of 20 Maxim guns.

Internal combustion engines were also applied to early attempts at sustained flight. In 1900 Ferdinand von Zeppelin (1838–1917) constructed a rigid airship—a *dirigible*—consisting of a fabric-covered aluminum frame that was kept aloft by the incorporation of bags filled with hydrogen gas and powered by two 16-horsepower engines. Zeppelin's airships thus became the ancestors of the blimps that even today still ply the airways. Perhaps more momentous was the marriage of the gasoline engine to the glider, thus creating the first airplanes. Though there were several claimants to this honor, the Wright brothers in Kitty Hawk, North Carolina, on December 17, 1903, are usually credited with the first sustained engine-powered flight. By 1909, the first flight across the English Channel had been completed; in 1911 the first transcontinental airplane flight across the United States took place, though by taking 82 hours of flight time within a span of 2 months it could scarcely compete with railroad travel. Still, the potential of both the automobile and the airplane were to be starkly revealed within a few years during the Great War.

The Weapons Revolution   The advances in chemistry and explosives, metallurgy, and machine tooling during the second half of the nineteenth century also contributed to a vastly enhanced lethality among weapons. The earlier advances from the 1830s to the early 1860s that had included the percussion cap, the conical bullet, the revolver, and the rifled musket—all of which had made the American Civil War so deadly—now provided the base for the next generation of ever more sophisticated firearms. Breech-loading weapons, in their infancy during the early 1860s, rapidly came of age with the advent of the brass cartridge. By 1865, a number of manufacturers were marketing repeating rifles, some of whose designs, like the famous Winchester lever-action models, are still popular today. Rifles designed by the German firms of Krupp and Mauser pioneered the bolt-action, magazine, and clip-fed rifles that remained the staple of infantry weapons through two world wars.

Artillery went through a similar transformation. Breech-loading artillery, made possible by precision machining of breech-locks and the introduction of metallic cartridges for artillery shells, made loading and firing large guns far easier, faster, and more efficient. By the early 1880s the invention of the recoil cylinder—a spring or hydraulic device like an automobile shock absorber—to cushion the force of the gun's recoil eliminated the necessity of reaiming the piece after every shot. Field artillery could now be anchored, aimed, and fired continuously with enhanced accuracy: It had become "rapid-fire artillery." Its effectiveness was enhanced further by the new explosives like guncotton, dynamite, and later TNT, available for use in its shells. Another innovation in this regard was the development of smokeless powder, or *cordite*, which, in addition to eliminating much of the battlefield smoke generated by black powder, was three times more powerful as a propellant. Thus, the range and accuracy of small arms and artillery were pushed even further.

By far, the most significant—and lethal—advance in weaponry during the later nineteenth century, however, was the invention of the machine gun, the deadliest weapon ever developed, responsible for more deaths than any other device in history. Though many quick-firing weapons had been developed with varying degrees of success during these years—the most famous being the Gatling Gun (1861)— the first fully automatic machine gun was conceived by Hiram Maxim (1840–1916), an American inventor and dabbler in electricity. How he designed and manufactured the gun, first fired in 1884, along with how it was received and adopted by European states is recounted in Maxim's autobiography, *My Life* (1915), from which the accompanying excerpt is taken. Near the end of his memoir Maxim also recounts, somewhat ruefully, that he was applauded more highly for inventing his "killing machine" than for inventing a steam inhaler for those suffering from bronchitis.

By the outbreak of World War I, every major army in the world was equipping itself with Maxim's guns, now manufactured in licensed factories in Europe and the United States. Perhaps more than any other single weapon, the machine gun made the western front in Europe from 1914 to 1918 the most devastating killing field in human history.

> ### Hiram Maxim on the Mechanics of His Machine Gun
>
> "I first made an apparatus that enabled me to determine the force and character of the recoil, and find out the distance that the barrel ought to be allowed to recoil in order to do the necessary work. All the parts were adjustable, and when I had moved everything about so as to produce the maximum result, I placed six cartridges in the apparatus, pulled the trigger, and they all went off in about half a second. I was delighted. . . . I had made an automatic machine gun with a single barrel, using service cartridges, that would load and fire itself by energy derived from the recoil over six hundred rounds in a minute."
>
> —Hiram Maxim. *My Life* (London: Methuen, 1915), p. 170.

The Social and Economic Impact of Industrialism, 1750–1914

All of these changes in modes of production, particularly the emergence of the factory system, resulted in wholesale transformations in the daily lives of millions around the globe. Along with new networks of transportation, new materials, and new sources of energy, the industrialized nations underwent significant changes in the way they viewed politics, social institutions, and economic relationships across the period of industrialization.

Demographic Changes

Changes in the demographics of industrialized nations followed the development of new industries and consequent transformations in the lives of millions. Perhaps most significantly, the populations of these countries grew at unprecedented rates and became increasingly urbanized. Indeed, Great Britain became by the latter half of the nineteenth century the first country to have more urban dwellers than rural inhabitants. This trend would continue among the industrialized nations through the twentieth century.

Population Surge and Urbanization   As data from 1700 to around 1914 reveal, the industrialized nations experienced a significant population explosion (see Map 23.3). Advances in industrial production, expansion of factories, and improved agriculture during the first industrial revolution combined to produce increasing

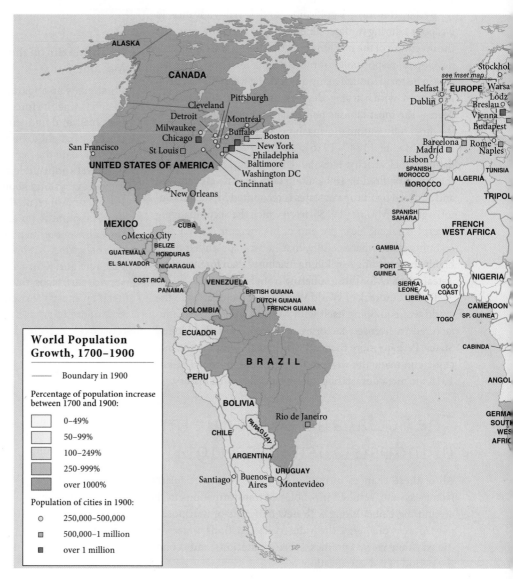

MAP **23.3 World Population Growth, 1700–1900.**

opportunities for jobs as well as more plentiful and nutritious food in order to sustain a larger population. In the second Industrial Revolution scientific advances in medicine, including medications and vaccinations, and notions of sanitation contributed to a declining mortality rate. For example, the population of Britain grew from around 9 million in 1700 to around 20 million in 1850. Then from 1871 to 1914 Britain's population soared from 31 million to nearly 50 million. Other industrialized states experienced similar population increases. In Germany much the same occurred: around 41 million in 1871 versus 58 million in 1914.

More revealing than overall population figures is the shift of populations away from rural areas and into urban areas. For example, in Great Britain in 1800 around 60 percent of the population lived in rural areas. By 1850, however, about

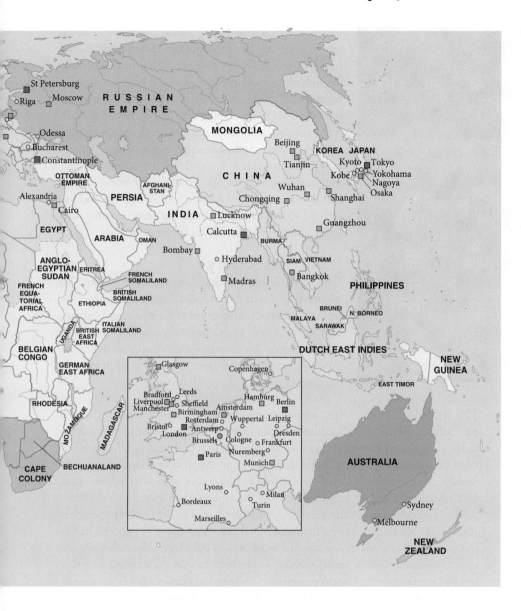

50 percent of the population lived in cities. In numerical terms, the population of London amounted to around 1 million in 1800, but by 1850 that figure had more than doubled to around 2.5 million. Moreover, in 1801 only 21 cities in Europe (including London) could boast of populations over 100,000. By 1850, this had more than doubled to 42. Significant in this respect were the appearance of new industrial and commercial centers such as Manchester, Liverpool, Birmingham, and Glasgow, as well as vast increases in the size of older capital cities such as Paris, Berlin, and St. Petersburg.

European Migrations   Another social change during the industrial era concerns emigrations of Europeans to foreign lands. In part, this movement was sparked

Italian Family at Ellis Island, New York, ca. 1905. This iconic photo of an Italian mother and her three children, taken by the photojournalist Lewis Hine and later hand colored, has come to portray the dreams of peace and prosperity that millions of immigrants to America brought with them in the late nineteenth and early twentieth centuries. The mother and her girls stare at the camera with dazed looks, but with a sack thrown jauntily on his back, the boy looks ready to explore his new world.

by the dramatic rise in population figures in industrialized areas of Europe. Another contributing factor, however, was the desire to escape the grinding poverty of underdeveloped regions of the West—particularly Ireland and southeast Europe—in order to seek better opportunities in developing industrial parts of the West. It should also be noted that advances in transportation, such as railroads and steamships, made it easier for Europeans to emigrate to foreign lands. In all, some 60 million Europeans left for other parts of the world (North and South America, Australia, and Asiatic Russia) between 1800 and 1914. Of these, the majority emigrated to the United States and Canada (see Map 23.4).

Industrial Society

Significant changes in the lower levels of society also occurred as a result of industrialization. Although the landed elites continued to enjoy their privileged status, they nevertheless began to lose ground to the rising middle classes. The principal alteration in social classes, however, was the appearance of a new class: the working class.

The Middle Classes   The prosperous middle classes, which included those in professional, administrative, educational, and commercial jobs, rose to prominence in the new age, thanks largely to their acquisition of liquid wealth. Distinguished from the landed aristocracy above them and from the working classes below, the middle classes themselves were divided into an upper class of wealthy industrialists, bankers, lawyers, and doctors at the top and tradespeople and handcrafters below.

These middle classes constituted around 15 percent of Europe's total population. It was this class that set the cultural and moral tone for most of the second half of the nineteenth century. What counted most in their eyes was "respectability"; not a hint of impropriety or sexual scandal was to be tolerated. As a measure of this, in 1867 the English Parliament passed the Obscene Publications Bill in an attempt to crack down on pornographic literature. The middle classes set themselves apart from the elites above and especially from those below by emphasizing what they considered their respectability, frugality, and industry. Indeed, with their emphasis on family and respectability, the morality of the middle classes during the reign of Britain's Queen Victoria inspired the adjective "Victorian" to describe a particular kind of prudish, self-disciplined—"earnest"—code of behavior. Determined to succeed at all costs, the middle classes eagerly consumed numerous self-improvement books, of which the most famous was Samuel Smiles's *Self Help* (1859). The book went through multiple editions in succeeding years and emerged as the most popular work on self-improvement in the Victorian era.

The Working Class   Urban factory workers were distinguished from farmers and workers in rural areas by their daily routine of regulation by the factory time clock and by selling their labor in return for cash wages. Among the working classes,

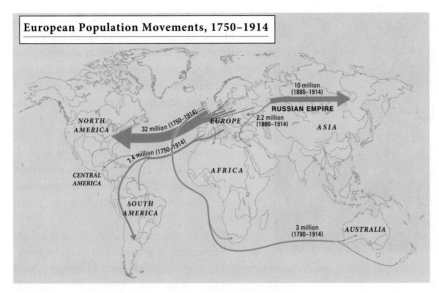

MAP 23.4 **European Population Movements, 1750–1914.**

divisions applied between skilled and unskilled workers, largely determined by familiarity with the intricacies of industrial machinery and its maintenance.

What were typical working conditions in British textile mills in the early 1800s? In a word, deplorable. In a new age when there were no traditional protective guilds or associations, workers were at the mercy of factory owners. The factory clock and the pace of factory machinery determined the day's work; the work was repetitive, dirty, and dangerous, not to mention dehumanizing. This was especially the case with young children—some as young 7 years—who either worked in factories alongside their parents as family units or had been orphaned or turned over to local parishes by parents who could no longer provide for their care. Working long hours—12- to 14-hour days were common in the early 1800s—children were constantly urged to speed up production and severely disciplined for "idling." Indeed, they were commonly beaten for falling asleep and to keep them from falling into the machinery, which, because of the lack of protection from its moving parts, could easily maim or kill them. In fact, until the 1840s in Britain, the majority of "hands," or factory workers, were women and children, who, by virtue of their inexperience and expendability, could be paid less than their male counterparts.

Conditions were often even worse in the mines. Children frequently began work in mines as early as age 6 or 7, most often as "trappers," responsible for opening and shutting ventilation doors in mineshafts. As they continued, they often moved up to "hurrying," or lugging newly dug coal along long, low underground passageways for conveyance to the surface. Girls were especially victimized in underground mines, where they not only had to drag heavy coal-filled carts by chains fixed to leather belts around their waists but also were frequently sexually abused by their supervisors.

Factory Towns   Because industrial cities expanded close to factories and mills, conditions there generally mirrored those of the factories themselves. Clouds of coal smoke tended to hang over them, blackening buildings, acidifying the rain and soil, and often causing respiratory ailments among the citizens—prompting William

Working-Class Tenements in English Industrial Cities. In this engraving, entitled *Over London by Rail*, the celebrated engraver Gustave Doré (1832–1883) depicts the overcrowded and squalid living conditions in working-class tenements during the early years of the Industrial Revolution. Notice the long rows of houses separated by walls and arranged in back-to-back fashion. Notice also the stretched lines for drying clothes, as well as the large number of occupants in each outdoor area.

Blake's famous allusion to "dark Satanic Mills." In addition to the acrid smell of coal, there were usually a variety of other stenches assaulting the nostrils of the inhabitants. Piles of coal ash and clinkers, pungent waste materials from coking or from gas works, and vile outpourings from tanneries and dye-works all lent their smells to the more prosaic ones of household waste, sewage, and horse manure. With the population exploding and only rudimentary waste disposal and access to clean water, it was little wonder that diseases like cholera, typhus, and tuberculosis were rampant.

Adding to the miseries of the inhabitants were their wretched living conditions. The working classes lived in crowded tenements consisting of row after row of shoddily built houses packed together in narrow, dark streets. One social activist, Friedrich Engels (1820–1895), the son of a wealthy mill owner and later collaborator with Karl Marx, was determined to call attention to such abysmal conditions. As a young man Engels was sent to his father's cotton-producing factory in Manchester, England, to learn the factory system. What Engels observed there compelled him to write a scathing attack on the industrial movement, *The Condition of the Working-Class in England in 1844* (1845), in which he described what he perceived as the horrors of workers' lives.

Critics of Industrialism

It was not long before the criticisms of Engels and other socially conscious observers began to draw attention to the obvious abuses of the industrial movement and to stimulate reform of working conditions. Efforts to improve these sordid conditions were launched in Great Britain in the 1820s and 1830s and carried over into the 1870s.

The Laboring Quarters

"[R]ight and left a multitude of covered passages lead from the street into numerous courts, and he who turns in thither gets into a filth and disgusting grime. . . . In one of these courts there stands directly at the entrance, at the end of the covered passage, a privy without a door, so dirty that the inhabitants can pass into and out of the court only by passing through foul pools of stagnant urine and excrement."

—Friedrich Engels. *The Condition of the Working-Class in England in 1844* (London: Allen Unwin, 1943) p. 37

Socialists   The plight of the working classes caught the attention of a variety of social activists who determined to take up the fight for reform. Into the fray stepped several French and English "utopian socialists"—a term originally used derisively to describe the presumed impracticality of their schemes. One of the earliest of these activists was Henri de Saint-Simon (1760–1825), who presented a view of humanity that flew in the face of industrial society's competition for individual wealth. In Saint-Simon's view, private property should be more equally distributed, according to the notion that "from each according to his abilities, to each according to his works." Louis Blanc (1811–1882) criticized the capitalist system in his *The Organization of Work* (1839). In the book Blanc urged workers to agitate for voting rights, called for radical ideas like the right to work, and reconfigured Saint-Simon's memorable phrase to read "from each according to his abilities, to each according to his needs." Charles Fourier (1772–1837) advocated the founding of self-sustaining model communities in which jobs were apportioned according to ability and interest, with a sliding scale of wages tailored to highly compensate those doing the most dangerous or unattractive jobs. Fourier's concept of such "phalanxes" was the one adopted by the North American Phalanx, in which Mary Paul spent time (see the vignette to this chapter).

Robert Owen (1771–1858), a factory owner in the north of England, led a movement to establish the Grand National Consolidated Trades Union. Its objective was to call for a national strike of all trade unions, but owing to a lack of participation among workers, the movement was disbanded. Owen had previously established a model community in Scotland called "New Lanark," where more humane living and working conditions for workers resulted in greater profits. After campaigning for the formation of workers' unions, Owen left for America, where he set up a model socialist community in Indiana called "New Harmony," which eventually dissolved amid internal quarrels when he returned to England.

Chartism was another organized labor movement in Britain. Taking its name from the Peoples Charter (1838), chartism was formed by the London Working Men's Association; and its purpose was, among other issues, to call for universal male suffrage. Millions of workers signed petitions, which were presented to Parliament in 1839 and 1842; both were rejected. Nevertheless, the chartist movement galvanized for the first time workers' sentiments and aspirations, and it served as a model for future attempts at labor reform.

Karl Marx. In this photo, taken in London in 1875, Marx displays many of the character traits for which he is best known. Following the publication of his *Das Kapital* in 1871, Marx had established his reputation as a scholar of economic theory. Notice his self-satisfied and confident demeanor as he stares at the camera in an almost defiant manner. Notice as well his attire, ironically suggestive of a successful member of the bourgeoisie. After Marx's death, his longtime friend Friedrich Engels distributed 1,200 copies of this photo to communists around the world.

Karl Marx   By far the most famous of the social reformers was Karl Marx (1818–1883). The son of a prosperous German attorney, Marx proved a brilliant student, eventually earning a PhD in philosophy from the University of Berlin. Marx's activities, however, resulted in his being exiled from Germany and then from France. During a visit to the industrial center of Manchester, where he met and befriended Friedrich Engels, Marx observed both the miserable lives of factory workers and the patent inequities of industrialism. From this, Marx developed his theory, which he termed "scientific socialism," that all of history involved class struggles. Borrowing the dialectical schema of the German philosopher Georg Wilhelm Friedrich Hegel (1770–1831), Marx replaced its idealism with his own materialist concept based on economic class struggle: *dialectical materialism*. Moreover, Marx saw revolution as the means by which the industrial working classes will ultimately topple the capitalist order: Just as the Third Estate and bourgeoisie had overthrown the aristocracy during the French Revolution, the current struggle between the working classes and the capitalist entrepreneurs would ultimately result in the demise of capitalism.

Convinced of the need for the overthrow of the capitalist system, Marx and Engels joined the nascent Communist Party in London. In preparation for a meeting in 1848, the two collaborators dashed off a pamphlet entitled *The Communist Manifesto* (1848), a book that later on emerged as the bible for worldwide communism. The slender work is really a propaganda piece designed to rally support among the working classes, or *proletariat*, and to encourage them to rise up and overthrow the capitalist factory owners, or *bourgeoisie*. Compiled from a variety of

French socialist, German philosophical, and personal interpretations of past history, the *Manifesto* reflects Marx's vision that "the history of all hitherto existing society is the history of class struggle" and that the time had come for the working classes to follow earlier examples and to overthrow the capitalists: "The proletarians have nothing to lose but their chains. They have a world to win. WORKING MEN OF ALL COUNTRIES, UNITE!"

Inquiries and Reforms   As critics of industrialism began to cry out against obvious abuses of the industrial movement, many called for government efforts and programs for the reform of working conditions. Efforts to improve these horrid conditions were launched in Great Britain in the 1820s and 1830s. In 1832 Parliament launched an inquiry into abuses within factories. In 1833 the Factory Act was passed, which set a minimum age of 9 for child employees and limited the workday to 8 hours for children between the ages of 9 and 13 and to 12 hours for those aged 13–18. Similar inquiries were conducted concerning working conditions within mines. As a result, the Mines Act of 1842 forbade the underground employment of all girls and women and set a minimum age of 10 for child laborers.

Improved Standards of Living

Although still a matter of debate among historians, contemporary data suggest that in overall terms living and working conditions began to improve in Britain from around the 1830s to the end of the century. Thanks to the series of reforms already mentioned, conditions in factories and mines were substantially better than at the beginning of the century. Textile factories were now located in urban areas, and housing conditions for workers were more amenable. Most important, wage levels increased across the nineteenth century for industrial workers. For example, from 1850 to 1875 wages of British workers increased by around one-third and by nearly one-half by 1900.

New Jobs for Women   As a result of the second Industrial Revolution, many women fared far better in terms of employment. In overall terms, women represented around one-third of the workers in later nineteenth-century industrial jobs. Mary Paul's experience, discussed in the vignette at the beginning of this chapter, is one example of opportunities for women. Again, the data from these textile mills offer supporting evidence. While fewer than 2,000 women were employed in the mills in 1837, that figure nearly doubled by 1865; and by around 1900 the number of female textile workers had increased to nearly 6,000. But factory work in textile mills was not the only avenue opened to women as the industrial era unfolded in the later years of the nineteenth century.

When new technologies and social trends created new employment possibilities, women constituted a readily available pool of workers. Inventions like the typewriter (perfected in the 1870s), the telephone (invented by Alexander Graham Bell in 1876), and calculating machines (in use in the 1890s), for instance, required workers to handle related jobs, the majority of which went mostly to single women and widows. As a result, women became particularly prominent in secretarial office jobs. In addition, the explosion of business firms created countless jobs for secretaries, while department stores opened up jobs for women as clerks.

Women Working as Telephone Operators. The first telephone exchange appeared in 1879. In this image from 1881, women operators are shown at work at an early pyramidal switchboard. Women were selected as operators because their voices were considered pleasing to the ear and because they were considered more polite than men.

Women's Suffrage Movement

Although many women were afforded new opportunities in business and in professions like nursing and education after 1871, in many other areas women remained second-class citizens. Women in both the United States and Europe did not begin to gain the right to own property or to sue for divorce until the third quarter of the nineteenth century, as exemplified by the passage of the English Married Woman's Property Act in 1882.

More pressing in the eyes of many female reformers was the right to vote. Throughout Europe during the late nineteenth and early twentieth centuries, women formed political activist groups to press for the vote. The most active of these groups was in Britain, where in 1867 the National Society for Women's Suffrage was founded. The most famous—and most radical—of British political feminists was Emmeline Pankhurst (1858–1928), who together with her daughters formed the Women's Social and Political Union in 1903. They and their supporters, known as *suffragettes*, resorted to public acts of protest and civil disobedience in order to call attention to their cause. Although these tactics were of no avail prior to 1914, the right to vote was extended to some British women after the war (taken over from the British colony of New Zealand, which granted the right in 1893).

Political feminists were also active on the Continent. The French League of Women's Rights was founded in the 1870s, and the Union of German Women's Organizations was formed in 1894; in neither country was the right to vote granted women until after World War I. Women in the United States pursued a parallel course with similar results: After decades of lobbying before the war, women's suffrage was finally granted by constitutional amendment in 1920.

Emmeline Pankhurst. Pankhurst was arrested numerous times for her militancy and aggressive actions against the British government and its refusal to extend the suffrage to women. In this photo, taken on May 21, 1914, Pankhurst is shown being arrested outside Buckingham Palace after attempting to present a petition to King George V.

Improved Urban Living

Living conditions within the major urban areas in industrialized nations underwent significant improvements during the late nineteenth and early twentieth centuries. Largely the result of the application of new technologies emerging from the industrial movement, there is no question that the lives of urban dwellers were improved in the second half of the nineteenth century.

Sanitation and Electricity   One measure of improved living conditions was in the provision of better sanitation. A first of its kind was the Public Health Bill (1848) in Britain, followed by a further measure in 1875. Beginning in the 1860s and 1870s large cities in Britain and Europe established public water services and began to construct underground sewage systems to carry waste from houses, outfitted with running water, to rivers and other locations beyond urban areas. By the latter part of the nineteenth century, the widespread use of gas lighting gradually began to give way to electrical varieties. Thomas Edison (1847–1931) perfected the incandescent lightbulb in 1879, making the lighting of homes and business interiors more affordable and practical and gradually replacing gas lighting.

Paris represents a good example of the implementation of these reforms. In the 1850s and 1860s Napoleon III (r. 1852–1870) appointed the urban planner Georges Haussmann (1809–1891) to begin a massive reconstruction of the city. Haussmann tore down close-packed tenements in order to provide modernized buildings for residential and commercial use and to construct wide boulevards. This was in part driven by a desire to beautify the city, but it was also driven by the necessity of providing better access for government troops in the event of public demonstrations; barricaded streets, a feature of the revolutions of 1830 and 1848, thus became a thing of the past. And, like most cities of the industrialized West by the turn of the

The Great Stink. In the summer of 1858 the combination of a heat wave and unusually slow flow in the Thames resulted in one of London's worst modern health threats. The smell was so vile that shades treated with carbolic acid had to be mounted in the Houses of Parliament. The situation was also fair game for cartoonists, as depicted here. Beyond this, the incidence of waterborne diseases skyrocketed. The result was the building of a new citywide sewer and treatment system that vastly reduced the amount of raw sewage in the river.

PUNCH, OR THE LONDON CHARIVARI.—July 3, 1858.

DIPHTHERIA.   SCROFULA.   CHOLERA.

FATHER THAMES INTRODUCING HIS OFFSPRING TO THE FAIR CITY OF LONDON.
(A Design for a Fresco in the New Houses of Parliament.)

twentieth century, Paris featured lighted and paved streets, public water systems, parks, hospitals, and police.

A dramatic symbol of both the newly redesigned city of Paris and the triumph of industry and science during the second Industrial Revolution was the Eiffel Tower, designed and erected by Alexandre Gustave Eiffel (1832–1923). Constructed for the Paris Exposition of 1889, the tower took years to construct and, at nearly 1,000 feet in height, was the tallest structure in the world until the construction of the Empire State Building in New York in 1931.

Big Business

As the scale of urban planning and renewal increased toward the end of the nineteenth century, together with the size of buildings and other constructions, so did business. As manufacturing, transportation, and financing matured, entrepreneurs and businessmen became concerned about competition and falling profit rates. Since governments generally pursued hands-off liberalism (*laissez-faire*, see Chapter 22) in the economy, except for protective tariffs, entrepreneurs sought to establish cartels and monopolies, creating big business enterprises in the process.

Eiffel Tower and Paris Exposition, 1900. Although it was reviled as an eyesore by many when it was first constructed, the Eiffel Tower emerged as one of the world's great symbols of industrial elegance. It was the centerpiece—along with the great globe next to it and the Palace of Electricity—of the Great Exhibition in Paris in 1900, pictured above.

Large Firms   When Britain industrialized, it gradually shifted from a closed mercantilist economy to the liberal free-trade policy Adam Smith advocated (see Chapter 22). Britain's competitors, especially Germany and the United States, by contrast, erected high tariff walls around their borders in order to help their fledgling industries. After the second wave of steel, chemical, and electricity industrialization in the second half of the nineteenth century, the scale of industrial investments rose exponentially. On domestic markets, governments did not interfere with business organization and practice, except for labor protection in Europe. As a result, in several branches of the economy, big businesses emerged during the second half of the nineteenth century that protected their profit rates through *cartels* (market-sharing agreements) or strove altogether for monopolies.

Large firms typically developed in Germany and the United States, the leaders of the second wave of industrialization. Corporations like the Krupp steelworks in Germany and Standard Oil Company in the United States had evolved by the 1890s, controlling large shares of their markets. Standard Oil at its height, for example, produced over 90 percent of the country's petroleum. Another example is the United States Steel Company, founded in 1901 by Andrew Carnegie (1835–1919), which dominated the production of American steel. Carnegie himself amassed a huge personal fortune of almost $250 million, making him the richest man in the world.

New Management Styles   In addition, new technologies in all industrial sectors offered more efficient means of production; the result was a series of significant changes in production processes during the second phase of European industrialism. One example is the implementation of the so-called American System, incorporating the use of interchangeable parts, which greatly enhanced mass production. A related development was the appearance of "continuous-flow production," wherein workers

The Assembly Line. The American System of interchangeable parts for muskets of the early nineteenth century had evolved into the assembly line by the early twentieth. Here, Ford Model T automobiles are moved along a conveyor to different stations, where workers assemble them in simple, repetitive steps, resulting in production efficiency and low prices for the cars.

performed specialized tasks at stationary positions along an assembly line. In addition, new "scientific management" tactics were employed in mass-production assembly plants. Since no more than basic skills were required on many assembly lines, labor costs could be kept low.

The best known of the new management systems was "Taylorism," named after Frederick W. Taylor (1856–1915), an American engineer. The objective was to measure each factory worker's production based on how many units were completed in an hour's time. The result was that workers were not only more carefully managed by their superiors but also paid in accordance with their productivity. The combined result was a rapid escalation in the speed of production, which in turn contributed to a marked increase in the production of goods for daily consumption and, therefore, in the development of a consumer market at the turn of the twentieth century.

Intellectual and Cultural Responses to Industrialism

The new society that industrialism was creating not surprisingly spawned entirely new directions in science, philosophy, religion, and the creative fields such as literature and art. It generated new kinds of popular expression, from dime novels to photography. The advent of *mass society* also led to the beginnings of a mass culture, in which widespread literacy and public education allowed a far greater percentage of the populace access to what had largely been the province of elites. It allowed artists, writers, composers, and musicians to have mass followings for the first time. Men and women like Charles Dickens, Harriet Beecher Stowe, and Richard Wagner, to name only three, were the popular equivalent of today's "superstars" in their own time. Yet, there was also a profound disquiet among scientists, intellectuals, and artists. With so many of the old standards falling by the wayside, tremendous uncertainty was present just underneath the surface of material progress. This disquiet would come to the surface with a vengeance in the immediate years after World War I.

Scientific and Intellectual Developments

The latter half of the nineteenth century saw advances in both theoretical and empirical sciences that laid the basis for many of the staples of the twentieth century. Among the most far-reaching were atomic physics and relativity theory, Darwinism and evolution, and the foundations of modern psychology. Scientists also laid the foundations for medicine, although here the most important breakthroughs had to await the twentieth century.

New Theories of Matter   Quests for understanding the nature of matter, under way since Galileo (see Chapter 17), became systematic with the foundation of technical universities and science faculties in existing universities in the second half of the 1800s. Researchers carried out extensive experiments and made important discoveries in the 1890s that would have far-reaching consequences in defining atomic physics and theories of relativity. In 1892 the Dutch physicist Hendrik Lorentz (1853–1928) demonstrated that the atom, far from being a solid billiard ball, actually contained smaller particles, which he named "corpuscles"; these were later renamed "electrons." A few years later, Wilhelm Roentgen (1845–1923) discovered a mysterious form of emission he called "X-rays." The ability to generate these rays would shortly lead to using them in medical diagnoses and creating the modern X-ray machine. The following year, 1896, saw the first experiments in assessing radioactivity in uranium and radium by Antoine Becquerel (1852–1908) and Marie Curie (1867–1934).

As a result of these experimental findings, theoretical physics advanced new theories on the nature of light and energy. In 1900 Max Planck (1858–1947) proposed that instead of the accepted notion that energy is emitted in steady streams or waves, it is issued in bursts, or what he termed "quanta." This idea, later developed into quantum theory, suggested that matter and energy might be interchangeable. Ernest Rutherford (1871–1937), interested in this interchangeability, demonstrated in 1911 that radioactive atoms release a form of energy in the process of their disintegration. Thus, nearly three centuries of speculation about atoms as the building blocks of nature led to experimentally verified theories of subatomic particles.

Albert Einstein   These discoveries in the physical sciences set the stage for the appearance of perhaps the most sensational of the turn-of-the-century scientific theories: Albert Einstein's (1879–1955) theory of relativity. In 1905 and then again in 1915 Einstein published papers in which he destroyed the Newtonian notion of a certain, absolute, and mechanistic universe that obeys unvarying and objectively verifiable laws. Instead, Einstein argued that there are no absolutes of time, space, and motion; rather, these are relative to each other and depend on the position of the observer.

Moreover, Einstein demonstrated that Newton was incorrect in thinking that matter and energy were separate entities; they were, in fact, equivalent and he developed the corresponding mathematical formula. In his equation $E = mc^2$, Einstein theorized that the atom contains an amount of energy equal to its mass multiplied by the square of the speed of light. In other words, relatively small amounts of matter could convert into massive amounts of energy. This discovery, developed further in the twentieth century, provided the foundation for a full understanding of the forces among subatomic particles and the construction of nuclear weapons.

Charles Darwin   The basis of modern theories of evolution was laid by Charles Darwin (1809–1882). Darwin's *On the Origin of Species by Means of Natural Selection* (1859) argued that in nature species gradually evolved from lower to higher forms. As a young man Darwin sailed on an exploratory mission on the H.M.S. *Beagle* from 1831 to 1836 to the waters off the South American coast in the Pacific. Observing the tremendous variability of species in the string of the isolated Galapagos Islands, he found himself at a loss to explain why so many different species cohabited within such close geographical areas.

It occurred to Darwin—and independently to another English naturalist, Alfred Russell Wallace (1823–1913)—that an explanation for the appearance of new

Charles Darwin as Ape.
Darwin's theories about the evolution of humankind aroused enormous scorn. In this scathing 1861 cartoon, Darwin, with the body of a monkey, holds a mirror to a simian-looking creature. The original caption quoted a line from Shakespeare's *Love's Labor Lost*: "This is the ape of form."

species in nature might lie in the struggle for food: Only those species equipped with the tools to survive in their environments would win out; those without these characteristics would become extinct.

In its essence, therefore, the Darwinian theory of evolution as spelled out in the *Origin* boils down to three main elements: (1) in nature more species appear than can be supported by existing food supplies, (2) there is a resultant struggle among species to survive, and (3) through inheritance subtle mutations within species are transmitted that render some more able than others to survive in the struggle for food. The most controversial part of this theory rests in the notion that characteristics are passed on by means of "natural selection." In other words, there is no intelligence or plan in the universe—only random chance and haphazard process, resulting in a pessimistic view of "nature red in tooth and claw."

Although the *Origin* said nothing about the theory of evolution as applied to humankind—this appeared later in the *Descent of Man* (1871)—there were those who quickly applied it to society and nations. As noted in other chapters in this section, the work of Herbert Spencer (1820–1903) was instrumental in proposing a theory that came to be called "social Darwinism," which sought to apply ideas of natural selection to races, ethnicities, and peoples. Spencer's ideas were frequently used to support imperial ventures aimed at the conquest and sometimes the "uplift" of non-European or American peoples as well as to justify increasingly virulent nationalism in the years leading to World War I.

Developments in Psychology   The first scientist to separate psychology from philosophy and to make it a serious scientific discipline was Wilhelm Wundt (1832–1920). A German physiologist and student of human behavior, Wundt established the first psychology laboratory in 1879, where he conducted early experiments on aspects of human behavior.

Increasingly important among psychologists was the topic of insanity. What especially concerned Victorians were apparently unconscious impulses for actions not subject to human will. The best known of the early psychologists was Sigmund Freud (1856–1939), an Austrian physician. After obtaining a degree in medicine in Vienna, Freud studied cases of emotionally disturbed patients in Paris, and then in 1886 he set up his own practice in Vienna. Freud specialized in treating patients suffering from what was then called "hysteria," which he treated using a technique he labeled "psychoanalysis." In 1900 Freud published his highly influential *The Interpretation of Dreams*, in which he drew connections between dreams and the unconscious in humans. Although controversial, and today largely discarded, Freud's theories stressed the dominance of unconscious urges and motivations—mostly sexual in nature—in determining human behavior. The sum total of Freudian psychological theories is that humans, so far from being rational creatures, are in fact irrational creatures, driven by subconscious, and not conscious, urges. Today, it no longer enjoys the unquestioned dominance it once did in the field and has largely become a branch of medicine and, in particular, the study of brain chemicals. But it still survives on the practical level in the form of lifestyle counseling and behavior modification.

The Meaning of the New Scientific Discoveries   Physics, biology, and psychology were not the only sciences contributing fundamentally to the emergence of scientific–industrial society at the end of the nineteenth century. Medicine began to acquire a scientific character, for example, with the discoveries of vaccines by Louis Pasteur (1822–1895). But it had to await the twentieth century before it reached maturity. With the arrival of the theories of relativity, Darwinian selection, and the psychological unconscious, however, enough of a transition toward the scientific–industrial age had occurred to throw people into deep philosophical and religious confusion.

In a sense, the path of reductionism begun in the seventeenth century and discussed in Chapter 17 was being reached. In previous centuries, the Hobbesian embodied mind, fear of death,"war of all against all," and the religious skepticism, secularism, and atheism of the Enlightenment were merely speculations that remained ultimately unproved. Now, the specter of a meaningless universe inhabited by beings devoid of free will and driven by biological forces over which they have no control seemed to many to be inescapable. Thus, the new era seemed to usher in a profoundly disturbing devil's bargain: The sciences had created so many useful things to ease the burdens of human life but had taken away the sense of purpose that made that life worth living. It was left to philosophers, religious leaders, intellectuals, and artists to wrestle with the implications of this central problem of scientific–industrial society.

Toward Modernity in Philosophy and Religion

Despite the impressive achievements of Western industrialized society during the late nineteenth century, there were many who felt uneasy about the results. Scores of detractors—mostly in the intellectual community of western Europe—decried the boastful claims of a "superior" scientific civilization. These voices ridiculed Western bourgeois values and advocated alternative approaches to personal fulfillment.

Friedrich Nietzsche   Easily the most celebrated of these detractors was the German philosopher Friedrich Nietzsche (1844–1900). A brilliant, but increasingly mentally unstable, professor at the University of Basel, Nietzsche railed against the conventions of Western civilization and criticized the perceived decadence of modern culture. Nietzsche represents a growing trend toward pessimism and doubt about the progress of Western culture near the end of the nineteenth century.

Nietzsche began his assault on Western culture in 1872 with the publication of *The Birth of Tragedy*, which was followed in later years by works like *Beyond Good and Evil* (1886) and *On the Genealogy of Morals* (1887). One object of derision for Nietzsche was the entire notion of scientific, rational thought as the best path toward intellectual truth. For Nietzsche, and for others of like mind, rational thought will not improve either the individual or the welfare of humankind; only recourse to "will" instead of intellect—what Nietzsche called the "will to power"—will suffice.

The individual who follows this path will become a "Superman" and will lead others toward truth.

Another target of Nietzsche's wrath was Christianity, which in his eyes led its believers into a "slave morality"; and in a famous quote, he declared that "God is dead."

Roman Catholicism   As might be expected, the various religious establishments of the West were forced into a defensive position by the growing prestige and influence of the sciences. Although mainstream Protestant leaders tended to urge accommodation with scientific progress—though they struggled considerably with the implications of Darwinism—the Catholic Church was more inclined to resist both the allure of science and the appeal of materialism and capitalism. Pope Pius IX for example, staunchly resisted the drift toward modernism by issuing the encyclical entitled "Syllabus of Errors" in 1864 and by convening the First Vatican Council in 1871.

With the death of Pius IX in 1878, however, the church adopted a new position under the leadership of Pope Leo XIII (r. 1878–1903). On the one hand, Leo mounted a full-scale offensive against what he considered an alarming trend toward secular materialism by urging Catholic workers to form socialist unions and workers' parties. In 1891 Leo XIII issued "De Rerum Novarum" ("On Modern Things"), in which he criticized capitalism for widening the gulf between the haves and the have-nots in the age of industrialism. On the other hand, Leo made slight concessions to science and the study of the sciences by Catholics and by establishing a Vatican office to look into scientific advances. Leo XIII's successor, Pope Pius X (r. 1903–1914), reversed these moves of moderation and criticized those who supported the church's reconciliation with science.

Toward Modernity in Literature and the Arts

As we have seen throughout this chapter, the creation of scientific–industrial society—modernity—was a slow and excruciatingly traumatic process. The social

Kulturkampf. The "conflict of cultures" between church and state in Germany reached its peak in the 1870s. In this cartoon from the period, the German chancellor Otto von Bismarck appears to have the upper hand in a game of political chess against Pope Pius IX.

which themes reflecting Freudian theories of the unconscious along with the noises and dissonances of engines, machines, and urban life would now dominate musical composition.

Putting It All Together

The series of dramatic and sweeping changes associated with the Industrial Revolution had profound implications for both the industrializing countries and the nonindustrialized world. Thanks in large part to new technologies and facilitated by advances in transportation and communication, the period from 1871 to 1914 saw world trade networks and empires dominated by the newly industrialized nations.

The Industrial Revolution began in Britain in the early eighteenth century and eventually spread to Europe and North America during the nineteenth century. Britain began the revolution when it harnessed steam engines to the rapid production of textiles. The subsequent development of the factory system along with more efficient transportation systems facilitated by railroads greatly expanded British manufacturing. Not everyone benefited, however, from the emergence of the factory system; capitalist entrepreneurs were reluctant to share with workers their slice of the economic pie, which in turn led to social unrest and calls for reform.

During the second Industrial Revolution in the later nineteenth century, advanced technologies led to the development of steel, electricity, and chemicals, which in turn greatly expanded the industrial economies of highly industrialized countries beyond Britain, including those of America and Germany. The daily lives of most citizens in industrialized nations were also improved by the application of industrial technologies to advances in transportation, communication, and even safety and sanitation.

These same advances also contributed to a new and greatly expanded surge of European imperialism. The explosive growth of industry and commerce, aided and abetted by new technologies and inventions, resulted in a quest among highly industrialized nations for raw materials, cheap labor, and new markets in order to sustain and expand their developing industries (see Concept Map). Moreover, Western industrial nations soon discovered that new needs forced the importation of not only raw materials but also foodstuffs. It is important to point out that nineteenth-century imperialism was made possible in the first place by technological innovations associated with advances in science and industrialism. Quinine prophylaxis, steam-powered gunboats, rapid-firing breechloaders, and the machine gun provided the overwhelming firepower to subdue nonindustrial societies and to open up interior regions of continents to Western colonialism. By the 1880s sailing ships were eclipsed by faster oceangoing ships powered by much more efficient compound engines and submarine cables provided for more efficient overseas communications and for the setting of more exact timetables. After 1871, the world's economy was increasingly divided into those who produced the world's manufactured products and those who both supplied the requisite raw materials and made up the growing pool of consumers.

Amid this process the basis for many of the patterns of twentieth-century modernity was being laid, as well as the foundations of its opposition. With the coming of World War I, and its aftermath, many of the cleavages created by modernity and its scientific–technological underpinnings were laid bare. Yet, as a new form of society,

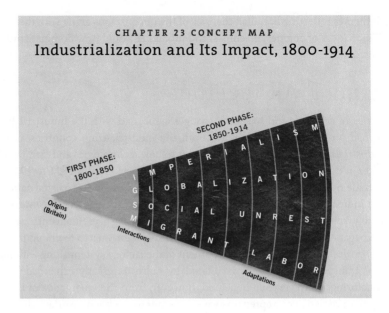

CHAPTER 23 CONCEPT MAP

Industrialization and Its Impact, 1800-1914

its interaction and adaptation with older forms continued unabated. Today, the two places that contain the largest number of "Mary Pauls" in world history—young women migrating from their farms to find work in urban factories—are the successors to the agrarian–urban religious civilizations that held out against the new order most tenaciously: India and China, both of whose economies now increasingly set the pace for twenty-first century industrial development. It is the story of the impact of modernity on these societies and others around the globe to which we now turn (see Concept Map).

Review and Respond

1. How was the steam engine originally used in the Industrial Revolution, and with what results?

2. How did industrialization improve daily life in Europe and the United States during the nineteenth century? What were the negative effects of industrialization?

3. Discuss the origin and development of negative reactions to the industrial movement.

4. Do you agree or disagree with the following statement: The expansion of Western imperialism in the nineteenth century reflects the positive contributions of inventions and technological advances emanating from industrialism.

5. Discuss and analyze ways in which the steady advance of industrialism during the second Industrial Revolution provoked responses from the scientific, intellectual, and cultural communities toward the turn of the twentieth century.

▶ For additional resources, including maps, primary sources, visuals, and quizzes, please go to www.oup.com/us/vonsivers. Please see the Further Resources section at the back of the book for additional readings and suggested websites.

Thinking Through Patterns

▶ **Where and when did the Industrial Revolution originate?**

Because of several advantageous factors, the Industrial Revolution began in Britain in the early eighteenth century. Among these were an earlier political revolution that empowered the merchant classes over the landed aristocracy, along with a prior agricultural revolution, and abundance of raw materials like coal.

Industrialization resulted in several social changes and adjustments. The capitalist middle classes were enriched and empowered by the growth of industrialism, as were the working classes, which did not exist as a group prior to industrialism. The benefits of industrialism were not evenly distributed across social strata; factory and mine workers were frequently exploited by the entrepreneurial and prosperous middle classes.

▶ **What were some effects of industrialization on Western society? How did social patterns change?**

▶ **In what ways did industrialization contribute to innovations in technology? How did these technological advances contribute to Western imperialism in the late nineteenth century?**

With the invention and perfection of the steam engine, capitalist entrepreneurs were able to substitute mechanical power for natural power and, thus, to develop the factory system. The factory system spread to the Continent and America as middle-class capitalism eclipsed mercantilism. Further advances contributed to a second Industrial Revolution after ca. 1850 that emphasized steel, chemistry, and electricity.

Progress in industrial technology during the second Industrial Revolution led to innovations ranging from practical inventions like the lightbulb to advances in communication and transportation. Inventions developed from industrial advances included the machine gun, new medicines, and startling developments in communications, to name a few. These tools facilitated the expansion of Western imperialism in Africa and Asia during the closing years of the nineteenth century

The new society that industrialism was creating not surprisingly spawned entirely new directions in science, philosophy, religion, and the creative fields such as literature and art. It generated new kinds of popular expression, from dime novels to photography. The advent of *mass society* also led to the beginnings of a mass culture, in which widespread literacy and public education allowed a far greater percentage of the populace access to what had largely been the province of elites. Yet, there was also a profound disquiet among scientists, intellectuals, and artists. With so many of the old standards falling by the wayside, tremendous uncertainty was present just underneath the surface of material progress. This disquiet would come to the surface with a vengeance in the immediate years after World War I.

▶ **What new directions in science, philosophy, religion, and the arts did industrialism generate? What kind of responses did it provoke?**

Chapter 24

1750-1910 | The Challenge of Modernity

EAST ASIA

> In Asia, our two countries, China and Japan, are the closest neighbors, and moreover have the same [written] language. How could we be enemies? Now for the time being we are fighting each other, but eventually we should work for permanent friendship . . . so that our Asiatic yellow race will not be encroached upon by the white race of Europe.

**EAST ASIA
1750–1900**

So commented Chinese statesman Li Hongzhang to his Japanese counterpart, Ito Hirobumi, as they discussed terms to end the Sino–Japanese War at the Japanese town of Shimonoseki in the spring of 1895. For Li it was the culmination of more than three decades of frustration as China's most powerful advocate of *self-strengthening*—using new foreign

Seeing Patterns

▶ What was the impact of Western imperialism on the "regulated societies" of China and Japan?

▶ Why did European empire building in Asia have such dramatically different effects on China and Japan?

▶ How have historians seen the nature of these outside forces and their influences in east Asia?

technologies and concepts to preserve China's Confucian society in the face of European and American intrusion. During Li's lifetime such intrusions had come with alarming frequency. Now, at 71, he was forced to go to Japan to sue for peace as Japanese troops occupied Korea and southern Manchuria. To add injury to insult, he had just narrowly survived being shot in the face by a Japanese fanatic while en route to the peace talks.

For Ito, one of the architects of Japan's astonishing rise to power, the victory over China was tinged with sadness and puzzlement as he responded: "Ten years ago when I was at Tientsin (Tianjin), I talked about reform with [you]. . . . Why is it that up to now not a single thing has been changed or reformed? This I deeply regret." As did Li, whose reply betrays a weary bitterness at China's deteriorating position: "At that time when I heard you . . . I was overcome with admiration . . . [at] your having vigorously changed your customs in Japan so as to reach the present stage. Affairs in my country have been so confined by tradition that I could not accomplish what I desired . . . I am ashamed of having excessive wishes and lacking the power to fulfill them."

The significance of this rueful exchange was not lost on the other countries with interests in east Asia, who viewed the war's outcome with a

Li Hongzhang and Ito at Shimonoseki. In this ukiyo-e print of the peace negotiations held in the Shunpanro Restaurant in the Japanese town of Shimonoseki in early 1895, Li Hongzhang, the chief Chinese diplomat is dressed in the reddish brown gown at the right side of the table. His Japanese counterpart, Ito Hirobumi, sits opposite him and wears a sash; to his left is the Japanese foreign minister Mutsu Munemitsu, also wearing a sash. John W. Foster, former U.S. Secretary of State and advisor to the Chinese during the negotiations, stands at the head of the table close to Li. Interestingly, the negotiations were conducted in English through interpreters.

mixture of fascination and alarm. Japan's surprisingly complete victory over China was cited as proof that it was now ready to join the ranks of the great powers. It also upset a shaky balance of power that required China's feeble Qing dynasty to not collapse altogether. Now Japan had dramatically raised the stakes. In addition to imposing a crippling indemnity on the Qing, reducing Korea to a client state, and annexing the island of Taiwan, the new Treaty of Shimonoseki called for the occupation by Japan of Manchuria's Liaodong Peninsula, which guarded the approaches to Beijing.

For Russia, France, and Germany, who saw their own interests threatened by this move, it was time to act. In what became known as the Triple Intervention, they threatened Japan with joint action if it did not abandon its claims to Liaodong. Unable to take on all three powers, the Japanese bitterly acquiesced. They grew more bitter the following year when the Qing secretly leased the territory to Russia in a desperate attempt to counter Japanese expansion. For the Japanese, this began a decade-long state of tension with Russia that would culminate in the Russo–Japanese War of 1904–1905. For the other powers in east Asia, it began a "race for concessions" in China that stopped just short of dismembering the empire.

For the Chinese, however, it marked the most dramatic and humiliating role reversal of the past 1,500 years. China had always viewed Japan in Confucian terms as a "younger brother." Like Korea and Vietnam, Japan was considered to be on the cultural periphery of the Chinese world, acculturating to Chinese institutions and following Chinese examples in those things considered "civilized." Now, after barely a generation of exposure to Euro-American influence, Japan had eclipsed China as a military power and threatened to extend its sway throughout the region.

This new east Asian order also pointed up the larger effects of one of the most momentous patterns of world history: the phenomenon of imperialism growing from the innovations that created scientific–industrial society—one of the foundations of modernity that we have examined in this part of the text. As we began to see in the previous two chapters, in less than a century, European countries and their offshoots—and now Japan— expanded their power so rapidly and completely that on the eve of World War I in 1914 more than 85 percent of the world's people were under their control or influence. How were a very few countries like Japan able to resist and adapt to the broad forces of modernity, while China struggled to cope with its effects through most of the nineteenth and twentieth centuries?

China and Japan in the Age of Imperialism

As we saw in Chapter 21, the reign of the Qing emperor Qianlong (r. 1736–1795) marked perhaps the high point of China's power in the early modern world and the period in which the first hints began to appear of trouble to come. Some of the problems facing the Qing began to emerge within a year after Qianlong stepped down from the throne in 1795. A Buddhist sect with secret-society connections called the White Lotus sparked a smoldering rebellion, which took years to suppress, while at the same time highlighting the limitations of the Manchu bannermen as a military force. Less obvious, but perhaps more debilitating for the agrarian imperial order as a whole, were the new directions in economics. China was steadily drawn into the emerging European global commercial system, but the increasing forces of free trade were eroding its tried and true systems of exchange control. Specifically, China's efforts to retain close control over its export trade in tea, porcelain, silk, and other luxury goods coupled with action to stamp out the new, lucrative, and illegal opium trade created a crisis with Great Britain in the summer of 1839, which led to the First Opium War, China's first military encounter with the industrializing West.

China and Maritime Trade, 1750–1839

By the 1790s, with the China trade at record levels and the French Revolution making European trade increasingly problematic, the British government sought to establish diplomatic relations with the Qing. In the summer of 1793, they dispatched Lord George Macartney, an experienced diplomat and colonial governor, to Beijing with a sizeable entourage and boatloads of presents. His mission was to persuade the Qianlong emperor to allow the stationing of diplomatic personnel in the Chinese capital and the creation of a system for the separate handling of ordinary commercial matters and diplomacy along the lines of European practices. Qianlong, however, politely but firmly rebuffed Macartney's attempts to establish a British embassy. In addition to observing that China really had "no need of your country's ingenious manufactures," Qianlong stated bluntly that permanent foreign embassies were contrary to the tradition of tribute missions and would "most definitely not be permitted." A second British mission in 1816 met with similar results.

> ### Possessing All Things
>
> "As your Ambassador can see for himself we possess all things . . . this then is my answer to your request to appoint a representative at my Court; a request that is contrary to our dynastic usage, which would only result in inconvenience to yourself. I have expounded my wishes in detail and have commanded your tribute Envoys to leave in peace on their homeward journey . . ."
>
> —The Qianlong emperor's rebuff of the Macartney Mission, in H.F. MacNair, *Modern Chinese History, Selected Readings*, Shanghai: Commercial Press, 1923, p. 2.

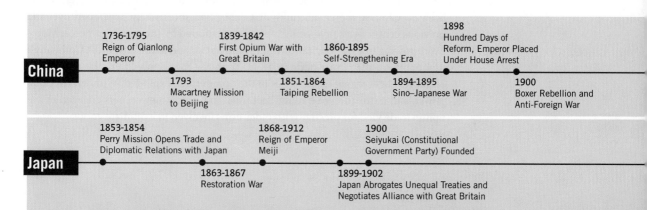

China

| 1736-1795 Reign of Qianlong Emperor | 1793 Macartney Mission to Beijing | 1839-1842 First Opium War with Great Britain | 1851-1864 Taiping Rebellion | 1860-1895 Self-Strengthening Era | 1894-1895 Sino–Japanese War | 1898 Hundred Days of Reform, Emperor Placed Under House Arrest | 1900 Boxer Rebellion and Anti-Foreign War |

Japan

| 1853-1854 Perry Mission Opens Trade and Diplomatic Relations with Japan | 1863-1867 Restoration War | 1868-1912 Reign of Emperor Meiji | 1899-1902 Japan Abrogates Unequal Treaties and Negotiates Alliance with Great Britain | 1900 Seiyukai (Constitutional Government Party) Founded |

The Imbalance of Trade?   One important reason that Europeans and Americans were anxious to bring the Chinese into their diplomatic system was the widespread perception that China was benefiting from a huge trade imbalance. Though recent scholarship has shown that China's economy actually supported much of the interconnected Eurasian commercial system, contemporary merchants and political economists were convinced that China's control of trade functioned in the same way as did European mercantilism. Thus, they believed that the money paid to Chinese merchants essentially stayed in the "closed" economy of the Qing Empire, draining the West of its stocks of silver. However, as Qianlong's reply to Macartney noted, European merchants offered little that the Chinese needed or wanted.

Thus, by the end of the eighteenth century, European and American traders had become increasingly anxious to find something that Chinese merchants would buy in sufficient quantities to stem the flow of Western silver into China. By the beginning of the nineteenth century, a growing number of merchants were clandestinely turning to a lucrative new commodity, with tragic consequences. When tobacco was introduced into China from the Americas, the innovation of smoking quickly spread. In southwestern China, tribesmen living in remote mountain villages began combining small quantities of powdered opium with tobacco. The Dutch, who briefly maintained bases on Taiwan, also introduced the practice there, from which it spread gradually to the maritime provinces of south China. Disturbed by the growing use of opium beyond normal medicinal practice in the area, the Qing banned the smoking of the substance as early as 1729. For the rest of the century opium use remained a strictly local problem in China's south.

Smugglers, Pirates, and "Foreign Mud"   By the end of the eighteenth century, the British East India Company's territory in Bengal had come to include the area around Patna, historically a center of medicinal opium production. While company traders were strictly prohibited from carrying opium to China as contraband, an increasing number of noncompany merchants willing to take the risk discovered that they could circumvent Chinese regulations and sell small quantities of the drug for a tidy profit. Initially, their customers were the wealthy of Canton society; and the exotic "foreign mud," as opium was nicknamed, soon became a favorite local diversion. With success came increased demand, and by the early decades of the nineteenth century, an elaborate illicit system of delivery had been set up along the south China coast. Heavily armed ships unloaded their cargo of opium on small, sparsely inhabited offshore islands, from which Chinese middlemen picked up the drug and made their rounds on the mainland (see Map 24.1). The ever-rising profits from this illegal enterprise encouraged piracy and lawlessness along the coast, and the opium trade soon became a major irritant in relations between China and the West.

The relationship that the British East India Company and the government-licensed Chinese merchant guild, or *Cohong* had so carefully developed over the previous century was now being rapidly undermined by the new commerce. Moreover, growing free trade agitation in England put an end to the East India Company's monopoly on the China trade in 1833. With the monopoly lifted, the number of entrepreneurs seeking quick riches in the opium trade exploded. With wealth came power, and in the foreign trading "factories" in Canton, newcomers engaged in the opium trade vied for prestige with older firms involved in legitimate goods.

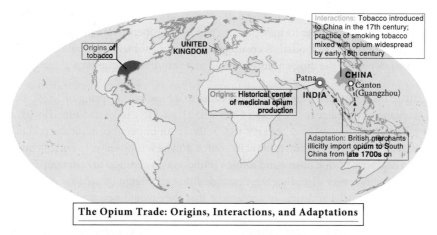

MAP 24.1 **The Opium Trade: Origins, Interactions, Adaptations.**

The push for legitimacy among the opium merchants coincided with an aggressive attempt by Westerners to force China to open additional trading ports for legal items. Chinese authorities, however, viewed this Western assertiveness as driven primarily by opium and Christian evangelism. The East India Company itself was now fatally compromised as well since an estimated one-quarter of its revenues in India were directly tied to opium production.

Far worse, however, were the effects on the ordinary inhabitants of south China. The huge rise in availability and consequent plunge in prices increased opium usage to catastrophic levels. Its power to suppress pain and hunger made it attractive to the

Commissioner Lin Destroys the Opium. This drawing depicts Lin Zexu burning 20,000 chests of opium surrendered by the foreign merchants. Because of the potency of the drug, Lin not only burned it but mixed the ashes with lime and flushed them in sluiceways out to sea. He then offered prayers to the spirits of the sea asking forgiveness for burdening them with this noxious poison.

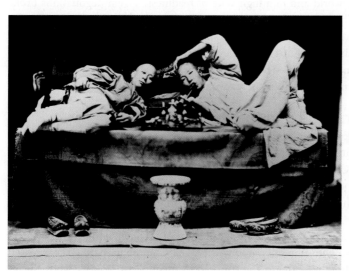

Chinese Opium Smoker. This photograph, taken in the early 1870s, shows the pervasiveness of the opium habit among ordinary Chinese. These men are smoking in the back room of a restaurant, a common practice, even here in British-controlled Hong Kong.

poor engaged in physical labor, though the dream-like state it induced often made it dangerous to work under its influence. Its addictive properties led people to seek it even at the expense of food, thus creating a health crisis for tens of thousands, made infinitely worse by the drug's notoriously difficult withdrawal symptoms.

Commissioner Lin Zexu   Matters came to a head in the spring of 1839. The Daoguang emperor sent Lin Zexu (1785–1850), a widely respected official with a reputation for courage and honesty, to Canton as an imperial commissioner. Lin's task was to cut off the opium trade at its source, and he was given wide-ranging powers to deal with both Chinese and foreign traffickers. In addition to setting up facilities for the recovery of addicts, he demanded that all foreign merchants surrender their opium stocks and sign an agreement that they would not, under penalty of death, deal in the drug anymore. When the foreign community balked at surrendering the goods, Lin blockaded the port and withdrew all Chinese personnel from Western firms. His determined stance finally cracked the stalemate, and the dealers eventually surrendered 20,000 chests of opium, with most also signing the pledge. Lin then publicly burned the surrendered opium and flushed the ashes into the sea. Following Lin's actions, however, the dealers appealed to the British government for compensation.

The British government decided to use the incident to settle the long-standing diplomatic impasse with the Qing over foreign representation and open ports. In a show of force, the British sent a fleet of warships to Canton to demand reparations for the burned opium, pressure the Qing to establish diplomatic relations, and open more ports. In sad contrast to the days four centuries earlier when Zheng He commanded his great fleets, the Chinese now had no real naval forces to contest the British. What vessels they had were modestly armed with seventeenth-century cannon and used for customs collection. The British fleet, on the other hand, was the most powerful in the world and in a high state of readiness. When negotiations broke down, a small Chinese squadron sailed out to confront the British men-o'-war. By an incredible chance, a rocket from a British ship hit the Chinese flagship in its powder magazine and blew it up. Such inauspicious circumstances marked the beginning of the First Opium War (1839–1842) and, with it, a long, painful century of foreign intrusion, domination, and ultimately revolution for China.

The Opium Wars and the Treaty Port Era

The hostilities that began in the fall of 1839 between China and Great Britain exposed the growing gap between the military capabilities of industrializing countries and those, like China, whose armed forces had fallen into disuse. The military had never been an honored profession in China, and the consequences of maintaining scattered Manchu banner garrisons, discouraging militia recruiting, and underfunding the Chinese regular forces (Armies of the Green Standard) were immediately put on painful display. The massive English ships of the line, mounting as many as 128 guns, moved with impunity among the small Chinese fleets of coastal vessels frantically sent to oppose them. The armored steam gunboat *Nemesis*, whose heavy pivot gun allowed it to dominate riverside batteries, landed the British expeditionary forces wherever they pleased.

Over the next 2 years, with a brief truce called in 1841, the British methodically attacked and occupied ports along the Chinese coast from Canton (Guangzhou)

Extraterritoriality: The immunity of a country's nationals from the laws of their host country.

Steam Power Comes to China.
The new technologies of the Industrial Revolution were on painful display in China in 1840 as the British gunboat H.M.S. *Nemesis* took on provincial warships down the river from Guangzhou (Canton). The *Nemesis* featured an armored hull put together in detachable sections, shallow draft and steam–powered paddle wheel propulsion for river fighting, and a large pivot gun to take on shore batteries. Its power and versatility convinced Lin Zexu and a growing number of Chinese officials over the coming decades that China needed, at the very least, the same kinds of "strong ships and effective cannon" if they were to defend their coasts and rivers. By the 1860s the first attempts at such craft were finally under way.

to Shanghai at the mouth of the Yangzi River, for the most part without serious opposition. As the British planned to move north to put pressure on Beijing, Chinese officials opened negotiations in August 1842. The resulting Treaty of Nanjing (Nanking) marked the first of the century's "unequal treaties" that would be imposed throughout east Asia by European powers.

The Treaty of Nanjing   Curiously, the treaty ending the First Opium War did not mention opium. In the final agreement, the British claimed the island of Hong Kong, with its excellent deep-water harbor; levied an indemnity on the Chinese to pay the costs of the war; and forced the Chinese to open the ports of Shanghai, Ningbo, Fuzhou, and Xiamen (Amoy), in addition to Guangzhou (Canton). The Chinese were also confronted with British insistence on **non-tariff autonomy**: By treaty they could now charge no more than a 5 percent tariff on British goods. Taking a page from arrangements in the Ottoman Empire, whereby merchants of particular countries were the responsibility of their respective consuls, the British also imposed the policy of **extraterritoriality** in the newly open ports: British subjects who violated Chinese laws would be tried and punished by British consuls.

Over the next several years, the Chinese signed similar treaties with France and the United States. An important addition in these later treaties was the *most-favored nation* clause: Any new concessions granted to one country automatically reverted to those who by treaty were "most-favored nations." Thus, the time-honored Chinese diplomatic strategy of "using barbarians to check barbarians" was dealt a near fatal blow (see Map 24.2).

Non-tariff autonomy:
The loss by a country of its right to set its own tariffs.

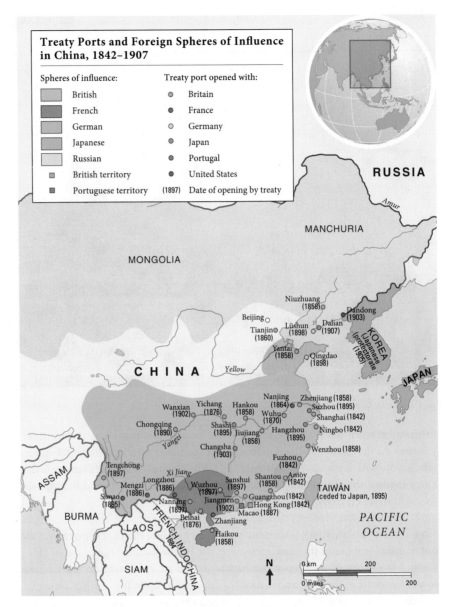

MAP 24.2 **Treaty Ports and Foreign Spheres of Influence in China, 1842–1907.**

The Taiping Movement, 1851–1864   In addition to the spread of the opium trade to the newly opened ports, long-established trade routes for more legitimate items swiftly shifted from Guangzhou to more convenient outlets. The growth of Shanghai was especially important in this regard because it served the Yangzi River, the greatest highway through China's heartland. Coastal trade also increased, while Hong Kong grew as the primary point of opium transfer to small smuggling vessels. The swiftness of all of these changes and their accompanying economic dislocation, along with smoldering discontent at the inability of the Qing government to resist foreign demands, made south China particularly volatile. In 1851 the region exploded in rebellion. Before it was over, this largest civil war in world history and its related conflicts would claim as many as 30 million lives.

The catalyst for revolt was in many ways symbolic of the diverse cultural influences penetrating the area. Though Christian proselytizing had been banned by the Qing since the early eighteenth century, missionary activity was protected in the foreign enclaves and now increased dramatically with the enactment of the new treaties. A candidate for the local Confucian examinations, Hong Xiuquan [HUNG SHIOO-chwahn] (1813–1864), had come upon some Christian missionary tracts passed on by a colleague. Not long after, he failed the examination for the third time and lapsed into a nervous breakdown. When he eventually recovered, Hong gradually came to believe that the Christian God had taken him up to heaven and informed him that he was in fact Christ's younger brother. Hong told his startled listeners that it had been revealed to him that he must now work to bring about the Heavenly Kingdom of Great Peace (*taiping tianguo*) on earth. The movement became known as the "Taiping Rebellion" and lasted from 1851 until 1864.

Hounded from their community, Hong and his group moved into a mountain stronghold and began to gather followers from the disillusioned and unemployed, anti-Manchu elements, religious dissidents, secret societies, and fellow members of south China's Hakka minority. By 1851 they had created a society based on Protestant Christian theology, Chinese traditions, and a vision of equality in which all goods were held in common; women worked, fought, and prayed alongside men; and foot binding, opium smoking, and gambling were forbidden. As a sign that they were no longer loyal to the Qing, the men cut their queues and let the hair grow in on their foreheads, prompting the Qing to refer to them as "the long-haired rebels." Repudiating Confucian tradition, the rebels targeted the scholar-gentry in their land seizures and executions.

By late 1851, the movement had gathered enough strength to stand against local government forces and began an advance to the north. By 1853 they had captured the city of Nanjing and made it their capital. That winter they were narrowly thwarted from driving the Qing from Beijing and pushed back to central China. For the next decade they would remain in control of the Chinese heartland, and the long, bloody contest to subdue them would leave thousands of towns and villages devastated for decades to come.

For the foreigners in China, the prospect of a Christian movement taking power seemed like a cherished dream about to come true. As time went on, however, missionaries and diplomats became less sure of where the movement was heading. On the one hand, Hong and his advisors talked about instituting Western-style administrative reforms and building a modern industrial base—something Western well-wishers had continually urged on Chinese officials. On the other hand, a powerful Taiping China might repudiate the unequal treaties and throw the new trade arrangements into disarray. Thus, the foreign powers in the end grudgingly elected to continue recognizing the Qing as China's legitimate rulers (see Map 24.3).

The Second Opium War, 1856–1860   At the height of the rebellion in 1856, a new dispute arose between the Qing and the British and French. After 4 years of intermittent fighting, it produced the next round of "unequal treaties" that greatly expanded foreign interests and control in the empire. Britain, France, and the United

The Taiping Rebellion, 1851–1864

Area controlled by rebels, ca.1861

Nanjing

Shanghai

Wuhan

Hangzhou

Nanchang

Wenzhou

GUANGXI
PROVINCE

Xiamen
(Amoy)

TAIWAN

Guangzhou

Hong Kong

0 km   200

0 miles   200

N

MAP 24.3 **The Taiping
Rebellion 1851–1864.**

States all felt by the mid-1850s that the vastly expanded trade in China—and now Japan—called for the opening of still more ports, an end to Qing prohibitions on missionary activity, and diplomatic relations along Western lines.

The catalyst came in late 1856. A Chinese customs patrol in Canton hauled down the British flag on the *Arrow*, a Chinese vessel whose registry had been falsified to take advantage of British trading privileges. The British seized upon this purported insult to their flag as an opportunity to force treaty revision. The French, who considered themselves the protectors of Catholic missionaries and their converts, saw an excellent opening to pressure China on the missionary issue and so joined the British.

The war itself was fought intermittently in a highly localized fashion. The British seized the walled city of Canton, captured the governor-general of the region's two provinces, and sent him into exile in India. As the conflict moved into 1857, however, the Great Rebellion in India consumed British attention through much of the year, while in China negotiations dragged on intermittently and the Qing remained preoccupied with the Taipings. In 1858, a draft treaty was worked out, but the Qing court refused it. Returning in 1860 with a large expeditionary force, British and French troops advanced to Beijing, drove the emperor from the city, and burned and looted his summer palace. The final treaty stipulated that a dozen ports be opened to foreign trade, that opium be recognized as a legal commodity, that extraterritoriality be expanded, and that foreign embassies be set up in the capital. A newly created Chinese board, the Zongli Yamen, was to handle Qing foreign relations; and the Chinese were invited to send their own ambassadors abroad.

Self-Strengthening   The end of the Second Opium War began a period lasting through the early 1870s sometimes referred to by historians as the "cooperative era." There were few major disputes between the foreign powers and the Qing; indeed, in several instances, foreigners worked closely with Chinese officials to help them in assessing ways to upgrade their defenses, lay the foundations of modern industrial concerns, and start programs that signaled institutional change. The motives of these men ranged from simple altruism to missionary devotion to what might be called "enlightened self-interest": the belief that a strong, modern China would be a more stable trade and diplomatic partner.

For their part, Chinese officials, desperate to roll back the foreign threat and suppress the Taipings, favored a diverse array of strategies. Few advocated simply fighting the foreigners with whatever means were at hand. Most, like the emperor's brother, Prince Gong, felt that over time these new peoples would be assimilated to Chinese norms, like invaders and border peoples of the past. In the meantime, however, they should be "soothed and pacified" but not unconditionally. As the prince later remarked to the British Ambassador, "Take away your opium and your missionaries and you will be welcome."

In order to do this, however, China needed to be able to halt further encroachments by the powers. Toward this end, a growing number of prominent officials advocated a policy that came to be called "self-strengthening." During the 1860s, the two most prominent were Li Hongzhang (1823–1901) and his senior colleague Zeng Guofan (1811–1872). Both men had distinguished themselves as Confucian scholars and as leaders of militia armies during the Taiping years. In 1864, their combined forces finally captured the Taiping capital at Nanjing and forced the suicide of Hong Xiuquan, bringing the movement to an end.

Like a number of leaders during these desperate times, Li and Zeng were also distinguished by the flexibility of their thinking and, increasingly, by their growing familiarity with the new weapons and techniques brought to China by foreign forces. By the end of the rebellion, they had begun to move toward a strategy of what a later slogan called "Chinese studies for the essence; Western studies for practical application." They sponsored an impressive array of projects in the 1860s and early 1870s: a foreign language and technical school, modern arsenals and factories at Nanjing and Jiangnan (Kiangnan), a modern navy yard at Fuzhou, initiatives to send Chinese students to the United States and Europe, a modern shipping concern (The China Merchants' Steam Navigation Company), and the first moves toward sending representatives abroad.

Opposition to such programs also mounted during the period and continued throughout the century. These were the people Li Hongzhang had cited as being "confined by tradition" in the vignette beginning this chapter. Often highly placed—including, ultimately, the Empress Dowager Cixi [SIH-shee] (1835–1908) herself—these opponents felt that any and all reforms of the kind advocated by Li and Zeng would bring down China's Confucian society. For them, the kind of change necessary to create an industrial base in China would erode the social, cultural, and economic ties that held that society together. In the end, they said, the people would cease to be Chinese in any meaningful sense and become like Europeans and Americans. As much as anything else, the lack of a clear strategy at the top and the ferocity of these debates among Chinese officials worked to frustrate the hopes of the "self-strengtheners" through the turn of the century.

Self-Straighteners. Two of the key figures in China's Self-Strengthening Movement were Zeng Guofan (top) and Li Hongzhang (bottom). The two men began working together during the last years of the Taiping Rebellion, both having formed and led militia armies in their home provinces of Hunan (Zeng) and Anhui (Li). Both men also pioneered the use of modern weapons by their troops. After Zeng's death in 1872, Li emerged as the most active proponent of self-strengthening and China's most powerful official.

Toward Revolution: Reform and Reaction to 1900

While China's efforts at self-strengthening seemed promising to contemporaries during the 1870s, the signs of their underlying weakness were already present for those who cared to look. As we have seen, the architect of many of these efforts, Li Hongzhang, was all too aware of the political constraints he faced. With the ascension of the infant Guangxu as emperor in 1874 came the regency of the Empress Dowager Cixi. Desperate to preserve Manchu power, Cixi constantly manipulated factions at court and among the high officials to avoid concentration of power in any particular area. Such maneuverings, sometimes favoring Li's colleagues and as often opposing them, severely hampered the long-term health of many self-strengthening

Patterns Up Close | Interaction and Adaptation: "Self-Strengthening" and "Western Science and Eastern Ethics"

Most of the important technical innovations taking place in China and Japan during the late eighteenth and early nineteenth centuries came from outside east Asia. This, of course, is not surprising since the Scientific and Industrial Revolutions were largely focused on developing labor-saving machinery, weaponry, and improving the speed and efficiency of transportation—things of lesser priority in these labor-rich societies. Confronted by the expansive, newly industrialized countries of Europe and America, their possible responses were largely confined to what might be called the "three R's"—Reaction, Reform, and Revolution. Perhaps most interesting in this regard is the middle path of reform taken by both countries in attempting to create a synthesis of tried and true Confucian social structures and what were considered to be the best of the new technologies and institutions.

As we have seen in past chapters, Chinese philosophical concepts tended toward the desire for correlation and the reconciliation of opposites. In this tradition, *ti* and *yong*, or "essence" and "function/application," became the two key terms in the popular self-strengthening formulation, *Zhongxue wei ti; Xixue wei yong* ("Chinese

Interaction and Adaptation in China and Japan Weapons on display at the Nanjing Arsenal in 1868 include an early Gatling-type rotary machine gun, a Congreve rocket, and a pyramid of round explosive shells. (*a*), while an 1890 lithograph of a Japanese seamstress (*b*) shows the delicate balance between "essence" and "function" that Japan has tried to maintain since the middle of the nineteenth century. The woman is attired in Western dress and she works a Western-style sewing machine. Has the "function" degraded the essence of what she is doing? It is a question that many in Japan still ask today.

studies for the essence; Western studies for the practical application"). Thus, Chinese thinkers were able to accommodate the need for new foreign technologies within historically and philosophically acceptable terminology. Similarly, the Japanese, also schooled in Neo-Confucianism, were able to justify an even more thoroughgoing transformation of society by means of the balanced formula they called "Western science and Eastern ethics."

However, the two sides of the concept were not equally balanced. As with many Neo-Confucian formulae, the "essence" and "ethics" elements were considered to be primary and the method of implementation—"function"—secondary. Thus, their proponents could argue that their chief aim was the preservation of the fundamentals of Confucian society, while being flexible about the appropriate means of attaining their goals. Opponents, however, argued that the formula could—and eventually would—be reversed: that "function" would eventually degrade the

(b)

"essence." Here, they pointed to the alleged Westernization of students sent abroad and the wearing of Western clothes in Japan as examples of the dangers of this approach.

Yet, in both countries, one can argue that this has remained a favored approach, even through war and revolution. Though societal and generational tensions over "tradition" and "modernity" have been present for nearly a century and a half in Japan, the Japanese have made foreign technologies and institutions their own, while retaining some of their most cherished Shinto and Buddhist practices alongside social customs still tinged with Neo-Confucianism. Similarly, in China, since the beginning of the Four Modernizations in 1978, coupling technological and institutional modernization with an effort to rediscover and preserve what is considered to be the best of traditional Chinese civilization has been the dominant approach. Thus, the present regime pursues a policy of "socialism with Chinese characteristics" and supports the founding of Confucian institutes alongside computer factories—all in the service of creating what the Communist Party calls "the harmonious society."

Questions

• How were the Chinese and Japanese adaptations to Western innovations similar? How were they different? What do these similarities and differences say about the cultures of these two countries?

• Do you believe that, over the course of time, the "function" of foreign innovations has degraded the "essence" in China and Japan?

measures. In addition, the new programs were costly, usually requiring foreign experts, and China's finances were continually strained by the artificially low treaty tariffs and the obligation to pay old indemnities.

China and Imperialism in Southeast Asia and Korea

By the 1880s foreign tensions exposed more problems. France had been steadily encroaching upon southeast Asia since the late 1850s. By the early 1880s, however, Vietnamese resistance led by a force called the Black Flags was on the verge of rolling back the French. Li Hongzhang supported the Black Flags, and in order to preempt outright Chinese intervention, the French launched a surprise attack on the modern Chinese naval facilities at Fuzhou, sinking the cream of China's steam fleet. Though Chinese forces gave a better account of themselves in other engagements, the French emerged from this conflict with control of the whole of Vietnam, which they promptly combined with Cambodia and Laos into the colony of French Indochina in 1885.

In 1885, as China was still involved with France, tensions with Japan over Korea threatened to dislodge that kingdom as a Qing client state. Japanese diplomats had exerted influence over the Korean court as it sought to deal with the smoldering Tonghak Rebellion (see later, "Creating an Empire"). China sent its own team of officials to keep watch on Qing interests, and both sides quickly threatened to send troops. In the agreement between Li Hongzhang and Ito Hirobumi at Tianjin (Tientsin) that year, both sides agreed not to take any action in the future without informing the other.

By the early 1890s, however, rising tensions surrounding the Korean court and intrigues by Japanese and Chinese agents involving various factions threatened war once again. Japan sent a force which was claimed to be diplomatic; troops of a Chinese counterforce were killed when a Japanese warship sunk their transport. By the fall of 1894, both sides were sending troops and naval forces to Korea and a full-scale war over the fate of Korea and northeast Asia was under way.

The Sino–Japanese War

As we noted at the beginning of this chapter, the war between China and Japan over control of Korea graphically exposed the problems of China's "self-strengthening" efforts. China's arms procurement, for example, was not carried out under a centralized program, as was Japan's. The result was that different Chinese military units were armed with a wide variety of noninterchangeable weapons and ammunition, making it difficult for them to support each other. China's rebuilt fleet, though impressive in size and armament, faced similar problems. Unlike the Japanese ships, China's largest warships had their components separately built at various shipyards in Europe. In one memorable incident during the Battle of the Yellow Sea in 1894, the recoil from the mismatched, oversized guns aboard the Chinese flagship destroyed its own captain's bridge. Worse still, Chinese gunners found to their dismay that many of the shells they were firing were filled with sand rather than explosive—the result of the empress dowager's diversion of naval funds to rebuild the summer palace destroyed in 1860.

While many of the land battles were hotly contested, superior Japanese organization and morale enabled them to drive steadily through Korea. A second force landed in southern Manchuria to secure the territory around the approaches to Beijing, while Japanese naval forces reduced the fortress across from it at Weihaiwei. By spring 1895, after some preliminary negotiations, Li made his humiliating trip to

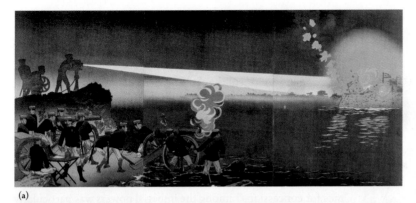

(a)

(b)

Scenes from the Sino–Japanese War. News accounts of the Sino–Japanese War aroused great interest and an unprecedented wave of nationalism in Japan. They also marked the last extensive use of ukiyo-e woodblock printing in the news media as the technology of reproducing photos in newspapers was introduced to Japan shortly after the conflict. Because few of the artists actually traveled with the troops, the great majority of these works came from reporters' dispatches and the artists' imaginations. In these representative samples from the assault on Pyongyang and the use of the new technology of the electric searchlight to illuminate an enemy fort (a), the pride in Japan's modernization and the disdain for China's "backwardness" are all too evident. Note the almost demon-like faces and garish uniforms of the Chinese as they are invariably depicted as being killed or cowering before the Japanese; note, too, the modern, Western uniforms and beards and mustaches of the Japanese (b).

Shimonoseki and was forced to agree to Japan's terms. The severity of the provisions, especially the annexation of Taiwan, the control of Korea, and, temporarily at least, the seizure of Liaodong, signaled to the Western powers in east Asia that China was now weak enough to have massive economic and territorial demands forced on it.

Thus, a "race for concessions" began in which France demanded economic and territorial rights in south China adjacent to Indochina; Great Britain did the same in the Yangzi River valley; Russia and Japan made demands in the north for rights in Manchuria; and a newcomer, Germany, demanded naval bases and rights at Qingdao [Ching-DOW] (Tsingtao) on the Shandong Peninsula. China's total dismemberment was avoided in 1899 when John Hay, the US secretary of state, circulated a note with British backing suggesting that all powers refrain from securing exclusive concessions and instead maintain an "open door" for all to trade in China.

The Hundred Days of Reform   Amid this growing foreign crisis, the aftermath of the war produced a domestic crisis as well. The terms of the Shimonoseki treaty had prompted patriotic demonstrations in Beijing and raised levels of discussion about reform to new levels of urgency. A group of younger officials headed by Kang Youwei (1858–1927) petitioned Emperor Guangxu, now ruling in his own right, to implement a list of widespread reforms, many modeled on those recently enacted in Japan. Guangxu issued a flurry of edicts from June through September 1898, attempting to completely revamp China's government and many of its leading institutions. Resistance to this "hundred days' reform" program, however, was

EN CHINE
Le gâteau des Rois et... des Empereurs

Dismembering China. The weakness of the Qing during the final years of the nineteenth century prompted the so-called Race for Concessions among the imperial powers in east Asia. In this French cartoon, China is depicted as a flatbread or pizza around which caricatures of the monarchs and national symbols of the various powers sit with their knives poised arguing over who should get the best pieces. A desperate Chinese official—perhaps Li Hongzhang himself—with his long fingernails and flapping queue, holds up his hands imploring them to stop. The French caption says roughly, "In China: The cake of kings and emperors."

extensive, and much of it was centered on the emperor's aunt, the empress dowager. With support from her inner circle at court, she had the young emperor placed under house arrest and rounded up and executed those of Kang's supporters who could be found. Kang and his junior colleague, the writer and political theorist Liang Qichao [LEEAHNG chee-CHOW] (1873–1929) managed to escape to the treaty ports. For the next decade they traveled to overseas Chinese communities attempting to gather support for their Constitutional Monarchy Party.

The Boxer Rebellion and War   The turmoil set off by the "race for concessions" among the imperial powers was particularly intense in north China, where the ambitions of Russia, Japan, and Germany clashed. With the stepped-up activity of German missionaries on the Shandong Peninsula came a new wave of antiforeign sentiment, increasingly centered on a group called the Society of the Harmonious Fists. Anti-Qing as well as antiforeign, the members' ritual exercises and name prompted the foreign community to refer to them as the "Boxers." By late 1899 the Boxers were regularly provoking the foreign and Christian communities with the aim of pushing their governments to pressure the Qing to suppress the movement, by which they hoped to stir up rebellion against them.

In the spring of 1900 matters came to a head. Boxers assassinated the German ambassador, and the Germans demanded that the Qing crush the movement once and for all, pay a huge indemnity, and erect a statue to their ambassador as a public apology. In the midst of this crisis, the empress dowager, who had been negotiating in secret with the Boxers, declared war on all the foreign powers in China and openly threw the court's support behind the movement. The result was civil war across northern China as Boxer units hunted down missionaries and Chinese Christians, many Chinese army units aided the Boxers in attacking foreigners, and the foreign diplomatic quarter in Beijing was besieged from June until August.

The foreign governments quickly put together a multinational relief force led by the Germans and British and largely manned by the Japanese but including units of nearly all the countries with interests in China. By August they had fought their way to the capital and chased the imperial court nearly to Xi'an. Amid considerable carnage in the mopping up of Boxer sympathizers, Li Hongzhang, in his last official duty before his death, was commissioned to negotiate the end of the conflict for the court. With Qing power utterly routed, the foreign governments were able to impose the most severe "unequal treaty" yet: They extracted the right to post troops in major Chinese cities, they demanded the total suppression of any antiforeign movements, and they received such a huge indemnity that China had to borrow money from foreign banks in order to service the interest on the payments. The only bright point in the Boxer Protocols of 1901 was that the United States agreed to return its share of the indemnity money to China on the condition that it would be used to send Chinese students to study in American institutions.

Toward Revolution   With the return of the imperial court to Beijing and the enhanced foreign presence in the capital, the Qing finally turned to institutional reform. During the first decade of the twentieth century, the old Confucian examination system was abolished and new curricula—including science and technology—were created. Similarly, the army was overhauled and modernized. Perhaps most dramatically, the government itself was to be restructured more or less along the lines envisioned by Kang Youwei and Emperor Guangxu—who was still under house arrest. An imperial commission was sent abroad to study the constitutional systems of the great powers, and upon its return a plan to turn the Qing into a constitutional monarchy was created. By 1910, 2 years after the deaths of both the empress dowager and Guangxu, the first limited elections were being held for a planned legislative body.

The Empress Dowager Cixi.
Following the rout of the Qing and Boxer forces in the fall of 1900, the empress dowager made herself more accessible to Western diplomats and photographers. There are numerous pictures of her in various royal poses; here, she sits with her court ladies-in-waiting. The legend above her throne reads from right to left: "The reigning Saintly Mother, Empress Dowager of the Great Qing, (may she rule) 10,000 years! 10,000 years! 10,000, 10,000 years!"—the last exhortation (*wan sui, wan sui, wan wan sui*) the Chinese rendering of the more familiar Japanese "Banzai."

While Qing reform efforts were proceeding apace, however, the plans of revolutionaries were moving even more rapidly. As we will see in Chapter 28, the central figure in this regard was Sun Yat-sen (1866–1925), a man in many ways emblematic of the changes in China during the nineteenth century. Born near Canton, Sun received the fundamentals of classical education but then undertook Western training in medicine in Hong Kong and developed a thriving medical practice in Canton. A student of European and American history, his political ideas were already germinating by the time of the Sino–Japanese War. Like growing numbers of Chinese, the war convinced Sun that the feeble and increasingly corrupt Manchu government was the biggest obstacle to China's regeneration. In the end, his movement would play the leading role in forcing it out.

In Search of Security Through Empire: Japan in the Meiji Era

As we have just seen, the close of the nineteenth century saw Japan looming larger and larger as China's chief threat. Yet, they both faced similar pressures and, as Li Hongzhang observed, shared a common culture and in many ways a common cause. How, then, was Japan, with only a fraction of China's population and resources, able to not only survive in the face of foreign pressure but join the imperial powers itself?

The Decline of Tokugawa Seclusion   Though the eighteenth century saw occasional attempts by foreign ships to put in at Japanese ports, Europeans generally honored Japan's seclusion policies. Moreover, since all maritime trade with China took ships along a southerly route to Canton, the opportunity to go to Japan seldom presented itself. By the first decades of the nineteenth century, however, the situation was changing. The vastly expanded legitimate trade with China and the development of the opium trade increased the volume of shipping closer to Japanese waters. Moreover, the rapid growth of the whaling industry in the northern Pacific increasingly brought European and American ships into waters adjacent to

Japan. From their perspective, the need for establishing relations for the disposition of shipwreck survivors and perhaps trade was therefore becoming ever more urgent.

By the 1840s the pressure to establish relations with the Tokugawa shogunate became even more intense for the Western powers with interests in China. The treaty ports created in the wake of the First Opium War included Shanghai, which was rapidly becoming east Asia's chief commercial enclave. Because of its geographical position, major shipping routes to Shanghai now ran directly adjacent to southern Japan. Moreover, the Mexican War (1846–1848) brought the Pacific coast of North America under the control of the United States. At the same time, the discovery of gold in California made boomtown San Francisco the premier port for all American transpacific trade. In addition, increasing numbers of Chinese sought passage to the gold fields and the promise of employment in the American West, while the infamous "**coolie** trade" continually increased human traffic to Cuba and Peru. Plans to open steamship service along the great circle route from San Francisco to Shanghai, and the need for coaling stations to supply it, now threatened to place Japan squarely across the path of maritime traffic (see Map 24.4).

Coolies: Poor migrant laborers from China and India who performed menial work in other parts of the world in the nineteenth century.

The Coming of the "Black Ships"

The Tokugawa were well aware of the humiliation of the Qing at the hands of the British in 1842 and watched nervously as foreign commerce mounted in the Chinese treaty ports. As pressure increased on Japan to open its ports, divided counsels plagued the shogunate. The influential Mito School, long exposed to "Dutch learning" (see Chapter 21), feared the growing military and technological power of the Europeans and Americans and advocated a military response to any attempt at opening the country. Others looking at the situation in China felt that negotiation was the only possible way for Japan to avoid invasion.

MAP **24.4** **Steamship Routes and Underwater Telegraph Cables, ca. 1880.**

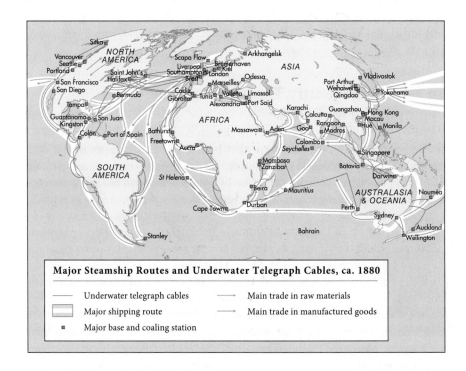

Major Steamship Routes and Underwater Telegraph Cables, ca. 1880

——— Underwater telegraph cables

▭ Major shipping route

▪ Major base and coaling station

⟶ Main trade in raw materials

⟶ Main trade in manufactured goods

The Americans, taking the lead in seeking diplomatic and commercial relations, put together a fleet of their newest and most powerful warships in arriving in July, 1853. Their commander, Matthew C. Perry, assembled multiracial and -ethnic crews for them in order to impress his Japanese hosts with the reach and power of the United States. Anxious to awe them as well with the new technologies available, he brought along as presents a telegraph set and a model railroad, both of which proved immediately popular. When negotiations flagged, the shogun's men gleefully amused themselves aboard the miniature train, smacking the engine and its operator with their fans to make it go faster.

On Perry's return trip in 1854 with even more of the "black ships," as the Japanese dubbed them, the Treaty of Kanagawa was signed, Japan's first with an outside power. Like China, Japan had now entered the treaty port era.

"Honor the Emperor and Expel the Barbarian!" The widely differing attitudes toward foreign contact expressed within the shogunate were reflected among the daimyo and samurai as well. The treaty with the Americans, and the rapid conclusion of treaties with other foreigners, tended to reinforce antiforeignism among many of the warrior elite, while emphasizing the weakness of the Tokugawa to resist further demands. Moreover, the new cultural contacts taking place in treaty ports like Yokohama and Nagasaki hardened positions and raised tensions further. Many samurai felt that dramatic gestures were called for to rouse the country to action. Hence, as with the Boxers later in China, they attacked foreigners and even assassinated Tokugawa officials in an effort to precipitate antiforeign conflict. By 1863, a movement aimed at driving out the Tokugawa and restoring impe-

rial rule had coalesced around the samurai of two southern domains, Satsuma and Choshu. Taking the slogan *sonno joi* ("Honor the emperor, expel the barbarian!") members of this "Satcho" (*Satsuma* and *Choshu*) clique challenged the shogunate and fought the smoldering Restoration War, which by the end of 1867 forced the Tokugawa to capitulate. In short order, the new regime moved to the Tokugawa capital of Edo and renamed it "Tokyo" (Eastern Capital).

The new emperor, 15-year-old Mutsuhito, took the reign name of Meiji (Enlightened Rule) and quickly moved to make good on its promise. As proof that the new regime would adopt progressive measures, the throne issued a charter oath in April 1868. A constitution was also promulgated, which spelled out in more detail how the new government was to be set up.

"Blue-eyed Barbarians." Japanese commonly referred to Westerners as "blue-eyed barbarians." In these sketches, part of a long series that artists made after Commodore Perry's four heavily-armed steamships sailed into Tokyo Bay in July 1853, Perry's son Oliver, who served as his father's personal secretary, is portrayed as jowly and slightly demonic looking *(a)*, while a group of US Marines are portrayed as both menacing and ridiculous at the same time *(b)*.

Emperor Meiji. A number of portraits and photographs of Emperor Meiji were done during his lifetime, particularly in his twenties and thirties. Here, in a portrait probably done in the late 1870s or early 1880s, he is shown as a vigorous and decisive man at the height of his powers. Note the European-style military uniform and Van Dyke beard of the kind frequently sported by Western monarchs and leaders.

Creating a Nation-State   While the Tokugawa had created an efficient warrior bureaucracy based on Neo-Confucianism, Japan was still dominated by regional loyalties and fealty to the daimyo of one's *han*, or feudal domain. The foreign threat and restoration of the emperor provided the opportunity as well as the necessity to forge a more thoroughgoing national unification. Thus, the new government quickly set about dismantling the feudal han and replacing them with a centralized provincial structure; the daimyo were replaced by governors, and the samurai were disbanded, given stipends, and encouraged to form business enterprises or to teach. In their place, a new conscript army modeled after that of Germany was created and a navy modeled on Great Britain's was established. In addition, the new order was to be held together by a national system of compulsory education in which loyalty to the emperor and state was carefully nurtured at every level.

The 1870s also marked the flourishing of government-managed social experimentation. Like the Chinese "self-strengtheners," Japanese senior advisors, or *genro* [hard "g": GEN-row], to the emperor sought to use new foreign technologies and institutions to strengthen the state against further foreign intrusion. Japan's planners, however, proved more systematic and determined in their efforts and, unlike their Chinese counterparts, had the full backing of the imperial court. Thus, Japan's proclaimed goals of using "Western science and Eastern ethics" in the service of "civilization and enlightenment" were seen as the primary tools in asserting eventual equality with the Western imperial powers and rolling back Japan's unequal treaties.

Adventures Abroad and Revolt at Home   Amid these dizzying changes, some senior advisors advocated an aggressive foreign policy in order to create a buffer zone around Japan. For these men, most prominently former samurai Saigo Takamori (1827–1877), Korea, which so far had resisted Western attempts to end its seclusion, was the obvious place to start. Saigo offered to sacrifice himself in order to create an incident in Korea that would justify Japanese action to "open" the so-called Hermit Kingdom. The Meiji court and inner circle, however, favored restraint. Instead, Japan contented itself with the expedition against Taiwan in 1874 and the purchase of the Ryukyu Islands in 1879.

The social turmoil at home and the tempering of Japan's ambitions abroad stirred discontent among many former samurai. In their view, Japan had abandoned its true character and was rapidly becoming a second-rate copy of the Western countries, fueled by greed, lack of honor, and international cowardice. In 1876, such sentiments helped spark a revolt among dissident samurai. Saigo, an imposing giant of a man much admired by the samurai, was persuaded to join them. Their movement, however, was crushed with brutal efficiency by the modern conscript army of Yamagata Aritomo (1838–1922), and Saigo himself committed suicide in April 1877. Though discontent at the direction of Japanese modernization continued to fester throughout the nineteenth century, it never again reached the level of open rebellion.

Creating an Empire   As we saw earlier in this chapter, rising tensions between Japan and China over the disposition of Korea ultimately led to the Sino–Japanese War of 1894–1895. The issue was temporarily held in abeyance by the Treaty of Tianjin of 1885, but continuing difficulties arising from the instability of the Korean government, feuding pro-Chinese and pro-Japanese factions within it, and the *Tonghak*, or "Eastern learning," movement, kept the region a volatile one. Combining elements of Confucianism, Buddhism, and a pronounced strain of antiforeignism, Tonghak-led peasant rebellions had erupted in 1810 and 1860. Though the rebellion had been suppressed in the 1860s, the forced opening of Korea to trade in the following decade and the constant intrigues of the Qing and the Japanese surrounding the Yi court in succeeding decades brought about the movement's revival in the 1890s.

As we have seen, Japan's successful showing in the war surprised and alarmed the Western powers in the region. The Triple Intervention, in which Russia, Germany, and France forced Japan to return the Liaodong Peninsula to China, only to have them lease it to Russia the following year, put that empire on a collision course with Japanese aspirations on the Asian mainland. Japan's control of Korea made it intensely interested in acquiring concessions in Manchuria. For Russia, it was vital to build rail links from the Trans-Siberian Railway to their new outposts of Port Arthur and Dairen (Dalian) in Liaodong and to extend the line across Manchuria to Vladivostok on the Pacific. As the twentieth century began, they pressured the Chinese into allowing them the rights to build the Chinese Eastern Railway across Manchuria and the South Manchurian Railway to Port Arthur, with a vital junction at Mukden, known today as Shenyang. Japan and Russia would shortly fight a war that would secure Japan's dominant position in northeast Asia and begin a long train of events that would end in revolution for Russia (see Map 24.5).

> **Enlightened Rule**
>
> "All matters [would be] decided by public discussion ... evil customs of the past shall be broken off ... [and] knowledge shall be sought throughout the world so as to strengthen the foundations of imperial rule."
>
> —From *Meiji boshin*, pp. 81–82. Quoted in Ryusaku Tsunoda, William T. De Bary, and Donald Keene, eds. *Sources of Japanese Tradition*, vol. 2, p. 137. New York: Columbia University Press, 1964.

Economics and Society in Late Qing China

The century and a half from 1750 to 1900 marked the structural, cultural, and economic decline of the great agrarian empires. Nowhere was this more evident than in Qing China. By 1900, China's treasury was bankrupt; its finances increasingly were controlled by foreign concerns; its export trade was outstripped by European and Japanese competitors; its domestic markets turned to factory-produced foreign commodities; and its land, ravaged by war, eroded by declining productivity, and squeezed by the world's largest population, grew less and less capable of sustaining its society.

The Seeds of Modernity and the New Economic Order

As we have seen a number of times in this chapter, the economic policies of late imperial China were increasingly at odds with those of the industrializing and

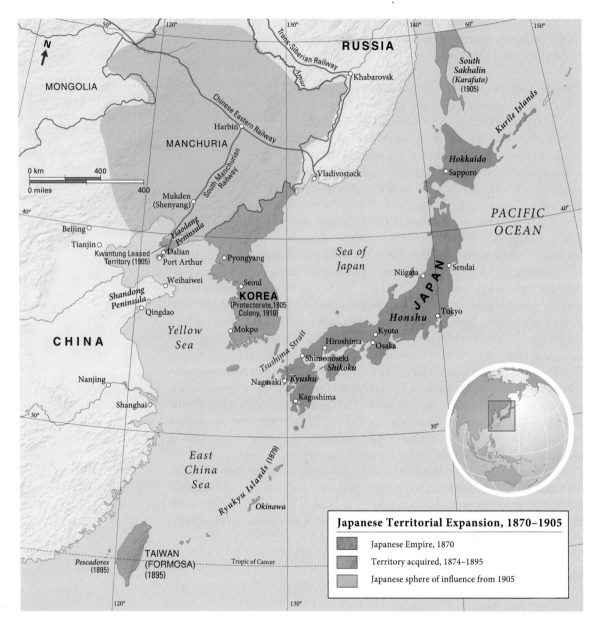

MAP **24.5** **Japanese Territorial Expansion, 1870–1905.**

commercially expanding West. For Chinese thinkers, this was considered sound in both ideological and economic terms. Confucianism held that agriculture was China's primary concern; that the values of humanity, loyalty, and filial piety were tied to agrarian society; and that the values of the merchant—particularly the drive for profit—were in direct opposition to these agrarian values. As the nineteenth century advanced, the opium trade provided ample evidence to Confucian officials of the correctness of this stance.

While opium was the great entering wedge, the building pressures on China and other regulated societies to lower their barriers to legitimate trade and the steps taken by those countries exerting the pressure to safeguard their own markets had equally severe long-term effects. Briefly, China was squeezed both ways in terms of trade. That is, the unequal treaties imposed artificially low tariff rates on the empire, making it increasingly difficult to protect its markets; at the same time, trading nations in the West increased tariffs on their own imports and, in some cases, developed their own substitutes for Chinese products.

Self-Strengthening and Economics   The programs to improve China's economics and trade were set up as "government-sponsored/merchant-operated" enterprises. One of the most initially promising of these was the China Merchants Steam Navigation Company, founded in 1873. The company's purpose was to recapture the carrying trade on China's rivers from foreign operators. With key purchases of foreign steamers and dock facilities during the early and mid-1870s, the company had gone far toward reclaiming a significant percentage of China's river traffic by 1880. However, renewed foreign competition, lackluster governmental support, and traditional avenues of graft eroded the company's position until it folded later in the decade. In many respects, the company's experience marked a crucial tension between the entrepreneurial instincts of the merchants and the expectations of officials in regulation and receiving regular payoff income. The government itself and officials critical of self-strengthening were quick to point out the high cost of such programs, their potential for corruption, and the futility of attempting to beat the Westerners at their own game.

Amid the halting attempts at government-sponsored innovation, however, other economic forces at work would also have a profound effect on China's later economic development. The first is that in the treaty ports themselves the economic climate created by the Western powers for their own benefit exposed much of China's urban population to aspects of modern industrial and commercial society. A substantial class of Chinese people who made a living mediating between Westerners and Chinese interests had developed by the end of the nineteenth century.

The other long-term process at work was the growing influx and popularity of European, Japanese, and American consumer goods diffused from the treaty ports to the interior. While foreign curiosities had been popular with Chinese elites since the eighteenth century, Qing efforts to safeguard domestic markets through the Canton system and internal transit taxes had been steadily beaten down. By the end of the nineteenth century, foreign machine-made cotton cloth dominated the Chinese interior, John D. Rockefeller's Standard Oil Company was giving away kerosene lamps to market their fuel, the British–American Tobacco Company had established its products in the empire, and even the Japanese invention of the rickshaw had become a popular mode of transport in China's cities. With the Qing finally committed to railroad and telegraph construction and modern deep mining and with China's commercial ports resembling more and more their foreign counterparts, the seeds of economic modernity had been at least fitfully planted.

Rural Economics and Society   While about 80–85 percent of China's population remained rural, the old structures of the empire's peasant-based society were slowly beginning to crumble. As we saw during the Taiping era, tensions among peasants, village headmen, scholar-gentry, and local officials were never far from the surface. Landlordism, especially the growing incidence of absentee landlordism, tended to stretch these tensions further. As some controversial economic studies of rural Qing society have suggested, even with the most advanced intensive farming techniques available and the introduction of better crops for marginal areas like corn, peanuts, and potatoes, the land was approaching the limits of its ability to support the population without the widespread introduction of power-driven machinery. Living on the edge of poverty in many areas, with old trade routes and handicrafts disrupted by the treaty ports, many peasants saw in the Taipings, the Nian, and other local rebellions a desperate way to change their situations. But in the end, the radical ideologies and ruthlessness of the rebels disillusioned the peasantry, while in many places their poverty increased due to the immense destruction caused by rebel clashes and the flight of many wealthy scholar-gentry to the treaty ports. As a result, by the beginning of the twentieth century, absentee landlordism had become an increasingly acute problem. As some scholars have noted, the land problems of China—and their parallels in India and the Ottoman Empire—were an important impediment to an effective response to the scientific–industrial challenge of Europe and America.

Chinese Family, ca. 1873. While the later nineteenth century marked changes on a number of fronts, the centrality of the family and its Confucian hierarchy remained largely intact. In the portrait here of the Yang family of Beijing, the father and eldest son occupy the places of honor under the central window of the ground floor, while the wives, concubines, infants, and servants are arrayed on the upper veranda. In most cases, the seclusion of such wealthy women was nearly complete. The photographer reported, however, that these women frequently moistened their fingertips and rubbed them on the paper windowpanes to make them transparent so they could secretly watch events outside.

Social Trends While changes were certainly noticeable in the family, in relationships between men and women, and in the confidence the Chinese displayed in the Confucian system—particularly among urban Chinese—the durability of long-standing traditions is probably far more striking. As we have seen in every chapter on China, the family remained the central Chinese institution. Within it, the father continued to be the most powerful figure and the Confucian ideal of hierarchical relationships between husband and wife, father and son, and elder brother and younger brother remained in force. Daughters, though most often treated with affection, were also considered a net drain on family resources because they would marry outside the family. Thus, the education they received was generally aimed at fostering the skills the family of their husbands-to-be would consider valuable—cooking, sewing, running a household, and perhaps singing and poetry. Enough literacy was also desirable for girls to read such classics as "Admonitions for Women," the "Classic of Filial Piety," and other guides to proper behavior. But the proverbial wisdom remained that "a woman with talent is without virtue." Hence, the daughters of the wealthy were kept secluded in the home, and most—with the exception of certain minorities like south China's Hakkas—continued the practice of foot binding.

The disruptions of the nineteenth century began to have some effect on this situation. Though there had been a slow trickle of foreign influence into China, particularly in the treaty ports, for much of the nineteenth century, the decade following the Sino–Japanese War saw an upsurge in it, particularly as the Qing moved belatedly toward reform and underground revolutionary movements began to gain adherents. Women in Taiping areas had had a brief taste of equality, though it had been undermined by Taiping excesses and the Confucian revival afterward. With wealthier Chinese beginning to send daughters abroad to be educated, the impressions they returned with began to erode some Chinese customs, though the full impact of this would not be felt until the 1920s and 1930s. Meanwhile, such customs as the selling of young girls and female infanticide continued to be common, particularly in economically hard-pressed areas.

Culture, Arts, and Science

Though the late Qing period is often seen by scholars as one more concerned with cataloging and preserving older literary works than innovation, there was nevertheless considerable invigoration due to foreign influences toward the end of the dynasty. Indeed, one could say that the era begins with one of China's great literary masterpieces and ends with China's first modern writers pointing toward a vernacular-language "literary renaissance" starting around 1915. Reversing the trend of thousands of years, the most significant Chinese developments in science and technology were those arriving from the West as products of the Industrial Revolution and the new kind of society emerging there.

The Dream of the Red Chamber   Though the novel during Ming and Qing times was not considered high literary work by Chinese scholars, the form, as with Europeans in the eighteenth and nineteenth centuries, proved immensely popular. During the mid-eighteenth century, what many consider to be China's greatest novel, *Hong Lou Meng* (*The Dream of the Red Chamber*) was written by the shadowy Cao Xueqin [SOW shway-CHIN] (ca. 1715–ca. 1764). Almost nothing is known of Cao, including exactly when he was born and who his actual father was. The novel itself chronicles the decline and fall of a powerful family over 120 chapters. Some scholars see in it a loose autobiography of Cao's own family and a thinly veiled account of events in the early days of the Qing. In fact, the novel has been so closely studied and analyzed that there is an entire field called "red studies" or "redology" (*hong xue*) devoted to examination of the work.

Poetry, Travel Accounts, and Newspapers   While the form of the interlocking "three excellences"—painting, poetry, and calligraphy—remained largely unchanged, their content increasingly treated subjects related to China's new position in the age of imperialism. Though sometimes confining himself to more traditional fare, Huang Zunxian (1848–1905), for example, wrote many poems based on his experience as a diplomat in Japan and the United States.

China's increasing need to understand the nature of the threat confronting it prompted a greater number of atlases, gazetteers of foreign lands, and by the 1860s the first eyewitness travel accounts. Many of the early attempts at compiling information about foreign countries were copies of Western works, whose sophistication gradually increased as the century wore on. The most significant of these were Wei Yuan's (1794–1856) *Illustrated Gazetteer of the Maritime Countries* of 1844 and Xu Jiyu's (1795–1873) *Record of the World* of 1848. These accounts, especially Xu's, formed the backbone of what Chinese officials knew about the outside world until the first eyewitness accounts of travelers and diplomats began to arrive in the late 1860s.

Though hundreds of thousands of Chinese had emigrated to various parts of the world by the mid-1860s, it was only in 1866 that the first authorized officials began to visit foreign countries and not until 1876 that diplomats began to take up their posts in foreign capitals and ports. All of these men, however, were required to keep

Li Gui (1842–1903) on the Philadelphia Exposition in 1876

"Considering that the intent of countries in holding expositions is primarily to display friendship and extend human talent, particular emphasis is placed on the four words 'expand and strengthen commerce.' For the most part, though, we Chinese have not seen this as advantageous nor, since so few of us have gone abroad, have we fully grasped its implications. Still, can it be the case that others do their utmost to understand the precise thoughts of foreigners and eagerly spend hundreds, thousands, tens, or even hundreds of thousands of dollars of their capital competing in enterprises that are not advantageous? We Chinese alone seem capable of thinking that the intent of the Westerners in undertaking these exhibitions rests on principles against which we should guard at any cost. Yet as a means of enriching the country on the one hand, and benefiting the people on the other, how could this . . . exposition attendance be considered wasteful?"

—Li Gui, *Huan you diqiu xin lu*, 10a; translated by Charles Desnoyers, in *A Journey to the East*. Ann Arbor: University of Michigan Press, 2004, p. 100.

journals of their experiences, and by the later part of the century China began to acquire a far more complete sense of what the outside world was like. The diaries of the diplomats Zhang Deyi (1847–1919) and Guo Songtao (1818–1891) were particularly significant in this regard.

A new popular medium also emerged in the treaty ports and eventually in most Chinese cities as well—the newspaper. For centuries newsletters tracking official doings at the capital had been circulated among the elites. However, the 1860s saw the first popular Chinese-language papers, the most prominent of which was *Shenbao*. By the turn of the century, Liang Qichao had emerged as China's most influential journalist and scholar, having started and edited five newspapers, each heavily influenced by his views on reform. Such publications and the growing numbers of journals and popular magazines, many started by missionaries anxious to use science and Western material culture as a vehicle for their work, were vitally important in the transfer of ideas between Chinese and foreigners.

Science and Technology   As we have seen, the most pressing need for China during the early nineteenth century was considered to be military technology. During the period between the Opium Wars, Chinese officials attempted with some success to purchase guns and cannon from European and American manufacturers to bolster their coastal defenses. It was quickly apparent to the self-strengtheners, however, that China must understand the basic principles behind these revolutionary weapons and begin to manufacture them on their own. Moreover, this would be impossible to do unless the infrastructure was in place and such supporting industries as mining, railroads, and telegraphy were also established. One early move in this regard was the founding of the All-Languages Institute (*Tongwen Guan*) in 1861. Founded to provide interpreters for the newly arriving diplomats in Beijing, the foreign experts employed soon allowed the school to become a kind of all-purpose science and technology academy as well. With the founding of arsenals and dockyards and their supporting infrastructures, the need for technical knowledge accelerated. Here, the Chinese Education Mission to the United States, as well as later student missions to England and Germany, was meant to create a nucleus of trained personnel to modernize Chinese industry and defense.

Despite the general animosity directed against them by Chinese officials, missionaries ironically were key players in science and technology transfers. Unlike the Jesuit missionaries of the seventeenth century, Protestant missionaries in the nineteenth century directed their efforts at ordinary Chinese but often did so by attracting them with the new advantages of science. Central to their efforts was the role of medical missionaries in setting up clinics and using their presence in the community to foster conversion. The missionary community was also active in popularizing developments in Western science and technology through journals like *The Globe Magazine*.

By the latter part of the century, increasing numbers of Chinese scholars were becoming involved in the study of foreign subjects, going abroad for education, and in the translation of Western works into Chinese. The Chinese mathematician Li Shanlan (1810–1882), for example, collaborated with Shanghai missionaries in translating works on algebra, calculus, and analytical geometry. Later, Liang Qichao and Yan Fu (1854–1921) studied and translated a wide range of foreign scientific and social science works by John Stuart Mill, Thomas Huxley, Herbert Spencer, and Charles Darwin, as well as such Enlightenment authors as Hobbes, Locke, Hume, Rousseau, and Bentham.

Thus, while China had not yet completed its move to the new scientific–industrial society, the momentum had already begun among the empire's intellectual leaders. Even so, nearly all agreed that the future would not lie in slavish imitation of the West. In the meantime, however, the example of Japan confronted them only a short distance away.

Zaibatsu and Political Parties: Economics and Society in Meiji Japan

Scholars of Japan's economic history have often pointed out that the commercial environment developing through the Tokugawa period was well suited to the nurturing of capitalism and industrialism in the nineteenth century. As we saw in Chapter 21, for example, the imposition of the law of "alternate attendance" created a great deal of traffic to and from Edo as daimyo processions made their biannual trips to the capital. This guaranteed traffic supported numerous hostels, restaurants, stables, supply stores, theaters, and all the other commercial establishments necessary to maintain the travelers in safety and comfort. The infrastructure of the major roads also required constant tending and improvement, as did the port facilities for coastal shipping and fishing industries. Towns and cities along the routes also grew, as did the regionally specialized crafts and industries they supported. By 1850, for example, Edo had well over 1 million inhabitants, while Osaka and Kyoto both had about 375,000. Finally, commercial credit establishments, craft guilds, and large-scale industries in ceramics, sake brewing, fine arts, fishing, and coastal shipping—all intensified by being compressed into a relatively small area—had already regularized many of the institutions characteristic of the development of a modern economy.

Commerce and Cartels

Perhaps because of the urgency of their situation following Perry's visits, the Japanese were quicker to go abroad to study the industrially advanced countries of Europe and the United States. In 1860, for example, they sent an embassy to America in which the participants—including the future journalist Fukuzawa Yukichi (1835–1901)—were expected to keep diaries of everything they saw. Even during the last days of the Tokugawa regime, Japanese entrepreneurs were already experimenting with Western steamships and production techniques.

Cooperation and Capitalism   When the Meiji government began its economic reforms, its overall strategy combined elements that still mark Japanese policy today. The first was to make sure that ownership, insofar as possible, would

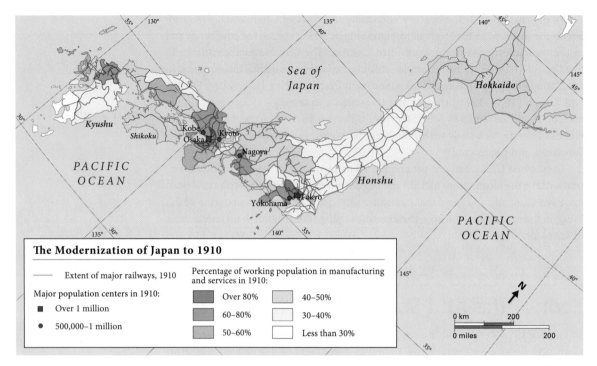

MAP **24.6 The Modernization of Japan to 1910.**

remain in Japanese hands. The second was that, taking its cue from the success of the leading commercial nations of the West, Japan would develop its exports to the utmost while attempting to keep imports to a minimum. Japanese entrepreneurship also received an enormous boost from the cashing out of the samurai. While many of the former warriors found anything to do with commerce distasteful, some took to heart the government's injunction that starting economic enterprises was a patriotic duty. By the end of the century, Japan's industrial statistics were impressive by any standards: Coal production had increased to six times its 1860 base, and iron, copper, and other mining industries expanded at a similar rate—but still could not keep pace with Japan's industrial needs. By the turn of the century Japan needed to import much of its raw material, a situation that has continued to this day.

Not surprisingly, families with long-standing connections to capital swiftly moved to unite their enterprises to gain market share. The Mitsui Company, for example, used its extensive brewing profits to fund a host of other enterprises, soon becoming one of Japan's largest industrial concerns. Similarly, the Mitsubishi Company expanded from coastal shipping to manufacturing—later creating military vehicles and famous aircraft during World War II as well as popular cars today. The encouragement of the government and the cooperation of social networks among elites in finance and industry led to the creation of a number of **cartels** called *zaibatsu*. By the end of the nineteenth century, the zaibatsu would control nearly all major Japanese industries.

Cartel: A group of domestic or international businesses that form a group to control or monopolize an industry.

The Transportation and Communications Revolutions

The rapid development of railroads and telegraphs was one of the most stunning transformations of the Meiji era. The Japanese pursued these devices with an enthusiasm scarcely paralleled anywhere else in the world. Even today, Japan's fabled "Bullet Train" remains the standard for high-speed ground transportation, while companies such as Sony and Motorola continue to dominate electronic communications markets. By the mid-1870s Japan had in place a trunk railroad line paralleling the main coastal road and several branches to major cities in the interior. Though Westerners found Japanese trains quaint—along with the custom of leaving one's clogs on the platform before boarding the cars—they were efficient and marked a trend for railroad building wherever the Japanese went. Similarly, telegraph—and, by the end of the century, telephone—lines were swiftly strung between the major cities and towns, followed by undersea cables to the Asian mainland and North America. By 1895, Japan was estimated to have over 2,000 miles of private and government railroads in operation and over 4,000 miles of telegraph wires in place (see Map 24.6).

The Meiji Constitution and Political Life   While the Charter Oath and Constitution of 1868 were instituted with considerable success, a debate had already begun among the genro concerning the liberalization of representative government in Japan. In 1881 the emperor approved a plan whereby Ito Hirobumi (1841–1909) and several senior colleagues would launch a painstaking study of the constitutional governments of the United States, Great Britain, France, Germany, and other countries, to see what aspects of them might be suitable for Japan's needs. The Meiji Constitution, as it came to be called, was promulgated in 1889 and remained in force until it was supplanted by the constitution composed during the Allied occupation of Japan after World War II.

While borrowing elements from the US and British models, Ito's constitution drew most heavily from that of Germany. Much of it was also aimed at preserving the traditions of Japan's Confucian society that Ito and the genro most valued. Chief among these was the concept of *kokutai*, the "national polity." In this view, Japan was unique among nations because of its unbroken line of emperors and the singular familial and spiritual relationship between the emperor and his people. Thus, the Meiji Constitution is presented, in Ito's words, as "the gift of a benevolent and charitable emperor to the people of his country." The sovereignty of the country is placed in the person of the emperor as the embodiment of kokutai; the emperor's Privy Council, the army and navy, and the ministers of state are answerable directly to him. There is also a bicameral parliamentary body called the

Visions of the New Railroads. The marvels of the new systems of railroads and telegraphs springing up in Japan provided practitioners of ukiyo-e woodblock art a host of new subjects to depict in the 1870s and 1880s. Here is one of a number of views of new stations, in this case, Ueno on the Ueno–Nakasendo–Tokyo Railway, with small commuter trains arriving and departing.

Progress and Reform

"Political reform and progress is the unanimous wish of our party and has ever been my abiding purpose. It must, however, be achieved by sound and proper means.... We differ categorically from those parties which fail to act when the occasion demands it, and which under the guise of working for gradual progress seek private advantage through deliberate procrastination."

—Okuma Shigenobu from Watanabe Ikujiro, *Okuma Shigenobu*, pp. 92–95; quoted in Tsunoda, DeBary, Keene, *Sources of Japanese Tradition*, vol. !!, p.187.

Diet, with an upper House of Peers and a lower House of Representatives. Like the House of Lords in Great Britain, Japan's House of Peers consisted of members of the nobility; the representatives were elected by the people. The primary purpose of the Diet in this arrangement is to vote on financing, deliberate on the everyday items of governance, and provide advice and consent to the Privy Council, Ministry of State, and Imperial Court.

As for the people themselves, 15 articles spell out "The Rights and Duties of Subjects." Duties include liability for taxes and service in the military, while the rights enumerated are similar to those found in European and American constitutions: the right to hold office, guarantees against search and seizure, the right to trial, the right to property, and freedoms of religion, speech, and petition. All of these, however, are qualified by such phrases as "unless provided by law," leaving the door open for the government to invoke extraordinary powers during national emergencies.

Political Parties   As constitutional government began to be enacted in the 1890s, the factional debates among senior advisors naturally began to attract followers among the Diet members and their supporters. In the preceding decades there had been political parties; but their membership was limited, and they were seen by many as illegitimate because of their potential opposition to the government. Now, two major parties came to the fore by the turn of the century. The Kenseito [KEN-say-toe], or Liberal, Party had its roots in the work of Itagaki Taisuke (1837–1919) and his political opponent, Okuma Shigenobu [OH-ku-ma SHIH-geh-no-bu]. The two merged their followers but later split into factions at the turn of the century. It later was reestablished as the Minseito.

The more powerful party during this time was the Seiyukai, or Constitutional Government Party, founded by Ito and his followers in 1900. Generally associated with the government and the zaibatsu, the Seiyukai dominated Japanese politics in the era before World War I; after World War II, its adherents coalesced into Japan's present Liberal Democratic Party.

Social Experiments   In addition to creating an industrial base and a constitutional government, Japan's rulers attempted to curb practices in Japan that were believed to offend foreign sensibilities as part of its program of "civilization and enlightenment." Bathhouses, for example, were now required to have separate entrances for men and women, and pleasure quarters were restricted in areas near foreign enclaves; meat eating was even encouraged in largely Buddhist Japan, resulting in the new dish *sukiyaki*. In the boldest experiment of all, the government mandated the use of Western dress for men and women, accompanied by a propaganda campaign depicting the advantages of this "modern" and "civilized" clothing. Criticism from a variety of quarters, however, including many Westerners, ultimately forced the government to relent and make the new dress optional.

In the same vein, traditional restrictions on women were altered. Though the home remained the primary domain for women, as it does even today, women were far more often seen in public. Concubines were now accorded the same rights as wives. Courtesans and prostitutes were no longer legally considered servants. Among elites, the fad of following all things Western established to some degree Victorian European standards of family decorum. More far-reaching, however, was the role of the new education system. Even before the Meiji Restoration, Japan had one of the highest levels of preindustrial literacy in the world—40 percent for males and 15 percent for females. With the introduction of compulsory public education, literacy would become nearly universal; and the upsurge in specialized women's education created entire new avenues of employment for women.

This same trend toward emancipation was evident among the rural population. The formal class barriers between peasants and samurai were eliminated, though informal deference to elites continued. In addition, some barriers between ordinary Japanese and outcast groups, such as the Eta, were also reduced. During the latter part of the nineteenth century, aided by better transportation, improved crops, maximum utilization of marginal lands, and the opening up of Hokkaido for development, Japan became the most intensely farmed nation in the world. Japan's already well-developed fishing industry contributed mightily by introducing commercial fish-based fertilizers that boosted yields enormously. The result was that although Japan's population increased to 40 million by 1890, it was a net exporter of food until the turn of the century.

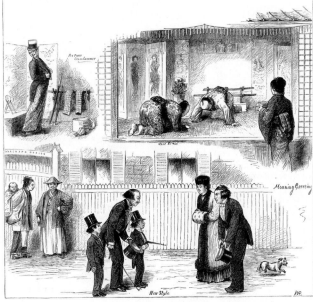

NEW YEAR'S DAY IN JAPAN

New Year's Day in Japan, ca. 1905. An important part of Japan's strategy to roll back its unequal treaties with the West was the campaign of *bunmei kaika*, or "civilization and enlightenment." The idea of this policy was to show Western observers in concrete terms that Japan accepted Western notions of what it meant to be a "civilized" nation. In this cartoon the contrast between the old Japan of the Tokugawa days and the new Japan of the "enlightenment and civilization" is graphically depicted. The upper panel, labeled "Old Style" shows two samurai bowing in greeting in a traditional room replete with screens and scrolls marking the occasion, and the wife of the host entertains the men. The lower panel shows the "new style," in which men and women wear Western fashions, with families greeting each other together on the street in front a Western house surrounded by a picket fence, while a pet dog romps nearby.

"Enlightenment and Progress": Science, Culture, and the Arts

As we saw in Chapter 21, while the Tokugawa sought seclusion, they were by no means cut off entirely from developments in other nations. Of particular importance in this regard was the requirement imposed on the Dutch merchants at Deshima to make their annual reports to the Shogun on the state of the world. By the time of Commodore Perry's visit the accumulated amount of "Dutch learning" was impressive. Much of it consisted of notes on scientific and technical developments.

Engaging "Western Science"　　Nevertheless, at the time of their initial contact with the Western powers, the Tokugawa were stunned at the degree to which the accelerating technologies of the Industrial Revolution had armed their adversaries. During Perry's visits Japanese sketch artists frantically sought to capture the details of the ships' gun ports and cannon and the outward signs of their steam power. As we have seen, the Japanese were immediately engaged with the notion of the railroad; just as quickly they sought to create oceangoing steamships. By 1860, they had built and manned steamers and insisted that their embassy to the United States travel aboard one the Japanese had built themselves.

Western Science. The Japanese were fascinated by the new and strange technology they found on Perry's ships, including the paddle wheel from one of his steamships, which they drew with scientific precision.

Journalism in Modern Society

"In editing the paper [*Jiji-shimpo*] I encouraged the reporters to write bravely and freely. I have no objection to any severe criticism or extreme statements, but I warned them that they must limit their statements to what they would be willing to say to the victim face to face. Otherwise, they are what I would call *kage-benkei* [shadow fighters] attacking from the security of their columns. It is very easy for *kage-benkei* to fall into mean abuses and irresponsible invectives which are the eternal shame of the writer's profession."

—Fukuzawa Yukichi. *The Autobiography of Fukuzawa Yukichi*, Kiyooka Eikichi, trans., Tokyo, 1934. Quoted in Tsunoda, DeBary, Keene, *Sources of Japanese Tradition*, p. 129.

The demand for industrial and military technology required large numbers of Japanese to seek technical education. During the initial stages of the Meiji era, thousands of Japanese students studied in Europe and the United States, and the Japanese government and private concerns hired hundreds of foreign advisors to aid in science and technical training. By the 1880s a university system anchored by Tokyo Imperial University and including Keio, Waseda, and Doshisha was offering courses in medicine, physics, chemistry, engineering, and geology, among other advanced disciplines. By the turn of the century, Japan's Institute for Infectious Diseases had become world famous for its pathbreaking work in microbiology. On the whole, however, the bulk of the nation's efforts went into the practical application of science to technology and agriculture in order to support the government's modernization efforts.

Culture and the Arts   As was the case a decade later in China, Japanese intellectuals eagerly absorbed copies of Western Enlightenment, philosophical, and social science works in translation—including Locke, Hobbes, Spencer, Darwin, and Comte, to name but a few. As was also true in China, journalism played a dominant role as a disseminator of information to the public. Here, Fukuzawa Yukichi, like Liang Qichao in China, held a central place both in fostering the growth of newspapers and in articulating the role of journalists in a modern society.

As were nearly all the arts in late nineteenth-century Japan, the novel was also heavily influenced by Western examples. In some respects, the culmination of this trend was *Kokoro*, by Natsume Soseki, (1867–1916) published in 1914. Soseki utilizes the wrenching changes in Meiji Japan set against traditional and generational values to create the tension and ultimate tragic end of the central character in his work.

More traditional arts such as Noh and kabuki theater and ukiyo-e printing survived but often in a somewhat altered state. Updated kabuki variations now featured contemporary themes and often had female actors playing female parts.

In addition, European plays such as Ibsen's *A Doll's House* enjoyed considerable vogue. As for ukiyo-e, it remained the cheapest and most popular outlet for depictions of contemporary events until the development of newspaper photography. Especially telling in this regard are ukiyo-e artist's interpretations of the Sino–Japanese War.

Putting It All Together

Scholars of China and Japan have long debated the reasons for the apparent success of Japan and failure of China. One school of thought sees the fundamental reasons growing from the cultural outlooks of the two countries. China, it is argued, assumed that outsiders would simply be won over to Confucian norms and modes of behavior because this is what China's historical experience had been for the last 2,000 years. When it became apparent that defensive measures were necessary, it was still assumed that China's superior culture would win out. Japan, on the other hand, because of its long history of cultural borrowing and its much smaller size, assumed a more urgent defensive posture. In addition, the Japanese had the advantage of watching events unfold in China before the threat reached their own shores. This allowed them to act in a more united and pragmatic fashion when resisting the Western threat.

Some historians, however, disagree with this approach. They argue instead that the cultural differences between China and Japan were secondary in the face of the foreign threat. According to this school of thought, the primary cause of the radically different outcomes for China and Japan was that China was victimized by foreign imperialism much earlier and much more thoroughly than Japan. Once Japanese modernization efforts were under way, they won for themselves a breathing spell with which to keep imperialism at bay and ultimately fought their way into the great power club themselves (see Concept Map).

Both China and Japan were to continue their relative trajectories for decades to come. Japan would achieve its ultimate military power in early 1942. At that point, during World War II, the Japanese Empire encompassed Korea, Manchuria, much of China, the Philippines, Indonesia, most of southeast Asia, and hundreds of Pacific Islands. In a little over 3 years, however, the empire was gone, the home islands were in ruins, and for the first time in its history Japan was under occupation. Since that time, however, its economic development has resumed with even more vigor, and is today the third largest economy in the world.

China's troubles would, despite a few bright points along the way, multiply. Throwing off the Qing, the Chinese republic would be plagued by warlordism, civil war, and invasion, until the triumph of the Communist Party and founding of the People's Republic of China in 1949. Yet, it is only since 1978 that its most significant progress in industrial and economic development has taken place. Ironically, much of China's newfound economic might was inspired by the approaches employed in Japan's postwar recovery. In the long sweep of China's history, however, this resurgence is seen with growing confidence by the Chinese as marking a return to their accustomed place and in 2010 it passed Japan to become the world's second largest economy.

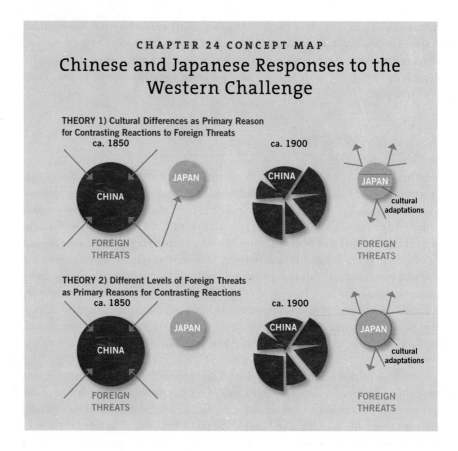

CHAPTER 24 CONCEPT MAP

Chinese and Japanese Responses to the Western Challenge

THEORY 1) Cultural Differences as Primary Reason for Contrasting Reactions to Foreign Threats

Review and Respond

1. How would you characterize the Western maritime countries' economic relationship with China during this period?

2. How did opium become such a problem between Britain and China? Was opium the real cause of the First Opium War? Why or why not?

3. Why did "self-strengthening" produce China and "Western science and Eastern ethics" in Japan as adaptations to modernity have such different results?

4. What do you see as the major strengths and weaknesses of the Meiji response to Western imperialism?

5. Why did Japan become an imperial power instead of simply strengthening its home islands?

> For additional resources, including maps, primary sources, visuals, and quizzes, please go to www.oup.com/us/vonsivers. Please see the Further Resources section at the back of the book for additional readings and suggested websites.

Thinking Through Patterns

▶ **What was the impact of Western imperialism on the "regulated societies" of China and Japan?**

The impact of the intrusion of Great Britain, France, the United States, and later Germany and Russia forced both China and Japan into defensive postures. Both countries had sought to keep out what they considered subversive foreign influences after an earlier period of exposure to Western traders and missionaries. China had created a tightly controlled system of overseas trade based in Guangzhou (Canton); Japan allowed only the Dutch to trade with them. But the expansion of trade in both legitimate goods and opium and the need of the British for regularization of diplomatic practices pushed Britain and China into a cycle of war and "unequal treaties" under which China was at an increasing disadvantage. Japan, suddenly thrust into international commerce and diplomacy by the young United States, now sought to protect its borders without pushing the Western powers into seizing any of its territory.

China's long history of absorbing and acculturating outside invaders to Confucian norms encouraged its leaders to assume that the Westerners would be no different. Though many officials realized the qualitative difference between the industrializing Euro-American countries and invaders from the Chinese past, they were of divided opinion about what to do. Thus, attempts at reform were often undercut by political infighting at court and in the bureaucracy. The Taiping Rebellion also played a central role in further depleting China's strength and resources. As time went on, increasing Western control of China's ports and tariffs, absentee landlordism, and declining agricultural productivity also played a role.

▶ **Why did European empire building in Asia have such dramatically different effects on China and Japan?**

For Japan, after a decade of indecision about how to handle the foreign intrusion, a civil war ended in the dismantling of the shogunate and the unification of the country under Emperor Meiji. With remarkable unity born of a deep sense of urgency, Japan embarked upon a thoroughgoing reform program aimed at remaking the country along avowedly Western lines. The focus and consistency displayed by Meiji and his advisors avoided many of the problems China experienced, and Japan's late Tokugawa economics to some degree had predisposed the country toward a smoother transition into that of scientific–industrial society.

▶ **How have historians seen the nature of these outside forces and their influences in east Asia?**

Historians have long debated the relative weight that should be assigned to cultural and material reasons for the differing paths of China and Japan. China's long history as the region's cultural leader, some have argued, made it difficult for the empire to remake itself to face the Western challenge; Japan, on the other hand, has a long history of cultural borrowing and, thus, found it easier to borrow from the Euro-American world. Some historians have argued that China's earlier experience with imperialism stunted the modernizing tendencies within the empire and kept it from responding; they argue that Japan had the advantage of being "opened" later and so could respond more effectively. Others have argued that Japan's tradition of military prowess played a role, still others that China's more complete incorporation into the modern "world system" crippled its ability to respond more independently.

Chapter 25
1683-1908

Adaptation and Resistance

THE OTTOMAN AND RUSSIAN EMPIRES

RUSSIAN AND OTTOMAN EMPIRES, 1683-1908

October 13, 1824, marked a most unusual event in Russia. On this date, Aleksander Nikitenko, born into serfdom, received his freedom at the young age of 20 from his lord, a fabulously wealthy landowning count. Even more remarkable is the subsequent course of Nikitenko's life and career. After earning a university degree, he went on to become a professor of literature at St. Petersburg University, a member of the distinguished Academy of Sciences, and a censor in the Ministry of Education.

Beginning in 1818 at the age of 14, the bright and precocious Nikitenko kept a diary. The account of events from this date until his emancipation in 1824 at the age of 20 was written as a retrospective memoir. The most important entries refer to the role of the European Enlightenment thinkers in shaping changing intellectual attitudes in Russia. For example, Nikitenko makes repeated reference to the works of Montesquieu, particularly *The Spirit of Laws*, which inspired the so-called Decembrists, leaders of an abortive proconstitutional uprising in 1825, with whom Nikitenko was in touch.

Nikitenko's diary provides deep insights into the role of **serfdom** in the Russian Empire. We are told that "when the inevitable happened," the errant serfs were turned over to a lackey in charge of meting out punishment in the form of flogging with birch rods: "Woe to the unfortunates who fell into [his] hands! He was a master and enthusiast of flogging, especially of girls, and they were terrified by the mere sight of him." Nikitenko also tells of his sadness when he had to part with his classmates upon graduating at age 13 from his country school: "But more painful than anything else was the knowledge that I would not be allowed to join the boys who were preparing to enter high school. For me its doors were inexorably closed.

Seeing Patterns

▶ Which new models did the Ottomans adopt during the nineteenth century to adapt themselves to the Western challenge?

▶ Why did the tsars and landholding aristocracy fear Western constitutionalism? Why did the Russian constitutionalists eventually lose out to the revolutionaries?

▶ How did the agrarian Ottoman and Russian Empires, both with large landholding ruling classes, respond to the western European industrial challenge during the 1800s?

▶ Why did large, well-established empires like the Russian and the Ottoman struggle with the forces of modernity, while a small, secluded island nation like Japan seemed to adapt so quickly and successfully?

Auction of Serfs. In this painting, *Auction of Serfs* (1910), the well-known Russian realist painter Klavdiy Vasilievich Lebedev (1852–1916) depicted the room of a Russian aristocratic landowning family as it auctioned off valuables as well as serfs (standing on the right). The 1861 decree ending serfdom in Russia was far less than what its name suggested since the peasants had to buy their land from the nonfarming landowners.

Serfdom: Legal and cultural institution in which peasants are bound to the land.

Here, for the first time, I had to face the terrible curse that hung over me because of my social status, which later caused me so much suffering and almost drove me to suicide." Nikitenko's curse, Russian serfdom, was scarcely different from plantation slavery in the Americas or from the status of untouchables in India. Slavery was also the common lot of many in the neighboring Ottoman Empire and, though limited to households, was no less demeaning. The end of serfdom in Russia would not come until 1861 and that of slavery in the Ottoman Empire not until 1890.

Serfdom and slavery were dramatic examples of the kinds of practices that the new Enlightenment constitutionalism, in theory at least, stood firmly against. As such, they were among the first of many challenges the world outside western Europe and North America faced from the West in the nineteenth century. Russia was an empire that had inherited Byzantine Christian civilization but had not adopted the New Science and its offspring, the twin revolutions of the Enlightenment and Industrial Revolution. For its part, the Ottoman Empire was heir to both Islamic and Byzantine traditions but had also not participated in the transition to the New Science, Enlightenment, and industrialization. Even though Enlightenment thought had produced and elaborated the political theories of the social contract and popular sovereignty, which were realized in the American, French, and Haitian Revolutions, shortly before the onset of the Industrial Revolution in Great Britain, it would be the campaigns of Napoleon in the early nineteenth century that sowed these ideas throughout Europe.

They also would fling these seeds at the initially unpromising soil of the Russian and Ottoman Empires. Napoleon's invasions of Ottoman Egypt in 1798 and Russia in 1812 drove home to their rulers that his new armies of mass conscripts, equipped with flintlock muskets and light, mobile artillery and drilled to fight in flexible formations, were superior to their own military forces. It became inevitable for the Ottomans and Russians, short of losing their independence, to update their armies and training and to respond somehow to the constitutional nationalism arising from the French Revolution and carried by Napoleon's armies, which now attracted rising numbers of adherents among their subjects.

At the same time, the two empires became mortal enemies: An expanding eastern [Orthodox] Christian Russia declared its goal to be conquest of the former eastern Christian capital Istanbul (Constantinople) and to drive a shrinking Ottoman Empire from Europe back into "Asia" (Asia Minor or Anatolia). Since both empires were members of the Concert of Europe, their profound conflict involved the other European powers as well. These powers found themselves increasingly drawn into a conflict, culminating in the Crimean War of 1853–1856, that was only partially European and increasingly involved Russia and the Ottomans in Asia. For the monarchs, politicians, and diplomats focused after 1815 on the balance of power in western and central Europe, such a power struggle between the Russians and Ottomans held little interest: For them, this contest was "Oriental" and therefore alien.

It is important that we keep this partially non-Western identity of the Russian and Ottoman Empires in mind for this chapter: As forcefully as Russia asserted itself in the European Concert in the early years after 1815 and again at the end of the nineteenth century, it was in reality—despite its Christian character—not any more or less "European" than the increasingly harried Muslim Ottoman Empire. Indeed, as we will see, both empires had far more in common with each other, and to some degree with the empire of the Qing in China, than they did with the evolving nation-states of western Europe. Furthermore, their reactions to the challenges posed by the new nation-states paralleled each other to a degree not often appreciated by students and scholars studying them outside of a world context. Therefore, we consider them together here as their own case studies in the overall patterns of constitutionalism, nation-state formation, and the challenge of modernity.

Decentralization and Reforms in the Ottoman Empire

Prior to the Russian–Ottoman rivalry in the 1800s, the traditional enemies of the Ottomans were the Austrian Habsburgs. This enmity had reached its climax in the second half of the 1600s. The Habsburgs ultimately won but in the course of the 1700s were increasingly sidelined by the rise of Russia as a new, Orthodox Christian empire, whose rulers, the tsars, saw themselves as representatives of the "third Rome," that is, Moscow as the successor of Rome and Constantinople. After consolidating itself on the fertile northeast European plains, Russia expanded eastward and southward, clashing with the Muslim Ottomans, conquerors of Constantinople. Because the Russians adapted themselves earlier than the Ottomans to new western European military tactics, the Ottomans found it increasingly difficult to defend themselves in the later 1700s. They

1683 Second Ottoman Siege of Vienna

1768-1774 First Ottoman–Russian War

1832 Greece Secures Independence from Ottomans

1762-1796 Catherine II of Russia

1798-1801 Napoleon's Occupation of Egypt

1839-1876 Tanzimat Reforms in Ottoman Empire

1853-1856 Crimean War of Great Britain, France, and Ottoman Empire Against Russia

1878-1885 Independence of Serbia, Montenegro, Romania, and Bulgaria

1908 Young Turks Rise to Power in Ottoman Empire

1861 Emancipation of Serfs in Russian Empire

1904-1905 Russo–Japanese War, Followed by Abortive Russian Revolution

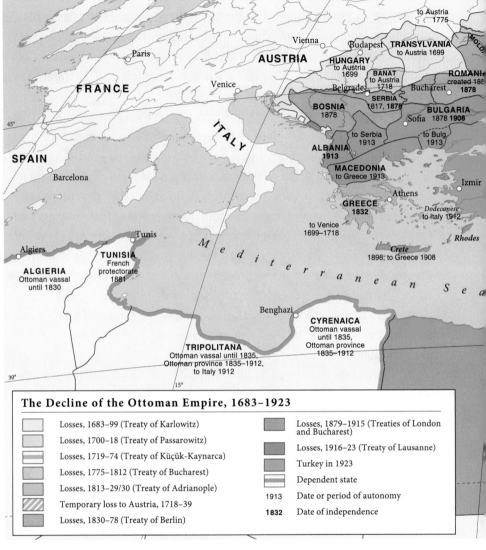

MAP 25.1 **The Decline of the Ottoman Empire, 1683–1923.**

sought to improve their defenses through military and constitutional–nationalist re-forms in the mid-1800s but were only half successful. Russia became the patron of nationalist movements among the Slavic populations in the European provinces of the Ottoman Empire. Although they strengthened themselves through reforms, the Ottomans were no match for the combined Russian–southern Slavic aggression. At the end of the Second Balkan War of 1913, they had lost nearly the entire European part of their empire to ethnic–nationalist liberation movements and were barely able to hang on to Istanbul (see Map 25.1).

Ottoman Imperialism in the 1600s and 1700s

In the period from 1500 to 1700 the Ottoman Empire was the dominant politi-cal power in the Middle East and North Africa, flanked by the two lesser realms

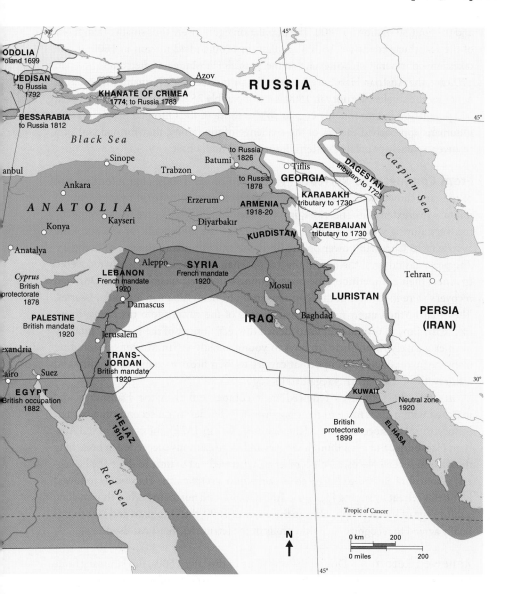

of Persia in the east and Morocco in the west. At that time, as we noted, the main enemy of the Ottomans was not yet Russia but the Habsburg Empire in Spain, Germany, and Austria. The two were fighting each other on dual fronts, the Balkans in the east and North Africa in the western Mediterranean, each gaining and losing in the process and eventually establishing a more or less stable disengagement. It was during this disengagement period that Russia began its expansion southward at the increasing expense of the Ottomans.

Demographic Considerations   As with the other agrarian–urban regions of Asia and Europe, the Middle East had experienced a sustained recovery of population figures after the Black Death of the mid-1400s. This recovery came to an end around 1600, with 25 million inhabitants, though with slow increases to 27 million by 1700 and to about 30 million by 1800. The population figures were thus smaller than those of the Habsburg countries, with 37 million in 1700 and 42 million in 1800. If one takes into consideration, however, that the Spanish Habsburg line died out in Spain in 1700 and the Austrian Habsburgs governed only indirectly in Germany, the resulting figure for the smaller territory in 1800 is a comparable 25 million. Russia, for its part, had population figures roughly comparable to those of the Ottoman Empire. As the Ottomans approached the era of the challenge of modernity, they formed part of a relatively sparsely populated eastern Europe and Middle East.

From Conquests to Retreats   At the end of the 1500s, after a long period of military showdowns, the Ottomans and Habsburgs were beset by problems of military overextension. Therefore, in 1606 they concluded a peace to gain time for recovery, during which the Ottomans recognized the Habsburgs for the first time as a de facto Christian power on the border of the Ottoman province of Hungary. The peace lasted until the end of the 1600s when both were sufficiently recovered to renew their competition. The main administrators responsible for the Ottoman recovery were the viziers of the Köprülü family, from an Albanian line of Janissaries. They transformed many military assignments of the cavalry into tax farms, to increase the flow of revenue, and broadened the recruitment of the Janissary infantry from exclusively rural Christian boys to young, mostly urban Muslims. By shifting from the increasingly less important cavalry to their firearm-equipped infantry and artillery, the Ottoman army regained its edge.

In 1683 the Ottomans renewed their competition with the Habsburgs and marched with a giant force to their northwestern border. For a second time in their history, they laid siege to Vienna (the first siege was in 1529), the capital of the Austrian Habsburgs. But even though sappers and siege cannons succeeded in breaching the walls in several places, a Polish relief army arrived just in time to drive the besiegers, who had neglected to fortify their camp, into a retreat. The Habsburgs followed up on this retreat by seizing Hungary, Transylvania, and northern Serbia, thus making a third siege of Vienna impossible. In the peace of 1699, the Ottomans and Habsburgs finally agreed to recognize each other fully in the territories they possessed.

Renewed Reforms   During the war years of the later 1600s, the Janissary force had swelled to some 70,000 soldiers. In the end, however, only about 10,000 were on active duty. Since they were all on the payroll and given renewed fiscal shortfalls, the money was often debased or in arrears, forcing them to earn a living as craftspeople. A brisk trade developed in which Janissaries and non-Janissaries alike exchanged pay tickets that entitled the holders not only to wages but also to fiscal and juridical exemptions. Coffeehouses near Janissary barracks became flourishing trade centers for pay tickets, food rations, and military supplies. In short, the Janissary force was in the process of becoming a collection of crafts guilds on a kind of government welfare.

New reforms were clearly necessary. In the early 1700s the sultan's government cut the Janissary rolls by half and enlisted Anatolian farmers to supplement the active Janissaries. In order to improve revenues with which to pay the Janissaries, the reformers introduced the new institution of the lifetime tax farm, or **life lease**, for agricultural rents from village farmers. As in France, which developed a similar tax farm regime at the time, the idea was to diminish the temptation—endemic among

Life lease: Lifelong tax farm, awarded to a wealthy member of the ruling class, in return for advances to the central imperial treasury on the taxes to be collected from village farmers.

the annual tax farmers—to squeeze farmers dry so that they would flee from the countryside to the cities. Wealthy and high-ranking courtiers, officers, administrators, and Islamic clerics in Istanbul bought these life leases. They numbered about 2,000, shifting the weight in the ruling class increasingly from the military to civilians. The large cash outlays necessary for the purchase of these life leases required access to liquid capital, which Armenian merchants with European connections provided. Thus, here in the early 1700s was the beginning of a development parallel to similar developments in France and England, with efforts to organize a kind of capital market. As a result of the reforms, in 1720, for the first time in a century and a half, the central budget was balanced again.

The Tulip Era The new ruling class, holding life leases, was less connected to the Topkapı, the sultan's palace, and its administrative quarters and invested its wealth in new constructions. A building boom ensued in the early 1700s, expressing itself in the erection of numerous office buildings and mansions in town as well as palaces and gardens along Istanbul's waterfront. Other construction included renovations, aqueducts, mosques, colleges, libraries, public baths, and fountains. In addition, villages in the provinces benefited from construction projects. Ruling-class members who remembered their modest rural origins competed in the capital and countryside for philanthropic recognition.

The new palaces and mansions were architecturally inspired by the long tradition of pre-Islamic Middle Eastern royal residences and parks, especially in Iran. In the salons of these residences, poets and musicians presented their compositions. Books, for the first time printed in Ottoman Turkish, became available: One of these books contained a summary of Copernicus's New Science, although there is no evidence of any intellectual impact made by heliocentrism in the empire. The gardens of the residences featured hundreds of varieties of flowers, plants, shrubs, and trees. (Many of these varieties, including tulips, had made their way earlier to Europe; and ever since the mid-1600s the Dutch have been *the* tulip specialists of the world.) Modern Turkish writers dubbed the time of cultural efflorescence in the first half of the 1700s the Ottoman "Tulip period."

The Tulip Period. During the "Tulip period," the Ottoman ruling class not only prided itself on its ability to breed ever new varieties of tulips, hyacinths, and roses (a) but also frequented coffeehouses and public parks for picnics (b).

Decentralization During the Tulip period, an accelerating transformation of cavalry-held lands into tax farms started a pattern of political decentralization in the Ottoman Empire. Agents responsible for the collection of taxes for their superiors succeeded in withholding increasing amounts from the treasury in Istanbul. By the mid-1700s, these agents were in positions of considerable provincial power as "notables" (*ayan*) in the Balkans or "valley lords" (*derebeys*) in western Anatolia. Starved for funds, the sultan and central administration were no longer able to support a large standing army of infantry and cavalry in the capital.

In 1768–1774 the notables and valley lords played a crucial role not only in financing a major war against Russia but also in recruiting troops—untrained and underarmed peasants—since the numbers of government forces in fighting order had shrunk to minimal levels. The war was the first in which the Russian tsars exploited Ottoman decentralization for a systematic expansion southward. When the sultan promptly lost the war, he was more or less at the mercy of these notables and lords in the provinces.

The Western Challenge and Ottoman Responses

Soon after this Ottoman–Russian war, the Ottoman Empire began to face the challenge of Western modernity. As with China and Japan, the increasing military, political, and economic strength of the West allowed it to force the traditional Asian empires to adapt to its challenges. This adaptation was extremely difficult and entailed severe territorial losses for the Ottoman Empire. But after initial humiliations, the ruling class was able to develop a pattern of responses to the Western challenge, by reducing the power of the provincial magnates, modernizing the army, introducing constitutional reforms, and eventually transforming its manufacturing sector.

External and Internal Blows   During the period 1774–1808, the Ottoman central government suffered a series of humiliations which were comparable in their destabilizing effects to those in the later Opium Wars and the Taiping and Boxer Rebellions in China. Russia gained the north coast of the Black Sea and Georgia in the Caucasus. Napoleon invaded Egypt and destroyed the local regime of Ottoman Mamluk vassals in 1798. But a British fleet sent after him succeeded in destroying his navy, and a subsequent land campaign forced him to return to France in 1801. As he was victimizing the Ottoman Empire, Napoleon apparently wanted to demonstrate the ineffectiveness of Great Britain's European continental blockade and teach it a lesson about the vulnerability of its control of India. Napoleon's sudden imperialist venture produced a deep shock in the Middle East: For the first time a Western ruler had penetrated deeply into the Ottoman Empire, cutting it effectively in half.

Internally, the lessening of central control in the second half of the 1700s left the provinces in virtual independence. Most notables and lords were satisfied with local autonomy, but a few became warlords, engaging in campaigns to become regional leaders. In other cases, especially in Egypt, Syria, and Iraq, *Mamluks*, that is, military slaves from the northern Caucasus whom Ottoman governors had previously employed as auxiliaries in the military, seized power. In eastern Arabia, a local Sunni cleric, Muhammad Ibn Abd al-Wahhab [Wah-HAHB], exploited Ottoman decentralization to ally himself with the head of a powerful family in command of a number of oases, Ibn Saud [Sa-OOD], to establish an autonomous polity in the desert, which today is the most powerful oil state in the world—Saudi Arabia. None of these ambitious leaders, however, renounced allegiance to the sultan, who at least remained a figurehead.

To take power back, the sultan and his viziers once more sought for ways to reform the empire. In 1792, they proclaimed a "new order" (*Nizam-i Cedid* [Nee-ZAHM-ee Jay-DEED]), defined as a reorganization of the army with the creation of a new, separate artillery and flintlock musket corps of some 22,000 soldiers alongside the Janissaries. The new corps was recruited from among Anatolian farmers, with the help of willing notables and lords, and financed through ad hoc measures, such as property confiscations, currency debasements, and tax increases. European officers trained these soldiers in drills, line fighting, bayonet combat, and formation marching. Officers received their education at the newly founded Land Engineering School. The corps underwent its baptism by fire when it defended Acre in Syria successfully against Napoleon.

The ad hoc financing of the new order, however, came to haunt the reformers. During a severe fiscal crisis in 1807, auxiliary Janissaries, refusing to wear new uniforms, assassinated a new order officer. Inept handling of this incident resulted in a quickly mushrooming, full-scale revolt of Janissaries as well as religious scholars and students, costing the sultan his life and ushering in the dissolution of the new troops. In a counterrevolt, thanks to the timely arrival of a Ukrainian-born notable from northern Bulgaria with his private army, a new sultan came to power in 1808. As a price for his accession, the sultan had to agree to power sharing with the provincial lords.

Renewed Difficulties   After a dozen years of careful maneuvering, during which the sultan reconstituted the nucleus for another new army and neutralized many notables and valley lords, he was able to crush the Janissaries in a bloody massacre (1826). But the new corps was in no shape yet to provide the backbone for a sustained recentralization of the empire. New internal enemies arose, in the form of Greek ethnic nationalists, whom the Ottomans would have defeated had it not been for the military intervention of the European powers. As a result, Greece became independent in a war of liberation (1821–1832). It was the first country, prior to Italy and Germany, in which ethnic nationalism was central to its foundation.

Russia, providing support for its fellow Orthodox Christian Greeks, acquired new territories from the Ottomans around the Black Sea. Several Balkan provinces achieved administrative autonomy. Algiers in North Africa was lost in 1830, falling to an invading French force. Worst of all, in 1831, the new Ottoman vassal in Egypt, the Albanian-born officer Muhammad Ali (r. 1805–1848), seeking greater influence within the empire, rose in rebellion. After occupying Syria (1831–1840), he would have conquered Istanbul had he not been stopped by Russian, British, and French intervention. Without the diplomacy of Great Britain, which carefully sought to balance the European powers after the end of the Napoleonic empire, the Ottoman Empire would not have survived the 1830s.

Life, Honor, and Property   The cumulative effect of these setbacks was a realization among Ottoman administrators that only a serious effort at recentralization would save the empire. In 1839, with a change of sultans, the government issued the Rose Garden Edict, the first of three reform edicts, plus more specific additional ones in between, which are collectively known as

Muhammad Ali. Muhammad Ali transformed Egypt during the first half of the nineteenth century more thoroughly than the Ottoman overlord sultan could in his far-flung empire. He astutely realized that long-staple cotton, bred first in Egypt, could make Egypt a wealthy state in the beginning industrial transformation of the world.

Tanzimat: Ottoman reforms inspired by constitutional nationalism in Europe, covering the adoption of basic rights, a legal reform, and a land code.

Tanzimat ("Reorganizations"). In the Rose Garden Edict, the government bound it-self to three basic principles: the guarantee of life, honor, and property of all subjects regardless of religion; the replacement of tax farms and life leases with an equitable tax system; and the introduction of a military conscription system, all in accordance with the Shari`a, the compendium of Islamic morality and law. The edict carefully avoided a definition of the position of the Christians and Jews in the empire before the law, offering them the rights of life, honor, and property while maintaining their inequality vis-à-vis the Muslims proclaimed in Islamic law.

The edict addressed the two fundamental problems of the empire, that is, taxes and the military, carefully emphasizing the Islamic justification. It also enumerated basic human rights, inspired by the American Declaration of Independence and the French Rights of Man. Here, we can see a first adaptation of the Ottoman Empire to the Western challenge: The Ottoman Empire adapted, at least in an initial and partial way, to constitutional nationalism, the outgrowth of Enlightenment thought.

Further Reforms   As these reforms were being implemented, a new European political initiative challenged the Ottoman Empire. The aggressively imperialistic Napoleon III (1848-1852 president, 1852-1870 emperor), self-declared emperor of France, challenged the Russian tsar's claim to be the protector of the Christian holy places in Palestine, a claim which the Ottoman sultan had granted after his defeat in 1774. As we saw in Chapter 24, the French joined the British during the Second Opium War for much the same reason: protection of Catholics and French mission-aries in China. While the French and Russian diplomats sought to pull a vacillating sultan back and forth toward their respective claims, the political situation turned increasingly tense. Through careful maneuvering, Ottoman diplomats were able to strengthen themselves in a coalition with Great Britain and France. In the Crimean War of 1853–1856 this coalition was victorious against an isolated Russia. It forced Russia in the subsequent peace to recognize the Ottoman Empire's right to full in-tegrity, provided the latter would continue the reforms announced in 1839.

Accordingly, the sultan promulgated the "Fortunate Edict" of 1856, in which he clarified the question of equality left open in the earlier edict: Regardless of religion, all subjects had the right to education, employment, and administration of justice. A number of subsequent measures spelled out this right and the earlier edicts in greater detail. To begin with, the reformers reorganized the judiciary by establishing law courts for the application of newly introduced commercial, maritime, and criminal legal codes, based on European models. Muslim law was collected in the 16 volumes of the *Mecelle* (Arabic "Code"), containing the Hanafi Islamic legal tradition that was constitutive for the empire since its foundation in 1300. Family law remained in the hands of the traditional Islamic judges as well as the heads of the Christian and Jewish communities (called *millets*). Since Muslims were obliged to a 5-year military service in the new army, the edict extended this obligation to Christians and Jews as well. Ironically, however, this extension was subsequently undercut by a regulation which exempted Christians and Jews from the service with the payment of a fee. Hence, de facto equality remained an ambiguous concept in the empire.

A further reform measure was the introduction of a system of secular schools, ini-tially for males, beginning with age 10 and culminating with high schools. But a lack of funds delayed building this system, which at the end of the 1800s still lagged far behind the traditional religious primary schools (*mekteps*) and colleges (*medreses*) as well as the more rapidly expanding Christian, Jewish, and foreign missionary schools. Literacy in the general population hovered around 10 percent in 1900, and thus, the edict had little to show even after half a century of efforts.

A measure that worked out quite differently from what was intended was the Land Code of 1858. The code reaffirmed the sultan as the owner of all land unless subjects or religious foundations possessed title to specific parcels of private property, such as urban real estate, suburban gardens, and endowments. But it also confirmed all users of the sultan's land, that is, farmers who produced harvests on family plots as well landowners collecting rents from the farmers of entire villages. Theoretically, the code subjected all users, family farmers as well as landowners, to taxation. But in practice the central administration had no money to appoint tax collectors (or even establish a land registry prior to 1908). It could not do without tax farmers, who still collected what they could get and transmitted to the government as little as they were able to get away with.

Highly uneven forms of landownership thus developed. In central and coastal Anatolia, as well as in the hill country of Palestine, family farmers received title to their individual plots. In Anatolian swamplands, tribal Kurdish steppe ranges, and Palestinian coastal strips large absentee landownership appeared. Syrian life leaseholders bribed officials to acquire a title to entire village districts. Similarly, Iraqi sheikhs succeeded in registering tribal lands in their name. Overall, tax yields remained as low as ever, improving only toward the end of the nineteenth century, long after the introduction of the Tanzimat. The much needed land reform remained incomplete.

Prohibition of Owning an Entire Village and Exemptions

"The land of an inhabited village cannot be given to one person independently in order to make a *çiftlik* [family plot]; but, as stated in Art. 72, if all the inhabitants of a village are scattered, and the *Tapu* [sovereign as supreme landowner] has acquired the right to its lands, if it is not possible to bring back that village to its original state by bringing fresh agriculturists to live there, and conferring on them the land separately, the land can be given in lots to one, two, or three persons …"

—F. Ongley, trans., with revisions by Horace E. Miller. *The Ottoman Land Code.* London: William Clowes and Sons, 1892. Article 130, Internet Archive, http://www.archive.org/details/ottomanlandcodeooturkuoft.

Constitution and War

Seen in the context of the centralization reforms in previous centuries, the Tanzimat decrees of 1839 and 1856 were little more than enactments of traditional policies. In the context of nineteenth-century constitutional nationalism, however, they appeared like autocratic dictates from above, lacking popular approval. In the 1860s, younger Tanzimat bureaucrats and journalists working for the first Ottoman newspapers, meeting in loose circles in Istanbul and Paris under the name of "Young Ottomans," became advocates for the introduction of a constitution as the crowning element of the Tanzimat, to end the autocracy of the sultan.

The idea of a constitution became reality in the midst of a deep crisis in which the empire found itself embroiled from 1873 to 1878. The crisis began when the Ottoman government defaulted on its foreign loans. In order to service the renegotiated loans, it had to increase taxes.

Ottoman Parliament. The constitutional reforms (Tanzimat) of the Ottoman Empire culminated in elections for a parliament and two sessions, uniting deputies from a multiplicity of ethnic backgrounds (1876–1878). It met during the Russian–Ottoman War of 1877–1878, which the Ottomans lost. The newly installed Sultan Abdülhamit used the war as an excuse for ending constitutional rule and governing by decree.

Patterns Up Close | From Constitutional to Ethnic Nationalism

The constitutional revolutions in the United States, France, and Haiti from 1776 to 1804 helped usher in the modern period of world history. They were rooted in two crucial developments in the preceding two centuries.

First, they were intellectually based on the concept of a fictive original state of individuals in nature giving up their independence in return for the establishment of a civilized state with a constitution. According to this constitution, individuals had rights and obligations resulting in elections of deputies, representation in a parliament, and an elected ruler under popular sovereignty.

Second, this intellectual constitutionalism did not

Visions of a New Order. The stirring events of 1848 produced visions of a new political order in which the peoples of Europe would form a "holy alliance" and a new "universal and social democratic republic," as shown in this lithograph where representatives from each nation march in solidarity with flags aloft past the rubble of toppled monarchs. In reality, the impulses of ethnic-linguistic nationalism sowed deep divisions among the very people depicted here.

remain on paper. It became a revolutionary reality thanks to the existing constitutional practice of England (later Great Britain), which in the Glorious Revolution of 1688 formalized the earlier constitutional practices of shared sovereignty between king and Parliament. In other words, because constitutionalism was functional in England/Great Britain, it became *the* aspirational model in the American colonies of Britain and later France.

As we saw in Chapter 22, however, in the course of the nineteenth century many constitutional nationalists began to add embellishments to the fundamental ideas of liberty, equality, and fraternity that had inspired the revolutions. Romantic thinkers in Germany, such as Johann Gottfried Herder (1744-1803), had already written voluminously on the concept of the "people" (*Volk*) prior to the revolutions. In their writings, the romantics assumed that there were ethnic, linguistic, literary, historical, and religious bonds that predated the formation of constitutional nations.

Byron Dressed as an Albanian. The famous Romantic English poet, George Gordon, Lord Byron (1788–1824) was one of many European intellectuals who came to the assistance of Greece and other Balkan countries in their liberation movements against the perceived tyranny of the Ottoman Empire. In this painting, Byron appears dressed as an Albanian—a backward corner of the Balkans that was then under Ottoman rule. His exotic dress shows his support for the ethnic-nationalist movements that were then bubbling up across the Balkans. Byron, in fact, died in Greece of 1824 of a fever, just a few years before Greece formally achieved independence.

This romantic thinking was highly speculative and largely undocumented. Above all, the requirement that a people—often dispersed and living among other peoples—should become a nation (requiring borders for the constitution) was often highly unrealistic. Ethnic–linguistic–religious nationalism was just as fictional as the assumption of an original state of individuals in nature.

As vague as it was, ethnic nationalism attracted groups of followers among many Europeans on the continent during the nineteenth century. They were typically students at the premier universities, graduating as lawyers, journalists, doctors, pharmacists, and other professionals. Much of the scholarship that university professors produced concerned the historical origins of European "peoples," their heroes, literary creations, and enemies against which they had to prevail. Many students, especially from eastern Europe, engaged in highly imaginative ethnic–linguistic–religious identity creation and, in the process, became nationalists who literally created the peoples whom they then wished to liberate from the yoke of their alien monarchs. Not surprisingly, the forces of ethnic-linguistic-religious nationalism would be particularly active within the large, multi-ethnic, multi-linguistic, and multi-religious empires of the Habsburgs, Ottomans, and Russia (see Map 25.2).

The first to proclaim a people entitled to become a nation under a constitution were the Greeks, who in 1821–1833 waged a war of liberation against the Ottoman sultan. They invoked a "Greekness" that was rooted in the assumption of a common Greek language, the history of the Greek city-states, Alexander the Great, the intellectual achievements of Plato and Aristotle, and a host of other real or imagined precedents.

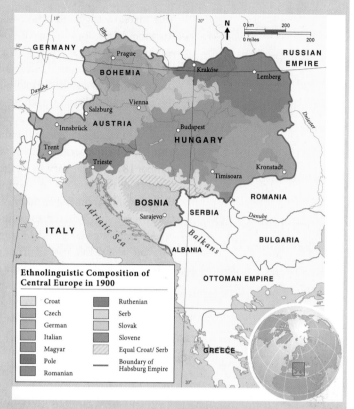

MAP 25.2 **Ethnolinguistic Composition of Central Europe, ca. 1900.**

When it came to adopting constitutions, however, the liberators did not aim to create of republics, as the Americans and French had done. They opted for constitutional monarchies, thereby revealing what subsequently became a trademark of ethnic–linguistic–religious nationalism (or, for short, "ethnolinguistic nationalism"): that culture, including that of kings, was more important than the principle of popular sovereignty.

This remains true today. "Peoples" who are supposed to be or become "nations" often seem to tolerate autocrats or dictators who hold constitutions in low regard. Conversely, constitutionally unified "nation-states" encompass ethnic groups which are unwilling to curb their identities and strive for secession. In short, many people in the world have yet to find a balance between the two types of constitutional and ethnic nationalism. Yet, the nation-state, as we have seen, has become nearly the only form of political organization in the world today.

Questions

- How do the origins of ethnic nationalism show the power of an imagined past in shaping people's group identity?

- In which places in the world today is this process still a force in shaping people's national consciousness?

This increase triggered ethnic–nationalist uprisings in Montenegro, Serbia, and Romania in the Balkans in 1875. The heavy-handed repression of these uprisings resulted in a political crisis, with a palace coup d'état by the Young Ottomans, during which a new sultan, Abdülhamit II (r. 1876–1909), ascended the throne and a constitution was adopted. Finally, in this sequence of events, the Russians exploited the perceived political weakness of the new constitutional Ottoman regime for a new Russo–Ottoman war in support of the Balkan nationalist uprisings.

Amid a rapid advance of Russian troops against a crumbling Ottoman army, the Ottomans held elections for the constitutionally decreed parliament between December 1876 and January 1877. Provincial and county councils elected 130 deputies to meet for two sessions in Istanbul. With the invading Russian forces practically at the gates of Istanbul in February 1878, the deputies engaged in a spirited criticism of the government. Irritated, the sultan dismissed the parliament and ruled by decree.

A few months later, at the Congress of Berlin, the sultan had to accept the loss of two-thirds of the empire's European provinces. Montenegro, Serbia, Romania, and (after a delay of 7 years) Bulgaria gained their independence. Bosnia-Herzegovina and Cyprus, although still Ottoman, received an Austrian administration and a British administration, respectively. Sultan Abdülhamit never reconvened the parliament, and the empire reverted back to autocratic rule.

Autocracy   Sultan Abdülhamit surrounded himself with capable second-generation Tanzimat bureaucrats who did not have the constitutionalist leanings of the Young Ottomans. He had very little financial leeway since the Public Debt Administration, imposed by the European powers in 1881, collected about one-third of the empire's income to pay for its accumulated foreign debt. Furthermore, the European price depression in the second half of the nineteenth century (1873–1896) was not favorable to foreign investments in the empire. Nevertheless, a few short-distance railroads connecting the fertile Anatolian valleys and their agricultural exports with Mediterranean ports were built thanks to French capital. A postal service and telegraph system connected all provinces, and steamship lines connected the ports. Once the depression was over, foreign investors enabled the government to build long-distance railroads across Anatolia (see Map 25.3). By the early 1900s, a basic communication infrastructure was in place in the Ottoman Empire.

MAP **25.3** **Railways in the Ottoman Empire, 1914.**

Given his fiscal limits, the sultan was all the more active as a propagandist, burnishing his credentials as the pan-Islamic caliph of Muslims in Eurasia, from Austrian Bosnia and Russian Asia to British India. He astutely sensed that the Balkan events of 1878 and subsequent Congress of Berlin had been a watershed in European politics. The Concert of Europe, with its Britain-supported concept of a balance of power, was no more. It was being replaced by the beginning of an imperial rivalry between Germany and Great Britain. France, Austria-Hungary, and Russia played their own subsidiary imperial roles. Since France and Great Britain, furthermore, carried out their imperialism against the Ottoman

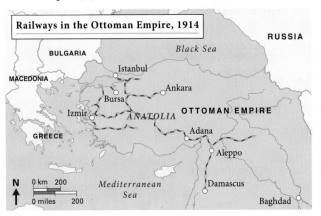

Railways in the Ottoman Empire, 1914

RUSSIA

BULGARIA   *Black Sea*

Istanbul

MACEDONIA

Ankara

Bursa

Izmir   *ANATOLIA*   OTTOMAN EMPIRE

GREECE   Adana

Aleppo

N   0 km   200   *Mediterranean*   Damascus
     0 miles   200   *Sea*
                                              Baghdad

Empire, with the conquests of Tunisia in 1881 and Egypt in 1882, respectively, Abdül-hamit was particularly affected. His pan-Islamism was therefore a carefully executed effort to instill the fear of jihad in the European politicians and their publics.

Although most of the Ottoman Balkan provinces had become independent nations by 1878, three ethnic–nationalist movements were still left inside the empire. Abdülhamit met them with an iron fist. The first movement consisted of Serb, Bulgarian, Vlah, and Greek nationalists agitating in Macedonia during 1893–1895. Without outside support, none of these feuding groups could impose itself on the province; and Ottoman troops were therefore able to repress them.

The next were the Armenians, who formed sizeable minorities in the six eastern provinces of Anatolia. Most Armenian farmers and craftspeople in these provinces were politically quiet, but urban-based and secularized Armenian ethnic nationalists organized terrorist incidents. In reaction, the sultan armed Kurdish tribal units, which massacred thousands of Anatolian Armenian villagers from 1894 to 1896. Finally, the Ottomans met a revolt in Crete in 1897, in favor of union with Greece, with an invasion and defeat of Greece itself, which had to pay an indemnity. Europe, busy with its imperialist competition in Africa and Asia, had no time to help the remaining ethnic–nationalist stirrings of the Macedonians and Armenians in the Ottoman Empire.

In the later years of his rule, Abdülhamit increasingly failed to suppress dissatisfaction with the lack of political freedom among the graduates from the elite administrative and military academies. As so often prior to revolts or revolutions, improved economic conditions—as they materialized after the end of the worldwide recession of 1893—stoked political ambitions to create a condition social scientists sometimes call a "revolution of rising expectations." In a pattern similar to that unfolding in Qing China at the same time, oppositional circles among Ottoman intellectuals abroad merged with secret junior officer groups in Macedonia and Thrace in 1907. Barely one step ahead of the sultan's secret service, the officers launched a coup d'état in 1908, which urban Ottomans generally received with great relief. The officers forced the sultan to reinstate the constitution of 1878 and, after elections, accept a new parliament.

The Young Turks   The officers, organized as the Committee of Union and Progress (CUP) and colloquially referred to as "Young Turks," did not initially force Abdülhamit from office. They did so in part because the wily sultan presented himself to the public as having engineered the reinstatement of the constitution, blaming his bureaucrats for not having done so earlier. Behind the scene, he did everything to get rid of the Young Turks. He had his courtiers arouse military and government employees, religious students, and religious brotherhood leaders into a countercoup in April 1909. The rebels demanded the reinstatement of the Sharia, which actually had never been suspended, as mentioned earlier. The government gave in to the demand, and the CUP leaders, unsure of army support in the capital, headed for the provinces to find more reliable troops. In short order, they returned at the head of trustworthy soldiers and this time deposed Abdülhamit, enthroning one of his brothers as his successor.

As the CUP consolidated its power against the conservative religious opposition, a weak imperial government fell into disarray. Members of the increasingly marginal (even if CUP-dominated) parliament as well as an array of provincial notables exploited the deposition of Abdülhamit for their own gains. Austria-Hungary and Bulgaria formally annexed Bosnia-Herzegovina and northern Rumelia, respectively, in 1908. Albania revolted in 1910 and Italy invaded Tripolitania in 1911, triggering a nearly 20-year guerilla war of resistance by members of the Sanusiyya brotherhood against the invaders. The CUP found itself in a near desperate position.

Even worse, the newly independent Balkan states of Serbia, Montenegro, Greece, and Bulgaria unified behind the Russian imperial idea of driving the Ottomans once and for all out of Europe. In 1912, they demanded sweeping reforms in Macedonia (where uprisings had been suppressed in 1895). When the Ottoman government rejected these demands, the four countries declared war against the empire. In response, the Ottoman general staff made the mistake of attacking the Balkan states on several fronts, instead of fighting a defensive war. Bulgarian troops broke through the Ottoman defenses, occupied Macedonia and Thrace, and advanced dangerously close to Istanbul. Once more, the survival of the empire hung in the balance.

In this extremely critical situation, the government was willing to give up on besieged Edirne, the second capital of the empire. Infuriated by this defeatism, a triumvirate of CUP officers staged another coup and assumed direct ruling responsibilities. Step by step, power had been narrowed, from the broad parliamentary coalition that had reinstated the constitution in 1908 to the CUP operating behind the scenes in 1909 to now three powerful men within the CUP supported by a cast of about 50 officers. Try as it might, however, the triumvirate was unable to prevent the fall of Edirne. At the subsequent conference in London, it had no choice but to accept the independence of Albania, the loss of Macedonia (with the city of Salonica, the birthplace of the CUP), Thrace, and nearly all of southern Rumelia, including Edirne.

Fortunately for the CUP, the four victorious Balkan states were unable to agree on the division of the spoils. The Ottomans exploited the disagreements and retook Edirne, succeeding in a new peace settlement to push the imperial border westward into Thrace. Nevertheless, the overall losses were horrendous: Except for a rump Rumelia, the Ottoman Empire had now been driven out of Europe, ending more than half a millennium of rule in the Balkans.

Economic Development

While the empire was disintegrating politically, the economic situation improved. The main factor was the end of the depression of 1873–1896 and a renewed interest among European investors in creating industrial enterprises in the agrarian but export-oriented independent and colonial countries of the Middle East, Asia, and South America. When Abdülhamit II was at the peak of his power in the 1890s and early 1900s, investors perceived the Ottoman Empire as sufficiently stable for the creation of industrial enterprises.

New research since the 1980s has considerably refined the concepts of less developed agriculture-based economies and industrialization during the 1800s. Prior to that time, scholars often compared the Ottoman Empire unfavorably to Japan, the only non-Western country that was successful in adopting the British model of industrialization. By 1900, Japan was essentially industrialized, producing its own iron and steel, heavy machinery, and machine-produced textiles. Historians had to free themselves from the fixation on the British and Japanese models and concede that more circuitous paths toward industrialization merited the same serious attention. For example, the Netherlands did not industrialize until the 1890s, and France continued to industrialize slowly from industrial "islands" in certain urban areas out

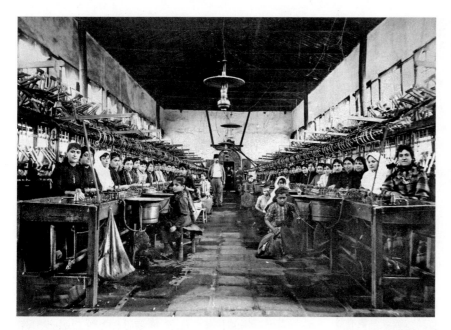

Silk Manufacture, Turkey, ca. 1892. Small textile factories were able to flourish in the nineteenth century, in spite of cheap English cotton goods. They did so on the basis of lowly paid workers and relatively coarse, low-quality goods affordable to the poor in cities, towns, and villages. Industrialization expanded in the 1890s with the foundation of textile factories, such as the silk manufacture in Bursa depicted here.

into the surrounding countryside and provincial centers until well into the twentieth century. Until the 1890s Latin American countries achieved high economic growth rates through commodity exports, without its leaders feeling a strong urge to industrialize. Thus, these countries all possessed viable economies in the second half of the nineteenth century even though their industries were still comparatively light.

With this notion of viable nonindustrial economies in the 1800s in mind, the Ottoman Empire in the 1800s can be described as a state in which the traditional crafts-based textile industry initially suffered under the invasion of cheap industrially produced English cottons in the period 1820–1850. But a recovery took place in the second half of the 1800s, both in the crafts sector and in a newly mechanized small factory sector of textile manufacturing, producing cottons, woolens, silks, and rugs. This recovery was driven largely by domestic demand and investments because the European price depression of 1873–1896 was not conducive to much foreign capital inflow. Operating with low wages and even more lowly paid female labor, domestic small-scale manufacturing was able to hold foreign factory–produced goods at bay.

Throughout the 1800s, the empire was also an exporter of agricultural commodities, particularly cotton, dried fruit, and nuts. But the recovery of the domestic textile production demonstrates that the Ottomans did not succumb completely to the British free market system. When foreign investments resumed in the 1890s and early 1900s, there was a base for industrialization to build on, similar to what people in the Netherlands, France, and Latin America had when they industrialized.

Iran's Effort to Cope with the Western Challenge

Iran (also called "Persia," in recognition of its long heritage) had risen in the 1500s as the Shiite alternative to the Sunni Ottomans. The two dynasties of kings (*shahs*) who ruled Iran, the Safavids (1501–1722) and Qajars (1795–1925), nurtured a hierarchy of Shiite clerics who formed an autonomous religious institution in their state. While

Isfahan, Ali Qapu (High Gate).
Entrance to the Qajar palace (*a*) from a large rectangular square around which major mosques and bazaars are also located (*b*). The palace contains rooms on several floors with richly plastered and decorated walls and ceilings such as the music room, with instrument motifs set in the plaster (*c*).

the Ottoman sultans always kept their leading Sunni religious leaders under firm control, the Iranian rulers had to respect a careful balance of power with their Shiite leaders. Therefore, when Iran in the 1800s faced the Western challenges, reformers had to establish an alliance with the Shiite clerics to bring about constitutional reforms.

Safavid and Qajar Kings   The Safavid Empire was a less powerful state than that of the Ottomans. It comprised Shiite Iran, the Caucasus, Sunni Afghanistan, and parts of Sunni central Asia. The Safavid kings, whose lands were limited in most provinces to oasis agriculture, were not wealthy enough to recruit a large firearm infantry to match the Janissaries. As a result, for most of the time the Ottomans were able to keep the Safavid rivalry within manageable proportions, especially from the mid-1600s onward.

At this time, the Safavids ruled Iran from their newly founded capital of Isfahan in the center of the country, which they embellished with palaces and mosques. One of its suburbs was inhabited by a group of Armenian merchants who controlled silk production along the warm and humid Black Sea coast. Safavid Iran was a major exporter of silk yarn and clothes, second in quality only to Chinese wares, and thus supplemented its limited agrarian revenues with an international trade of silk.

The Safavids were vulnerable not only to the military challenges of their Ottoman neighbors to the west but also to those of tribal federations in the Sunni provinces to the east. In Afghanistan, one of the two major Pashtu tribal federations revolted repeatedly against the efforts of the Safavids to convert them to Shiite Islam. Eventually, in 1722, this federation succeeded in conquering Iran and ending Safavid rule, at a time of advanced decentralization in the empire. The Afghanis, however, were unable to establish a stable new regime. Instead, provincial Iranian rulers reunified and even expanded the empire for short periods during the 1700s. Stabilization finally occurred in 1796, with the accession of the new Qajar dynasty.

The Qajars had been among the founding Shiite Turkic tribal federation of the Safavids, but in contrast to their brethren, they had no Shiite aspirations of their own. Instead, they paid respect to the clerical hierarchy that had become powerful in the aftermath of the Afghani conquest in the 1700s. The clerics supported themselves through their own independent revenues from landholdings in the vicinity of their mosques and colleges, and the Qajars were not powerful enough to interfere.

During the 1800s, two developments dominated Iran's historical evolution. First, like the Ottoman Empire, primarily agrarian Iran was subject to oscillating periods of decentralization and recentralization, following the decline or rise of tax revenues from the countryside. Second, the increasingly hierarchical and theologically rigid Shiite clerics were challenged by the popular, theologically less tradition-bound Babi movement. This movement, begun in 1844, rallied around a figure who claimed to be the promised returned Twelfth Imam or Mahdi (Messiah) with a new law superseding the body of legal interpretations of the Shiite clergy. A combination of Qajar troops and clerically organized mobs succeeded in suppressing this widespread movement, which subsequently evolved into the Baha'i faith.

The Qajars not only faced an unstable internal situation but also suffered from Russian imperialism. The declared Russian goal of liberating Constantinople implied the conquest of the central Asian Turkic sultanates as well as the north face of the Caucasus Mountains astride the land bridge between the Black and Caspian Seas. Accordingly, Russian armies sought to drive the Qajars from their Caucasus provinces. In response, the Qajar kings embarked on centralizing military and

In the Gardens of the Caucasus. Tiflis (modern-day Tbilisi), the capital of Georgia, was the crossroads of the contested and strategically vital Caucasus region that Persia, the Ottomans, and Russia all fought over incessantly for centuries. Though today we tend to think of Georgia as a "post-Soviet" state and part of Russia's "near abroad," for millennia Georgia and its neighboring countries of Armenia and Azerbaijan looked southward toward the Middle East, as reflected in the dress of the Georgian ladies and the musical instruments seen in this lithograph from 1847. But while the Georgian language contains many loan words from Persian, Arabic, and Turkish that reflect this long association with the Middle East, it has always retained deep and ancient Christian roots, as evidenced by the thirteenth-century church perched on a high cliff in the background.

administrative reforms, which were similar to those of the Ottomans though less pervasive. In the absence of sizeable groups of reformers of their own and bowing to Russian pressures, they hired Russian officers to train a small corps of new troops, the Cossack Brigade. (The tsar, although bent on expanding into the Caucasus, did not want Iran to collapse as a counterweight to the Ottomans.) Swedish advisors trained the police force, in an effort to improve civil peace. British subjects acquired economic concessions, such as monopolies for minerals and telegraph connections or the manufacture of tobacco. The increasing foreign influence in Iran aroused the ire of the conservative clerical hierarchy, and the kings had to withdraw the concessions. The Qajar ruling class was acutely aware of the Western challenge, but its reformist power vis-à-vis the clerical establishment was limited.

Perceptive Iranian constitutional nationalists from among the educated younger ruling class were less numerous than their Young Ottoman colleagues. They therefore founded a tactical alliance toward the end of the 1800s with conservative clerics and merchants. In 1906, after widespread revolts against tax increases to cover a lavish European trip by the shah, this alliance mounted a successful constitutional revolution, imposing parliamentary limits on the Qajar regime. The constitutional-nationalist alliance with the clerics was, however, inherently unstable and parliamentary rule failed to become a reality. As World War I drew near, Iran reverted to autocratic rule by the shahs. Nevertheless, the memory of the abortive Constitutional Revolution of 1906 lived on, becoming decisive in the later twentieth century with the formation of the Islamic Republic in 1979 and the enactment of a hybrid Islamic–democratic constitution.

Westernization, Reforms, and Industrialization in Russia

The Russian Empire that expanded during the 1800s southward at the expense of the Qajar and Ottoman Empires had arisen in 1547 as a tsardom in Moscow, succeeding the Byzantine eastern Christian "caesars" (from which the Russian term "tsar" or "czar" is derived). It was a relatively late empire, succeeding that of the Mongols; and it spanned eastern Europe as well as Asia. Given this geographical location at the eastern edge of Europe and outside western Christian civilization, Russia developed along an uneven pattern of relations with western Europe. The western European Renaissance and Enlightenment did not spread to Russia. Western culture became a force only around 1700 when the tsar Peter the Great (r. 1682–1725) became its advocate. The idea of constitutionalism arrived in the wake of the French Revolution and Napoleon's failed invasion of Russia (1812). But it remained weak and was diluted by pan-Slavic ethnic nationalism, an ideology whereby Russians sought unification with the Slavic peoples of the Balkans. Multiple small political groups competed with each other, with no single united reformist force emerging. These groups rose amid the social dislocations that followed the Russian industrialization effort at the end of the nineteenth century, but none was able to take over leadership in the abortive revolution following the disastrous defeat at the hands of a modernizing Japan in 1905. Although this uprising produced a weak Russian parliament, the Duma, the autocratic tsarist regime tottered on until collapsing under the unbearable strain of World War I.

Russia and Westernization

In 1768 George Macartney, British envoy to Russia (whom we met as the leader of Britain's attempted diplomatic overture to Qing China in Chapter 24 and the man generally credited with saying that Britain had an empire on which "the sun never sets"), observed that Russia was "a great planet that has obtruded itself into our system, whose place is yet undetermined, but whose motions most powerfully affect those of every other orb." The states of western Europe were, of course, aware of a large empire on their eastern flank but did not consider it fully European. Indeed, at a time when feudal practices were dying in western Europe, Russia under the Romanov dynasty *institutionalized* serfdom. Half a century earlier, Tsar Peter the Great, attempting to travel incognito—despite his six-foot eight-inch frame—went on a mission of investigation to western Europe and began a reform and urbanization process from the top, against an often fierce resistance in both the ruling class and the population at large, to bring Russia closer to the western European norms. His legacy was the new capital of St. Petersburg, extensive military reorganization, and concerted attempts to reign in the power of Russia's high nobility, the *boyars*—including physically cutting off their beards so that they would be clean-shaven like their Western counterparts. But another legacy was a deep-set resistance on a political and cultural level to any such measures coming from outside Russia, not unlike the cultural resistance that would plague Chinese reformers in the nineteenth century.

The German-born "enlightened despot" Tsarina Catherine II, the Great (r. 1762–1796), continued the reform process from the top, which by its very nature, however, was slow to trickle down. When the constitutional-nationalist revolutions broke out in the United States, France, and Haiti, the Russian Empire was an autocratic, fiscal–military state that had expanded in all directions. And its expansion did, indeed, affect many other "orbs."

Catherine II's Reforms   Catherine the Great was the dominant figure of tsarist Russia during the eighteenth century. By origin, she was the princess of a minor German family in the service of Prussia. Early on she learned the art of aristocratic discretion and later in life set a record with her string of lovers in the recesses of her palace in St. Petersburg. Also early in life she developed an abiding intellectual engagement with the Enlightenment trends that proliferated not only in academies and salons but also among the European courts. According to the courtly version of this thought, called "the royal thesis (*thèse*)," rulers were to remain firmly committed to absolute rule but should also pursue administrative, judicial, and educational reforms in order to increase the welfare of their subjects. Catherine subscribed to a digest reporting on the latest trends in Parisian Enlightenment thought. In correspondence with Voltaire, a supporter of the royal thesis, and even Diderot, whom she subsidized (ignoring his atheism and antimonarchical impulses), she kept abreast of who was in and who was out of fashion among the leading *philosophes*. With her Enlightenment engagement,

Aristocratic Charter. The charter that Empress Catherine II of Russia granted to the Russian nobility in 1785 consolidated the Russian aristocracy as a class with its own set of rights and privileges. The charter also contained ideas of liberty that later were interpreted as extending to the other ranks of society as well. Shown here is frontispiece, with the coats of arms of the various provinces of the Russian Empire extending along the edge of the document, while the empress's official title is handwritten in gold in the center.

Catherine was far ahead of the Russian aristocracy, not to mention the small urban educated upper strata, both of which were still much beholden to eastern Christian traditions.

As much an activist as Peter the Great but more subtle, the energetic Catherine pushed through a number of major reforms. Urban manufactures, especially of linen and woolen cloth, had greatly expanded in the early 1700s; and Catherine strengthened urban development with a provincial reform in 1775 and a town reform in 1785 that allowed local nonaristocratic participation. But in 1785 she also strengthened the aristocracy with a charter that exempted its members from the poll tax and increased their property rights, including the purchase of serfs. This was largely a measure to head off a repetition of the terrible peasant rebellions of 1762–1775, which had culminated with Pugachev's Cossack revolt. In a reform of the educational system (1782), the government set up a free, mostly clergy-staffed educational system, from urban primary schools to high schools. Catherine's legal reform project, however, apart from a police ordinance issued in 1782, remained incomplete; and the codification and humanization of Russia's laws had to wait for another 80 years.

In foreign affairs, Catherine was determined to revive Peter the Great's expansionism. She first undertook the dismemberment of the kingdom of Poland, accomplished together with Prussia and the Austrian Habsburgs in three stages, from 1772 to 1795. Then, in two wars with the Ottoman Empire (1768–1792), Catherine waged a successful campaign to end the Ottoman alliance with the Tatars, a Turkic-speaking population of mixed ethnic descent that had succeeded the Mongols of the Golden Horde (ca. 1240–1502) in Crimea and adjacent northern Black Sea lands. Catherine's modernized infantry forces were successful in humbling the considerably larger but disorganized Ottoman army and navy. In the first war, Russia gained access to the Black Sea, ending the Tatar–Ottoman alliance and gaining free access for Russian ships to the Mediterranean. In the second war, Russia absorbed the Tatars within its imperial borders, which now advanced to the northern coast of the Black Sea.

Russia in the Early Nineteenth Century

The ideas of the French Revolution made their first fleeting mark on Russia in the form of the Decembrist Revolt in 1825, several decades before they did in the Ottoman Empire. But since in the pattern of traditional empire formation the personality of the ruler still counted more than the continuity of the administration, the reign of the deeply monarchical Nicholas I for a generation in mid-1800 Russia meant that whatever the Decembrists had set in motion could only spread under the surface. Above the ground, Nicholas pursued an aggressive foreign policy of expansion, in the tradition of Catherine the Great (see Map 25.4).

Russia and the French Revolution   In her old age, Catherine was aghast at the monarchical constitutionalism of the French Revolution, not to mention its republicanism and radicalism. In an abrupt about-face, her government had Voltaire's books burned and other Enlightenment books banned. Alexander Radishchev (1749–1802), a Russian landed aristocrat and prominent author with sympathies for the revolution, was forced into exile in Siberia. The situation eased under Catherine's grandson, Alexander I (r. 1801–1825), who was educated in Enlightenment ideas. He initially showed inclinations toward constitutionalism, coaxed by his

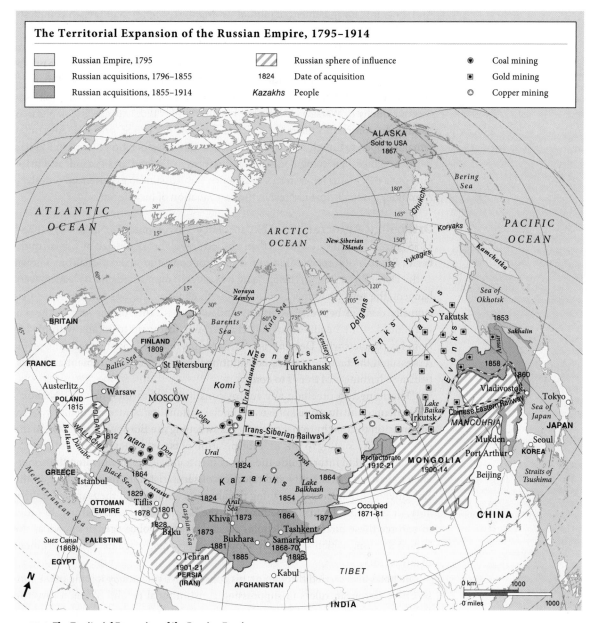

MAP 25.4 **The Territorial Expansion of the Russian Empire, 1795–1914.**

discreetly constitutionalist minister Mikhail Speranskii (1772–1839); but Napoleon's imperial designs interrupted any idea of implementation.

Russia emerged as a key power in efforts to prevent Napoleon's takeover of Europe. In 1805 Russia joined Britain and Austria in the Third Coalition against France; but Napoleon's smashing victory at Austerlitz in December 1805—where Alexander personally commanded the Russian troops—doomed the coalition. Napoleon followed up on his victorious campaigns by defeating Russian forces in June 1807. This was followed by a dramatic meeting between Napoleon and Alexander on a raft anchored in the River Niemen on July 27, 1807. Napoleon forced

Alexander into an agreement of mutual aid and the recognition of French conquests on the European continent.

However, after the defeat of Napoleon during his disastrous Russian campaign of 1812, Alexander rebounded. At the Congress of Vienna in 1815 he assumed a prominent role in the negotiations for the territorial settlements and reestablishment of peace, advocating a "holy alliance" of monarchs to be its guarantors. As a result, Napoleon's duchy of Warsaw became the kingdom of Poland, with the Russian tsar as its king. In contrast to his monarchical colleagues in Europe, however, Alexander remained open to Enlightenment reforms, initiating the liberation of serfs in Russia's Baltic provinces, pursuing constitutional reform in Finland and Poland, and mapping out a new status for eastern Christianity. But Russia also experienced unrest, so Alexander gradually lost interest in the continuation of his reforms.

Orthodoxy, Autocracy, and Nationality   No sooner did Nicholas I (1825–1855) ascend the throne in 1825 than a bloody revolt broke out, led by a small number of Russian officers exposed to the ideas of constitutional nationalism. Known as the Decembrist Revolt, the uprising was quickly suppressed and its leaders were hanged. The revolt had few connections with civilians and was furthermore intellectually divided between federalists and unionists. The former serf Nikitenko, introduced at the beginning of this chapter, was fortunate to escape with his life from his contacts with Decembrists. Despite this relative lack of impact, the revolt represented the first anti-tsarist, constitutional-revolutionary movement and, thus, became a harbinger of things to come.

Determined to preclude any future constitutional revolts, in 1833 Nicholas implemented the doctrine known as "official nationality," aimed particularly at the suppression of constitutional movements sweeping the European continent in the early1830s. According to this new formulation of tsarist policy, three fundamental theories would in future guide the government: *orthodoxy*, reaffirming the adherence to eastern Christianity and rejection of secularist notions originating in the Enlightenment; *autocracy*, meaning the absolute authority of the tsar; and *nationality*, or the equivalent of something like the "spirit" of Russian identity. In order to enforce these directives, Nicholas created a secret police agency known as the "Third Section," which vigorously suppressed dissidence against the government in any form.

Nicholas also carried through on his conservative policies by joining other conservative European rulers in suppressing constitutional revolts. When a revolt in Poland in 1830 threatened to topple the viceroy (meaning ultimately the tsar himself as overlord), Nicholas intervened by suppressing it and abolishing the country's autonomy. Then, during the widespread agitation of revolutionary constitutional movements across Europe in 1848, Nicholas supported the Austrian emperor in suppressing the Hungarian nationalists. The failure of the attempted constitutional revolutions of 1848 was largely attributable to Nicholas's determined intervention.

In larger terms, Nicholas was determined to continue Russia's drive toward Constantinople (Istanbul). In the Russo–Ottoman War of 1828–1829 Russia succeeded in helping the Greeks achieve independence. With Russian help Serbia attained autonomy, while Moldavia and Wallachia—technically still within the Ottoman Empire—became protectorates of Russia. However, when Napoleon III of France in 1853 demanded recognition as protector of the Christians in Palestine under Ottoman rule, Russia did not fare as well. After Nicholas responded by insisting that the Ottomans honor their agreement with the Russian tsars as the actual protectors, the ensuing diplomatic wrangling ended in the outbreak of the Crimean War between Britain, France, and the Ottoman Empire, on one side, and Russia, on the other.

Poor planning, missed opportunities, language barriers, and a lack of coordination between soldiers and officers plagued both sides in the Crimean War. One of the first products of the mid-nineteenth century industrial weapons revolution, the French Minié ball, whose hollow expanding base allowed for ease of ramming in muzzle-loading rifles, quadrupled the effective range of infantry weapons and vastly increased their accuracy. As they would a few years later during the American Civil War, armies fighting with increasingly obsolescent tactics would suffer fearful losses from these new weapons. French steam-powered and iron-hulled floating batteries inaugurated the age of ironclad navies. Telegraph lines permitted correspondents to send frontline reports to their London newspapers. And the nascent technology of photography was there to document the conflict. To lessen the sufferings of the wounded, doctors and nurses on both sides staffed field hospitals—including the English nurse Florence Nightingale (1820–1910), the founder of modern medical care on battlefields and the first prominent advocate of nursing as a profession for women. The new scientific–industrial age had manifested itself for the first time in war.

Hospital Ward, Scutari, Ottoman Empire, 1856. This airy, uncluttered, warm hospital room shows injured and recovering soldiers. Florence Nightingale is depicted in the middle ground, in conversation with an officer.

The Ottomans, still in the initial stages of their military reform, did not acquit themselves well, suffering from a weak officer corps and the absence of noncommissioned officers. They would have been defeated, had it not been for allied participation. The Russians did not perform well either, except for their navy with its superior shells. The Russian army suffered from overextending its battle lines on too many fronts, from the Danube and Crimea to the Caucasus. Thus, as far as the two imperial foes, the Russian and Ottoman Empires, were concerned, the war was a setback for both in their effort to meet the challenges of the West. Like their counterparts in China during the Second Opium War, also fought in the mid-1850s, however, they did receive a renewed taste of the state of the art in military technology and usage. This would mark many of the reform efforts of all three empires in the coming decades.

The Golden Age   During the period 1810–1853, in spite of times of censorship and repression, Russia enjoyed an outburst of intellectual and cultural activity. Taken as a whole, this period was considered the golden age of Russian culture. Inspired by European romantics, a Russian *intelligentsia*—Western-educated intellectuals predominantly from the ranks of the landowner nobility—met in the salons of Moscow and St. Petersburg, where they considered and debated issues related to religion and philosophy, as well as Russian history. A significant development was the appearance of literary journals, which spread the ideas and appeal of new literary forms as well as new ideas. Many of these ideas were potentially seditious since they concerned ways to end the autocracy of the tsars and to reform serfdom. More importantly, the first stirrings of reform movements emanated from these circles.

Alexander Sergeyevich Pushkin (1799–1837) stood at the forefront of the new intellectual movement. His lineage included old aristocratic forebears and an African-descended servant of Peter the Great, and he committed himself early on to the cause of reform with his poems, novels, as well as political activism, which brought him into conflict with the authorities. Best known among his works are his fairy tale poem "Ruslan and Lyudmila" (1820), the historical drama *Boris Godunov* (1825), and the novel in verse *Eugene Onegin* (1837) about a St. Petersburg dandy. Another prominent figure was Pyotr Chaadayev (1794–1856), also of aristocratic parentage. His sharply critical *Philosophical Letters* (1836) began the debate between constitutionalist "Westernizers" and conservative "Slavophiles." Westernizers considered Western models of governance, exemplified by constitutional government, along with industrial development and urbanism, as good models for progress in Russia. Slavophiles, by contrast, clung to traditional Russian institutions like the eastern Christian Church and the village commune. Nikolai Gogol (1809–1852), of Ukrainian Cossack descent, for example, felt that the distinguishing feature of Russia was its devotion to the Russian Orthodox Church, which served as the focal point of existence for the peasantry. With their determined opposition to Westernization, Slavophiles developed an early form of Russian ethnic nationalism that later evolved into the movement of pan-Slavism.

The Great Reforms

The Russian defeat in the Crimean War convinced the newly enthroned Alexander II (r. 1855–1881) of the need for reforms. Russia, so he believed, lost the war because of a technologically inferior army, a lack of infrastructure, and the unwillingness of the serf-owning aristocracy to shift from subsistence to market agriculture. He implemented major reforms, which, however, took time to produce the intended effects. Many Russians did not want to wait, and the empire entered a time of social destabilization, balanced abroad to a degree by successes against the Ottoman Empire.

The Emancipation of Serfs   Nicholas tackled serfdom first. In 1861, Alexander (the "tsar liberator") issued the Emancipation Edict, in which peasants were ostensibly freed from their bondage to their villages and their dues and labor services to the Russian landowning aristocracy. The traditionally unfree status of the serfs is usually explained on the one hand by the sparse population of the empire, with few cities and poor communication, and on the other hand by the relatively high level of fertility of Russia's humus-rich "black soil" (*chernozem*). On the face of it, the edict ended the centuries-old system of serfdom, affecting some 50 million serfs. But the edict fell far short of liberating the peasantry and satisfying critics. For one thing the decree of emancipation did not go into effect immediately but took 2 years to be fully enacted. For another, peasants were not given land titles per se; the land was turned over to the control of local communities (*mirs*), which then in turn allocated parcels to individual serfs. Finally, serfs had to redeem their new holdings by making annual payments to the state in the form of long-term government loans, the proceeds from which were then used to compensate the landowning nobility. Even worse, these payments were often higher than the former dues which serfs had owed the aristocracy. In effect, then, tens of millions of farmers remained mired in poverty-stricken agricultural self-sufficiency.

Following Western models, Alexander enacted further reforms. For example, in 1864 the administration of government at the local level was reorganized by the establishment of regional councils known as *zemstva*. Each zemstvo was in reality controlled by the local aristocracy, although peasants had a say in their election. Whatever their drawbacks, it must be said that zemstva achieved advances in education, health, and the maintenance of roads within their regions. Legal reforms were enacted shortly afterward; these provided all Russians access to courts, trial by jury, and especially the concept of equality before the law. Then, in 1874, a series of reforms aimed at modernizing the military and bringing it closer to Western standards was enacted. Among these was the reduction of active duty service in the military from 25 to 6 years, followed by several years of service in the reserves, along with an overall improvement in the quality of life in the ranks. Planned infrastructural reforms, however, remained limited for lack of funds. As in the Ottoman Empire, the reforms brought important changes to Russia; but in many cases, their effects would not be known until years later. Yet, just as the Ottoman Empire was increasingly called, after the example of Nicholas, the "Sick Man of Europe," it remained an article of faith among many in the West that, despite its reforms, "Russia could always be beaten for her backwardness."

Radicalization Among Intellectuals   The incompleteness of the reforms and the glaring absence of constitutionalism among what reforms did come expressed itself in a transition from peaceful demands to radicalism. Many Russians perceived this transition as a generational change. The aristocrat turned liberal Ivan Turgenev (1818–1883) observed this transition most astutely. In his aptly named *Fathers and Sons* (1862), a novel still widely read today, he declared that the new generation was dominated by "nihilists" (from the Latin *nihil*, meaning "noth-ing"). The term **nihilism**, coined in Germany a century earlier and popularized by Turgenev, was meant to signify the inevitable end result of Enlightenment thought, if driven to its extremes. Nihilists, forming small underground circles, were devoted to individual freedom above all else, rejecting society's institutions and morality.

> **Nihilism:** Intellectual and political movement of the late nineteenth century that rejected the institutions and morality of society.

Other circles of radical intellectuals espoused *populism*, an ideology that romanticized rural peasant communities and their allegedly thriving autonomy. Members of these circles demanded that intellectuals go to the villages and stir them up into a socialist revolution from which the empire would be overthrown. In reality, however, the years after 1861 saw tensions arising between more well-to-do villagers able to buy their lands (called *kulaks*) and poor villagers unable to do so. The urban populists, unable to relate to these tensions, found few followers in the countryside, from either the kulaks or the poor.

> **The New Generation of Nihilists**
>
> "Well," replied Pavel Petrovich, "very well. You have discovered all that and you are not less decided not to undertake anything seriously."
>
> "Yes, we have decided not to undertake anything seriously," replied Bazarov in a brusque tone. He reproached himself all at once for having said so much before that gentleman.
>
> "And you confine yourself to insult."
>
> "We insult at need."
>
> "And this is called nihilism."
>
> "This is what is called nihilism," repeated Bazarov, but this time in a tone peculiarly provoking.
>
> Pavel Petrovich winced a little.
>
> "Very well!" he said with a forced calm that was rather strange.
>
> —Ivan Sergheïevich Turgenev. *Fathers and Sons: A Novel*, trans. Eugene Schuyler, p. 61. New York: Leypoldt & Holt, 1867.

Later groups, inspired by the writings of the aristocrat turned anarchist Mikhail Bakunin (1814–1876) and seeking to learn from the failures of the populists, sought to bring together the urban and rural poor for the organization of small, self-administering communities without the need for a state with a central government and bureaucracy. Action-oriented splinter groups among these anarchists devoted themselves to bringing the state down through terrorism, trying to assassinate Alexander II seven times before finally succeeding in 1881. No spontaneous revolutions from below, however, materialized; and the tsar's secret service found it relatively easy to keep the small revolutionary circles under surveillance, except for its final fatal lapse.

Pan-Slavism: Ideology that espoused the brotherhood of all Slavic peoples and gave Russia the mission to aid Slavs in the Balkans suffering from alleged Ottoman misrule.

Pan-Slavism   Concurrently with the appearance of radical ideologies on the left, a new right-wing ideology known as **pan-Slavism** emerged in the 1870s. Pan-Slavism proclaimed the brotherhood of all Slavic peoples and gave Russia the mission to aid Slavs in the Balkan territories who were suffering from alleged Ottoman misrule. Pan-Slavism took on a religious identity, that is, a commitment to Russian eastern Christianity. One of the best-known proponents of this ideology was the novelist Fyodor Dostoyevsky (1821–1881), son of a military surgeon. Dostoyevsky advocated the idea of a Russian "spiritual community" (*sobornost*), whose members would devote themselves to bringing about the unity of all humankind in the name of Christianity. As a writer, he transcended his Russian environment and became one of the most outstanding nineteenth-century authors on the Eurasian continent, with such psychologically refined novels as *Crime and Punishment* (1866) and *The Brothers Karamazov* (1879–1880).

Balkan Affairs   Two issues contributed to mounting Russian pan-Slavic engagement in the Balkans. First, across the nineteenth century the Ottomans had been forced to relinquish control of large areas of their empire in the Balkans, and an end was not in sight. Second, the increasingly popular appeal of ethnolinguistic nationalism in Europe—Italian unification in 1870, followed by German unification in 1871—strengthened the assertiveness of the Balkan nationalities. In 1875 Bosnia-Herzegovina revolted against the Ottomans, and the rebellion then spread to Bulgaria, Serbia, and Montenegro. What would happen if these provinces did in fact break away from the Ottoman Empire? Which of the European powers might then take them over and, thus, increase its presence in this vital region? Thus, the Balkans became an area of increasing attention for the leading powers, while at the same time representing a powder keg ready to ignite.

The Russo–Ottoman War   Encouraged by Russian popular pan-Slavic support and sensing an opportunity to exploit rising anti-Ottoman sentiments among ethnic national movements in the Balkans, the tsar reopened the war front against the Ottomans in July 1877. The pretext was the Ottoman repression of tax revolts in Bosnia-Herzegovina and Bulgaria, which had led to a declaration of war by neighboring Montenegro and Serbia in June 1876 and a call for Russian military aid. The Russians invaded across the Danube and by December had advanced as far as Rumelia. Serbia, claiming complete independence, and Bulgaria, under Russian tutelage, were now poised to gain control of Istanbul. The other European powers stood by, anxiously waiting to see whether Russia would advance on the Ottoman capital.

In 1878, alarmed over what appeared to be an imminent Russian occupation of Istanbul, Austria and Britain persuaded Germany to convene the Congress of Berlin. In order to preserve peace among the great powers and to diffuse rising tensions over this "eastern question," the Congress decided to amputate from the Ottoman Empire most of its European provinces. For its part, Russia agreed to give up its designs on Istanbul in return for maintaining control over lands it had secured in the Caucasus Mountains. Serbia, Romania, and Montenegro became independent states. Austria acquired the right to "occupy and administer" the provinces of Bosnia and Herzegovina. There things stood for the rest of the nineteenth century, as the European powers began their imperial scramble; and Russia, forced to deal with renewed internal unrest, turned its attention away from the Balkans.

Russian Industrialization

Following the assassination of Alexander II in 1881, the next Romanov tsars reaffirmed autocratic authority and exercised tight political control, harkening back to the policies of Nicholas I. They surrounded themselves with conservative advisors and buttressed their hold on absolute rule by connecting loyalty to the state with adherence to eastern Christianity. These tsarist policies provoked renewed calls for constitutional reforms and generated new movements opposed to the autocracy of the regime. At the same time, when the depression of 1873–1896 began to ease in the 1890s, the country enjoyed a surge in industrialization, aggravating the political and social contradictions in Russia.

The Reassertion of Tsarist Authority   In the face of increasing demands by constitutionalists and social reformers, Alexander III (r. 1881–1894) unleashed a broad program of "counterreforms" in order to shore up autocratic control over the country. These actions turned Russia into a police state, in which political trials

Aristocratic Splendor. This oil painting of the wedding of Nicholas II in 1894, by the Danish painter Laurits Regner Tuxen (1853–1927), completed in 1898, shows the rich glory of the eastern Christian Church and the empire in ascendancy, with their iconic art, ermine furs, veiled ladies in waiting, and decorated officers.

before military courts were commonplace. Anyone who opposed Alexander's policies was subjected to intimidation at best, exile or death at worst; revolutionaries, terrorists, and opponents among the intelligentsia were especially targeted. Outside Russia, Alexander insisted on a program of *Russification*, or forced assimilation to Russian culture, especially language, by Poles, Ukrainians, and the Muslim populations of central Asia. For the time being, the regime maintained its grip on power.

Nicholas II (r. 1894–1917), a narrow-minded, unimaginative, and ultimately tragic figure, followed in his father's footsteps. Nicholas's paramount concern was loyalty not only to the state but also to the church. Any deviations were considered treasonous. He held a special contempt for revolutionary groups and individuals, who therefore retaliated with increasingly strident demands for the overthrow of the tsarist government. In addition to continuing the repressive policies of his father, Nicholas held an enduring distrust of Russian Jews as unpatriotic, which climaxed in the pogroms of 1903–1906. These pogroms, a repetition of earlier ones in 1881–1884 following the assassination of Alexander II, triggered mass emigrations to the United States and smaller ones to Britain, South America, South Africa, and Palestine as Russian Jews sought to escape persecution (see Map 25.5).

Industrialization   Industrial development was as slow in Russia as in the Ottoman Empire and for many of the same reasons. For one thing, the empire suffered from a poor transportation infrastructure. Although canal construction had started under Peter the Great, road construction did not follow until the early 1800s. Railroad construction was even slower, owing to the great distances in the empire which made large capital investments from abroad necessary. The first line, from St. Petersburg to Moscow, opened in 1851; but only a few thousand miles of track were laid until 1890 when the European depression of the previous three decades lifted. A major reason for the defeat in the Crimean War was the absence of railroad connections from Moscow

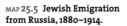

MAP **25.5** **Jewish Emigration from Russia, 1880–1914.**

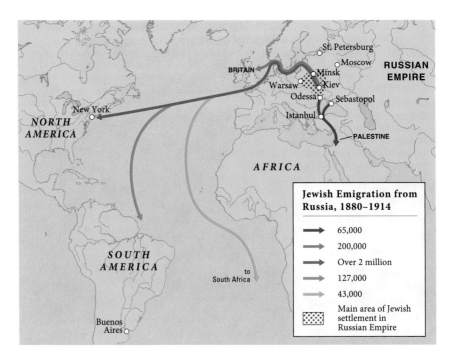

Jewish Emigration from Russia, 1880–1914

→	65,000
→	200,000
→	Over 2 million
→	127,000
→	43,000
▨	Main area of Jewish settlement in Russian Empire

to the Black Sea, forcing the army to rely on water transport and horse-drawn carts. Moreover, even into the twentieth century, Russian railroads never adopted the standard gauge of their Western counterparts, necessitating costly and time-consuming changes of carriages and rolling stock at border crossings.

Still, in the 1890s, British, French, and Belgian capital poured into the empire and helped in building railroads, mining ventures, iron smelters, and textile factories. It is estimated that during this decade Russia's industrial output increased at an annual rate of nearly 8 percent. Among other factors driving the push toward accelerated industrialization was the dawning recognition of the regime that Russia was falling behind the industrialized nations of Europe in the race for economic—and thus political—global political influence.

The driving force in Russia's push for industrialization in the 1890s was the minister of finance, Sergei Witte (1849–1915, in office 1892–1903). Of German–Baltic descent from the Russian province of Estonia, Witte held a degree in mathematics and was a railroad official before becoming responsible for the Russian finances. His "Witte system" included an acceleration of heavy industrial output, the erection of import tariffs, increased taxes on the peasantry, and conversion to the gold standard in order to stabilize the currency. Although historians debate the overall success of Witte's reforms, there is no question that Russia made tremendous progress in heavy industrialization during the late nineteenth century. Dramatic increases in the miles of rail laid, tons of coal and steel produced, and square yards of textiles woven attest to Witte's vigor.

Witte's crowning achievement was the Trans-Siberian Railroad, built during 1891–1905 and connecting Moscow with Vladivostok on the Pacific coast. During Catherine's time, it took 3 years for communications to be sent to and from Vladivostok; now, the distance was covered in 8 days. Witte's objective was not only to make Russia more competitive but also to extend Russia's reach into the rich agricultural and mineral resources of Siberia, while at the same time extending Russia's influence in east Asia. Russia's policy of opening east Asia was the equivalent of Western imperialism in Asia and Africa and designed to ensure that Russia enjoyed a share of the global race for empire.

The Russo–Japanese War The dramatic surge in industrialization, in conjunction with imperial ambitions in east Asia, brought Russia into conflict with Japan. As we saw in Chapter 24, with the Meiji Restoration in 1867–8, Japan had embarked on a concerted and systematic program of modernization and industrialization. Like western Europe and Russia, it developed imperial ambitions in the 1890s, seeking to replace China as the dominant power in east Asia. To this end Japan provoked war with China and in the Sino–Japanese War (1894–1895) occupied Taiwan and the Liaodong Peninsula of Manchuria. Although successful in defeating China and replacing it as the protector of Korea, the European powers forced Japan to give up the Liaodong Peninsula in the Triple Intervention (1895), which was in turn leased to Russia the following year. Determined to continue Russian expansion in east Asia, Witte completed the construction of a railway spur from the Trans-Siberian Railroad through Manchuria to the warm-water fortress city of Port Arthur on the southern tip of Liaodong.

The construction of this spur was the final straw for Japan, whose imperial goals seemed suddenly threatened by Russian expansion. Already smarting from what they considered Russia's double-dealing in helping to engineer the Triple Intervention and leasing the naval base at Port Arthur from the Qing, in early 1904 Japanese naval forces suddenly attacked the Russian fleet moored at Port Arthur, destroying several of its ships and laying siege to the fortress. The Japanese had had the foresight several years before of signing a treaty with Great Britain of "benign neutrality" in which the British agreed passively to help Japan in the event of war with a third party. They thus refused the Russian Baltic fleet passage through the Suez Canal on its voyage to raise the Japanese siege of Port Arthur. Following a decisive Japanese victory over Russian forces at Mukden in March 1905, Japanese forces finally cracked the stalemate at Port Arthur just as the Russian fleet, forced to sail around South Africa and across the Indian Ocean, attempted to run the narrow Straits of Tsushima. Here, the Japanese fleet was waiting for them and annihilated them in one of the most lopsided naval victories of the modern era. In the peace settlement, Japan gained control of the Liaodong Peninsula and southern Manchuria, as well as increased influence over Korea, which it finally annexed in 1910.

The Abortive Russian Revolution of 1905

In addition to Russia's mauling by the Japanese in the war of 1904–1905, a variety of factors coalesced in the early 1900s that sparked the first revolution against tsarist rule. One of these was a rising discontent among the peasantry, who continued to chafe under injustices such as the redemption payments for landownership. Another was the demand from factory workers for reform of working conditions: The workday ran to 11.5 hours and wages were pitifully low. Although the government had allowed for the formation of labor unions, their grievances fell on deaf ears. In response, workers in major manufacturing centers across the country, especially in St. Petersburg, mounted massive protests and occasional strikes.

Revolutionary Parties   The discontent among workers and peasants pumped new life into calls for reforms, resulting in the creation of two new political parties. One of these was the Social Democratic Labor Party, formed in 1898 by Vladimir Ilyich Lenin (1870–1924), a staunch adherent of Marxism (discussed in Chapter 23). This group sought support from workers, whom they urged to stage a socialist revolution by rising up and overthrowing the bourgeois capitalist tsarist government. The other group, the Social Revolutionary Party, was formed in 1901. Comprised mostly of liberal reformers among the intelligentsia, the Social Revolutionary Party advocated populism as a way to energize the peasantry, upon which they counted to lead the revolutionary effort.

During its meeting in London in 1903 the Social Democratic Labor Party split into two competing factions. The more moderate group, the Mensheviks ("minority," though they were actually numerically in the majority), was willing to follow classical Marxism, which allowed for an evolutionary process from fully evolved capitalism to social revolution and then on to the eventual overthrow of capitalism and tsarist rule. The more radical faction, known as Bolsheviks ("majority"), led by Lenin, was unwilling to wait for the evolutionary process to unfold and instead called for revolution in the near term. In 1902 Lenin had sketched out his agenda in *What Is to Be Done?* which laid out the principal Bolshevik aims. Foremost among these was a demand for the overthrow of the tsar, which could be accomplished only by relying on a highly disciplined core of dedicated revolutionaries leading the masses, whom Lenin distrusted as unwieldy and potentially unreliable. Even after the split in the Social Democratic Labor Party, however, the Bolsheviks were still a long way away from the kind of elite "vanguard of the revolution" party Lenin envisaged.

The Revolution of 1905 Events moved toward a violent climax in the Revolution of 1905. Amid mounting calls for political and economic reforms during the early 1900s, two concurrent events in 1904 shook the government to its foundations. First, reports of the humiliating defeats during the ongoing Russo–Japanese War began to filter to the home front. These made apparent the government's mismanagement of the war. Second, in January 1905, 100,000 workers went on strike in St. Petersburg, resulting in massive disruptions and loss of life commemorated later by Lenin.

The events of Bloody Sunday triggered further protests across the country during the spring and summer of 1905 (see Map 25.6). Then, from September to October, workers in all the major industrial centers staged a general strike, which brought the country to a standstill. Finally forced to make concessions, Nicholas issued the "October Manifesto," in which he promised to establish a constitutional government. Among other things, the Manifesto guaranteed individual civil liberties, universal suffrage, and the creation of a representative assembly, the Duma. During 1905–1907, however, Nicholas repudiated the concessions granted in the Manifesto, especially an independent Duma, which remained a rubber stamp parliament until Nicholas abdicated in 1917. Its momentum sapped, the revolution petered out.

What factors account for this deflation of revolutionary fervor? One event that enabled Nicholas to renege on his earlier promises was disagreement among the opposition parties; each had its own goals and ambitions, resulting in disagreement on how to bring down the tsarist government. More than that, each of the major political factions was unable to convince its followers among the workers and the peasants that its plans would in the end really address their specific concerns. Nicholas was therefore able to play off one group against the other and to reverse the reforms.

The revolution showed that the generational shift from constitutionalists to revolutionaries seeking to overturn the existing social order, which Turgenev had observed in the 1860s, was nearly complete. This shift made the formation of broader reformist coalitions, perhaps even with military participation, as in the Ottoman Empire, impossible. The tsarist regime, though humbled by Japan, still had enough military resources to wear down the combination of small groups of Marxist revolutionaries and street demonstrators. Without sympathizers in the army, a determined tsarist regime was impossible to bring down. But like Qing China during these years, whatever belated

Lenin on Bloody Sunday

"Today is the twelfth anniversary of 'Bloody Sunday,' [January 9 or 22, 1905, depending on different calendars] which is rightly regarded as the beginning of the Russian revolution.

"Thousands of workers—not Social-Democrats, but loyal God-fearing subjects—led by the priest Gapon, streamed from all parts of the capital to its centre, to the square in front of the Winter Palace, to submit a petition to the tsar. The workers carried icons. In a letter to the tsar their then leader, Gapon, had guaranteed his personal safety and had asked him to appear before the people.

"Troops were called out. Uhlans [Polish light cavalry] and Cossacks [southern Russian regiments] attacked the crowd with drawn swords. They fired on the unarmed workers, who on their bended knees implored the Cossacks to allow them to go to the tsar. The indignation of the workers was indescribable..."

—Vladimir I. Lenin. *Collected Works*, vol. 23, p. 236. Moscow: Progress Publishers, 1964. Accessible through http://www.marxists.org/archive/lenin/works/1917/jan/09.htm.

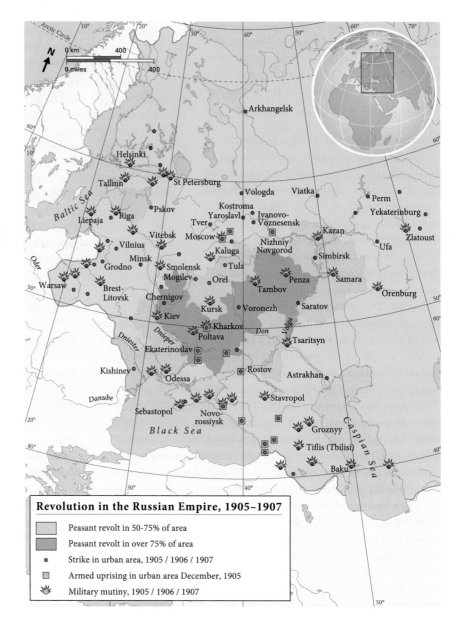

MAP **25.6 Revolution in the Russian Empire, 1905–1907.**

reforms were initiated by the government would increasingly be seen as irrelevant. It was now perceived that nothing short of changing the system would be effective. For both empires, the revolutionaries would now dominate the scene.

Putting It All Together

Both the Ottoman and Russian Empires faced the initial Western military and constitutional challenges directly on their doorsteps, not from across the ocean, as China and Japan did. Of course, once military technology had undergone its own industrial transformation in Europe during the first half of the 1800s, China was no longer too far away for British steam-powered gunboats and rifled breech-loading weapons. The Ottoman Empire, as a mature empire struggling to regain its traditional centralism, fought largely defensive wars. Russia, still a young empire, expanded aggressively against the defensive Ottomans and its weaker Asian neighbors (except Japan), all the while suffering occasional military and diplomatic setbacks. India failed to master the Western military challenge altogether. China, the Ottoman Empire, and Qajar Iran survived it at the price of diminished territories. The Western challenge was pervasive across the world.

Western constitutional nationalism was another powerful and corrosive pattern. The transformation of kingdoms or colonies into nations in which subjects would become citizens,

Vladimir Egorovic Makovsky (1846–1920), *Death in the Snow* (1905). This dramatic oil painting of the crowd protesting against the tsarist regime during the abortive revolution of 1905 is one of the greatest realist paintings. Makovsky was one of the founders of the Moscow Art School and continued to paint after the Russian Revolution of 1917.

regardless of language or dialect, social rank, or religion, was difficult enough in Europe. France, with its uneasy shift between monarchy and republic during the 1800s, demonstrated this difficulty. In the Ottoman Empire, a wide gap existed between constitutional theory and practice, especially as far as religion was concerned. Russia, plagued by the reluctance of its aristocracy to give up serfdom even after emancipation, left its constitutionalists out in the cold. Japan created a constitutional state but, like Germany, left the great majority of real power in the hands of its emperor and advisors. China's bid for a constitutional monarchy died once in 1898 and was never fully reborn before its revolution in 1911. Sultans, emperors, and kings knew well that none of their constitutions would fully satisfy the demands for liberty, equality, and fraternity.

To complicate matters for both the Ottoman and Russian Empires, in the second half of the 1800s, many members of the rising educated urban middle class deserted constitutional nationalism and turned to ethnic nationalism (in the Ottoman Empire) or to pan-Slavism, revolutionary socialism, and Marxism (in the Russian Empire). Marxism would eventually carry the day in Russia in the course of World War I. By contrast, both the Ottoman and Russian Empires met the Western *industrial* challenge—cheap, factory-produced cotton textiles—without completely surrendering their markets. Once they were able to attract foreign capital for the construction of expensive railroads and factories at the end of the 1800s, they even started on their own paths to industrialization—the seemingly stable Russia faster than the apparently sick Ottoman Empire. In spite of wrenching transformations, the two were still empires in control of themselves when World War I broke out. Neither would survive the war. Instead, they would be transformed by the forces that had beset them throughout the nineteenth century: Turkey would become a modern, secular nation-state, though always running somewhat behind its European contemporaries in economic development. Russia would be transformed into the world's first Marxist state, pursue breakneck industrial and economic development at a tragic cost, and emerge after World War II as one of two "superpowers" with the United States (see Concept Map).

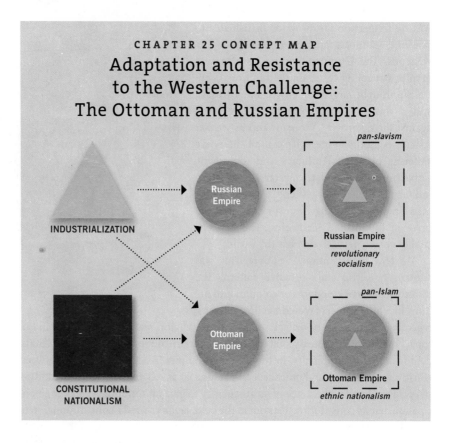

Review and Respond

1. What was the significance of Napoleon's invasion of Egypt in 1798?

2. How would you summarize the Tanzimat decrees in the Ottoman Empire.

3. What did the Committee of Union and Progress in the Ottoman Empire stand for, and what did it accomplish between 1908 and 1914?

4. Which features characterized Iran in this period, and how did the country adapt to the Western challenge?

5. What were the patterns of agrarian life in Russia during the nineteenth century?

6. Why did the tsars in Russia face a fractured opposition to their autocratic rule?

> For additional resources, including maps, primary sources, visuals, and quizzes, please go to www.oup.com/us/vonsivers. Please see the Further Resources section at the back of the book for additional readings and suggested websites.

Thinking Through Patterns

▶ **Which new models did the Ottomans adopt during the nineteenth century to adapt themselves to the Western challenge?**

The traditional model for reform in the Ottoman Empire was based on the Islamic concept of the divinely sanctioned, absolute authority of the sultan: Officials could be appointed or dismissed at will. The later history of the Ottoman Empire is significant in world history because it shows the *adaptation pattern* to the Western challenge, in this case, the borrowing of constitutional nationalism and modern military technology from Europe.

As agrarian polities with large landowning classes collecting rents from tenant farmers or serfs, the Ottoman and Russian Empires found it difficult to respond to the European industrial challenge. Large foreign investments were necessary for the building of steelworks, factories, and railroads. Given the long economic recession of the last quarter of the 1800s, these investments—coming from France and Germany—went to expanding Russia, more than the shrinking Ottoman Empire, as the safer bet.

▶ **How did the agrarian Ottoman and Russian Empires, both with large landholding ruling classes, respond to the western European industrial challenge during the 1800s?**

▶ **Why did large, well-established empires like the Russian and the Ottoman Empires struggle with the forces of modernity, while a small, secluded island nation like Japan seemed to adapt so quickly and successfully to them?**

This is in many respects a tantalizing question for world historians. Aside from philosophical debates about what actually constitutes "success," one avenue of inquiry is cultural: How receptive were the Russians and Ottomans—or the Qing, for that matter—toward the ideas of the Enlightenment? The short answer must be, "not very." Even the most willing leaders in these empires risked alienating a host of entrenched interests by attempting the most modest reforms. They therefore walked a very fine political line in what they attempted and often found that the reforms disrupted traditional routines but left little or nothing to replace them effectively. In addition, such large multiethnic empires as those of Russia and the Ottomans found it difficult to rally subjects around a distinct "nationality" since they encompassed so many divergent ones. In contrast, the Meiji reformers had the advantage of a unity derived from outside pressures. With the old shogunate gone, the emperor could formulate completely new institutions and count on the loyalty of subjects who had seen him as a semidivine figure. Moreover, the new regime commenced immediately in creating an ideology of Japaneseness—a form of ethnic nationalism—and institutionalized it in education and national policy. There was, to be sure, opposition; but it was scattered, class-based, and not effective against the modern army and industrial power the new regime created. Japan's legacy of cultural borrowing may also have been an advantage, as well as a nascent capitalist system developing in the late Tokugawa era. Finally, the goal of using its progress toward "enlightenment and civilization" according to Western standards could be measured along the way, as were the power and prestige of its new programs.

Riz: Mise en terre des plantes

Riz: Fleur et fruit

Tabac: Mise en terre

Tabac: Plante de tabac

Chapter 26

1750-1914

The New Imperialism in the Nineteenth Century

THE NEW IMPERIALISM

At the end of the Muslim month-long observance of Ramadan in 1827, Hussein (1815–1830), the ruler (*dey*) of the autonomous Ottoman province of Algeria in North Africa, held a celebratory reception for the diplomatic corps of consuls at his palace in the capital, the port city of Algiers. When he saw the French consul, Pierre Deval, Hussein signaled him to come up to the throne. In a quite undiplomatic harangue, the dey accused the consul of deliberately defrauding him of a large sum of money owed him by France for wheat deliveries between 1793 and 1798. He then demanded immediate payment of this long overdue debt. To emphasize his demand, the dey struck the consul with his fan and declared him *persona*

nsion pour
hage

Riz: Battage par

lte

Tabac: Indigène brésilien, fumant

Seeing Patterns

▶ What new patterns emerged in the transition from trade-fort imperialism to the new imperialism?

▶ How did European colonizers develop their colonies economically, given that they were industrializing themselves at the same time?

▶ What were the experiences of the indigenous people under the new imperialism? How did they adapt to colonialism? How did they resist?

non grata, which, in terms of diplomatic protocol, meant that he had to leave the country immediately.

France's restored Bourbon king, Charles X (r. 1824–1830), found this insult by the Algerian dey to an appointee of the French court intolerably injurious to his own divinely-ordained dignity. He dispatched a naval detachment to Algiers in 1828, demanding an apology, declaring the debt liquidated, and asking for reparations for a number of piracy depredations that had occurred in the preceding years. When the dey rejected the demands, the French mounted a blockade of the port. In 1830, they followed up on this blockade with an expeditionary force that conquered Algiers, deposed the dey, and sent him into exile. Less than two decades later Algeria became a colony of France.

The events that preceded the "fan slap," as it became known, were rooted in a drought in southern France toward the end of the French Revolution. The government at the time, the Directory, was chronically short of finances and received the Algerian relief shipments without having to pay immediately. They were made on trust, thanks to the services of a

Imperial Bounty. The material benefits of empire—at least for the colonizer—are colorfully illustrated in these panels from a 1910 French school textbook. The stages of cultivation for rice and tobacco are graphically illustrated, from first planting to taking to market. No white people toil in the fields, but the scenes nonetheless exude an idyllic sense of peace and prosperity under the "civilizing" effects of Western rule.

Colonialism: A system in which people from one country settle in another, ruling it and maintaining connections to the mother country; term now used most often to describe the contemporary exploitation of weaker countries by imperial powers.

prominent Italian–Algerian Jewish banking business, Bacri Brothers and Busnach [Boos-NASH].

Repayment was delayed by Napoleon's Mediterranean campaign. Napoleon had toyed with a conquest of Algeria but then decided to go for Egypt instead (1798–1801), possibly to frighten the British in India. After Napoleon fell from power, France made two payments, which were sufficient to satisfy some creditors of Bacri-Busnach but not Hussein—hence the fan slap nearly 30 years after the wheat shipments.

Among other things, the incident illustrates the changing fortunes of those countries that were the beneficiaries of the new forces of modernity—in this case, France—and those like the Ottoman Empire and its territories in Algeria that largely were not. In this chapter, our focus will be on those parts of the world outside east Asia (see Chapter 24) that were unable to preserve, even in a tenuous fashion, their political independence while adapting to the colonial challenge through military, constitutional, and economic reforms. Here, we will study the victims of conquest and occupation in south and southeast Asia, the Middle East, Africa, and the Pacific Ocean that most clearly make visible the underlying patterns of imperialism and colonialism.

Two patterns characterize the evolution of imperialism–colonialism in the period 1750–1900. The first was a shift from coastal trade forts under chartered companies—the old imperialism on the cheap—to government takeover, territorial conquest, and **colonialism**. Great Britain pioneered this "new imperialism" in India but also prevented the other European countries for a century from following in its footsteps.

The second pattern was the rise of direct territorial imperialism–colonialism by European countries in the course of the disintegration of the Ottoman Empire, under assault by Russia since the end of the eighteenth century and, in the course of the nineteenth century, in Asia and Africa. The Europeans first protected the Ottomans from Russia, only later to help themselves to Ottoman provinces, beginning with the capture of Algeria by France. Thus the dey's fan slap in Algeria may be viewed as the unlikely catalyst that set in motion competitive European imperialism–colonialism in Asia and Africa that characterized the remainder of the nineteenth century.

The British Colonies of India, Australia, and New Zealand

The transition in India from European trade-fort activities to governmental colonialism coincided with the decline of the Mughal dynasty (see Chapter 20). The British East India Company exploited the Mughal decline to evolve into a government in all but name. Its notorious corruption and ultimate inability to conduct military affairs, however, forced the British government to assume direct control. As a result, Britain became a colonial power in the Eastern Hemisphere, making India its center for the delivery of the cotton on which early British industrialization depended. Later on, sparsely inhabited Australia and New Zealand began as small British settler colonies, the former as a penal colony and the latter against fierce indigenous resistance.

The British East India Company

As with so many developments that helped to shape the later eighteenth century and its legacy, an important factor in the rise of British power in India was the Seven Years' War. As we have seen, the Seven Years' War resembled in many respects a kind of "first" world war in that fighting took place in Europe, in the Americas, on the high seas, and in India. It was the result of the war in India, along with the deepening political difficulties of the Mughals, that enabled the rise of the British to supremacy not only on the subcontinent but later in Burma and Malaya as well.

The Seven Years' War   The seeds had long been planted for a vibrant British commercial community among the European trading companies by the early eighteenth century. As we saw in Chapter 20, the British had joined forces at Surat on the west coast of India with the Dutch in the lucrative spice trade. But they had also established their own posts in provincial cities that would over time be transformed into India's greatest metropolises: Madras (Chennai), Bombay (Mumbai), and one created from scratch: Calcutta (Kolkata). By 1750 their chief commercial competitors were the French, who were aggressively building up both trade and political power from a base in Pondicherry in the southern part of peninsular India.

For the British East India Company, its evolution into a kind of shadow government in the area around Calcutta in Bengal on the northeast coast would now bear dividends. The decline of Mughal central power meant that regional leaders were being enlisted as French or British allies. If they were more powerful, they sought to use the Sepoy (from Persian *sipahi* [see-pa-HEE], "soldier") armies of the European companies as support in their own struggles. Out of this confused political and volatile military situation, the East India Company leader, Robert Clive (1725–1774), who

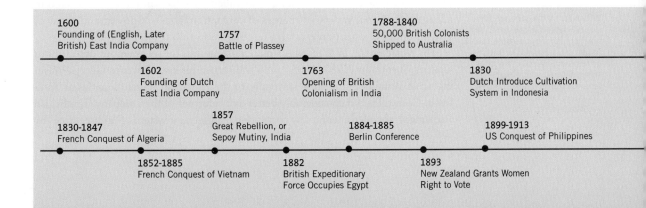

1600 Founding of (English, Later British) East India Company	1757 Battle of Plassey	1788-1840 50,000 British Colonists Shipped to Australia
	1602 Founding of Dutch East India Company	1763 Opening of British Colonialism in India	1830 Dutch Introduce Cultivation System in Indonesia
1830-1847 French Conquest of Algeria	1857 Great Rebellion, or Sepoy Mutiny, India	1884-1885 Berlin Conference	1899-1913 US Conquest of Philippines
	1852-1885 French Conquest of Vietnam	1882 British Expeditionary Force Occupies Egypt	1893 New Zealand Grants Women Right to Vote

Nabob: A person who acquired a large fortune in India during the period of British rule.

was ambitious, ruthless, and finely attuned to the vagaries of the shifting political landscape, won a signal victory over the Indian French allies at Plassey in 1757 and soon eliminated the French from power in the subcontinent. By the terms of the treaty ending the war in 1763, the East India Company ended up as the sole European power of consequence in India; and Clive set about consolidating his position from Calcutta.

Perceptions of Empire. The British East India Company's real ascent to power in India began with Robert Clive's victory at Plassey in 1757, the symbolism of which is depicted here. Note the deference with which the assorted Indian princes treat the conqueror (*a*). Below, the second from last Mughal emperor, Akbar Shah II (r. 1806–1837), receives the British resident, ca. 1815 (*b*). Despite the fact that the British East India Company had extended its sway over much of northern India by this time, the Indian artist depicts the British government official in a pose of supplication to Akbar Shah—in almost a mirror image of the imagined Indian princes in the painting of Clive.

Going Native—the Nabobs   Clive's aggressive style of economic aggrandizement set the style for what Indian scholars have often called "the Rape of Bengal" in the latter eighteenth century. The East India Company set about expanding its holdings across northern India, dealing, plundering, and extorting funds from pliant local princes. The company men had no interest in changing India or reforming Indian institutions. Indeed, many, inspired by Enlightenment ideals of cosmopolitanism, became great admirers of Indian culture. Some took this to the point of what became known as "going native": After gathering their fortunes, they took Indian wives, dressed as Indian princes, and on occasion wielded power as local magnates or **nabobs** (from Urdu *nawwab* [naw-WAHB], "deputy," "viceroy").

The period of the nabobs perhaps reached its height under the company directorship of Warren Hastings (1732-1818), Clive's successor. Where Clive was brutal and aggressive, Hastings, though acquiring immense wealth, developed an intense scholarly interest in Indian culture. The first translations into English of many of the classics of Indian literature took place during his governor-generalship from 1773 to 1785. Moreover, the first exposure of the Vedas to European scholars yielded the earliest hints that Sanskrit was a branch of the family of languages that came to be called "Indo-European." Over the coming decades additional scholarship on the Vedas contributed mightily to the first linguistic theories on the origins of some of Eurasia's earliest peoples—work that continues today.

The vast distances separating the company's London directors from operations in India, southeast Asia, and China tended to make its local activities more or less autonomous. Its power, organization, and, most importantly, army increasingly became the determining factors in local disputes across northern India, while its attractiveness to ambitious young men on the margins of British society—particularly among the Scots and Irish—wishing to "make their pile" in a few short years, left it vulnerable to corruption on a grand scale. This was particularly true because of the company's policy of paying low wages but winking at employees trading locally on their own behalf. Thus, Hastings was called back to London and subjected to a lengthy trial on a variety of charges of corruption, abuse of power, and abuse of Indians under company rule.

His replacement, in 1785, was a man most famous for ignominious defeat: Lord Charles Cornwallis (1738–1805), who had turned his sword over to George Washington in Britain's humiliating surrender to the American Revolutionaries at Yorktown. Cornwallis did considerably better as a reformer of the company. The British Parliament, appalled at company corruption, had set up a system of "indirect rule" by which the company's actions were to be supervised by a governor-general selected by the British government, rather than by the East India Company directors in London. Cornwallis labored to curb the worst excesses of private trading by increasing salaries and attempted to unify and rationalize the tax structure of the company's holdings.

By 1800, through the company's efforts to pacify turbulent territories adjacent to its holdings, British possessions extended across most of northern India (see Map 26.1). The irregular manner in which this was accomplished prompted many to say that the British Indian empire was created "in a fit of absence of mind." This extension also prompted a shift in the variety of trading goods as the eighteenth century wore on and as the new century dawned. Spices had been replaced by cotton goods as the most lucrative commodity and increasingly by raw cotton to be processed in Britain's mechanized textile revolution. Indian cotton would later be supplemented and eventually supplanted by cotton from the American South, Egypt, and Sudan.

The Perils of Reform   While we have become accustomed to seeing the nineteenth century as the period marking the beginning of Western supremacy, it is well

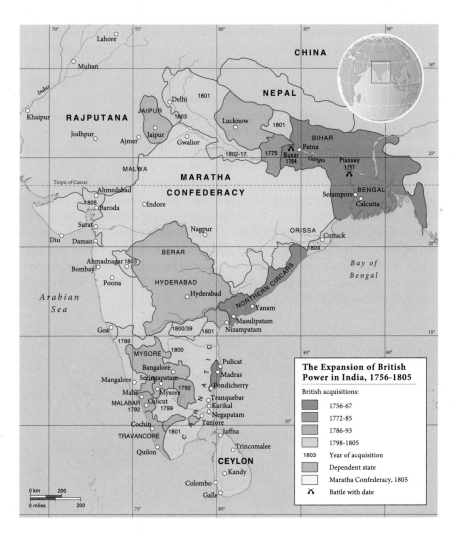

MAP **26.1 The Expansion of British Power in India, 1756–1805.**

The Expansion of British Power in India, 1756-1805

British acquisitions:
- 1756-67
- 1772-85
- 1786-93
- 1798-1805

1803 Year of acquisition

Dependent state

Maratha Confederacy, 1805

⚔ Battle with date

to remember—as we have noted in previous chapters—that even at this late date India and China were still the primary economic engines of Eurasia. As late as 1800, for example, Indian goods and services (what we call today the "GDP" or gross domestic product) accounted for perhaps 20 percent of the world's output, while Britain's came to only 3 percent. As the Industrial Revolution kicked into high gear by the mid-1800s, however, these numbers began to reverse (see Figure 26.1). As Britain's share of India's economy grew, moreover, the British increasingly sought to create markets for their own goods there and to shunt Indian exports toward the exclusive use of the British domestic market. As we saw in Chapter 24, the early acquisition of Patna by the British enabled the creation of the Chinese opium trade, which by 1830 accounted for nearly one-quarter of company revenues in India. In addition, the officials of "John Company," as the East India Company was nicknamed, were busily arbitrating disputes among Indian rulers, taking over their lands as payment for loans, and strong-arming many into becoming wards of the British. Because of this continuous attrition, by the end of the Napoleonic Wars, the Mughal emperor's lands had been reduced to the region immediately surrounding Delhi and Agra.

India's history, however, had long been marked by outsiders conquering large parts of the subcontinent, and while many chafed at company rule, its policy of non-interference with Indian customs and institutions softened the conquest somewhat. The period following the Napoleonic Wars, however, saw changes in this regard that had far-reaching consequences, by bringing the British government into a more direct role.

The economic slowdown, clashes between factory owners and labor, and drive for political reform in Britain during the period following the Napoleonic Wars found echoes in policy toward India. From the opening decades of the century, increasing numbers of Protestant missionaries, especially those of the new Evangelical denominations, saw India as promising missionary ground. As was the case in China, many missionaries brought with them practical skills, particularly in medicine, education, and engineering. Many of those active in mission-based reform in India had also been involved with the abolition of slavery, industrial workers' rights, and electoral reform movements in Britain. By 1830 many of these individuals were driving the agenda on British policy in India, which increasingly asserted that India should be reformed along the lines they envisioned for Britain: better working conditions for the poor, free trade, the abolition of "barbaric" customs, and a vigorous Christian missionary effort.

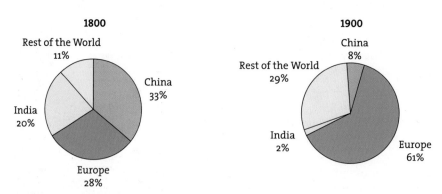

Figure 26.1 **Share of World Manufacturing Output, 1800 and 1900.**

Their opponents, many of them longtime company veterans, saw the pushing of such policies in India as unwarranted interference in their territory and largely unneeded as far as the Indians themselves were concerned. Nonetheless, missionaries mounted successful campaigns against female infanticide; against *sati*, the self-immolation of widows on their husbands' funeral pyres; and *thugee*, real or (many suggested) imagined ritual murders of travelers on Indian roads. Missionary efforts also increasingly used medicine and education as wedges for the introduction of Christianity to the Indian populace.

In addition, the company reformed the tax system into a money-based land fee for greater efficiency of collection. At the same time, new industrial enterprises and transport and communication advances—steamboats, railroads, and telegraph lines—were being constructed, benefiting the economy at large but also disrupting the livelihoods of many. Coupled with these changes was a perception on the part of opponents, and even some supporters, of these efforts in both India and England as characterized by smug righteousness—the clichéd and often caricatured middle-class "earnestness"—and arrogance of the English toward Indian society. Perhaps the most famous expression of this was found in the parliamentary reformer and historian Thomas B. Macaulay's 1835 "Minute on Education in India," where he asserted that "a single shelf of European books is worth more than all the literatures of Asia and Arabia."

Christian Missionary. The diverse crowd gathered around the young Christian preacher, who is most likely a Methodist, includes Muslims, Hindus, women, a mendicant, and at least one child. But the spectators all share one thing in common: they regard the preacher with a mixture of curiosity and amazement.

The Great Mutiny

The grim result of several decades of such wholesale change exploded in northern India in 1857. General disillusionment with the pace of change and the fear that British missionaries were, with government connivance, attempting to Christianize India came to a head among the company's Sepoy troops. With the introduction of the new Enfield rifle, which required its operator to bite the end off of a greased paper cartridge to pour the powder down its muzzle and ram the new conical bullet home, a rumor started that the grease had been concocted of cow and pig fat. Since this would violate the food restrictions of both Hindus and Muslims, the troops saw this as a plot to leave the followers of both religions ritually unclean and thus open to conversion to Christianity. Though the rumors proved untrue, a revolt raced through many of the Sepoy barracks and in short order became a wholesale rebellion aimed at throwing the British out of India and restoring the aged Mughal emperor, Bahadur Shah Zafar (r. 1837–1857), to full power. The accumulated rage against the perceived insults to Indian religions and culture pushed the troops and their allies to frightful atrocities, with even more that were rumored but never substantiated.

Execution of Indian Rebels. After British troops and loyalist Indian Sepoys had restored order in northern India, retribution was unleashed on the rebels. Here, the most spectacular mode of execution is being carried out. Mutineers are tied across the mouths of cannons and blown to pieces while the troops stand in formation and are forced to watch.

The Great Mutiny (also known by the British as the Sepoy Mutiny and by the Indians as the Great Rebellion, or First War of Independence) swiftly turned into a civil war as pro- and anti-British Indian forces clashed. The British frantically shipped troops just sent to China for the Second Opium War back to India in a desperate attempt to crush the insurgency. Through a number of hard-fought engagements they were ultimately able to reassert control but not without conducting frightful atrocities of their own in retribution for the rebels' excesses. The occupation of many towns was accompanied by mass hangings and indiscriminate shootings of suspected rebels and collaborators. In other areas, British commanders revived the old Mughal punishment of tying the victims to cannons and blowing them to bits in front of the assembled troops. Since this was thought to scatter the karmic "soul" of the victim as well as his body, it was meant to deprive the offender of his next life as well as his present one.

Direct British Rule

After assuming direct rule (Hindi *raj*, hence the term "Raj" for the colonial government), the British were crucially concerned to keep their apparatus of civilian administrators as small as possible but maintain an army large enough to avoid a repeat of 1857. These administrators made use of Indian administrators who, however, did not have any real decision-making powers. The raj functioned because of a "divide and rule" policy that exploited the many divisions existing in Indian society, which prevented the Indians from making common cause and challenging British rule.

Creation of the Civil Service   Even as the pacification was winding down, the British government, stunned by the course of events, conducted an investigation which led to sweeping reforms in 1858. The East India Company was dismantled, and the British government itself took up the task of governing India. In a proclamation to England and India, Queen Victoria announced that British policy would no longer attempt to "impose Our convictions on any of Our subjects." An Indian civil service was created and made open to British and Indians alike to administer the subcontinent's affairs. The incorporation of India as the linchpin of the British Empire was completed when Queen Victoria assumed, among her many titles, that of "Empress of India" in 1877. India had now become, it was said, "the jewel in the crown" of the empire (see Map 26.2).

Less than a decade later, the fruits of the new civil service and the Indian schools feeding it were already evident, though perhaps not in the way its creators envisioned or desired. In 1885, Indians first convened the National Congress, the ancestor of India's present Congress Party. The Congress's ongoing mission was to win greater autonomy for India within the structure of the British Empire and, by the opening decades of the twentieth century, to push for Indian independence.

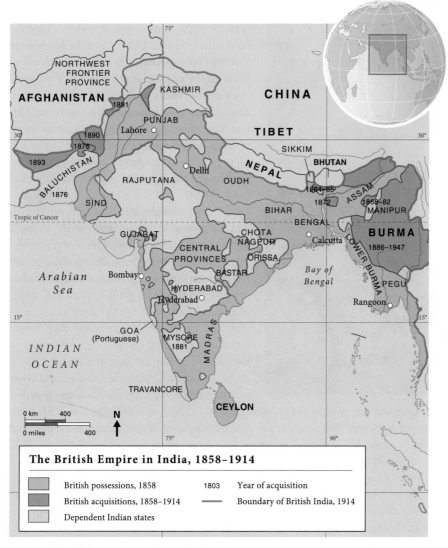

MAP **26.2** **The British Empire in India, 1858–1914.**

Already by the early 1890s, a young British-trained lawyer named Mohandas K. Gandhi (1869–1948) was actively campaigning for the rights of Indians in British-controlled South Africa. There, he honed the skills and developed the techniques that would make him among the most recognized world figures of the twentieth century as he pursued his quest to oust the British from India through nonviolence and noncooperation.

The Civil Service Caste   In the final decades of the nineteenth century the British community in India, rarely more than about 100,000 at any given time (in a population of some 270 million in 1900), increasingly set itself up as a caste and race apart. During the heyday of company rule, few wives and families moved from England to what was considered a hardship post. India's unrelenting summer heat and constant rain during the monsoon season took a considerable toll on those not fully acclimated, as did its array of tropical diseases, particularly malaria. One of the

Lord Curzon. Following the Great Rebellion, the British government dissolved the East India Company and inaugurated direct rule of the subcontinent through a civil service. Here, Lord Curzon, the British resident, or governor-general, and Lady Curzon preside over a tiger they bagged during a hunting trip. Curzon was famous for mounting flamboyant spectacles to enhance British prestige during government-sponsored durbars and was responsible for building the modern Indian capital of New Delhi.

reasons young company men were so eager to "make their pile" in a hurry was the knowledge that their life expectancy in India was rather low.

With the coming of reformers and missionaries in the 1820s and 1830s, the number of English families and dependents grew rapidly, and this increased further with the assumption of direct British rule at the end of the 1850s. The older practice of company men marrying Indian women and leaving them and their children behind when they left for home was now replaced by the professional bureaucrat or businessman and his proper Victorian family living in India for long stretches of time. This was made less physically arduous by the widespread use of quinine to treat the fevers of malaria—and popularizing the famous drink gin and tonic (the "tonic" including quinine water). In places where there were concentrations of Europeans, they tended increasingly to mingle almost exclusively among themselves, setting up their own social circuits, clubs, literary and theatrical societies, and other activities and groups. Many vacationed together during the hot months at the "hill stations" in the cooler upland areas. Thus, with the exception of their servants and civil service subordinates, European families had little contact with ordinary Indians.

"Never the Twain Shall Meet"   This, of course, was by now a familiar pattern at other outposts in European colonial empires. But this social segregation also coincided with the rise of social Darwinism and pseudoscientific theories of race that increasingly encouraged the British to see the Indians as inferior and became an additional inducement toward segregation. These attitudes can be seen in bold relief in much of Rudyard Kipling's literary work, in which, although there is much he finds admirable about things Indian, in the end concedes that "East is East and West is West and never the twain shall meet." For Kipling, the inability of these two peoples to connect suggests the superiority of the white Europeans over their Indian "charges."

Divide and Rule   The Indian civil service, among the most difficult bureaucracies in the world in which to gain admission, seldom had more than 1,000 "Anglo-Indian" (ethnically British subjects who were either born in India or longtime residents there) and Indian officials to govern a quarter of a billion people. The civil service was intended as a showpiece of British incorruptibility and professionalism, in stark contrast to the perception of endemic graft and petty bribery customary among the Indian princes. Some of the ablest men in the British Empire, particularly those whose class or ethnic background might have proven a hindrance at home, passed the grueling examinations and entered the service as "readers." With so few officials, the workload was very heavy and demanded a sophisticated understanding of local conditions and sensibilities. The numbers of civil service members increased markedly in the twentieth century as Britain began to implement a gradual devolution to a kind of federated Indian autonomy. Even at this point, however, the numbers were only slightly above 3,000.

How did such a small government apparatus and expatriate population control such a large and populous country? In many respects it was done by bluff and artifice. The Indian Army of Great Britain, "the thin red line" as it was called in the days before the uniforms were khaki, was small, well trained, but made up mostly of Indians. The British officers and noncommissioned officers included substantial numbers of Scots and Irish, themselves minorities often subject to discrimination at home. But the incipient threat of the army to suppress rebellion

> ### Kipling on the Indian Civil Service
>
> "Until steam replaces manual power in the working of the Empire, there must always be the men who are used up, expended, in the mere mechanical routine. For these promotion is far off and the mill-grind of every day very instant.... The older ones have lost their aspirations; the younger are putting theirs aside with a sigh. Both learn to endure patiently until the end of the day. Twelve years in the rank and file, men say, will sap the hearts of the bravest and dull the wits of the most keen."
>
> —Rudyard, Kipling. "The Education of Otis Yeere." In: *Under the Deodars, The Phantom Rickshaw, Wee Willie Winkie*, p. 16. Garden City, NY.: Doubleday, 1911.

and the fruits of the weapons revolution of the late nineteenth century—machine guns, rapid-fire artillery, repeating rifles—made any small revolt unthinkable, while the tactics of British divide and rule made large-scale organization across caste, religious, ethnic, and linguistic lines extremely problematic.

Though the bureaucracy and political structure of British India served to unite the country for administrative purposes, the British secured their rule locally and regionally by "divide and rule" tactics. A key divide they utilized was the obvious one between Hindus and Muslims. British policy had encouraged Muslims to see the British as their protectors, while also often leaning toward them in matters contested with the Hindus. Thus, Muslims often felt they had a stake in the Raj, particularly when the alternative that presented itself was a Hindu-controlled India should independence from Britain ever come. In the end, this fear translated itself into the partition of India into India and West and East Pakistan—as Muslim-dominated territories. East Pakistan later became Bangladesh.

Other divides exploited differences among the Hindus. Rajputs and Gurkhas, for example, as military castes, were widely employed in the army in areas away from their home regions; this was also true of the Sikhs. In order to undermine the power bases of local Brahmins, lower castes were sometimes subtly given favorable treatment. Depending on the circumstances, different regions might be given preferential treatment as well.

One other area that the British exploited with success was to appeal to the sense of grandeur of the Indian elites by staging elaborate durbars (see Chapter 20) at the Raj's showpiece capital of New Delhi, built during the early twentieth century under the aegis of the British Resident, Lord Curzon (1859–1925). His vision was to use these occasions to bolster the prestige, if not the actual power, of the Indian maharajas, who held about one-third of the country, and to reinforce traditional notions of deference and hierarchy.

The British administration created new systems of honorary ranks and revived older ones, all in the service of what some British jokingly called "Tory-entalism" because of Curzon's Conservative ("Tory") Party ties. By identifying British rule

Patterns Up Close | Military Transformations and the New Imperialism

French Defeat of the Mamluks at the Battle of the Pyramids, 1798. This painting shows the clear advantage of the military innovation of the line-drill. The orderly French forces on the right, commanded by officers on horseback, mow down the cavalry charges of the Mamluks.

As we have seen in earlier chapters, between 1450–1750 firearm-equipped infantries rose to prominence throughout Eurasia. Many rulers throughout Eurasia even reconstituted their states as *fiscal–military* polities in order to pay either mercenaries or standing infantries under their command, ready to march in short order. Recently, scholars have hotly debated the significance of the differences among the infantries and military organization more generally during this age of empire.

An answer to this question is important because historians believed for a long time that western Europeans had superior firearms, cannons, and cannon-equipped ships that enabled them to embark on overseas expansion, establish trade-fort mercantile empires, and eventually achieve imperial conquest and colonization of the Middle East, Africa, and southeast Asia. (The Americas were a different case since here the superiority of European arms is beyond doubt, even if their importance during the conquest is questionable.)

The debate is unresolved, although most scholars are now of the opinion that, beginning in the late seventeenth century, the flintlock muskets, bayonets, and line drill that distinguished western European infantries from other armies in Asia and Africa gave the Europeans an advantage. (*Line drill* was the Swedish-introduced innovation of training infantry soldiers stretched out in long lines five or six deep to fire, step back, allow the next line to fire, reload their muzzle-loaded flintlock muskets, and so on with the third to sixth lines.) These advantages were manifested in the Ottoman–Russian War of 1768–1774 and in Napoleon's invasion of Egypt in 1798.

In the early 1730s, the Ottomans realized that they could not match other powers with their matchlock muskets and that their infantry, the Janissaries, lacked sufficient discipline. Although their gunsmiths switched to flintlocks, the largely

Ethiopian Forces Defeating an Italian Army at Adowa, 1896. A hundred years after Napoleon's victory, the tables were turned when an Ethiopian army equipped with repeating rifles, machine guns, and cannon routed an Italian invasion force. In response to the defeat, the *Times* of London bemoaned that "the prestige of European arms as a whole is considerably impaired."

part-time and lowly paid Janissaries resisted all efforts at drills. Lack of finances caused these military reforms to grind to a halt. The Russian military, by contrast, learned much from the Seven Years' War (1756–1763), in which it was allied with Austria and France against Prussia and Great Britain. Its sizeable line infantries were of great importance during the war of 1768–1774 against the Ottomans. The victory was not easy, given the long supply lines south to the Black Sea and Danube. But in the end the sizeable Russian line infantry regiments prevailed over the un-coordinated and untrained Ottoman foot soldiers. Similarly, Napoleon successfully employed his small, highly mobile, and flexible units (composed of mixed infantry, cavalry, and artillery) in his victory against the lopsidedly cavalry-dominated Egyptian Mamluks in 1798.

The Mughals in India and the Qing in China did not have to worry about flintlock, bayonet, and line infantry attacks in the eighteenth century, either from their neighbors or from the far-away Europeans. Like the Ottomans, who continued to maintain large cavalry forces against their nomadic neighbors in the Middle East and central Asia, the Mughals and Qing privileged their cavalries and treated their ethnically indigenous and not very mobile firearm-equipped infantries as secondary. However, once British East India Company officers elevated indigenous infantry soldiers to the privileged ranks of the Sepoy regiments, as Karl Marx astutely observed, their discipline ultimately created such problems for the company that the British Crown had to take over the governance of India in 1858.

When European innovators introduced workable breech-loading rifles and artillery in the late 1850s, the technological balance shifted decisively toward Europe. The addition of rapid-firing mechanisms in the second half of the 1800s to these improved weapons further cemented Europe's technological superiority. They amplified western Europe's ability to subdue and colonize all but the largest states of the Middle East, Africa, and Asia by World War I. In addition to infantries, cavalries could be equipped with rapid-fire rifles and pistols, enabling detachments to land on Middle Eastern, African, and Asian coasts and quickly sweep through the interior. The French in particular made use of this improved cavalry capability in their conquests of Africa south of the Sahara.

Thus, in this shift from an initially slight to an eventually pronounced superiority of European arms during this period, the new imperialism and the Industrial Revolution were parallel developments engendered by the same modernity that also saw the rise of constitutional nationalism and the formation of a new type of polity, the nation-state. Certainly, industrially produced weapons in the later nineteenth century greatly enhanced Europe's ability to dominate much of the Middle East, Africa, and Asia. But modernity is a complex bundle of many different interacting elements. In short, there is—if you will excuse the pun—no "smoking gun."

Questions

- Examine the photo showing French forces defeating the Mamluk cavalry. Are the military advantages of the line drill evident? If so, what are they?

- Does the photo of Ethiopian forces defeating an Italian army in 1896 show that indigenous peoples could adapt Western innovations to their own purposes? If so, how?

Subaltern: A person or thing considered subordinate to another.

with India's historic past, it was hoped that the perception of strength and legitimacy would be enhanced. This effort to co-opt local rulers into upholding the British government as the historically destined status quo is sometimes called by historians a **subaltern** relationship. Yet, a small but growing elite of Western-educated, often accomplished, Indian leaders began to use the arguments of empire against their occupiers. By the 1920s many of these people would make up the burgeoning national movement associated with Gandhi's strategy of noncooperation and the Indian National Congress's outlines for government when Britain was finally forced to "quit India."

The British Settler Colonies of Australia and New Zealand

India was merely one area in Asia and the Pacific where the British advanced from exploration and trade forts to imperial expansion and colonial settlement. In the continent of Australia and on the islands of New Zealand they colonized indigenous forager and agrarian populations as well as—in contrast to India—encouraged large-scale immigration of European settlers.

White Settlement in Australia and New Zealand   Dutch navigators, blown off course on their way to Indonesia, initially discovered the western coast of Australia in 1606; but when profitable trade opportunities with the forager Aborigines (the name given to the indigenous Australians) failed to materialize, they did not pursue any further contacts. The British navigator James Cook (1728–1779), during one of his many exploratory journeys in the Pacific, landed in 1770 on the Australian east coast and claimed it for Great Britain. After the United States wrested its independence from Britain in 1783, the British government looked to Australia as a place where it could ship convicts. Between 1788 and 1840, some 50,000 British convicts were shipped to the penal colony.

The Making of Australia. British Army redcoats register convicts disembarking in Australia at Sydney Cove. As a result of poverty and crime accompanying the early industrialization in Britain, prisons were so overcrowded that the authorities sought relief by sending prisoners to penal colonies overseas. About 25 percent of the prisoners were Irish, mostly arrested on political charges.

Immigration by free British subjects, begun a decade before the end of convict shipments, led to a pastoral and agricultural boom. Settlers pioneered agriculture in south Australia where rainfall, fluctuating according to dry and wet *El Niño/La Niña* cycles, was relatively reliable and provided the population with most of its cereal needs. Sugar and rice cultivation, introduced to the tropical northeast in the 1860s, was performed with indentured labor recruited from Pacific islands. Even during penal colony times, sheep ranching in the east and the exportation of wool developed into an early thriving business, with half of the wool needed by the British textile industry being supplied from Australia. Even more important for the evolution of the Australian colony was the mining of gold and silver, beginning in the east in 1851 and continuing thereafter in nearly all parts of the continent. Although a colony, Australia was very similar to independent Latin America (see Chapter 27) in that it was a labor-poor but commodity-rich region, seeking its wealth through export-led growth (see Map 26.3).

Mining generated several gold rush immigration waves, not only from Britain but also from China, as well as internal migrations from mining towns to cities when the gold rushes ended. Cities like Sydney and Melbourne expanded continuously during the 1800s and encompassed more than two-thirds of the total white population of about 5 million by 1914. The indigenous population of Aborigines, who had inhabited the continent since 65,000 BCE, shrank during the same time from several hundred thousand to 67,000, mostly as a result of diseases but also after confrontations with

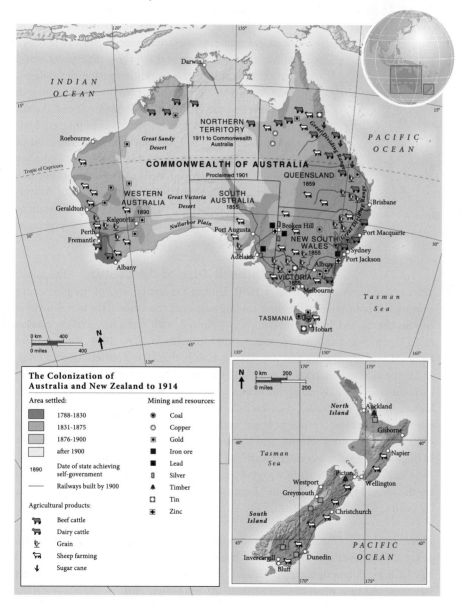

MAP 26.3 **The Colonization of Australia and New Zealand to 1914.**

The Colonization of
Australia and New Zealand to 1914

Area settled:

	1788–1830
	1831–1875
	1876–1900
	after 1900

1890   Date of state achieving self-government

—   Railways built by 1900

Agricultural products:
- Beef cattle
- Dairy cattle
- Grain
- Sheep farming
- Sugar cane

Mining and resources:
- Coal
- Copper
- Gold
- Iron ore
- Lead
- Silver
- Timber
- Tin
- Zinc

Racial Harmony in Australia. The government's attempts to encourage cooperation between natives and settlers found little success, as shown in this 1816 oil painting. At top, whites and Aborigines, dressed in European clothing, mingle harmoniously. Harmony prevails in the second panel from the top, in which uniformed soldiers and a government official greet the Aborigines courteously. Things begin to deteriorate in the third panel, however, as an Aborigine spears a white man and is hung for his infraction. A cycle of violence takes over in the bottom panel as a white man shoots an Aborigine and is in turn hung by soldiers.

ranchers intruding on their hunting and gathering lands. As in North America, whites were relentless in taking an allegedly empty—or expected soon to be empty—continent into their possession.

The Long Boom As it did in Latin America, a long boom favored Australia in the second half of the nineteenth century, up until the 1880s. A wet La Niña cycle, strong wool and gold exports, and the inflow of investments for the construction of railroads supported growth. An Australian-born generation of whites came into its own during this boom, which, on the one hand, was still strongly colonial in outlook, cherishing the metropolitan ties, but, on the other hand, was proud of its Australian pioneer differences. In early stirrings of Australian literature and art, these differences stood out. The writers of the weekly magazine the *Bulletin*, founded in 1880, discussed the harshness of farming in the bush and the virtues of republicanism; and the so-called Heidelberg painters (after their camp near Melbourne) in the 1880s developed their own version of impressionism, emphasizing shades of ochre and olive green. The legislative councils of the colonies became veritable battlegrounds between native white Australians and the colonial government over issues such as "free selection" (the Australian equivalent of homesteading), land-squatting, and tariffs.

The Difficult Turn of the Century The boom years ended for Australia around 1890. During the last quarter of the nineteenth century, the economies of the three leading industrial countries of the world—Great Britain, the United States, and Germany—slowed, with first a financial depression in 1873–1879 and another more economy-wide one in 1890–1896. Australia had been able to ride out the first depression, mainly thanks to continuing gold finds. But in the 1890s, construction as well as banking collapsed and factories closed. Coincidentally, a dry El Niño cycle devastated free selection farming. Labor unrest followed: Although widespread strikes failed, the newly founded Labor Party (1891) immediately became a major political force. The country adopted labor reforms, an old-age pension, fiscal reforms, and a white-only immigration policy. The discovery of huge gold deposits in western Australia in 1892–1894 helped to redress the economy. In 1900, Australia finally adopted a federal constitution, which made the country the second fully autonomous "dominion," after Canada (1867) but before New Zealand (1907), Newfoundland (1907), South Africa (1910), and Ireland (1922).

New Zealand Fourteen hundred miles southeast of Australia lies the archipelago of New Zealand. Both the north and south islands had been settled around 1200 CE by Polynesians called "Maori," farmers who brought along yams, sweet potatoes, and taro. Most of their settlements were on or close to the coasts on the northern island, where agriculture was most productive. After initial hostile and even bloody encounters between Maoris, numbering about 100,000, and Europeans, the British negotiated a controversial treaty in 1840, which entitled the Maoris to their land and status as British subjects. The governor, however, disregarded the treaty; and white settlements proceeded apace, with Maoris pushed off their land. In a series of clashes from 1860 to 1872, a number of Maori groups retaliated with violence, slowing down white settlement severely but also eventually ending Maori independence. Disease reduced Maori numbers to a low of 40,000 in the 1890s.

Large-scale immigration began only in 1870, and within a decade the white population doubled to 200,000. As in Australia, wheat farming made New Zealand self-sufficient and wool and gold sustained export-led growth. High-quality coal, mined from 1873, added to the exports. Refrigeration (introduced in 1882) initiated New Zealand's specialization in lamb meat and butter production for export. In the wake of rapid urbanization and the rise of a textile industry, far-reaching social legislation was set in motion, which culminated in 1893 with New Zealand becoming the first country in the world to grant voting rights to women. Thus, a small British settler colony far away from either Europe or the United States set the pace for women's emancipation at the end of the nineteenth century.

Maori Meeting House. Shown here is the entrance, made of carved wood, to the oldest tribal meeting house of the Maori, built in 1842. The chief carver, Raharuhi Rukupo, portrayed himself on the right. When the British colonial government proceeded with its land confiscations in 1860–1872, it transferred the house from the tribe to what is today the Museum of New Zealand. After lengthy litigations by the Maori, the government admitted in the 1990s to the illegality of the seizure.

European Imperialism in the Middle East and Africa

The British role in the Middle East during the eighteenth and early nineteenth centuries was much more modest, as was that of Europeans in general. Their function was limited to that of merchants, diplomats, or military advisors in an Ottoman Empire with a long tradition of conquering European lands. The situation changed at the end of the eighteenth century when Russia adopted a plan of southern expansion designed to drive the Ottomans back into Asia, take Istanbul, and convert it back into an eastern Christian capital. The other European powers sought to slow the Russian advances, with Great Britain assuming the lead role in protecting the Ottomans. In the long run, this policy of containment failed. Under Russian pressure, Ottoman territory shrank, the Europeans joined Russia in dismembering the Ottoman Empire, and a general imperialist competition for carving up other parts of the world—notably south and east Asia as well as Africa—ensued.

The Rising Appeal of Imperialism in the West

Empires (multiethnic, multi-linguistic, and multi-religious polities) were, as we have repeatedly seen in this book, of old lineage in world history. Their current embodiments were the Ottoman, Habsburg, and Russian Empires. The Russian Empire, a latecomer, saw its mission as replacing the Ottoman Empire as the dominant eastern

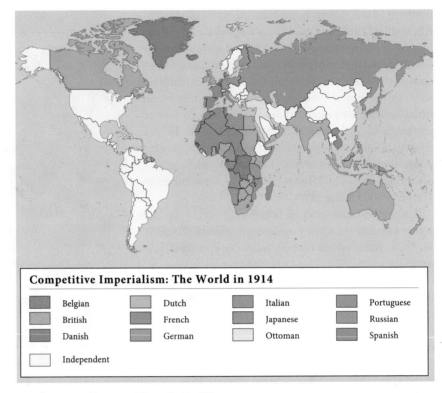

Competitive Imperialism: The World in 1914

▨	Belgian	▨	Dutch	▨	Italian	▨	Portuguese
▨	British	▨	French	▨	Japanese	▨	Russian
▨	Danish	▨	German	▨	Ottoman	▨	Spanish
▨	Independent						

MAP **26.4** **Competitive Imperialism: The World in 1914.**

European power and, by expanding eastward across the steppe, the leading Asian power. Its ambition became the catalyst for France, Great Britain, Belgium, Germany, and even late-industrializing Italy to embark on competitive imperialism in other parts of the world (see Map 26.4).

The Ottoman, Russian, and British Empires After the failure in 1815 of Napoleon's imperial schemes in both Egypt and Europe, Great Britain was the undisputed leading empire in the world. No country had a navy that could rival it, British trade posts and colonies were widely distributed over the world, and British colonialism in India was geared toward growing and exporting Indian cotton to fuel British industrialization. On the European continent, Britain worked to restore the monarchies of France, Austria, Prussia, and Russia so that they would balance each other as "great powers" in a **Concert of Europe**. Under no circumstances would Britain tolerate any renewed European imperialism of the kind that Napoleon had pursued. Meeting more or less regularly in congresses, the great powers were actually remarkably successful at maintaining peace in Europe. For an entire century not a single war engulfed the continent as a whole, throwing Europe into turmoil as had happened during the Napoleonic era.

The Concert of Europe, however, was less successful with curbing the imperial ambitions of its members reaching for lands outside the western European core. Russia did not hide its goal of throwing the Ottoman Empire (admitted to the Concert

Concert of Europe: International political system that dominated Europe from 1815 to 1914 and which advocated a balance of power among states.

for better protection of its integrity in 1856) back into "Asia," that is, Asia Minor or Anatolia. Great Britain, although it made itself the protector of the integrity of the Ottoman Empire, could at best only slow the ambitions of Russia. The movement to secure the independence of Greece (1821–1832) is a good example of this pattern. Russia, as the Greeks' coreligionist and protector, was centrally involved in initiating a pattern of ethno-linguistic nationalism that replaced constitutional nationalism as the organizing ideology for many Europeans in the nineteenth century.

The French Conquest of Algeria   Britain, unable to prevent an early spark of renewed French imperialism, directed outside Europe against Ottoman Algiers. The French naval expedition—the circumstances of which were described at the beginning of this chapter—conveniently took place in 1830 while British attention was still focused on the negotiations for Greece's independence. In its North African expedition, France followed an earlier short-lived blueprint of Napoleon's, which envisaged the creation of a Mediterranean empire encompassing Algeria and/or Egypt, prior to his lightning imperialism in Europe, possibly to signal to Britain the ease of reaching India via the Mediterranean.

Algeria was the crucial first step of a European power toward seizing provinces of the Ottoman Empire in competition with the Russians, while officially protecting its integrity. This first step was still full of hesitations and counter maneuvers. At first, the French stayed on a small coastal strip around Algiers and other places, encouraging the rise of indigenous leaders to take over from the Ottoman corsairs and Janissaries and share the country with the French. The British discreetly supported Algerian leaders with weapons to be used against the French.

In the longer run, however, coexistence proved impossible and the French military—against strong Algerian resistance—undertook an all-out conquest. The civilian colonial administration after 1870 encouraged large-scale immigration of French and Spanish farmers, who settled on small plots, as well as French corporate investments in vineyards and citrus plantations on the coast. The indigenous population of Arabs and Berbers, decimated by cholera epidemics in the 1860s, found itself largely reduced to less fertile lands in the interior.

The Conquest of Algiers. Algiers fell to France in 1830, a development driven in part by the efforts of King Charles X (1824–1830) to salvage his regime. Charles, a younger brother of Louis XVI (executed in the French Revolution), had sought a restoration of absolutist rule. Although Napoleon had fleetingly thought of conquering Algeria, Charles had no plans beyond the defeat of the Algerian dey. In spite of the French victory, republican revolutionaries overthrew Charles and established the constitutional monarchy of Louis-Philippe (r. 1830–1848).

Britain's Containment Policy   Great Britain adhered longer to the policy of protecting what remained of the Ottoman Empire. It also opposed Russia in its own backyard of central Asia, inaugurating what was called the **Great Game** against Russia in Asia with the first Anglo–Afghan war in 1838. Although Great Britain failed to occupy Afghanistan and make it an advance protectorate against the approaching Russians, it eventually succeeded in turning Afghanistan into a buffer state, keeping Russia one country away from India. A little later, in 1853–1856, Britain and France teamed up in the Crimean War to stop Russia from renewing its drive for Istanbul. This defeat, demonstrating the superiority of industrially produced new rifles and breech-loading artillery, chastened Russia for the next two decades.

In the second half of the nineteenth century, however, the ethnic–nationalist unification of Germany in 1870–1871, engineered by Prussia through a successful war against France (the Franco–Prussian War), destroyed the balance of the European Concert. Germany, much larger than Prussia and strengthened further through the annexation of the French industrializing region of Alsace-Lorraine, was now the dominant power in western Europe. Russia promptly exploited the new imbalance in Europe during anti-Ottoman uprisings in the Balkans in 1876. Leaving the humiliation of the Crimean War behind, Russian troops broke through Ottoman lines of defense and marched within a few miles of Istanbul. However, Great Britain, although no longer the arbiter of the European Concert, still had enough clout to force Russia into retreating.

British Imperialism in Egypt and Sudan   To prevent a repeat of the Russian invasion, Britain and the Ottomans agreed in 1878 to turn the island of Cyprus (off the Syrian coast) over to the British as a protectorate. This protectorate would have British advisors and troops, ready to defend Istanbul against a renewed Russian invasion. Thus, in the name of curbing Russian imperialism, Great Britain became an imperial power itself in the Mediterranean.

Events after the occupation of Cyprus, however, followed a dramatically different course. Instead of watching Russia, the commanders of the British navy squadron in Cyprus had to turn their attention to Egypt. This province was the wealthiest part of the Ottoman Empire. It was governed by a dynasty of autonomous rulers, beginning with Muhammad Ali (r. 1805–1848), an Albanian officer in the Ottoman army who assumed political control after Napoleon's troops had evacuated Egypt. An energetic statesman, Muhammad Ali reorganized the Nile-irrigated agricultural lands into large estates, producing Egyptian-bred long-staple cotton, and created his own independent army of conscripted Egyptians. Efforts to create a textile industry failed because he was unable (as an Ottoman governor) to establish high tariff barriers against British imports. Similarly, efforts to use his new army for a conquest of Istanbul and take over the Ottoman Empire were thwarted by a Great Britain anxious to protect the sultans. Even in failure, however, Muhammad Ali had a huge impact on Egypt. In a major cultural renewal, similar to the Tanzimat constitutional reforms in Istanbul, Cairo and Alexandria became centers of adaptation to European arts and letters as well as a reformed Islam.

Muhammad Ali's successors were less able rulers who incurred considerable debts, in part for the French-led construction of the Suez Canal in 1869. Britain took over a large part of the canal shares from the debt-ridden Egyptian ruler in 1857. A year later, Britain and France imposed a joint debt commission that garnished a portion of Egyptian tax revenue. Opposition in Egypt to this foreign interference grew in the following years, both inside and outside the Egyptian government. It culminated in 1881 with a revolt in the Egyptian army, endangering the continuation of the debt repayments.

British-initiated negotiations between the Ottoman sultan and the leader of the army revolt, Col. Ahmad Urabi (1841–1911, an early Egyptian—as opposed to foreign-descended—officer), over the issue of the debt collapsed after riots in Alexandria and a careless British bombardment of the port in response to Egyptian fortification efforts. Interventionists in London, fearing for their bonds and eager for more cotton imports from Egypt for the British textile industry, gained the upper hand. Overcoming the fiercely resisting Egyptian army, a British expeditionary force occupied Egypt in 1882.

The Ottoman sultan acquiesced to the occupation because the appointment of a British-appointed high commissioner, charged with the reorganization of the Egyptian finances, was announced to be only temporary. Costly campaigns by British-led Egyptian troops in Sudan during 1883–1885, however, derailed any early departure plans. Egypt had occupied Sudan in the 1820s and, as in Egypt, had made cotton a major export crop for the British textile industry. Sudanese resentment over the occupation and anxiety over the accompanying social changes became focused when Britain occupied Egypt and were expressed in a religiously inspired uprising in Khartoum in 1883.

> ### Strengthening the Empire
>
> "I have always, and do now recommend it [the purchase of the Suez Canal shares] to the country as a political transaction, and one which I believe is calculated to strengthen the Empire. That is the spirit in which it has been accepted by the country, which understands it though the two right honourable critics may not."
>
> —Benjamin Disraeli, Prime Minister of Britain (in office 1874–1880) addressing Parliament. In *The Nation. A Weekly Journal Devoted to Politics, Literature, Science and the Arts*, 22 (1876), p. 193.

Scottish Troops at the Sphinx, 1882. The British occupied Egypt as a means to secure the Suez Canal and guarantee the repayment of Egyptian debts. Subsequent negotiations with the Ottoman sultan for the status of Egypt failed, and the province became an unofficial protectorate of Britain. Although granted internal independence in 1922, Egypt remained in a semi-colonial relationship with Britain until 1956.

The leader of the uprising was Muhammad Ahmad Ibn Abdallah (1844–1885), head of an Islamic Sufi brotherhood and self-styled Mahdi ("rightly guided" or "Messiah"), sent to establish a realm of justice. After the Mahdi succeeded in driving the British–Egyptian forces from Sudan and establishing an independent state, he was left alone for the next decade.

Until the British slaughtered his forces at the Battle of Omdurman in 1898, Egypt's finances, aggravated by problems in Sudan, were sufficiently in disarray to keep the British focused on Egypt. On the one hand, the British wanted to put the Egyptian finances on a sound footing again, but, on the other hand, they wanted out so as to not be responsible for the country's governance. They had no plans yet for a full-fledged Mediterranean imperialism. As a compromise, they conceived of a conditional departure, with the right of return at times of internal unrest or external danger. The Ottoman sultan, however, refused to sign this compromise. He was grateful to Britain for recognizing Ottoman sovereignty but sought to avoid the responsibility of governance. A veritable dance around the question of governance developed. The two sides exchanged notes concerning the issue no fewer than 66 times, with neither side budging. In the end, Britain stayed for almost three-quarters of a century, running Egypt as an undeclared colony for the first 40 years. Without a clear plan, Britain had nonetheless transplanted the pattern of imperialism–colonialism it had first experimented with in India.

France's Tunisian Protectorate   The quid pro quo for Britain's acquisition of Cyprus in 1878 was for France to gain title to Tunisia. Similar to Algeria and Egypt, Tunisia was an autonomous Ottoman province, ruled by its own dynasty of *beys*. The dynasty had been founded by a Janissary officer in 1705 when the military ruling class began to shift from corsair raids against Christian shipping to the fiscal exploitation of the villages and nomadic tribes of the interior. Fertile northern Tunisia provided limited but fairly reliable tax revenues from olive oil, barley, wheat, fruits, and nuts. Annual tax expeditions to the south among the semi-nomadic sheep and camel tribes usually yielded few taxes and served mostly to demonstrate the dynasty's sovereignty.

The beys responded to the Western challenge early, being the first in the Muslim Middle East and North Africa to modernize their military and adopt a constitution (1857). With their more limited revenues, they hit the debt ceiling already in 1869, much earlier than the Ottomans and Egyptians, and had to accept a British–French–Italian debt commission for the reorganization of the country's revenues. When the French took over in 1881, they began with the same thankless task of balancing the budget as the British had in Egypt. Only later did they benefit from the French and Italian settlers they called in to the protectorate to intensify agriculture.

The Scramble for Africa

Competitive European imperialism exploded beyond the Mediterranean in early 1884 as Germany claimed its first protectorates in Africa. Conveniently, after having secured lands for his country, the German chancellor Otto von Bismarck (in various offices 1862–1890) called a conference in Berlin, which met from late 1884 to early 1885. The main agenda of the Berlin conference was a discussion on how the 14 invited European countries and the United States should "define the conditions under which future territorial annexations in Africa might be recognized." Bismarck's proposal of the main condition was "effective occupation," with the creation of "spheres of influence" around the occupied places. The first "protectorates," confirmed at the conference, were Cameroon in west central Africa for Germany and Congo as a private possession of King Leopold II of Belgium. The **scramble for Africa** was on (see Map 26.5).

Explorers, Missionaries, and the Civilizing Mission

Sub-Saharan Africa was still little known in Europe and poorly misunderstood to most Europeans in 1880. The Enlightenment had instilled curiosity about the geography, flora, fauna, and ethnology of Africa among the European reading public. But to endure the hardships of traveling in the savanna, rain forest, and desert required strong commitment. David

Scramble for Africa: Competition among European powers from 1884 to 1912 to acquire African colonies.

MAP 26.5 The Scramble for Africa.

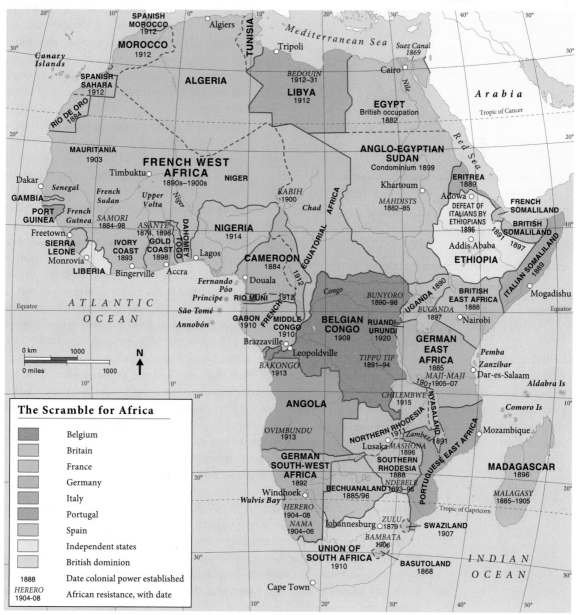

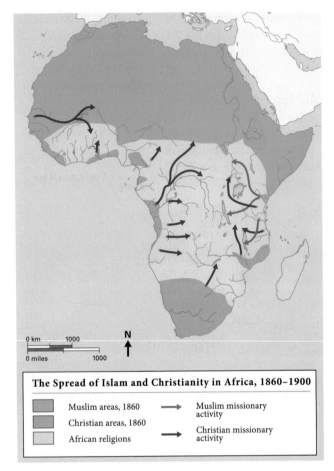

The Spread of Islam and Christianity in Africa, 1860–1900

▓ Muslim areas, 1860	→	Muslim missionary activity
▓ Christian areas, 1860		
░ African religions	→	Christian missionary activity

MAP 26.6 **The Spread of Islam and Christianity in Africa, 1860–1900.**

Civilizing mission:
Belief that European colonizers had a duty to extend the benefits of European civilization to "backward" peoples.

Livingstone (1813–1873), a tireless missionary and passionate opponent of slavery, was the best known among the pioneers who explored much of south central Africa. The European middle class was fascinated with the early explorers' tales of exotic and mysterious lands and peoples.

The generation of explorers after Livingstone was better equipped, led larger expeditions, and composed more precise accounts. Here, the outstanding figure was Henry Morton Stanley (1841–1904), a Welsh journalist who worked in the United States and became famous for his encounter with Livingstone ("Dr. Livingstone, I presume?") at Lake Tanganyika in east central Africa. Still, in spite of extensive explorations, European politicians at the end of the century had only the vaguest idea of the geography of the "dark continent."

Christian missionaries contributed little to the knowledge of Africa but through their preaching shaped a sense of both responsibility for and superiority to the Africans in the European public. They were at the forefront of the **civilizing mission**, the belief prevalent in the West in the nineteenth century that colonists had a duty to extend the benefits of civilization, that is, European civilization, to the "backward" people they ruled. In the earlier 1800s, the danger of malaria and yellow fever still confined missionaries to the coasts of Africa. Supported by missionary societies in Europe, they trained indigenous missionaries to translate tracts and scriptures for the conversion of Africans in the interior. When quinine (made from the bark of a Brazilian tree) became available in the middle of the 1800s, allowing for treatment of malaria, missionaries were able to follow their indigenous colleagues into the interior (see Map 26.6). At that time, tensions often arose between the two groups. African converts preached the gospel in the spirit of Christian equality, as did the former slave and later Anglican bishop Samuel Adjai Crowther (ca. 1809–1891); but many Western missionaries considered African Christianity to be contaminated by animist "superstitions" and did not accept Africans as equal. Malaria was one infectious disease that could be overcome, but the rising racism of the Victorian period went largely unchecked.

Conquest and Resistance in West Africa Colonialism on the coast of West Africa after 1885 was an outgrowth of the traditional trade-fort system. By the 1800s, the British had ousted the Dutch and the French from most of the trading forts and had become the dominant European presence in the region. Ghana is a particularly instructive example of the pattern of conquest and resistance. Ghana, previously known as the Gold Coast, was the land of the Ashante kingdom. The Ashante had emerged back in the time of the empire of Songhay, when they mined the gold of the Alkan fields that caravans carried across the Sahara. When gold declined in importance, the kingdom turned to the Atlantic slave trade and benefited handsomely from it. After the 1807 British prohibition of slavery, Ashante merchants switched to commodities, especially palm oil, used for the greasing of machinery and for making soap, that were in great demand in industrializing Europe.

But the Ashante and British traders were in constant conflict over the terms of trade in the forts. Disciplined and well-armed Ashante troops defeated the British repeatedly. Only in 1896, when the British sent regular troops with breech-loader rifles and machine guns to put down the Ashante with their now antiquated muskets, was Ghana finally turned into a protectorate. Later on, after well over a half-century of colonialism, the memory of Ashante nineteenth-century prowess was an important factor in the Ghanaian struggle for independence.

France lost its West African trade forts after the Seven Years' War (1756–1763) to Britain but later received one of them back, a fortified island at the mouth of the River Senegal. It was from this base that career-hungry French officers after 1850 carried out expeditions into the interior of the river rain forest, for alliances and trade purposes. In 1857 they came into conflict with Al-Hajj Umar (ca. 1791–1864), an Islamic reformer in the interior savanna who was in the process of building a state in what are today Guinea, Senegal, and Mali. The French barely survived a siege in a border fort and for decades were in no state to advance any further. Once the scramble was on, however, the West African Islamic state was doomed. In 1891, in the teeth of stiff resistance from the Islamists, the French began to carve out their huge colony in the steppe and savanna of West Africa that formed the core of their colonial empire.

Al-Hajj Umar was one of several West African Muslim religious scholars who became holy warriors (jihadists). Like other Middle Eastern and North African reformers, Umar was dismayed by the decline of Ottoman power. The reformers sought to rejuvenate Islam through a return to the study of the original Islamic sources. In the footsteps of what they perceived as the Prophet Muhammad's original state in Mecca, rising among the defeated unbelievers, the West African reformers forcibly converted black animists to Islam. In contrast to the Islamic kings and emperors of the previous centuries who made no efforts to convert their subjects, the jihadists of the 1800s succeeded in making Islam the dominant religion of West Africa.

Conquest and Resistance in East Africa

The arrival of colonialism in East Africa differed from the pattern in West Africa. Here, as early as the sixteenth century, the Portuguese had established trade forts in the south to acquire gold and ivory for their spice purchases in India. When Swahili patricians in the city-states

A Slave Who Became Bishop. The remarkable life of Samuel Adjai Crowther (ca. 1809–1891) shows that Africans and Asians also participated in the "civilizing mission." Born in Yorubaland in present-day West Africa, Crowther was enslaved as a young man but was rescued by the British navy and freed in 1821. He then converted to Christianity, and after training in London he was ordained an Anglican priest in 1841. He was appointed the first African Anglican bishop in 1864 and went on to produce Yoruba translations of the Bible and the Book of Common Prayer.

Ivory Merchants. Besides slaves, Zanzibar imported elephant tusks from the interior to be marketed for the carving of ivory jewelry and art objects. Principal buyers of the tusks were British, German, and Arab traders.

farther north resisted this intrusion into their traditional Indian Ocean trade, the Portuguese responded with piracy and the construction of coastal forts in their midst. But the arrival of the Dutch with more powerful and numerous ships in the 1630s to take over the spice trade forced the Portuguese to curtail their East African engagement. An Omani Arab expeditionary force exploited the reduced Portuguese presence in 1698 by conquering the Swahili city-state of Mombasa after a 2-year siege. Oman had long-standing trade relations with East Africa and seized its opportunity to expand its limited domestic agricultural base on the Arabian peninsula. Once in control, the Omanis developed a flourishing plantation system for sugar, rice, grain, and cotton on the coastal islands, along with slaves imported from the African interior. In the 1820s, the Omanis—by now under their separate sultan residing on the island of Zanzibar—began to specialize in cloves, becoming the main exporters of this precious spice on the world market. Thanks to the Omanis, the Swahili coast was prosperous again.

Zanzibar was the staging ground for adventurers, explorers, and missionaries in the nineteenth century to enter the African interior. It was here that they vied for places to occupy and spheres of influence to declare. Accordingly, in 1886 Germany received the lion's share on the coast and in the interior, Belgium gave up its claims in return for being recognized in the Congo, and Zanzibar somewhat later became a British protectorate. In its colony of Tanganyika (in current Tanzania), Germany used forced labor for the growing of cotton, provoking the fierce but in the end brutally suppressed Maji Maji rebellion of 1905–1907.

Atrocities and Genocides   Similar atrocities stalked the European civilizing mission. As Germany was quelling rebellion in Tanganyika, it led a ferocious campaign on the other side of the continent against the Herero and Nama people of southwest Africa (modern Namibia). In their determination to establish colonial rule in the region, the German general staff ordered the extermination of the Herero in terms that can be described only as genocide: "I believe that the nation as such must be destroyed," commented General Lothar von Trotha (1848–1920 [TROW-tah]). From 1904 to 1908 the war on the Herero resulted in 80,000 deaths. North of Namibia, King Leopold II (r. 1865–1909) of Belgium turned his personal colony of the Congo into a vast forced-labor camp for the production of rubber. The rubber tree, native to South America, gained great importance in Europe for a variety of industrial applications. Leopold was particularly sadistic in his exploitation of the native workforce, using beatings and mutilations if collection quotas were not filled. An astonishing 3,000,000 Congolese were either killed or starved to death. The horror of the Belgian Congo was the setting for Joseph Conrad's *Heart of Darkness* (1902), perhaps the most powerful anti-imperialist novel of the time and still widely read today. It was also the catalyst for Mark Twain's virulently satirical attack on the Belgian exploitation of the Congolese, *King Leopold's Soliloquy* (1905).

Colonial Atrocities. The German garrison at Windhoek, in present-day Namibia, was besieged by the native Herero people in 1904. Retaliation was swift and violent, with the colonial authorities encaging prisoners in concentration camps, which in turn led to reprisals, such as the massacre of railroad workers shown here.

The scramble finally ended in 1912 with the French declaration of a protectorate over Morocco. By this time, the political competition in Europe had narrowed to the struggle between Germany and Great Britain for political predominance in western Europe. Italy's imperialist dreams were stymied by its crushing defeat at the battle of Adowa in 1896, in which one-third of its army was killed by Ethiopian forces (see Patterns Up Close). Ethiopia emerged from the scramble as the only non-colonized state in Africa. French and British rivalry in Africa, which had cropped up during the scramble and had even led to a confrontation at Fashoda over the control of Sudan in 1898, ended between 1905 and 1911, when Britain allied with France to counterbalance Germany. As a result of this alliance, Britain recognized France's interests in Morocco, adjacent to the two French territories of Algeria and Tunisia, over protests by Germany.

Western Imperialism and Colonialism in Southeast Asia

Parallel to developments in Africa, the new imperialism made its appearance also in southeast Asia, specifically Indonesia, the Philippines, Vietnam, Cambodia, and Laos. While the new imperialism in southeast Asia was an outgrowth of the earlier trade-fort presence of Portugal, Spain, and the Netherlands, it also included the return of France to imperial glory.

The Dutch in Indonesia

The Dutch were heirs of the Portuguese, who had set up forts that traded for spices in Indonesia during the sixteenth century. For 100 years, they were the middlemen for the distribution of spices from Portugal to northern Europe. But after liberating themselves from Habsburg–Spanish rule, the Netherlands displaced Portugal from its dominant position as a spice importer to Europe. From 1650 to 1750, the Netherlands was the leading naval power in the world. After 1750, they shifted from the trade of spices in their trade forts in Indonesia to the planting of cash crops, such as sugar, cacao, coffee, and tobacco—the mild warm weather commodities to which Europeans were addicted and which they consumed in ever larger quantities. The aim of the full colonization of Indonesia during the nineteenth century was to profit from European industrial demand for agricultural and mineral commodities.

Early Indonesia   The western part of southeast Asia, comprising today's Indonesia, is a complex of well over 17,000 islands, fewer than half of which are inhabited. The term "Indonesia" dates to the eighteenth century, denoting sparsely inhabited large and small tropical islands to the southeast of India. The five largest and today most densely populated islands are, from west to east, Sumatra, Java, Borneo, Sulawesi (Celebes), and New Guinea. The earliest inhabitants were prehistoric foragers; the first agrarian–urban settlers were speakers of Austronesian languages. The Austronesians were intrepid sailors across the Pacific and Indian Oceans who settled islands as far away as Hawaii off the Americas and Madagascar off of Africa.

In Sumatra and the Malay Peninsula, chieftainships gave way to a first kingdom around 700 CE, organized around Buddhist religion and law. The kingdom was mostly coastal and commercial, trading pepper, nutmeg, cinnamon, cardamom, cloves, ivory, gold, and tin to the Middle East and China. In the following centuries, it extended its influence to islands as far as the Philippines in the east and the mainland in the north.

Islam gained converts in Indonesia only slowly in the face of stiff Buddhist opposition, but from about 1300, indigenous Indonesian rulers began to convert to Islam. The leading Islamic sultanate was Aceh [AT-shay] (1496–1903) on the western island of Sumatra, a major producer of pepper. In the sixteenth century, when the Portuguese rose to dominance in the Indian Ocean, the Ottomans supported it with firearms.

Portuguese and Dutch Trade Forts   Portuguese sailors arrived in the strategic Strait of Malacca (separating Sumatra from the Malay Peninsula and dividing the Indian Ocean from the Chinese Sea) in 1511, defeating the local sultanate and establishing a fort in the Malaysian capital, Malacca. Their main interest, however, given the power of Aceh on Sumatra, was to push onward to the spice islands of Maluku (today the Maluccas) in eastern Indonesia (between Sulawesi and New Guinea), where they established a trade fort in 1522, amid several Islamic island lords. From there, the Portuguese pushed on to China and Japan, where they arrived in the mid-1500s. Overall, their role in the Indonesian spice trade remained small, and indigenous Islamic merchants maintained their dominance.

After declaring their independence from Spain in 1581, the northern provinces of the Netherlands formed the Republic of the United Netherlands and pushed for their own overseas network of trade forts. In 1602, the Dutch government chartered the Dutch United East India Company (VOC), which spearheaded the expansion of Dutch possessions in India and southeast Asia. After a slow start, the company erected outposts on many Indonesian islands and in the mid-1600s founded Batavia (today Jakarta) on the island of Java as its main southeast Asian center. The VOC was by far the largest and wealthiest commercial company in the world during the seventeenth century, with a fleet consisting of nearly 5,000 merchant ships supported by large naval and land forces.

When the Dutch *stadhouder* (ruler) of the Netherlands, William of Orange (1650–1702), became king of England after the English Glorious Revolution of 1688 that imposed constitutional limits on monarchical rule, the Dutch and English overseas trade interests were pooled. Great Britain (as the country was known after

England's union with Scotland in 1707) deepened its Indian interests through the English East India Company, and the Dutch pursued their engagements in Indonesia. Like the British Company in India, the VOC was increasingly drawn during the early 1700s into dynastic wars. Supported by some 1,000 Dutch soldiers and 3,000 indigenous auxiliaries, the VOC established peace in 1755 in the fragmenting Islamic sultanate of Banten (1527–1808). Thereafter, it became the de facto government on the island of Java over a set of pacified Islamic protectorates.

Several decades earlier than its British counterpart in India, the VOC fell on hard times. Governing and maintaining troops was expensive. VOC employees often paid their expenses out of their own pockets since contact with the Netherlands in pretelegraph times was slow and sporadic. In the late eighteenth century, trade shifted from spices to bulk commodities, such as sugar, cacao, coffee, tobacco, indigo, and cotton. The inability of the VOC to shift from spices to commodities, requiring investments in plantations and accompanying transportation infrastructures, was the decisive factor which led, in 1799, to the liquidation of the VOC. Similar to the British experience in India, the government of the Netherlands then became the ruler of Indonesian possessions that had grown from trade forts into small colonies, surrounded by dependent indigenous principalities as well as independent sultanates.

Cultivation system: Dutch colonial scheme of compulsory labor and plantation of crops imposed on indigenous Indonesian self-sufficiency farmers.

Dutch Colonialism

The Dutch government took the decisive step toward investments in 1830 when Belgium separated from the large Dutch kingdom created after the Napoleonic Wars to form an independent Catholic monarchy. Faced with severe budgetary constraints and cut off from industrializing Belgium, the Dutch government adopted the **cultivation system** in Indonesia. According to this system, indigenous Indonesian subsistence farmers were forced into compulsory planting and labor schemes which required them to either grow government crops on

Indonesia in the Nineteenth Century. A traditional house in north Sumatra, with animal stables in the bottom and human living quarters on top. (*a*) Dutch judges meting out harsh sentences, including death by hanging, against Indonesians. (*b*) Workers in Batavia (today Jakarta), ca. 1830, stacking tropical wood for export in the harbor. (*c*)

(a)

(b)

(c)

20 percent of their land or work for 60 days on Dutch plantations. Overnight, the Dutch and collaborating Indonesian ruling classes turned into landowners. They reaped huge profits while Indonesian subsistence farmers, having to replace many of their rice paddies with commercial crops, suffered in many places from famines. In the course of the nineteenth century, Indonesia became a major or even the largest exporter of sugar, tea, coffee, palm oil, coconut products, tropical hardwoods, rubber, quinine, and pepper to the industrial nations.

To keep pace with demand, the Dutch pursued a program of systematic conquest and colonization. In a half-dozen campaigns, they conquered the Indonesian archipelago, finally subduing the most stubborn opponents, the Muslim guerillas of Aceh, in 1903 (see Map 26.7). Even then, the conquest was incomplete and inland rain forests remained outside Dutch government control. Conquered lands were turned over to private investors who established plantations. To deflect criticism at home and abroad, the Dutch government also introduced some reform measures. In 1870 they liberated farmers from the compulsory planting of government crops, and in 1901 they issued an "ethical policy," announcing measures such as land distribution, irrigation, and education. Severe underfunding, however, kept these measures largely on paper; and it was clear that the profits from colonialism were more important than investment for indigenous people.

Spain in the Philippines

Adjacent to the Indonesian islands in the northeast were the Philippines. Here, the Spanish had built their first trade fort of Manila shortly after conquering Mexico from the Aztecs. Manila served as a port from which to trade with China. Using

MAP **26.7** **Western Imperialism in Southeast Asia, 1870–1914.**

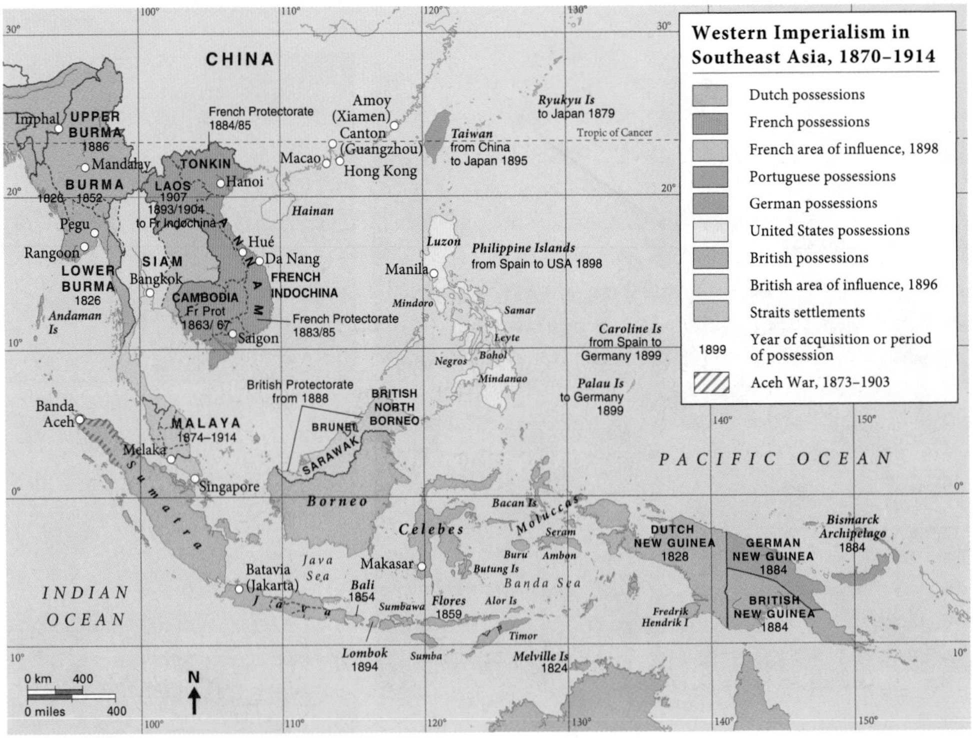

Mexican silver, Spanish merchants bought Chinese luxury manufactures. Manila expanded only slowly, suffering from constant raids by indigenous highlanders from the interior, Islamic rulers from the southern islands, and Dutch interlopers. Imperial conquest had to await the later eighteenth century, and colonization followed in the middle of the nineteenth century with the introduction of sugarcane.

Galleons and Trade with China   Spain expanded early on from the Americas farther west in order to prevent Portugal from claiming all the lucrative spice islands of Indonesia. A Portuguese explorer in Spanish service, Ferdinand Magellan (d. ca. 1480–1521), successfully crossed the sea channels at the southern tip of South America in 1520 and, on a journey that took his fleet eventually around the entire globe, discovered what later became known as the "Philippines," in honor of King Phillip II of Spain. It took another half-century, however, before Spain could spare ships and men for the implantation of a first trade fort and small colony. This fort, Manila, became the base for subsequent biannual silver fleets from Mexico. Spanish merchants based in Mexico, from where Manila was administered, benefited greatly from the trade of silver for Chinese silk, porcelain, and lacquerware. Thus, Manila began as a small sub-colony of the large Spanish colony of Mexico or New Spain.

The Philippines are a collection of some 7,000 islands, with the four largest, from north to south, being Luzon, Visaya, Mindanao, and Sulu. The earliest inhabitants were prehistoric islanders, followed ca. 2000 BCE by Austronesians who settled mostly on the coasts, growing rice and exploiting maritime resources. Similar to the inhabitants of the Indonesian islands, the Filipinos were animists influenced to varying degrees by Indian and Chinese cultures. As the Spanish gradually expanded their hold on the coastal lowlands outside Manila on Luzon and Visaya (where the local king had converted to Christianity), they established estates, thus advancing from trade-fort imperialism to the beginnings of territorial expansion.

Incipient Colonialism   The indigenous farmers on the Philippine estates were obliged to deliver rents, paid in kind, in the form of rice and animals, to ensure the food supply for some 30,000 inhabitants of Manila, mostly merchants of Spanish, Chinese, and Japanese origin. Warrior chieftains outside Spanish lands who converted were confirmed as owners on their lands and transformed themselves into a Hispanicized landowner class. By the early eighteenth century, the Spanish controlled enough of a critical mass on the two islands of Luzon and Visaya that they were able to establish a regular administration for fiscal and juridical matters. The beginnings of colonialism in the Philippines had emerged.

The balance sheet for the colonial administration was always in the red, however, since the fiscal revenue did not yield surpluses and villagers produced only small quantities of exportable ginger, cinnamon, and gold. Much money had to be invested in defending the Spanish-controlled territory from attacks by independent Filipinos in the mountainous upland interiors of Luzon and Visaya who resisted conquest and conversion. Even more vexing were raids supported by Islamic sultanates which had formed in the south on the basis of trading hardwoods for luxuries with China.

To make matters worse, a brief British occupation of Manila during the Seven Years' War (1756–1763) demonstrated that Spain lacked the means to protect itself against the rising naval and merchant power of Great Britain in the China trade.

On Filipino Ethnic Nationalism

"Does your Excellency know the spirit of (my) country? If you did, you would not say that I am 'a spirit twisted by a German education,' for the spirit that animates me I already had since childhood, before I learned a word of German. My spirit is 'twisted' because I have been reared among injustices and abuses which I saw everywhere, because since a child I have seen many suffer stupidly and because I also have suffered.... And 'twisted' like my spirit is that of hundreds of thousands of Filipinos who have not yet left their miserable homes, who speak no other language except their own, and who, if they could write or express their thoughts, would make my *Noli me tangere* [one of Rizal's novels] very tiny indeed, and with their volumes there would be enough to build pyramids for the corpses of all the tyrants ..."

—José Rizal. *La Solidaridad*, a newsletter published by the Propaganda Movement, February 15, 1890. In Diosdado G. Capino, Minerva A. Gonzalez, and Filipinas A. Piñeda, *Rizal's Life, Works and Writings: Their Impact on Our National Identity*, p. 104. Quezon City, Philippines: Publisher's Association of the Philippines, 1977.

Using Indian cottons and Chinese middlemen, the British diverted much of the American silver trade to India, calling into question the entire rationale for Spanish trade-fort commerce and limited colonialism in the Philippines. The last galleon bringing silver from Mexico sailed in 1815.

Full Colonialism   Major reforms, shifting the economy from silver to commodity exports, began at the same time, motivated by the Spanish loss of Mexico to independence. These reforms resulted in the liberalization of trade and the beginnings of commercial agriculture for export. Ports were opened to ships from all countries, discrimination against Chinese settlements ended, and Spanish administrators and churchmen lost their trade privileges. Foreign entrepreneurs cleared rain forests and exported hardwoods. On the new land they grew cash crops, such as sugar, tobacco, hemp (for ropes and sacks), indigo (as a dye), coffee, and cotton. Large-scale rice farms replaced a great number of small-scale village self-sufficiency plots, and thus, commercialization even invaded subsistence agriculture.

Strong resistance by landowners against a reform of the land regime and tax system until the very end of the nineteenth century, however, assured that Spain did not benefit much from the liberalization of trade. Additionally, Philippine society stratified rapidly into a wealthy minority and a large mass of landless rural workers and urban day laborers. Manila had over 100,000 inhabitants in the early nineteenth century. This stratification, however, was very different from that in the Americas. There was no real Creole class, that is, a Spanish–Philippine upper stratum of landowners and urban people. Although the French Revolution and subsequent Napoleonic upheavals in Spain had their impact on the islands, agitation for independence and constitutionalism was largely limited to urban intellectuals. The Philippines remained a colony, producing no revenue and still demanding costly administrative—especially fiscal—reforms and infrastructural investments, both of which Spain was unable to afford.

The first stirrings of Filipino nationalism, primarily among Hispanicized Filipinos of mixed Spanish and indigenous or Chinese descent, made themselves felt in the second half of the nineteenth century. The principal spokesman was José Rizal (1861–1896), whose subversive novels were a response to the Spanish justification of continued colonialism.

Colonial authorities promptly arrested Rizal for his activities, banishing him to Hong Kong; but he returned to Manila in 1892, inspiring both overt and underground resistance groups. One of these groups, Katipunan, operated in secret, advocating Filipino independence through armed struggle. In 1896 the government discovered the existence of the organization in Manila and executed hundreds of revolutionaries, including Rizal, before firing squads. But it was unable to destroy Katipunan in the provinces, and the two sides agreed in 1897 to a truce which included the end of armed revolt in return for exile of the leadership in Hong Kong.

Philippine–American War   Although it appeared that the colonial government was successful in suppressing the Filipino revolt for independence, events took a dramatic turn when the Spanish–American War broke out in 1898. A mysterious explosion of an American warship in Cuba—newly autonomous under Spanish suzerainty—had led to mutual declarations of war. The two sides fought their first battle in Manila Bay, where the United States routed a Spanish squadron. An American ship fetched the exiled Filipino rebel Emilio Aguinaldo (1869–1964) from Hong Kong, and he quickly defeated the Spanish and declared independence. Over four centuries of Spanish colonialism in the Pacific had come to an end.

American Soldiers in the Philippines. The victory of the United States over Spain in 1898 and its decision to annex the Philippines created for the first time an American overseas empire. Resistance was immediate, and a brutal war against Philippine fighters lasted from 1902 until 1913, with isolated outbreaks continuing until Philippine independence in 1946. Here, American troops dig in and fortify an outpost in Luzon.

After 4 months of fighting, Spain was defeated not only in Cuba, Puerto Rico, and Guam but also in the Philippines. The United States and Spain made peace at the end of 1898, ignoring the independent Philippine government in their agreement. Accordingly, US forces took possession of Manila in 1899 and within a year defeated the troops of the protesting Filipino government under the elected president, Emilio Aguinaldo. The Filipinos shifted to guerilla war, but US troops were able to capture Aguinaldo in 1901. The United States declared the war over in 1902 but had to fight remnants of the guerillas as well as southern rebels until 1913. Thus, the United States had joined the European race for imperial and colonial control of the non-Western world.

The French in Vietnam

North of Indonesia and west of the Philippines is Vietnam. Indochina, the peninsula on which Vietnam is located, also includes Cambodia, Laos, and Thailand. Portuguese monks were the first western Europeans to go to Indochina in the sixteenth century, seeking converts among the Buddhist, neo-Confucian, and animist indigenous inhabitants. French imperial and colonial involvement began in 1858, a time when Europe was industrializing and competition in the Concert of Europe was beginning to spill over from the Balkans and Middle East into Africa. At first focusing on the south of Indochina, France gradually expanded northward, establishing protectorates over the Nguyen royal dynasty, which was the last of a succession of kingdoms that had begun in the third century CE.

French Interests in Vietnam   As discussed in earlier chapters, in the later first and early second millennia CE Vietnam was intermittently part of China, from where the country received strong Buddhist, Confucian, and Daoist cultural impulses. Independent dynasties reemerged after 1400, and by the later eighteenth century a royally sponsored Vietnamese culture developed, replacing the original

Saigon Street Scene, 1915.
As they did in other areas in their empire, the French pursued what they termed their "civilizing mission." What this meant in practical terms was the importation of French culture, and urban planning including architecture as well as language, education, and literature. The French increasingly looked at their empire as "overseas France" and took it for granted that their subjects would want to adopt French culture and practices.

Chinese script with its own reformed script. French royal efforts in the seventeenth and early eighteenth centuries to sponsor Catholic missions and trading companies were largely unsuccessful and ended altogether after the lost Seven Years' War (1756–1763). When France renewed these efforts after the French Revolution and Napoleon, it was rebuffed by the Vietnamese kings, who shared Chinese concerns about the Western challenge. Both China and Vietnam adopted a policy of isolationism as their first answer to Western patterns of challenge.

The French, however, were not deterred. Napoleon had toyed with the idea of a Mediterranean empire that included either Algeria or Egypt before embarking on his campaign of European imperialism. The French then actually conquered Algeria in 1830–1847, as we have seen earlier in this chapter. The ruler who was subsequently most active in pushing for the renewal of Napoleon's imperialism outside Europe was his nephew, Napoleon III (r. 1848–1870). This self-styled emperor involved himself in a variety of short-lived ventures in Mexico, China, and Japan. His one enduring conquest was that of "Cochinchina," that is, southern Vietnam, in 1858–1862. Taking as a pretext the renewed torture and execution of French missionaries and Vietnamese converts, the French dispatched a squadron that occupied the sparsely inhabited Mekong River delta in 1858–1862, annexing it as a protectorate.

Conquest and Colonialism   Serious colonization efforts by the French had to await the scramble for the division of Africa and what remained of Asia in the mid-1880s. After Napoleon III's fall from power as a result of the lost war against Prussia and the establishment of the Third Republic, opinions among politicians about the wisdom of a French empire were divided. But when pro-imperialists came to power in 1883, the French challenged China a year later in a successful war for the control of northern Vietnam. In contrast to the thinly settled south, the Red River estuary with the capital of the kingdom, Hanoi, in the north was densely populated. When the imperialist frenzy was at its peak during the Berlin conference of 1884–1885 for the partition of Africa, the French conquerors united southern and northern Vietnam into the French colony of Indochina. Two members of the deposed Vietnamese dynasty took to the mountains and waged a guerilla war against the occupation, called the Black Flag Revolt. But by the early twentieth century the French had captured both and were in full control.

The French government and French entrepreneurs invested substantial sums in the Mekong delta. They established plantations for the production of coffee, tea, and rubber. Indigenous rice farmers had to deliver 40 percent of their crops to the colonial government. Hanoi was made the seat of the colonial administration in 1902 and was enlarged as an architecturally French city. The port of Haiphong, downriver from Hanoi, became the main entry point for ships to load agricultural commodities for export. The commodities for the world market, which French West Africa largely lacked, existed in Vietnam, Cambodia, and Laos (the latter two added in 1893–1904).

Early Nationalism Given Vietnam's long tradition of Confucian scholar-administrators, it was only a question of time before the pre-1858 spirit of anti-foreign Vietnamese patriotism reasserted itself. The driving force in this reassertion was Phan Boi Chau (1867–1940), trained by his father and other scholars and an eyewitness of the crushing by the French of a protest by scholars in 1885. Initially a royalist harking back to the glory of the last dynasty, in 1904 Phan Boi Chau founded the first of a number of small groups, mostly abroad, devoted to driving out the French. He spent some time in Japan, where he was active among Vietnamese students for a number of years, buoyed by the Japanese victory over Russia in 1904–1905 and seeking support from Japanese politicians.

Phan Boi Chau's activities and writings inspired antitax demonstrations and a provincial uprising in Vietnam in 1908–1909, which the French suppressed harshly. Under French pressure, the Japanese expelled Phan Boi Chau from Japan in 1909. By 1912, he had given up his royalism, and from then on a newly formed nationalist grouping favored the expulsion of the French and the formation of a Vietnamese democratic republic.

> ### Creating a Revolutionary Party
>
> "Inukai [Inukai Tsuyoshi, leader of the Progressive Party in Japan] went on to ask me: 'Have you organized a revolutionary party?' At that moment I felt so ashamed I wished to die, knowing that there was not yet any real revolutionary party in our country. Reluctantly, however, I replied: 'An organization there is, but its influence is negligible, as if it did not exist.'"
>
> —Phan Boi Chau. *Overturned Chariot: The Autobiography of Phan-Boi-Chau.* Translated by Vinh Sinh and Nicholas Wickenden, SHAPS Library of Translations, p. 89. Honolulu: University of Hawaii Press, 1999.

Putting It All Together

Ever since Vladimir Lenin, the founder of the Soviet Union, declared in his famous 1916 work that imperialism was "the highest stage of capitalism" (adopting a similar thesis first suggested by the English historian John A. Hobson in 1902), scholars have hotly debated the topic of whether or not the capitalist industrialization process in Europe, North America, and Japan needed colonies to sustain its growth. Most recent historians, beginning with David K. Fieldhouse in 1984, have come to the conclusion that imperialism and colonialism were not needed and that all the mineral and agrarian commodities crucial for industrialization during the first and second Industrial Revolutions could have been bought from independent countries on the world market. It so happened, of course, that Great Britain had transformed India from trade-fort imperialism to territorial imperialism just prior to its industrialization and used Indian cotton as raw material for its textile factories. But this raises the reverse question: Would industrialization have happened had Great Britain not conquered India? This counterfactual question has no easy answer.

Perhaps a better approach to finding an answer is to think of trade-fort and territorial imperialism as world-historical patterns of long standing. By contrast, industrialization was a much later phenomenon that arose out of the application of the New Science to practical mechanical uses, of which steam engines and textile factories were the first examples, appearing around 1800. Thus, old patterns of imperialism continued to exist during the rise of the new pattern of industrialization. These old patterns received a tremendous amplification as a result of the new power that industrialization bestowed on the European countries. Therefore, the new imperialism of

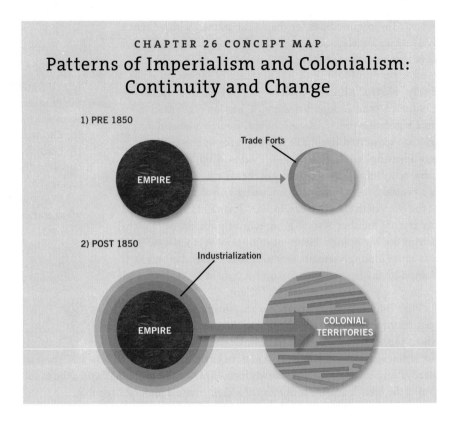

CHAPTER 26 CONCEPT MAP
Patterns of Imperialism and Colonialism: Continuity and Change

the nineteenth century and the colonialism which followed in its wake can be seen as phenomena in which old patterns continued but were superimposed on and enlarged by the patterns of industrial power (see Concept Map).

Review and Respond

1. What were the role and activities of the British East India Company, and why was this company important in the rise of British imperialism?

2. How did Australia and New Zealand evolve as British settler colonies?

3. What was the European Concert, and how did it affect the new imperialism?

4. How did the "scramble for Africa" originate, how did it evolve, and what were its results?

5. Compare and contrast Dutch, Spanish, and French imperialism and colonialism in southeast Asia.

▶ For additional resources, including maps, primary sources, visuals, and quizzes, please go to www.oup.com/us/vonsivers. Please see the Further Resources section at the back of the book for additional readings and suggested websites.

Thinking Through Patterns

▶ **What new patterns emerged in the transition from trade-fort imperialism to the new imperialism?**

During the early modern period, European monarchs commissioned merchant marine companies, such as the British East India Company and the Dutch United East India Company (VOC), to avoid military expeditions of their own but still receive a share of the profits of trade. The mariner-merchants built coastal forts for storage and protection, granted to them by the local rulers with whom they traded. In the seventeenth and eighteenth centuries, much larger trading companies were formed, in which investors pooled their resources and large numbers of mariner-merchants now served in dozens of trade forts overseas. In India and Indonesia, these companies became too big to fail and resorted to their governments in England and the Netherlands to rescue them. Thus, through the back door, governments found themselves forced to conquer and to colonize—they had become imperialist-colonizers.

Great Britain was the pioneer in the development of exportable agricultural and mineral commodities in its colonies for the support of its expanding industries. By the middle of the nineteenth century, other industrializing countries either embarked on imperial conquests or shifted to full colonialism in order to obtain necessary commodities. As a rule, labor for the production of these commodities was scarce. Workers had to be recruited forcibly and were routinely paid low wages.

▶ **How did European colonizers develop their colonies economically, given that they were industrializing themselves at the same time?**

▶ **What were the experiences of the indigenous people under the new imperialism? How did they adapt to colonialism? How did they resist?**

Many imperial conquests involved protracted campaigns that claimed many indigenous victims. If one of the goals of the ensuing colonization was commodity production, the indigenous population was recruited, often forcibly and with low wages. Resistance to European colonialism manifested itself in ethnic nationalism, as demonstrated by the examples of José Rizal, Phan Boi Chau, and Emilio Aguinaldo discussed in this chapter. In Australia and New Zealand and other colonies where European settlement was encouraged, colonial governments or settlers ousted the indigenous population from the most fertile lands, often in the face of fierce resistance.

Chapter 27 | Creoles and Caudillos

1790-1917 | LATIN AMERICA AND THE CARIBBEAN IN THE NINETEENTH CENTURY

LATIN AMERICA AND THE CARIBBEAN

When the French Revolution broke out in 1789 a young Caribbean mulatto named Vincent Ogé (ca. 1755–1791) was on business in France. His extended family of free *Creoles*—inhabitants born in the Caribbean or Louisiana—owned a coffee plantation and a commercial business with slaves on Saint-Domingue [SAN-dow-MANG] (later Haiti). Caught up in the excitement of 1789, Ogé embraced the French revolutionary principles of liberty, equality, and fraternity with great enthusiasm and quickly became an adherent of French constitutional nationalism: As we saw in Chapter 22, the former absolute monarchy in France was swiftly

Seeing Patterns

▶ Which factors in the complex ethnic and social structures of Latin America were responsible for the emergence of authoritarian politicians or caudillos?

▶ Why did Latin American countries, after achieving independence, opt for a continuation of mineral and agricultural commodity exports?

▶ How do the social and economic structures of this period continue to affect the course of Latin America today?

reorganized to incorporate a written constitution and an elected National Assembly. As part of the general atmosphere of emancipation so prevalent during the early part of the revolution, he joined the antislavery Society of the Friends of Blacks in Paris and demanded that French constitutionalism be extended to Saint-Domingue.

In a short time the society's efforts appeared to bear fruit. In March 1790, the National Assembly granted self-administration to the colonies, and Ogé returned to Saint-Domingue full of hope that he would be able to participate as a free citizen in the island's governance. But the governor stubbornly refused to admit mulattoes as citizens of the new order. Ogé and a group of friends therefore joined a band of 250–300 freedmen and took up arms to carve out a stronghold for themselves in the north of the island by arresting plantation owners and occupying their properties. One plantation owner later testified that the rebels looted and killed during their uprising but that Ogé himself was a man of honor who treated his prisoners fairly and even left him in the possession of his personal arms.

After only a few weeks of fighting, however, government troops pushed the rebels into the Spanish part of the island. Ogé and his followers

To Preserve Their Freedom. The great African American painter Jacob Lawrence (1917–2000) depicted the Haitian Revolution in a series of 41 paintings between 1937–1938. The painting here shows the defeat of Napoleon's efforts to restore slavery by force in 1802.

surrendered after being guaranteed their safety. But the Spanish governor, washing his hands of his prisoners, turned them over to the French. After a trial for insurrection in February 1791, Ogé and 19 followers were condemned to death. Ogé suffered particularly barbaric tortures before expiring: He was condemned to perhaps the old French regime's most painful mode of public execution: being broken on the wheel. Executioners strapped him spread-eagle on a wagon wheel and systematically broke his bones with an iron bar until he was dead.

The Ogé insurrection was the opening chapter of the Haitian Revolution, which began in August 1791 and culminated with the achievement of independence under a black government in 1804. It was the third of the great constitutional-nationalist revolutions—after the American and French Revolutions—that inaugurated, with the Industrial Revolution, the modern period of world history. While the other two revolutions were events in which aristocratic rule ended and the middle classes assumed power, the Haitian Revolution was a much more radical movement in which the underclass of slaves liberated itself from both aristocratic and middle-class control. Indeed, the presence of a free, black republic in the New World both haunted slave owners in the Americas and lent itself to strengthening abolitionist sentiment. Thus, it presaged the eventual arrival of full emancipation of blacks in the United States and other states in the region.

After Haiti, Latin America followed with its own wars of independence, which took place during and immediately after the Napoleonic era and also produced constitutional revolutions. In some Spanish colonies Creoles and mulattoes collaborated, but in most colonies the Creoles—like the white colonists in the North American colonies—were by far the chief beneficiaries of the fruits of independence. Given their European cultural and intellectual connections, many Creoles found it relatively easy to adapt to the new challenges of modernity. After independence, wealthy Creoles often traveled to Europe, sent their children to France or England for education, and imported industrial consumer goods from Great Britain. Moreover, most of the Latin American regimes—with the prominent exception of Brazil—abolished slavery before mid-century. As in the United States, however, the lower classes of *mestizos* (mixed Native Americans and Europeans) and mulattoes and the underclasses of Native Americans and blacks were for the most part excluded from the benefits of modernization. For much of the nineteenth century, too, authoritarian **caudillo** regimes allied with landowners and army generals governed under the pretense of constitutional nationalism.

In the economy, the Creole landowners themselves had little interest in industrialization, which would have meant a shifting of scarce labor from

Caudillo: Latin American strongman or dictator.

the estates to factories in cities. They found it much more profitable instead to adopt the role of suppliers to the industrial states through mineral and agricultural exports until the very end of the nineteenth century. Latin America thus took a path of development that diverged substantially from that of Europe and most of North America after the initial constitutional-nationalist revolutions.

Independence, Authoritarianism, and Political Instability

As in the United States and France, the growth pattern of constitutional nationalism in Latin America was slow, full of reverses, and uneven. Historians now give greater weight to the participation of urban craftspeople, of both Iberian and African descent, in the independence movements; but it is generally agreed that the leadership was for the most part in the hands of the Creole landowning class. The revolutionary potential of urban mass participation, so visible in the United States and France, was relatively weak in Latin America. No changes in social structures occurred except in Haiti, from which the white Creole settlers had largely fled after the revolution. The outcome of the independence movements in Latin America was not a single federal or central, constitutionally defined *nation* but a multiplicity of states defined by more or less the same constitutional nationalism of the Creoles, unwilling to share power very broadly.

Independence and Political Development in the North: Haiti and Mexico

The French Revolution in 1789 had two very different consequences for Latin America. In Saint-Domingue, or Haiti, the revolution triggered a direct and immediate adaptation process among the large majority of slaves, who quickly embraced the radical concept of *égalité* for acquiring their freedom. They eliminated their competitors, the white Creoles, and pushed the adaptation process to its ultimate conclusion, independence and constitutionalism for what was now fundamentally a nation of blacks. By contrast, in Mexico, the adaptation to the French Revolution was indirect, limited largely to the Creoles, and never broadened to include much of the non-Creole population prior to the twentieth century. It was indirect insofar as it came only by way of Napoleon's invasion of Iberia and its consequences. And it

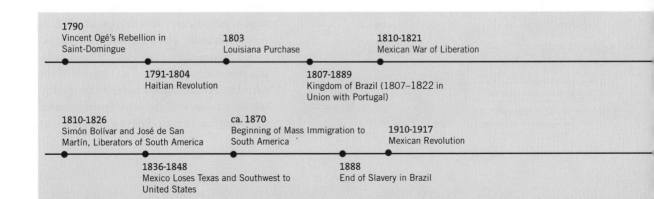

1790
Vincent Ogé's Rebellion in Saint-Domingue

1803
Louisiana Purchase

1810-1821
Mexican War of Liberation

1791-1804
Haitian Revolution

1807-1889
Kingdom of Brazil (1807–1822 in Union with Portugal)

1810-1826
Simón Bolívar and José de San Martín, Liberators of South America

ca. 1870
Beginning of Mass Immigration to South America

1910-1917
Mexican Revolution

1836-1848
Mexico Loses Texas and Southwest to United States

1888
End of Slavery in Brazil

remained a stunted revolution, in part because the urban, small-propertied, entrepreneurial, and professional classes that provided so much of the momentum of the American and French Revolutions were much smaller than in the United States and France. Thus, the impulse toward radicalism and social leveling characteristic of France in early 1790 never really took deep roots during the independence movement in Mexico.

Death Is Preferable to Slavery

"All men are born free and equal; any man born into arbitrary servitude has the right to kill his oppressor. The slave's insurrection against his master is a natural right; death is preferable to slavery."

—A black protagonist in a play written by an anonymous white author during the Haitian Revolution. In Jeremy D. Popkin, trans., *Facing Racial Revolution: Eyewitness Accounts of the Haitian Insurrection*, p. 248. Chicago: University of Chicago Press, 2007.

Sugar and Coffee in Haiti   The Caribbean island of Hispaniola, today Haiti and Santo Domingo, was one of the earliest and richest European colonies, based on plantations that produced vast amounts of sugar, coffee, and cotton for export to the Old World from the 1700s onward. At the time of the French Revolution, the French part of the island produced half of the world's sugar and coffee. Originally, the entire island had been a Spanish colony. But as Spain's power slipped during the seventeenth and eighteenth centuries, France took advantage of the situation and assumed control of the western end of the island in 1697. In the following century, settlers enjoyed French mercantilist protectionism for splendid profits from their slave plantations. By 1789, some 30,000 white settlers, 28,000 mulattoes (holding about one-third of the slaves), and about 500,000 black plantation and household slaves formed an extremely unequal colonial society in which fear and violence reigned supreme.

Revolt of the Slaves   After the failure of Ogé's uprising, discussed in the vignette that opens this chapter, resentment continued to simmer among the mulattoes and blacks in the north of Saint-Domingue. Resentment turned into fury, however, when the French revolutionary Constitutive Assembly in May 1791 began to debate the issue of citizen rights for propertied mulattoes (for which Ogé had been fighting), while the settlers in Saint-Domingue continued to refuse any debate. Plantation slaves chafing under a dehumanizing regime of exploitative owners and managers exploded in August 1791 with a collective rage not previously seen in an American colony. Within weeks, the slave rebellion numbered 100,000 followers and encompassed the entire northern province of the island. The settlers were well-armed but suffered heavy casualties under the onslaught of overwhelming numbers.

With the rebellion taking an increasingly severe toll on the economy, the Legislative Assembly of the new French Republic sent commissioners and troops in 1792 to reestablish order. But when war broke out between France and its neighbors in the following year, the possibility of an invasion of the island by Britain and Spain, and of their forming an alliance with the slave leaders, caused the commissioners to abolish slavery. This act

MAP **27.1 The Haitian Revolution.**

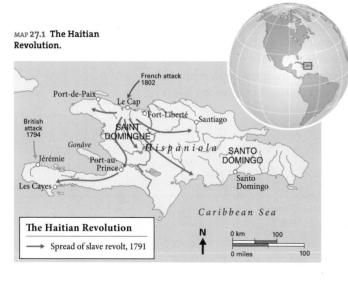

The Haitian Revolution

→ Spread of slave revolt, 1791

of abolition, confirmed in France by February 1794, enabled the most powerful slave leader, François-Dominique Toussaint Louverture (ca. 1743–1803), to end foreign interference and make peace with the few thousand remaining French forces and settlers (see Map 27.1).

Nation-State Building   To repair the plantation economy—sugar production, for example, had fallen by 75 percent—Louverture dispatched his officers, who forced former slaves to resume production. In 1801, Louverture was sufficiently strong to assume the governorship of Saint-Domingue and proclaim a constitution that incorporated the basic principles of French-inspired constitutional nationalism. Napoleon Bonaparte, in control of France since 1799, however, was determined to rebuild the French overseas empire and now revoked the abolition of slavery. He dispatched a military force to the island, which succeeded in capturing Louverture in 1802. Louverture died shortly thereafter in 1803.

Defending the Revolution. When Poland ceased to exist after the Third Partition of the Polish Commonwealth (1795) between Russia and Prussia, thousands of Polish soldiers joined Napoleon's forces. Napoleon sent some of the Polish soldiers to Haiti in 1802 to reconquer it; but even though the soldiers fought bravely, as depicted in *Battle on Santo Domingo* by the Polish painter January Sucholdoski (1797–1875), the Haitian Republic defeated Napoleon's troops and gained full independence in 1804.

His deputy, the former slave Jean-Jacques Dessalines (r. 1802–1806), was able to defeat Napoleon's troops and in 1804 declared the colony an independent nation. Subsequently, Dessalines made himself emperor and renamed the country "Haiti," its supposed original Native American name. When he changed the constitution in favor of autocratic rule, he provoked a conspiracy against him, which culminated in his assassination in 1806. In the aftermath, the state split into an autocratically ruled north with a state-run plantation economy and a democratic south with a small-farm privatized economy (1806–1821).

A subsequently reunified state annexed neighboring Spanish Santo Domingo for a short time (1822–1842) before losing it again. This loss touched off a period of political instability in the middle of the century before constitutional rule and the agricultural commodity economy were stabilized (1874–1911). Despite all its difficulties, Haiti entered the twentieth century as the first successful black constitutional state—and one with nearly one hundred years of independence behind it. Together with the United States and France, Haiti created the pattern of constitutional nationalism in the nineteenth century, which became part of the modern challenge to the traditional kingdoms and empires of the world.

Napoleon's Conquest of Iberia and Its Impact on the Americas   Napoleon's defeat in Haiti ended France's efforts to rebuild its overseas empire. Instead, the French embarked on the conquest of Europe for the end of absolutism and a new revolutionary empire from Portugal to Russia. The effect of this policy of European conquest, however, was a decisive weakening of Iberian colonialism in the Americas. Ironically, the first step in this weakening was unintended. In the Battle of Trafalgar off the southwestern coast of Spain in 1805 France and Spain lost a substantial part of their combined sea power. Great Britain, the victor, entered the nineteenth century as the unchallenged maritime power in the world.

Then, during the Peninsular War in 1807–1808, Napoleon Bonaparte conquered Portugal and Spain in a bid to put his brother on the Spanish throne. The Portuguese

Land and Liberty. This enormous mural by Diego Rivera (1886–1957), in the National Palace in Mexico City, shows Father Hidalgo above the Mexican eagle, flanked by other independence fighters. Above them are Emiliano Zapata and Pancho Villa, the heroes of the Revolution of 1910, holding a banner, "Tierra y Libertad." The other parts of the mural show historical scenes from the Spanish conquest to the twentieth century.

heir apparent, Prince Joâo (later Joâo VI of Brazil and Portugal, r. 1816–1826), and his family fled to Brazil; and the French ruled by military decree. In Spain, Napoleon forced the king, Fernando VII (r. 1808 and 1813–1829), to abdicate and placed his own brother, Joseph Bonaparte (r. 1808–1813), on the throne. Joseph ruled tenuously, dependent on generals under his brother's command as the Spanish mounted a determined guerilla campaign against their occupiers, and eventually abdicated with alacrity. An interesting legacy of this struggle is that the Spanish term *guerilla* for this kind of irregular warfare stuck and is the name we still use today for popular insurgencies against larger conventional forces.

As a consequence of Napoleon's conquest of Iberia, the Creoles of the Spanish colonies rejected Joseph Bonaparte's rule and declared their loyalty to the deposed king Fernando. But since Napoleon held the king captive in France, this declaration meant for all practical purposes independence for the American colonies. Once the Spanish had chased the French army out of Iberia and King Fernando returned to his throne in 1813, however, the American colonies had to fight in order to remain independent.

Mexican Independence   In New Spain (modern Mexico), Miguel Hidalgo y Costilla (1753–1811), son of a Creole hacienda estate administrator, launched his movement for independence from Bonapartist Spain in 1810. A churchman since his youth, Hidalgo was broadly educated, well versed in Enlightenment literature, and on the margins of strict Catholicism. Later in his life he became a parish priest and devoted himself to creating employment opportunities for native Americans or Amerindians in a province southeast of Mexico City. He had earlier participated in a conspiracy of Creoles, some of them members of the military, to overthrow a group of Spanish colonial military officers who had staged a successful coup d'état against the civilian colonial administration in 1808. On the point of being discovered, the conspiracy launched a popular rebellion in 1810, declaring itself in favor of Fernando VII, whom they considered to be Spain's legitimate ruler, as opposed to Joseph Bonaparte.

Under the leadership of Hidalgo, tens of thousands of poor Creoles, mestizos, and Amerindians who had suffered in a drought marched on Guanajuato, looting and killing *peninsulares* (Spaniards from Europe) and Creoles without distinction. They were initially successful in defeating the Spanish troops marching against them. When Hidalgo, shocked by the violence, avoided an attack on Mexico City, however, the rebellion began to sputter and was eventually defeated in 1811. Spanish forces ultimately captured and executed Hidalgo.

Under militarily experienced mestizo and Creole leaders, the war of independence continued in several southwestern provinces of Mexico but failed to make a comeback in the heartland around Mexico City. Here, monarchists intent on retaining the union between Spain and Mexico appeared to retain the upper hand. But during a constitutionalist uprising in Spain (1820–1823) King Fernando VII came close to defeat. The Mexican Creole monarchists, not wishing to submit to a Spanish republic, made the colony a regency ready to receive Fernando in order for him to continue Spanish colonial rule. Fernando, however, overcame the uprising in Spain. When he then declined to take up his American regency, the Creoles made Mexico an independent empire of its own in 1821, thereby provoking declarations of independence from Mexico in the southern provinces of El Salvador, Nicaragua, Costa Rica, and Honduras. Mestizo and Creole independence fighters in Mexico redoubled their efforts for an independent republic as well. In 1824, they succeeded with the declaration of the Republic of Mexico and a constitution broadly following the US and French models (see Map 27.2).

Early Independence   Initially, Mexico had a number of advantages as an independent nation. It had abundant natural resources, and its northern territories—Texas, Colorado, and California—contained much valuable pasture and agricultural

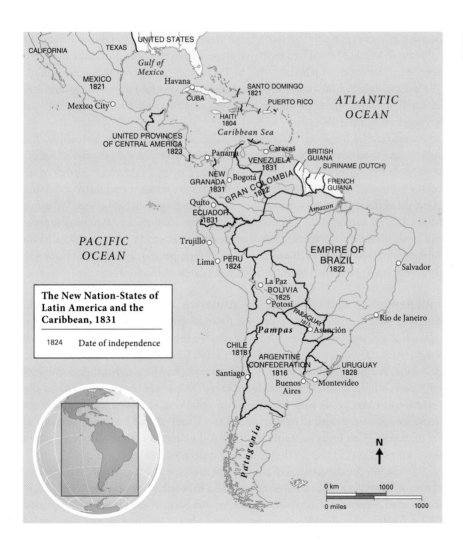

MAP **27.2 The New Nation-States of Latin America and the Caribbean, 1831.**

land. The great dying of the indigenous population of Amerindians from European mass diseases in the sixteenth and early seventeenth centuries, however, had radically depopulated much of the land. Thus, while Mexico's territory was vast, it was doomed to stay largely undeveloped unless a policy of open immigration was encouraged.

From the early 1820s, Mexico therefore encouraged immigration, gave generous terms for the purchase of land to settlers, and allowed them to be largely self-governing as long as taxes were duly paid. At the same time, Mexico's rapidly expanding northern neighbor, the United States, went through a protracted period of growth. Settlement of the rich agricultural areas of the formerly French Ohio and Mississippi valleys moved with astonishing speed. The new demand for American cotton in British and American factories drove a frenetic expansion into Alabama, Mississippi, Louisiana, and Arkansas. Cotton exhausted the soil quickly, and the availability of cheap land made it more efficient to abandon the depleted lands and keep pushing the realm of "King Cotton" ever westward.

As North American settlement drew closer to Mexico's territories, many North Americans emigrated to Mexico to take advantage of its land policies and autonomy. The Mexican province of Texas was particularly attractive, especially to southerners, because of its nearness to the settled southern states and its suitability for cotton cultivation. While Mexico had outlawed slavery from the time it became independent, most slave owners who migrated to Texas tended to ignore these restrictions. The increasingly blatant violation of the antislavery laws and the swelling numbers of immigrants seeking opportunity in Texas came to alarm the Mexican national government by the 1830s.

Moreover, the huge size of Texas, the habit of local autonomy fostered by the settlers, and their ties to the United States made many Texans view themselves as essentially independent. The perception in Mexico City of a Texas on the brink of seceding prompted the government to send the army to crush any incipient rebellion. Here, the actions of the president, General Antonio López de Santa Anna (in office from 1833, off and on, until 1855), in dissolving the congress and assuming the role of a caudillo had already sparked rebellion in several other Mexican provinces. Santa Anna confronted these rebellions in turn, and then personally led 4,000 troops to deal with Texan pro-independence militias in March of 1836.

Independence and Growing US Influence   For the Texan militias Santa Anna's actions became the cause of a war for independence, particularly as the caudillo's ruthlessness toward the militias convinced them that negotiation was out of the question. Santa Anna's men besieged a small Catholic mission in San Antonio called the "Alamo" in which several hundred Texans had barricaded themselves, determined to hold out until a relief force came. The Texans were bolstered by the presence of some celebrated volunteers from the United States, among them the Tennessee frontiersman and congressman Davy Crockett, and Jim Bowie, the inventor of the knife that bears his name. In the end, the defenders were all killed, though the circumstances of their deaths are still hotly debated today.

For Texans, the dead men became instant martyrs and the Alamo became "the shrine of Texas liberty." Santa Anna's army had suffered heavy casualties, and Texan forces soon defeated it in the battle of San Jacinto. Santa Anna himself was captured on the battlefield and, having narrowly escaped being lynched on the spot, ceded

Texas to the insurgents. Mexico's largest province now became an independent state. Santa Anna, after being taken to the United States and meeting with President Andrew Jackson (in office 1829–1837), was repatriated to Mexico and served as president six more times in his long career as that nation's most famous caudillo.

Mexico's Dismemberment

After some 30 years of not doing much with its right to govern Louisiana—the huge land on both sides of the Mississippi in the center of today's United States—Spain had returned its territorial rights there to France. Napoleon, for his part, sold the rights to the United States in 1803, in the hope of strengthening the latter against Great Britain, his main opponent in his European imperial conquests. By the early 1840s, American settlement of the territory of this so-called Louisiana Purchase on both sides of the Mississippi was proceeding rapidly. Settlers bought some land from the indigenous Amerindians, whose opinions had not been consulted during the purchase, and gained even more land from wars against them. Moving farther west, American settlers made claims on the Oregon Territory along the northern Pacific Coast. These claims now meant that the young US republic's ambitions were swiftly making it a continental power.

During the administration of President James K. Polk (1845–1849), the idea of "Manifest Destiny"—that it was the evident fate of the United States to be the dominant power of the North American continent, with territory stretching from the Atlantic to the Pacific—was becoming an article of faith. Both the British in Canada and the Mexican government were increasingly alarmed by this new aggressive US posture. Moreover, Texas, insecure as an independent republic between the United States and Mexico and dominated by Americans, now applied for annexation to the United States.

MAP 27.3 **Mexico's Loss of Territory to the United States, 1824–1854.**

For Santa Anna, president once again of Mexico, such a move meant a war for survival; for Polk and many Americans, it meant a potential opportunity to expand the republic's borders directly to the Pacific. When Texas was admitted to the union, therefore, the United States and Mexico went to war. Despite vigorous protests against this war as one of conquest—including a spirited condemnation by a young Illinois congressman named Abraham Lincoln—the war was prosecuted by the United States with vigor. A small but well-trained expeditionary force, launching a seaborne invasion of central Mexico, fought its way to Mexico City. Other American troops fought in what were to become New Mexico and California. By 1848 Mexico sued for peace and gave up most of what is now the southwestern and western United States: Texas, New Mexico, Arizona, Colorado, Nevada, and California (see Map 27.3).

To make the territorial losses even harder to swallow for Mexico, the richest gold strike in the continent's history began almost immediately in California. The boomtown of San Francisco

Mexico, 1824–1854

— Boundary of Mexico, 1824

▢ Texas, independent republic 1836–45, 1845 to US

▢ Ceded 1845, 1850

▢ Ceded by Treaty of Guadalupe Hidalgo, 1848

▢ Ceded 1853 (Gadsden Purchase)

▢ Mexico, 1854

attracted tens of thousands of newcomers—"Forty-Niners"—seeking riches, and California entered the union as a state in 1850. Santa Anna stayed on in Mexico as caudillo until 1855. Then, even his supporters could no longer take his lavish crony-ism and payoffs to the military and deposed him. In a strange historical footnote, Santa Anna spent his last years of exile in the United States, where his efforts at im-porting *chicle*, the base for modern chewing gum, ultimately led to one of his associ-ates starting the Chiclets Chewing Gum company. In 1876, under a general amnesty, Santa Anna went back to Mexico and soon after passed away.

The French Interlude in Mexico   The Latin American independence move-ments had inspired the declaration of the US Monroe Doctrine in 1823. According to this policy, the US government would not tolerate European attempts to recolo-nize the new republics of the Western Hemisphere. For four decades the doctrine had been remarkably successful at deterring the European powers, largely because it suited British policy as well. Mexico easily beat back two attempts by small ex-peditionary forces at invasion, one from Spain in 1829 and another from France in 1838. With the American Civil War raging in the mid-1860s, however, the tempta-tion to create an empire in Mexico proved too much for Louis-Napoleon Bonaparte (in office 1848–1852 as president; r. 1852–1870 as emperor) of France to resist. As a nephew of Napoleon, he yearned to return France to imperial glory.

After staging a coup d'état in 1852 and becoming Emperor Napoleon III, he pursued imperial campaigns in North Africa, West Africa (Senegal), and In-dochina (Vietnam), apart from flexing France's military muscle in Russia, Italy, China, and Korea. His opportunity to intervene in Mexican affairs came after the downfall of Santa Anna in 1855 and the subsequent uprising of con-servatives against the liberal constitution of 1857, with its separation of church and state. The liberals under the lead-ership of Benito Juárez, the first Amerindian to become president (1861–1864, 1867–1872), thus defeated the conservatives.

But the state that Juárez inherited was bankrupt, and when he found himself forced to suspend payments on the state debt, the international repercussions were disastrous for Mexico. Napoleon III seized on the payment issue and, with an eye on the Mexican silver mines, set into motion an ambitious plan of imposing a pliable ruler from the outside. In 1862, he provided military backing to the Austrian prince Maximilian, well liked by Mexican conservatives, to install himself as the emperor of Mexico (1864–1867).

With the defeat of the Confederate states in April 1865, however, and the Union army ballooning to over a million men, many of whom had just been sent to Texas to suppress the last Confederate holdouts, Maximilian's position was suddenly in grave danger. In the following year, after some discreet aid from the US government under the aegis of the Monroe Doctrine, an uprising broke out in Mexico. Cut off from any hope of effective support from France, Mexican

Birth and Death of Constitutions

"With good reason the public now feels that constitutions are born and die, that governments succeed each other, that codes are enlarged and made intricate, that pronouncements and plans come and go, and that after so many mutations and upheavals, so much inquietude and so many sacrifices, nothing positive has been done for the people, nothing advantageous for these unhappy classes, from which always emerge those who shed their blood in civil wars, those who give their quota for armies, who populate the jails and labor in public works, and for which were made, finally, all the evils of society, and none of its goods."

— Special vote (report) of Ponciano Arriaga in the Mexican Assembly, June 23, 1856. In Kenneth L. Karst and Keith S. Rosenn. *Law and Development in Latin America: A Case Book.* UCLA Latin American Studies Series, vol. 28, p. 275. Berkeley: University of California Press, 1975.

liberal forces defeated Maximilian, captured him, and executed him by firing squad in 1867.

Porfirio Díaz's Long Peace   With the withdrawal of most US government troops from Texas at the end of Reconstruction—ending the potential threat of invasion or border incursions—and the rise of Mexico's next conservative caudillo, Porfirio Díaz (in office 1876–1880 and 1884–1911), a period of relative peace came at last. Díaz's lengthy hold on power allowed a degree of conservative stability to settle in on Mexico's turbulent politics. Moreover, the period also coincided with the defeat of the last Amerindians north of the border and the settlement and development of the American West. In addition, Díaz, like his contemporary, President José Balmaceda (1886–1891) of Chile, favored some initial industrial and infrastructural development in Mexico. The basic lines of Mexico's major rail, telegraph, and telephone systems were laid during this time; textile factories and some basic heavy industry were set up; and modest agricultural improvements were made.

The Execution of Emperor Maximilian of Mexico, June 19, 1867. Édouard Manet has been characterized as the "inventor of modernity" not only for his technique, but for the way he portrayed events, even significant political events, in a calm and composed manner. The soldiers who dispatch the hapless Emperor come across as cool and professional—what they are doing is all in a day's work.

Most of this investment, however, came from British and American firms in return for Mexican mineral, precious metal, and fruit and vegetable exports. Toward the end of Díaz's dictatorship, the first petroleum drilling enterprises were set up, an industry that, although nationalized today, still has proved disappointing at consistently generating revenue. In assessing Mexico's relative lack of economic development since the late 1800s, poverty, and ongoing tensions with the industrial colossus to the north, it is no wonder that he once exclaimed so poignantly, "Alas, poor Mexico! So far from God, so close to the United States!"

The Mexican Revolution   Díaz's long presidency and Mexico's halting development tended to foster discontent, particularly among the poor urban workers and *peons*—agricultural laborers on large estates, who were held in conditions of virtual serfdom. In 1910, half of the Mexican population worked on estates and 20 percent of the farmland was foreign-owned. The reform-minded Francisco Madero, from a wealthy northern family, drove Díaz from power and through elections legitimized his own presidency (1911–1913); but he was unable to gain control over the country. Two additional movements now vied for power in different parts of Mexico: Emiliano Zapata (1879–1919) advocated for plantation land reform in the south and Pancho Villa (José Doroteo Arango Arámbula, 1878–1923) for hacienda land reform in the north. In addition, a seesaw struggle for the presidency erupted between reformers from wealthy backgrounds and conservative pro-Díaz officers, each seeking to gain a grip on the movements by Zapata and Villa as well as other provincial rebels.

During a short-lived interval in the middle of this struggle, a group of reformers were able to convene a constitutional congress, which passed a new, revolutionary

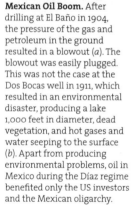

Mexican Oil Boom. After drilling at El Baño in 1904, the pressure of the gas and petroleum in the ground resulted in a blowout (a). The blowout was easily plugged. This was not the case at the Dos Bocas well in 1911, which resulted in an environmental disaster, producing a lake 1,000 feet in diameter, dead vegetation, and hot gases and water seeping to the surface (b). Apart from producing environmental problems, oil in Mexico during the Díaz regime benefited only the US investors and the Mexican oligarchy.

constitution with paragraphs establishing land reform, limits to foreign ownership of resources, a labor code, and a secular, compulsory educational system (1917). It took altogether at least 2 million and possibly in the vicinity of 3.5 million victims in the struggle for and against the revolution, as well as one more military coup, before a moderate general, Álvaro Obregón (in office 1920–1924), was able to stabilize the presidency and begin the implementation of the constitution. In contrast to the 1824 and 1857 constitutions, the new one of 1917 stood out for its socialist programs, creating greater equality in the distribution of farmland and ending the grip of the Catholic Church on land as well as education.

Independence and Development in Northern South America

The viceroyalty of New Granada in northern South America, with today's countries of Venezuela, Colombia, Ecuador, and Panama, had far fewer Creoles than that of New Spain, from which independent Mexico issued. For its struggle for independence to succeed, leaders had to seek support from the *pardos*, as the majority population of free black and mulatto craftspeople in the cities was called. Independence eventually came through the building of strong armies from these diverse elements, mostly by Simón Bolívar, the liberator of northern South America from renewed Spanish colonialism. After independence, however, the Creoles quickly moved to dissolve their coalitions with the lower classes and embraced the same conservative caudillo politics that Mexico practiced for most of the nineteenth century.

Comuneros and Pardos In contrast to New Spain, with its relatively large Creole and mestizo populations in the cities and countryside, New Granada's Creole population was small in relation to mestizos and pardos. The latter constituted over half of the urban and two-thirds of the rural people. Unrest began early, expressing itself in loyalty to the Spanish king but also in fury against the high taxes collected by the peninsular administrators: The *comunero* revolt of 1781–1782—together with the Túpac Amaru revolt of 1780–1781 in Peru—was a harbinger of things to come during the independence struggle a generation later. The comuneros were urban and

Revolutionary Women.
Women, such as these
soldaderas taking rifle practice,
played many significant roles
in the Mexican Revolution,
1910–1920.

rural Creoles and mestizos whom the hard-pressed authorities placated with promises, only to renege once their assemblies dissipated.

In 1810, the battle cry was again loyalty to the Spanish king, the deposed Fernando VII, and outrage against the peninsulars, although this time it was more massive, bringing together Creoles and pardos. In 1810 they created *juntas*, or committees, among which the junta of Cartagena in what was to become Colombia was the most important, and drove the peninsulars from their administrative positions. Initially, they agreed on the equality of all ethnicities and worked on constitutions that provided for elections by all free men. But they were also suspicious of each other, denouncing their allegedly aristocratic versus democratic aspirations.

In 1811, cooperation broke down and the pardos assumed power in a coup. The Creoles struck back a year later when they declared the First Republic of Cartagena. Their power was limited by the pardo-dominated militias however, and in a compromise they agreed on the continuation of full voting rights. In the long run, during the 1800s, this revolutionary achievement did not last and the Creoles established oligarchic rule. But Cartagena, together with Mexico under Hidalgo, proved that Latin American independence was not exclusively the work of a conservative Creole class consolidating its privileges.

Bolívar the Liberator　　The junta of Cartagena, together with other juntas, formed the federation of the United Provinces of New Granada in 1811, with a weak executive unable to prevent squabbling among the juntas. Fernando VII, after returning to Spain in 1813, was determined to reestablish colonial control by dispatching armies to Latin America. The largest forces, comprising some 10,000 troops, landed in the United Provinces in 1814, taking Cartagena after a siege, and resurrected the viceroyalty of New Granada.

The eventual liberator of northern South America from renewed Spanish rule in 1819 was Simón Bolívar (1783–1830). Bolívar was born in Venezuela, into a wealthy Creole background; his family owned cacao plantations worked by slaves and was engaged in colonial trade. Venezuela, like Colombia, was a part of New Granada. Although lacking a formal education, thanks to his tutor Bolívar was familiar with Enlightenment literature. In 1799, he visited Spain, where he met his future wife; and he later returned to Europe after her death. In 1804, he was deeply impressed when he watched Napoleon's lavish spectacle of crowning himself emperor in Paris. These European visits instilled in Bolívar a lasting admiration for European ideals of liberty and popular sovereignty, and he longed to create a constitutional republic in his homeland.

In 1810, as in Cartagena, Venezuelan cities formed Creole-led juntas with pardo participation. A young Bolívar participated in the congress of juntas that declared outright independence for Venezuela in 1812, against the resistance of royalists who remained faithful to Fernando VII. A civil war ensued, which made Bolívar's tenure in Venezuela insecure and, after the arrival of the Spanish expeditionary force of 1815, impossible. He went into exile first to British Jamaica and then to revolutionary Haiti. In 1816 Bolívar returned from exile to Venezuela with a military force, partly supplied by Haiti. After some initial difficulties, he succeeded in defeating the Spanish troops. In 1822, he assumed the presidency of "Gran Colombia," an independent republic comprising the later states of Colombia, Venezuela, Ecuador, and Panama.

The Bolívar–San Martín Encounter

After their defeat in Gran Colombia, Spanish troops continued to occupy Peru in the Andes, where an independence movement supported by Argentina was active but made little progress against Spanish and royalist Creole troops. In the face of this situation, the Argentinian general and liberator José de San Martín (ca. 1778–1850) and Bolívar met in 1822 to deliberate on how to get rid of the Spanish and to shape the future of an independent Latin America. As for fighting Spain, they agreed that Bolívar was in a better geographical position than San Martín to send military forces to Peru. But even for Bolívar that task was daunting. His troops were unaccustomed to high-altitude fighting and were hindered as much by mountain sickness as by enemy resistance. One of Bolívar's lieutenants finally got the better of the fiercely resisting Spanish in 1824. Two years later, Spanish colonialism in Latin America finally ended when the last troops surrendered on the Peruvian coast.

The content of the discussion for the future of Latin America between San Martín and Bolívar never became public and has remained a bone of contention among historians. San Martín, bitterly disappointed by endless disputes among liberal constitutionalists and royalists, federalists and centralists, as well as Creole elitists and mestizo and mulatto populists, favored monarchical rule to bring stability to Latin America. Bolívar preferred republicanism and Creole oligarchical rule, although he always sought limited pardo and mestizo collaboration, especially in his armies. Clearly, there was not much common ground between the two independence leaders.

San Martín's sudden withdrawal from the Andes after the meeting and his subsequent resignation from politics, however, can be taken as an indication of his realization that the chances for a South American monarchy were small indeed. Bolívar, also acutely aware of the multiple cleavages in Latin American politics, more realistically envisioned the future of Latin America as that of relatively small independent republics, held together by strong, lifelong presidencies and hereditary senates. He actually implemented this vision in the 1825 constitution of independent upper Peru, renamed after him "Bolivia." Ironically, in his own country Bolívar was denied the role of strong president. Although he made himself a caudillo, he was unable to coax his recalcitrant politicians into an agreement on a constitution for Gran Colombia similar to that of Bolivia. Eventually, in 1830 Bolívar resigned, dying shortly after of tuberculosis. In 1831 Gran Colombia fell apart into its component parts of Colombia, Venezuela, Ecuador, and (later) Panama.

Revolving-Door Caudillos Independent Venezuela, as perhaps the poorest and most underpopulated of northern South America's newly independent countries, acquired the dubious distinction of being among its most politically turbulent. In Carácas, the capital, caudillos displaced each other at an astonishing rate. By one estimate, there were 41 presidencies and 30 insurrections in the period 1830–1899. Although many of these presidents sought foreign financial support for development, little was accomplished and much of the money went into the private coffers of the leaders. The main issue that kept rival factions at odds was federalism versus tighter central control, with at least one all-out war being fought over the issue during the 1860s. Following this so-called War of the Caudillos, the official name of the country was changed from the "Republic of Venezuela" to the "United States of Venezuela," a name which it retained into the middle of the twentieth century.

Venezuela's neighboring countries traversed a similar pattern of caudillo politics. Though enjoying longer periods of stability, Colombia—the name adopted in 1861 to replace that of New Granada—also saw a continuing struggle between federalists and centralizers, liberals and conservatives, with each party seeking the support of the Catholic Church. From 1899 until 1902, the "War of a Thousand Days" was conducted, leaving the country sufficiently weak for Panamanian rebels to establish an independent state of Panama, supported by the United States. After independence, the administration of Theodore Roosevelt (1901–1909) swiftly concluded a treaty with the new country to control a 10-mile-wide strip bisecting the narrow isthmus and began the construction of the Panama Canal, completed in 1914.

Machines in the Garden. The first railroads in Latin America were constructed in Mexico in 1836. Initially, construction was supported by state funds, with private and foreign participation. A railway bridge spans the Rio Grande River in Costa Rica, 1902 (a). In the 1870s and 1880s, once profitable railroads were privatized and expanded. The United States built the 51-mile Panama Canal in 1904–1914 with Treasury bonds, after encouraging Panama to secede from Colombia and appropriating the land for construction (b).

Independence and Development in Southern and Western South America

Independence movements also began in 1810 farther south in South America. Under the guise of remaining loyal to the deposed Fernando VII of Spain, Creoles in Buenos Aires seized the initiative to establish a junta rejecting the viceregal peninsular authorities. By contrast, Creoles along the Andes similarly avoided declarations of loyalty to Napoleon but supported the existing colonial administration, even after 1814 when fresh Spanish troops arrived. The figure who eventually broke the logjam between the two sides of pro- and antipeninsular Creole parties in 1816–1822 was José de San Martín.

Independence in Argentina   The viceroyalty of La Plata, comprising the modern countries of Argentina, Uruguay, Paraguay, and Bolivia, was the youngest of Spain's colonial units. In the course of the Bourbon reforms, Spain decided in 1776 to separate it from the viceroyalty of Peru, where declining silver exports diminished the importance of the port of Lima. La Plata, with the rising port of Buenos Aires, had grown through contraband trade with Great Britain; and the Bourbon reformers wanted to redirect its trade more firmly back to Spain. Buenos Aires was so important to the British even after the reform of 1776, however, that a naval commander and British merchants exploited the destruction of the Spanish navy by Britain in the battle off Trafalgar in southwestern Spain (1805) to occupy Buenos Aires in 1806–1807, until they were driven out by Spanish colonial forces.

Creoles in La Plata had far fewer Amerindians, African slaves, mestizos, and mulattoes to deal with—or fear—than in any of the other viceroyalties. But in 1810, when the first independence movements formed, there was a clear distinction between the proindependence Creoles of Buenos Aires, or *porteños*, and the Creoles of the *pampas*, or grasslands of the temperate interior of Argentina and Uruguay, and the subtropical plains and hills of Paraguay favoring continued colonialism. The latter either were royalists or strove for separate independence. Uruguay, furthermore, was initially claimed by Brazil and eventually achieved its own independence only in 1828. Upper Peru, or modern Bolivia, with its high-elevation plains, lowland Amazon basin rain forest, large Amerindian population, and Potosí silver mines, was heavily defended by colonial and peninsular Spanish troops. Given these various urban–rural and geographical circumstances, the porteño independence movement fought to no more than a standstill during the initial period 1810–1816.

As in the northern tier, the breakthrough eventually came via an experienced military figure, the highly popular José de San Martín. San Martín was a Creole from northeastern Argentina. His father, an immigrant from Spain, was a military officer and administrator of a Jesuit-founded Amerindian mission district. The son, educated from an early age in a Spanish military academy, began service in the porteño independence movement in 1812, where he distinguished himself in the Argentinian independence struggle.

During his service, San Martín realized that the final success for independence in the south also required the liberation of the Andes provinces. Accordingly, he trained the Army of the Andes, which included mulatto and black volunteers, with which he crossed the mountains to Chile in 1818, liberating the country from royalist forces. With the help of a newly established navy composed of ships acquired from the United States and Britain, he conquered Lima in Peru but was defied by the local Creoles when he sought to introduce social reforms, such as an end to the Amerindian tribute system, the *mit'a*, and the emancipation of the children of black slaves. When he was also unable to dislodge Spanish troops near the city, he traveled north for his meeting with Bolívar. As discussed, it was Bolívar who completed the liberation of the Andes lands and, thereby, also helped Argentina to defeat the peninsulars and royalist Creoles in the south.

Independent Peru   Peru's independence came following the defeat of Spanish forces in 1824–1826. As with the other new states in South America, it took decades for Peru, Chile, and Bolivia to work out territorial disputes. The most serious of these by far was the War of the Pacific from 1879 to 1884, resulting in a victorious Chile annexing Peruvian and Bolivian lands. Most devastating for Peru was the destruction that Chilean troops wrought in southern Peru. The economy, which had made modest progress by using nitrate exports in the form of guano to fund railroad building and mining, was only painfully rebuilt after the destruction of war. Political stability for several decades returned under the presidency of Nicolás de Piérola, who introduced a number of belated reforms during his terms (1879–1881 and 1895–1899). As the presidency from this time until the 1920s was held by men from the upper landowning Creole class, it is sometimes called the period of the "Aristocratic Republic."

Caudillos and Oligarchic Rule   During the later 1820s the independence junta in Buenos Aires solidified into an oligarchy of the city's wealthy Creole elite, but the vast, largely undeveloped areas of the pampas with their small floating population of Amerindian peoples and Creole *gauchos*, or cowboys, remained largely outside the new state. A war with Brazil drained the country of much of its manpower and resources. The political circles in Buenos Aires began to solidify around those favoring a strong central government to conduct a strong foreign policy and exercise control over the provinces, which advocated a looser federal system. By the 1830s these unsettled conditions gave rise to the first of many Argentine caudillos, Juán Manuel de Rosas (in office 1829–1852).

De Rosas was descended from a wealthy ranching family and tended to identify with the gauchos. But he saw himself as a champion of national unity rather than one who sought to limit the role of the government in regional affairs. After becoming governor of Buenos Aires in 1829, he systematically extended his personal influence (*personalismo*) over his fellow governors until he was named caudillo in 1835, imposing a severe and fundamentally conservative brand of autocratic rule on the country.

Ultimately, his centralism and appetite for expansion helped in his downfall. Fierce in his opposition to British annexation of the Malvinas Islands—or Falklands, as the British called them—though frustrated by not being able to reverse it, he unwisely intervened in a civil war in Uruguay in 1843. His popularity flagged as the war dragged on for 9 years. Finally, the unsuccessful war, coupled with his unwillingness to lend his support to a constitution favorable to the provinces, led to his ouster in 1852.

The Settling of the Pampas   The victor was a provincial governor named Justo José de Urquisa, who became the new caudillo. Urquisa swiftly extricated Argentina from Uruguay, defeated an army of de Rosas loyalists, and successfully sponsored a constitutional convention in 1853, lessening political centralism. In 1854 he

> **"In My Country I Am Like a Princess"**
>
> "Marriages were made among a small number of families, **endogamously**. Their children's education began in exclusive schools. Playmates continued as schoolmates and as classmates in the universities.... Families were generally large with an abundance of servants, who were sometimes treated as if they belonged to the same family circle. There were drawing rooms where only those with certain surnames could enter and which were closed to those who had only the power of money; there were families before which one knelt with respect, awe, and adulation. The daughter of one of these once said in Europe, 'In my country I am like a princess.'"
>
> —Peter F. Klarén, trans. "The Origins of Modern Peru, 1880–1930." In *The Cambridge History of Latin America*, vol. 5, c. *1870 to 1930.* Edited by Leslie Bethell, p. 613. Cambridge: Cambridge University Press, 1986.

Endogamy: Custom of restricting marriage to a local community, clan, or tribe.

was elected president, and it seemed for the moment that Argentina was on the road to a more open, representative government. But the presidency remained the property of a small Creole oligarchy from the provincial elite. Not surprisingly, renewed conflict broke out with Buenos Aires over the issue of a strong centralized regime versus a projected new federal arrangement. In 1861, the forces of Buenos Aires defeated Urquisa's provincial forces and the country was reintegrated, with Buenos Aires as the national capital.

In the following years, many of the same forces that were shaping the North American West were also actively transforming the pampas. The land was opened to settlement, driving the gauchos from their independent existence into becoming hired hands. The railroad was spurring settlement, and the remaining Amerindians were driven south to Patagonia or exterminated. In contrast to the homesteading policies in the United States, however, the pampas were divided up into huge *estancias*, or estates, of tens of thousands of acres, aided by the introduction of barbed wire to fence in the ranges. Thus, the old system of rounding up essentially wild livestock and driving it to market now gave way to the ranching of cattle, sheep, and goats. As in other areas of South America, the new landed Creole elites dominated politics and economics long into the twentieth century.

Toward Party Politics   Despite the cozy arrangement of nineteenth-century Argentine politics, the growing urban center of Buenos Aires and the waves of Spanish and Italian immigrants grew restless under the rotating presidency that characterized the period 1880–1900. Spurred by the development of radical politics in Europe, especially those adopting versions of Marxism and socialism, two major urban opposition parties took shape in the 1890s: the Radical Party and the Socialists. As the influence of these parties grew, electoral reforms were forced on an unwilling landed oligarchy. In 1912, universal male suffrage was passed, and voting would take place by secret ballot. By 1916, the closed oligarchy was at last cracked open by the arrival of a new president, Hipólito Yrigoyen (1916–1922, 1928–1930). He relied for support mostly on an urban constituency, which dominated politics in the early twentieth century.

Brazil: From Kingdom to Republic

During the late colonial period, Brazil underwent the same centralizing administrative, fiscal, and trade reforms as the Spanish possessions. These reforms were resented as much by the Brazilian planter and urban Creoles as by their Spanish counterparts, but their fear of rebellion among the huge population of black slaves held them back from openly demanding independence. As it happened, independence arrived without bloody internecine wars, through the relocation of the monarchy from Portugal to Brazil in the wake of Napoleon's invasion of Iberia in 1807. Brazil had since become an empire and when the second emperor, Dom Pedro II (r. 1831–1889), under pressure from Britain, finally abolished slavery in 1888, the politically abandoned plantation oligarchy avenged itself by deposing him and switching to a republican regime under the military in 1889. Given the enormous size of the country, as well as the split of the Creole oligarchy into mining, sugar, and coffee interests, the regime became solidly federal, making it difficult for caudillos to succeed and allowing eventually for the rise of civilian presidents.

Transfer of the Crown from Portugal to Brazil   Portugal's royal family fled the country in advance of Napoleon's armies in 1807. Escorted by British ships, it took refuge in Brazil and elevated the colony to the status of a coequal kingdom in union with Portugal but governed from Brazil after Napoleon's defeat in 1815. The arrival of some 15,000 Portuguese together with the dynasty, however, created resentment among the Brazilian Creoles, sharpening the traditional tension between Creoles and Portuguese-born reformers. A crisis point was reached in 1820 when rebels in Portugal adopted a liberal constitution, which demanded the return of Brazil to colonial status as well as the transfer of the dynasty back to Portugal. The reigning king returned but left his son, Pedro I (r. 1822–1831), behind in Brazil. On the advice of both his father and courtiers, Pedro uttered in 1822 his famous "*fico*" ("I remain"), and proclaimed "Independence or Death!" thereby making Brazil an independent kingdom.

Pedro I's Authoritarianism   On acceding to the throne, Pedro declared Brazil an empire because of its size and diversity. His rule, however, embodied many of the same characteristics as that of the caudillos in the Spanish-speaking South American countries. In addition, like the restoration monarchs of Europe in the early 1800s, he firmly adhered to his belief in divine right, which was incompatible with more than token constitutionalism. Consequently, he rejected an attempt by the landed Creole oligarchy to introduce limited monarchical rule. Instead, he issued his own constitution in 1823 that concentrated most powers in his hands as well as a council of state, with a weak lifetime senate and a legislative chamber based on severely limited voting rights. Since he also reserved to himself the nomination and dismissal of ministers, the dissolution of the chamber, and, above all, the appointment of provincial governors, his rule was far too authoritarian even for the conservative planter elite.

In reaction, in 1824 six northeastern provinces attempted to secede. They proclaimed the republican Federation of the Equator and, somewhat illogically, demanded more central government support for the traditional northern sugar and cotton plantations, neglected by a rising emphasis on south-central coffee plantations. Increased British patrols in the Atlantic to suppress the slave trade had increased the price for slaves. The sugar planters could ill afford the increased prices, but the expanding coffee market enabled its planters to pay (see "Patterns Up Close").

Given the close ties between Britain and Brazil, Pedro found it difficult to resist mounting British demands for the abolition of slavery. As a result, early signs of alienation between the crown and the Creole planter elite crept in. It also did not help that Pedro supported the open immigration to Brazil of skilled foreigners, as well as foreign loans and investments for development. Like their counterparts in the American South, the plantation elites sought to limit immigration except for servile labor and control the courts to assure severe punishments for infractions by slaves; and they voiced their opposition to internal improvements like railroads, for fear of disrupting the stability of the plantation system. Ultimately, a succession crisis in Portugal in 1830 led to a conservative revolt against Pedro. In 1831, he lost his nerve and abdicated, sailing back to Portugal. He left the throne for his 5-year-old son, Pedro II (r. 1831–1889), who required a regent. Given a temporarily weak monarchy, the plantation oligarchy exploited the situation by renewing its demands for federalism.

Patterns Up Close | Slave Rebellions in Cuba and Brazil

The successful slave revolt in Haiti was the most inspiring event for blacks in the first half of the nineteenth century. Blacks had gained little from the American and French Revolutions, and the pattern of brutal exploitation continued in many parts of the Americas. Not surprisingly, therefore, blacks sought to emulate the example of Haiti during the first half of the 1800s. Through careful and systematic preparation, they sought to tap into the repressed fury of the plantation slaves. However, none of the subsequent Haiti-inspired revolts was any more successful against the well-prepared authorities than previous revolts had been in the 1700s, as a look at rebellions in Cuba and Brazil during the first half of the nineteenth century shows.

In Cuba, the decline of sugar production in Haiti during the revolution encouraged a rapid expansion of plantations and the importation of African slaves. As previously in Haiti, a relatively diversified eighteenth-century society of whites, free mulattoes, and blacks, as well as urban and rural black slaves, was transformed into a heavily African-born plantation slave society, forming a large majority in many rural districts. The black freedman José Antonio Aponte (ca. 1756–1812), militiaman and head of the Yoruba confraternity (*cabilde*) in Havana, led an abortive revolt in 1812 that drew support from both sectors. In the subsequent revolts of 1825, 1835, and 1843, the urban element was less evident. Authorities and planters, invested heavily in new industrial equipment for sugar production and railroads, and exhausted by the unending sequence of uprisings, unleashed a campaign of sweeping arrests of free blacks and mulattoes that cut the urban–rural link once and for all.

Brazil, like Cuba, also benefited from the collapse of sugar production on Haiti in the 1790s and the first half of the 1800s. It expanded its plantation sector,

Slave Revolt Aboard Ship. Rebellions aboard ship, such as the famous 1839 mutiny aboard the *Amistad* shown here, were common occurrences. The *Amistad* was engaged in intra-American slave trafficking, and the slaves overpowered the crew shortly after embarkation in Cuba. After protracted legal negotiations, the slaves were eventually freed and retuned to Africa.

particularly in the province of Bahia, and imported large numbers of slaves from Africa. But here distrust divided African-born from Brazilian slaves, freedmen, and mulattoes. Many freedmen and mulattoes served in the militias that the authorities used to suppress the revolts. Furthermore, in contrast to the narrow island of Cuba, plantation slaves could run away more easily to independent settlements (called *quilombos*) in the wide-open Brazilian interior, from where revolts were more easily organized than either in cities or on plantations. In fact, no fewer than a dozen quilombo revolts extending into plantations occurred in Bahia during 1807–1828, revolts which the militias found difficult to crush, having to march into often remote areas.

Two urban revolts of the period were remarkable for their exceptional mix of insurgents, unparalleled in Cuba or elsewhere in Latin America. The first was the Tailor's Rebellion of 1798 in Salvador, Bahia's capital. Freedmen, mulattoes, and white craftspeople cooperated in the name of freedom and equality against the Creole oligarchy. The second was the Muslim uprising of 1835, also in Bahia, organized by African-born freedmen as well as slaves with Islamic clerical educations that they had received in West Africa before their enslavement.

The impact of Islam on African American slave societies has not been sufficiently studied. West African Muslims, including clerics, were frequently enslaved in the early 1800s during the many conflicts and the civil wars in what is today coastal Nigeria. These clerics represented an African strand of Islam that was tolerant of West African animism, to which the majority of slaves in Salvador adhered. Distinguished by their knowledge of Arabic, white gowns, and protective amulet necklaces, the clerics converted slaves in Salvador and surrounding areas to Islam and took up arms as freedom fighters during the short-lived rebellion in 1835. The role of Islam as an alternate ideology to that of constitutionalism, as symbolized by the Haitian Revolution, is an important reminder that American slaves, far from being culturally dependent, had the freedom to carve out their own unique identities.

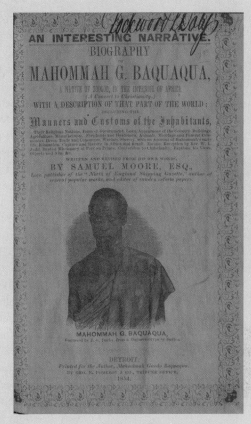

Man of Many Worlds. The life of Mahommah G. Baquaqua demonstrates the way in which some enslaved Africans could forge their own identities in the New World despite the daunting obstacles they faced. Captured and enslaved in West Africa in 1845 at about the age of 20, Baquaqua was taken to Pernambuco, Brazil, and then later to Rio de Janeiro, where a ship's captain bought him. He eventually escaped, made his way to New York City and then Haiti and then back to New York and finally on to Canada where he wrote his autobiography, the cover of which is shown here. He last shows up in the historical record in Britain, where seems to have lived out his remaining days.

Questions

• Do the slave rebellions in Cuba and Brazil in the early nineteenth century confirm or complicate the pattern of slave revolution that was first manifested first in Haiti?

• Why would Islam be attractive to many slaves in the Americas?

The Federalist Interlude   After lengthy debates, in 1834 the government granted the provinces their own legislative assemblies with strong tax and budget powers, effectively strengthening the provincial landholding elites with their various regional interests. It also abolished the council of state but created a national guard to suppress slave revolts and urban mobs. This mixed bag of reforms was not enough for some provinces. The most dangerous one was that of 1835 in Rio Grande do Sul, a southern province led by cattle owners who commanded military forces composed of gauchos. These owners established an independent republic that attracted many domestic and foreign radicals opposed to slavery, including Giuseppe Garibaldi, the Italian nationalist who played a crucial role in the unification of Italy. In reaction to the coexistence of a now weak and decentralized monarchy with an antislavery republic offering a refuge to runaways on Brazilian soil, the centralists reasserted themselves. In 1840 they proclaimed the 14-year-old Pedro II king and curbed the powers of the provincial assemblies, and in 1845 they negotiated a return of Rio Grande do Sul to Brazil.

The End of Slavery   The 1830s and 1840s coincided with a transition in Brazil from sugar to coffee as a major export commodity on the world market. The old sugar plantation elite lost clout, and a newer coffee planter oligarchy ascended to prominence. Both needed slaves, and as long as the crown did not seriously fulfill its promises of 1831 to the British to curb the importation of slaves, there was no more than unease about the mutual dependence of the king and the oligarchy on the continued existence of slave labor. But when the British in 1849 authorized warships to enter Brazilian waters to intercept slave ships, the importation of slaves virtually ceased. A serious labor shortage ensued, leading to a movement of slaves from the north to the center. For different reasons, sugar, cotton, and coffee plantation owners began to think of ridding themselves of a monarchy that was unable to maintain the flow of slaves from overseas.

In the 1860s and 1870s, anti-monarchy agitation gathered speed. Brazilians, especially professionals and intellectuals in the cities, became sensitive to their country being isolated in the world on the issue of slavery. After the United States, the Spanish colonies of Puerto Rico and Cuba ended slavery for all aged slaves and newborn children. Brazil was now left as the only unreformed slave-holding country in the Western Hemisphere. In the following decade and a half, as the antislavery chorus increased in volume, the government introduced a few cosmetic changes and it fell on the provinces to take more serious steps. Planters began to see the demise of the system on the horizon and encouraged their provinces to increase the flow of foreign immigrants, to be employed as wage labor on the coffee plantations. The political situation neared the point of anarchy in 1885, with mass flights of slaves from plantations and armed clashes to keep them there. Only then, in 1888, did the central government finally end slavery.

The Coffee Boom   Predictably, given the grip of the planter oligarchy on the labor force, little changed in social relations after the abolition of slavery. The coffee growers, enjoying high international coffee prices and the benefits of infrastructure improvements, through railroads and telegraph lines since the 1850s, could afford low-wage hired labor. The now free blacks received no land, education, or urban jobs, scraping by with low wages on the coffee and sugar plantations. Economically, however, after freeing itself from the burdens of slavery, Brazil expanded its economy in the 5 years following 1888 as much as in the 70 years of slavery since independence.

The monarchy, having dragged its feet for half a century on the slavery issue, was thoroughly discredited among the plantation elite and its offshoot, the officer corps in the military. By the 1880s, officers were also drawn from professional and intellectual urban circles. Increasingly, they subscribed to the ideology of *positivism* coming from France, which celebrated secular scientific and technological progress (see Chapter 22). Positivists, almost by definition, were liberal and republican in political orientation. In 1889, a revolt in the military supported by the Creole plantation oligarchy resulted in the abolition of the monarchy and proclamation of a republic, with practically no resistance from any quarter.

Two political tendencies emerged in the constituent assembly 2 years after the proclamation of the republic. The coffee interests of the south-central states favored federalism, with the right of the provinces to collect export taxes and maintain militias. The urban professional and intellectual interests, especially lawyers, supported a strong presidency with control over tariffs and import taxes as well as powers to use the federal military against provinces in cases of national emergency. The two tendencies were embodied in a compromise with a tilt toward federalism, which produced provincial caudillos, on the one hand, but regularly elected presidents, on the other.

Following this tilt, in the 1890s the government was strongly supportive of agricultural commodity exports. Coffee, rubber, and sugar exports yielded high profits and taxes until 1896, when overproduction of coffee resulted in diminishing returns. The State of São Paulo then regulated the sale of coffee on the world market through a state purchase scheme, which brought some stabilization to coffee production. At the same time and continuing into the early twentieth century (and without much state or central government support), immigrants and foreign investors laid the foundation for **import-substitution industrialization**, beginning with textile and food-processing factories. The comparative advantage from commodity exports had run its course by the late 1800s and early 1900s and now had to be supplemented with industrialization.

Children Picking Coffee in Brazil, ca. 1900. The first coffee bush was planted in Brazil in 1727. With the decline of the slave trade in the late nineteenth century, Brazil increasingly had to rely on immigrants—such as the children shown here—to provide labor for its booming coffee industry, which was centered in the hilly region near Rio de Janeiro and in the Paraíba Valley in the state of São Paulo.

Latin American Society and Economy in the Nineteenth Century

Independence brought both disruptions and continuities in the economy as well as in politics. In Spanish America, four colonial regions broke apart into eventually 21 independent republics, organized around the pattern of constitutional nationalism. Trade with Europe was thus radically altered. What continued were deep divisions

Import-substitution industrialization: The practice by which countries protect their economies by setting high tariffs, and construct factories for the production of consumer goods (textiles, furniture, shoes; followed later by appliances, automobiles, electronics), and/or capital goods (steel, chemicals, machinery).

between the small landowning elites and the urban masses of officials, professionals, craftspeople, and laborers. Although many members of the elites and urban lower classes had collaborated in the drive for independence, afterward they broke apart into conservative and liberal wings, unable to establish a consensus and stable state institutions. When trade with Europe resumed, a lowest-denominator pattern of export-led growth based on mineral and agricultural commodities evolved (see Map 27.4).

MAP 27.4 The Economy of Latin America and the Caribbean, ca. 1900.

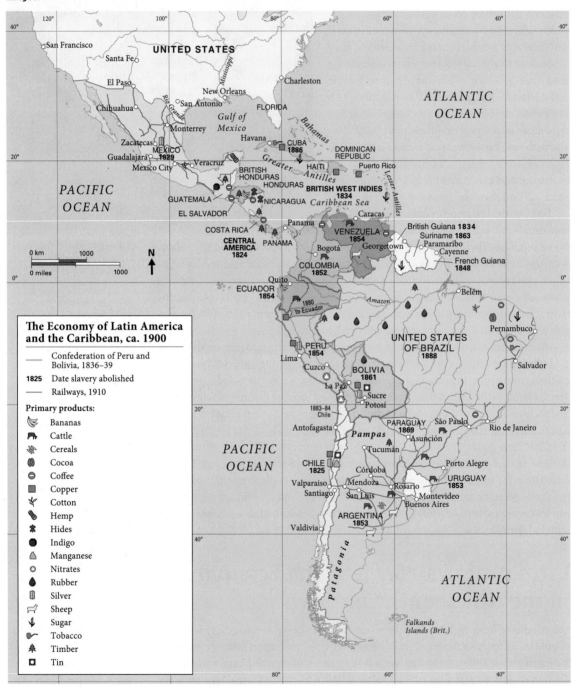

The Economy of Latin America and the Caribbean, ca. 1900

— Confederation of Peru and Bolivia, 1836–39

1825 Date slavery abolished

—— Railways, 1910

Primary products:
- Bananas
- Cattle
- Cereals
- Cocoa
- Coffee
- Copper
- Cotton
- Hemp
- Hides
- Indigo
- Manganese
- Nitrates
- Rubber
- Silver
- Sheep
- Sugar
- Tobacco
- Timber
- Tin

Rebuilding Societies and Economies

Reconstruction in the independent republics and the Brazilian monarchy took several decades. Mercantilist trade was gone, and in its place, free trade had to be built. Social structures changed little, and constitutional disagreements took some time to be settled. Production in the mines and on the estates had to be restarted with fresh capital. All this took time, and it was only by mid-century that Latin America had overcome the aftereffects of the wars of independence.

On the Eve of Independence   During the colonial period, the economies of Spain and Portugal in the Americas followed a pattern of mercantilism. In mercantilist theory, as we have seen a number of times, the Spanish and Portuguese colonies could purchase only goods manufactured in Iberia and had to pay with gold, silver, sugar, cocoa, indigo, or other goods from the colonies. In practice, as Spain and Portugal reformed colonial administration and trade in the 1700s, it became easier for the colonies to buy from European countries via transit through Iberia. Contraband trade similarly mitigated and undercut Iberian mercantilism. Interregional trade increased during the reform period, especially for foodstuffs and cattle, Mexican and Ecuadorian textiles, and Argentinean and Chilean wine. Overall, however, interregional trade remained a poor cousin of the export trade.

Taxes were considerably higher in the Americas than in Iberia, with estimates of a 40–70 percent differential. But since tax surpluses from rich regions, such as Mexico, had to subsidize poor regions for administrative, judicial, and military costs, Spain did not earn much from its American colonies. Portugal was luckier with its colony of Brazil, which more or less consistently yielded a tribute. But, in contrast to earlier centuries, during the 1700s Iberia as a whole did not earn much from its American conquests.

After Independence   The achievement of independence in the 1820s, after lengthy struggles with Spain and local and internal conflicts, had a number of far-reaching consequences. The most important result was the end of Spain's mercantilist monopoly. The Latin American republics were free to buy or sell and to borrow money anywhere in the world. Among trading partners, this freedom benefited Great Britain most directly. Its merchants had already established themselves in several Latin American cities during the continental boycott of Napoleon, which had shut out Great Britain from trade with the European continent.

Initially, however, for Latin Americans the freedom to trade was more hope than reality. Dislocations from the struggle of independence were considerable. Capital had fled the continent and left behind uncultivated estates and flooded mines. The Catholic Church held huge, uncollectable debts. In many areas taxes could not be collected. Troops helped themselves to payment through plunder. In Mexico, where the struggle between republicans and royalists was the fiercest, the disruptions were worst and reconstruction took longest. Chile also experienced violent struggles but stabilized itself relatively quickly. On average, though, it took until about 1850 for Latin America to fully recover.

Constitutional Nationalism and Society   The Creoles were everywhere the winners in the wars of independence. Many were ardent constitutional nationalists, finding it easy to adapt to conservative versions of this form of the Western

> ### State and Religion
>
> The Religion of the Mexican Nation is, and will be perpetually, the Roman Catholic Apostolic. The Nation will protect it by wise and just laws, and prohibit the exercise of any other whatsoever.
>
> —Federal Constitution of the United Mexican States (1824), article 3. Accessible through the Jamail Center for Legal Research, Tarlton Law Library, University of Texas at Austin, http://tarlton.law.utexas.edu/constitutions/text/1824index.html.

challenge of modernity. The most powerful among them were large landowners, that is, owners of grain-farming self-sufficiency estates, cattle ranches, and sugar, indigo, cacao, coffee, or cotton plantations. Independence did not produce much change in agrarian relations: Landowners of self-sufficient estates and plantations in many parts of Latin America continued to employ tenant farmers and slaves.

The large majority of the Creoles were urban administrators, professionals, craftspeople, and laborers. Their leaders, ardent constitutional nationalists, tended toward political and economic liberalism. In many areas they were joined by mestizos, mulattoes, and black freedmen, also largely craftspeople and laborers. The main issue dividing the liberals and conservatives, as in the French Revolution, was the extent of voting rights: Liberals wanted to extend it to all males, while conservatives sought to limit it through literacy and property requirements to a minority of males. No influential group at this point considered extending voting rights to women.

Deep Political Divisions   Once independence was won, distrust between the two groups with very different property interests set in and the political consensus fell apart. Accordingly, landed constitutional conservatives restricted voting rights, to the detriment of the urban constitutional liberals. The exceptions were Argentina and, for a time during the mid-century, Peru: The one had few mestizos and mulattoes but a relatively large urban Creole population that gained the upper hand, and the other had large numbers of urban mestizos and Amerindians who could not be ignored. Nevertheless, even if constitutionalism was submerged for periods of time under caudillo authoritarianism, as we have seen, adaptation to constitutionalism, in its conservative or liberal variation, remained a permanent fixture. It was this early adoption of constitutionalism which distinguished Latin America from the Ottoman Empire, Russia, China, and Japan.

Split Over State–Church Relations   Among the many issues over which conservatives and liberals split, the relationship between state and church was the deepest. Initially, given the more or less close collaboration between republicans and conservatives during the struggle for independence, Catholicism remained the national religion for all. Accordingly, education and much property remained under church control.

But the new republics ended the powers of the Inquisition and claimed the right of *patronato*, that is, of naming bishops. At the behest of Spain, however, the pope left bishoprics empty rather than agree to this new form of lay investiture. In fact, Rome would not even recognize the independence of the Latin American nations until the mid-1830s. The conflict was aggravated by the church's focus on its institutional rather than pastoral role. The Catholic clergy provided little guidance at a time when industrial modernity, even if only indirectly via urbanization, was crying out for spiritual reorientation. At the same time, papal pronouncements made plain the church's hostility toward the developing capitalist industrial order.

This hostility of the church was thus one of the factors that in the mid-1800s contributed to a swing back to liberalism, beginning with Colombia in 1849. Many countries adopted a formal separation between church and state and introduced secular educational systems. But the state–church issue remained bitter, especially in Mexico, Guatemala, Ecuador, and Venezuela, where it was often at the center of political shifts between liberals and conservatives. In Colombia, for example, it even led to a complete reversal of liberal trends in the mid-1880s, with the reintroduction of Catholicism as the state religion.

Economic Weakness   Given the difficulties of arriving at a political and cultural consensus during the period of recovery after independence (ca. 1820–1850), the reconstruction of a fiscal system to support the governments remained contradictory and problematic. For example, governments resorted to taxation of trade, even if this interfered with declared policies of free trade. The yields on tariffs and export taxes, however, were inevitably low and made the financing of strong central governments difficult. Consequently, maneuvering for the most productive mix of the two taxes trumped official pronouncements in favor of free trade and often eroded confidence among trade partners.

This maneuvering had little effect on the domestic economy—self-sufficiency agriculture and urban crafts production—which represented the great bulk of economic activities in Latin America. Grain production on large estates and small farms, especially in Brazil where gold production declined in late colonial times, had escaped the turbulence of the independence war and recovery periods relatively unscathed. Land remained plentiful, and the main bottleneck continued to be labor. The distribution of marketable surpluses declined, however, given the new internal borders in Latin America with their accompanying tariffs and export taxes. Self-sufficiency agriculture and local economies relying on it thus remained largely unchanged throughout the 1800s.

The crafts workshops, especially for textiles, suffered from the arrival of cheap British factory-produced cottons, which represented the majority of imports by the mid-1800s. Their impact, however, remained relatively limited, mostly to the coasts, since in the absence of railroads transportation costs to the interior were prohibitively expensive. Only Mexico encouraged the financing of machine-driven textile factories, but the failure of its state bank in 1842—from issuing too many loans—ended this policy for a number of decades. On the one hand, there was a definite awareness in most countries of the benefits of factories, using domestic resources, and linking the self-sufficiency agricultural sector to modern industrial development. On the other hand, its necessity in the face of traditional opposition was not demonstrated until later in the nineteenth century.

Export-Led Growth

The pursuit of a policy of commodity exports—export-led growth—from about 1850 led to expanding rates in the standard of living for many Latin Americans. The industrializing countries in Europe and North America were voracious consumers of the minerals and materials that Latin America had in abundance and of its tropical agricultural products. More could have been sold, had there not been a chronic labor shortage.

Raw Materials and Cash Crops   Mining and agricultural cash crop production recovered gradually so that by the 1850s, nearly all Latin American governments had adopted export-led economic growth as their basic policy. This was about

Loading Nitrate into Rail Cars, Chile, 1915. In the 1830s, farmers realized the value of nitrate as a fertilizer and an export boom to industrializing Europe ensued. Most of the deposits were located in what were then coastal lands of Peru and Bolivia. In 1879, Bolivia raised its taxes on nitrate mining, and in response Chile declared war on Bolivia. Chile won the war against Bolivia (and Peru, which sided with the latter) in 1884; as a result, Bolivia became landlocked. The nitrate boom eventually collapsed in World War I when Germany began making synthetic fertilizer.

all the conservatives and liberals were able to agree on since land distribution to poor farmers and a system of income taxes were beyond any consensus. Mexican and Peruvian silver production, the mainstay of the colonial mercantilist economy, became strong again, although the British adoption of the gold standard in 1821 imposed limits on silver exports. Peru found a partial replacement for silver with guano mining. Guano, seabird excrement accumulated over the millennia and fossilized, was mined by laborers using simple implements, such as pickaxes and shovels. It was exported for use as an organic fertilizer and as a source of nitrates for explosives. Chile hit the jackpot with guano, nitrate, and copper exports, of crucial importance during the chemical- and electricity-driven second Industrial Revolution.

In other Latin American countries, tropical and subtropical cash crops defined export-led economic growth during the mid-1800s. In Brazil, Colombia, and Costa Rica, labor-intensive coffee growing redefined the agricultural sector. In Argentina, the production of jerked (dried) beef, similarly labor-intensive, refashioned the ranching economy. The main importers of this beef were regions in the Americas where plantation slavery continued into the second half of the 1800s, especially the United States, Brazil, and Cuba. The latter, which remained a Spanish colony until 1895, profited from the relocation of sugarcane plantations from the mainland and a number of Caribbean islands after the British outlawing of the slave trade (1807) and slavery itself (1834) and the Latin American wars of independence (1810–1826).

In the long run, however, like silver, cane sugar had a limited future, given the rise of beet sugar production in Europe. Minerals and cash crops were excellent for export-led economic growth, especially if they required secondary activities such as the processing of meat or the use of mining machinery. But competition on the world market increased during the 1800s, and thus, there was ultimately a ceiling, reached in the 1890s.

Broadening of Exports   With their eyes increasingly focused on exports, Latin American governments responded quickly to the increased market opportunities resulting from the Industrial Revolution in Great Britain, the European continent, and the United States. Peru broadened its mineral exports with copper, Bolivia with tin, and Chile with nitrates. Brazil and Peru added rubber, Argentina and Uruguay wool, and Mexico *henequen* (a fiber for ropes and sacks) to its traditional exports. Luxuries from tropical Latin America, like coffee, cacao (for chocolate bars, invented in 1847), vanilla, and bananas, joined sugar after 1850 in becoming affordable mass consumer items in the industrialized countries. Argentina, with investments in refrigeration made by Britain, added frozen meat to this list in 1883. This commodity diversification met not only the broadened demand of the second Industrial Revolution, with its demand for chemicals and electricity, but also the demand for consumer goods among the newly affluent middle classes.

Since the choice among minerals and crops was limited, however, most nations remained wedded to one commodity only (50 percent of exports or more). Only two, Argentina and Peru, were able to diversify (exports of less than 25 percent for the leading commodity). They were more successful at distributing their exports over the four main industrial markets of Great Britain, Germany, France, and the United States. On the eve of World War I the United States had grown to be the most important trading partner in 11 of the 21 Latin American countries. Given its own endowments and under the conditions of world trade in the second half of the nineteenth century, the continent's trade was relatively well diversified.

The prices of all Latin American commodities gyrated substantially up and down during the second half of the nineteenth century. This fluctuation was in contrast to the imported manufactured goods, primarily textiles, metal utensils, and implements, which became cheaper over time. In fact, Brazil's government was so concerned about fluctuating coffee prices in the 1890s that it introduced the Taubaté coffee valorization scheme in 1906. As the largest producer, it regulated the amount of coffee offered on the world market, carefully adjusting production to keep market prices relatively stable in much the same way that oil-producing countries would later do with petroleum. Since coffee trees need 5 years to mature, Brazil was largely successful with its scheme until World War I, when worldwide conditions changed. An American oligopoly (the United and Standard Fruit Companies) in control of banana production in Central America from the 1890s similarly controlled prices. A careful investigation of commodity prices by economic historians has resulted in the conclusion that in spite of all fluctuations commodity prices rose overall during 1850–1914.

Rising Living Standards   From all evidence, in the period from the middle of the 1800s to the eve of World War I, the governments can be judged as having been successful with their choice of export-led growth as their consensus policy. Living standards rose, as measured in gross domestic product (GDP). At various times during 1850–1900, between five and eight Latin American countries kept pace with the living standards in the industrialized countries. Argentina and Chile were the most consistent leaders throughout the period. Thus, although many politicians were aware that at some point their countries would have to industrialize in addition to relying on commodity export growth, they can perhaps be forgiven for keeping their faith in exports as the engine for improved living standards right up to World War I.

Labor and Immigrants   As in the industrialized countries, the profitable exports were achieved through low wages. Together with the rest of the world, Latin America experienced high population increases during the 1800s. The population grew sevenfold, to 74 million, although it remained small in comparison to the populations of Europe, which doubled to 408 million, and Africa and Asia, which each grew by one-third to 113 and 947 million, respectively. The increases were not large enough to dent the favorable land–person ratio, so it is not surprising that the high demand for labor continued during the 1800s. This demand, of course, was the reason the institution of forced labor—revolving labor duties (mit'a) among Amerindians in the Andes and slavery—had come into existence in the first place.

Not surprisingly, mit'a and slavery continued during the 1800s, liberal constitutionalism notwithstanding, in a number of countries. Even where forced labor was abolished early, however, low wages continued. One would have expected wages to rise rapidly, given the continuing conditions of labor shortage and land availability. Mine operators and landowners, however, were reluctant to raise wages because they feared for the competitiveness of their commodities on the world market. Governments, doing their bidding, preferred to resort to selective and mass immigration from overseas to enlarge the labor pool.

Typical selective immigration examples were *coolies* (from Urdu *kuli*, hireling), that is, "indentured" laborers recruited from India and China on 5- or 10-year contracts and working off the costs of their transportation. During 1847–1874, nearly half a million East Indians traveled to various European colonies in the Caribbean. Similarly, 235,000 Chinese came to Peru, Cuba, and Costa Rica, working in guano pits and silver mines, on sugar and cotton plantations, and later on railroads. If the experience of five Caribbean islands can be taken as a guide, only about 10 percent of the coolies returned home. Coolie migration to Latin America, therefore, can be described as a major part of the pattern of massive migration streams across the world that typified the nineteenth century (see Map 27.5).

Immigration to Latin America from Europe was on an even bigger scale. In Argentina, Uruguay, Brazil, and Chile, Italians and Spaniards settled in large numbers from around 1870 on. In Argentina, nearly one-third of the population consisted of immigrants, a share much higher than at any time in the United States. The Italian population of Argentina numbered close to 1 million by the turn of the century. Most immigrants settled in cities, and Buenos Aires became the first city on the continent with more than a million people. Only here did a semi-regular labor market develop, with rising urban and rural wages prior to World War I. Elsewhere in Latin America, governments, beholden to large landowners, feared the rise of cities with immigrant laborers who did not share their interests. They, therefore, opposed mass immigration.

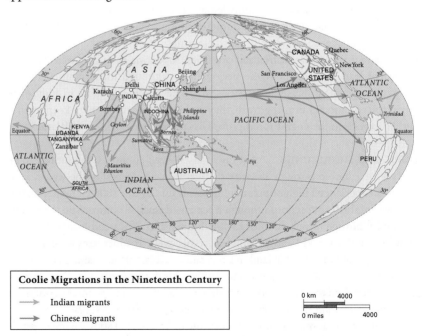

Coolie Migrations in the Nineteenth Century

→   Indian migrants

→   Chinese migrants

MAP **27.5 Coolie Migrations in the Nineteenth Century.**

Dining Hall for Recently Arrived Immigrants, Buenos Aires. Immigrants, all male, and more than likely all Italian, rub shoulders sometime around 1900 in a dining hall in Buenos Aires set up for newly arrived immigrants. By 1914, 2 percent of the population of Buenos Aires—about 300,000 people—had been born in Italy, most from the poor southern regions of Campania, Calabria, and Sicily.

Self-Sufficiency Agriculture   Except for Argentina, Chile, and Uruguay, the levels of commodity exports did not rise sufficiently to reduce the size of the rural labor force not working for exports, a major condition for improved living standards across the board. On the eve of World War I, two-thirds to half of the laborers in most Latin American countries were still employed as tenant farmers or farmhands on large estates. In much smaller numbers, they were indigenous villagers who owned their small farmsteads. Their contribution to the national GDP, for example, in Brazil and Mexico was less than one-quarter. Toward the end of the century, observers began to realize that export-led growth—even though it looked like an effective economic driver—did not have much of a transformative effect on the rural masses in most countries.

The absence of such transformative effects was visible, for example, in the high levels of illiteracy among rural inhabitants. Adult illiteracy rates of up to 80 percent were not uncommon, even in relatively diversified countries, such as Brazil and Mexico. Only Argentina and Chile after 1860 invested heavily in primary education, on levels similar to the United States and Britain, followed by Costa Rica in the 1890s. Literate self-sufficiency farmers, knowledgeable in plant and animal selection as well as fertilizers, were practically nonexistent north of the southern end of Latin America.

Governments paid greater attention to the improvement of rural infrastructures from about 1870 onward, with the development of railroads. Almost everywhere, they looked to direct foreign investment, given the low-yielding and highly regressive trade taxes on which the relatively slim central domestic revenues depended. The foreign investors or consortiums built these railroads primarily for the transportation of commodities to ports. Many self-sufficiency farmers or even landlords, therefore, received little encouragement to produce more food staples for urban markets. Argentina and Chile, followed by Costa Rica and Uruguay, built the most railroads, with between 2.8 and 1.5 miles per 1,000 heads of population. Correspondingly, with fertilizers and better implements available via railroads, corn yields quintupled

Mexican Textile Factory.
Cocolapam in the state of Veracruz was the site of the first Mexican cotton textile factory, founded in 1836 by Lucas Alamán, a Mexican government minister and investment banker. Its machinery, imported from Great Britain, was water-driven. The textiles it produced remained inferior to imports, but they were cheap and satisfied the needs of most Mexicans.

in Argentina. Conversely, these yields changed little in Mexico, which had only 1.2 miles per 1,000 heads. Overall, the Latin American railroad network represented only about one-fifth to one-third of that in other Western developing settler countries, such as Australia, Canada, and New Zealand.

Factories Until about 1870, the handicrafts sector met the demands of the rural as well as low-earning urban population. It produced cheap, low-quality textiles, shoes, soap, candles, tools, implements, cutlery, and horse tack. As is well known, this sector failed in most parts of the world during the 1800s or 1900s to mechanize itself and establish a modern factory system. Latin America was no exception. Most crafts shops were based on family labor, with a high degree of self-exploitation, unconnected to the landowning elite and deemed too small by lending banks. There was no path from workshops to factories.

However, even entrepreneurial investors interested in building factories for the manufacture of yarn or textiles were hampered in their efforts. They had little chance for success prior to the appearance of public utilities in the 1880s, providing water during the dry season and electricity as an energy source, in the absence of high-quality coal in most parts of Latin America. Even then, the risk of engaging in manufacturing, requiring long-term strategies with no or low profits, was so great that the typical founders of factories were not Creoles but European immigrants.

In Argentina and Chile these immigrants labored hard during their first years after arrival and saved the start-up capital necessary to launch small but modern textile, food-processing, and beverage factories. Argentina, Chile, Mexico, and Peru made the greatest advances toward factory industrialization, producing import-substituting consumer goods to the tune of 50–80 percent. Prior to World War I, the only country that took the step from consumer goods to capital goods (goods for factories) was Mexico, with the foundation of the Fundidora Iron and Steel Mill in 1910 in Monterrey, which, however, was unprofitable for a long time. Full capital goods industrialization had to await the postwar period.

Culture, Family, and the Status of Women
Economic growth and urbanization added considerably to the growth of constitutional-nationalist modernity in Latin America. But the absence of industrialization until the end of the nineteenth century impeded the transformation of society and its cultural institutions. The law and custom represented by the Catholic Church remained pervasive. In the second half of the nineteenth century, however, the idea of separating church and state gained adherents, with some major legal consequences for social institutions.

Legal Changes In most countries, repeated attempts by governments after independence to reduce the role of the Catholic church in society remained unsuccessful. The church resisted the efforts of the constitutional nationalists to carry out land expropriations and to separate state and church in social legislation. In a number of civil codes women's rights in inheritance and property control improved, but overall husbands retained their patriarchal rights over their families. Typically, they were entitled to the control over the family budget, contractual engagements, choice of husbands for their daughters (up to age 25 in some countries), or residence of unmarried daughters (at home, up to age 30). Only from the middle of the nineteenth century did the influence of the Catholic Church diminish sufficiently to allow legislation for secular marriages and divorce in a number of countries. Catholicism remained doctrinally unchanged.

"Men in the Street and Women at Home"

As it also developed in the Euro-American Victorian world, on the cultural level there was a popular ideal in nineteenth-century Latin America of nuclear family domesticity. But, as research has also shown, in both places this was often honored more in the breach than in the observance. That is to say, in Mexico and South America, despite the long-standing proverb *El hombre en la calle, la mujer en la casa* ("Men in the street, women in the home"), it was often the case that the two roles were intermingled. In urban areas, women frequently ran shops, managed markets, were proprietors of *cantinas*, and performed a host of skilled and unskilled jobs, particularly in the textile and food trades. In rural areas, farm work on small holdings and peonages was often shared by men and women, though a number of individual tasks—plowing, for example—were most frequently done by men.

As in Europe and North America, too, there was a remarkably high level of widowhood and spinsterhood. In areas where the predominant form of employment was dangerous—mining, for example—the incidence of widowhood was very high. Widows often could not or chose not to remarry, especially if they had relatives to fall back on or were left an income. The stereotype of the stern patriarchal husband was also pervasive enough so that many middle-class women, often to the consternation of their families, chose not to marry at all. Both of these conditions were common enough so that by one estimate one-third of all the households in Mexico City in the early nineteenth century were headed by women. Widows were entitled to their dowries and half of the community property, while boys and girls received equal portions of the inheritance. Thus, despite society's pressures to marry and raise children, many women did not marry or, after becoming widowed, remained single. In this sense, they achieved a considerable degree of autonomy in a male-dominated society. Thus social realities and legal rights diverged in early independent Latin America, even before legal reform.

The Visual and Literary Arts

To try to encapsulate the culture and arts of more than a continent—and one so vast and diverse as Latin America—is far beyond the scope of this textbook. In general terms, the legacy of European baroque and romantic-era paintings remained alive throughout the nineteenth century as a background current until giving way to the influences of European impressionists and painters.

The trend in all of Latin America colonial-era high culture under the aegis of Spanish and Portuguese influences after independence was toward "indigenization": Much like the way the United States attempted during this time to break away from European art and literary influences, a similar movement pervaded the Latin American world. Along with attempts to form national and regional styles of their own, many countries also engaged in art as a nation-building exercise—artistic and literary celebrations of new national heroes or famous historic instances through portraiture and landscape painting. Finally, there were also periodic engagements with the popular or folk arts of Amerindian peoples, mulattoes, mestizos, and Africans in celebration of regional uniqueness.

Literature to some extent paralleled the trajectory of the other arts. In the latter eighteenth and early nineteenth centuries, a style had developed called *criollo* (Creole), for its inception and popularity among that class. The most famous of work in this style was José Joaquin Fernández Lizardi's *The Mangy Parrot* (*El Periquillo Samiento*), published in 1816. Though ostensibly a tale of children's stories, it is more in the vein of Voltaire's *Candide* in lampooning the venality, corruption, and incompetence of the late colonial world. Initially, there was little nostalgia for the pre-independence years.

Following independence, as in painting, literature often turned to themes befitting countries trying to establish themselves as nations with distinct historic pasts and great future potential. In some cases, as with sometime newspaper crusader and later Argentine president Domingo Faustino Sarmiento (in office 1868–1874), critique of the present was the order of the day. Sarmiento relentlessly criticized the authoritarian rule and arbitrary ways of the caudillo Juán Manuel de Rosas in his book *Facundo: Civilization and Barbarism*. The book, written while Sarmiento had been forced into exile by Rosas in 1845, is an indictment of Rosas thinly disguised as a biography of the brutal gaucho leader Juán Facundo Quiroga. It is also, however, a meditation on the meaning of "civilization" and "barbarism" as exemplified by Europe, Asia, Africa, and Latin America. As such, it has been called by some the most important book to be published in the nineteenth century in Latin America.

The themes of the social sciences and reportage merged in much of the work of the Brazilian writer Euclides da Cunha (1866–1909). In his most famous work, *Os Sertões* (*The Rebellion in the Backlands*, 1902), he examines with a critical eye the social demography of Brazil, its racial composition and conflicts, and weighs them against the claims of the new Brazilian Republic. The vehicle for this is the attempt by the government to crush a rebellion of isolated settler outcasts in Bahia, during the 1890s, who, despite the odds against them, repeatedly defeat the government forces and become regional heroes. The book acquired considerable popularity in Brazil and was also championed by a number of leading writers in Europe and the United States. In Brazil as in the Spanish-speaking Americas, authors in the nineteenth century had a keen eye for society caught between tradition and modernity.

> ## Civilization and Barbarism
>
> "No, we are not the lowest among Americans. Something is to result from this chaos; either something surpassing the government of the United States of North America, or something a thousand times worse than that of Russia—the Dark Ages returned, or political institutions, superior to any yet known."
>
> —Domingo F. Sarmiento. *Life in the Argentine Republic in the Days of the Tyrants: Or Civilization and Barbarism*, p. 247. New York: Hurd and Houghton, 1868.

Putting It All Together

The term "banana republic" appeared for the first time in 1904. The American humorist O. Henry (1862–1910) coined it to represent politically unstable and economically poor Latin American countries, governed by small elites and relying on tropical exports, such as bananas. O. Henry had spent several years at the end of the nineteenth century in Honduras, hiding from US authorities. Thus he knew whereof he spoke.

Today, political stability is much greater; but many parts of Latin America are still poor and underindustrialized. Consequently, banana republics still resonates. Were Latin American elites, therefore, wrong to engage in a pattern of export-led growth, and did they collude with elites in the industrial countries to maneuver the continent into permanent dependence on the latter? Indeed, an entire generation of scholars in the second half of the twentieth century answered the question in the affirmative and wrote the history of the 1800s in gloomy and condemnatory tones. They called their analysis "dependency theory."

Contemporary historians are less certain about many of these conclusions. They compare Latin America not with the United States or western Europe but with the settler colonies of South Africa, Australia, and New Zealand or the old empires of the Middle East and Asia. In these comparisons, Latin America did very well and was not any more dependent on the industrializing countries than the latter were on Latin America.

Dependence increased only at the very end of the 1800s when industrial countries like the United States and Britain began to make significant capital investments. It was then that foreign companies, such as those that owned railroads in Nicaragua and Honduras, succeeded in exploiting and controlling production and export. The question we may need to ask then is not why Latin America failed to industrialize in the 1800s but, rather, did Latin America, choosing from the available choices, make

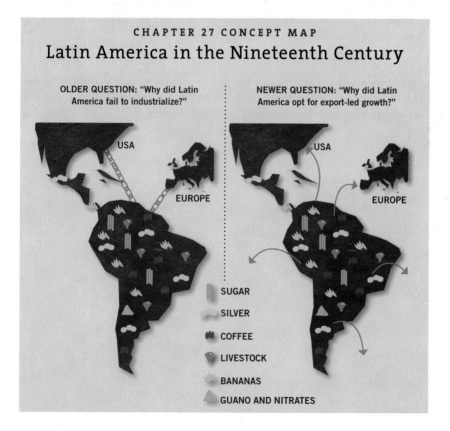

CHAPTER 27 CONCEPT MAP
Latin America in the Nineteenth Century

OLDER QUESTION: "Why did Latin America fail to industrialize?"

NEWER QUESTION: "Why did Latin America opt for export-led growth?"

USA

EUROPE

USA

EUROPE

SUGAR

SILVER

COFFEE

LIVESTOCK

BANANAS

GUANO AND NITRATES

the right decision when it opted for export-led growth up to about 1890? Did such a choice represent a "third way" toward economic growth, separate from industrial capitalism and tenacious attempts to keep economies closed off from the vagaries of world trade? Perhaps it did (see Concept Map).

Review and Respond

1. Define the concept of constitutional nationalism, and explain how and why it became a pattern of state formation in Latin America in the nineteenth century.

2. Compare Vincent Ogé and Toussaint Louverture. How are these two revolutionaries similar? How are they different?

3. Compare the political development of Haiti and Mexico in the early nineteenth century.

4. Why did the Creoles not become radical constitutional nationalists? Which kind of constitutionalism did they espouse?

5. Why did slavery persist for so long in Brazil? How is Brazilian slavery an example of the origins-interactions-adaptations model that informs this book?

6. Who were Simón Bolívar and José de San Martín, and what brought them together?

7. What distinguished the political development of Brazil from a colony to an independent country in Latin America?

8. Compare and contrast the dependency theory model and the export-led growth model for understanding patterns of development in Latin America in the nineteenth century.

> For additional resources, including maps, primary sources, visuals, and quizzes, please go to www.oup.com/us/vonsivers. Please see the Further Resources section at the back of the book for additional readings and suggested websites.

Thinking Through Patterns

▶ **Which factors in the complex ethnic and social structures of Latin America were responsible for the emergence of authoritarian politicians or caudillos?**

Similar to the United States and France, which also underwent revolutions in the late 1700s and early 1800s, Latin America's independence movements (1810–1824) did not extend the constitutional revolution beyond a small number of property owners who inhabited the highest levels of the social strata. The dominant class of large landlords and plantation owners was conservative and did not favor land reform for the benefit of small farmers. Urban professionals and craftspeople, divided in many places by ethnicity, did not share common interests that allowed them to provide an effective opposition to the landed class. Landowning and plantation interests thus protected themselves through authoritarian caudillo politics and sought to keep the opposition weak.

In colonial times, Latin America was the warm-weather extension of Europe, sending its mineral and agricultural commodities to Europe. When it acquired its independence and Europe industrialized during the 1800s, these commodities became even more important and the continent opted for a pattern of export-led development. This meant the systematic increase of mineral and agricultural commodity exports, with rising living standards not only for those who profited directly from the exports but also for many in the urban centers. Even with rising living standards it became clear by the turn of the century that a supplementary policy of industrialization had to be pursued.

▶ **Why did Latin American countries, after achieving independence, opt for a continuation of mineral and agricultural commodity exports?**

▶ **How do the social and economic structures of this period continue to affect the course of Latin America today?**

Many countries in Latin America are barely richer than they were in the 1800s. Even though industry, mineral, and commodity exports, as well as services, expanded in urban centers in the early part of the twentieth century, poor farmers with low incomes continued to be a drag on development. This phenomenon still characterizes many parts of Latin America today.

PART SIX

From Three Modernities to One

1914–PRESENT

World War I and the Interwar Period

The first great crisis in the evolution of modern scientific–industrial society was World War I (1914–1918). Although imperial competition in the Balkans indirectly triggered the war, there were even stronger forces playing their part in the background, together with other reasons still hotly contested by historians today.

For our purposes, the most dramatic effect of the war was that the single nineteenth-century pattern of modernity—constitutional and ethnic–linguistic nationalism and scientific–industrial society—splintered into the three subpatterns: capitalism–democracy, socialism–communism, and supremacist nationalism. The countries representing these subpatterns of modernity formed camps that were bitterly hostile to each other:

- Capitalist democracy (most notably the United States, Britain, France, and parts of Latin America): support for the concepts of freedom (especially the free market), capitalism, and international institutions for maintaining peace.

- Communism–socialism (the Soviet Union): professed support for equality over freedom and a command economy originating from the top.

- Supremacist nationalism (Italy, Germany, and Japan): contempt for both democracy and communism, the celebration of racial supremacy and authoritarian/dictatorial rule, a state-controlled economy, and territorial expansion through military conquest.

In the period after World War I, the countries representing these three modernities moved in very different directions:

- The democratic victors, Great Britain and France, expanded their colonial empires by acquiring, under the rubric of "mandates," new territories taken from the liquidated Ottoman Empire in the Middle East and German possessions in Africa. Since a variety of ethno–linguistic nationalisms in these territories were forming at the same time, future conflicts were inevitable.

1908
Oil Discovered in the Middle East

1914–1918
World War I

1919
Versailles Treaty, Founding of League of Nations

1937–1945
World War II in China and the Pacific

1947
Indian and Pakistani Independence

1950–1953
Korean War

1958
Great Leap Forward in China

1911–1912
Revolution in China, Fall of Qing Dynasty

1917
Bolshevik Revolution

1929–1933
Stock Market Crash and Great Depression

1942
Nazis Implement the Final Solution

1948
State of Israel Founded, First Arab–Israeli War

1957
Soviet Union's Launch of Sputnik Satellite, Decolonization Begins in Africa

1962
Cuban Missile Cr

- In Russia, a small but highly disciplined communist party managed to engineer a political takeover, withdraw from the war, and build a communist state: the Union of Socialist Soviet Republics (USSR or Soviet Union). The Soviet Union acquired full industrial strength in the 1930s.
- The loser of World War I, Germany, together with Italy and Japan (both of which had joined the Allies in hopes of territorial gains), turned toward supremacist nationalism.

World War II and the Rise of New Nations

In contrast to World War I, the Second World War was actively planned by the supremacist nationalists and was far less avoidable. Both World War I and the Great Depression effectively ended the global free trade that had characterized the nineteenth century. All countries, including the capitalist democracies, now subscribed to the idea that the future of industry lay in economic "spheres" each dominated by one *autarkic*—that is, self-sufficient—industrial power. With the victory of the Allies, the United States and Soviet Union emerged after World War II as the leading examples of the two surviving patterns of modernity: capitalist democracy and socialism–communism. The proponents of each of these patterns competed with the other during the Cold War (1945–1991):

- The first, or "hot," phase, 1945–1962: The United States and Soviet Union surrounded themselves with allies in Europe and Asia and fought one another militarily through proxies, that is, smaller allied states. They also sought to align the new nations, emerging in the wake of decolonization, into their respective camps. The Cold War climaxed during the Cuban Missile Crisis of 1962.
- The second, "cooling" phase, 1962–1991: During this time, the two nuclear powers reduced tensions ("détente") and agreed on a mechanism to limit, and then to reduce, their nuclear arsenals. But they continued their proxy wars, in particular in Vietnam and Afghanistan.

Capitalist-Democratic Modernity

Perhaps the most significant event that put the United States on course for eventual victory over the Soviet Union in 1991 was the computer revolution—the third industrial revolution after the steam engine (ca. 1800) and steel, electricity, and chemicals (ca. 1865). After fully adapting itself to this revolution, the United States became the unrivaled superpower, deriving its strength from its advanced computer technology, powerful financial services, and unmatched military strength.

Thinking Like a World Historian

▶ How are the three patterns that emerged after World War I different adaptations to modernity? Despite their marked differences, what common features do they share?

▶ Why, after World War II, was socialism–communism in many ways a more attractive pattern to decolonizing countries than capitalism–democracy?

▶ Why was the United States better able to adapt to technological innovation than the Soviet Union?

▶ How do consumerism and the widespread use of social networking show the emergence of a global culture in the twenty-first century? Can we predict what future patterns will look like?

1963
Nuclear Test Ban Treaty

1966–1969
Cultural Revolution in China

1968–Present
Rise of "Women's Liberation" and Modern Feminism

1979
Shah of Iran Overthrown, Soviet Union Invades Afghanistan

1989
Tiananmen Square Demonstrations in China, Berlin Wall Torn Down, and German Unification

1989–1991
Collapse of Communism in Soviet Bloc

1965–1973
Vietnam War

1968
Massive Student Demonstrations in Europe, the United States, and Mexico

1978
Deng Xiaoping Announces "Four Modernizations" in China

1985–1989
Perestroika and Glasnost in the Soviet Union

1991
Collapse of the Soviet Union and End of the Cold War

1990–2000
Civil War and Ethnic Cleansing in Former Yugoslavia

4
d of Apartheid and Election of Nelson ndela as President in South Africa, u Genocide Against Tutsis in Rwanda

2001
Al-Qaeda Attack on United States

2007–2011
Global Financial Crisis and Economic Recession

2010
Number of Cell Phones Reaches 5 Billion Worldwide

2011
"Arab Spring," Nuclear Crisis in Japan, World Population 7 Billion

Chapter 28

1900-1945

World War and Competing Visions of Modernity

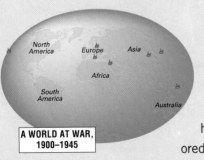

Professor Minobe seemed clearly rattled. For 30 years he had been Japan's leading jurist and constitutional theorist. His decades of work in the law school of Japan's leading academic institution, Tokyo Imperial University, were celebrated not just in Japan but among scholars throughout the world. Indeed, such was his prestige that he had received a noble rank and occupied an honored place in Japan's House of Peers, the upper chamber of its Diet, or

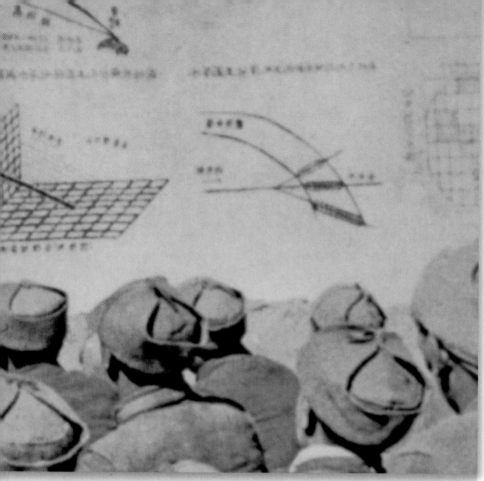

Seeing Patterns

▶ Which three patterns of modernity emerged after World War I? How and why did these patterns form?

▶ What were the strengths and flaws of each of the three visions of modernity?

▶ Why did supremacist nationalism disappear in the ashes of World War II?

parliament. A self-confident, even combative, man, he was not ordinarily given to suffering fools or meekly taking a dressing down.

But today was different, and only later would Minobe Tatsukichi (1873–1948) realize what a dramatic turning point it was for him and for the direction of Japanese law and politics. On this bleak February day in 1934, his fellow peer, Baron Takeo Kikuchi, had taken the floor and publicly denounced Minobe's most famous legal theory. Decades earlier, Minobe had posited that the relationship of the emperor to the constitution was one in which the emperor was an "organ" of the state. More than a generation of Japanese lawyers and scholars had internalized and practiced law according to this "organ theory." But now, the baron had accused Minobe of belittling the emperor's role in Japan's unique *kokutai*, or "national polity/essence." This concept, as we shall see, played a key role in Japanese supremacist nationalism during the 1930s.

Though Minobe defended his position skillfully, reminding his colleagues that to say the emperor was an organ of the state simply means that he rules for the state and not for himself, the damage had been done.

Tracing Modernity's Path. Members of the People's Liberation Army undergo artillery training during the civil war between the Nationalists and Communists, which ended with Communist victory in 1949.

Following more attacks in the Diet, Minobe resigned from his position, narrowly escaped being tried for his views, and was nearly assassinated in 1936. Already, however, in their drive to "clarify" the meaning of the "national essence," the cabinet had eliminated all of Minobe's writings and banned his works from study or circulation.

Minobe's experience personalizes a struggle to come to grips with new visions of modernity not only in Japan but in much of the world as well. By the 1930s, the liberal principles of modernity—constitutionalism, capitalism, science, and industry—were being tested in the crucible of the Great Depression and increasingly found wanting. In Japan, these values were already giving way to what we call "supremacist nationalism," offering close parallels to the ideologies of Nazism in Germany and fascism in Italy. In Russia, Communism represented another new subpattern of modernity. Other nations—Spain, Portugal, and China, for example—struggled with variations of one or more these competing ideologies.

In this chapter we will explore how the conflicts of spreading modernity spawned these new visions and how each fared through two world wars and the largest economic depression in history. We will also see how the supremacist nationalism that haunted Minobe, as embodied in the Axis powers, was utterly destroyed by the alliance of Communism and capitalist democracy. Their interlude of victory, however, was destined to be short-lived. Within a few years the remaining two divisions of modernity renewed the struggle for supremacy against each other under the shadow of potential nuclear annihilation.

The Great War and Its Aftermath

On July 27, 1914, the nations about to plunge into the abyss of total war the following day represented a host of different conditions with regard to modernity. As we saw in the preceding chapters, some, like Great Britain, Germany, and France, were, along with the United States, among the world leaders in the development of what we call "scientific–industrial society." Others, like Austria-Hungary, Ottoman Turkey, the newly independent Balkan nations, Russia, and even Japan, were at various stages of industrialization, more or less along the lines of the leading powers. In most cases, this latter group had come to this condition somewhat reluctantly, often after violent interactions with the new industrial powers. In terms of political modernity, all of these initial members of what would shortly be known as the Allies and Central powers—with the exception of France—were monarchies, though a number had become modified over the course of the nineteenth century with the

addition of constitutions and legislative assemblies. The larger powers were also imperial powers which, collectively, had reduced much of Asia and effectively the entire continent of Africa to the status of colonies. Over the next 4 years, this picture would change so completely that the old order would be dimly glimpsed only through the fog of memory of the diminished numbers who could recall it.

Once the war was on, science and industry made it far more lethal than any previous conflict had ever been; and when it ended, peace turned out to be elusive. Though the old empires of Germany, Austria-Hungary, and Ottoman Turkey were broken up, the new nations that arose from their wreckage emerged with their own sets of problems. Moreover, the new international order embodied by the League of Nations lacked the power to resolve conflicts and enforce its sanctions. Finally, the contradictions inherent in modernity between constitutionalism, imperialism, and emancipation were powerfully brought home to inhabitants of the colonial empires of the victors. For many, it meant using the ideas of nationalism—both ethnolinguistic and constitutional—and those of the new subpattern of communism as tools to achieve autonomy or independence.

Total War. By 1918, large swaths of northern France and Belgium resembled moonscapes from four years of destruction and carnage. One of the unluckiest places was the Belgian city of Ypres, which suffered three battles and was all but completely obliterated by war's end.

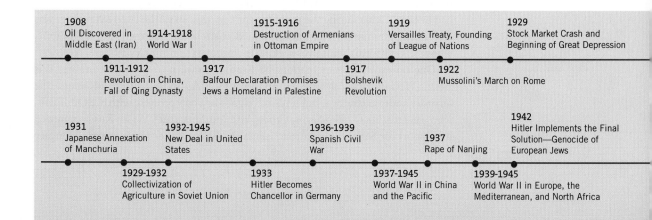

| 1908 Oil Discovered in Middle East (Iran) | 1914-1918 World War I | 1915-1916 Destruction of Armenians in Ottoman Empire | 1919 Versailles Treaty, Founding of League of Nations | 1929 Stock Market Crash and Beginning of Great Depression |

| 1911-1912 Revolution in China, Fall of Qing Dynasty | 1917 Balfour Declaration Promises Jews a Homeland in Palestine | 1917 Bolshevik Revolution | 1922 Mussolini's March on Rome |

| 1931 Japanese Annexation of Manchuria | 1932-1945 New Deal in United States | 1936-1939 Spanish Civil War | 1937 Rape of Nanjing | 1942 Hitler Implements the Final Solution—Genocide of European Jews |

| 1929-1932 Collectivization of Agriculture in Soviet Union | 1933 Hitler Becomes Chancellor in Germany | 1937-1945 World War II in China and the Pacific | 1939-1945 World War II in Europe, the Mediterranean, and North Africa |

A Savage War and a Flawed Peace

Time-honored imperial politics, tempered by the need for a balance of power among the major states, dominated Europe during the century following the Napoleonic Wars. This intersected with the two trends of nineteenth-century modernity we have identified in the last several chapters: the political patterns of constitutional nationalism and ethnolinguistic nationalism and the pattern of industrialization. The rise of the new imperialism in the nineteenth century, itself part of the growth of nationalism and industrialism accompanying modernity, carried a logic of its own that seemed destined to disrupt the ongoing efforts of statesmen to adjust the balance of power to ever-shifting political conditions. Here was the desire for naked conquest for a variety of reasons: markets, raw materials, strategic advantage, and national prestige, to name only the most prominent. For the moment, the victims of these conquests were the peoples of Africa, Asia, and Oceania, though the lesser European powers saw that they could be victims as well. Hence, as nationalism, imperialism, and industrialization moved forward, powers great and small sought alliances for protection and maintenance of the balance of power.

Empires and Nations in the Balkans   The causes of World War I have been endlessly debated from the moment the first shot was fired. Indeed, the role of Germany, rightly or wrongly, was enshrined in the Versailles Treaty ending the war as the famous "war guilt" clause. After decades of consensus and revision, modern scholars have begun to emphasize German aspirations for expansion into Eastern Europe as one of the prime catalysts for its support of Austria against Serbia in 1914. For its part, France had sought at various times *revanche*—revenge—for Germany's annexing of its "amputated provinces" of Alsace and Lorraine in 1870, though this was tempered by the painful awareness of Germany's superior might. In the first decade of the twentieth century, however, the key to the preservation of peace in Europe was seen as maintaining the balance among the three unequal empires that met in the Balkans.

The shrinking Ottoman Empire, beset by continuing demands from ethnic-nationalist minorities for independence, struggled to survive. The expanding Russian Empire, despite having suffered a defeat at the hands of Japan and an abortive revolution in 1904–1905, was rapidly recovering its aggressiveness, if not its military strength. For its part, the opportunistic Habsburg Empire of Austria-Hungary opposed Russian expansionism but also sought to benefit from Ottoman weakness. Germany had largely replaced Great Britain as the protector of the Ottomans and assisted the latter in strengthening their army. Though it had taken Mediterranean territories from the Ottomans, Britain still had a stake in keeping the rest of the Ottoman Empire in existence, as did the other powers, all of whom feared the results of a territorial scramble if the Ottoman Empire collapsed altogether. Hence, as there had been in China during the scramble for concessions of the late 1890s, there was also a rough community of interest aimed at strengthening the Ottoman Empire, whose leaders were themselves seeking to improve their military posture.

One unresolved ethnic-nationalist issue of concern to the three empires was Bosnia-Herzegovina. After the Balkan war of 1878, Austria-Hungary had become the territory's administrator—but not sovereign—as a compromise with the Ottomans, who were unable to keep Serbs, Croats, and Muslims apart. When Russia renewed its support for Serb ethnic nationalism in the Balkans after 1905, Austria-Hungary felt compelled to assume sovereignty of Bosnia-Herzegovina in a protective move in 1908. This in return offered Russia support for its demand for open shipping through the Bosporus. Britain and Germany, however, forced Russia to withdraw this demand. Russia, committed to a policy of pan-Slavism—support for the aspirations of Slavs everywhere—avenged itself by stirring up Serb nationalists. On June 28, 1914, members of a Bosnian Serb nationalist group assassinated the Austrian heir to the throne, Franz Ferdinand, and his wife while they toured the Bosnian city of Sarajevo. This assassination began the tragic slide of the two rival alliances that maintained the balance of power into the cataclysm of World War I. Yet even this occurred only after a month of intense diplomacy and increasing desperation among most of the politicians involved. In the end, each country's perceived military necessities were invoked to trump any diplomatic solution to the crisis.

The Early Course of the War

In contrast with past conflicts, this war was no longer limited and localized but comprehensive from the start: **total war**. In addition, the contingency plans of the combatants' general staffs in many cases relied on precise timing and speedy mobilization of their forces. Here, the most dramatic example was that of Germany. In order to avoid a two-front war, Germany, with its allies Austria-Hungary and the Ottoman Empire (the Central powers), had to defeat France before Russia's massive army was fully mobilized. The German Schlieffen Plan therefore called for a massive assault on northern France through Belgium that would take Paris in 6 weeks, while trapping and isolating the Allied armies aimed at invading Alsace and Lorraine, taken by Germany after the Franco–Prussian War of 1870.

Though the German plan came close to succeeding, it ultimately failed after the desperate French–British victory in the first Battle of the Marne in early September 1914, a more rapid Russian mobilization than expected, and a poor showing of the Austrians against Russia. After several months of seesaw fighting along the lines of the initial German advance into France, the Germans and the French and British dug in. By 1915 the two sides were forced to conduct grinding trench warfare in northeastern France and an inconclusive war in the east. The Germans, with superior firepower and mobility, were able to keep the Russians at bay and inflicted heavy losses on their troops—many of whom marched into battle without weapons, being expected to pick them up off their dead comrades. For its part, the Ottoman Empire suffered a crushing Russian invasion in the Caucasus, prompting it to carry out a wholesale massacre of its Armenian minority, which was alleged to have helped in the invasion. From official Turkish documents published in 2005 it can be concluded that the number of Armenians killed was close to 1 million. This planned

Total war: A type of warfare in which all the resources of the nation—including all or most of the civilian population—are marshaled for the war effort. As total war became elaborated, all segments of society were increasingly seen as legitimate targets for the combatants.

War of Annihilation

"I got to my position and looked over the top. The first thing I saw in the space of a tennis court in front of me was the bodies of 100 dead or severely wounded men lying there in our own wire . . . I sent my runner 200 yards on my right to get into touch with our right company, who should have been close beside me. He came back and reported he could find nothing of them. It subsequently transpired that they never reached the front line as their communication trenches had caught it so much worse than mine, and the communication trench was so full of dead and dying, that they could not get over them. . . . Those three battalions [2,500 men] who went over were practically annihilated. Every man went to his death or got wounded without flinching. Yet in this war, nothing will be heard about it, the papers have glowing accounts of great British success . . . 60 officers went out, lots of whom I knew. I believe 2 got back without being wounded . . ."

—Quoted in Michael Kernan. "Day of Slaughter on the Somme." *Washington Post*, June 27, 1976. From the diary of Captain Reginald Leetham, a British soldier who fought in the Battle of the Somme, July–November 1916. Nearly 60,000 British soldiers were killed in the first day of battle.

massacre, the one large-scale atrocity of the war, still requires a full accounting today and is hotly debated by scholars, lawyers, and politicians.

As the war dragged on, both camps sought to recruit new countries to their sides. Italy, Greece, and Romania entered on the Allied side with the hope of gaining territory from Austria-Hungary and the Ottomans; Bulgaria joined the Central powers in the service of its own territorial ambitions. Japan declared war on Germany in 1914 as part of a previous alliance with Britain but used its occupation of German territories in the Pacific and China as a step toward expanding its own empire. The Allies also recruited volunteers from among their dominions and colonies in considerable numbers, some 800,000 from India alone. Thus, with soldiers from the mostly white dominions of Australia and New Zealand, as well as the African and Asian colonies of Britain and France fighting and dying in the trenches, the war became a true world war. With the token entrance of China in 1917 and the pivotal entrance of the United States that same year the war now involved every major state in the world.

The Turning Point: 1917   By early 1917 the ever-intensifying slaughter took its first toll. In March 1917, tsarist Russia collapsed in the face of horrendous casualties, crippled industry, extensive labor unrest, government ineptitude, and general internal weakness. This February Revolution (actually in March, so called because it took place during February in the old-style Julian calendar still in use in Russia at the time) forced Tsar Nicholas II to abdicate and created a provisional government. The new social-democratic government committed itself to carrying on the war, which now grew even more unpopular and untenable for Russia to manage. The communist Bolshevik Party of Vladimir Lenin (1870–1924), now liberated from persecution by the provisional government, steadily campaigned against continuing the war and in early November (October in the Julian calendar) launched a takeover of the government in the capital of Petrograd—as St. Petersburg had been renamed

Supporting the Empire. The colonies were drawn into the conflicts of their rulers. One million Indian troops, such as the ones shown here, fought with the British during World War I.

at the beginning of the war. Capturing the reins of government, the Bolsheviks began tortuous negotiations with the Germans, which resulted in the disastrous Treaty of Brest-Litovsk in March 1918. Roughly one-third of the Russian Empire's population, territory, and resources were handed over to the Germans in return for Russia's peaceful withdrawal from the conflict. They had now come close to what the Supreme Army Command (*Oberste Heeresleitung*, OHL) had secretly declared as its war goal: the creation of *Lebensraum* (living space) for Germany in the industrialized European part of Russia.

The United States had declared neutrality at the outset of the war, but despite President Woodrow Wilson's plea to Americans to stay "neutral in thought" as well as action, the course of the war had shifted US opinion decidedly toward the Allied side. The German violation of Belgian neutrality in the opening days of the war and extensive German use of the new technology of the submarine swung Americans toward a profound distaste for German actions. The German torpedoing and sinking of the British liner *Lusitania* on May 7, 1915, cost the lives of more than 100 Americans and brought the United States to the brink of war. German guarantees to abandon their policy of "unrestricted" submarine warfare contained the crisis for the time being. Still, the ties of American banks and industries to France and Britain continued to tilt the United States increasingly toward the Allies.

Several key decisions prompted the Germans to risk and ultimately bring on war with the United States. With each side increasingly desperate to gain a decisive advantage over the other and the British naval blockade of Germany wreaking increasing hardships on their economy and populace, the German naval staff calculated that they could starve England into submission with an all-out campaign of submarine warfare. Knowing this would bring the United States into the war, they concluded that they could accomplish their task before the Americans could draft and train a large army. They also felt that their submarines could sink many American troop ships and stifle any US efforts to bolster the Allies. However, they then made a singularly clumsy diplomatic overture to Mexico to join the Central powers if the United States declared war on Germany. The British intercepted this so-called Zimmerman note and gleefully passed it on to the Americans. When Germany announced resumption of unrestricted submarine warfare, Wilson had no choice but to ask Congress to declare war, which it did on April 6, 1917.

The entrance of the United States added the critical resources needed by the Allies to ultimately win the war. More importantly, Wilson's war aims, embodied in his Fourteen Points, sought to transform the conflict from one of failed diplomacy and territorial gain to a war "to make the world safe for democracy." He called for freedom of the seas, the rights of neutral powers, self-determination for all peoples, and peace "without annexations or indemnities." These new causes represented not only American war aims but now were presented as the Allies' war aims as well. For peoples in all the world's empires yearning for independence and self-determination, it appeared, briefly at least, that one side decisively championed their desires.

It was not until early 1918, however, that American troops began to land in France in appreciable numbers. This coincided with the last spring offensive mounted by Germany. Bolstered by the addition of troops from the now peaceful Russian front, the Germans threw everything they had at the Allies and once again came close to seizing Paris. But the new American troops in France gave the Allies the advantage they needed to stop the German effort, and it soon collapsed. By June, more than 1 million Americans had arrived; by September, nearly 2 million; by the end of fighting in November, 4 million more Americans were in various stages of progress to the western front. Faced with these new conditions and reeling from the Allies' September counteroffensive that now threatened to advance into Germany, the Germans agreed to an armistice on November 11, 1918.

The Versailles Peace   As the staggering war toll sank in, the Allies settled down to make peace. About 20 million soldiers and civilians were dead, and 21 million were wounded. Military deaths were 5 million for the Allies and 4 million for the Central powers. Many more millions perished in the world's worst influenza pandemic, abetted by the massive transportation of goods and soldiers at war's end. The settlement, signed at Versailles on June 28, 1919—the fifth anniversary of the assassination of Franz Ferdinand—has been described unflatteringly as a "victor's peace."

In the peace treaty, the German, Austro-Hungarian, and Ottoman Empires were all dismantled and new nation-states were created in their stead. Germany lost its overseas colonies, Alsace-Lorraine, and East Prussia. The Allies declared Germany responsible for the war and condemned it to substantial military restrictions and huge reparation payments. France did not prevail with plans to divide Germany again into its pre-1871 components but succeeded in acquiring temporary custody of the Saar province with its coal reserves and steel factories as a guarantee for the payment of war reparations. For a long time, historians considered the Allied-imposed reparations excessive but more recent research has come to the conclusion that Germany, not destroyed by war, had the industrial-financial capacity to pay. A new supranational **League of Nations** was entrusted with the maintenance of peace. But since one of its clauses required collective military action in case of aggression, the US Senate refused ratification, rejecting this infringement on American sovereignty. Altogether, the Versailles peace was deeply flawed. Instead of binding a Germany that could not be diminished economically into a common western European framework, the Allies actually encouraged it to go it alone by flanking it in the east with small and weak countries that could be dominated in the future (see Map 28.1).

America First: The Beginnings of a Consumer Culture and the Great Depression

The United States emerged from the war as by far the strongest among the Allied democracies. From a debtor country, it had turned into a creditor country; a majority of Americans now lived in nonrural environments; and the war economy shifted relatively easily into a sustained peacetime expansion. Far less hampered by old traditions than its European counterparts, it espoused modernity with a brusque enthusiasm, although its writers and intellectuals were often all too aware of modernity's contradictions.

Modernity Unfolding in the United States   Increased mechanization in industries such as construction materials, automobile assembly lines, and electrical appliance manufacturing spurred the economic expansion. A new dream arose among Americans: to move from countryside to city and to own a house (with running water and sewage), car, refrigerator, radio, and telephone. Once in the city, during the "Roaring Twenties," as the decade came to be called, Americans wanted

League of Nations:
An international body ultimately numbering 58 states created as part of the Versailles Treaty and functioning between 1919 and 1946 that sought to ensure world peace by curbing secret diplomacy, settling international disputes through negotiation, supervising colonial dependencies under a mandate system, and punishing aggressor nations through the practice of "collective security."

Europe, the Middle East, and North Africa, 1914

0 km   400
0 miles   400

N

NORWAY
SWEDEN
North Sea
DENMARK
BRITAIN
NETH.
GERMANY
BEL.
LUX.
ATLANTIC OCEAN
FRANCE
SWIT.
AUSTRIA-HUNGARY
RUSSIAN EMPIRE
ITALY
MONT.
ALB.
SERBIA
ROMANIA
BULGARIA
Black Sea
PORTUGAL
SPAIN
GREECE
OTTOMAN EMPIRE
SPANISH MOROCCO
Mediterranean Sea
ALGERIA (to France)
TUNISIA (to France)
DODECANESE (to Italy)
CYPRUS (to Britain)
PERSIA
MOROCCO (to France)
LIBYA (invaded by Italy, 1911)
EGYPT
ARABIA

Europe, the Middle East, and North Africa, 1923

0 km   400
0 miles   400

N

FINLAND
NORWAY
SWEDEN
ESTONIA
LATVIA
LITHUANIA
North Sea
DENMARK
BRITAIN
REPUBLIC OF IRELAND (after 1932)
GER.
SOVIET UNION
NETH.
GERMANY
BEL.
LUX.
POLAND
SAAR
CZECHOSLOVAKIA
ATLANTIC OCEAN
FRANCE
SWIT.
AUSTRIA
HUNGARY
ROMANIA
ITALY
YUGOSLAVIA
BULGARIA
Black Sea
GEORGIA
ALB.
ARMENIA
AZERBAIJAN
PORTUGAL
SPAIN
GREECE
TURKEY
SPANISH MOROCCO
Mediterranean Sea
TRANS-JORDAN (Brit. mandate)
SYRIA (French mandate)
IRAQ (British mandate)
IRAN
ALGERIA (to France)
TUNISIA (to France)
PALESTINE (Brit. mandate)
MOROCCO (to France)
LIBYA (to Italy)
EGYPT
SAUDI ARABIA (after 1932)

MAP 28.1 Europe, the Middle East, and North America in 1914 and 1923.

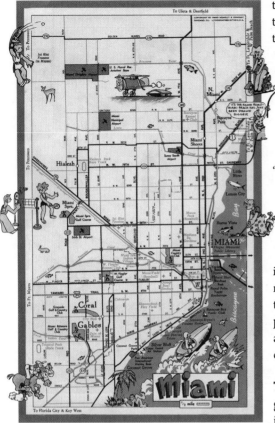

A Vision of American Modernity. This detail from a ca. 1930 Gulf Gasoline "Florida Info Map" vividly captures the American pattern of modernity—miles of roads and highways stretching in all directions, ample leisure opportunities, and a natural environment where the sun always shines.

to be entertained. A remarkable efflorescence of popular culture accompanied the rising urban prosperity. City and small-town dwellers alike were caught up in the mania of the movies, which, after 1927, came with sound. Americans frequented ballrooms to experiment with a large variety of dance steps and to listen to bands playing popular tunes. Jazz music with a large variety of styles found avid listeners. One could now listen to recorded sound on convenient 78-rpm records played on gramophones. The film industry of Hollywood and a recording industry came into being, churning out "hit" after "hit" as their popular products came to be called.

As far-reaching as both of these were, the growth of radio went one step further. From a primitive system of sending Morse-code messages via electrical "spark–gap" transmissions at the turn of the century, radio received vacuum tube amplification and by the time of the war was capable of sending sound and voice messages. In 1919, the first commercial radio station in the United States began broadcasting; by 1930, the number of radios was in the tens of millions. Moreover, experimental work on an even more advanced technology was also under way during the 1920s, though its impact would not come for nearly 30 years: television.

The New Woman   The Nineteenth Amendment of 1920 gave American women the right to vote, enormously expanding the promise of constitutional nationalism by half the population. In addition to winning political rights, American women heightened their social profile. Many colleges and universities went co-ed, although women often majored in education to become teachers, or home economics to become good housewives for the husbands they met at school. Alternatively, they became secretaries skilled in shorthand and typing or nurses in hospitals. Indeed, the typewriter, developed in the latter nineteenth century, directly contributed to the shift from employing mostly men as secretaries to making it an overwhelmingly female profession. Its ease of operation and speed of copying and reproduction (through the use of carbon paper) was ideally suited to what were perceived to be "women's skills" and abilities. Similarly, women swiftly dominated the new occupations of telephone operator and switchboard operator as the new century advanced. By the 1920s it was rare indeed if one picked up the telephone to make a call in the United States and did not hear a female voice ask, "Number please?"

For people of color, however, the situation was far different. Black women, if they were not agricultural laborers, rarely were able to become more than domestic servants or laundry workers in the growing urban economy. In larger segregated areas with more diversified economies, however, African American women often found similar kinds of opportunities as white women, though far more limited in scope and availability. Hence, although emancipation was real for white women, it clearly remained gendered, while the situation for black women continued to be additionally hampered by racism.

Nevertheless, women on the whole became consumers and participants in pop culture in their own right. The new female ideal—or troubling stereotype, depending on your perspective—for many young women was the "flapper." Wearing lipstick and other cosmetics (which were no longer considered signs of being "of ill repute"), having her hair "bobbed" under her cloche hat, wearing dresses above the knee, and throwing away her corset, she drank and smoked cigarettes—and might even drive her own car. She might go to jazz clubs and indulge in such daring dances as the Charleston or the Black Bottom. Sex was also becoming something that she might openly talk about in public, and sexual satisfaction was no longer an emotion to be suppressed. One can still see this contemporary vision of the flapper and her successors in the cartoon series *Betty Boop* from the early 1930s. Liberal social values, as they were called, including premarital sex, divorce, and tolerance for homosexuality, made inroads, although mostly among the relatively small number of white-collar, educated people in the cities.

Inevitably, there was also a conservative backlash, expressing itself most directly in the ratification of the Eighteenth Amendment. From 1920 to 1933, the commercial production of alcohol was prohibited in the United States, primarily for the purpose of reducing public drunkenness among the largely immigrant working classes. Since it did not outlaw noncommercial home brewing or bars, however, widespread production of "moonshine," "bathtub gin" and other "bootleg liquor" and discreet sale of liquor in "speakeasies" (bars where one spoke softly so as not to draw attention) made Prohibition the subject of ridicule and impossible to enforce effectively. The rise of organized crime in America was greatly abetted by its domination of the illegal alcohol industry in the 1920s and 1930s.

High Artistic Creativity   American intellectuals, writers, and artists viewed consumer and pop culture modernity with mixed feelings. On the one hand, they hailed what they viewed as the progress of liberal values. But, on the other hand, they were often uneasy about what they perceived as an increasing superficiality and materialism in modernity, furthered by ads, fashions, and fads. Prior to World War I, Europeans continued to consider themselves culturally superior, as reflected in a quip from Oscar Wilde's play *A Woman of No Importance*, where one character remarks that when good Americans die they go to Paris and another character replies that when bad Americans die they go to America. But after World War I, the ambiguities of modernity engendered a veritable explosion of creativity in American culture.

The shattered illusions of the pre–world war era and search for a new beginning in modernity fueled much of this creativity. An entire cohort of artists and intellectuals viewed themselves as belonging to a "lost generation," a term referring to the generation that had lost its best years of life, or even life altogether, to a senseless world war. Such figures as Gertrude Stein (1874–1946), a writer and poet who coined the term, and Wallace Stevens (1879–1955), Sinclair Lewis (1885–1951), Ezra Pound (1885–1972), T. S. Eliot (1888–1965), Eugene O'Neill (1888–1953), F. Scott Fitzgerald (1896–1940), Thornton Wilder (1897–1975), William Faulkner (1897–1962), and Ernest Hemingway (1899–1961)—five among them recipients of the Nobel Prize in Literature—defined the new American style of "modernism" and are still widely read and taught today. For African Americans, a new cultural touchstone was the Harlem Renaissance, featuring the leading innovators in jazz and the writers Claude McKay (1889–1948), Langston Hughes (1902–1967), James Weldon Johnson (1871–1938), and Zora Neale Hurston (1891–1960).

Few later authors plumbed modernity with the breadth of education as these "modernists" did, analyzing its contradictions, exposing its follies, articulating its inner emotional tensions in a "stream of consciousness," or offering countermodels of spirituality, naturalness, Greek classicism, or Chinese monism. Not only did the United States give mass culture to the world; it also provided many of the literary tools to grapple with modernity and attempt to understand it, either by loathing it or by living with it critically.

Business and Labor   Just as much energy characterized American business. Business tycoons and probusiness politicians were integral parts of the Roaring Twenties. Presidents Harding, Coolidge, and Hoover along with the Congress exercised a minimum of political control, illustrated by the slogan "Less government in business and more business in government." President Calvin Coolidge (in office 1923–1929), legendary as "Silent Cal" for his taciturn manner—when the famous wit Dorothy Parker (1893-1967) told him of a bet she had made that she could make him say more than two words, his reply was "You lose"—expressed the spirit of the day with characteristic succinctness: "The business of America is business."

While business boomed, trade and industrial unions stagnated. The American Federation of Labor (AFL), founded in 1886, was the largest trade union pushing for improved labor conditions. But, in contrast to European labor unions, it was always hampered by the problem that its members were unskilled workers of many ethnic, linguistic, and religious backgrounds and, therefore, difficult to organize. Business easily squashed widespread strikes for the right to unionize in 1919. An anti-immigration hysteria followed, with laws that cut immigration by half. The hysteria, mixed with anticommunism, climaxed in 1927 with the trial of Ferdinando

A Klan Lynching. Outside the South, Indiana was the state that experienced the greatest surge in Klan activities in the period immediately after World War I. In 1925, the governor and half the state assembly were Klansmen and about 30 percent of the state's white population were members. In this photo from August 1930, a crowd gathers to gawk at Tom Shipp and Abram Smith, two African American men who were lynched by a mob for allegedly committing robbery and rape.

Nicola Sacco and Bartolomeo Vanzetti, two Italian anarchist immigrants who were convicted and executed for murder on contradictory evidence.

The Backlash   The antiforeigner and anticommunist hysteria was part of a larger unease with modernism. Fundamentalist religion, intolerance toward Catholics and Jews, and fear and violence directed at African Americans rose visibly. The revival of the Ku Klux Klan was at the center of repeated waves of lynchings in the South and attempts to control the local politics of a number of states, most prominently Indiana. The Klan remained a powerful force in the South and Midwest until World War II.

The most startling offenses against the modern principles of liberty and equality, however, came from ideologues wrapping themselves in the mantle of modern science. Researchers at the leading private universities lent respectability to the pseudoscience of **eugenics**, conceptualizing an ideal of a "Nordic" race and searching for ways to produce more athletic, blond, and blue-eyed Americans. Foundations such as the Carnegie Endowment and businessmen such as Henry Ford financed research on how to prevent the reproduction of genetically "inferior" races. California and other states passed laws that allowed for the sterilization of nearly 10,000 patients—mostly women (black and white)—in state mental hospitals, and the Supreme Court in 1927 upheld these laws. Ironically, some of the practices that would inspire Hitler and the Nazis were already quietly in place during the 1920s in the United States and actually seen by many as progressive.

Eugenics: The supposed study of hereditary breeding of better human beings by genetic control. Beginning in the 1920s, a well-financed social movement in the US succeeded in sterilizing thousands of women considered to be mentally and/or racially inferior.

The Great Depression   The Roaring Twenties came to a screeching halt in 1929, when saturation of the market for consumer goods behind high tariff walls during the later 1920s led to falling profit rates. Many of the wealthy had begun to shift their money from investments in manufacturing to speculation on the stock market. In addition, stocks began to be seen as a viable outlet for ordinary investors due to widespread margin borrowing with little money down. As long as the market boomed, investors made money; but if stocks went down, the margin calls went out, and investors could be wiped out. By the late 1920s, a general slowdown in production shifted attention to unsustainable debt levels. Farmers were particularly deep in debt, having borrowed to mechanize while speculating wrongly on a continuation of high prices for commodities. In October 1929, the speculators panicked, selling their stock for pennies on the dollar. The panic rippled through both the finance and manufacturing sectors until it burst into a full-blown cascade. As banks began calling in loans at home and abroad, the panic swiftly became a worldwide crisis: the Great Depression of 1929–1933. Harrowing scenes of unemployment and poverty put the American system of capitalist democratic modernity to a severe test.

Americans largely blamed their probusiness president, Herbert Hoover (in office 1929–1933), for failing to manage the crisis and in 1932 elected Franklin D. Roosevelt (in office 1933–1945). Hoover's approach had been one that previous administrations had turned to in times of economic crisis: cut government spending, raise tariffs to protect US industries, and let market forces correct themselves. But such measures seemed only to make things worse, while the Smoot-Hawley Tariff of 1930—with the highest tariff rates in American history—encouraged retaliatory tariffs in other countries and discouraged world commerce, thus contributing to a world-wide economic collapse. Under Roosevelt's prodding, Congress immediately enacted what he called the "New Deal," in which the government engaged in deficit spending to enact measures designed to help the unemployed and revive business and agriculture. Among the most ambitious of these were the National Recovery Act (1933) aimed at fostering competition, safeguarding the rights of labor, and discouraging monopoly practices; and the Agricultural Adjustment Act (1933), which began the use of subsidies to stabilize the prices of farm commodities Other notable programs included the Civilian Conservation Corps (CCC) in 1933, which enlisted large numbers of the unemployed to conduct improvements in the country's national parks and nature preserves; and the Works Progress Administration (WPA) in 1935, which utilized the talents of the nation's creative community by subsidizing the arts and literature.

One showpiece of the New Deal was the Tennessee Valley Authority, a government-owned corporation for the economic development of large parts of the southeastern United States particularly hard hit by the Depression. In addition, a social safety net was created for the first time, with unemployment benefits and the Social Security Act. Finally, a Securities and Exchange Commission (SEC) was created in 1934 to supervise and enforce regulations governing the stock market in order to prevent a number of the practices that had led to the collapse of 1929.

To finance the New Deal, Roosevelt took the United States off the gold standard, a monetary system that linked currencies to the value of gold, and went deep into deficit spending. In 1937, however, a Congress frightened by the deficit slackened efforts to reduce unemployment, while the Supreme Court declared several of the new programs unconstitutional. The result was a new slump, from which the economy finally recovered only with America's entry into World War II.

Great Britain and France: Slow Recovery and Troubled Empires

While the impact of World War I on the United States was relatively slight, Britain and France suffered severely (see Map 28.2). A lack of finances hampered the recovery, as did the enormous debt both countries contracted during the war. Conservative politicians relinquished the state capitalism of the war period and returned to politics favorable to private investors, without, however, allowing for the same uncontrolled speculations as in the United States. Although socialist politicians gained in importance, they did not succeed in improving working-class conditions or the safety net. Britain benefited from the discovery of oil in its mandates in the Middle East, and the demands of the League of Nations mandate system, in which the colonies were to be prepared for future independence, were not pursued vigorously by either France or Britain.

Weak British Recovery   As the economy shifted from state control during the war back to free enterprise, industry was still in a leading role; but Britain was also heavily dependent on world trade, carried by its merchant fleet. Unfortunately for Britain, world trade declined dramatically after the war. In addition, the country owed a war debt of $4.3 billion to the United States for war materiel, which the United States insisted on receiving back (relenting only during the Depression). Since much of Britain's ability to repay these debts rested upon Germany's ability to pay its reparations, the entire European economic system remained problematic throughout the 1920s.

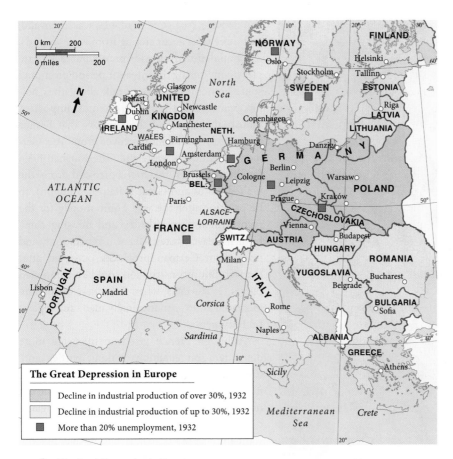

MAP 28.2 **The Great Depression in Europe.**

With the restructuring of Germany's debts under the Dawes Plan in 1924, some stability finally came to the international capital markets. Still, close to half of the annual British budgets in the interwar period went into paying off the war debt. In this situation, industrial investments were low and unemployment was high, dipping below 10 percent of the workforce only once during the 1920s. In addition, business lowered wages, causing labor to respond with a massive general strike in 1926. The strike collapsed after only 9 days, but business, without capital to make industry competitive again, did not benefit either. The British economy remained stagnant.

The dominant conservatives in the government could not bring themselves in the 1930s to accept deficit spending. At a minimum, however, they went off the gold standard and devalued the currency to make exports competitive again. World trade, of course, had declined; but by lowering tariffs within the empire, Britain created the equivalent of the **autarky** that Nazi Germany and militaristic Japan were dreaming of with their planned conquests. A semblance of prosperity returned to the country in the 1930s.

Autarky: The maintenance of a self-supporting state economic system.

France: Moderate Recovery

Together with Russia, France suffered devastating human losses and destruction of property during the war. For every 10 men of

Down and Out in Wales. The 1930s' prosperity was largely limited to southern England. Most of the rest of the British Isles, such as this unemployed miner in Wales, who totters from either drink or depression and is consoled by his two children, were largely left out. George Orwell (1903–1950) published his investigations of British poverty in *The Road to Wigan Pier* (1937), a widely read essay in which he castigated the Conservatives for their lack of a job-creating policy. A strong advocate for social democracy, he became well known after World War II for his opposition to antidemocratic regimes, expressed in his novels *Animal Farm* (1945) and *Nineteen Eighty-Four* (1949).

working age, two were dead, one was an invalid, and three were recuperating from their wounds. The population drop and consequent lack of replacement during the interwar period prompted some French observers to talk about the "hollow years." Alsace-Lorraine, the most important industrial region and the territory that France desperately wanted to recover from the Germans, was now a wasteland. The war had been fought with war materiel borrowed from the United States and Great Britain ($5 billion), to be paid for after the war. Some money for the reconstruction of industry and housing came from increased taxes, German reparations, and taxes from German provinces occupied after the war. But reconstruction could be completed only in 1926–1929, when taxes were once more increased and Germany finally made full reparation payments.

Although French governments were more dependent on coalitions among parties and, therefore, less stable, labor was more often than not represented in the governments. France did not suffer a traumatic general strike like England did, and even though it also returned to the gold standard (1928–1936), it wisely avoided the prewar parity, thereby making the low wages for its workers a bit more bearable. Since it had to reconstruct so much from the ground up, France modernized more successfully in many ways than Britain in the interwar period.

Thanks to its successful reconstruction, France weathered the Depression until 1931. Even then, conservative politicians found the idea of deficit spending as a way to get out of the Depression too counterintuitive. Instead, like the Hoover administration in America, they slashed government spending and refused to devalue the currency. Unrest in the population and rapidly changing governments were the consequences which, in 1933–1934, made supremacist-nationalism an attractive model, especially for business, which was afraid of labor strife. When fascist–communist street fighting broke out in Paris, the Communist Party initiated the formation of a Popular Front coalition with the Socialist Party and others (1936–1938). Although this coalition prevented a further slide into supremacist nationalism, it was too short-lived to allow for the centrist middle-class core to broaden, with disastrous consequences for France's ability to resist Hitler in World War II.

"The Crazy Years"   American pop culture, with its music, dance, movies, and fashions, swept both Britain and France during the 1920s. As in the United States, the ambiguities of modernity also provoked a burst of artistic creativity. The *années folles* ("crazy years") produced in Britain the Bloomsbury Group (after a district in London), a loose collection of modernist writers, such as Virginia Woolf (1882–1941) and E. M. Forster (1879–1970), intellectuals, philosophers, and the economist John Maynard Keynes (1883–1946). Woolf is remembered for her interests in the literary tool of inner monologue, parallel to Faulkner. In addition, the Irishman James Joyce (1882–1941) and D. H. Lawrence (1885–1930) left their permanent imprint on modernity. Joyce employed the stream-of-consciousness approach with extreme formal variations and precision of description. Lawrence became notorious among conservatives for his modernist interests in human intimacy while endearing himself to them with his doubts about the blessings of democracy. A majority of these modernists, reflective of the contradictions of modernity, practiced liberal ethics and expressed socialist leanings.

In France, the 1920s produced *surrealism*, an artistic movement that took its inspiration from the theory of the subconscious popularized by the contemporary Austrian psychiatrist Sigmund Freud. Prominent surrealist painters in Paris were the German Max Ernst (1891–1976) and the Spanish Salvador Dalí (1904–1989). Surrealist poets were André Breton (1896–1966) and Louis Aragon (1897–1982). Ernst famously declared himself dead in 1914 and resuscitated in 1918, a declaration reminiscent of Gertrude Stein's

Surrealism. Surrealist painters allowed their Freudian subconscious to flow into their creations. (*a*) Marcel Duchamp, *Fresh Window* (1920). (*b*) Max Ernst, *Two Children Are Threatened by a Nightingale* (1924). (*c*) Salvador Dalí, *Ghost of Two Automobiles* (1929).

term the "lost generation." Both followed Freud's assertion that the unconscious dominates the artist's creativity: Dreams and myths are stronger influences than reality. Many members, coming originally from the earlier movement of Dadaism in Zurich, also celebrated accident and coincidence as elements in their work, especially in poetry. *An Andalusian Dog* (*Un chien andalou*, 1929) by the Spanish director Luis Buñuel (1900–1983) was a stunning short movie, a visual companion to the surrealist game of "exquisite corpse," the sequential utterance of sentences in free association. In the view of surrealists, the Freudian subconscious typically produced spontaneous, uncontrolled creations. With their playful and often ironic stances, often disdainful of the modernists' adherence to "rational" form, the surrealists anticipated postmodernism, which dominated the arts and humanities during the last quarter of the century.

Colonies and Mandates   The carefree consumer modernity in France and Britain during the 1920s contrasted sharply with the harsh reality of sustaining expensive colonial empires covering much of the world's land mass. After World War I, the British Empire grew by 2 million square miles to 14 million, or one-quarter of the earth's surface, adding 13 million to its 458 million subjects, or one-quarter of the world population. The French Empire at the same time measured 5 million square miles, with a population of 113 million. Although the wisdom of maintaining empires was widely debated in the interwar period, in view of increased subsidies that had to be given many of the colonies, conservatives held fast to the prestige that square mileage was presumed to bestow on their holders. Defense of these far-flung empires, interpreted as the "strategic interest" of the colonial powers, dominated the policies of Britain and France toward their dependencies and mandates during the interwar period (see Map 28.3).

The most important area strategically for both the British and the French after World War I was the Middle East. Under the postwar peace terms, the British and

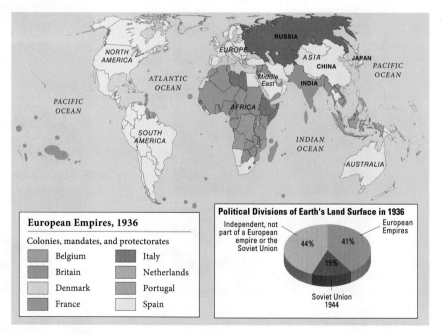

MAP 28.3 European Empires, 1936.

French had received the Arab provinces of the former Ottoman Empire (other than Egypt and Sudan, acquired in 1881) as *mandates*—that is, as territories to be prepared for independence. Since a British geologist had in 1908 discovered oil in southwestern Iran, however, Britain and France put a high premium on their new Middle Eastern imperial possessions. Neither was in a hurry to guide its mandates to independent nationhood.

Twice-Promised Lands   As would be expected, Arab leaders were strongly opposed to the British and French mandates. Nationalism was on the rise, ironically encouraged by the British during the war as they were searching for regional allies against the Ottomans. Their agent, T. E. Lawrence (1888–1935), the famous "Lawrence of Arabia," fluent in Arabic and Islamic customs, helped the members of a prominent family, the Hashemites from Mecca in western Arabia, to assume leadership of the Arabs for a promised national kingdom in Syria and Palestine in the so-called McMahon–Sharif Hussein correspondence of 1915–1916.

Since the British, to rally support among Jews in Britain as well as Germany, Poland, and Russia, also promised the Jews a "national home" in Palestine in the Balfour Declaration of 1917, Arab nationalism was stymied even before it could unfold. The French ended a short-lived Arab-declared kingdom in 1920 in Damascus, and the British moved the Hashemites into their mandates of Iraq and Transjordan in 1921, in accordance with the Sykes–Picot agreement (1916) concerning the imperial division of the Middle East between the Allies. As Iraq was divided by majority Shiites and minority Sunnis, the British inaugurated a policy of divide and rule in their Middle Eastern mandates, while dangling the prospect of eventual independence in front of their populations.

In Palestine, the contradiction between the promises to Arabs and Jews during the war forced Britain to build an expensive direct administration under a high commissioner. In 1920, Palestine was inhabited by nearly 670,000 Arabs and 65,000 Jews. Many religious Jews had arrived as refugees from anti-Semitic riots or pogroms in Russia in the early 1880s and 1890s and the difficult postwar years in eastern Europe. When the Austrian Jewish journalist Theodor Herzl (1860–1904) made ethnic nationalism the ideology of secular Jews, early pioneers of **Zionism**, as secular Jewish nationalism was called, began to arrive as well. A Jewish National Fund collected money from Jews worldwide to buy land from willing Palestinian absentee landlords residing in Beirut and Jerusalem. As a consequence, Jewish settlers evicted the landlords' Palestinian tenant farmers. These evictions were the root cause of two Palestinian–Arab nationalist uprisings, in 1929 and 1936–1939, for which the British had no real answer except force and belated efforts in 1939 to limit Jewish immigration.

The Balfour Declaration

Foreign Office
November 2nd, 1917

Dear Lord Rothschild:

I have much pleasure in conveying to you, on behalf of His Majesty's Government, the following declaration of sympathy with Jewish Zionist aspirations which has been submitted to, and approved by, the Cabinet:

His Majesty's Government view with favor the establishment in Palestine of a national home for the Jewish people, and will use their best endeavors to facilitate the achievement of this object, it being clearly understood that nothing shall be done which may prejudice the civil and religious rights of existing non-Jewish communities in Palestine, or the rights and political status enjoyed by Jews in any other country.

I should be grateful if you would bring this declaration to the knowledge of the Zionist Federation.

Yours,
Arthur James Balfour

—*The Times* (London), November 9, 1917. Arthur James Balfour was the British foreign secretary; Lionel Walter de Rothschild (1868–1937) was the leader of the Jewish community in Britain.

Zionism: The belief, based on the writings of Theodor Herzl, that European Jews—and by extension all Jews everywhere—were entitled to a national homeland corresponding to the territory of Biblical Israel. It grew into a form of ethnolinguistic-religious nationalism and ultimately led to the formation of the state of Israel in 1948.

Arab–Jewish Violence. British police step in to separate Palestinians and Jewish immigrants fighting each other in November 1933 in Jaffa. Continued unrest led to the Palestinian Arab Revolt of 1936–1939, a nationalist uprising confined initially to urban areas and later spreading to the countryside. The British authorities suppressed the revolt brutally, by most estimates killing perhaps as many as 5,000 Arab Palestinians. Jews aided the British through self-defense forces, both the official Haganah and the clandestine Irgun. In 1939 the British issued a white paper that deplored the hostilities between the two national communities and restricted Jewish immigration.

Egypt and Turkey   After 1882, the Suez Canal acquired vital importance for the British in India and relinquishing it was unthinkable. They rejected a demand in 1919 by a delegation of Egyptian nationalists for independence out of hand and exiled its leader, Saad Zaghlul (ca. 1859–1927). After deadly riots and strikes, the British relented and invited Zaghlul to the peace negotiations in Paris. But the independence the British granted in 1923 was of modest proportions: Both military defense and control of the Suez Canal were withheld from Egypt. A year later, Zaghlul and the Wafd Party won the first independent elections with 90 percent of the vote. The ruling class, as in Iraq, was composed of landlords and urban professionals and, with few exceptions, was uninterested in industrial development. Thus, at the onset of World War II, Egypt was still entirely dependent on agricultural production and exports, though its strategic position was absolutely vital to the British Empire.

The severe punishment meted out to the Ottoman Empire by the Allies provoked the rise of local grassroots resistance groups in Anatolia. These groups merged under the leadership of General Mustafa Kemal "Atatürk" ("Father of the Turks," 1881–1938) into a national liberation movement, driving out the Greeks from western Anatolia, occupying one-half of Armenia (the other half was taken by the new Soviet Union), and ending the Ottoman sultanate (1921–1923) altogether. Atatürk, son of an Ottoman customs official in Salonika, was among the few militarily successful officers in World War I, most notably in his defense of Gallipoli against the British. Atatürk was the driving force behind the creation of a modern, secular Turkey that was able to stand up against the European powers.

Although he was authoritarian, Atatürk saw to it that the new Turkish parliament remained open to pluralism. Parliament adopted the French model of *laicism* (separation of state and religion), European family law, the Latin alphabet, the Western calendar, metric weights and measures, modern clothing, and women's suffrage. During the Depression, Atatürk's economic advisors launched *étatism*, the Turkish version of deficit spending. State capitalism, rather than private domestic or foreign capital, provided for the construction of steel and consumer good factories, including textile plants. Both modernism and étatism showed only modest successes by 1939, and the rural masses in Anatolia remained mired in small-scale self-sufficiency farming and wedded to religious tradition. But the foundation was laid in Turkey not only for a Westernized ruling class but also for a much larger urbanized middle class.

Indian Demands for Independence   The compromises negotiated during the Versailles Peace Conference, as we have seen, had a profound effect on the colonial world. Nowhere was this truer than in India. In April 1919, frustrated by a British crackdown on political protest, a large crowd gathered in a walled square in the Sikhs' sacred city of Amritsar. The British responded with a wholesale slaughter of the assembled men, women, and children by an elite unit of Gurkha troops. As the international furor over this "Amritsar Massacre" raged, the British, giving in to the inevitable, reformed the Indian Legislative Assembly by enlarging the portion of elected members to nearly three-quarters and the property-based franchise to 5 million, out of a population of 250 million. The Indian National Congress was infuriated by this minimal improvement and called for full self-rule (Hindi **swaraj**), urging nonviolent noncooperation, which, among other measures, called for a refusal to pay the land tax, for a boycott of British goods, and for people to spin and weave textiles at home.

Secularizing Turkey. Atatürk was a committed educational reformer who sought to create a "public culture," and he was advised by the famous American philosopher of education, John Dewey (1859–1952). Here, in 1928, dressed in a Western-style suit and necktie he gives a lesson on the new Turkish alphabet, a variant of the Latin alphabet, whose use was mandated throughout the Republic.

Inevitably, civil disturbances accompanied the congress' push for self-rule. Mohandas Gandhi (1869–1948), a trained lawyer and the most prominent advocate of nonviolence, suspended the push in 1921. The leaders—lawyers, doctors, journalists, and teachers—exited the cities and, with the help of a large influx of party workers, scoured the countryside preaching renunciation. It was during the 1920s and 1930s that the National Congress transformed itself from a small Westernized elite into a broad urban as well as rural mass party.

In Britain, the Labour Party attained a majority of seats in Parliament for the first time in 1929. The Labour government explored the possibility of changing India to dominion status, but there was strong opposition from the other parties. When Labour could not deliver, Gandhi responded with the demand for complete independence and, on March 12, 1930, embarked on his famous 24-day Salt March to the sea in order for his followers to pan their own salt, which the government refused to free from taxation. Crowds in other places also marched to the sea. Disturbances accompanied the marches, and in a massive crackdown, with 100,000 arrests, the government succeeded in repressing the National Congress.

Swaraj: Literally, "self-rule" (*swa-raj*). Gandhi interpreted this term as meaning "direct democracy" while the Congress Party identified it with complete independence from Great Britain.

Nevertheless, after lengthy discussions in three roundtables during the following years—accompanied by much unrest, many jailings (including that of Gandhi), and a rising split with unsupportive Muslims—the British government in 1935 passed the Government of India Act, which devolved all political functions except defense

Gandhi Leading the Salt March. Perhaps the most famous act of civil disobedience in Gandhi's career was the Salt March in 1930 to protest the British salt monopoly in India. It was a perfect embodiment of Gandhi's belief in nonviolent civil disobedience, which he called *satyagraha*, "soul-" or "truth-force." Though it failed to win major concessions from the British, it focused worldwide attention on the Indian independence movement.

and foreign affairs to India. The members of the National Congress were unhappy, however, because of the decentralized structure of the reformed Indian government and particularly because the act recognized the Muslim League of Muhammad Ali Jinnah (1876–1948), not the congress, as the representative of the Muslims. The British viceroy further inflamed matters in 1939 when he declared India in support of the British World War II effort, without even asking the congress. As in Egypt and Iraq, with their similar forms of "independence," there was a profound reluctance by the Western colonial powers to relinquish colonialism. The legacy of this unwillingness would haunt the capitalist democracies well into the later twentieth century.

Latin America: Independent Democracies and Authoritarian Regimes

Like Britain and France, Latin America remained faithful to its constitutional-nationalist heritage throughout the nineteenth century, though with a preference for strong authoritarian rule. In addition, a pattern of narrow elite rule had evolved in which large estate owners controlled the elections and politics of their countries and, through the military, kept rural black and indigenous Amerindian peoples, as well as the mixed urban populations, in check. Politicians in some countries realized the voting potential of the urban populations after World War I and pursued a new type of autocratic politics, called "populism," in conjunction with more or less extensive industrialization programs. Estate owner politics and populism, together with industrialization programs, characterized Latin America during the later interwar period.

Postwar Recovery At the beginning of the 1900s, Mexico had enjoyed a long period of political stability and economic growth. It had a relatively diversified array of mineral and agricultural export commodities and began to exploit its mineral wealth in the early 1900s to set up an iron and steel industry. But no change had taken place in agriculture, where the traditional oligarchy of rich ranching and plantation landowners continued to keep wages low. Thanks to American investments, railroad construction had progressed but more to support mining interests than agriculture as there was no desire to improve the mobility of either the landless workers on landlord properties or the indigenous Native American population engaged in subsistence farming.

Latin America During the Depression In Mexico, a rapid urbanization process, begun in the late 1800s, continued during the interwar period. Immigration from overseas, mostly southern and eastern Europe, as well as rural–urban migration fueled this process. In 1929 the newly created Institutional Revolutionary Party (Partido Revolucionario Institucional, PRI) brought the revolution of 1910–1917 to an end. A sufficiently strong government was in place again to complete land distribution to poor farmers, expand education, and begin social legislation. The PRI weathered the Depression with some difficulty, but thanks to increased state control of economic investments, it was able to maintain its footing until European and east Asian war preparations increased demand for commodities again.

Like Mexico, the countries with the largest internal markets, such as Argentina and Brazil, rode out the Depression more successfully than others. Nevertheless, overall the impact was substantial, with a reduction of commodity exports by over 50 percent (see Map 28.4). Luckily, the countries which were unable to pay back their foreign loans no longer had to fear gunboats and debt commissions but could make more equitable arrangements. Still, the Depression resulted in urban unrest, especially in countries with newly expanded mines or oil wells, such as Chile, Peru, and Venezuela, or expanded administrative bureaucracies, as in Brazil. At no time except the period of independence were there more coups, attempted coups, and uprisings than during 1930–1933.

Thereafter, the political situation remained unstable, except for Argentina and Uruguay under a tenuous constitutionalism. But an important shift away from landed oligarchies began to appear in the ruling classes. Millions of people now lived in urban environments, although in the absence of sizeable import-substitution industries, they did not have the clearly delineated social classes of workers and the nonindustrial lower classes that could be organized by communists, socialists, fascists, and militarists. Instead, a new generation of military officers, with urban backgrounds and no longer tied to the traditional oligarchy, appeared. They offered populist authoritarian programs that mixed elements from the prevailing European ideologies.

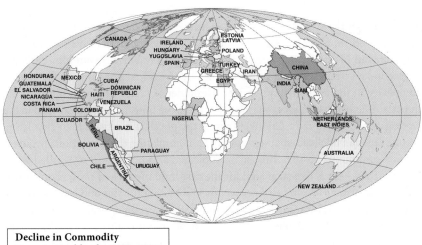

Decline in Commodity Exports Worldwide, 1929–1933

Decline in exports of primary goods by:

- Over 80%
- 70%–80%
- 60%–70%
- 50%–60%
- 30%–50%

MAP 28.4 **Decline in Commodity Exports Worldwide, 1929–1933.**

New Variations on Modernity I: The Soviet Union and Communism

After capitalist democracy, communism was the second pattern of modernity that arose out of the ashes of World War I. Following their communist coup in November 1917, the Bolsheviks under Lenin overcame a debilitating civil war and established the Union of Soviet Socialist Republics. Lenin's successor, Joseph Stalin (1879–1953), built the Communist Party into an all-powerful apparatus that violently shifted resources from agriculture into industry and dealt ruthlessly with opposition to its policies. By World War II, Stalin's brutal policies had lifted the Soviet Union into the ranks of the industrialized powers.

The Communist Party and Regime in the Soviet Union

Proletariat: A term for the industrial working classes popularized by Marx and Engels in the *Communist Manifesto* and other works.

As we saw in Chapter 23, Karl Marx (1818–1883), the leading ideologue of communism—which he also referred to as "scientific socialism" or simply "socialism"—believed that capitalist democracy would ultimately be overthrown by an ever-expanding working class—the **proletariat**. For this to happen, however, countries had to be in an advanced stage of industrialization. He did not think that the underdeveloped Russian Empire, with its large majority of peasants, would be ready for a communist revolution for a long time to come. It was the achievement of Vladimir Lenin, however, as the leader of the Bolsheviks, the Russian Communist Party, to adapt communism to his circumstances. For him, the party was the disciplined, militarily armed vanguard that ruled with monopoly power and instilled the ideology of communism in a gradually expanding working class.

The Bolshevik Regime   Lenin was from a well-educated middle-class family with Swedish, German, Russian, and Jewish ancestry. Both of his parents were teachers, and his father had been given a patent of nobility; Lenin himself had a degree in law. The execution of his brother by the tsarist government for alleged complicity in the assassination of Tsar Alexander II (1881) imbued him with an implacable hatred for Russian autocracy. At the same time, he became steeped in the writings of Marx and radical thinkers across the political spectrum then circulating around Russia's intellectual underground. Contemplating the revolutionary potential of a communist party in Russia, he published a pamphlet in 1903, called *What Is To Be Done?* Here, he articulated for the first time the idea of professional revolutionaries forming an elite strike force. By eliminating the tsar and seizing control of the government, he argued, Russia's highly centralized political structure would make it possible for an ideologically trained mass communist party to implement its program of equality and industrialization from the top down.

The fall of the tsar's government in the spring of 1917 allowed Lenin and his fellow Bolsheviks to return from political exile, including Leon Trotsky (1879–1940), the well-educated son of an affluent Ukrainian Jewish family, and Joseph Stalin, the hardnosed son of an impoverished Georgian cobbler who had escaped exile in Siberia seven times before the outbreak of World War I. Well aware of Lenin's subversive potential, the German government provided Lenin safe passage from Switzerland to Petrograd. In the words of Winston Churchill, Lenin emerged "like a bacillus" from his special passenger car. By the summer of 1917, the Bolsheviks were mounting massive demonstrations with the slogans "Land, Peace, Bread" and "All Power to the Soviets" (councils of workers and soldiers that helped maintain order as the nation struggled to create a constitution). The collapse of a disastrous Russian summer offensive emboldened the Bolsheviks, who controlled the Petrograd Soviet, which included a "Red Guard" that consisted of some 20,000 armed factory workers in the capital, to make a bid for power. In early November 1917, the Bolsheviks staged a successful coup d'état in Petrograd.

Civil War and Reconstruction   The takeover of Russia by a tiny radical minority unleashed a storm of competing factions all across the political spectrum. For the Bolsheviks the first necessity became building an army from scratch. Here, Trotsky proved a genius at inspiration and ruthless organization. From his armored train flying the new "hammer and sickle" red flag, he continually rallied his forces against the far more numerous but utterly disunited "White" armies arrayed against his "Red" forces. From 1918 to 1921, the Ukraine, Georgia, Armenia, and Azerbaijan were each forced back into the new Bolshevik state. The price for communist victory in the civil war was a complete collapse of the economy, amid a coincidental harvest failure. Lenin had initiated a policy of "war communism"—sending the Red Army into the countryside to requisition food, often with unrestrained brutality. Peasants fought back, and by 1922 a second civil war threatened. Only then did Lenin relent by inaugurating the temporary New Economic Policy (NEP), with a mixture of private and state investment in factories and small-scale food marketing by peasants. At the same time, however, the party—now several hundred thousand members strong—established an iron grip, with no deviation allowed. By 1928, a successful NEP had helped the Soviet Union to return to prewar levels of industrial production.

The Collectivization of Agriculture and Industrialization

Lenin suffered a stroke in 1922 and recovered only for short periods before he died in 1924. His successor was Joseph Stalin, who had garnered the key position of general secretary of the Communist Party in 1922. He had to fight a long struggle, from 1924 to 1930, to overcome potential or imagined rivals, a struggle which left him with a deep reservoir of permanent suspicion. His chief victim was Trotsky, whom he outmaneuvered, forced into exile, and removed altogether by ordering hitmen to assassinate him in Mexico in1940.

"Liquidation of the Kulaks as a Class"   When Stalin finally felt more secure, he decided that industrialization through the NEP was advancing too slowly. The most valuable source of funds to finance industrialization came from the sale of grain on the world market. But farmers had lost all trust in the communist regime after the forcible requisitions during the civil war and hoarded their grain. Grain production had fallen off from predictions and created a so-called "Crisis of 1928." In November, 1929, therefore, the party Central Committee officially decreed the collectivization of agriculture as the necessary step for an accelerated industrialization. Over the next two years , in a carefully laid out plan, 3–5 percent of the "wealthiest" farmers on grain-producing lands, called *kulaks* (Russian for "fist," meaning tightfistedness of wealthier farmers vis-à-vis poor indebted ones) were "liquidated"—selected for

Marching for Modernity. Farmers of a *kolkhoz* behind their party boss prepare to march with their rakes to their fields in May 1931, under a banner propagandizing their success. In reality, Russian peasants experienced the collectivization program of 1929–1940 as a second serfdom, especially in the Ukraine, where private rather than collective village farming was widespread. They resisted it both passively and actively, through arson, theft, and especially the slaughtering of livestock.

execution, removal to labor camps, or resettlement on inferior soils. Their properties were confiscated and the remaining peasant masses were regrouped as employees either of state farms (*sovkhozy*) or of poorer collective farms (*kolkhozy*). Animals were declared collective property, with the result that farmers slaughtered their cherished livestock rather than turn them over to the collectives. Altogether, it is estimated, that between 6 and 14 million farmers were forcibly removed, with the majority killed outright or worked and starved to death.

Stalinism   The impact on agriculture was appalling. Grain, meat, and dairy production plummeted and failed to regain 1927 levels during the remainder of the interwar period. Food requisitions had to be resumed, bread had to be rationed on farms as well as in cities, and real wages on farms and in factories sank. On the other hand, the one-time transfer of confiscated wealth from the kulaks to industry was substantial. Income from accelerated oil exports and renewed grain exports from state farms in the 1930s was similarly plowed into factory construction. By 1939, the rural population was down from 85 to 52 percent and, for all practical purposes, industrialization had been accomplished, though at an unparalleled human cost (see Map 28.5).

The industrial and urban modernity which the Soviet Union reached was one of enforced solidarity without private enterprises and markets. The communist prestige objects were huge plant complexes producing the industrial basics of oil, coal, steel, cement, fertilizer, tractors, and farm combines (see Patterns Up Close). Little investment was left over for textiles, shoes, furniture, and household articles, not to mention cars, radios, and appliances. Consumers had to make do with shoddy goods, delivered irregularly to government outlets and requiring patient waiting in long lines.

The disaster of collectivization had made Stalin even more concerned about any hidden pockets of potential resistance in the country. Regular party and army purges decimated the top echelons of the communist ruling apparatus. In 1937

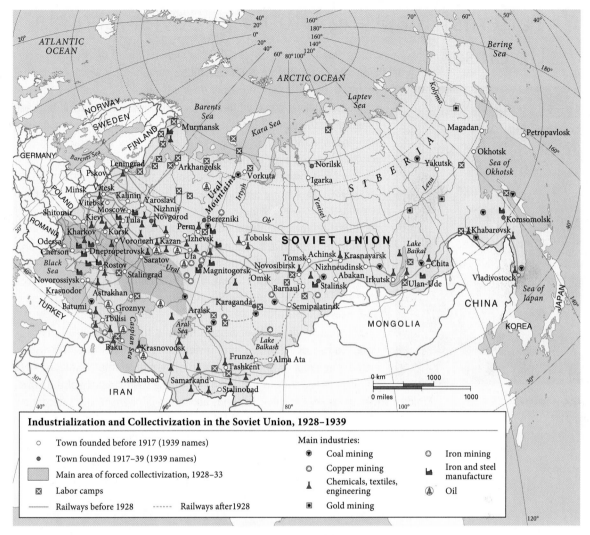

MAP 28.5 Industrialization and Collectivization in the Soviet Union, 1928–1939.

alone, Stalin had 35,000 high-ranking officers shot, with disastrous effects for the conduct of World War II a few years later. Thus, in view of the enormity of Stalin's policies, scholars have since wondered about the viability of this attempt at accelerated modernity.

New Variations on Modernity II: Supremacist Nationalism in Italy, Germany, and Japan

The third vision of modernity, underlying the development of the three countries of Italy, Germany, and Japan, was an ideology of nationalist supremacism. In contrast to communism, which was a relatively coherent ideology, the systems of fascism,

Patterns Up Close | Mapping Utopia in Soviet Georgia

When most of us think of "utopias" we tend to imagine far-off or fictional places, such as Thomas More's sixteenth-century island community for which he first invented the word (from the Greek for "not place"). Or we may think of social or religious communities whose members seek to seclude themselves from the corrupting influences of the outside world: the Shakers, who flourished in New England in the early part of the nineteenth century, may immediately come to mind.

Few of us probably consider the Soviet state during the late 1920s and 1930s as sharing anything remotely similar to the impulses guiding nineteenth-century utopias (including Marx's own original utopia of a proletarian revolution ushering in a state-less and class-less society). Stalin's ruthless drive to industrialize was accompanied by extreme violence. Millions perished from hunger, and thousands lost their lives in the political purges of the "Great Terror." Certainly, the upheavals associated with Stalinism make it difficult for us today to view them as part of a utopian enterprise.

However, if we shift our perspective and transport ourselves back in time, we can begin to see how Soviet policymakers regarded their mission as the creation of a type of utopia. Central to this "revolution from above" was the transformation of space. The vast expanses of the Soviet Union were to be improved, civilized, and, above all, industrialized. "We conquer space and time/We are young masters of the land" was a popular refrain from the 1930s. On the right, a map of the Soviet republic of Georgia, from *The Great Soviet*

Utopian Paradise. The Georgian city of Batumi, located on the Black Sea, was developed by the Soviets into a subtropical vacation resort, famed for its tea, citrus, and pleasure beaches.

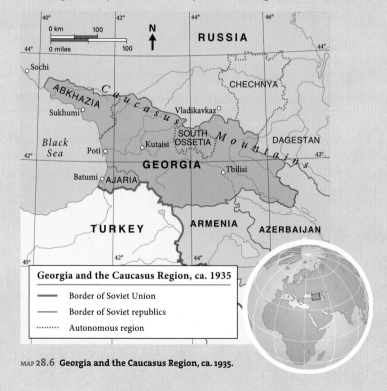

MAP 28.6 **Georgia and the Caucasus Region, ca. 1935.**

The civilizing effects of socialism are brought to the Georgian people by the Georgian-Military Highway, which runs through the Caucasus Mountains and connects the country with Russia.

Georgia's strides toward utopia are charted by the number of automobiles it produces each year, as well as the level of production of its petroleum, timber, manganese, cement, and silk and wool industries.

Energy production is a key metric for determining conformity with the socialist pattern of modernity. The colored stars stand for different types of energy sources.

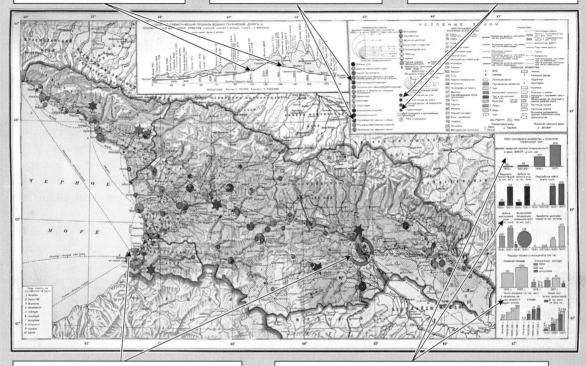

The design of the map is highly original, laying out industrial production in giant circles, subdivided by color according to the type of industry, with the size indicating the amount of the output. For the power needed to run various industries, the map designers employed a six-sided star whose size corresponded to an exact amount of output. Different color stars correspond to the type of energy--coal, petroleum, or hydroelectric.

The map celebrates Soviet agricultural and industrial successes through a "Growth Chart." Each row of graphs is devoted to an area of success: The top row shows increased agricultural output, the second and third improved industrial production, and the fourth and fifth rows the increase in the number of people attending school as well as the growing number of books printed. Just like agriculture or industry, the progress of human culture can be scientifically and precisely graphed.

World Atlas of 1937–1939, provides a vivid demonstration of this utopian impetus. Through its innovative use of symbols, the map shows how Soviet technocrats visualized their socialist utopia—literally, on paper.

Questions

- Does the map above confirm or alter the way you think about the goals that animated the socialist–communist pattern of modernity? Do you believe that the term "utopian" can also be applied to those who strove to implement the democratic-capitalist and nationalist-supremacist patterns of modernity? If so, why?

- What does this map say about the Soviet Union as an empire? What dynamics between the center (Russia) and the periphery (Georgia) can you see revealed in this map?

What Was Fascism?

"Fascism replaces ... the old atomistic and mechanistic state theory that was at the basis of the liberal and democratic state theory with an organic and historical concept ... Instead of the liberal and democratic formula, 'society for the individual,' we have 'individuals for society,' with this difference, however: that while the liberal doctrines eliminated society, fascism does not submerge the individual in the group. It subordinates him but does not eliminate him, the individual as part of his generation ever remaining an element of society however transient and insignificant he may be."

—Alfredo Rocco, "The Political Doctrine of Fascism," *International Conciliation* 223 (October 1926): 393-415. Reprinted in Schnapp, Jeffrey Thompson, Olivia E. Sears, and Maria G. Stampino, ed. and trans. *A Primer of Italian Fascism*, p. 111. Lincoln, NE: University of Nebraska Press, 2000. Rocco was minister of justice (1925–1932) under Mussolini.

Nazism, and Japanese militarism were far more diffuse, and cobbled together from a wide variety of nineteenth-century intellectual sources. Fascism became a persuasive alternative to democracy and communism in Italy right after World War I. The much more brutal German Nazi and Japanese militarist ideologies became acceptable only once the Depression hit and discredited capitalist democracy as being capable of weathering the crisis.

From Fascism in Italy to Nazism in the Third Reich

Benito Mussolini (1883–1945), son of a blacksmith with anarchist leanings and a teacher, was well read in nineteenth-century philosophy and held positions as a journalist at various socialist newspapers. His support for the war as an instrument of radical change brought him into conflict with the majority of socialists, who bitterly opposed the war. As a result, he grew disillusioned with Marxism and founded the "Italian Combat Squad" (*Fasci italiani di combattimento*). War veterans, dressed in black shirts and organized in paramilitary units, roamed the streets and broke up communist labor rallies and strikes. The symbol of the movement was the *fasces* [FAS-sees]—derived from the old Roman emblem of authority with a bundle of sticks and an ax, tied with a ribbon.

With their street brawls, the fascist "Blackshirts" contributed mightily to the impression of a breakdown of law and order, which the democratic government allegedly was unable to control. Anticommunism thus was accompanied by denunciations of democracy as a chaotic form of government incapable of decisive action. Although Mussolini's party was still woefully behind the Socialist, Christian Democrat, and Conservative Parties in the parliament, he demanded and received the premiership by threatening a march on Rome by 10,000 Blackshirts. This turned into a victory parade, with the king acquiescing to the fascists' "third way" between democracy and socialism.

Mussolini's Dictatorship   Once given his chance, Mussolini transformed the Blackshirts into a militia for national security, paid for by the state. In 1923 he used the threat of their violence again when he led his coalition government in the passing of a law that gave two-thirds of the seats in parliament to the party that garnered the most votes (at least 25 percent). A year later, "Il Duce" ("The Leader"), as he now styled himself, won his two-thirds and began to implement his fascist **corporate state**.

By 1926, elections were abolished, strict censorship of the press was in place, and the secret police kept a close eye on the population. Fascist party officials, provincial governorships, and mayors were appointed from above and labor unions closed down. In the Ministry of Corporations, industrialists and bureaucrats, representing labor, met and sharply curtailed wages and labor conditions. The Lateran Accords of 1926–1929 made Catholicism the Italian state religion in return for full support by the Vatican. Youth and women's organizations instilled authoritarian behavior. The new vision of Italian efficiency prompted observers to say admiringly of Mussolini that "he made the trains run on time." In architecture and art, as well as the new technologies of automobiles and aircraft, Italy, long seen as backward, now became a world pacesetter.

Depression and Conquests   Italy weathered the Depression through deficit spending and state investments. In 1933, Mussolini formed the Industrial

Reconstruction Institute, which took over the industrial and commercial holdings of the banks that had failed earlier. This institute was crucial in efforts to revive the Italian industrial sector, which was still much smaller than elsewhere in Europe. Only in the mid-1930s did the urban population, concentrated mostly in the north, acquire majority status. In spite of a few swamp-reclamation and grain-procurement reforms, the fascists had no answer for the endemic underdevelopment of southern Italy, which remained profoundly rural and poor.

Nevertheless, Italy's military industry was sufficiently advanced for Mussolini to proclaim a policy of autarky with the help of overseas territories. First, the conquest of formerly Ottoman Libya was completed with utmost brutality in 1931. Declaring Libya to be the "Fourth Shore," the fascists encouraged emigration into the largely infertile Sahara colony, which eventually numbered some 100,000 settlers. The other major colony was the proud Christian kingdom of Ethiopia, conquered by Italy in 1935–1936 and merged thereafter with the earlier territories of Italian Eritrea and Somalia into Italian East Africa. Eager to avenge Italy's defeat by the Ethiopians forty years before, Mussolini's forces invaded with airplanes, tanks, and poison gas and, after crushing Ethiopian resistance, pacified the new colony with the settlement of 200,000 Italians.

The Ethiopian conquest prompted protests by the League of Nations. Although these were ineffective, Mussolini felt sufficiently isolated to seek closer relations with Adolf Hitler and the Nazis. He had formerly treated Hitler as a junior colleague but now found him to be a useful counterweight against international isolation. An increasingly close cooperation began between the two dictators, who formed the nucleus of the later Axis powers, joined in 1941 by Japan.

The Foundation of the Weimar Republic

In September 1918, the German Supreme Army Command came to the conclusion that Germany had lost World War I. In the subsequent 2 months unrest broke out in the navy and among workers. German soldiers melted away from the western front, and communist worker councils formed in a number of major cities. Alarmed civilian politicians in Berlin did everything in their power to bring about a peaceful transition from empire to republic. When the emperor eventually abdicated, his last chancellor (head of the government) appointed Friedrich Ebert (1871–1925), a prominent member of the German Social Democratic Party, on November 9, 1918, as his successor. This appointment was not quite legal, but Ebert immediately contacted the OHL for armed support; and in the following months the two cooperated in crushing well-organized and armed communist workers' councils.

The first test for the new republic (founded in nearby Weimar during the height of communist unrest in Berlin) came in the summer of 1919 when the Allies presented their peace settlement. The French, concerned about both their military security and the future economic power of their more populous and industrially advanced German neighbor, would have liked to have Germany divided again, as it was before 1871. The British and Americans, however, were opposed to such a drastic settlement. Germany was let off with what historians now see in retrospect as relatively moderate reparations for civilian casualties and the loss of two western provinces, although it was also forced to accept responsibility for the beginning of the war. The compromise settlement was satisfactory to no one: France's security remained unresolved, German conservatives and nationalists screamed defiance, and

Corporate state: Sometimes called an "organic state"; a philosophy of government that sees all sectors of society contributing in a systematic, orderly, and hierarchical fashion to the health of the state, the way that the parts of the body do to a human being. In practice, it was a polity in which a dictator or an authoritarian leader orchestrated the single state party and all ministries, business corporations, associations, and clubs, while other parties and organizations such as labor unions were outlawed.

Play Money. German children in 1923 playing with bundles of money in the streets. Hyperinflation had made money in the Weimar Republic worthless: Printed overnight, it was practically worthless before it even hit the market in the morning. At the height of inflation, $1 US was worth 4.2 million reichsmark.

the democrats of Weimar who accepted the settlement were embittered by its immediate consequence: inflation.

Asked to begin the payments immediately, Germany was unable to correct the general inflation which also occurred in other countries in 1918–1919, when pent-up consumer demand exploded with the onset of peace. Instead, the inflation accelerated to a hyperinflation in which the German mark became virtually worthless and Germany had to suspend payments. France and Belgium responded by occupying the industrial Ruhr province in 1923. German workers in the Ruhr retaliated with passive resistance, and a deadlock was the result.

Faced with this crisis, the new Weimar Republic made peace with the French by recognizing the new borders. Recognizing, too, the dire financial implications of an economically crippled Germany, the American-crafted Dawes Plan of 1924 had US banks advance credits to European banks to refinance the now considerably reduced German reparation payments. France and Belgium withdrew from the Ruhr, inflation was curtailed, and the currency stabilized. The newly solvent Weimar Republic then experienced a considerable economic and cultural efflorescence during the rest of the decade.

The Golden Twenties   In these years, Germany produced more movies than the rest of Europe combined, with such classics as *Metropolis*, by the director Fritz Lang (1890–1976). Sports fans followed the career of the boxer Max Schmeling (1905-2005), world champion in 1930, and watched car races on the Avus in Berlin, the first freeway (*Autobahn*). The *Kabarett* ("cabaret"), with its biting political satire, attracted major literary figures who wrote sketches for this new popular art form. Playwrights probed the conflicts of social class, which were more pronounced in Germany than elsewhere. Perhaps best known was *The Threepenny Opera* of 1928, with lyrics by Bertolt Brecht (1898–1956) and music by Kurt Weill (1900–1950).

Painters and architects probed the geometrical and detached style they assumed was the essence of modernity at the Bauhaus school in Weimar, which became an international trendsetter for art, architecture, and design. The Russian Wassily Kandinsky (1866–1944) and the Swiss Paul Klee (1879–1940) taught the new style of abstract painting, which they had pioneered at the school. Similarly, the pioneer of modern glass, steel, and concrete architecture, Ludwig Mies van der Rohe (1886–1969), began his career at the Bauhaus, before he designed some of the best-known skyscrapers of the Chicago cityscape.

The Rise of the Nazis   The Golden Twenties disintegrated quickly in the months after the US stock market crash of 1929. American banks, desperate for cash, began to recall their loans made to Europe. Beginning in 1931 in Austria, European banks began to fail; and in the following 2 years world trade shrank by two-thirds, hitting an exporting nation like Germany particularly hard. Unemployment soared at the same time to 30 percent of the workforce. Once more, as during the hyperinflation of 1923, millions of Germans were cast into misery. The number of people voting for extremist opponents of democracy—communists and nationalist supremacists—rose from marginal to more than half of the electorate by July 1932. Among them, the National Socialist German Workers' Party (NSDAP), or Nazi Party, achieved 38 percent, becoming the largest party in parliament.

In early 1933, the Nazi leader, Adolf Hitler (1889–1945), a failed artist and son of an Austrian customs official, could look back on a checkered postwar political career. He had led a failed uprising in 1923, done time in prison, and in *Mein Kampf* (*My Struggle*), a book published in 1925, openly announced a frightening political program. Hitler advocated ridding Germany of its Jews, whom he blamed for World War I, and communists, whom he blamed for losing the war, and sought to punish the Allies for the peace settlement they had imposed on Germany. In its most grandiose sections he supported the German conquest of a "living space" (*Lebensraum*) in Russia and eastern Europe for the superior "Aryan" (German) race, with the "inferior" Slavs reduced to forced labor. No one who followed politics in Germany during the 1920s could be in doubt about Hitler's unrestrained and violent supremacist nationalism. Throughout the decade, however, he remained marginalized and ridiculed for his extreme views.

Function and Simplicity. The architect Walter Gropius (1883–1969) founded the Bauhaus movement. Its emphasis on function and simplicity still exerts great influence.

The Nazis in Power   When the Nazis won a plurality in parliament, however, not only in spring 1932 but again in the fall (albeit with a loss of 4 percent, while the communists gained nearly 3 for a total of nearly 17 percent), Hitler demanded the chancellorship. Upon the advice of his counselors, President Paul von Hindenburg (in office 1925–1934), one of Germany's heroes as a leading general during World War I, nominated Hitler to the post on January 30, 1933, in an effort to neutralize Nazism and keep Hitler under control. Hitler, however, wasted no time in escaping all restraints. Following a major fire in the Reichstag (German parliament) building in February 1933, the causes of which have never been fully explained, but which Hitler blamed on the communists, the president allowed his new chancellor the right to declare martial law for a limited time. Two months later, the Nazi Party in parliament passed the Enabling Act with the votes of the mostly Catholic Centrist Party: Its leaders calculated that they could control Hitler while receiving a much desired agreement between the Vatican and Germany parallel to the one of Mussolini. According to the constitution, Hitler now had the power to rule by emergency decree for 4 years.

Taking their cue from Mussolini's policies, the Nazis abolished the federalist structure of the Weimar Republic, purged the civil service of Jews, closed down all parties except the NSDAP, enacted censorship laws, and sent communists to newly constructed concentration camps. Other inmates of these camps were Roma (Gypsies), homosexuals, and religious minorities. In order to gain the support of Germany's professional army, Hitler replaced his *Sturmabteilung* (SA) militias of thugs with the smartly outfitted *Schutzstaffel* (SS). A new secret police force (abbreviated *Gestapo*) established a pervasive surveillance system in what was now called the Third Empire (*Drittes Reich*), following that of the Holy Roman Empire and Germany after its unification in 1871.

At the same time, Hitler succeeded in gaining enthusiastic support from among the population. Aided by a general recovery of the economy, within 1 year of coming to power he lowered unemployment to 10 percent. He had the support of able economists who advised him to reduce unemployment through deficit spending

A Fatal Error

"I really thought that it was [Hitler's] earnest desire to comply in matters of religion. In his speeches in the Reichstag to March 1933, he said that he respected Christian fundamentals and would do everything to uphold them. It was I who asked Hitler to include this point in his speeches."

—Franz von Papen, interviewed by Leon Goldensohn, *Nuremberg Interviews: A Psychiatrist's Conversations with the Defendants and Witnesses*, p. 180. New York: Vintage, 2004. Papen was a Centrist deputy, former chancellor, and one of the advisors of Hindenburg urging the appointment of Hitler.

and build a mixed economy of state-subsidized private industrial cartels. Enthusiastic Germans built freeways, cleared slums, constructed housing, and, above all, made arms, for minimal wages. A once mediocre artist and aspiring architect, Hitler also pronounced upon the "decadence" of modern art and pushed his planners to create monumental buildings in older neoclassical or art-deco styles. In all of these endeavors he advocated a personal vision of a stridently "nationalist" German art. In his appeal to the patriotic and economic aspirations of so many Germans, Hitler thus succeeded in making himself a genuinely popular leader (*Führer*) among the great majority of Germans.

German rearmament was initially secret but, after 1935, public knowledge, with the introduction of the draft and the repudiation of the peace settlement cap on troop numbers. During 1935–1939, the army grew from 100,000 to 950,000 men, warships from 30 to 95, and, most startling of all, the air force from 36 to over 8,000 planes. France, realizing the danger this rearmament signified for its security, signed a treaty of mutual military assistance with the Soviet Union, which Hitler took as a pretext for the remilitarization of the Rhineland (one of the German provinces temporarily occupied by France after World War I) in 1936.

This first step of German military assertion was followed with the unofficial air force support of General Francisco Franco (1892-1975) who rose against the legitimate Republican government in the Spanish Civil War (1936–1939) and incorporation of Austria in 1938. Now alarmed at Germany's growing appetite for expansion and committed by treaty to defend the eastern European states created after the war, the heads of state of Britain and France met with Hitler and Mussolini in Munich in the summer of 1938 to hammer out a general agreement on German and Italian territorial claims. In the Munich Agreement, Hitler was allowed to occupy the Sudetenland, an area largely inhabited by ethnic Germans in Czechoslovakia, with the understanding that it represented his final territorial demand. The British prime minister, Neville Chamberlain, (in office 1937–1940) seeking to mediate between the less compromising France and Hitler, claimed that this appeasement of Germany represented "peace in our time." Hitler went to war, however, in little more than a year.

World War II in Poland and France

In 1939 Hitler decided that the German armed forces were ready to begin the quest for Lebensraum in eastern Europe. In a first step, Poland needed to be taken; and in order to do so, Stalin had to be led to believe that it was in the best interest of the Soviet Union and Germany to share in the division of eastern Europe. Stalin, of course, was under no illusions about Hitler's plans but needed time to rebuild his army after the purges of 1937 and found the idea of a Russian-dominated Polish buffer against Germany appealing. Accordingly, the two signed a nonaggression pact on August 23, 1939; and German troops invaded Poland on September 1, triggering declarations of war by Poland's allies Britain and France 2 days later. World War II had begun in Europe.

Having removed the two-front problem that had plagued Germany in World War I, Hitler had to eliminate Britain and France before turning to the next phase in the east. This he did by attacking France on May 10, 1940. The German army in Poland had pioneered a new kind of warfare: "lightning war," or *Blitzkrieg*. Using aircraft to cripple rear area defenses and harass enemy troops, while smashing enemy lines with tanks and motorized infantry, the Germans turned warfare from the stagnant defensive posture of World War I into a fast, highly mobile form of conflict. The French, bled dry of manpower in the previous war, had since relied largely on the highly elaborate but fixed defenses of their Maginot Line. Now, the German troops simply went around these fortifications on a broad front, from the Netherlands and Belgium to Luxemburg. After breaking through the thick unprotected Ardennes Forest in southern Belgium, to the great surprise of the French and British, the German troops turned northward, driving the Allies toward the Atlantic coast. Establishing a desperate defensive perimeter at Dunkirk, the encircled French and British troops used every available vessel to escape across the English Channel to Britain as the Germans regrouped for their final thrust.

France had no choice but to agree to an armistice. Hitler divided the country into a German-occupied part, consisting of Paris and the Atlantic coast, and a small unoccupied territory under German control, with its capital in Vichy. The German follow-up effort of an invasion of Britain failed when the air force, having suffered more losses than anticipated in the invasion of France, was unable to deliver the final blow. During the worst air raids the conservative politician Winston Churchill (in office 1940–1945) replaced Neville Chamberlain as prime minister. Churchill's inspirational and unbending will during the aerial Battle of Britain proved to be a turning point in rallying the Allied cause.

The Eastern Front   A year after finishing with France, and with Britain only desperately hanging on, Hitler launched an invasion of the Soviet Union on June 22, 1941, to the surprise of an unprepared Stalin. Although the Soviet forces were initially severely beaten, they did not disintegrate, thanks in part to a force of new T-34 tanks that proved superior to German models and were four times more numerous than the Germans expected. The Soviets held out against the German attacks on Leningrad (the renamed St. Petersburg/Petrograd), Moscow, and the Ukraine. Neither side made much progress in 1942, until the Soviets succeeded in trapping a large force of Germans in Stalingrad on the lower Volga, near the vital Caspian oil fields. The Soviet victory on February 2, 1943, became the turning point in the European war. Thereafter, it was an almost relentless and increasingly desperate retreat for the Germans, particularly after the western Allies invaded the continent in Italy and France.

The Final Solution   As Hitler's *Mein Kampf* foretold, the war in the east became an ideological war of annihilation: Either the supremacist or the communist vision of modernity would prevail. The Soviets began early with their killings, when they massacred nearly 22,000 Polish prisoners of war in the forest of Katyn and sent hundreds of thousands of eastern Europeans to their eventual deaths in labor camps. The German SS and army, driven by their racism against Slavs, murdered soldiers and civilians alike; and German business tycoons worked their Slavic slave laborers to death. The so-called **Final Solution** (*Endlösung*), the genocide of the European Jews, was the horrendous culmination of this struggle. After Poland and the western Soviet Union were conquered, the number of Jews under

Genocide. The specters of the Holocaust that haunt us usually involve the infamous extermination camps—Auschwitz, Treblinka, Majdanek, Sobibor—but millions of Jews and other "undesirables"—Slavs, gypsies (Roma), and homosexuals—were shot, such as this man calmly waiting for the bullet to penetrate his brain while SS stooges accomplices look blithely on.

Final Solution: German nationalist-supremacist plan formulated in 1942 by Adolf Hitler and leading Nazis to annihilate Jews through factory-style mass extermination in concentration camps; resulting in the death of about 6 million Jews or roughly two-thirds of European Jewry.

German authority increased by several million. The Final Solution, set in motion in January 1942, entailed transporting Jews to eight extermination camps, the most infamous of which was at Auschwitz, in Poland, to be gassed in simulated shower stalls and their corpses burned in specially constructed ovens. In its technological sophistication in creating a kind of assembly line of death and the calm, bureaucratic efficiency with which its operators went about their business, the Holocaust (Hebrew *Shoa*) marks a milestone in twentieth-century inhumanity. It has since become the standard of genocide against which other planned mass murders are measured.

The Turn of the Tide in the West   The first counteroffensives of the Allies in the west after their defeat in 1940 came in November 1942. After fighting a desperate rearguard action against the German general Erwin Rommel (1891–1944), "The Desert Fox," British forces in Egypt and American forces landing in occupied French North Africa launched a combined offensive, capturing Rommel's forces in a pincer movement and driving them to capitulate 6 months later. But it took another 2.5 years of long campaigning to grind down the forces of the Axis powers. Here, the industrial capacity of the United States proved to be the determining factor. For example, between 1942 and 1945 American factories produced 41,000 Sherman M4 tanks alone, which was more than the production of all German tank types taken together. German aircraft production peaked in 1944 at 44,000 planes; US manufacturers produced more than 100,000 the same year. The United States enjoyed similar advantages in manpower. By war's end, over 16 million American men and women, or 10 percent of the entire population, had served in the armed forces. Finally, the natural barriers of the Atlantic and Pacific Oceans and American naval power ensured against invasion, while the lack of a long-range strategic bombing force prevented Axis air attacks on North America.

Furthermore, starting in 1943, the US Army Air Force and Britain's Royal Air Force began a furious campaign of "around-the-clock" bombing of military and civilian targets in Germany. Despite heavy Allied losses in planes and men, by war's end, there was scarcely a German city of any size or industrial center that had not been reduced to rubble by air attack—quite a contrast to World War I, when Germany's interior was unscathed. With the landing of troops in Sicily in July 1943 and Normandy in June 1944, combined with the steady advance of Soviet forces in the east, the eventual unconditional German surrender on May 8, 1945 ("Victory in Europe," or "VE," Day) was inevitable (see Map 28.7).

Japan's "Greater East Asia Co-Prosperity Sphere" and China's Struggle for Unity

The Japanese ruling class that implemented the Meiji industrialization consisted for the most part of lower-ranking samurai "oligarchs." After World War I, this generation retired and for the first time commoners entered politics. These commoners formed two unstable conservative party coalitions, representing small-business and landowner interests, but were financed by big-business cartels, the zaibatsus (see Chapter 24) By the mid-1920s Japan's interwar liberalizing era had reached perhaps its high point, with universal male suffrage for all over the age of 25. Thereafter, however, and at an accelerated pace during the Depression of 1929–1933, the military increased its power and ended the liberalizing era.

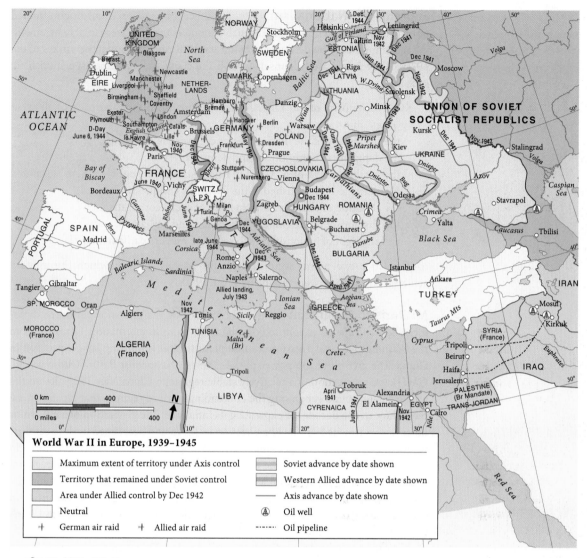

MAP **28.7** World War II in Europe, 1939–1945.

Liberalism and Military Assertion

In the midst of the middle-class ferment of "Taisho Democracy," as Japan's politics during the reign of Emperor Taisho (r. 1912–1926) was known, the government not only broadened the suffrage but also enacted the first of what would be a long line of security laws. Worried about communist influence, the Peace Preservation Law of 1925 drew a line against frequent labor strikes and general leftist agitation. Anyone violating the "national essence" (*kokutai*) not only through action but also thought could be arrested. A branch of the secret services, the *Tokko*, made widespread use of this law, with some 70,000 mostly arbitrary arrests during 1925–1945. The law was a turning point as Western-inspired liberalism began to swing toward militarism. Nowhere was this more dramatically on display than in the saga of Professor Minobe, described at the beginning of this chapter, who would go in a few short years from being Japan's leading legal theorist to being denounced as a traitor.

Supremacist Nationalism   Military officers of modest rural origin, trained prior to World War I and without much general education, were unable or unwilling to comprehend the democracy, cultural transformation, and labor strikes of the 1920s. They intoxicated themselves with the staples of supremacist nationalism, such as

- the superiority of the Yamato "race" of Japan and the inferiority of all other "races" in Asia;
- the supremacy of the "national essence" over the individual;
- the depravity of communism and democracy;
- the establishment of a "Greater East Asia Co-Prosperity Sphere" (*Dai-to-a Kyoeiken*) to be established in the Pacific by conquest;
- the abolition of class divisions in favor of social corporatism;
- the absolutism of the emperor, above law and parliament;
- and the right of junior officers to refuse to execute parliamentary laws.

The latter two points were decisive for actions through which the military achieved dominance over parliament in the 1930s.

Militaristic Expansion   The early 1930s saw the end of a period of diplomacy by which Japan sought to consolidate its gains in international prestige from the Washington Naval Treaty and subsequent treaties stabilizing Japan's position in China. The growth of the power of the Chinese Nationalist Party (Guomindang, GMD) and its creation of a relatively stable regime in China after 1927 altered the fragile balance of power among the contending warlord regimes that Japan had exploited for over a decade for expanding its influence. The generation of rural junior officers who frowned on the liberalization of Japan and hearkened back to samurai values also found a home and opportunity in the colonial armies of Manchuria. In addition, nationalist radicals like Kita Ikki (1883–1937) expounded a complete reorganization of Japan based on a stricter interpretation of the kokutai. Finally, the long-standing maneuverings of semimilitary groups advocating further expansion in the Asian heartland, such as the Black Dragon Society, kept the situation in Japan's Asian possessions in turmoil.

The first step in this new direction was taken in 1928 when the Japanese Kwantung Army (the name for Japan's force in Manchuria) blew up the train of Chinese warlord Zhang Zuolin because of his leanings toward the GMD. This was followed by the Mukden Incident of 1931, in which the Japanese military engineered another railroad bombing, which was blamed on local warlords and used as the pretext for the annexation of Manchuria. Politicians in Tokyo, cowed by the aggressiveness of supremacist nationalist ideologues, and by the select assassinations of political opponents of Japan's expansion, acquiesced. By way of making it a puppet state, they installed the last Manchu Qing Chinese emperor (Henry) Pu-Yi (r. 1908–1912; 1932–45), deposed in the Chinese Republican Revolution of 1911–1912. Over the next several years, the Japanese army in Manchuria systematically moved into northern China. In July 1937, after a clash between Chinese and Japanese forces near the Marco Polo Bridge outside Beijing, Japan launched a full-scale invasion of China.

The Republican Revolution in China   The Qing dynasty had failed to develop a sustained effort at reform in response to the Western challenge during the

1800s. Following belated attempts at institutional reform in the wake of the Boxer uprising in 1900, a variety of radical groups, aided by the growing numbers of overseas Chinese, began to work for the overthrow of the Qing. The most important figure among these groups was Sun Yat-sen (1866–1925), a medical doctor and son of peasants in south China, with his Revolutionary Alliance of 1905. Making common cause with a number of local revolutionary groups and Chinese secret societies, Sun's group formed an umbrella organization for a wide array of political ideas. Sun's core ideas, however, were relatively straightforward and given as the Three Principles of the People (*san min zhuyi*):

- Nationalism: Expulsion of the Manchus and later all Western interests.
- Democracy: Representative institutions based on a constitution. One-party tutelage until the Chinese people grow used to the new forms of democratic institutions.
- "People's livelihood": Sometimes rendered as "socialism," this principle called for comprehensive land reform and a government commitment to safeguard the economic well-being of the people.

On October 10, 1911, an explosion in a Wuhan barracks signaled a takeover of the base. The movement quickly spread, and by the end of the year three groups of Qing opponents—provincial warlords, scholar-gentry, and nationalists—staged separate uprisings which reduced the Qing to a small territory in the north. The Qing commander, Yuan Shikai (1859–1916), struck a deal with the insurgents whereby he came over to them in return for the presidency of the new republic, formed upon the abdication of the Qing in February 1912. Sun was thus elbowed aside by the revolution he had done so much to begin. With Yuan's death in 1916, the remaining warlords feuded with each other for control of the country for the next decade.

Reemergence of Nationalism   Sun Yat-sen, however, was not quite finished. With the republic in shambles and the provinces hijacked by the warlords, Sun remained a profoundly inspirational figure for Chinese nationalists, mostly through his numerous publications issued from exile in the Western treaty port of Canton (Guangzhou). Meanwhile, the decision announced on May 4, 1919, by the Allies at Versailles to allow Japan to keep the German territory in China it had seized at the beginning of the war set off mass demonstrations and a boycott of foreign businesses. This May Fourth Movement, as it came to be called, is often cited as the modern beginning of Chinese nationalism. Shortly thereafter, inspired by the Bolshevik Revolution in Russia, the Chinese Communist Party (CCP) was founded in 1921.

By 1923, encouraged by support from the Third Communist International (Comintern), Sun's Nationalist Party was being reorganized and supplied with Russian help, in return for which the party agreed to allow members of the CCP to join with them to form what became known as the First United Front (1924–1927). The Nationalist Party organized the National Revolutionary Army in the south, and the CCP fomented communist-inspired strikes in the industrial cities of the Yangtze delta, including Shanghai. Sun died in 1925, and a year later Chiang K'ai-shek (1887–1975) ascended to the leadership of the army. Chiang came from a wealthy salt merchant family and was a military officer trained in the Nationalist Party academy and in Moscow. The most pressing objective in 1926 was the unification of China. The two parties mobilized an army of some 85,000 men, and the so-called

Mao. The images of Mao that dominate our consciousness are usually the old Mao, when his health was failing, his youthful vigor was long gone, and his political power diminished. But it is in the young Mao, such as this photo from 1938, that we can best see his leadership skills in action. As Mao's longtime associate Zhou Enlai (1898–1976) observed in 1943, "The Comrade's style of work incorporates the modesty and pragmatism of the Chinese people; the simplicity and diligence of the Chinese peasants; the love of study and profound thinking of an intellectual; the efficiency and steadfastness of a revolutionary soldier; and the persistence and indomitability of a Bolshevik."

Northern Expedition of 1926–1927 became a remarkably successful effort which brought about the unification of southern China as far north as the Yangzi River.

In the middle of the campaign, however, the bonds between the GMD and CCP ruptured. The socialist wing of the GMD and the CCP had taken the important industrial centers of Wuhan and Shanghai in the Yangtze delta from warlords, setting the stage for a showdown with the nationalist wing. Though he had been trained in Moscow, Chiang had grown intensely suspicious of Comintern and CCP motives and, thus launched a preemptive purge of communists in nationalist-held areas. Though much of the leftist opposition was eliminated, a remnant under Mao Zedong (1893–1976) fled to the remote province of Jiangxi in the south to regroup and create their own socialist state. Mao, a librarian by training from a wealthy peasant family, was an inspiring rural organizer; and he set about developing his ideas of Marxist revolution with the heretical idea of having peasants in the vanguard.

By the early 1930s Mao's Chinese communists had developed this crucial variant of rural communism, which Marx and Lenin had found impossible to envisage. Mao replaced the capitalists with the landlords as the class enemy and promised a much needed land reform to the downtrodden peasants. Moreover, the peasants would be the leading participants in the "People's War"—a three-stage guerilla conflict involving the entire populace and borrowing from sources as diverse as Sun Zi's *Art of War* and American tactics against the British in the War for Independence.

Believing the communist threat to be effectively eliminated, Chiang resumed his Northern Expedition in 1928, submitting Beijing to his control but failing to eliminate the strongest northern warlords. Nevertheless, China was now at least nominally unified, with the capital in Nanjing, the National Party Congress functioning as a parliament, and Chiang as president. Chiang made substantial progress with railroad and road construction as well as cotton and silk textile exports. Thanks to the silver standard of its money, rather than the fatal gold standard of most other countries, the financial consequences of the Depression of 1929–1933 remained relatively mild. Chiang made little headway, however, with land reform. Furthermore, the volatile relations with the remaining warlords made the government vulnerable to border violence and corruption. Hovering above all after 1931 was the Japanese annexation of Manchuria and creeping encroachment on northern China.

The Long March and the Rape of Nanjing   In the early 1930s, Chiang knew that Japan was the enemy to watch, but he was painfully aware of the need to completely eliminate his internal opponents. Following the old proverbial advice of "disorder within, disaster without" he resolved to eliminate the remaining threat from Mao's "Jiangxi Soviet." He mounted increasingly massive "bandit extermination" campaigns from 1931 to 1934, but each one was defeated by the superior mobility, local loyalty, and guerilla tactics of Mao's growing People's Liberation Army. With the help of German advisors, Chiang turned to encircling the CCP areas with a ring of trenches and blockhouses to eliminate the mobility of his opponents. By the fall of 1934 he had tightened the noose around the communists and almost succeeded in destroying their army.

But Mao and about 100,000 soldiers broke out in October 1934, thanks to the negligence of one of the warlords entrusted with the encirclement. Once free, the majority of the Red Army embarked on its epic Long March of 6,000 miles, describing a semicircle from the south through the far west and then northeast toward Beijing. Along the way harassment by nationalist troops, warlords, and local people as well as hunger, famine, heat, swamps, bridgeless rivers, and desertion decimated the bedraggled marchers. In the fall of 1935 some 10,000 communists eventually straggled into the small enclave of Yan'an (Yenan), out of Chiang's reach. Living in caves cut into the loess soil, they set up communes and concentrated on agricultural production and reconstituting their forces.

The communists had seized upon Japan's aggression as a valuable propaganda tool and declared war against Japan in 1932. Chiang's obsession with eliminating his internal enemies increasingly made him subject to criticism of appeasement toward Japan. By 1936, a group of warlords and dissident nationalist generals arrested Chiang outside the city of Xi'an and spirited him off to CCP headquarters at Yan'an. After weeks of fraught negotiations, Chiang was released as the leader of a China now brought together under a Second United Front, this time against Japan.

The Rape of Nanjing. Of the many horrors of the twentieth century, few can match the Rape of Nanjing for its sadistic brutality, in which perhaps as many as 300,000 people lost their lives in a killing orgy.

Seeing their prospects for gradual encroachment quickly fading, Japan seized on the so-called Marco Polo Bridge Incident and launched an all-out assault on China. The bridge was a key point along the frontier between Japanese and Chinese forces just outside Beijing, and on the night of July 7, 1937, a brief exchange of fire accidentally took place between the two sides. When a Japanese soldier seeking to relieve himself during the exchange did not return to post, the Japanese used this as a pretext to move against the Chinese. Though Chinese resistance was stiff in the opening months, the Japanese were able to use their superior mobility and airpower to flank the Chinese forces and take the capital of Nanjing (Nanking) by December 1937. Realizing the need to defeat China as quickly as possible in order to avoid a war of attrition, they subjected the capital to the first major atrocity of World War II: "the Rape of Nanjing." Though scholars are still debating the exact number of casualties, it is estimated that between 200,000 and 300,000 people were slaughtered in deliberately gruesome ways: hacked to death, burned alive, buried alive, and beheaded. Over and above this brutality, however, rape was systematically used as a means of terror and subjugation.

The direct message of all of this was that other Chinese cities could expect similar treatment if surrender was not swiftly forthcoming. Like the British and Germans under aerial bombardment a few years later, however, the destruction only stiffened the will to resist of the Chinese. Continually harassed as they retreated from Nanjing, the Chinese adopted the strategy of trading space for time to regroup, as did the Soviets a few years later. In an epic mass migration, Chinese soldiers and civilians stripped every usable article possible and moved it to the region of the remote city of Chongqing (Chungking), which became the wartime capital of China until 1945. Thereafter, both nationalists and communists used the vast interior for hit-and-run tactics, effectively limiting Japan to the northeast and coastal urban centers but themselves incapable of mounting large offensives.

World War II in the Pacific   While Japan had used its control of Manchuria, Korea, and Taiwan in its support of autarky and economic stability in the 1930s, its bid for empire in the Pacific was portrayed as the construction of "The Greater East Asia Co-Prosperity Sphere." This expansion was considered essential because oil, metals, rubber, and other raw materials were still imported in large quantities from the United States and the Dutch and British possessions in southeast Asia. After Hitler invaded the Netherlands and France in 1940, the moment arrived when the Japanese could plan for extending their power and removing the United States from the Pacific. Moreover, the stalemate in China was increasingly bleeding Japan of vital resources, while mounting tensions with the United States over China were already resulting in economic sanctions. Accordingly, in the summer of 1941, the Japanese government decided on the extension of the empire into the Dutch East Indies and southeast Asia, even if this meant war with the United States. Under the premiership of General Tojo Hideki (in office 1941–1944), Japan attacked Pearl Harbor, Hawaii; the Philippines; and Dutch and British territories on December 7–8, 1941. Within a few months, the Japanese completed the occupation of all the important southeast Asian and Pacific territories they had sought (see Map 28.8).

Japan's newfound autarky did not last long however. Within 6 months, in the naval and air battle of Midway, American forces regained the initiative. The Japanese now

MAP 28.8 **World War II in the Pacific, 1937–1945.**

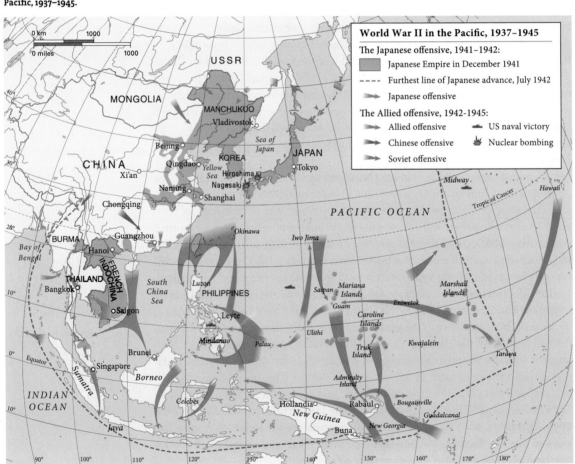

exploited the populations of their new territories for their raw materials with increasing urgency. As the American forces slowly deprived the Japanese of these resources through their highly effective "island-hopping" strategy, they came within bombing range of the Japanese home islands by late 1944. Starting in March 1945, they subjected Japan to the most devastating firebomb attacks ever mounted. Finally, President Harry S Truman (in office 1945–1953) made the fateful decision to have two experimental atomic bombs dropped on Hiroshima and Nagasaki (August 6 and 9, 1945), effectively obliterating both cities. With the Soviets declaring war against Japan on August 8 and advancing into Manchuria, the Japanese were finally convinced that the war was lost and surrendered on August 14, 1945, with the final ceremony taking place aboard the US battleship *Missouri* on September 2, 1945.

Putting It All Together

As discussed in previous chapters, the patterns of constitutional nationalism and industrialization in the late eighteenth and early nineteenth centuries were most visibly manifested in Great Britain, the United States, and France. Subsequently, two further patterns complicated the evolution of nations joining in the pursuit of modernity: ethnolinguistic nationalism and the rise of the industrial working class. Abetted by the imperialistic tendencies inherited from before 1800, all of these patterns collided in the First World War. After the war, they recombined into the three ideologies of modernity analyzed in this chapter: capitalist democracy, communism, and supremacist nationalism (see Concept Map).

For the most part, only democracy and communism are considered to be genuine ideologies of modernity, in the sense of being based on relatively coherent programs. More recent historians, however, have come to the conclusion that nationalist supremacism was a genuine variety of modernity as well, though one defined more by what it opposed than by what it supported. The adherents of the three modernities bitterly denounced the ideologies of their rivals. All three considered themselves to be genuinely "progressive" or modern.

What is very difficult to understand in a country like the United States, still deeply loyal to its foundational national constitutionalism, is that someone could be an ardent ethnic nationalist, have little faith in constitutional liberties, find the conquest of a large and completely self-sufficient empire perfectly logical, and think of all this as the wave of a future modernity. Indeed, historians have customarily thought of these views as revolts *against* modernity. Yet, as we have seen so often, innovations frequently create a "gelling" effect in which opposition to the new clarifies and solidifies, often in unexpected ways. The "modern" notion of ethnolinguistic nationalism thus created

> **Emperor Hirohito's (r. 1926–1989) Surrender Message to the Japanese People, August 14, 1945**
>
> "We declared war on America and Britain out of Our sincere desire to ensure Japan's self-preservation and the stabilization of East Asia, it being far from Our thought either to infringe upon the sovereignty of other nations or to embark upon territorial aggrandisement. But now the war has lasted for nearly four years. Despite the best that has been done by everyone—the gallant fighting of the military and naval forces, the diligence and assiduity of Our servants of the State and the devoted service of Our one hundred million people, the war situation has developed not necessarily to Japan's advantage, while the general trends of the world have all turned against her interest. Moreover, the enemy has begun to employ a new and most cruel bomb, the power of which to damage is indeed incalculable, taking the toll of many innocent lives. Should We continue to fight, it would not only result in an ultimate collapse and obliteration of the Japanese nation, but also it would lead to the total extinction of human civilization. Such being the case, how are We to save the millions of Our subjects; or to atone Ourselves before the hallowed spirits of Our Imperial Ancestors? This is the reason why We have ordered the Acceptance of the provisions of the Joint Declaration of the Powers."
>
> —Transmitted by Domei Tsushinsha (Japanese Federated News Agency) and recorded by the US Federal Communications Commission, August 14, 1945

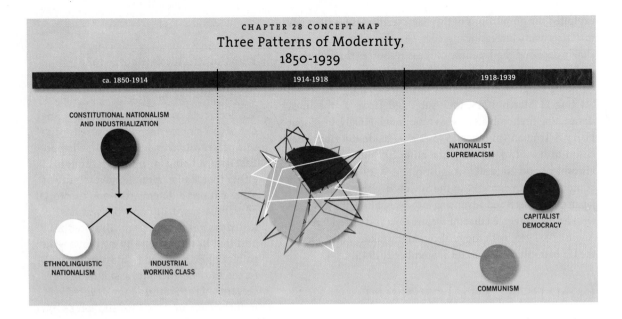

CHAPTER 28 CONCEPT MAP
Three Patterns of Modernity, 1850-1939

ca. 1850-1914 | 1914-1918 | 1918-1939

CONSTITUTIONAL NATIONALISM
AND INDUSTRIALIZATION

ETHNOLINGUISTIC
NATIONALISM

INDUSTRIAL
WORKING CLASS

NATIONALIST
SUPREMACISM

CAPITALIST
DEMOCRACY

COMMUNISM

ways of opposing other modern innovations such as constitutionalism and industrialism—with their messy uncertainties and feelings of rootlessness—by insisting on a purer, more mystical bond for the modern nation-state that, ironically, hearkened back to a simpler, reimagined past. But Mussolini, Hitler, and the Japanese generals all aspired to the same scientific–industrial future as Roosevelt, Churchill, Stalin, Chiang K'ai-shek, and Mao Zedong.

Review and Respond

1. How did the Allies deal with Germany after its defeat in 1918, and how did it recover?

2. Explain the shift from capital goods to consumer goods investment in the capitalist economies after World War I. How did this shift express itself?

3. Which factors contributed to the Great Depression of 1929–1933?

4. What role did the protagonist play in the communist vision of modernity? Why was industrialization central to the Soviet communist pattern of modernity?

5. Trace the steps through which Hitler advanced from prisoner to dictator.

6. How did a version of constitutionalist modernity arrive in Japan, and which factors limited its impact?

7. What reasons limited constitutional nationalism in China after the creation of the republic in 1912?

8. What were some of the artistic responses to modernity? How did they reflect the anxiety of the period?

For additional resources, including maps, primary sources, visuals, and quizzes, please go to www.oup.com/us/vonsivers. Please see the Further Resources section at the back of the book for additional readings and suggested websites.

Thinking Through Patterns

▶ **Which three patterns of modernity emerged after World War I? How and why did these patterns form?**

Ethnic nationalism was difficult to accommodate in the nineteenth century, which began with the more inclusive constitutional nationalism of Great Britain, the United States, and France. New nations like Italy, Germany, and Japan were formed on the basis of an ethnic nationalism that in a sense created nations but not necessarily ones with the ideals of equality embodied in constitutional nation-states. World War I set back Germany, Italy, and Japan, but afterward they inflated their ethnic nationalism into supremacist nationalism and adopted imperialism, all under the banner of modernity. In Russia, communists seized the opportunity offered by the turmoil of World War I to turn a constitutionally as well as industrially underdeveloped empire into a communist one-party, industrial empire. The United States, Britain, and France, each based on variations of constitutionalism, industry, and smaller or larger empires, became advocates of a capitalist democratic modernity.

Capitalist democracy was a modernity that upheld free enterprise, the market, and consumerism. It succeeded in providing the modern items of daily life, but it suffered a major setback in the Depression and had to be reined in through tightened political controls. It also withheld freedom, equality, and the staples of daily life from minorities and the colonized. Communism succeeded in industrializing an underdeveloped empire and providing the bare necessities for modern life; it did so with untold human sacrifices. Supremacist nationalism was attractive to nationalists who were not workers and therefore afraid of communism. Supremacist nationalists held democracies in disdain because they considered constitutions meaningless pieces of paper.

▶ **What were the strengths and flaws of each of the three visions of modernity?**

▶ **Why did supremacist nationalism disappear in the ashes of World War II?**

Supremacist nationalism was a modernity that failed because the conquest of new, self-sufficient empires proved to be an impossible goal. The advocates of democratic capitalist and communist modernity—most notably the United States, Great Britain, France, and the Soviet Union—were dangerously threatened by Germany, Italy, and Japan and came together to destroy these supremacist national countries.

Chapter 29 | Reconstruction, Cold War, and Decolonization

1945-1962

By any standard the event seemed symbolic of a new world order, one in which the emerging nonaligned nations would set the pace of innovation. Appropriately enough, it also marked the beginning of a new decade, one that would begin full of promise and peril and end in conflict and confusion for much of the world. The event was the 1960 election of the world's first female prime minister, Sirimavo Bandaranaike (1916–2000), of what was then called Ceylon (renamed Sri Lanka in 1972), a large island off the southeastern coast of India.

Her country had achieved independence from Great Britain only a dozen years before and had maintained close ties to its former colonial

THE COLD WAR AND DECOLONIZATION

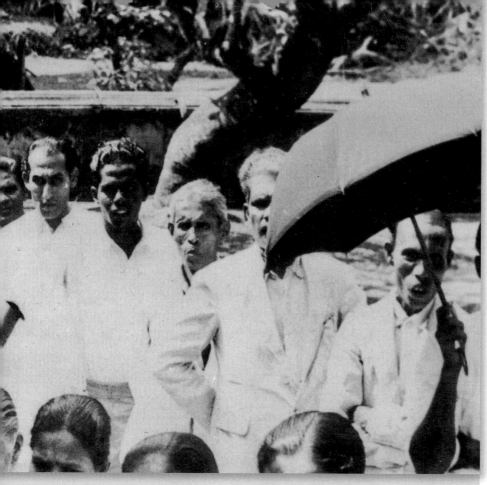

Seeing Patterns

▶ Why did the pattern of unfolding modernity, which offered three choices after World War I, shrink to just capitalist democracy and socialism–communism in 1945? How did each of these two patterns evolve between 1945 and 1962?

▶ What are the cultural premises of modernity?

▶ How did the newly independent countries of the Middle East, Asia, and Africa adapt to the divided world of the Cold War?

overlord. In 1956, however, Bandaranaike's husband Solomon was elected prime minister with a pronounced nationalist and socialist platform, in the newly assertive spirit of the nonaligned nations reflected in the Bandung Conference the year before. As prime minister, he replaced English with Sinhalese as the country's language and evicted the British military from its bases. When a Buddhist monk opposed to Western medicine assassinated him in 1959, she succeeded her husband, winning an election in 1960, becoming prime minister in her own right, and serving her first term from 1960 to 1965.

Coming from a prominent Buddhist family, she held the same deep political convictions as her husband, believing in a strong national foundation for her country as an independent nation beholden to neither West nor East. As a socialist, she continued the nationalization of the banking, insurance, and petroleum sectors begun by her husband; ordered the state to take over all Catholic schools; and joined the Nonalignment Movement in 1961. The movement sought to bring India, Egypt, Yugoslavia, Indonesia, and a number of other states together as a bloc to retain their independence from the pressures of the Cold War between the two superpowers of the United

Democracy in Action. One important element in the spread of representative government in Asia was the right of women to vote and hold office. Here, in a remote village on the island of Ceylon (now Sri Lanka) men and women line up separately to cast their votes in the general election of March 22, 1960. The victor in the race for prime minister, Sirimavo Bandaranaike, became the world's first woman prime minister.

United Nations: Successor of the League of Nations, founded in 1945 and comprising today about 200 countries; with a Secretary General, a General Assembly meeting annually, and a standing Security Council composed of permanent members (United States, China, Russia, Great Britain, and France) as well as 5 rotating temporary members.

States and the Soviet Union and their allies. Her strong commitment to a Sinhalese-only language policy, however, aroused considerable resistance in the country, especially from the Tamil minority in the north. The Theraveda Buddhist Sinhalese comprise about 74 percent and the Hindu Tamils 17 percent of the population. Only 2 years into Bandaranaike's tenure, the country was gripped by a Tamil civil disobedience campaign and it rapidly became apparent that Ceylon was entering a time of political turbulence. Ultimately, anti-Tamil discrimination led to the abortive Tamil Tiger liberation war (1976–2009), pursued on both sides with the utmost brutality.

During her four terms as prime minister (1960–1965, 1970–1972, 1972–1977, and 1994–2000), Bandaranaike was a prominent leader on the world stage. Like her fellow female prime ministers Benazir Bhutto in Pakistan and Indira Gandhi in India and first-generation nonaligned leaders like Jawaharlal Nehru of India, Sukarno of Indonesia, and Gamal Abdel Nasser of Egypt—Bandaranaike spent much of her time and scarce resources trying to navigate the turbulent waters of ethnic and religious conflict, superpower pressure, and nation-building in an increasingly competitive economic arena. The backdrop against which all these nonaligned nations acted was woven from two main developments in the unfolding pattern of scientific–industrial modernity: the Cold War and decolonization. The capitalist–democratic and the socialist–communist spheres competed with each other for political, military, and economic dominance; at the same time, the West rid itself of what was now seen as its biggest curse—colonialism—which bedeviled it and had severely detracted from its appeal during the interwar and early postwar periods.

The early Cold War, discussed in the first half of this chapter, dominated world politics during this time because the contest between the two superpowers allowed practically no escape. The one partial exception was China, which presented itself as a nonaligned country as it distanced itself from the Soviet Union but was viewed with ambivalence by its nonaligned colleagues. Decolonization, discussed in the second half of this chapter, was a subsidiary political process; but it nevertheless played a major role in the dynamics of the Cold War because it created many of the new nations over which both superpower blocs sought influence and so many tried to escape. By the 1962 Cuban Missile Crisis, during which the superpower confrontation reached its climax, the configuration of the two superpower blocs and the camp of the nonaligned nations was still in flux. Over the coming years, the tilting to one camp or another of India, Pakistan, Indonesia, and ultimately China, to name only a few, would loom large in the superpower struggle. And the role of Bandaranaike and other nonaligned leaders as spoilers between the superpowers, for a time at least, was secure.

Superpower Confrontation: Capitalist Democracy and Communism

World War II was the most destructive war in human history. Nearly 6 years of fighting in Europe and 9 years in Asia resulted in casualties on a scale scarcely conceivable in the past. The total loss of life, including combatants, civilians, and victims of the Holocaust, is estimated at over 50 million, three times as many as in World War I. With the exception of the continental United States, which was unreachable by enemy aircraft, all combatant countries in World War II suffered widespread destruction. Most ominous was that the final days of the war also ushered in the nuclear age. The use of the first atomic weapons by the United States against Japan meant that future general wars would almost certainly be nuclear ones. Yet, while the war was still on, the foundations of a new world organization to replace and fix the shortcomings of the old League of Nations—the **United Nations**, whose charter was later signed by 51 nations in October 1945—were being laid in San Francisco. Thus, the year 1945 was simultaneously one of hope that the war's end might result in a better world and one of grim assessment as the full extent of the global damage began to be understood. Remarkably, within a few years, out of the ruins, the world's remaining strains of modernity—capitalism–democracy and socialism–communism—would reemerge stronger than ever, each according to its own vision.

Destruction and Despair in the Nuclear Age. World War II was the most destructive human conflict in history, far exceeding the damage of what had only a short time before been considered to be "the war to end all wars"--World War I. Nowhere was the damage more complete than in Japan, where an aerial campaign of firebombing Japanese cities by American B-29s had destroyed nearly every major Japanese center. The culmination of this campaign was the first—and to date, last—use of nuclear weapons in warfare on the Japanese cities of Hiroshima and Nagasaki in August, 1945. Here, a mother and child who survived the nuclear destruction of Hiroshima sit plaintively amid the utter devastation of their city in December, 1945.

The Cold War Era, 1945–1962

As the world rebuilt, the United States and the Soviet Union promoted their contrasting visions of modernity—capitalist-democratic and communist—with deep missionary fervor. For the next 45 years the two powers were locked in a prolonged struggle to determine which approach would eventually prevail in the world. While each on occasion engaged in brinkmanship—pushing crises to the edge of nuclear war—as a rule both sought to avoid direct confrontation. Instead, they pursued their aims of expanding and consolidating their respective systems, dubbed the "Cold War," through ideological struggle and proxy states (that is, states acting as substitutes against each other). Two phases can be discerned in the early Cold War. The first lasted from 1945 to 1956, when the Soviet Union continued to pursue Stalin's prewar policy of "socialism in one country," which was now extended to include Eastern Europe. The second comprised the years 1956–1962, when Stalin's

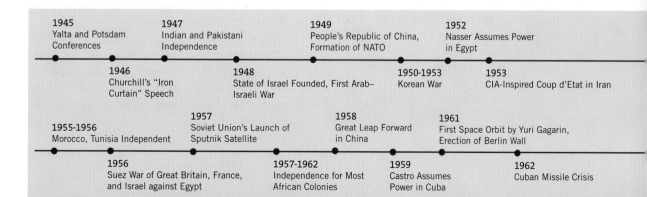

1945 Yalta and Potsdam Conferences	**1947** Indian and Pakistani Independence	**1949** People's Republic of China, Formation of NATO	**1952** Nasser Assumes Power in Egypt
	1946 Churchill's "Iron Curtain" Speech	**1948** State of Israel Founded, First Arab–Israeli War	**1950-1953** Korean War	**1953** CIA-Inspired Coup d'Etat in Iran
1955-1956 Morocco, Tunisia Independent	**1957** Soviet Union's Launch of Sputnik Satellite	**1958** Great Leap Forward in China	**1961** First Space Orbit by Yuri Gagarin, Erection of Berlin Wall
1956 Suez War of Great Britain, France, and Israel against Egypt	**1957-1962** Independence for Most African Colonies	**1959** Castro Assumes Power in Cuba	**1962** Cuban Missile Crisis

Cold War: Ideological struggle between the United States and its allies and the Soviet Union and its allies that lasted from 1945 to 1989.

Containment: U.S. foreign policy doctrine formulated in 1946 to limit as much as possible the spread of communism.

successor Nikita Khrushchev (1894–1971, in office 1953–1964) reformulated the policy to include spreading aid and influence to new nationalist regimes in Asia and Africa that had won their independence from Western colonialism, even if these regimes were not (yet) communist. This new policy, applied to Cuba, produced the near disaster of the Cuban Missile Crisis in 1962 during which the United States and the Soviet Union almost came to blows (see Map 29.1).

Cold War Origins   The origins of the **Cold War** have been bitterly debated and minutely studied since the 1940s, with apologists for each side tending to see its inception in the actions of the other. While it may not be possible at this point to establish an exact time or event for the beginning of the Cold War, we can point to certain mileposts in its development. One such milepost that most scholars point to came in the spring of 1945, when the Soviet Red Army occupied German-held territories in Eastern Europe and communist guerillas made rapid advances in the Balkans. In a secret deal between British Prime Minister Churchill and Soviet leader Josef Stalin in May 1944, Greece became part of the British sphere, in return for Romania and Bulgaria being apportioned to the Soviet sphere of responsibility for occupation at war's end.

Later, at the Yalta Conference in February 1945, Churchill, Stalin, and a haggard and ill American president Franklin Roosevelt agreed that the armies of the Allies would each undertake the occupation of the territories they held at war's end and hold free elections in those areas as soon as possible. Stalin also agreed that the Soviet Union would enter the war with Japan after the surrender of Germany. At the Potsdam Conference in July 1945, American interests were represented by Roosevelt's former vice president, Harry S Truman, who had assumed the office of president following Roosevelt's death in April.

Truman (in office 1945–1953) was more openly skeptical of Stalin's motives than Roosevelt, and he now had an edge that his predecessor lacked: On July 16, scientists at the "Manhattan Project," the US effort to develop an atomic weapon, had succeeded in detonating a plutonium test device in New Mexico. Armed with the astonishing results of the device's power and the knowledge that bombs were already being constructed for use against Japan, Truman felt confident he could deal firmly with Stalin's demands. His assessment of Stalin's motives was not reassuring; he felt the Russians had no intention of either withdrawing from Eastern Europe or allowing for democratic elections. By early 1946, Churchill, in a speech at Fulton, Missouri, coined the phrase that would define the communist sphere for decades to come in the West: the "Iron Curtain."

Accordingly, the United States formulated a policy designed to thwart Soviet expansion known as "**containment**." First spelled out in 1946 by George F. Kennan, a diplomat in the State Department, the proposed policy served as the foundation for the administration's determination to confront communist expansion.

Containing the Soviet Threat

"It is clear that the main element of any United States policy toward the Soviet Union must be that of long-term, patient but firm and vigilant containment of Russian expansive tendencies.... It is clear that the United States cannot expect in the foreseeable future to enjoy political intimacy with the Soviet regime. It must continue to regard the Soviet Union as a rival, not a partner, in the political arena. It must continue to expect that Soviet policies will reflect no abstract love of peace and stability, no real faith in the possibility of a permanent happy coexistence of the Socialist and capitalist worlds, but rather a cautious, persistent pressure toward the disruption and weakening of all rival influence and rival power."

—George F. Kennan. "The Sources of Soviet Conduct." *Foreign Affairs* 24, no. 4 (1947): 566–582. www .historyguide.org/europe/kennan.html.

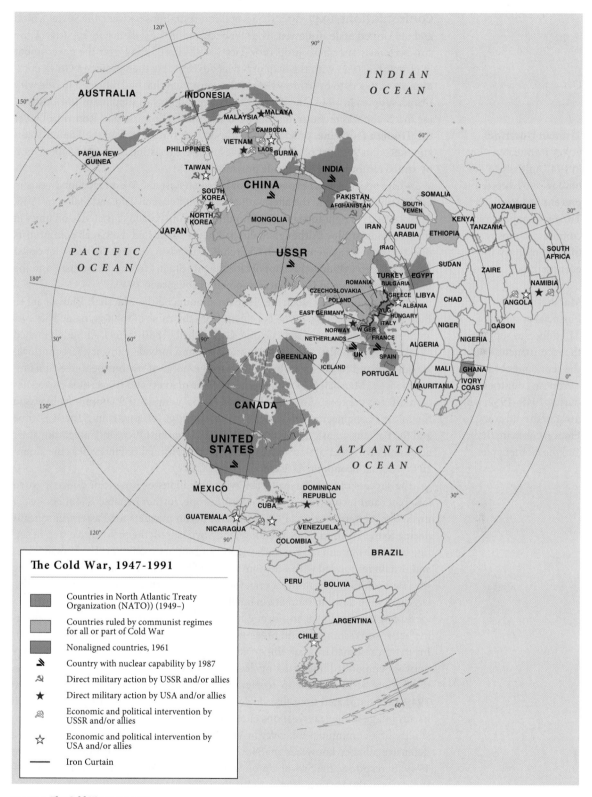

The Cold War, 1947-1991

- Countries in North Atlantic Treaty Organization (NATO)) (1949–)
- Countries ruled by communist regimes for all or part of Cold War
- Nonaligned countries, 1961
- ⟍ Country with nuclear capability by 1987
- ☭ Direct military action by USSR and/or allies
- ★ Direct military action by USA and/or allies
- ☭ Economic and political intervention by USSR and/or allies
- ☆ Economic and political intervention by USA and/or allies
- — Iron Curtain

MAP 29.1 **The Cold War, 1947–1991.**

Confrontations, 1947–1949   Several confrontations between the Soviet Union and the United States followed. The first occurred in the Balkans. In Yugoslavia, the anti-Nazi resistance hero Josip Broz Tito (1892–1980) took over the government in November 1945 with the help of Soviet advisors. He then provided Greek communists with aid, to overthrow the royal government that had returned to rule with British support in 1946. The United States stepped in with supplies in 1947, assuming that Stalin was orchestrating aid from Yugoslavia, Bulgaria, and Romania. Under the **Truman Doctrine**, proclaimed in a speech of the same year, the United States announced its support of all "free peoples who are resisting attempted subjugation by armed minorities or by outside pressures."

What appeared like a proxy civil war between East and West raged for 2 years in Greece until it ended in the aftermath of the split between Tito and Stalin. In 1948, Tito claimed his right to regional communism, against Stalin's insistence on unity in the Communist Bloc. Although Stalin had never supported the Greek communists directly, given his agreement with Churchill, a surprising majority of the latter opted for Stalin. Tito withdrew his support for the pro-Stalin Greek communists, and the bid for communism in Greece was doomed to collapse in 1949.

Following up on his doctrine, Truman announced the **Marshall Plan** of aid to Europe, for the recovery of the continent from the ruins of the war, named after its architect, the secretary of state George C. Marshall (1880–1959). Although invited to take part, Stalin flatly rejected American aid and forbade Hungary, Czechoslovakia, and Poland to ask for it. In addition to the political reasons behind Stalin's injunction, the Marshall Plan's requirement of free markets and convertible currencies contradicted the communist ideology of a central command economy. Stalin was in the midst of engineering his fledgling communist governments in Eastern Europe and the Balkans, transforming them into the Communist Bloc, and integrating their economies with that of the Soviet Union. This was formalized in 1949 as the Council for Mutual Economic Assistance (COMECON).

The success of the Marshall Plan, with its billions of American dollars poured into relief and reconstruction in Western Europe, further irritated Stalin because it made the Western sectors of Germany and Berlin magnets for Eastern Europeans fleeing to the West. In 1948, therefore, the Soviets took the provocative step of setting up a highway and rail blockade of food and supplies to Berlin. The United States and Britain responded with a demonstration of technological prowess by mounting the "Berlin Airlift." For nearly a year, food, fuel, and other supplies required by this large city were flown in until Stalin finally gave up the blockade.

So far, the Cold War in Europe had been confined to diplomatic maneuvering between Washington and Moscow. During the Berlin crisis, however, the confrontation assumed military dimensions. Thanks in part to an elaborate espionage network embedded inside the nuclear programs of Britain and the United States, the Soviets had been able to accelerate their efforts to build a nuclear bomb. In 1949, they detonated their first device 4 years earlier than anticipated. Now, with its advantage in nuclear weapons eliminated and concern increasing over the possibility of a communist takeover in Western Europe, the United States formed a defensive alliance known as the North Atlantic Treaty Organization (NATO) in 1949. In response, the Soviet Union later formed the Warsaw Pact in 1955 among the states of the Eastern Bloc.

Truman Doctrine:
Policy formulated in 1947, initially to outline steps directed at preventing Greece and Turkey from becoming communist, mostly through military and economic aid.

Marshall Plan:
Financial program of $13 billion to support the reconstruction of the economies of 17 European countries during 1948–1952, with most of the aid going to France, Germany, Italy, and the Netherlands.

The Berlin Airlift. During nearly 1 year from June 1948 to May 1949 US, British, and British Commonwealth airplanes delivered more than 2 million tons of food and supplies to Berlin after Stalin had blocked all land access to the city. Berlin children eagerly await the next delivery of supplies.

Hot War in Korea   Emboldened by the development of the nuclear bomb and the victory of the Chinese communists over the nationalists in October 1949, Stalin ratcheted up the Cold War. After a series of raids and counterraids between communist North Korea and nationalist South Korea and Stalin's blessing for an invasion by the north, the Cold War turned hot. In June 1950, large numbers of communist troops crossed over into South Korea in an attempt at forcible unification. South Korean troops fought a desperate rearguard action at the southern end of the peninsula. Under US pressure and despite a Soviet boycott, the United Nations (UN) Security Council branded North Korea as the aggressor, entitling South Korea to UN intervention. At first, in July 1950, the North Korean invaders trapped US troops arriving from Japan and what remained of the South Korean defense forces in the southeast. But by October US troops, augmented by troops from a number of UN members, had mounted a surprise amphibious invasion and fought their way into North Korea, occupied the capital (Pyongyang), and advanced to the Chinese border.

In the meantime, the United States had sent a fleet to the remnant of the Chinese nationalists who had formed the Republic of China on the southern island of Taiwan, to protect it from a threatened invasion by a newly communist China. Thwarted in the south at Taiwan, Mao Zedong took the pronouncements of General Douglas MacArthur, the commander of the UN forces in Korea, about raiding Chinese supply bases on the North Korean border seriously. Stalin, on the other hand, opposed an escalation and gave Mao only token support.

Secretly marching to the border in October 1950, communist Chinese troops launched a massive surprise offensive into the peninsula, pushing the UN forces back deep into South Korea. Over the next 3 years, the war seesawed back and forth over the old border of the 38th parallel, while negotiations dragged on. Unwilling to expand the war further or use nuclear weapons, the new Eisenhower administration and the North Koreans agreed to an armistice in 1953. The armistice has endured from that date, and no official peace treaty was ever signed. For more than half a century, the border between the two Koreas has remained a volatile flashpoint, with provocative incidents repeatedly threatening to reopen the conflict.

McCarthyism in the United States   The strains of a "hot war" in Korea produced troubling domestic fallout in the United States as well. Amid the general atmosphere of anticommunism, Joseph McCarthy (1908–1957), a Republican senator from Wisconsin, rose to prominence almost overnight when he revealed in a 1950 speech that he had a lengthy list of members of the Communist Party employed by the State Department. Though he never produced the list, his smear tactics, together with denunciations made by the House Committee on Un-American Activities, ruined the careers of hundreds of government employees, movie actors and writers, and private persons in many walks of life. McCarthy went as far as accusing Presidents Truman and Eisenhower of tolerating communist "fellow travelers" in their administrations. For 4 years hysteria reigned until finally enough voices of reason arose in the Senate to censure McCarthy and relegate him to obscurity in 1954. The legacy of bitterness engendered by the "McCarthy era" remained for decades and generated abundant political accusations on both sides.

Revolt in East Germany   As the McCarthy drama unfolded in the United States and the frustrating Korean armistice negotiations at Panmunjom dragged on, Stalin died of a stroke in April 1953. The death of this all-powerful, inscrutable, and paranoid dictator was profoundly unsettling for the governments of the Eastern Bloc. This was especially the case in the German Democratic Republic (East Germany), where the government was nervously watching the rising wave of defections to the Federal Republic (West Germany)—nearly a million persons during 1949–1953. It had sealed off the border through a system of fences and watchtowers, but Berlin—also divided into East and West sectors—was still a gaping hole. The population was seething over rising production quotas, shortages resulting from the shipment of industrial goods to the Soviet Union (in the name of reparations), and the beginnings of a West German economic boom in which it could not share.

In June 1953, a strike among East Berlin workers quickly grew into a general uprising, encompassing some 500 cities and towns. East German police and Soviet troops, stunned at first, quickly moved to suppress the revolt. The Politburo (the Communist Party's Central Committee Political Bureau) in Moscow, still trying to determine Stalin's succession, refused any concessions, except for a few cosmetic changes in the reparations. The German Stalinist government obediently went along.

Stalin's eventual successor in the fall of 1953 was Nikita Khrushchev, a metalworker from a poor farmer's family on the Russian–Ukrainian border who had worked his way up through the party hierarchy during the war years. It took Khrushchev a year and a half to consolidate his power as party secretary and premier, during which he made substantial investments in agriculture, housing, and consumer goods. In February 1956 he gave a much-noted speech in which he denounced Stalin's "excesses" during collectivization and the purges of the 1930s. Thousands were released from prisons and the labor camps in Siberia (*gulags*) and other remote areas. In the Communist Bloc Khrushchev pushed for the removal of Stalinist hard-liners and the arrival of new faces willing to improve general living conditions for the population. To balance the new flexibility within the Soviet Bloc, Khrushchev was careful to maintain toughness toward the West. He alarmed leaders of the West when he announced that he was abandoning Stalin's doctrine of socialism in one country for a new policy that supported anticolonial nationalist independence movements around the globe even if the movements were not communist. The policy sent shivers down the spines of the cold warriors in the West.

Revolt in Poland and Hungary   Khrushchev's speech and reforms awakened hopes in Eastern Europe that new leaders would bring change there as well. In Poland, where collectivization and the command economy had progressed only slowly and the Catholic Church could not be intimidated, Khrushchev's speech resulted in workers' unrest similar to East Germany 3 years earlier. Nationalist reformists gained the upper hand over Stalinists in the Polish Politburo, and Khrushchev realized that he had to avoid another Tito-style secession at all costs. After a few tense days in mid-October, pitting Soviet troops and an angry population against each other, Poland received its limited autonomy.

In Hungary, the Politburo was similarly divided between reformers and Stalinists. People in Budapest and other cities, watching events in Poland with intense interest, took to the streets. The Politburo lost control and the man appointed to lead the country to a national communist solution similar to that of Poland, Imre Nagy [Noj] (1896–1958), felt emboldened by popular support to go further by announcing a multiparty system and the withdrawal of Hungary from the Warsaw Pact. These announcements were too much for Khrushchev, who unleashed the Soviet troops stationed in Hungary to repress the by now fully blossoming grassroots revolution.

Aware of British, French, and American preoccupation with the Suez Crisis, the Soviets crushed the uprising in November 1956. Nagy, finding sanctuary in the Yugoslav Embassy and promised safe conduct out of the country, was duped and found

Unrest in the Soviet Bloc. In the Hungarian uprising from October to November 1956, some 2,500 Hungarians and 700 Soviet troops were killed, while 200,000 fled to neighboring Austria and the West. Here, a young boy and older man watch with a surprising degree of nonchalance while a Soviet tank rumbles through an intersection with barricades set up by Hungarian "freedom fighters."

Aiming for the Stars. New scholarship sheds light on Sputnik's role in Russian cultural history. As this commemorative postcard from 1958 reveals, the connection between the technological achievement of Sputnik and popular interest in space travel was strong. The legend reads in Russian: "4 October, the USSR launched Earth's first artificial satellite; 3 November, the USSR launched Earth's second artificial satellite."

himself arrested. The new pro-Moscow government executed him in 1958. During the brief uprising, perhaps a quarter of a million Hungarian citizens escaped to the West. For those who stayed, in the hopes of experiencing greater freedom, the events were a crushing blow.

ICBMs and Sputniks The suppression of anticommunist unrest in the Eastern Bloc decreased the appeal of communism among many Marxists and revolutionary socialists in the West. But steady advancement in weapons technologies and by extension in missiles and space flight, revealed that there was a powerful military punch behind Soviet repression. In 1957 the Soviet Union announced the development of the world's first intercontinental ballistic missile (ICBM), with a range of around 3,500 miles, making it capable of reaching America's East Coast. In the same year, the Soviet Union launched the world's first orbiting satellite, named "Sputnik," into space. Then, in 1961, Russian scientists sent the world's first cosmonaut, Yuri Gagarin (1934–1968), into space, followed 2 years later by Valentina Tereshkova (b. 1937), the world's first female cosmonaut.

These Soviet achievements duly frightened the Eisenhower administration and Congress as the implications of nuclear weapons falling from space with no practicable defense against them began to set in. Politicians played up the apparent technological leadership of the Soviet Union to goad Congress into accelerating the US missile and space program even at the risk of reheating the Cold War with the Soviet Union. Thus, in 1958 the United States successfully launched its first satellite, Explorer I, and the following year its first ICBM, the Atlas. The space and missile races were now fully under way.

Communism in Cuba In 1959, Fidel Castro (b. 1926), a nationalist guerilla fighter opposed to the influence of American companies over a government generally perceived as corrupt, succeeded in seizing power in Cuba. A trained lawyer, Castro was the son of a Spanish immigrant who had become a wealthy planter. About 6 months after the coup, Cuba was the new symbol of the Khrushchev government's widely hailed openness toward national liberation movements worthy of communist largesse. The Soviet Union lavished huge sums on the development of the economy of the island. Khrushchev's instincts were proven right when Castro openly embraced communism in 1960.

To counter Khrushchev's overtures to national liberation movements, President Eisenhower and the head of the American Central Intelligence Agency (CIA), Allen Dulles (1893–1969), secretly supported and trained anticommunist dissidents in the Middle East, Africa, and Latin America. In the case of Latin America, a group of Cuban anticommunists trained in Guatemala with CIA support for an invasion and overthrow of Castro in Cuba. President John F. Kennedy (in office 1961–1963) inherited the initiative and, against his better judgment, decided to steer a middle course, sanctioning an invasion of Cuba by seemingly independent freedom fighters with no direct US armed forces support. The so-called Bay of Pigs invasion in April

1961 (named for the small bay in southern Cuba where the anticommunist invasion began) was promptly intercepted and easily defeated by Castro's forces, to the great embarrassment of Kennedy.

The Berlin Wall   Fortunately for the United States, Khrushchev suffered a severe embarrassment of his own. East Germany, which retained its Stalinist leadership, pressured Khrushchev to close the last loophole in Berlin through which its citizens could escape to West Germany. Between 1953 and 1961, the East German "brain drain" reached 3 million defectors or nearly one-fifth of the population, most of them young and ambitious people whose talent and skills the regime coveted. The East German Stalinists, allied with a few remaining Stalinists in the Politburo, prevailed over Khrushchev's opposition and built the Berlin Wall in 1961, effectively turning the German Democratic Republic into a prison.

The playing field between East and West was now level, with setbacks on both sides, when the two reached the climax of the Cold War: the first direct confrontation between the Soviet Union and the United States nearly two decades after the end of World War II. In October 1962 US spy planes discovered the presence of missile launching pads in Cuba. In October 1962 President Kennedy demanded their immediate destruction and then followed up with a naval blockade of the island to prevent the arrival of Russian missiles. In defiance, Khrushchev dispatched Russian ships to Cuba; when it was discovered that they were bearing missiles, President Kennedy demanded that Khrushchev recall the ships. The world held its breath for several days as the ships headed steadily for Cuba, raising the very real possibility of a nuclear exchange between the world's superpowers (see Map 29.2).

In the face of American determination, Khrushchev recalled the ships at the last minute. Kennedy, for his part, agreed to remove American missiles from Turkey. Realizing just how close the world had come to World War III, Kennedy and Khrushchev signed the Nuclear Test Ban Treaty in 1963, an agreement banning the aboveground testing and development of nuclear weapons. The treaty also sought to prevent the spread of these technologies to other countries. After this dramatic climax in the Cold War, relations gradually thawed.

Society and Culture in Postwar North America, Europe, and Japan

As in many other wars, World War II was followed by years of conservatism during which the generation of war veterans, deprived of some of their best years because of military service, sought to pursue civilian lives of normalcy and comfort. Intellectuals and artists again cast a critical eye on the modernity that was relentlessly evolving around them, not unlike the previous generation had after World War I. Now, however,

MAP **29.2 The Cuban Missile Crisis.**

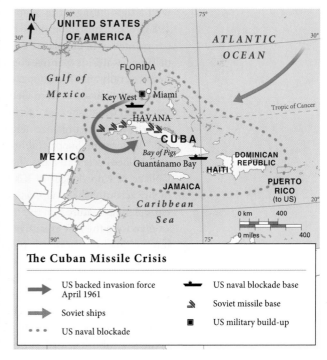

The Cuban Missile Crisis

→ US backed invasion force April 1961

→ Soviet ships

• • • US naval blockade

⊢ US naval blockade base

⬊ Soviet missile base

■ US military build-up

The G.I. Bill for African Americans. Staff Sergeant Herbert Ellison explains the G.I. Bill to members of his company. The bill, enacted in 1944, provided soldiers returning from the war with support for training and education as well as subsidized home loans. Some 7.8 million veterans benefited from the training and education it provided.

the political and ideological options were narrower. Supremacist nationalism in the form of fascism, Nazism, or militarism had been thoroughly bankrupted; and choices had shrunk to communism and capitalist democracy. Still, among the emerging nations, artists and intellectuals struggled to forge new paths, often with attempts at synthesis among indigenous culture and socialist and democratic ideas.

Mass Consumption Culture As discharged American soldiers returned to civilian life, they married and had children. The "babyboomer" generation appeared on the scene between 1945 and 1961. Families with four to six children were almost the norm. Medical advances and improved diet and nutrition helped in the health and survival of parents and children. The growing population triggered increased consumer demand, not only for the basics of living, such as food, clothes, shoes, and shelter, but also for consumer durables which increased the comfort of living, such as refrigerators, dishwashers, vacuum cleaners, radios, televisions, telephones, and cars. In the United States, the G.I. Bill supported not only the middle-class lifestyle but also university studies for better-paying jobs. In Europe, the Marshall Plan helped to provide Europeans with similar, if still somewhat lower, living standards. Americans increasingly took on credit to move into their middle-class lives, while Europeans tended to save first before spending their money on consumer goods.

One convenience symbolic of the new era was the innovative plastic container with a tight-fitting lid to keep food fresh in the refrigerator. Earl Tupper (1907–1983), a subcontractor of the chemicals conglomerate DuPont during the war, experimented with the plastic compound polyethylene and in 1947 launched his line of Tupperware, inexpensive containers of all sizes and shapes. Sales began to pick up, however, only after the Tupperware company hired Brownie Wise (1913–1992), an eighth-grade dropout from Georgia who sold household products through a home party plan which she had developed. This plan provided suburban housewives with the motivation to organize neighbors at parties where they could demonstrate and sell Tupperware. Successful housewives rose in the sales-force hierarchy, and annual jubilees celebrated the champion saleswomen of the year at the "Tupperware College of Knowledge" in Kissimmee, Florida. Tupperware sales took off, and a highly accomplished Wise went on to become vice president and the first female entrepreneur featured on the cover of *Business Weekly*. Wise and a half-dozen other women were the first executives to break into the male-dominated corporate structure of American business, pioneers of a trend that is only now becoming more commonplace.

In addition to the Tupperware parties, the Avon lady and the encyclopedia man were fixtures of American suburban life. In the idealized family of the 1950s and early 1960s, husbands worked downtown from 9:00 to 5:00, while mothers and grandmothers were responsible for the household and children. Shopping was done in the new suburban mall, and everybody went to church or synagogue on weekends

Suburban Convenience. Three suburban housewives examine the latest in food container design and utility at what had become a fixture in the postwar landscape—the Tupperware party. Tupperware sparked and reinvigorated a host of other women-dominated, door-to-door businesses like Avon, Amway, Herbalife, and Mary Kay Cosmetics. Note that while middle-class hair styles and clothing have undergone fashion cycles over the intervening decades, the differences between the styles of these women from the early 1960s is not dramatically different from styles of the early 2000s.

and occasionally treated themselves with a trip to the downtown department store and movie theater. This gendered and spatially segregated life was highly structured, corresponding to the yearning of the expanding middle classes for regularity and order after the years of economic depression and war. In Europe and Japan, with variations due to cultural differences and a later suburbanization process, similar changes in consumer culture took place. An important minority of baby boomers found this middle-class life eventually so stultifying that they revolted in the 1960s, as we will see in Chapter 30.

American Popular Culture Dominates the World   Thanks to US leadership in the entertainment industry first established during the Roaring Twenties, American pop culture spread again across the world. American shows produced for television in the 1950s were wildly popular and constituted over one-half of televised shows played in British and Western European homes. Westerns were exemplified by the long-running success of *The Lone Ranger*, which was broadcast from 1949 to 1957. Some of the most successful film directors were John Ford (1894–1973), Alfred Hitchcock (1899–1980), and Joseph Losey (1909–1984), who recruited internationally known stars such as Marlene Dietrich (1901–1992), Clark Gable (1901–1960), James Stewart (1908–1997), Marilyn Monroe (1926–1962), and Elizabeth Taylor (1932–2011) to their productions. American music had a similar influence in shaping the development of popular culture on both sides of the Atlantic. Blues and, especially, jazz resumed their pre-1930s dominance of

Popular Culture and Rock and Roll

Perhaps the most successful musical genre and export of twentieth-century popular culture was rock and roll. Today, rock and roll and its descendents—disco, rap, and hip-hop, among many—are all-pervasive on the world scene, appearing in tiny cafes in Congo and remote villages in South America and spawning a host of local artists and imitators worldwide. As part of an identifiable global youth culture, it has also inspired most of the fashions associated with youth and rebellion since the mid-1950s.

Music scholars avidly debate who actually "created" the music, and a host of pioneers have been cited. The origins of the music may be found in blues, rhythm and blues, and jazz. By the late 1940s many African American musicians were performing in small groups featuring combinations of recently developed electrically amplified guitars and basses, drums, horns, and keyboard instruments. This kind of group allowed for a loud, hard-driving music with a more economical configuration than the large jazz groups that dominated the war years. Some scholars have cited Ike Turner's 1951 "Rocket 88" as the first rock and roll record; more conventionally, Bill Haley and the Comets' "Rock Around the Clock" (1954) is considered to be the breakout song that took African American musical forms and made them accepted by a larger—and mostly white—teenage audience.

Rock Around the Clock. The breakthrough success of the new form of popular music called "Rock and Roll" by the mid-1950s was unmistakable, though its origins in African American music forms led many conservative white parents to view it as dangerous and subversive—while their sons and daughters took to it with enthusiasm. Here, the first rock-and-roll group with cross-over success, Bill Haley and the Comets, wails away with exuberance.

Within short order, Elvis Presley, Buddy Holly, Little Richard, Jerry Lee Lewis, and a host of other performers also came to dominate the charts; their recordings sold in the millions from the mid-1950s onward. By the early 1960s the influence of this music in Great Britain led to the famous "British Invasion" of the United States by such groups as the Beatles, the Rolling Stones, the Yardbirds, the Kinks, the Who, and others. By the late 1960s the international appeal of what was now being called "rock music" or simply "rock" and its successful transplantation far and wide had created rock culture throughout Europe, Latin America, and Asia. Despite vigorous efforts to ban it or create substitutes for it in Soviet-Bloc nations, it also achieved major cult status as underground music for a variety of political and lifestyle dissidents. Since the 1950s, each successive generation has sought to use a variation of the music to push its own ideas of rebellion and outrageousness in distancing itself from its predecessors. But in the end, they all seem to agree with the Rolling Stones, who sang "It's only rock and roll but I like it!"

Questions

- How is rock and roll a cultural expression of the capitalist-democratic pattern of modernity?

- Does rock's global impact show that cultural forms of expression are in many ways more enduring than political ones?

Rock Around the World. Over the succeeding decades, rock-and-roll—later shortened to simply "rock"—became a kind of world music, with local variants. By the end of the twentieth century there was probably no place on earth where the music had not become established. In this startling scene an image of the wildly successful performer Madonna graces a van door window in the city of Jenné-Jeno, in Mali in West Africa.

European popular music. A new musical form, rock and roll, arose from the older musical forms and appealed to the baby-boom generation as it entered its teenage years in the later 1950s. Parents were generally aghast at this "noise," but the teenagers prevailed—and rock and roll conquered the world (see "Patterns Up Close").

Existentialism   Consumerism was a central element in the capitalist-democratic order and was based on the belief in the autonomous individual as the basic component of society. The Enlightenment ideas of materialism and the social contract continued to dominate the Anglo-American cultural sphere, but their reductionist vision, which diminished everything to nature and atoms, had prompted Kant and Hegel to reintroduce the transcendence of mind into continental European thought in the early nineteenth century.

The effect of these different orientations was that when the broad nineteenth-century movements of early modernity—first romanticism and then realism—gave way to the twentieth-century **modernism**, the great majority of Anglo-American thinkers and artists continued their broad modernist approaches. By contrast, European thinkers and artists, dissatisfied with the nineteenth-century solutions to modernity's materialist shortcomings, remained more strongly committed to finding new ideological solutions to materialism. In philosophy, the most important modernist thinker was Martin Heidegger (1889–1976), who saw himself as a prophet offering a non-materialist future in his work *Being and Time* (1927). His ideas became constitutive not only for the ideology of existentialism, which swept continental Europe in the 1950s and early 1960s, but also for the ideologies of poststructuralism and postmodernism which became dominant in the world after the mid-1970s.

In Germany, Heidegger was tainted by his support for the Nazis. But in France, his castigation of what he viewed as a modernity of meaningless materialism exerted a powerful attraction on intellectuals, such as Jean-Paul Sartre (1905–1980) and Albert Camus (1913–1960). Sartre was a communist enthralled by the egalitarian core of socialism; Camus was an anticommunist who was appalled at the barbarity of Stalin as revealed by Khrushchev after Stalin's death in 1953. Sartre, in *Being and Nothingness* (1943) and other essays and plays, described life as a material existence without God amid the horrors of a gaping nothingness in space and time. For him, the only way of living in such a bleak reality was to espouse the absurdity of existence in the here and now as intensively as possible, choosing whatever would give one authenticity from among equally relative possibilities.

For Camus, who rejected the label of **existentialism**, the absurdity of life in a purely material universe without God was nevertheless also a point of departure. He pinned his hope not on socialist egalitarianism but on rebellion against the denial of human rights in any form of mass politics. His novel *The Stranger*, essay *The Rebel* (1951), and other essays and plays were pleas for a spirited engagement of the individual in an existence of honesty and justice as a way out of modernity's materialist absurdity. The Irish playwright Samuel Beckett (1906–1989) and the Romanian playwright Eugène Ionesco (1909–1994), both writing in French, were less optimistic about humanity's ability to escape absurdity. For them, even more than Sartre and Camus, the only point of one's existence was to uncover modern life's abundant moments of pointlessness, often presented in a hilarious way in their scripts, so as to make existence less hypocritical and more honest.

Modernism: Any of various movements in philosophy and the arts characterized by a deliberate break with classical or traditional forms of thought or expression.

Existentialism: A form of thought built on the assumption that the scientific–industrial society of modernity is without intrinsic meaning unless an answer to the question of what constitutes authentic existence is found; in the later 1970s this question was renewed in the intellectual movement known as postmodernism.

Poetry and Literature   Not surprisingly, the basic materialist problem of modernity was fertile ground not only for existentialists in philosophy and the theater but in a more generalized form also for writers and film directors, the two often collaborating. With cultural variations, typically modern themes (individualism, loneliness, and alienation; conformism, freedom, and personal fulfillment; family bonds and parental relations; class, race, and gender sensibilities; political persecution, torture, and mass murder), all provided fodder for rich national literary and cinematographic post–World War II cultures in Western countries. As culture-specific as many authors and filmmakers were, by not merely dwelling on the reductionism of modernity but rather confronting it with their rich inherited premodern traditions, they created works that could be understood across cultures. In many cases, they created classics that are today as fresh and relevant as they were then.

A few representative examples illustrate the breadth of global culture in 1945–1962. In the United States it was the rich premodern culture of the South which produced figures such as William Faulkner (1897–1962) and Tennessee Williams (1911–1983), who explored in different ways the complexities of southern family life. The influential southern journal *New Criticism* revolutionized the understanding of literary works on their own formal and substantive merits, without recourse to biography and social environment. The poets Wallace Stevens (1879–1955) and Elizabeth Bishop (1911–1979) emerged from interwar modernism with fresh approaches. Stevens focused his attention on the autonomy and depth of modern imagination, while Bishop wrote a carefully crafted formal poetry that obscured more than it revealed about her search for belonging in the modern world.

Poetry in Great Britain was similarly oriented toward personal struggles with the emotional effects of modernity, as in the work of the Englishman (later American citizen) W. H. Auden (1907–1973) and the Welshman Dylan Thomas (1914–1953). By contrast, German-language authors, such as the Swiss playwright Max Frisch (1911–1991), the Romanian-born Jewish poet–essayist Paul Celan (1920–1970), the Austrian Ingeborg Bachmann (1926–1973), and the German Günter Grass (b. 1927)—albeit in their own different ways—focused on social themes such as identity, suffering, guilt, and the truth of language. Similar social themes within different cultural contexts are found in the works of the Italian Alberto Moravia (1907–1990), the Japanese Shohei Ooka [OH-kah] (1909–1988), the Russian Aleksandr Solzhenitsyn (1918–2008), and the Spaniard Jorge Semprún (1923–2011). Latin America was a microcosm of the varieties of modernism, coming to the fore in such different authors as the Argentine Jorge Luís Borges (1899–1986), the Chilean Pablo Neruda (1904–1973), and the Mexican Octavio Paz (1914–1998). Strikingly, in all of these authors the ebullient and often strident modernism of the early twentieth century gives way to a more reflective, sometimes distant, and always more personal encounter with the ambiguities and contradictions of modernity.

Sartre on Consciousness

"Thus it amounts to the same thing whether one gets drunk alone or is a leader of nations. If one of these activities takes precedence over the other, this will not be because of its real goal but because of the degree of consciousness which it possesses of its real goal; and in this case it will be the quietism of the solitary drunkard which will take precedence over the vain agitation of the leader of nations."

—Jean-Paul Sartre. *Being and Nothingness.* Translated by Hazel E. Barnes, p. 797. New York: Philosophical Library, 1956.

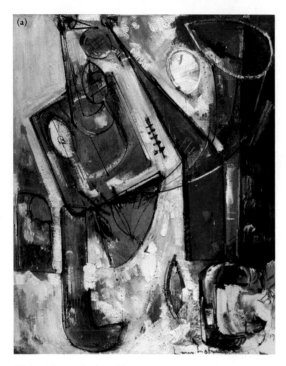

Abstract Expressionism. (*a*) Hans Hofmann (1880–1966), *Delight*, 1947. (*b*) Willem de Kooning (1904–1997), *Montauk Highway*, 1958. Abstract expressionism was a New York–centered artistic movement that combined the strong colors of World War I German expressionism with the abstract art pioneered by the Russian-born Wassiliy Kandinsky and the artists of the Bauhaus school. Before and during the Nazi period, many European artists had flocked to New York, including Hofmann and de Kooning. The movement caught the public eye when Jackson Pollock, following the surrealists, made the creation of a work of art—painting a large canvas on the floor through the dripping of paint—an art in itself.

Film, Painting, and Music   Many literary works, including some by the aforementioned authors, made their way into film, in the hands of directors who elevated the pop-culture entertainment movie into an art that sought to visualize the multifaceted literary modernity of 1945–1962. The pioneers of the "art flick" were Erich von Stroheim (1885–1957) and Jean Renoir (1894–1979, son of the impressionist painter Pierre-Auguste Renoir), who made their main contributions during the modernist interwar period. After World War II, two broad movements emerged: the neorealist school of Italian filmmakers that dealt with the harsh life in post–World War II Italy and the related New Wave (*Nouvelle vague*) in France, beginning in the late 1950s, that featured free-wheeling baby boomers breaking loose from the regimented post-war life.

Similar to the movements in film, two artistic developments swept through painting and music in the post–World War II period: abstract expressionism and serialism. The proponents of these two movements presented their works as existentialist reflections of conflicted emotions, expressed in art as pure color without form and in music as sound without harmony or traditional form. Abstract expressionism began in the United States with Mark Rothko (1903–1970) and Jackson Pollock (1912–1956) and swiftly spread across the world.

Latin America, by contrast, continued to follow social realism, a version of early twentieth-century modernism which, especially in Mexico, fit well within the cultural approach of the dominant revolutionary party. Here, the outstanding representatives were the Mexican husband and wife team Diego Rivera (1889–1957) and Frida Kahlo (1907–1954). Rivera executed many commissioned murals celebrating important historical episodes from the Aztec and early independence periods. Kahlo's folk art approach masks a deep and often troubled self-exploration, which has had a strong impact both in Mexico and the world.

Serialism, based on the pioneering "atonal" music of the Austrian American composer Arnold Schoenberg (1874–1951), was international from the start, with such representatives as the Italian Luigi Nono (1924–1990), the French Pierre Boulez [Boo-LEZ] (b. 1925), and the Germans Werner Henze (b. 1926) and Karlheinz Stockhausen (1928–2007). The 12–tone octave allows for 66 pitches, or sound frequencies, and is no longer organized around a key, or central tone, characteristic of all music from the Renaissance to Romanticism. Compositions after the middle of the twentieth century were, typically, mathematically related series of pitches (hence "serialism"). The works of both abstract expressionism and serialism require considerable understanding to be enjoyable, and for many people they remain unknown cultural territory.

Populism and Industrialization in Latin America

Given its large Creole and European immigrant populations, Latin America's dominant social classes had participated since the time of the constitutionalist revolutions in the pattern of unfolding cultural modernity. But Latin America also had a large population of Amerindians and blacks, who participated only marginally in this modernity and large majorities of whom were mired in rural subsistence. Since these populations increased rapidly after World War II, the region faced problems that did not exist in North America or Europe, where industry and its related service sector employed an overwhelmingly urban society. Latin America began to resemble Asia and Africa, which also had massive rural populations, small middle classes, and limited industrial sectors. Populist leaders relying on the urban poor thus sought to steer their countries toward greater industrialization, although with limited success.

Slow Social Change

Latin America had stayed out of World War II. The postwar aftermath therefore neither disrupted nor offered new opportunities to the pattern of social and economic development. The region had suffered from the disappearance of commodity export markets during the Depression of the 1930s, and politicians realized that import-substitution industrialization, replacing imported manufactures with domestically produced ones, had to be seriously taken up as a postwar policy. Tackling industrialization, however, was not easy since landowners opposed it and the great majority of rural and urban Latin Americans were too poor to become consumers.

Rural and Urban Society   Prior to 1945, the rural population had been decreasing, though very slowly. It still comprised about two-thirds of the total population. But during 1945–1962, the pace of urbanization picked up, with the proportions nearly reversed (see Map 29.3). Overall population growth during this period accelerated, but the poverty rates remained the same or even increased, making Latin America the one world region with the greatest income disparities. The inequalities were exacerbated by the continuation of sizeable indigenous Amerindian farming populations in Guatemala, Ecuador, Peru, Bolivia, and parts of Mexico, as well as blacks in Brazil. Landowners continued to thwart efforts at land reform: Except for Mexico (in spurts after 1915) and Bolivia (1952) no country abolished landlordism

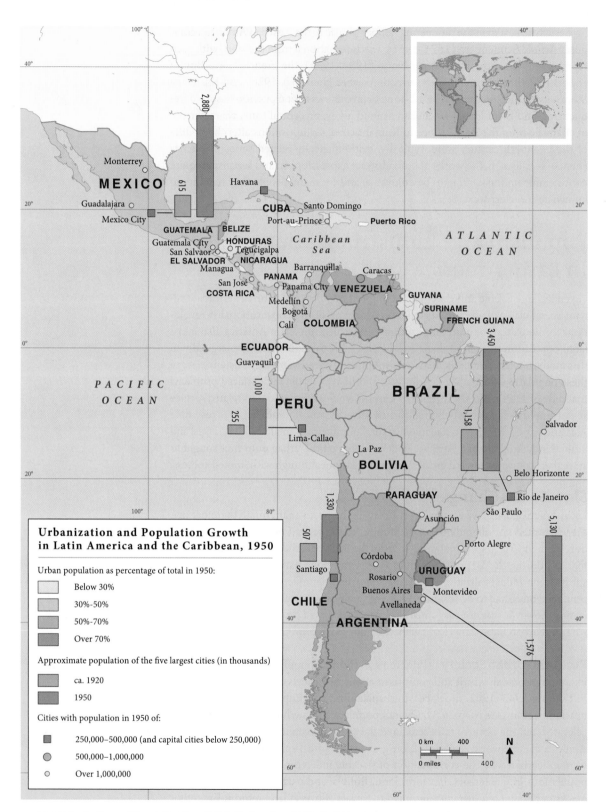

MAP 29.3 Urbanization and Population Growth in Latin America and the Caribbean, ca. 1950.

prior to 1962. Cuba's land reform (1959) and the threat of local peasant revolutions made the issue urgent again, but agrarian reforms picked up only in the 1960s.

Much of the landless population migrated to the cities, making up nearly half of the arrivals. They settled in sprawling shantytowns with no urban services. Some migrants found employment in the expanding industrial sector, but more often than not they survived through occasional labor in the so-called informal sector, a new phenomenon of peddling, repairing, and recycling which comprised about one-third of the urban population. In contrast to the villages, rural–urban migrants benefited at least marginally from the health and education benefits which populist politicians introduced. The industrial labor force grew to about one-quarter of the total labor force, a growth that was far behind that of the East Asian "Tigers" or "Little Dragons" of Korea, Taiwan, and Hong Kong in the 1950s and reflected the hesitant attitude of the politicians toward industrialization in view of rebounding commodity exports in the 1950s.

At the end of World War II, industrialism was still confined mainly to food-processing and textile manufacturing; only Mexico and Brazil had moved into basic goods, such as steel and chemicals. In the later 1940s and early 1950s, the larger Latin American countries moved to capital goods and consumer durables, such as machinery, tools, cars, and refrigerators. Smaller countries, like Bolivia, Peru, and Paraguay, overextended themselves with industrial import substitution and, after a few years of trying, had to return in the early 1950s to a primacy of commodity exports. Very little private capital was available on the domestic market for risky industrialization ventures, and therefore, the state jumped into the fray to allocate the necessary funds.

Populist Guided Democracy

As we have seen, the period 1945–1962 was the time when the siren songs of fascism and Nazism faded and only democracy and communism remained as political and ideological choices. The attraction of democracy in its constitutional-nationalist North American and European forms, however, was limited since the United States, in the grip of the Cold War, was primarily interested in the professed loyalty of autocratic rulers in its Latin American backyard. Communism was initially also of limited appeal, given Stalin's preference for large, obedient communist parties that toed his line, and flourished only once Khrushchev supported national liberation movements, as in Cuba. **Populism** was an intermediate form of governance that found strong, albeit brief, support in Latin America from 1945–1962.

The Populist Wave   Democracy in Latin America during this time was represented by the three countries of Venezuela (1958), Colombia (1953–1964), and Costa Rica (1953–). Democratic politicians, however, were unable to put Venezuela's oil to productive use or bring about land reform in Colombia, resulting eventually in the formation of a communist guerilla underground in the latter country in 1964. Eight Latin American countries had populist regimes for varying periods from the mid-1940s onward: Guatemala (1944–1954), Argentina (1946–1955), Brazil (1946–1954), Venezuela (1945–1948), Peru (1945–1948), Chile (1946–1952), Costa Rica (1948–1953), and Ecuador (1948–1961). In Guatemala, the Cold War and the banana plantation interests of the United Fruit Company formed the background for a CIA-fomented military coup d'état which ended the rule of the elected populist Jacobo Arbenz and was the prelude to a vicious civil war (1960–1996). The

Populism: Type of governance in which rulers seek support directly from the population, through organizing mass rallies, manipulating elections, and intimidating or bypassing parliament.

The Ambition for Social Progress

"The ambition for social progress has nothing to do with its noisy partisan exploitation, neither can it be achieved by reviling and lowering the different types of men. Mankind needs faith in his destiny and in what he is doing and to possess sufficient insight to realise that the transition from the 'I' to the 'we' does not take place in a flash as the extermination of the individual, but as a renewed avowal of the existence of the individual functioning in the community. In that way the phenomenon is orderly and takes place during the years in the form of a necessary evolution which is more in the nature of 'coming of age' than that of a mutiny."

—Juan Perón. *An Organized Community*, p. 53. Buenos Aires: Club de lectores, 1954.

remaining countries similarly moved in and out of coups d'état and authoritarian or dictatorial regimes from 1945 to 1962.

Peronism is the best-known form of the populist interlude in Latin America that characterized the period of 1945–1962. Colonel Juan Perón (1895–1974), of modest rural background, was a member of a group of officers who staged a coup in 1943 against the traditional landowners and their conservative military allies. They sympathized with the urban population of workers in the nascent food-processing industries as well as the poor in the traditional crafts, service employments, and the informal sector of street vending, repairing, mending, and trash collecting. Perón became minister of labor in the junta. In this position, he entered into an alliance with labor unions and improved wages, set a minimum wage, and increased pensions. After an earthquake, as the junta solicited donations from celebrities, Perón met Eva Duarte (1919–1952), a movie actress. An attractive, popular person in her own right, she headed a variety of social organizations and charities; and the two together became the symbol of Peronism. In elections in 1946, at the head of a fractious coalition of nationalists, socialists, and communists, Perón gained a legitimate mandate as president.

After the elections he started a 5-year plan of nationalization and industrialization—the characteristic state socialism pursued also in Asia and Africa. Banks, phone companies, railroads, and streetcars, mostly in the hands of British and French capital, were nationalized, as was the entire export of agricultural commodities. A year later, construction of plants for the production of primary and intermediate industrial goods, such as iron, steel, farm machinery, ships, and airplanes, got under way. Interestingly, Perón's state socialism stopped short of the automobile sector in order to avoid a confrontation with US investors. During Perón's tenure, the economy expanded by 40 percent.

To get the national factories going, however, they had to be equipped with imported machinery. Initially, Perón paid for these imports with reserves accumulated from commodity exports during World War II. But soon the costs for the imported machinery exceeded the internal reserves and revenues of Argentina. Inflation and strikes plagued the country. What eventually derailed Perón, however, was the Cold War. President Truman refused to include Argentina in the list of recipients for Marshall Plan aid. He disliked a populist regime in his own hemisphere that strove to leap into full industrialization through state socialism. Plagued by chronic deficits and unable to pay its foreign debts, Perón was overthrown by a conservative-led coup against him in 1955. Thus, Argentina, instead of leaping into industrialization, stumbled—not unlike China in the later 1950s.

The End of Colonialism and the Rise of New Nations

Like Latin America, Asia and Africa also experienced rapid population growth and urbanization in the period 1945–1962. But in contrast to the politically independent American continent, colonialism was still dominant in Asia and Africa at the end of World War II. The governments of Great Britain and France had no inclination to relinquish their empires at this point, but both were too exhausted by the war to hold them completely. Thus, in a first wave after the end of war, a few independence movements succeeded in more or less forcibly prying themselves loose, notably in the Middle East and Asia. A major shift in the perception of the benefits of colonialism during the mid-1950s, however, had to take place before Britain and France were willing to relinquish their colonial grip in Africa.

"China Has Stood Up"

Japan maintained a short and brutal colonial regime from 1937 to 1945 in China. Given Japan's defeat in World War II by the Allies, the Chinese did not have to fight for their independence; but they were not spared conflict. In 1949 the communists finally prevailed over the nationalists after 4 more years of a civil war that had begun over a decade earlier. China was still fundamentally a peasant-based economy with scant industrial resources. Mao's theories of revolution had adopted Marxist principles to put peasants instead of industrial workers at the forefront of the movement toward socialism. For Mao, this reinterpretation of Marxism opened up fresh possibilities of development, with the expropriation of landlords, the construction of communal farms, and the eventual leap into decentralized village industrialization. During the Stalin years, China depended heavily on Soviet material aid and advisors. After Khrushchev introduced his consumer-oriented reforms in the mid-1950s and refused to share nuclear and space technology, estrangement set in, culminating in the Soviet Union's withdrawal of all advisors from China in 1960.

Victory of the Communists   China emerged from World War II on the winning side but was severely battered militarily, economically, and politically. The brutal war with Japan had taken 10–20 million lives, according to various estimates. Moreover, the shaky wartime alliance between the communists under Mao Zedong and the nationalists under Chiang K'ai-shek unraveled in the later civil war. The communists, who had entrenched themselves deeply in the countryside, were at a strategic advantage in China's overwhelmingly rural society. Despite the nationalists' superiority, resulting from modern arms and American support, the communists were able to systematically choke the cities, causing hyperinflation in Shanghai and other urban centers in 1947.

By 1948 the size of the two armies had reached parity; but Mao's People's Liberation Army had unstoppable popular momentum, and the United States cut back on its aid to Chiang as he faced imminent defeat. By 1949, Chiang and most of his forces had fled to Taiwan, Mao's forces took Beijing, and the new People's Republic of China set about reshaping the country according to the Maoist vision of the communist pattern of collectivist modernity. For millions of Chinese Mao's pronouncement on October 1, 1949, from atop the Gate of Heavenly Peace in Beijing that "China has stood up" and would never be a victim of imperialism again was a source of enormous pride. What would follow in the next decade, however, would be welcomed with more selective enthusiasm.

Land Reform   During the 1950s, a central aspect of Mao's thinking was the idea that Chinese peasants were the only reliable resource the country possessed. Lacking a workable industrial and transportation base, the early Maoist years thus were

Land Reform with a Vengeance, 1952. A Chinese farmer kneels at gunpoint before a Communist court enforcing land redistribution policies. Like thousands of others, the landowner was convicted of being a "class enemy" and was executed.

marked by repeated mass mobilization campaigns. Aside from the "Resist America/ Aid Korea" campaign in support of Chinese intervention in Korea, the most important of these was the national effort at land reform. Party cadres moved into the remaining untouched rural areas and proceeded to expropriate land and divide it among the local peasants. Landlords who resisted were "struggled"—abused by tenants who were egged on by party cadres—and often lynched. By some estimates, land reform between 1950 and 1955 took as many as 2 million lives. As hoped for, peasant landownership caused agricultural productivity to increase.

Several years into the land reform program, party leaders decided it was time to take the next step toward socialized agriculture. Mao desperately wanted to avoid the mass chaos and bloodletting that had accompanied Soviet collectivization of agriculture in 1930–1932. The party leadership felt that by going slowly they could greatly ease the transition. Thus, in 1953 peasants were encouraged to form "agricultural producers' cooperatives" in which villages would share scarce tools and machinery. Those who joined were given incentives in the form of better prices and tax breaks. By 1956, agricultural production had recovered to pre–World War II levels and was registering impressive gains.

"Let a Hundred Flowers Bloom"

By 1957, Mao was ready to take the temperature of the nation's intellectuals. Many had been initially enthusiastic about the reforms, but Mao was not sure whether these people were really behind the programs or simply being circumspect. The party therefore invited intellectuals to submit their criticisms and suggestions. Adopting a slogan from China's philosophically rich late Zhou period, "Let a hundred flowers bloom, let a hundred schools of thought contend," officials threw open the door to public criticism of the party's record, assuring the intellectuals that offering their critique was patriotic.

By mid-1957 the trickle of criticisms had become a torrent, but when some critics suggested forming an opposition party, Mao acted swiftly. The "Hundred Flowers" campaign was terminated and the "Anti-Rightist" campaign was launched. Calls for an opposition party were denounced as the worst kind of right-wing thinking—as opposed to the "correct" left-wing thinking of the monopoly Communist Party. Those accused of "rightism" were rounded up and subjected to "reeducation." Even Deng Xiaoping (1904–1997), an old companion of Mao's and later the architect of China's present market economy, was forced to endure 5 years on a hog farm. In addition to being imprisoned and made to endure endless "self-criticism" sessions, many intellectuals were sentenced to long stretches of "reform through labor" in remote peasant villages.

The Great Leap Forward   At about the same time, Mao was growing impatient with the pace of Chinese agricultural collectivization. If production could be ramped up sufficiently, the surplus agricultural funds could then be used to fund 5-year plans for industrial development along the lines of those in the Soviet Union. Moreover, China had been borrowing heavily from the Soviet Union through the 1950s and had availed itself of Soviet technicians and engineers. All of the progress of the decade might be radically slowed or halted if agricultural revenues could not keep pace.

Mao therefore prodded the Communist Party into its most colossal mass mobilization project yet: the Great Leap Forward (1958–1961). The entire population of the country was to be pushed into a campaign to communalize agriculture into self-sustaining units that would function like factories in the fields. Men and women would work in shifts and live in barracks on enormous collective farms. Peasants were to surrender all their iron implements to be melted down and made into steel to build the new infrastructure of these "communes." The most recognizable symbol of the campaign was the backyard steel furnace, which commune members were to build and run for their own needs. Technical problems were to be solved by the "wisdom of the masses" through politically correct "red" (revolutionary) thinking. The entire country would therefore modernize its rural areas and infrastructure in one grand campaign.

Predictably, the Great Leap was the most catastrophic policy failure in the history of the People's Republic. Knowledgeable critics had been cowed into silence

Great Leap Backward. Workers at the Shin Chiao (Xin Jiao) Hotel in Beijing, in the process of constructing a small steel furnace in October 1958, during the Great Leap Forward. Mao Zedong's plan was to transform China within 15 years and 600,000 furnaces from an agrarian–urban into a scientific–industrial country. Instead, the policy became a total disaster, costing China some 30 million deaths.

by the anti-rightist campaign, and the initial wave of enthusiasm that greeted the mobilization swiftly ground to a halt as peasants began to actively resist the seizure of their land and implements. So many were forced into building the communal structures and making useless steel that by 1959 agricultural production in China had plummeted and the country experienced its worst famine in modern times over the next several years. By 1962 an estimated 30 million people had died in its wake.

Conditions became so bleak that Mao stepped down from his party chairmanship in favor of "expert" Liu Shaoqi (1898–1969) and retreated into semiretirement. Liu, from a well-off peasant background in south-central China, and the rehabilitated Deng Xiaoping were now reinstated. Together they tackled the task of rebuilding the shattered economy and political structures, made worse by the Soviet withdrawal of its advisors, who had become useless during the Great Leap. The next 5 years saw impressive gains in China's technical, health, and education sectors as the country returned to something like normalcy. But Mao was soon plotting his return.

Decolonization, Israel, and Arab Nationalism in the Middle East

Parallel to China ridding itself of Japanese colonialism after World War II, independence movements arose in the Middle East and North Africa against the British and French colonial regimes. Here, countries achieved their independence in two waves, the first following World War II and the second during 1956–1970 (see Map 29.4).

MAP **29.4** Decolonization in Africa, the Middle East, and Asia Since 1945.

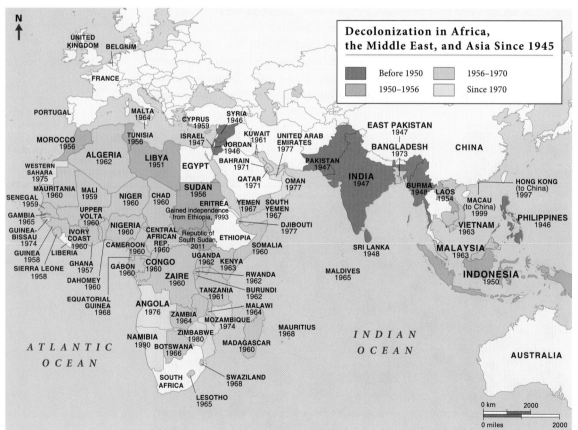

The first wave was the result of local pressures, which colonial authorities found too costly to resist, as in the cases of Syria, Lebanon, Iraq, Jordan, and Israel. The second wave had to await the realization of the British and French governments that they were no longer powerful enough in a world dominated by the United States and the Soviet Union to maintain their empires.

Palestine and Israel As World War II ended, Britain found itself in a tight spot in Palestine. After the suppression of the uprising of 1936–1939, the Arab Palestinians were relatively quiet; but Zionist guerilla action protesting the restrictions on Jewish immigration and land acquisitions had begun in the middle of the war. Sooner or later some form of transition to self-rule had to be offered, but British politicians and the top military were determined to hold on to the empire's strategic interests (oil and the Suez Canal), especially once the Cold War heated up in 1946.

When it became impossible to find a formula for a transition acceptable to the Arabs, in February 1947 Britain turned the question of Palestinian independence over to the United Nations. After the collapse of the Soviet Union in 1991, documents surfaced showing that—interestingly, given the Soviet Union's later animosity toward the Jewish state and support of the Arabs—during the 1940s Stalin had used the United Nations to push for a weakening of the British imperial position in the Middle East by favoring the creation of the state of Israel. Accordingly, the United Nations adopted a partition plan worked out with American assistance in November and Israel declared its independence on May 14, 1947 (see Map 29.5).

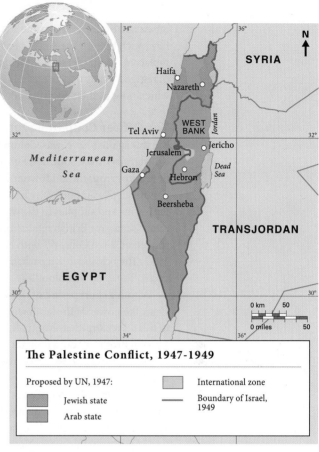

MAP 29.5 The Palestine Conflict, 1947–1949.

The map legend reads:

The Palestine Conflict, 1947-1949

Proposed by UN, 1947:
- Jewish state
- Arab state
- International zone
- Boundary of Israel, 1949

The Soviet Union backed up its tactical, Cold War–motivated support for Israel to release 200,000 Jewish emigrants from the Soviet Bloc and have Czechoslovakia deliver rifles, machine guns, and World War II vintage planes to Israel. Israel was victorious against the Arab armies that invaded from surrounding countries, which, although determined to contest the new state, were unable to obtain weapons as the result of British and American embargoes. Only Jordan was successful, conquering the West Bank and Old Jerusalem. Between November 1947 and the end of fighting in January 1949, the territory in and around the new state experienced, albeit on a smaller scale, the same kind of tragic and chaotic population shift that took place at about the same time in India and Pakistan. Some three-quarters of a million Palestinians were either forced from their villages or fled, leaving only 150,000 in an Israeli territory now substantially larger than that of the original partition plan. In response, the Arab countries expelled about half a million Jews during the next decade from their countries. In the end, Stalin's early Cold War tactics were a grave miscalculation: Israel became a staunch Western ally. But the Western camp did not fare much better: The Arab "catastrophe" (Arabic *nakba*), as it was called, led to the replacement of liberal, landowning Arab nationalists by ardent military hard-liners of refugee background determined to end what remained of Western colonialism—which now, in their eyes, included the state of Israel.

The Officer Coup in Egypt   One Egyptian officer serving with distinction in the war against Israel was Colonel Gamal Abdel Nasser (1918–1970), eldest son of a postal clerk from southern Egypt. Nasser had benefited from the opening of the officer corps from the landowner elite to commoners. He was bitter toward the Egyptian royalty—supported by landowners who had done little to support the country with arms and supplies in the war. In the middle of a declining internal security situation—massive British retaliation against acts of sabotage in the Suez Canal Zone—the secret "Free Officers," with Nasser at their head, assumed power in a coup in July 1952. They closed down parliament and sent the king into exile on his private luxury yacht. The coup was bloodless, and there was little reaction in the streets.

Within a short period of time, Nasser tightened the rule of his military regime. To break the power of the landowners, the Free Officers in 1952 initiated the first round of a land reform that eventually eliminated large estates. A rival for power was the Muslim Brotherhood, a militant organization founded in 1928 by the preacher Hasan al-Banna (1906–1949), who propagated a reformed Islam in place of the traditional Sufi Islam to poor and rural–urban migrants in the cities with some success and advocated the establishment of an Islamic regime. Accusing the Brotherhood of an assassination attempt, Nasser outlawed it in 1954, driving it underground. In a plebiscite in 1956, Nasser made himself president, with a largely rubber-stamp parliament.

Once firmly in power, Nasser espoused the Arab nationalist cause. Palestinian Arab "freedom fighters" carried out raids against Israel from refugee camps in the Arab countries, which inevitably provoked Israeli reprisals. After the first raid and reprisal involving Egypt in February 1955, Nasser realized that the Egyptian military needed urgent improvements. When the United States would not sell weapons readily, Khrushchev jumped in 6 months later, based on his new Soviet strategy of supporting anticolonial nationalists. Where Stalin had failed, Khrushchev succeeded: After its failure in Israel, the Soviet Union was in the Middle Eastern Cold War struggle again.

At the same time, Nasser laid early plans for infrastructural improvements in advance of a later state-industrialization plan: He asked the World Bank for a loan to finance the Aswan High Dam. Initially, the United States and Britain, main underwriters of the World Bank, were in support. But they withdrew this support in spring 1956 when Nasser pressured his neighbor, Jordan, into dismissing the British commander of its crack troops, the Arab Legion. Now the gloves were off: Nasser responded with the nationalization of the Suez Canal (but with compensation of the shareholders) and closure of the Strait of Tiran (used by Israel for Indian Ocean shipping) in July 1956. Without the necessary loans, Nasser had to put the construction of the High Dam on hold.

Israel considered the closure of the Strait of Tiran an act of war and, with French participation, prepared for a campaign to reopen the straits. France, anxious to punish Nasser for weapons deliveries to the Algerian war of liberation that had begun in 1954, persuaded Britain to join in a plan that would be initiated with an attack on Egypt by Israel. If Nasser would close the Suez Canal, France and Britain would occupy it, ostensibly to separate the combatants but actually to reestablish Western control. The plan was hatched in secret because of US opposition to the use of force against Nasser. It unraveled badly when Israel ended its canal campaign victoriously on November 2 but the British and French troops were unable to complete the occupation of the Canal Zone before November 4, the day of the ceasefire called by the UN General Assembly and the United States. Although defeated militarily, Nasser scored a resounding diplomatic victory, effectively ending the last remnants of British and French imperialism in the Middle East.

After the Suez War, Nasser rode high on waves of pan-Arabism, nonalignment, and Arab socialism. The monarchical regimes in Arabia were on the defensive and maintained themselves only thanks to the United States, heir of the strategic oil interests of Britain after the demise of the latter's empire. Although unification with Syria as the United Arab Republic (1958–1961) did not work out, Egypt succeeded in establishing a cultural hegemony from North Africa to Yemen based on propaganda, movies, and music. The relationship with the Soviet Union

Contrasting British and US Votes in the UN Security Council on the Suez Crisis. Although the Western powers agreed to keep the Soviet Union out of the Middle East, the United States viewed a Suez Canal under Egyptian control as the lesser evil. In spite of having been defeated in the war, Nasser emerged as the diplomatic victor. He kept his distance from the United States and became a leader of the Nonalignment Movement. This photo starkly contrasts the different votes of the British and American ambassadors during the UN Security Council session on the crisis.

deepened: Thanks to the Soviets, the Aswan Dam was completed, Soviet military and technical support grew, and Egyptian students received advanced educations in the Eastern Bloc. In 1961, the regime cofounded the **Non-Alignment Movement**, together with Indonesia's Sukarno, India's Nehru, Yugoslavia's Tito, and Ceylon's Bandaranaike. In the same year, Nasser announced his first 5-year plan, which included the nationalization of all large businesses and the construction of heavy steel, aluminum, cement, and chemical plants. Egypt espoused industrial modernity but under the aegis of state investments similar to what Stalin had originally pioneered in 1930. Nasser called this "Arab socialism."

Decolonization and the Cold War in Asia

Nationalist forces similar to those in the Middle East arose also in south and east Asia as a consequence of World War II. The war had either thoroughly destroyed or considerably diminished the colonial holdings of Great Britain, France, the Netherlands, and Japan in Asia. With the destruction of Japan, the Greater East Asia Co-Prosperity Sphere around the Pacific Rim and its islands dissolved. In several colonies, existing independence movements established nationalist governments or fought against the attempted reimposition of European rule. In quick succession India and Pakistan (1947), Burma (1948), Malaysia (1948), Ceylon (1948), Indonesia (1950), and Vietnam (1954) achieved independence from the British and French. India and Vietnam merit a closer look as countries that played important roles during the Cold War competition between the two modernities of communism and capitalist democracy on which this chapter focuses.

Independence and Partition on the Subcontinent   India, Pakistan, and Bangladesh form a prime example of the trials and tribulations encountered by the newly independent ethnic–religious nations in Asia. As the Indian crown colony emerged from the war, to which it had once again contributed huge numbers of volunteer soldiers, nationalists demanded nothing less than full independence. Gandhi, Nehru, and the majority of the Indian National Congress envisaged an Indian nation on the entire subcontinent in which a constitution, patterned after that of Britain, would trump any ethnic, linguistic, and/or religious identities, of which there were literally hundreds. For the congress, to be an Indian meant adherence to the constitutional principles of equality before the law, due process, and freedom from oppression.

The Muslim minority, however, beginning in the 1930s, had drifted increasingly toward religious nationalism, demanding a separate state for themselves in regions where they formed a majority. The main advocate for this separatism was the Muslim League, led by Muhammad Ali Jinnah (1876–1948). Not surprisingly, there was also a small minority of Hindu religious nationalists who had already in the 1920s published pamphlets advocating independence under the banner of "Hindu-ness" (*hindutva*). To the dismay of the Indian National Congress, the British negotiators lent an ear to the demands of the Islamic religious nationalists and prevailed on Gandhi and Nehru to accept independence with partition—and the possibility of widespread disruption, given that even the northwest and northeast, with their Muslim majorities, were home to sizeable minorities of millions of Hindus.

When, on August 15, 1947, the two nations of India and Pakistan ("Land of the Pure") became independent, the jubilation for being free at last was immediately mixed with the horrors of a population exchange on a scale never seen before. Desperate to save themselves and a few belongings, more than 2 million panicked people fled hundreds of miles on foot, by cart, or by railroad to settle in their respective countries. More than 100,000 Indians died in the accompanying communal violence. Gandhi himself fell victim 5 months later to an assassin from the hindutva supremacist-nationalist minority who was enraged by both the partition and Gandhi's principled adherence to constitutional nationalism, to which Hindu nationalism was to be subordinated.

Predictably, while India settled into a freewheeling, boisterous, and rough-edged federal parliamentary democracy, Pakistan's constitution became disposable and the regime authoritarian. From the start, it was clear that religious nationalism was insufficient to define the identity of Pakistanis, distributed over two physically separated regions of the nation, Punjab in the west and East Bengal in the east. The capital, Islamabad, was in the west and Urdu became the national language, relegating Bengali in the east to secondary status (to the dismay of its speakers, who eventually seceded in a bloody civil war and formed the nation of Bangladesh in 1971).

A decade into independence, a military officer, Field Marshal Ayub Khan (1907–1974) from the Pashtu minority in Waziristan on the western border, assumed power in a bloodless coup. Subsequently, he abrogated the 1948 British-style constitution and in 1962 imposed a new constitution, providing for a "guided democracy" of elected village councilors who voted for the president and the members of the national assembly. The constitution's definition of Islam as a national identity and its relationship to subsidiary ethnic and linguistic identities in the country, however, were so contentious that they remained unresolved in the constitution.

Worst of all, given the role of Islam as the religious–nationalist foundation principle, Pakistan was in conflict with India over Kashmir, a province lying in the north between India and Pakistan. In 1947, its Hindu prince hesitated to join Pakistan, while its majority Muslim population demanded incorporation. In the ensuing first war between Indian and Pakistan, India succeeded in conquering most of the province, with Pakistan holding on to only a small sliver, but Kashmiri Muslims remained restive. As in so many other postcolonial territorial disputes, clashes between constitutional and ethnic–linguistic–religious nationalism became irresolvable.

Srinagar. This 1948 color photo shows Srinagar on the Jelhum River in Kashmir, a northern province disputed between Pakistan and India. The river, flowing in and out of a chain of lakes, is surrounded by the Himalayas and empties into the Indus. The majority population of Kashmir is Muslim, but its former Hindu prince inclined in 1947 toward Indian sovereignty, thereby touching off a conflict that has yet to be resolved.

Independent India   As a newly independent India embraced its "tryst with destiny," as its first prime minister, Jawaharlal Nehru (in office 1947–1964), called it, his powers of negotiation and firmness served him well. Tying the subcontinent's disparate constituencies together into a united government was a formidable task. Within the British system, perhaps one-quarter of the territory had remained under the nominal rule of local princes, who now had to surrender their realms to the national government. The bewildering array of castes and the social inequalities built into the system also posed a powerful obstacle, especially since the British had, in many cases, played upon these inequalities to divide and rule. The new government was itself in the uncomfortable situation of constitutionally mandating equality for women and outlawing caste discrimination, while being forced to acquiesce to the de facto absence of the former and continuation of the latter. In the end, the British parliamentary and court systems were adopted and the old civil service was retained, while the economy of the new government would officially be a modified, nonrevolutionary kind of socialism. Nehru's admiration for Soviet successes persuaded him to adopt the 5-year plan system of development. Not surprisingly, India's first 5-year plan (1951–1955), like the early efforts in the Soviet Union and China, was geared toward raising agricultural productivity as a precondition for industrial development.

The most formidable problem was poverty. Though the cities were rapidly expanding beyond the ability of their local governments to keep pace with services, India, like China at the same time, was still fundamentally rural. The new nation's village population was second only to China's in size. The strains upon the land and reliance on the monsoon cycle could spell famine at any time. In the 1950s, India launched a family planning program, to encourage a slowing of the demographic expansion. As a democratic country, however, India had to rely on the voluntary cooperation of the villagers, a cooperation which was difficult to achieve as long as urbanization and industrialization were in their initial stages. For poor families, children were either important laborers in agriculture or, among the landless and the poor in city slums, crucial additional breadwinners as soon as they were old enough to work.

Political and Economic Nonalignment

Similar to the governments of the Soviet Union, China, and Egypt, Nehru and the Congress Party argued that the pressing rural poverty could be overcome only through rapid industrialization undertaken by the state. A hybrid regime of capitalist-democratic constitutionalism with private property (on a small scale) and guided "socialist" state investments came into being, which was officially aligned with neither the West nor the East. This nonalignment (Nehru coined this term in 1954) became the official policy of India and under its initiative also the founding principle of an entire organization, the Non-Alignment Movement, informally established in Bandung, Indonesia, in 1955, and formally inaugurated in 1961. The Nonaligned Movement, still in existence today, sought to maintain neutrality in the Cold War. It predictably incurred the wrath of Western Cold War warriors but was generally successful in maintaining its own course independent from the Western and Soviet Blocs.

Indian state socialism began with the state's second 5-year plan (1956–1961), which focused on state investments in heavy industry. Existing private enterprises were nationalized, and an immense hydroelectric complex and five steel plants were built, along with numerous cement works and an ambitious expansion of coal mines and railroads. In 1958, the Atomic Energy Commission was formed, to pursue both peaceful and military applications of nuclear fission. With the iron, aluminum, cement, and chemicals from heavy industry, so the planners

The Strains of Nonalignment. India's determined stance to navigate its own course between the superpowers was a difficult one, especially during the height of the Cold War. Here, however, a degree of diplomatic warmth appears to pervade the proceedings in Geneva, Switzerland, as People's Republic of China Foreign Minister Chen Yi (left) toasts his Indian colleague, Defense Minister V.K. Krishna Menon (right), and Soviet Foreign Minister Andrei Gromyko (center background) smiles on them both. The date of this conference, however, formally convened to discuss issues between the Soviet and American sides over influence in the Southeast Asian nation of Laos in July, 1962, also coincided with rising border tensions between India and China. This photo was specifically released to show that both sides were still on friendly terms. Within a few months, however, they were shooting at each other.

hoped, private Indian investors, still minute in number but recipients of compensation for factories lost to nationalization, would buy the heavy industrial goods—iron, aluminum, and chemicals—to construct housing and build factories for the production of basic consumer goods, such as textiles, shoes, soap, and toothpaste. The giant domestic market of India was to become fully self-sufficient and independent of imports.

Though begun with much hope at a time of prosperity, the second plan failed to reach its goals. The government debt, owed both to domestic banks and to foreign lending institutions, grew astronomically. Tax collection was notoriously difficult and unproductive, and chronic national and federal budget deficits drove up inflation. Bad monsoon seasons caused food shortages. In democratic India it was not possible to use the draconian dictatorial powers a Stalin had employed. India ran into difficulties that were experienced time and again in other countries after independence.

Southeast Asia   In contrast to India, where the postwar British imperialists gave in to the inevitable, the French under Charles de Gaulle (1890–1970) in 1944–1946 were determined to reconstitute their empire. De Gaulle and a majority of French politicians found it inconceivable that this new republic would be anything less than the imperially glorious Third Republic. To de Gaulle's chagrin, military efforts to hold on to Lebanon and Syria failed against discreet British support for independence and the unilateral establishment of national governments by the Lebanese and Syrians in 1943–1944. After these losses, the politicians of the Fourth Republic were determined not to lose more colonies.

Unfortunately for the French, however, when they returned to Indochina (composed of Vietnam, Laos, and Cambodia) in the fall of 1945, the prewar independence communist movement had already taken over. With covert American assistance, the communists had fought the Japanese occupiers in a guerilla war; and on September 2, 1945, the day of Japan's surrender to the United States, Ho Chi Minh, the leader, read a Vietnamese declaration of independence to half a million people in Hanoi.

Following protracted negotiations in early 1946 between Ho and the French, a stalemate ensued. Ho did not budge from independence, while the French insisted on returning to their "colony." The Vietminh promptly relaunched their guerilla war. Because of the rapid escalation of the Cold War, particularly the communist victory in China, the Soviet atomic bomb, and the Korean War, the French were successful at persuading the American administration that a victory of the Vietminh was tantamount to an expansion of communism in the world. By the early 1950s, the United States was providing much of the funding and the French and allied Vietnamese troops did the actual fighting.

In May 1954, however, the Vietminh defeated the French decisively. Having created an isolated base at Dien Bien Phu in the northwest, the French allowed Vietminh forces to encircle them and pound them with heavy artillery from surrounding hills in their now indefensible

> **Undeniable Truths**
>
> "The Declaration of the French Revolution made in 1791 on the Rights of Man and the Citizen also states: 'All men are born free and with equal rights, and must always remain free and have equal rights.' Those are undeniable truths. Nevertheless, for more than eighty years, the French imperialists, abusing the standard of Liberty, Equality, and Fraternity, have violated our Fatherland and oppressed our fellow citizens. They have acted contrary to the ideals of humanity and justice ..."
>
> —Ho Chi Minh. *On Revolution: Selected Writings, 1920–1966.* Translated by Bernard B. Fall, p. 143. New York: Praeger, 1967.

camp beneath. Resupply through airdrops eventually became impossible. During the Geneva negotiations carried out later that year, the French surrender resulted in a division of Vietnam into north and south along the 17th parallel, pending national elections, and the creation of the new nations of Laos and Cambodia.

The elections, however, never took place and instead Ngo Dinh Diem [No Deen Jem, in office 1955–1963], an authoritarian politician with a limited power base primarily composed of Catholics, emerged in the south. He legitimized his rule in 1955 through a fraudulent plebiscite. Although the new Kennedy administration (1961) was well aware of Diem's shaky and unscrupulous rule, concerns about military successes being achieved by Laotian and South Vietnamese communists receiving North Vietnamese support, led to the fateful American decision to carry the Western Cold War into Indochina. President Eisenhower had already sent several hundred military advisors to Diem but President Kennedy, faced with the Bay of Pigs disaster in Cuba (April 1961) and the East German wall in Berlin (August 1961), increased the military to 16,000 personnel by 1963. Since Diem was corrupt and unwilling to carry out much-needed land reforms, the United States engineered a coup in November 1963 that put a military government in place. This proxy regime was soon propped up by a growing American military presence that would reach a half-million men by 1967.

Decolonization and Cold War in Africa

Only 7 months after their defeat at Dien Bien Phu, the French had to face the declaration of a war of independence by the Algerian Front of National Liberation (November 1, 1954). Algeria, a French colony of 10 million Muslim Arabs and Berbers, had a European settler population of nearly 1 million. The French army was determined to prevent a repeat of the humiliation it had suffered in Indochina. But that is precisely what happened only 2 years later in the Suez war of 1956, and British and French politicians began to realize that the maintenance of colonies was becoming too costly. France hung on to Algeria and was even able to largely repress the liberation war by the later 1950s. But in the long run, Algerian independence (in 1962) could not be prevented, even though French military elements and settlers did everything (including two revolts in 1958 and 1961 against Paris) to keep the country French. France's colonial interests were too costly to be maintained and the United States took over the West's strategic interests in the world. Since the colonies required immense expenditures to support newly burgeoning populations, and the reconstruction of Europe was still far from complete, both Britain and France were forced to rethink the idea of colonialism.

Amid much soul-searching, European governments began to liquidate their empires, beginning in 1957. Only Portugal and Spain continued to maintain their colonies of Angola, Mozambique, and Rio de Oro. South Africa introduced its apartheid regime (1948–1994), designed to segregate the white Afrikaner (Dutch-descended) ruling class from the black majority. As the British, French, and Belgians decolonized, however, they ensured that the governments of the newly independent African countries would remain their loyal subalterns. For them, African independence would be an exchange for support in the Cold War and continued economic dependence.

The Legacy of Colonialism   Between 1918 and 1957, even though the governments of Britain, France, Belgium, and Portugal had invested little state money in their colonies, vast changes had occurred in sub-Saharan Africa. For one thing, the population had more than doubled from 142 to 300 million, mostly as a result of the reduction of tropical diseases through better medicine. Urbanization was accelerating, reliance on commodity exports alone was becoming too narrow, and an emerging small middle class of merchants, lawyers, doctors, pharmacists, and journalists was becoming restless. Heavy investments were required, not merely in mining and agriculture but also in social services to improve the lot of the growing African population. Faced with this financial burden, most of the colonial powers decided to grant independence rather than divert investments badly needed at home.

Ghana, the African Pioneer   Once Britain had decided to decolonize, the governmental strategy toward African independence was to support nationalist groups or parties that adopted British-inspired constitutions and the rule of law, guaranteed existing British economic interests, and abided by the rules of the British Commonwealth of Nations. The first of these to fit the criteria was Ghana in 1957. Its leader was Kwame Nkrumah (1909–1972), a graduate with a master's degree in education from the University of Pennsylvania who appeared to be a sound choice.

Ghana made an initial bid to be the pioneer of sub-Saharan independence and development. It had a healthy economy based on cocoa production as well as some mineral wealth. Its middle class was perhaps the most vital of any African colony. Nkrumah had had a long career as an activist for African independence and a leading advocate of pan-African unity. Jailed during the 1950s for his activism in the Convention People's Party and therefore viewed with some concern, the British nevertheless also realized that Nkrumah wielded genuine authority among a majority of politically inexperienced Ghanaians.

Only 2 years into his rule, however, Nkrumah discarded the independence constitution. Exploiting ethnic tensions among Ashante groups, where an emerging opposition to his rule was concentrated, he promulgated a new republican constitution, removing the country from the British Commonwealth. A year later, he turned to socialist state planning, similar to that of Egypt and India.

The construction of a massive hydroelectric dam on the Volta River, begun in 1961, was supposed to be the starting point of a heavy industrialization program, including aluminum, steel, glass, and consumer goods factories. But the country soon ran into financing problems since cocoa, the main export commodity, was fetching declining prices on the world market and large foreign loans were required to continue the program. On the political front, Nkrumah in 1964 amended the already once-changed constitution by making Ghana a one-party state with himself as leader for life. An unmanageable foreign debt eventually stalled development, and an army coup, supported by the CIA in the name of Cold War anticommunism, ousted Nkrumah in 1966.

> **True Freedom**
>
> "Capitalism is too complicated a system for a newly independent nation. Hence the need for a socialistic society. But even a system based on social justice and a democratic constitution may need backing up, during the period of independence, by emergency measures of a totalitarian kind. Without discipline true freedom cannot survive."
>
> —Kwame Nkrumah. *Ghana: The Autobiography of Kwame Nkrumah*, p. XVI. London: Panaf Books, 2002.

The Struggle for the Congo's Independence   Among the large group of sub-Saharan colonies achieving independence between 1957 and 1960, the Belgian Congo is an important case study because, like Vietnam, it became a battleground of the Cold War. The Belgian Congo had been under the authority of the Belgian government since the beginning of the century, when it took over from the king, who had exploited the colony as his personal property with scandalous brutality. During the interwar period, concession companies invested in mining, especially in the southern and central provinces of Katanga and Kisaï, where huge deposits of copper, cobalt, iron, uranium, and diamonds were discovered. Little money went into human development until after World War II when Catholic mission schools, with state support, expanded the health and the primary school systems. The urban and mine worker populations expanded considerably, but no commercial or professional middle classes to speak of existed.

Serious demands for independence arose in the Congo only after Ghana became independent in 1957. Several groups of nationalists, some advocating a federation and others a centralized state, competed with each other. The urban and mine worker–based National Congolese Movement (*Mouvement National Congolais,* MNC), founded in 1958 by the former postal clerk and salesman Patrice Lumumba (1925–1961), was the most popular group, favoring a centralized constitutional nationalism that transcended ethnicity, language, and religion. After riots in 1959 and the arrest of Lumumba, accused of stirring up the riots, Belgian authorities decided to act quickly so as not to lose control over events: They needed compliant nationalists who would continue existing economic arrangements. A Brussels conference with all nationalists—including Lumumba, freed from prison—decided to hold local and national elections in early 1960. To the dismay of Belgium, the centralists led by the gifted firebrand orator Lumumba won. On June 30, 1960, the Congo became independent, with Lumumba as prime minister and the federalist Joseph Kasa-Vubu (ca. 1910–1969) from Katanga as president.

Lumumba's first political act was the announcement of a general pay raise for state employees, which the Belgian army commander countermanded by spreading the rumor that the Congolese foot soldiers would be left out. Outraged, the soldiers mutinied; and amid a general breakdown of public order, Katanga declared its independence. Lumumba fired the Belgian officers, but for the restoration of order he had to ask for help from the United Nations. Order was indeed restored by the United Nations, but Belgium made sure that Katanga did not rejoin the Congo. To force Katanga, Lumumba turned for support to the Soviet Union, which airlifted advisors and equipment into the country. The Cold War had arrived in Africa.

Kasa-Vubu and Lumumba dismissed each other from the government on September 5, giving the new Congolese army chief, Mobutu Sese Seko (1930–1997), the opportunity to seize power on September 14. Mobutu was a soldier turned journalist and member of the MNC whom Lumumba had appointed as army chief, even though it was general knowledge that he was in the pay of the Belgians and the CIA. (Mobutu went on to become the dictator of the Congo, renamed "Zaire," and was a close ally of the United States during the period he held power, 1965–1996.) He promptly had Lumumba arrested. Eventually, Belgian agents took Lumumba to Katanga, where they executed him on January 17, 1961.

At the time, as it is now known from documents studied in the 1990s, the Belgian government and the Eisenhower White House were deeply convinced that Lumumba was another Castro in the making, a nationalist who would soon become a communist, falling prey to Khrushchev's charm offensive among the African nationalists about to achieve independence. In the Cold War between the United

States and the Soviet Union the fierce but inexperienced Lumumba was given no chance by the Belgian and American governments acting with mutual consultation. At all costs, the Congo had to remain in the Western camp as a strategic, mineral-rich linchpin in central Africa.

Putting It All Together

Rapid, dizzying change characterized the pattern of modernity as it unfolded in the middle of the twentieth century. After only 150 years of constitutionalism and industry, 75 years of worldwide imperialism, and 15 years of a three-sided competition among the modernist ideologies of capitalist democracy, communism, and supremacist nationalism, the world changed drastically once more. An intense Cold War competition between the proponents of the ideologies of capitalist democracy and communism ensued. Imperialism and colonialism collapsed within a mere 17 years. And nearly 200 nations came to share the globe in the United Nations. Compared to the slow pace of the agrarian–urban period of world history for 5,300 years, the speed of development during a mere 145 years of scientific–industrial modernity was dizzying (see Concept Map).

Perhaps the most noteworthy series of events characterizing the 17 years of the early and intense Cold War between capitalist democracy and communism in 1945–1962 was the sad fate of many countries as they emerged into independence or as they struggled to accommodate themselves as best they could in the Western camp, Eastern Bloc, or Non-Aligned Movement. As we have seen in this chapter, US and Soviet leaders were ruthless wherever they perceived communists, communist fellow travelers, or heretics of the Communist Party line in their ranks. But even when new nations could not easily be brought into line and instead pursued a policy of nonalignment, there were subtler ways through which both West and East could apply financial pressures with devastating consequences: Egypt lost its finances for the Aswan Dam, and China lost its Soviet advisors during the Great Leap Forward.

Not that capitalist democracy and communism were on the same plane: The former, even if it did not readily offer meaning or equality to its adherents, provided greater political participation than the latter, which paid only lip service to its notions of equality, as became obvious by 1991. But the period of the early, active Cold War and decolonization from 1945 to 1962 was far less brutal than the preceding interwar period. Although several confrontations between East and West were hot, and nuclear war on one occasion posed a serious threat, humanity was spared the cataclysms of World War II. Change was rapid but less horrific.

Review and Respond

1. What was the Cold War? Sketch the salient moments in its evolution.
2. Describe the differences in Stalin's and Khrushchev's approaches to communism.
3. Why did the United States issue the Marshall Plan, who benefited, and what were the results?
4. Why was the Cuban Missile Crisis the major turning point in world history during the second half of the twentieth century?

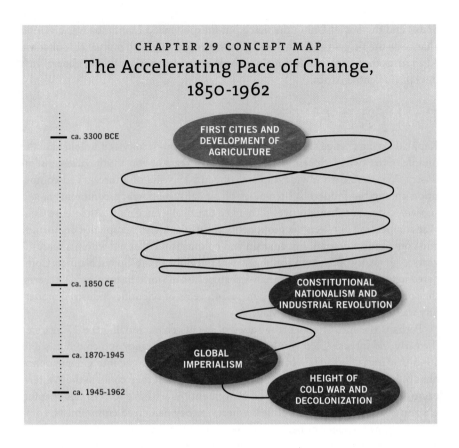

CHAPTER 29 CONCEPT MAP
The Accelerating Pace of Change, 1850-1962

- ca. 3300 BCE — **FIRST CITIES AND DEVELOPMENT OF AGRICULTURE**
- ca. 1850 CE — **CONSTITUTIONAL NATIONALISM AND INDUSTRIAL REVOLUTION**
- ca. 1870-1945 — **GLOBAL IMPERIALISM**
- ca. 1945-1962 — **HEIGHT OF COLD WAR AND DECOLONIZATION**

5. Discuss the basic tenets of existentialism, and explain why understanding this philosophy is important for modernity during the middle of the twentieth century.

6. Explain the different paths of evolution between India and Pakistan after independence in 1947.

7. Why was populism such an attractive mode of governance in Latin America after 1945?

8. Outline the sequence of policies which Mao Zedong pursued in communist China after 1949.

9. Discuss the significance of Ghana and the Congo for understanding decolonization in Africa.

> For additional resources, including maps, primary sources, visuals, and quizzes, please go to www.oup.com/us/vonsivers. Please see the Further Resources section at the back of the book for additional readings and suggested websites.

Thinking Through Patterns

▶ **Why did the pattern of unfolding modernity, which offered three choices in 1918 after World War I, shrink to just capitalist democracy and communism in 1945? How did each of these two patterns evolve between 1945 and 1962?**

The pattern of modernity evolved in the nineteenth century with four major ingredients: constitutional nationalism, ethnic–linguistic–religious nationalism, industrialism, and communism. However, traditional institutions such as monarchies and empires from times prior to 1800 continued to flourish. World War I wiped out most monarchies, but capitalist democracy continued, communism came into its own in the Soviet Union, imperialism and colonialism survived, and supremacist nationalism attracted all those who found democracy and communism wanting. World War II eliminated supremacist nationalism and, after a delay of 17 years, also imperialism and colonialism. The remaining choices of capitalist democracy and communism were divided between two power blocs, which during the early Cold War period of 1945–1962 almost evenly shared the world among themselves.

Modernity grew out of the philosophy of the New Science in the 1600s, with its assumptions of materialism and the social contract. After acquiring mass support, modernity with its twin ideologies of constitutional nationalism and industrialism evolved into scientific–industrial modernity with profound cultural consequences. On the one hand, wave after wave of ever more modern ideologies and artistic movements appeared, from early nineteenth-century romanticism to mid-twentieth-century existentialism. On the other hand, these consecutive waves of newness could at best only paper over the basic materialist flaw of modernity, which in each generation gave rise to the question of the meaning of it all. Did a modern world without transcendence, rampant consumer choices, and gaping social inequities have intrinsic meaning even if people continued to find ever new and thrilling possibilities in material and intellectual–artistic life? The question still haunts us today.

▶ **What are the cultural premises of modernity?**

▶ **How did the newly independent countries of the Middle East, Asia, and Africa adapt to the divided world of the Cold War?**

During 1945–1962 the number of nations on earth quadrupled to eventually (in 2011) comprise about 200. The new nations, emerging from colonialism, were in theory, like the older nations of early modernity in the nineteenth century, countries with ethnic–linguistic–religious cores and functioning constitutional institutions. In fact, many were not. Since most, furthermore, were still overwhelmingly agrarian, industrialism was beyond reach. With great hope, the ruling elites in a number of large new nations embraced a mixed capitalist-democratic and socialist regime, with heavy state investments in basic industries, such as textiles, steel, chemicals, cement, and fertilizer. However, in contrast to Stalin, who first introduced these type of investments under the label of state-guided socialism, none of the elites in the new nations had the will to collect the money for these investments from their rural population. Instead, they borrowed heavily from the capitalist-democratic countries. True independence remained an elusive goal.

Chapter 30

1963-1991

The End of the Cold War, Western Social Transformation, and the Developing World

THE WORLD,
1963–1991

The machine made an aggressive, rapid thudding sound as it slowly worked its way through the air by the dun-colored, snow-capped mountain. The fighter recognized it immediately, and his stomach tightened on seeing what it was: *Shaitan Arba*—"Satan's Chariot," the Soviet MI-5 "Hind" attack helicopter. This new, heavily

Seeing Patterns

▶ How did the political landscape of the Cold War change from 1963 to 1991?

▶ Why did such radically different lifestyles emerge in the United States and the West during the 1960s and 1970s? What is their legacy today?

▶ Why did some nations that had emerged from colonialism and war make great strides in their development while others seemed to stagnate?

armed, and armored helicopter gunship was more like a flying tank and had proven largely impervious to the rifle and small arms fire the fighter and his *mujahideen* Afghan warriors had used in their usually vain attempts to down it. Worse still, it carried a devastating array of rockets and machine cannon; the fighter had seen these gunships wipe out entire squads of his comrades. In this desperate fight in the Afghan high country, the Soviets, it appeared, had acquired a decisive technological edge as they sought to eliminate resistance to the client regime they had installed in the capital of Kabul nearly 8 years before, in 1979.

Just as he took a last look before seeking cover, he heard a peculiar sound, a kind of *whoosh*. He raised his eyes just in time to see the machine explode into a lurid red and orange fireball and plummet swiftly into the mountainside, its rotor blades windmilling helplessly without lift. A rapidly dissolving vapor trail marked a spot about 200 meters away from where it appeared a rocket had been fired. A small group of men shouted "God is great!" and cheered lustily at their victory.

This scene was to be repeated more than 300 times during the coming years. The weapon that had downed the helicopter was a new American

Mujahideen Soldiers Standing on a Destroyed Soviet Helicopter. The determination of Afghan resistance to secularism and Soviet-style communism is vividly portrayed in this photograph of the momentary triumph of a small unit of fighters celebrating the downing of a Russian helicopter. The technological disparity between the sides is clear as well: Note that all of the Afghan fighters hold long-obsolescent bolt-action rifles, many of them British models dating from before World War I. The arrival and capture of large quantities of automatic weapons and the secret supplying of American shoulder fired antiaircraft missiles would soon decisively change this situation.

"Stinger" shoulder-fired missile, which the United States was now clandestinely supplying to the Afghan Muslim fighters attempting to expel the Soviet forces occupying their country. Perhaps more than any other weapon, the Stinger neutralized the Soviet technological advantage in airpower and enabled an international force of mujahideen to ultimately push the Soviets out of Afghanistan in this last contest of the Cold War, in much the same way that the United States had been forced from South Vietnam. In fact, as we will see in more detail in this chapter, the immense cost of the Soviet–Afghan War, added to the even higher price of trying to match the American effort to create a missile defense system against intercontinental ballistic missiles (ICBMs), helped to grind the Soviet economy into a state of collapse by the end of the 1980s and led to the end of the Eastern Bloc and the Soviet Union itself. It thus appeared that the West and its version of modernity—capitalist democracy—had convincingly won both the physical and ideological contests of the Cold War.

In this chapter we will trace the progress of this struggle and the immense social changes associated with the period from 1963 to 1991 in the West and the progress of the struggle in the developing world. Although the end result was an apparent victory for democracy and capitalism—both of which were to be introduced into the successor states of the Soviet Union in the 1990s—the contest in the developing world was still active even beyond this time. From the seedbed of Muslim resistance to the secular communist vision of modernity in Afghanistan would sprout a new worldwide movement of resistance to the secular West, democratic capitalism, and the sole remaining vision of modernity itself: al-Qaeda and its affiliates.

The Climax of the Cold War

The Cold War continued through several phases into the 1980s when the power of the Soviet Union began to markedly ebb. During the 1960s, despite the progress of the Nuclear Test Ban Treaty, the United States and the Soviet Union remained bitter ideological enemies and both the Soviet Union and the People's Republic of China sent aid to Ho Chi Minh's forces fighting the Americans in Vietnam. The Soviets also supported the Arab efforts against United States–backed Israel in 1967 and 1973. Moreover, both sides continually upgraded and expanded their nuclear arsenals. Despite this continuing hostility, the late 1960s and early 1970s also witnessed the era of *détente*: a downplaying of overt aggression toward one another and the pursuit of competition through diplomatic, social, and cultural means. The Soviet invasion of Afghanistan in 1979, however, ushered in a final phase of openly hostile competition and covert warfare. In the end, the Soviet Union's resources were simply not sufficient to outlast those of the West in the struggle.

The Soviet Superpower in Slow Decline

In 1963, only a few months after the Cuban Missile Crisis, it still appeared that the Soviet Union was an adversary more or less equal to the United States. In fact, in many respects, it seemed to have the momentum of history on its side. Marxism and socialism more broadly were gaining popularity in the world as means of rapid development; the United States did not seem particularly successful at stopping the expansion of Soviet influence in Southeast Asia, Latin America, or Africa; and the Soviet Union still seemed to be setting the technological pace in the "space race." Yet, in less than 30 years the Soviet Union would fall apart, to be replaced by its core political unit of Russia and a host of newly independent former Soviet republics. What forces were at work in setting this unexpected course of events in motion?

From the Brink of War to Détente While Nikita S. Khrushchev had developed an earthy, peasant-flavored popularity in the Soviet Union and, to some extent, on the international stage, his initial success in rolling back some of the worst abuses of Stalinism had been overshadowed by two signal failures during the early 1960s. The first was allowing the Sino–Soviet split of 1960 to become a complete break. By 1963, the Soviet response to Chinese displeasure with Khrushchev's lack of notice prior to his denunciation of Stalin and Chinese criticism of Khrushchev's more temperate approach toward the United States and the West were met by the wholesale withdrawal of Soviet advisors from China. Moreover, Khrushchev's building of the Berlin Wall, though largely effective in its immediate objective of stopping the flood of refugees from East Berlin, had been a propaganda failure. His American

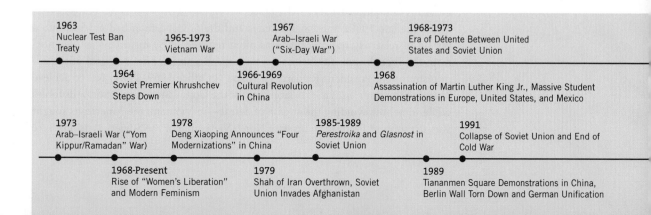

| 1963
Nuclear Test Ban
Treaty | | 1967
Arab–Israeli War
("Six-Day War") | 1968-1973
Era of Détente Between United
States and Soviet Union |
| 1965-1973
Vietnam War | | | |

1964
Soviet Premier Khrushchev
Steps Down

1966-1969
Cultural Revolution
in China

1968
Assassination of Martin Luther King Jr., Massive Student
Demonstrations in Europe, United States, and Mexico

1973
Arab–Israeli War ("Yom
Kippur/Ramadan" War)

1978
Deng Xiaoping Announces "Four
Modernizations" in China

1985-1989
Perestroika and *Glasnost* in
Soviet Union

1991
Collapse of Soviet Union and End of
Cold War

1968-Present
Rise of "Women's Liberation"
and Modern Feminism

1979
Shah of Iran Overthrown, Soviet
Union Invades Afghanistan

1989
Tiananmen Square Demonstrations in China,
Berlin Wall Torn Down and German Unification

Soviet N-1 Being Rolled Out to Its Launching Pad. The power of Soviet rocket boosters and ICBMs was a source of great anxiety to American military planners and those in NASA involved in US space initiatives. In this rare photograph, a Soviet booster developed specifically for the Russian manned lunar program is wheeled out to its launching area in the 1960s.

counterpart, the youthful, charismatic President John F. Kennedy (in office 1961–1963), had rallied world support against the wall when he proclaimed before it, "Ich bin ein Berliner" ("I am a Berliner")!

But Khrushchev's key blunder had been in appearing to back down during the Cuban Missile Crisis in October 1962. Seeking to test the resolve of the young American president by installing nuclear missiles on America's doorstep, the premier instead was forced to dismantle their bases in Cuba. Though the United States also agreed to the face-saving gesture of dismantling its own medium-range missiles in Turkey, the Soviet Politburo shortly acted to oust Khrushchev, who duly resigned in October 1964. The succession was remarkably smooth for the Soviet system, which tended toward intrigue and occasional violence when leaders left. Into the position of power stepped Leonid Brezhnev (in office 1960–1964, 1977–1982), who would preside over the Soviet Union as first secretary of the Communist Party until 1982, with Aleksey Kosygin (1964–1980) as premier.

The Brezhnev years were noteworthy in a number of areas. Both the United States and the Soviet Union had been shaken by how close they had come to all-out nuclear war in October 1962. One way that this danger had been partially defused was by the Nuclear Test Ban Treaty, signed in October 1963. Alert to the toxic effects of nuclear fallout and the possibility that tests may raise false alarms about attacks, the signatories agreed to abandon all aboveground nuclear testing. Nonnuclear nations were severely discouraged from developing their own weapons in subsequent "nonproliferation" treaties. Additional safeguards were built into the detection and early warning systems both sides used as part of missile defense. The last, and most famous, link in this chain was the installation of the Hot Line—a direct telephone link between the White House and the Kremlin—for American and Soviet leaders to alert each other if an accident or false attack signal had been issued. Nonetheless, the mood of the 1960s remained one of nuclear tension on both sides, and American popular culture was rife with doomsday fantasies of the catastrophic effects of nuclear war. Moreover, new types of weapons systems, such as submarine-based ICBMs that could be launched close to enemy shores and independently guided multiwarhead ICBMs (multiple independent reentry vehicles, or MIRVs) that could hit several targets simultaneously, raised tensions on both sides. Not surprisingly, from the early 1970s on, the two sides engaged in a series of Strategic Arms Limitation Treaty (SALT) talks.

By the late 1960s, the United States and the Soviet Union had entered into a period of relatively tranquil relations often referred to by historians as "détente," from the French term for "release of tension." Because a principal goal of the administration of President Richard M. Nixon (in office 1969–1974) was to achieve "peace with honor"—that is, a viable way for the United States to withdraw its forces while somehow avoiding the stigma of defeat—in Vietnam, the Americans sought Russian support for peace talks with North Vietnam. For the Soviets, tensions were

Détente. Following closer diplomatic contact between the United States and the Soviet Union in the wake of the Arab–Israeli War in the beginning of June 1967, President Lyndon Johnson and Soviet Premier Aleksey Kosygin met at Glassboro State College (now Rowan University). The talks centered around the US position in Vietnam and the possibility of opening talks on lessening nuclear tensions. Here, President Johnson and Soviet foreign minister Andrei Gromyko are engaged in a frank discussion.

swiftly mounting with the People's Republic of China over disputed borders along the Amur River and the rising chaos of the Cultural Revolution. At several points, military engagements took place; and at least once, the Americans were approached by the Soviets about the possibility of a preemptive nuclear strike against China.

The era of détente abruptly ended in the fall of 1973, however, with the Egyptian and Syrian surprise attack on Israel, which coincided with both the Jewish holy day of Yom Kippur and the Muslim month of Ramadan and sparked the largest Arab–Israeli conflict to date. While the Soviets had been supplying equipment and advisors to Arab countries during the earlier "Six-Day War" in 1967, that conflict had ended too quickly for either the US or USSR to contemplate intervention. The more protracted fighting of the 1973 war and the support of the United States for Israel, which finally defeated its opponents, raised superpower tensions for the next several years. The Soviets actively supported the largely Arab Organization of Petroleum Exporting Countries (OPEC) boycott of oil shipments to the United States during the mid-1970s and resumed support for North Vietnam's final drive to conquer South Vietnam after the American withdrawal in 1973.

"Prague Spring" and "Solidarity" in Poland

The Brezhnev years were also marked by a growing incidence of dissent, both in the Soviet Union and, even more markedly, in its Eastern European client states (see Map 30.1). Since the uprising in Hungary in 1956, for example, the government efforts to stifle dissent and reform had been increasingly difficult and threatened to stir up latent nationalistic feeling. One result was the evolution under János Kádár (in office 1956–1988), Hungarian party secretary, of what came to be called "goulash communism": a relatively relaxed attitude toward criticism of the regime, the introduction of limited market reforms, some attention to consumer demands, and limited trade with the West.

In 1968, dissent took a more direct course in Czechoslovakia, in what came to be called the "Prague Spring." With the rise to power of Alexander Dubček (in office

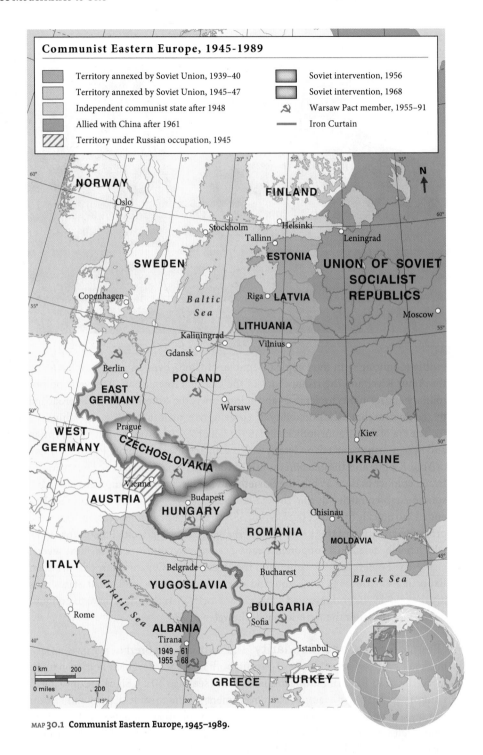

MAP **30.1** Communist Eastern Europe, 1945–1989.

1968–1969) in January 1968, a sweeping set of reforms, more extensive than those by Kádár in Hungary, was introduced. Calls for a new decentralized administrative structure, relaxation of censorship, free speech, and opposition political parties were voiced; and an atmosphere of excitement and expectation prevailed in the capital of Prague. Brezhnev's government, however, saw this as evidence of the Czech Communist Party slipping in power and entered into negotiations in order to bring the country back into line. By August, as the push for reform became more and more persistent, the Soviets sent Warsaw Pact forces into Czechoslovakia, where they ousted Dubček, installed Gustáv Husák (1913–1991), and promptly dismantled the reforms of the previous 7 months. The Soviet move became known as the "Brezhnev Doctrine"—the right of the Soviets and Warsaw Pact to forcibly hold in line any member country attempting to abandon socialism and the alliance with the Soviet Union.

With the shadow cast by the Brezhnev Doctrine, dissent once again went underground. In 1980, however, it reemerged in Poland, this time with more lasting results. Several factors were at work. One of these was the still prominent position of the Roman Catholic Church in Poland, which the local Communist Party was never able to totally suppress. The election of a Polish pope, John Paul II, in 1978 galvanized Polish Catholics even further. In addition, Poland had been undergoing a long economic crisis in the late 1970s, with consumer goods reduced to a minimum and many workers laid off. In 1980, a strike by electrical workers at the Lenin Shipyard in Gdansk was called, which quickly spread to other port cities. A labor union was formed called "Solidarity," led by an electrician named Lech Walesa (b. 1943), which called for an end to censorship, the lifting of economic restrictions, and the right of workers to organize outside of the Communist Party. Despite numerous arrests and government threats, by the end of 1980 one-fourth of Poland's population had joined the movement, including 80 percent of the country's workers.

The Polish government declared martial law in an attempt to stave off Soviet invocation of the Brezhnev Doctrine. Still, a massive general strike crippled the country, while international sympathy for the movement increased. This became even more intense after a visit by the pope and Walesa's selection for the Nobel Peace Prize in 1983. With the installation of Mikhail Gorbachev as the new Soviet leader in 1985, and his liberalizing policies of *glasnost* and *perestroika* in the Soviet Union, the future of Solidarity as a political movement became more assured. In 1989 Solidarity was finally relegalized, and it became the largest political party in Poland during the 1990s. Not surprisingly, Walesa was elected president of Poland, serving from 1991 to 1995.

The 1980s: Afghanistan and "Star Wars"   Despite the tensions following the collapse of détente and the Brezhnev Doctrine, some genuine progress on strategic arms limitation was achieved between the superpowers. During the late 1970s, the

Lech Walesa and Solidarity. The strike at the Gdansk shipyard in Poland in 1980 brought to the fore an obscure electrician but able leader named Lech Walesa. Here, he is shown at a 1981 meeting of the organization he helped found, Solidarity, which ultimately helped topple Poland's communist government. Walesa himself went on to win the Nobel Peace Prize and was elected president of Poland in 1991.

United States sought to counter the overwhelming conventional power of the Soviet ground forces in Europe with medium-range ballistic missiles armed with the new technology of the "neutron bomb"—a nuclear weapon designed for minimal blast damage but maximal radiation lethality. The idea was that such weapons would leave many structures intact but devastate the personnel of an invading army. During the ongoing SALT II talks from 1977 to 1979, a historic agreement was reached in 1979 that would, for the first time, require the United States and the Soviet Union to limit certain types of nuclear weapons and begin a process of actually reducing them—a process that would later be known as START (Strategic Arms Reduction Talks/Treaty).

Much of the feeling of progress achieved by this breakthrough was checked, however, by the Soviet invasion of Afghanistan in December 1979. The Egyptian–Israeli treaty of 1979, the tilting of Saudi Arabia and Iraq toward the United States, and the Iranian Revolution had altered the Middle Eastern landscape radically in favor of the West. Fearful of having a weak, nominally communist Afghan government on its flank, adjacent to pro-American Pakistan and a China that appeared to have shifted toward the United States, the Soviets launched a swift coup in Afghanistan and installed a strong communist leader with a massive military force to back him up. The Soviets were immediately subjected to international condemnation, and the United States announced that it would boycott the 1980 Summer Olympics, scheduled to take place in Moscow.

More concretely, the resistance to Afghan communism, led chiefly by idealistic Afghan Muslims and an increasingly large volunteer force of mujahideen, armed with small arms funneled through North Atlantic Treaty Organization (NATO) countries, battled the Soviets for a decade. As the fight wore on, Soviet morale deteriorated, especially with the introduction of more sophisticated weapons capable of countering the immense Russian advantage in armor and airpower. The key weapon is this regard was the shoulder-fired antiaircraft missile we encountered in the vignette at the beginning of this chapter.

At the same time, the new administration of President Ronald Reagan (in office 1981–1989) in the United States sought to adopt a more assertive policy toward the Soviet Union. The administration felt that the previous president, Jimmy Carter (in office 1977–1981), had been somewhat soft toward both the Iranian taking of American hostages and the Soviet invasion of Afghanistan. At the same time, breakthrough technologies in computers and satellite communications made it theoretically possible for the United States to create an antiballistic missile system in outer space. Such a system was in violation of the antiballistic missile provisions of the 1969 SALT I accords, but the advantages of having a reliable missile defense hundreds of miles in space—while at the same time retaining "first strike capability"—were overwhelming to American defense planners. Thus, over Soviet protests, the United States began to develop its Strategic Defense Initiative (SDI), nicknamed "Star Wars" from the popular movie of the same name.

From the mid-1980s, both superpowers thus began an enormously expensive strategic arms development race. For the Soviets, however, the drain of this new arms race, combined with the increasingly expensive and unpopular war in Afghanistan, was simply unsustainable for very long. As we will also see in the next chapter, the Soviet Union's increasing inability to reap the advantages of the computer revolution, and American economic dominance of the world economy through the "dollar regime" proved to be central factors in the decline of the USSR. By 1985, moreover, a new factor was also at work to undermine the old order.

Glasnost and Perestroika   The death of Leonid Brezhnev in 1982 ushered in two short-lived successors before the relatively young Mikhail Gorbachev (b. 1931) took office as first secretary in the Politburo in 1985. Faced with growing dissent in Poland and other Eastern Bloc countries, an increasingly inefficient economy (the problems of which seemed highlighted by successful Chinese experiments with market economics), the endless war in Afghanistan, and now the expensive arms race with the United States, Gorbachev called for large-scale structural reforms in the Soviet system.

What's for Dinner? Not much, if you are one of the miserable-looking shoppers eyeing the meager selection of meat at a Moscow market in early December 1991, just a few weeks before the dissolution of the Soviet Union. By the final days of the Soviet Union, consumer goods and food had become so scarce that many items had to be imported from abroad.

Up until the 1980s, the Soviet economy had functioned as a giant command economic pyramid. Some 100 ministries in Moscow and 800 in the provinces oversaw some 50,000 enterprises, which produced some 24 million individual products. At that time, the Soviet Union had some 200,000 computers compared to the United States with 25 million. With entire roomfuls of computers, the army of ministerial bureaucrats crunched every figure connected with the production and distribution process, figured out prices and wages, and saw to it that the books were balanced at the end of the budget year. The bureaucrats could never count on accurate figures, however, since both workers and managers had every incentive to overreport production figures and produce shoddy consumer goods manufactured as cheaply as possible. Periodic shortages were inevitable, and at any given time a percentage of workers were out in the streets with shopping bags, searching for stores where rumor had it that a fresh consignment of goods had arrived. As the saying on factory floors went, "They pretend to pay us and we pretend to work."

By the mid-1980s, however, Soviet planners had realized that their command system was delivering diminishing returns. Overall growth rates—in the 1950s and 1960s ranging around an impressive 10 percent—had declined to 3 percent. Several factors were responsible for the decline: fewer people were migrating to the factories, lack of investment in new technologies and labor-saving machinery meant that factories were becoming less productive, and the percentage of people over 60 years of age had doubled between World War II and the mid-1980s, requiring the increasingly unproductive labor force to support more and more retirees. In addition, raw materials were less abundant and had to be shipped in from farther away, on top of which bad weather in the later 1970s and early 1980s kept agricultural production low and required large purchases, with dollars, of foodstuffs on the world market. Soviet economic planners therefore asked themselves with increasing urgency how they could return to high growth rates and find the finances to do so.

Two years after becoming secretary of the Politburo in 1985, Gorbachev launched his two trademark economic and political programs, "restructuring" (**perestroika**)

Perestroika: "Restructuring" of the Soviet bureaucracy and economic structure in an attempt to make it more efficient and responsive to market demand.

Glasnost: "Openness"; an attempt to loosen restrictions on media in the Soviet Union with an aim at more accurate reporting of events and the creation of "socialist pluralism."

and "openness" (**glasnost**), which were intended to revitalize communism. Restructuring entailed the partial dismantling of the command economy. Gorbachev drastically reduced the Politburo's oversight function. He slashed the planning bureaucracy by nearly half. Partially freed from the planners' oversight, managers could sell up to one-third of what their factories produced on the market, instead of delivering everything to the state. Citizens were free to establish "cooperatives," the communist euphemism for private business enterprises. By the end of the 1980s, the law permitted co-ops in practically all branches of the economy, including agriculture. Gorbachev sold the new mixed command and market economy as a "socialist" or "regulated" system, advertising it as the same order once pursued by Lenin (then called the New Economic Policy, or NEP).

In practice, perestroika did not work out as intended. Market production rose to a meager 5 percent of total production. Many managers were stuck with the manufacture of unprofitable goods, such as soap, toothpaste, matches, and children's clothes. Consumers complained about continued or even worse shortages in the stores. Other managers, eager to increase production, granted irresponsible wage increases to their workers as incentives. People of modest means founded stores, restaurants, repair shops, construction firms, and software and engineering offices. They charged outrageous prices and did everything to evade paying taxes. Support structures for the co-ops, such as credit, banking, contract law, wholesale distribution centers, and wage bargaining mechanisms, were lacking. Gorbachev's measures, therefore, did little to get the state factories out of stagnation and encouraged the rise of wild "carpetbagger" capitalism.

Parallel to economic restructuring, Gorbachev introduced political "openness," or glasnost. The catalyst for glasnost was the nuclear accident at Chernobyl in the Ukraine in April 1986. When it became impossible to conceal the magnitude of the disaster, reporting in the media became remarkably frank, quickly turning to other hitherto suppressed topics. Journalists, writers, filmmakers, historians, and social scientists proceeded to unmask the taboos and hypocrisies of the previous decades. Gorbachev's glasnost was supposed to produce a "socialist pluralism," but the unintended result was a more genuine pluralism, reducing communism to just one of many competing ideologies in the rapidly evolving Soviet political scene.

Transformations in the Soviet Bloc

The countries of the Soviet Bloc, which were not oil producers, had borrowed heavily from the West in the 1970s and early 1980s for their costly oil imports and the renewal of their industrial base at the beginning of the electronic revolution. Others borrowed to build oil and gas pipelines from Russia via their territories to Western Europe. But the oil price collapse of 1985–1986 forced all Soviet Bloc countries to reschedule their debts and cut their budgets, especially expenditures for their social safety nets and subsidies for basic consumer goods. Popular protests against these cuts rose up from the grass roots in 1989 and 1990 in Poland, Hungary, and Czechoslovakia, accompanied by demands for power sharing.

In the German Democratic Republic (GDR, East Germany), a particularly dramatic shift occurred. Germans, at the end of their summer vacations at the Black Sea in 1989, refused to return home. They massed at the Hungarian border with Austria in hopes of being permitted to leave. Hungary, at that moment in search of its own reforms, including the introduction of democracy, let the vacationers cross the border. Back in the GDR, massive demonstrations led to the fall first of the communist government and then of the infamous Berlin Wall on the night of November 9, 1989. A year later, with Gorbachev's blessing, the two Germanys united, ending nearly a half-century of division.

Communist governments now fell in other Soviet Bloc countries as well (see Map 30.2). Before too much pressure built up from below, the governments of the Baltic states of Estonia, Latvia, and Lithuania, as well as that of Bulgaria, gave way

MAP **30.2** **The Fall of Communism in Eastern Europe and the Soviet Union.**

The Fall of Communism in Eastern Europe and the Soviet Union

Former republics of the Soviet Union gaining independence in 1991	Independence from Soviet Union declared 1991; at war with Russia, 1994-2000	─── Boundary of the former Soviet Union to 1991
Boundary of Russian Federation after December 1991	Former Warsaw Pact country holding free elections, 1990-1992	☙ Violent ethnic conflicts

more or less voluntarily to democracy. Albania followed suit in 1992. The only exception was Romania, where Nicolae Ceauşescu [Chow-CHESS-coo] (in office 1974–1989) had built a strong personality cult and had put family members into key party and government offices. The botched eviction by the police of a protestant Hungarian minority pastor from his parish in western Romania in November 1989 resulted in scores of deaths. Following a mass demonstration in Bucharest protesting the deaths, portions of the army defected and arrested the fleeing Ceauşescu and his wife Elena. Army elements assembled a tribunal, sentenced the two to death, and summarily executed them on December 25, 1989. Subsequently, however, the army and the Communist Party reconciled and the country returned to a dictatorship. It was not until 1996 that Romania adopted a democratic system.

The dissolution of communism in the Eastern Bloc eventually caught up with the 15 states making up the Soviet Union. Most of these states declared their sovereignty or even independence in the course of 1990. Gorbachev alienated his supporters by allowing the Soviet army to harass or even kill demonstrators in Georgia and Lithuania, in a vain attempt to salvage the Soviet Union. Meanwhile, elections in several Soviet states brought legitimate presidents to power. One of the presidents was Boris Yeltsin (in office 1991–1999), who was elected in Russia, the largest of the union states. As the president elected by a newly created but feeble Soviet Union parliament, Gorbachev did not have the popular mandate Yeltsin had within Russia and he resented the latter's grassroots support.

After arduous negotiations, Gorbachev agreed with Yeltsin and the other state presidents to a new federal union treaty for the Soviet Union in spring 1991, to be signed in August. This treaty triggered an abortive plot by eight communist hardliners who briefly succeeded in arresting Gorbachev as he was vacationing for a few days in his dacha on the Black Sea. The conspirators, however, showed thier ineptitude by failing to arrest Yeltsin. In a tense showdown with troops sent to occupy the Russian parliament, Yeltsin and a large crowd of Muscovites forced the hardliners to blink. Officially, the Soviet Union ended on Christmas Day, 1991, replaced by the Commonwealth of Independent States with a democratic Russia under Yeltsin at its center.

With the establishment of the new commonwealth, the Cold War and the epic struggle of competing modernities that had colored so much of the twentieth century quickly and quietly faded away. Russia's transformation to capitalism and democracy, however, was destined to be fraught with corruption, false starts, tension with former enemies, and pressure to return to a more authoritarian ethnolinguistic nationalist system.

Transforming the West

While North America and Western Europe certainly enjoyed an era of impressive growth and social change from the late 1940s through the early 1960s, scholars of popular culture have singled out the period from 1963 through the early 1970s as particularly intensive. Social movements that had long been germinating, such as the African American civil rights movement in the United States, moved to the center of the national agenda; the long-term drive for equal rights for women similarly moved into prominence, as did those of other historically marginalized groups such as the disabled, gays and lesbians, and a host of ethnic groups. Nearly all of these movements borrowed strategies and tactics from the movement for African American civil rights. Most of them also involved peaceful protests and civil disobedience, some borrowing directly from the strategies and philosophy of Gandhi. Some, however, advocated violent confrontation.

Civil Rights Movements

As we saw in Chapters 22 and 29, the story of African Americans since the end of the American Civil War had been one of emancipation from slavery and acquisition of the formal rights of citizenship in the constitutional order, but considerable opposition to their social integration, especially in the southern states. Indeed, by the time of World War II, all of the southern states had laws mandating segregation, and even some northern states and cities had formal and informal restrictions on such things as where African Americans could live and work. The "great migration" of blacks from the rural south to the industrial north during this time and the lobbying by such organizations as the National Association for the Advancement of Colored People (NAACP; founded 1909) increased the pressure for more civil rights for black people. In this respect, the war proved a decisive turning point in their struggle.

The Postwar Drive for Civil Rights   The massive mobilization during World War II began the process of greatly accelerating civil rights efforts on a number of fronts. The vast numbers of African Americans serving in the armed forces, along with professed US and Allied war aims regarding Nazi racial policies, made segregation in the military increasingly untenable. In 1947, therefore, President Truman signed an executive order desegregating the American armed forces. Repeated anti-lynching and civil rights bills now began to appear before Congress. In 1954, the Supreme Court reversed its earlier stand on segregation in education in the momentous *Brown v. Board of Education* ruling. Overturning the 1896 *Plessey v. Fergusson* decision that "separate but equal" facilities were constitutional, the court now ruled that the "separate" facilities were by definition not equal. Schools were therefore ordered to desegregate "with all deliberate speed." This met with determined resistance in many communities; in 1957, President Dwight D. Eisenhower (in office 1953–1961) was compelled to send in the military to Little Rock, Arkansas, to enforce the ruling. Still, by the early 1960s there was a dramatic movement under way for civil rights and equal treatment for African Americans in the American south.

In addition to the new domestic sense of urgency that desegregation was long overdue, international conditions played a role in pushing it forward. One of these conditions was postwar anticolonialism, particularly in Africa, where former European colonies (e.g., Ghana in 1957) secured their independence. The Cold War also played a vital role. Soviet propaganda had long played up the discrepancies between American claims of freedom and equality and its treatment of black people. Thus, the argument was increasingly made that desegregation and civil rights would give the lie to Soviet claims and thus be patriotic. When the accelerating pressure of civil rights marches and protests resulted in violence against the protesters in the early 1960s, President John F. Kennedy sponsored civil rights legislation to end discrimination.

A high point occurred in August of 1963 when the Reverend Martin Luther King Jr. (1929–1968) delivered his electrifying "I Have a Dream" speech before a huge crowd at the Lincoln Memorial in Washington, D.C. After the assassination of Kennedy that November, his successor, Lyndon B. Johnson (in office 1963–1969),

(a)   (b)

(c)

The Civil Rights Struggle. One of the first major contests for desegregation of public transportation in the American South was the Montgomery, Alabama, bus boycott of 1955. Here, Rosa Parks, by refusing to sit in the back of the bus in the area reserved for African Americans, sparked the boycott of Montgomery's bus lines by people of color (a). As the 1960s began the further desegregation of public areas, in this case, lunch counters were taken over by students "sitting in" and refusing to leave. (b) The career of the charismatic minister Dr. Martin Luther King Jr. was launched during the Montgomery bus boycott. By the early 1960s he had emerged as America's preeminent civil rights leader. Here, he is shown at the peak of his influence, delivering his famous "I Have a Dream" speech on the Capital Mall in Washington, D.C., in August 1963 (c).

secured the passage of the Civil Rights Act of 1964, which provided significant protections for African Americans, not least of which was the prohibition of segregation in public places. This was followed by the 1965 Voting Rights Act, aimed at outlawing the poll taxes, literacy tests, and other means by which states attempted to limit their citizens' ability to vote.

With many legal remedies now in place for past discrimination, civil rights leaders increasingly turned their attention to economic and social justice. The Johnson administration had created a comprehensive program, called "The Great Society," aimed at eliminating poverty in America. Civil rights advocates lobbied vigorously to make sure the proper proportion of jobs and poverty-relief programs were aimed at their constituents. Since that time, the emphasis has been largely on job equity, affirmative action (weighing one's minority status in hiring to make up for past group injustices), and ongoing efforts to improve education in largely African American or minority inner-city areas.

While the drive for African American civil rights was perhaps the most sweeping movement of the 1960s and early 1970s, it also generated many others. Taking their cue from the prominence and media attention of African American efforts, a host of ethnic groups facing discrimination of various kinds mounted their own drives for recognition and rights. Mexican Americans, Asian Americans, Puerto Ricans, the disabled, and gays and lesbians all borrowed heavily from the methods of the African American and the women's movements. In all of these cases, their drives resulted in legislation and social changes aimed at making up for past discrimination and protection from future reversals.

The Antiwar Movement   For many of the thousands of idealistic students who had taken part in civil rights demonstrations and programs to register African American voters in southern states in the early 1960s, it seemed to be a natural transition from political activism in favor of civil rights to activism for other causes. By 1965, the building American military effort in Vietnam began to attract protests against US involvement in southeast Asia. This was particularly true for young people of draft age, whether they had college deferments or not. The antiwar movement, initially limited to college campuses and other centers of left or liberal political leaning, increasingly became more mainstream over the next several years. At the same time, the movement generated considerable hostility among the previous generation, who had fought in World War II and felt that the protesters were shirking their duty to defend the country against communist expansionism.

By 1968 an additional factor adding to tensions on both sides was the assassinations of civil rights leaders Martin Luther King Jr. and antiwar presidential candidate Robert Kennedy in the spring of that year. In addition to anger and despair about creating change in the United States, student demonstrations now shook much of the Western world. The most serious of these took place in Paris, where rioting students calling for major education reforms at the University of Paris took to the streets, a movement that spread beyond the students to the laboring sector and threatened the downfall of the French government. Massive demonstrations also took place in Mexico City in advance of the Olympic Games there that summer. In the wake of the quelling of these riots in Europe and the frustration felt by American radicals at their failures in stopping the war, many now called for revolutionary violence directed against the government and programs funded by the military.

Groups like the Weather Underground staged robberies, planted bombs, and prodded demonstrators to be more aggressive in their protests in the belief that the United States and the West more generally were on the brink of revolution and required only some well-placed acts of violence to make it happen. In Italy and West Germany, some students joined violent revolutionary organizations such the Red Brigades and the Baader-Meinhof Gang. Along the way the most radical students expressed solidarity with Third World revolutionary efforts and such as colorful revolutionaries as Ernesto "Che" Guevara (1928–1967), Ho Chi Minh and the Vietnamese communists, and Mao Zedong and the Cultural Revolution in China. With the end of American involvement in the war and the draft in the early 1970s, however, most of these groups broke up, went totally underground, or were dismantled by the authorities.

Women's Rights and the Sexual Revolution

Encouraged by the success of the strategy and tactics of the civil rights and antiwar movements, a new assertiveness also marked the drive for women's rights. While suffragist agitation and mobilization during World War I had led to voting rights for women in both Great Britain and the United States, the more sweeping social changes brought on by World War II and the Cold War pushed the movement for equality in gender relations even further. A leading voice was that of Simone de Beauvoir (1908–1986), whose work *The Second Sex* (1949) challenged women to take more self-assertive actions in order to gain full equality with their male counterparts. De Beauvoir and other influential feminists also contributed to the so-called sexual revolution of the 1960s. European and American women now openly demanded changes in restrictions placed upon their reproductive and sexual freedoms. Laws prohibiting contraception and abortion were overturned in several Western countries during the 1960s and 1970s. The development and widespread use of oral contraceptives became commonplace, and the 1973 Supreme Court decision in *Roe v. Wade* protected a woman's right to have an abortion. The loosening of postwar moral standards, along with relaxed censorship in the media as well as its

Patterns Up Close | From Women's Liberation to Feminism

As we have seen in this chapter and several previous ones, the emancipation of women, the acquisition of rights in civil society, and changing mores in the family and in the workplace have all been part of a long and difficult process in Europe and America. While the nineteenth and early twentieth centuries witnessed vitally important benchmarks in this regard—the Seneca Falls Convention of 1848, the suffrage movements in the United States and Britain, and the movement of women into the workforce in World War I and World War II—historians often single out the 1960s and 1970s as particularly important. Indeed, the period is often considered to mark the beginning of "second-wave feminism," a renewal of the push that crested with "first-wave feminism's" achievement of suffrage and full political rights (see Map 30.3).

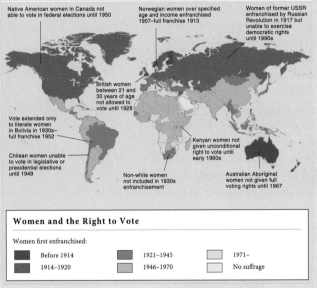

Native American women in Canada not able to vote in federal elections until 1950

Norwegian women over specified age and income enfranchised 1907—full franchise 1913

Women of former USSR enfranchised by Russian Revolution in 1917 but unable to exercise democratic rights until 1990s

British women between 21 and 30 years of age not allowed to vote until 1928

Vote extended only to literate women in Bolivia in 1930s–full franchise 1952

Chilean women unable to vote in legislative or presidential elections until 1949

Kenyan women not given unconditional right to vote until early 1960s

Non-white women not included in 1930s enfranchisement

Australian Aboriginal women not given full voting rights until 1967

Women and the Right to Vote

Women first enfranchised:

■ Before 1914	■ 1921–1945	□ 1971–	
■ 1914–1920	■ 1946–1970	□ No suffrage	

MAP 30.3 **Women and the Right to Vote.**

In addition to the work of Simone de Beauvoir, one reason for this is the influence of such theorists as Betty Friedan (1921–2006), whose 1963 book *The Feminine Mystique* applied many of the same critiques cited by de Beauvoir to a postwar America that treasured a return to home and hearth for women after they had played such a vital role in the workforce during World War II. Another key reason for the importance of the period is that women seeking change had the examples of the African American civil rights movement and the growing antiwar movement on which to draw. Within both of these movements some attention was given to women's rights as part of a larger rubric of emancipation, but it remained largely a secondary issue.

By the mid-1960s growing numbers of women were becoming dissatisfied with what they perceived as the latent *sexism*—the gender equivalent of racism—of other progressive organizations. In response, they founded the National Organization for Women (NOW) in 1966. At about this time the term "women's liberation" began to appear, first in the radical media and shortly thereafter in more mainstream publications and on television and radio. As leaders of the movement like Friedan, Gloria Steinem, and Kate Millett became nationally recognized spokespeople, they agitated for such things as equity in the workplace. In the cultural realm, they led the call for women's studies, "herstory" (instead of the perceived bias of "*his*tory"), and less gendered forms of address like "Mrs." and "Miss" in favor of the more neutral "Ms." As time went on and the stakes of the movement turned toward more personal issues in women's lives, these became political issues as well. The availability of birth control and abortion and laws governing marriage, for example, all became hot-button issues, reflected in the movement's motto claiming that "the personal is political!" Numerous demonstrations calling for everything from legalization of abortion to protesting the Miss America pageant demonstrated the widespread political agenda of this diverse movement.

By the 1970s the women's liberation movement had become firmly anchored in the national consciousness and had inspired similar movements in Europe and many other areas around the world. A new, more radical edge within the movement began to advocate increasingly extreme positions. For example, some argued that marriage itself was essentially sexist and should not be pursued by women; others went so far as to characterize all heterosexual activity as rape under a different name; still others argued for "cultural lesbianism" for women—proposing that women form a distinct community from men and pursue activities within that culture as exclusively as possible.

Although a "third wave" of feminism has taken hold from the 1990s in coexistence with the older ones and often projects a less restrictive attitude toward sexuality of all types than much second-wave feminism, all three waves have become part of the ordinary political landscape of many countries. Indeed, "feminism" has completely supplanted "women's liberation" as the term for a constellation of values and causes that includes equal pay in the workplace, free and full reproductive rights, greater sexual freedom for women, and a thoroughgoing lack of discrimination in society on the basis of gender. In many places, there are still quite specific causes that women seek to champion: an end to female genital mutilation, the abolition of "honor killings" of rape victims, an end to the total domination of males in marriages and arranged marriages, the elimination of female bond slavery, outlawing selective abortion of female fetuses, ending female infanticide, greater emphasis on the prevention of HIV/AIDS transmission, and so on. During the 1980s an evolving movement among scholars from India, Africa, and Southeast Asia (including Gayatri Spivak, Gloria Anzaldua, Chandra Talpade Mohanty, and Trinh Minh-ha), called "postcolonial feminism," explicitly linked sexism and patriarchy to latent colonial racism and its effects among its indigenous "subalterns." During this period, too, there was much theoretical groundwork laid for the problem of the "feminization of poverty" in the developing world: According to a recent United Nations report, women do 66 percent of the world's work, produce at least half of the food, but make only 10 percent of the income and own a scant 1 percent of the property. Thus, female poverty is intricately linked with the patriarchy embedded in long-standing cultural practices.

As the 1990s dawned and the Soviet Bloc collapsed, the problems of women in those countries were also brought to the fore. Thus, feminism as a worldwide movement, despite the many institutional, cultural, and religious obstacles facing it, has grown into perhaps the world's most widespread and influential phenomenon. It promises to be the great emancipation movement of the twenty-first century.

Women's Liberation in the US and India. Taking a page from the success of demonstrations for African American civil rights and the anti–Vietnam War movements, various women's activist organizations mounted their own marches to protest discrimination based on patriarchy and male domination. In this demonstration from 1968 the focus is on eliminating gender discrimination and artificial, male-dictated standards of beauty (*top*). Post-colonial feminism in action: members of the National Federation of Dalit Women demonstrate in support of rights for women of the Dalit ("untouchables") caste in New Delhi, India in 2008 (*bottom*). While discrimination against Dalit is proscribed by law in India, bias against Dalit women is still widespread.

Questions

- How does the women's liberation movement demonstrate many of the characteristics of evolving modernity?

- Why does feminism promise to be the great emancipation movement of the twenty-first century?

Woodstock. The iconic event of the "hippie" or "counterculture" era of the late 1960s was the Woodstock music and art festival held in August 1969 in upstate New York. It was a massive event, attended by perhaps as many as 400,000 people—as this aerial photo dramatically shows (*a*). Of the dozens of performers playing over the 3 days of the event, one of the most electrifying was the guitarist Jimi Hendrix. Hendrix pioneered a wild, free-form, jazz-inflected style that is still widely admired and imitated today (*b*).

increased emphasis on sex and eroticism, also played a part in new attitudes toward female sexuality. By the late 1960s, a "women's liberation" movement aimed at such things as equal pay for equal work, more social freedom for women to pursue careers outside the home, and, among the most radical, the pursuit of woman-centered values had come to the fore.

"Tune In, Turn On, Drop Out"   At the same time as this political transformation was taking place, students were increasingly engaged in protest against what they perceived as the excessive materialism, conformism, and sexual prudishness of the previous generation. Many of this "permissive generation" of "baby boomers" (those born during the postwar "baby boom" between 1945 and 1961) repudiated the rigidity of their parents by growing their hair long—in imitation of the Beatles and other rock bands—wearing jeans, T-shirts, and "workers'" clothing; dabbling in Asian philosophies; taking drugs and engaging in a variety of forms of sexual experimentation.

The early center for this movement of "hippies" was San Francisco, in which 1967 was proclaimed the "summer of love." The growing popularity of drugs like marijuana and the hallucinogenic compound lysergic acid diethylamide (LSD) encouraged many to experiment with mind-altering substances. Perhaps the most famous advocate of these allegedly "mind-expanding" drugs was Timothy Leary (1920–1996), a former Harvard University psychologist who advised people to "tune in, turn on [i.e., take LSD], and drop out [of society]." Musical groups espousing hippie values—often crudely summed up as "sex, drugs, and rock and roll"—also arose and dominated much of the popular music scene during this time. Among the most influential were The Grateful Dead, Jefferson Airplane, and, from England, Pink Floyd. Perhaps the peak of this movement came in August 1969, when the Woodstock Festival in New York State drew an estimated 300,000–500,000 attendees and sparked a decade of giant music and culture festivals attempting to capture the spirit of what became known as the "Woodstock generation." Though the hippie movement as a force for "liberation" from mainstream values had largely spent itself by the early 1970s, its influence in fashion, sexual attitudes, music, and drug use continues to some extent even today.

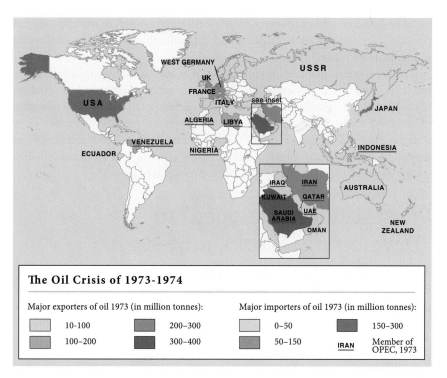

MAP 30.4 **The Oil Crisis of 1973–1974.**

Economics and Politics in the 1970s and 1980s   Whereas the 1950s and 1960s represented unprecedented growth and prosperity, a sudden economic downturn in the early 1970s initiated a prolonged period of economic stagnation. Several factors were at work here. One cause was the ramping down of the Vietnam War effort, which had driven the US defense industry. Another cause stemmed from renewed hostilities between Arab and Israeli factions in 1973. In retaliation against American support of Israel, the newly formed OPEC, led by Arab states, dramatically increased the price of oil for export to America. The price per barrel of oil rose dramatically from $1.73 in 1973 to nearly $35 in 1981 (see Map 30.4). The consequences of these economic downturns were at first inflation and then by the late 1970s **stagflation**. The emergence of developing economies in Asia and South America also began to lure American manufacturers to relocate to these countries in order to take advantage of lower labor costs, resulting in the decline of major industries in the United States.

The combined effect of these economic fluctuations and restrictions caused corresponding realignments in politics in the 1970s and 1980s. In many Western countries—the United States, Britain, and Germany—the trend shifted toward the adoption of more conservative policies. The most notable examples of what has been termed the "New Conservatism" were the policies of the American president Ronald Reagan and Britain's prime minister Margaret Thatcher (in office 1979–1990). Reagan's fiscal policies, by way of example (sometimes termed "Reaganomics") featured lower taxes as a way to increase jobs, lower interest rates, and offset deficit spending. Although the subject of considerable debate, these policies have been credited with producing a sustained period of economic growth during his presidency. Both leaders orchestrated cutbacks in governmental spending for

Stagflation: Increased prices and record high interest rates but a stagnant economy overall.

social services and welfare programs, and in both countries industrial strikes and the power of labor unions were restricted and the nationalization of major industries was replaced by privatization.

Other countries, like France, took an opposite approach. They rejected conservatism as a way to solve economic problems. The election of François Mitterand (in office 1981–1995) resulted in the adoption of socialist policies like nationalization of banks and industries, increases in wages, and increased spending on social welfare programs. Instead of improving the French economy, however, Mitterand's policies created an economic downturn, resulting in the election of a more conservative leader, Jacques Chirac (in office 1995–2007) at the end of his term.

From "Underdeveloped" to "Developing" World, 1963–1991

As the Cold War reached it peak in the 1960s, the drive for independence in Africa also crested, with the last colonies finally achieving nationhood in the 1970s. At the same time the drive for economic development, national prestige, and national power continued to grow among all of the newly independent nations everywhere. The 1960s through the 1980s marked in many ways the height of the contest among the nonaligned nations for preeminence between our two competing modernisms: market capitalism with democratic governments and variants of communism, based on the Soviet or Chinese model. Some newly independent governments attempted assorted combinations of both forms of modernity as paths to development. Although many countries remained in dire poverty and scarred by internal and external wars, the period also witnessed many more moving from the catchall category of "underdeveloped" to the more optimistic one of "developing."

While the unsurpassed prosperity of the West in this period mightily impressed leaders in the developing world, many, if not most, continued to question whether capitalism was appropriate for their nations as an economic basis. There were several reasons for this, both practical and historical. On a practical level it was considered that capitalism had developed in the West over a long time and with great suffering among the working classes. Putting a newly independent nation into competition with developed nations thus placed the latter at an unfair advantage. Additionally, capitalism encouraged continued economic dominance of the former colonial powers and thus skewed the economies of developing nations toward supporting the economies of their former occupiers. Moreover, the perceived connection between capitalism and imperialism was distasteful to many who had fought to rid their countries of colonialism. Finally, for decades after the end of imperial rule, the legacy of imperialism was blamed for many of the remaining problems of struggling developing countries.

As we saw in Chapter 29, the socialist road for many of these same reasons had a powerful theoretical appeal to many leaders in these emerging nations. The examples of the Soviet Union and China, and implicitly the "Communist Bloc" countries, appeared to show that formerly poor countries could become rich and powerful—even to the point of being superpowers. Moreover, they appeared to be able to do it far more quickly than capitalist countries. Finally, they were without the fatal stain of having been colonialists—at least in the sense that they had not created overseas empires—and thus could be perceived to be without a long-standing ulterior motive.

One key development that is worth considering in this regard revolves around the ideological approaches of the rival camps. Marxist theorists had long argued that underdevelopment was *caused* by capitalism and imperialism. That is, by taking control of the economy of a new colony, imperialism plugged it into the world capitalist system and shunted its products into areas useful to the mother country rather than the people of the colony. This disturbed the natural balance of the colony's economic life and retarded its further development according to its own needs. When the colony becomes independent, therefore, it remains at a disadvantage because its economy still depends on that of the mother country and has no way of breaking away cleanly and reestablishing an independent economy. The only way this can be done, said the theorists, was through a thoroughgoing political and social revolution.

> ### Germs of Rot
>
> "Violence is man re-creating himself.... Imperialism leaves behind germs of rot, which we must clinically detect and remove from our land, but from our minds as well.... The starving peasant ... is the first among the exploited to discover that only violence pays. For him there is no compromise, no possible coming to terms; colonization and decolonization are simply a question of relative strength."
>
> —Frantz Fanon. *The Wretched of the Earth*, p. 71. New York: Grove Press, 1961.

Economists and political thinkers in the West eager to combat this Marxist view asserted that underdevelopment was caused by a lack of modern institutions, basic industries, and infrastructure that would support a market economy. Their *modernization theory* argued that, although the modern elements in the former colonies had certainly not been set up for the benefit of the colonized, they were precisely those needed for survival in the modern world and should therefore be used as the modern base upon which new nations should build. Thus, instead of imperialism being seen as creating underdevelopment, it was viewed as the force that, however grudgingly, created the basis for modern development.

China: Cultural Revolution to Four Modernizations

Of all the major world powers, the People's Republic of China experienced perhaps the most wrenching policy changes during the period 1963–1991. Having just emerged from the first Maoist era of the 1950s, it entered into a less frenetic few years of more Soviet-style socialist development, only to be catapulted into the frenzy of the Cultural Revolution in the late 1960s. The death of Mao in 1976, however, ushered in a complete reversal of economic course. In 1978, the Four Modernizations of Deng Xiaoping called for opening the country to foreign experts, aid and investment, and creating a market economy—that is, to introduce capitalism. To this day, China's economic policy is officially called "Socialism with Chinese characteristics."

China's "Thermidorean Reaction," 1960–1966

The turbulence of the first round of the Maoist years ebbed considerably under the leadership of Liu Shaoqi. The decade began, however, with the "Sino–Soviet split," in which Soviet apprehensiveness about China's radical programs and Mao's distrust of Soviet policy changes under Khrushchev led to a complete withdrawal of Soviet aid and advisors in 1960. For Western observers accustomed to seeing the communist world as a "monolith," this was the first real divide among ideological allies since Tito's independent stance in Yugoslavia in 1948. By the end of the decade, Chinese and Soviet forces would be exchanging fire along several disputed border crossings.

Nonetheless, the early 1960s saw a reassertion of the need for education and technical training in China under Liu, and China made several important technological advances. Chief among these was the detonation of China's first nuclear device in October 1964. This was quickly followed by the testing of a thermonuclear (hydrogen) device in 1966. Chinese scientists also synthesized insulin and made advances in missile technology that would yield the first Chinese satellites in the following decade. Extensive studies of China's natural resources also disclosed large coal deposits and led to the discovery of oil fields at Daqing and in the extreme west. In addition, Liu's regime engaged in a more assertive policy of border rectification. Chinese forces had entered Tibet in 1959 to suppress an independence movement, resulting in the flight of the Dalai Lama to India. In securing Tibet, however, disputes arose regarding the actual border with India. In 1962, Chinese forces moved into the disputed regions and fought a brief undeclared war until withdrawing and submitting the issue to negotiation. This kind of display of force in order to make a point would be seen again in China's attack on Vietnam in 1979, though with far less effectiveness.

The Cultural Revolution   As China's Communist Party and government assumed a more Soviet-style approach to running the People's Republic, Mao Zedong grew increasingly uneasy about the direction of policy. For Mao, the party was reverting to a bureaucracy, increasingly unresponsive to the needs of pushing the revolution forward toward a pure communism. Mao's position of politics taking command was in direct opposition to the increasingly technocratic stance he saw in Liu Shaoqi's policies. Thus, Mao spent several years writing widely circulated essays extolling the virtues of devoted communists and plotting his comeback. An important step along the way was the publication of his famous "little red book," *Quotations from Chairman Mao Zedong*, in 1964. His ideological ally, Lin Biao (in office 1954–1971), as Vice-Premier and head of the People's Liberation Army, made it required reading for the troops and helped Mao establish an important power base.

In the spring of 1966, Mao launched a violent critique of the new direction of the party and called on the nation's youth to rededicate themselves to "continuous revolution." They were encouraged to criticize their elders and form their own pure "red" ideological path to socialism. Mao announced the launching of the Great Proletarian Cultural Revolution, the purpose of which was to stamp out the last vestiges of "bourgeois" and "feudal" Chinese society. Students formed themselves into squads of "Red Guards" with red armbands and attacked their teachers and elders. By August, millions of Red Guards converged on Beijing, where Mao addressed over 1 million of them in Tiananmen Square and symbolically donned their red armband as a show of solidarity.

From 1966 until 1969, when the Cultural Revolution was officially declared over, millions of people were hounded, tortured, killed, or driven to suicide by Red Guards and

A Revolution Is Not a Dinner Party

"People of the world unite and defeat the U.S. aggressors and their running dogs!"

"Every Communist must grasp the truth, 'Political power grows out of the barrel of a gun...'"

"A revolution is not a dinner party, or writing an essay, or painting a picture, or doing embroidery; it cannot be so refined, so leisurely and gentle, so temperate, so kind, courteous, restrained and magnanimous. A revolution is an insurrection, an act of violence by which one class overthrows another..."

—Mao Zedong. *Quotations from Chairman Mao Zedong. Mao zhuxi yulu*, 1964. English language version by Foreign Languages Press, Quotations from Chairman Mao Tsetung (Peking: 1972), pp. 82, 11, 59.

Red Guards on the March.
Mao Zedong's injunction to the youth of China to question the authority of party bureaucrats had swift effects on everything from the school system to factory production. The students banded together into Red Guard units and challenged their elders, often violently, on their adherence to Mao's thought as expressed in the famous "little red book," *Quotations from Chairman Mao Zedong.* In this photo from 1967, Red Guards parade with a portrait of Mao, while many carry the red book in their hands.

their allies. The "little red book" became the talisman of the movement, with people struggling to interpret it correctly to prove their ideological fitness. China's official ideology was now listed as "Marxism–Leninism–Mao Zedong Thought." A cult of personality surrounding Mao and the book sprang up as people waved it at mass rallies and even attributed magical powers to it. By 1968 the country was in complete chaos as pro– and anti–Cultural Revolution factions battled each other in several regions. It was chiefly to end this endemic civil war that Mao declared the Cultural Revolution over in 1969. Its aftermath, however, continued until Mao's death in 1976.

"To Get Rich Is Glorious": China's Four Modernizations   The final years of Mao's tenure as party chair saw at least one important change in policy. Despite the Sino–Soviet split, the People's Republic had maintained a strong anti-American posture in its domestic and foreign policy. This was matched by American Cold War antipathy toward "Red China" as a linchpin of the communist bloc. By the early 1970s, however, with the Vietnam War winding down and Soviet–Chinese tensions still high, President Nixon made a bold visit to the People's Republic, which resulted in the Shanghai communiqué of 1972. In this document, the United States and the People's Republic of China announced plans to begin formal diplomatic and cultural relations (which went into effect in 1979), the United States pledged to no

longer block the People's Republic's bid for a seat in the United Nations, and the United States agreed to downgrade its diplomatic presence in Taiwan.

The death of Mao Zedong in September 1976 opened the way for a new generation of Communist Party leadership in China. The end result was a repudiation of the Cultural Revolution and those who promoted it and an entirely different direction in strategy for building a new China. After some jostling among the party factions, the hardy Deng Xiaoping (in office 1978–1992) emerged on the scene in 1978 with the title of "vice premier" but, in fact, held the real power in the regime. The ascendancy of the pragmatic Deng, whose motto was "It doesn't matter whether the cat is black or white, as long as it catches mice," swiftly led to the unveiling of the fundamental policies that remain in force in China to the present: the Four Modernizations.

Painfully aware of the difficulties of pursuing socialism in a country with little wealth to share, Deng's strategy was bent on upgrading the quality of agriculture, industry, science, technology, and the military. China would pursue a new "open-door" policy with regard to foreign expertise from the West; it would allow its own students to study abroad and, most tellingly, allow the market forces of capitalism to

MAP 30.5 **Open Cities and Special Economic Zones in China, 1980–2000.**

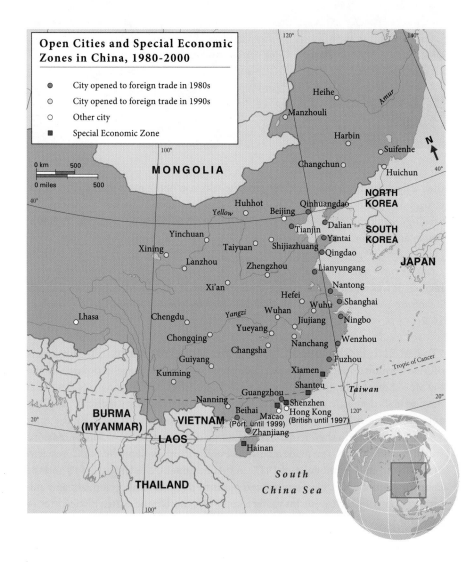

create incentives for innovation in all sectors of the economy. The new motto thus became "To get rich is glorious!"

The "responsibility system," as it was called, was introduced in a special economic zone set up in south China at Shenzhen to take advantage of capital and expertise from Hong Kong. The experiments in capitalism would then be expanded to the country at large once the flaws had been worked out. Peasants were among the first beneficiaries as the communes were disbanded, individual plots assigned, and market incentives introduced. By the mid-1980s China, which had long been a byword in the West for hunger, was rapidly approaching self-sufficiency in food production and, by the 1990s, would register surpluses (see Map 30.5). Through the 1980s and 1990s China's gross domestic product (GDP) would grow at an astonishing double-digit rate. In 2010 it surpassed Japan as the second largest economy in the world, after the United States.

Another more controversial innovation was the "one-child policy." Mao felt that China's huge and growing population was an advantage because of its potential manpower and as a hedge against catastrophic losses from nuclear war. But population pressures were also a powerful brake on China's development. Thus, a policy was inaugurated in 1979 mandating that families (excluding those of most minorities) were to have only one child. A second child would result in loss of subsidies for childrearing; a third pregnancy would result in mandatory abortion. Despite the many problems in enforcing such a policy, and its severe cultural impact on the male-centered traditional Chinese family structure, China's population has remained remarkably stable since the 1980s at around 1.3–1.5 billion. It has, however, abetted problems of selective female abortion, giving up girl babies for adoption, and even, in extreme cases, female infanticide. Moreover, all of these conditions have lent themselves to a large and growing gender imbalance: China currently has 117 male births for every 100 female births.

The "Fifth Modernization" and Tiananmen Square

The heady atmosphere of the early days of these sweeping changes brought political reformers temporarily out of hiding. In the so-called Peking Spring of 1979, thousands of demonstrators called for a wide array of democratic reforms by hanging "big-character" posters on the walls near Tiananmen Square, the site of China's most important government buildings and Mao's mausoleum. This "democracy" movement calling for a "fifth modernization: democracy" was shortly suppressed, but political agitation calling for a more open society, crackdowns on corruption, and even a multiparty system continued in muted form throughout the decade.

For its part, the government managed a delicate balance between allowing foreign technology to come into China while preventing cultural items "injurious to public morals" to enter. Hence, IBM computers were welcome, but MTV was not. Repeated campaigns against such "spiritual pollution" were conducted throughout the 1980s, though with less and less effect. Prodemocracy protests again took place in Beijing following the death of the popular moderate leader Hu Yaobang in 1989. The gatherings grew in size and force as the seventieth anniversary of the May Fourth nationalist movement grew closer. At one point students even constructed a large statue they called "the Goddess of Democracy," which dominated the center of the square near the Monument to the People's Revolutionary Martyrs. By the beginning of June the movement had turned into generalized protest of workers and

Tiananmen Square Demonstrations. At their peak in May 1989, the demonstrations by students seeking greater government accountability and a more open political system were joined by workers and people from all walks of life. Here are two memorable images from this event: (*a*) the "goddess of democracy," taken from behind in a pose that seems to confront the portrait of Mao Zedong on the Gate of Heavenly Peace, and (*b*) the suppression of the demonstration—a lone man confronting a tank. The driver of the tank tried to get around the man and eventually stopped, together with the other tanks. At that point, demonstrators pulled the man back to safety. His subsequent fate is unknown. Both images were widely broadcast throughout the world.

ordinary citizens in addition to students. When they refused to disperse, the government sent in the army on June 4 to crush what to many in the party had become incipient rebellion. One arresting image was flashed in various media around the world and became an instant icon of the movement: television footage of a lone man attempting to stare down an approaching tank. To this day, the number of killed and injured is unknown.

Vietnam: War and Unification

As we noted in Chapter 29, by the early 1960s Vietnam, having finally thrown off French colonialism in the 1950s, had failed to achieve final unification because of Cold War politics and remained divided into North and South Vietnam. The development of communist guerrilla fighters, the Vietcong, in South Vietnam and similar guerrilla threats in Laos had prompted the United States to send aid and military advisors to the shaky government of the Republic of Vietnam (South Vietnam) through the late 1950s. Rocked by clashes between Catholics and Buddhists, the government of South Vietnam was ousted in a coup with help from the American Central Intelligence Agency (CIA) in late 1963. Several weak governments took its place until a more stable one under Nguyen Van Thieu emerged and lasted from 1965 to 1975.

The American War   In the summer of 1964 several alleged attacks on American ships in the Gulf of Tonkin (the authenticity of these allegations is still murky today) resulted in the United States radically ramping up its presence in Southeast Asia, effectively beginning what became known in Vietnam as the American War and in the United States as the Vietnam War. In retaliation for the attacks, American planes bombed sites in North Vietnam. By 1965 tens of thousands of American combat troops were being sent to support the South Vietnamese against the Vietcong. But, as in Korea, the Americans and their allies were plagued by unclear goals and the impatience of a public hoping for quick, decisive results. The task of "winning the hearts and minds of the people," as the slogan went, however, was a long and torturous one at best and always vulnerable to the problem of being a foreign presence in someone else's land. Thus, American forces were increased until they reached a high of over a half-million by 1967. Despite official optimism, there was little evidence that the war was being won (see Map 30.6).

In February 1968, during the Vietnamese lunar new year (*Tet*), the Vietcong, supported by North Vietnamese forces, launched an all-out assault on the South Vietnamese capital of Saigon and a number of other cities. American and Army of the Republic of Vietnam (South Vietnam) forces reeled for several days but launched a successful counterattack, finally destroying the Vietcong as an effective fighting force. In the United States, however, the "Tet Offensive," as it came to be called, was seen as an American defeat. In the wake of massive protests against the war, President Johnson announced he would not seek reelection; and the way was clear for the United States to begin negotiations to end the war by political means. With the election of Richard Nixon in 1968, a combination of massive bombings of North Vietnam and Cambodian supply lines for North Vietnamese forces and peace talks in Paris over the next 5 years finally brought the war to an end.

Though South Vietnam survived the peace treaty in 1973, the American withdrawal spelled its demise within 2 years. Though the country was now finally united, much of Vietnam, Cambodia, and Laos lay devastated from fighting and bombing. Over the next 2 years a Cambodian revolutionary group, the Khmer Rouge (Red Khmers), launched a radical program of depopulating the cities, forced labor, and genocide against religious and political opponents that killed perhaps one-third of the country's population. The ideas and practices of the Khmer Rouge leader Pol Pot (1925–1998) were so radical and brutal that in 1977 Vietnam invaded the state and initiated his overthrow in favor of a more moderate and pliable candidate. In response, China briefly invaded northern Vietnam in 1979 but was soon repulsed by Vietnamese forces, the last and least successful of the many Chinese invasion attempts launched over two millennia.

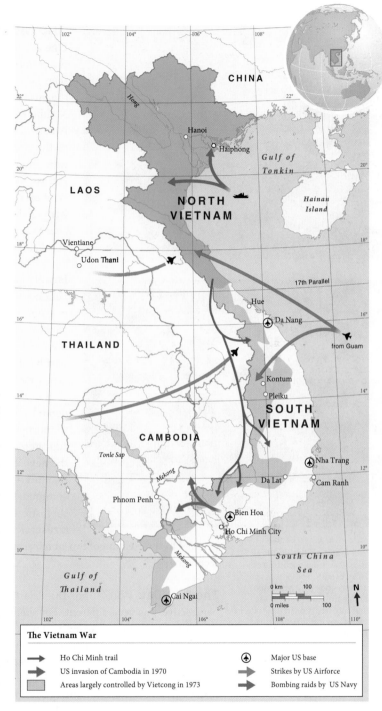

MAP 30.6 **The Vietnam War.**

(a)

(b)

The Arab-Israeli War of June 1967. The stunning victory of Israel over the combined armies of Syria and Egypt generated both admiration in the West and consternation in the Arab world and the Soviet Bloc. The Israelis' preemptive use of air power against Egyptian and Syrian tank and troop concentrations and their expert use of armor proved the deciding factors in the conflict. Here, Egyptian prisoners (in white underclothes in the truck to the right) are being transferred to holding camps (a). The war also led to a dramatic rise in the popularity of the Palestinian cause in the Arab and communist spheres. Here, Yassir Arafat marches with members of Al Fatah in 1970 (b).

The Middle East

One of the most troubled areas of the world during the twentieth century was also one that, as we have seen over the course of this book, has been perhaps the most prolific producer of influential religions: the Middle East. Since 1945, the area encompassing the Arabian Peninsula, Iran, Iraq, and the eastern shores of the Mediterranean has seen a number of major wars and minor conflicts; innumerable guerilla raids and assaults; and attacks directed against the religious symbols of Judaism, Christianity, and Islam. As of this writing, despite peace talks that have been conducted over the course of decades, no comprehensive settlement has been reached.

Israeli and Arab Conflict   In addition to competition arising from the increasing demand for petroleum as a strategic commodity, and Shia–Sunni conflict within the context of Persian–Arab competition, by far the most contentious issue in the Middle East has been the presence of the Jewish state of Israel. Israel during the 1950s and 1960s was largely seen in the West as a plucky young country fighting democracy's battles against a vast array of Arab states supported by the Soviet Union. The number of highly educated immigrants in the postwar decades helped the new state immensely in building an efficient agriculture—often through the socialist device of the communal farm, or *kibbutz*—and an increasingly sophisticated manufacturing sector. Mandatory military service and generous American support also contributed to the creation of top-notch armed forces equipped with the latest military technology.

The "Six-Day War"   For the Palestinian Arabs and their allies, however, the perspective was very different. For them it was "the disaster." Hundreds of thousands displaced since 1948 awaited their return in surrounding countries—often in camps—for decades, a situation that grew worse when new refugees arrived after every Arab–Israeli conflict. In the polarized Cold War climate, the Arab states viewed Israel as simply a new Western imperial outpost in what was rightfully Arab territory. Consequently, many subsequent attempts at Arab unity were premised on war with Israel. While Arab nationalism was largely secular, and often socialist-leaning with Soviet support, Muslim fundamentalist groups such as Egypt's Muslim Brotherhood gained adherence, despite government repression, as Western secular values came to be seen as causes of Muslim difficulties.

In 1964, Yassir Arafat (1929–2004) and other like-minded Palestinian nationalists formed the Palestinian Liberation Organization (PLO), whose militant wing, Al Fatah, began a guerilla war against Israel and its backers. Matters soon came to a head in June 1967. Following an Egyptian military buildup along the Sinai border and the expulsion of UN forces there, Iraq sent troops to Jordan at its invitation and local Muslim leaders began to call for holy war against Israel. The Israelis launched a massive preemptive air assault to neutralize the Egyptian and Syrian air forces. With an overwhelming advantage in number and quality of aircraft, Israel took out the Arab armor and ground troops with astonishing skill. The Six-Day War, as it came to be called, established Israel's reputation for military prowess and enlarged the state by the annexing of territories on the eastern side of the Jordan River, known since that time as the Occupied Territories. For many observers, Israel had now moved from a state simply fighting for its existence to one bent on expansion.

The Yom Kippur/Ramadan War

For the two superpowers, the Arab–Israeli conflict provided valuable data on the performance of the weapons systems they supplied to their respective allies. Thus far in these "proxy wars" (as they were sometimes called), American and European weapons—and increasingly, Israeli-made arms like the famous Uzi submachine gun—had tended to outperform the Soviet ordnance supplied to the Arab states. This was almost reversed in 1973 however. In early October

The Arab-Israeli Wars of 1967 and 1973

- Israel, before 1967 war
- Territory occupied by Israel, June 1967
- Territory occupied by Israel, Oct 1973
- Territory occupied by Egypt, Oct 1973

MAP 30.7 The Arab–Israeli Wars, 1967 and 1973.

1973, Egypt, Syria, and a coalition of Arab states, stung by their defeat in 1967, launched a massive attack during the Jewish holy day of Yom Kippur, which in 1973 coincided with the Muslim holy month of Ramadan. This time, with Israel, the United States, and the Soviet Union caught unawares, Egyptian tanks crossed the Suez Canal on pontoon bridges and attacked Israel (see Map 30.7). Syria attacked the Golan Heights and put pressure on Israeli forces at the other end of the state. After taking severe losses and giving ground for a week, Israeli forces managed to take the initiative and ultimately defeat the combined Arab armies once again. Having trapped Egyptian forces along the Suez Canal, Israeli units occupied the west bank of the Canal, pushing within 63 miles of Cairo. Other units drove 25 miles into Syria. A ceasefire was brokered by the United Nations, but the intensity of the fighting and the resupply efforts by the United States and Soviet Union moved both countries dangerously close to direct confrontation. For their part, the Arab oil producers and Iran immediately launched an oil boycott of the United States. Stringent measures and a degree of rationing and vastly higher gasoline prices drove home to Americans how dependent they had now become on foreign oil. (Much of the interest in solar and other alternative energy thus stems from this period.)

For Egypt, the defeat resulted in a transformation of policy toward Israel. Under President Anwar el-Sadat (in office 1970–1981), Egypt took the initiative in undertaking peace talks by visiting Israel in 1977. The following year, the two sides reached an understanding about a basic framework for peace; and with the backing of the American president Jimmy Carter, Egypt and Israel signed the first treaty between an Arab country and the Jewish state at Camp David, Maryland, in 1979. Egypt and Jordan are the only Arab states to date to maintain diplomatic and cultural relations with Israel. While Egyptian–Israeli relations remained relatively cordial on the surface, no other Arab countries followed suit. Syria remained hostile, having lost the Golan Heights, while the PLO stepped up its efforts throughout the 1980s. Profound resentment against Sadat for signing the treaty festered among many Egyptians. Despite some concessions to increasingly vocal fundamentalist Muslim groups—for example, agreeing to base Egyptian legislation on Islamic Shari`a law—Sadat was killed by assassins in 1981.

Africa: From Independence to Development

During the period 1963–1991, the main struggles in Africa moved from those mainly concerned with independence to those revolving around development. As with other parts of the postcolonial world, vigorous internal debates were conducted about strategies for economic development, how best to deploy scarce resources, and the relative merits of a planned economy versus one centered on market forces. But in nearly all cases, the economies of the newly independent states, regardless of which economic system they favored, were problematic. In most cases they were tied to their former colonial regimes by means of the same raw materials—minerals, petroleum, agricultural or forest products—that had been exploitatively extracted during their colonial days. Moreover, they were more frequently than not competing in these products with other former colonies. Thus, they were at the mercy of world commodity prices but not insulated from the worst ups and downs by their former colonial regimes.

In addition, the newly independent states now had to use the revenues generated to support governmental, transport, and military infrastructures, whose costs had formerly been underwritten by the colonial governments. Since many of the new countries, acculturating to the norms of ethnolinguistic nationalism, also wanted to rectify border problems or expand their borders to include ethnic regions ignored by the colonists, their militaries often consumed substantial portions of their budgets. In many cases, too, the first and second generations of government officials and business leaders, smarting from decades of colonial exploitation, felt entitled to reap the benefits of their new status and simply skim the profits from their new positions. Such regimes were often derisively referred to as "kleptocracies." As some scholars have also pointed out, instead of fostering an entrepreneurial middle class, opening up new and innovative areas of investment, all too many members of this "caretaker bourgeoisie" were simply content to milk the enterprises they had to their maximum capacity. Hence, they became far more reliant on foreign aid and investment, which all too often the volatile political environments of their countries made unattractive. For those countries trying to mount socialist policies of land reform and nationalization of businesses, corruption of this type was also an ongoing problem, coupled with little real wealth to share among their growing populations.

As in Chapter 29, far too many new nations emerged in Africa during this period for this chapter to cover them all. Therefore, we will center our examination on Nigeria, Zimbabwe, and South Africa as representative of the problems and prospects of the era.

Nigeria: Civil War and Troubled Legacies

While in the Congo the Cold War played out in fairly dramatic fashion with the United States supporting the overthrow of Patrice Lumumba in favor of Mobutu Sese Seko in the early 1960s, Nigeria's independence started in more promising fashion. With a large and fairly prosperous population, sound agriculture, and abundant resources, it started its postcolonial era as a republic with a British parliamentary system, commonwealth membership, and a federal-style constitution. Like many former African colonies, however, it soon became apparent that Nigeria was also saddled with ethnic and religious conflicts that were its legacy from the old colonial divisions in the continent. Thus, its growing pains were marked by clashes between its established system of constitutional nationalism and the desires of its major constituent groups for their own nation-states more reflective of Nigeria's ethnic, linguistic, and religious makeup.

The new nation brought together three major antagonistic groups, the Yoruba, Igbo, and Hausa, divided by history, culture, religion, and language. The largest, the Yoruba, who controlled most of the national offices, were predominantly Muslim. The Igbo, mostly living in the eastern region where valuable oil deposits had been recently discovered, were predominantly Christian or animist. Starting in 1966, the central government under strongman Yakubu Gowon (in office 1966–1975) had authorized raids to bring Igbo areas under greater control. In 1967, the eastern Igbo region declared itself independent as the state of Biafra under Colonel Chukwuemeka Odumegwu Ojukwu (b. 1933). What followed was perhaps the bloodiest civil war of the era. Both sides fought determinedly, and when a military stalemate was reached the Nigerian forces attempted to starve Biafra into submission. More than 1 million Biafrans died, mostly of starvation and malnutrition, before Biafra surrendered in early 1970. In the remainder of the period to 1991, Nigeria was ruled by a series of military strongmen, each in turn attempting to stabilize the volatile political situation of the central government. By 1991, the prosperity that seemed so promising in 1960 had vanished as a probability to all but the most optimistic observers.

Nigerian Civil War. The attempt by the region of Biafra to secede from Nigeria resulted in one of the bloodiest and most desperate confrontations of the 1960s. In its attempt to starve the Biafrans into surrender, Nigeria blockaded food supplies to the breakaway region with the result of mass malnutrition, starvation, and, ultimately, a sizeable UN relief effort. In this picture relief workers dish out scarce rations to Biafran women and children.

Zimbabwe: The Revolution Continued

Some of the former European colonies in Africa came to independence with substantial populations of white settlers, some of whose families had been there for several generations. Accustomed to a life of relative privilege, they had, in many cases, opposed independence; and when it came, they sought guarantees from the new governments against expropriation of land, discrimination, and reprisals. In 1964 the old colony of Northern Rhodesia gained independence as Zambia, breaking up a federation of the two colonies and Nyasaland, which subsequently became independent as Malawi.

Threatened by the independence of nearby black African nations and confident of support from apartheid-based South Africa, the white leaders of what now called itself simply "Rhodesia" declared unilateral independence in 1965 and set up a government in the colonial capital of Salisbury under Ian Smith (in office 1965–1970). Distressed at this move, Britain refused to recognize the new government and expelled Rhodesia from the commonwealth. Few countries outside of South Africa recognized the regime, which now faced international sanctions and a guerilla movement from within.

Two rival groups, the Zimbabwe African National Union (ZANU) under Robert Mugabe (b. 1924) and the Zimbabwe African People's Union (ZAPU) led by Joshua Nkomo (1917–1999) struggled to bring Smith's regime down and create a majority rule state. The war was a long and bitter one, lasting throughout the 1960s and 1970s, until Mugabe and ZANU finally triumphed and created a new state called "Zimbabwe" in 1980. Mugabe's regime pledged fairness to the remaining white settlers and, after changing the name of the capital to Harare, set about creating a socialist state. In this sense, despite constant condemnation of Africa's imperial legacy, Mugabe has been in constant need of the economic power of the country's white minority and, thus, initially trod fairly lightly on their rights. By the 1990s, however, vigilante seizures of white lands by "revolutionary veterans" became a regular occurrence. By the early-2000s, the chaotic agricultural sector combined with repression of challenges to ZANU one-party rule had plunged the country into a serious economic crisis.

South Africa: From Apartheid to "Rainbow Nation"   South Africa, the richest of the continent's countries, was also the one with the most complex and restrictive racial relations. From the seventeenth century, first Dutch, then English, settlers came to service the maritime traffic around the Cape of Good Hope. By the nineteenth century, the Dutch-descended *boers* had moved inland from Cape Town and begun setting up farms, ranches, and vineyards, pushing the local people before them. The expansion of Zulu power at roughly the same time forced the British

Black Commuters in South Africa. The regime of apartheid (the strict separation of the races) that had been inaugurated by the white minority government in South Africa in 1948 obliged all black citizens, such as these workers congregating in a Johannesburg train station in the late 1950s, to carry "passbooks" that specified what areas they were permitted to enter. Resentment at the passbook requirement prompted mass demonstrations that resulted in the Sharpeville Massacre of March 21, 1960, which in turn sparked widespread protests against the apartheid system.

rulers and Dutch settlers into protracted Zulu wars that, climaxing in 1879, broke the last black empire in the region. By the end of the nineteenth century, the discovery of vast mineral wealth in gold and diamonds led to both the expansion of the colony's holdings and an influx of immigrants, including Chinese and Indians.

By the early twentieth century, the social divisions among whites, Africans, and "coloreds"—south and east Asians and peoples of mixed descent—were hardening into legal classifications. The Indian nationalist leader Mohandas Gandhi, for example, developed his successful nonviolent strategies leading protests in South Africa for Indian rights. After 1910, immigration restrictions on Asians went into effect along with ever more restrictive laws governing relations between whites and Africans. The climax of this trend was the creation of the institution of **apartheid** (Afrikaans, "apartness") in 1948. Africans were relegated to a legal second-class status, they were to live in designated "townships" and tribal "homelands" or "Bantustans," they were required to carry passes when traveling, those commuting to work in white urban areas had to leave by sunset, and even in the townships they were subject to curfew regulations.

Through the 1950s South Africa faced international criticism for its policies, which the white government justified as necessary to maintain its rule, since whites made up less than one-sixth of the population. Moreover, as newly independent black majority countries came into being, the white government felt itself increasingly besieged. It pointed with some justification to a number of these emerging states as Marxist and, thus, claimed that it was fighting the free world's battle against the expansion of the Soviet Bloc in Africa. Nonetheless, it withdrew from the British Commonwealth in 1961, and a number of black political organizations—most prominently the African National Congress (ANC)—campaigned for the dismantling of apartheid. The brutality of the white armed forces and police and the constant harassment of dissenters, both white and black, added to the oppressive atmosphere.

By the 1980s it was clear that events on the continent would sooner or later force the breaking up of apartheid. International boycotts of South Africa had gained momentum, particularly after the public calling for sanctions by the African Episcopal bishop Desmond Tutu (b. 1931), who was awarded the Nobel Peace Prize in 1984. In the townships, the ANC, through a political and guerilla campaign, was making gradual gains. Massive strikes by black workers in 1987 and 1988 also led to increasing paralysis of the government. Finally, in 1990, the newly elected president, F. W. de Klerk (b. 1936), began a sweeping set of reforms aimed ultimately at dismantling apartheid. In quick succession, the ANC was legalized and became South Africa's largest political party; its leader—soon to be the country's president—Nelson Mandela (b. 1918) was released from prison; in 1991 all of the apartheid laws were repealed; and finally, in 1992 white voters elected to amend the constitution to mandate racial equality among all citizens. By 1994, the first multiracial elections were held, and Mandela became the first president of the new South Africa, which Archbishop Tutu dubbed the "Rainbow Nation" in its newly recognized diversity.

> **Apartheid:** System of social and legal segregation by race enforced by the government of South Africa from 1948 until 1994.

Latin America: Proxy Wars

The 1960s in Latin American politics were marked in many ways by the forces contending for dominance against the backdrop of the Cold War. Here, however, because the countries in question had long since achieved their independence—if not yet long-term stability in government—the issues guiding the respective sides were largely ideological and economic, as well as centering around revolutionary politics. This was particularly true for the rural poor, who in many cases continued to live in virtual peonage on large estates, with little hope for economic advancement and little effort on the part of their landlords to improve their lot. In this respect, the appeal of a Marxist movement drawing on such diverse sources as Maoism—with its emphasis on peasants as a revolutionary force—and the recent example of Cuba standing up to the United States and pursuing its own brand of land reforms were often attractive. Cuba, particularly its most visible and charismatic exponent of Latin American revolution Che Guevara, was active throughout this era, though Guevara's execution in Bolivia set the Cuban efforts back somewhat.

By the 1970s, dissatisfaction with the authoritarian regimes of the region, particularly in Central America, resulted in several revolutionary efforts, the most notable being in Nicaragua and El Salvador. Since the mid-1930s, the United States had supported the family of the authoritarian strongman Anastasio Somoza Garcia (collectively in office from 1936–1979). Landlordism and rural poverty had been particularly acute problems in Nicaragua, and from the early 1960s a guerilla insurgency called the Sandinista National Liberation Front (FSLN) had sought to overthrow the Somozas and mount a socialist land-reform scheme. The Somoza regime fell in 1979, and a new government under the Sandinistas (so-called to invoke the name of Emilio Sandino, one of the original Somoza opponents) was formed led by Daniel Ortega (in office 1979–1990; 2007–). The socialist direction of the new regime prompted the American administration of President Ronald Reagan to cut off aid to Nicaragua, begin a covert operation to destabilize Ortega through funding and arming of opposition groups know collectively as the "Contras," and boycott trade with the regime. With US support and fading aid from Cuba and the Soviet Bloc in the late 1980s, the two sides agreed to elections in 1990. These resulted in the presidency of the conservative opposition candidate, Violeta Barrios de Chamorro (in office 1990–1997). In similar fashion, guerilla groups in El Salvador fought United States–backed government forces, whose actions were sometimes directed against Catholic clergy believed to support the insurgents, in a bloody conflict throughout the 1980s, until elections were finally held in 1992. The death toll in this tiny country is estimated to be as high as 75,000. By the early 1990s, however, the two sides, as in Nicaragua, had resolved to work within the new political system.

The commitment of the United States to oppose any groups espousing Marxist or communist aims in Latin America also revealed itself in covert policy toward governments recognized as legitimate. As we saw in Chapter 29, for example, the CIA helped engineer a coup against Guatemalan leader Jacobo Arbenz (in office 1951–1954) in 1954 because he allowed a communist labor union to exist in his country. The most spectacular instance of American Cold War covert action, however, was directed at Chilean President Salvador Allende (in office 1970–1973) in 1973. Allende had led a coalition of socialists, communists, and liberal Christian Democrats to a plurality win in 1970. Many of his policies met opposition within Chile, while his ideology and nationalization of American interests in Chile's mines pushed the Nixon administration to back his opposition. With American blessings and CIA help, Allende was overthrown and the repressive but friendlier regime of General Augusto Pinochet (in office 1973–1990) installed. After Pinochet's term of 16 years in power, his rule remained repressive; but Chile also became increasingly economically vibrant and slowly began to move toward a more open and democratic government. In 1998 Pinochet was arrested in London on charges of human rights violations and torture. After a lengthy court battle, he was ultimately released and returned to Chile, where he died in 2006.

Liberation Theology   In addition to the Marxist-inspired revolutionary movements in Latin America during this period, there were religiously based, activist ideologies animating a host of issues from land reform to protest against human rights violations. These are usually lumped under the heading of "liberation theology." The idea itself is an old one dating back to the Catholic Church's frequent role as champion of the Amerindians and the poor during the colonial and national periods. The calls during the Vatican II Council for a more activist and relevant place for the church resonated with many clergy—Catholic and Protestant—who had formed a vision of Christ's historical and religious role as one of social change. Though particularly active in Latin America, by the early 1970s it had become a worldwide movement within Catholicism and received cautious endorsement of the papacy, though with the caveat that the liberation of the poor and oppressed should not be seen as an endorsement of Marxism. Still, as the decade wore on, increasing numbers of clergy became involved in grassroots organizing, in preaching and pastoral care aimed at propagating a socially active Christianity, and in denouncing the inequities of the economics and politics of authoritarian regimes. The line between such activism and revolutionary work could be thin indeed—Daniel Ortega and his wife, for example, were married by a priest who had become a Sandinista guerilla. The regimes and local elites that were the targets of liberation theology advocates thus often struck back with violence against outspoken priests and nuns. But with the demise of many of these regimes in the 1980s and 1990s and the end of the Cold War, much of the momentum ebbed from the movement, though it is still directed against inequity and poverty among the rural poor even today.

Liberation Theology Service.
The historical role of the Catholic Church at various times as advocate for the poor and oppressed in Latin America reemerged with vigor in the 1960s and 1970s against the backdrop of revolutionary turmoil and a new emphasis emanating from the Vatican on social activism. In the accompanying photo, a Mass is being celebrated in Brazil in the 1970s with a distinct message embodying themes associated with Liberation Theology: The banner reads in Portuguese, "The Church of Maranhao prays and fasts for peace and justice in the countryside."

"The Dirty War" and the "Disappeared"   As we have seen in this section, the damage inflicted by the Cold War and the actions of its combatants, real and proxy, upon Latin America was considerable. One of the most tragic and internationally condemned episodes of this struggle was the "Dirty War" (*Guerra Sucia*) carried out in Argentina from 1976 to 1983. The tangled politics of the post-Perón era resulted in a series of guerilla groups ranging from Peronists to radical communists conducting a smoldering guerilla war against various regimes from the 1960s onward. By the early 1970s, many of these groups had coalesced into the Peronist Montoneros and the Marxist People's Revolutionary Army (ERP). While the Montoneros were essentially crushed in 1977, the ERP remained active; and under the cover of "Operation Condor" pursued by the juntas of Jorge Raphael Videla, Roberto Viola, and Leopoldo Galtieri, tens of thousands of Argentinians were kidnapped, imprisoned, and killed. Many, if not most, of these men and women were not guerillas but writers, editors, labor organizers, teachers, and others suspected of having left-wing leanings or whom the government sought to eliminate for other reasons.

These victims became know as the "disappeared." Their plight is still poignantly brought to light by the Mothers of Plaza de Mayo, a group of women who have kept vigil for lost friends and relatives in that plaza in Buenos Aires since 1977 and whose movement has grown into an internationally recognized human rights organization. Already by 1979 the wholesale imprisonments prompted US President Carter to offer asylum to those languishing in Argentine jails.

In 1983, having deeply miscalculated in provoking and losing the Falklands War with Great Britain, the junta stepped down, elections were held, and a National Commission of the Disappearance of Persons (CONADEP) was established in December. While the figures vary greatly, from 15,000 to perhaps 30,000 "disappeared," the progress of the commission and its findings of torture, killing, and indefinite incarceration caused an international sensation. Today, most of the surviving military and political leaders held responsible are in prison themselves or have already served lengthy terms. As with so many other aspects of the Cold War era, the consequences for those involved have far outlived the conflict itself.

Putting It All Together

During the years 1962 to 1991, from the Cuban Missile Crisis to the dissolution of the Soviet Union, the Cold War contest between the two remaining twentieth-century versions of modernity—capitalist democracy and the different varieties of communism-socialism—reached its climax. At the beginning of the period it seemed at the very least that communism was competing evenly, perhaps even winning, in its appeal to so many developing nations and their leaders. But in the end, the wealth and power of the West, particularly the United States, ultimately wore the Soviet Bloc down. Along the way, the most populous communist state, China, abruptly changed from extreme radical leftist programs during its Cultural Revolution to a very capitalist style of market economics by 1991. Many other countries were now looking for some mixture of the two systems or a third way between the two for their own development. As the period drew to a close, it was, ironically, the two iconic communist regimes, the Soviet Union and the People's Republic of China, that were pioneering the way *out* of Marxist socialism. The Chinese sought to do this by retaining a powerful authoritarian government while embracing market economics.

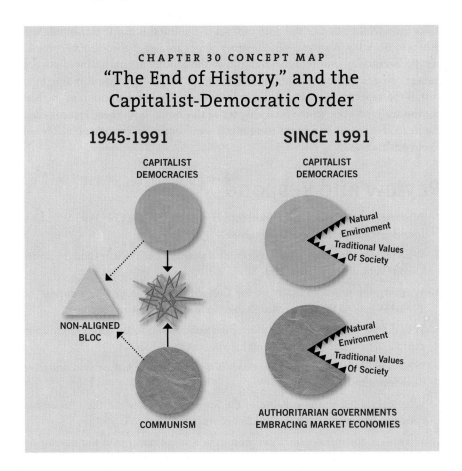

CHAPTER 30 CONCEPT MAP
"The End of History," and the
Capitalist-Democratic Order

The former Soviet Union adopted democratic political values and guardedly introduced capitalism.

For the people of the world observing these changes it might indeed have seemed as if the triumphant words of Francis Fukuyama's 1989 essay "The End of History?" actually did sum up the age:

> a remarkable consensus concerning the legitimacy of liberal democracy as a system of government had emerged throughout the world over the past few years, as it conquered rival ideologies like hereditary monarchy, fascism, and most recently communism. More than that, however . . . liberal democracy may constitute the "end point of mankind's ideological evolution" . . . and as such . . . the end of history.

The next two decades, however, would see the emergence of new and unanticipated challenges to the domination of the capitalist-democratic order. For many, its secular character and its breaking down of traditional norms of family, gender, and sexuality in the West convinced them that the evolving culture of this surviving version of modernity would undermine the core values of their own societies. Hence, like the reformers in many of the old empires of the nineteenth century, they engaged in an erratic struggle to acquire the material advantages of modernity while isolating themselves from the cultural threat it presented. Still others in both the West and various other places around the world had come to see the forces of modernity as breaking down the delicate natural balance between human beings and the environment (see Concept Map). They therefore sought to curtail the rapacity of capitalist-democratic countries and corporations in their contest for resources. In the final chapter of this book, both these trends—and the devil's bargain they present to so many—will occupy a considerable amount of our attention.

Review and Respond

1. What were some of the most important turning points of the Cold War? Why have historians designated these as important?

2. What factors ushered in the era of *détente* between the United States and the Soviet Union? Why did this period end?

3. What are the principal causes of the Cultural Revolution in China during the 1960s? What was the role of Mao Zedong in inaugurating it and ending it?

4. Why did the Soviet leadership launch their policies of glasnost and perestroika in the mid-1980s? Did these programs help or hurt the USSR?

5. What is meant by feminism? How do we distinguish among first, second, and third wave feminism?

6. What causes led to the collapse of the Soviet bloc? How did the relationship between the Soviet Union and its allies contribute to this collapse?

7. What were the main political, economic, and social patterns in the developing world from 1963 to 1991? How does the Marxist theory of underdevelopment differ from the modernization theory?

8. Some have claimed that the end of the Cold War spelled the end of ideological struggle—even the "end of history." Do you think this argument has merit on its own terms? Why or why not?

> For additional resources, including maps, primary sources, visuals, and quizzes, please go to www.oup.com/us/vonsivers. Please see the Further Resources section at the back of the book for additional readings and suggested websites.

Thinking Through Patterns

▶ **How did the political landscape of the Cold War change from 1963 to 1991?**

Perhaps the biggest changes came in the 1980s. Though the United States had been defeated politically in Vietnam and was facing a recession at home, it still was the world's largest economy and could weather a protracted arms race. Though it was not fully perceived at the time, the Soviet Union was far more economically fragile—which ultimately made it ideologically fragile as well. The strains of Polish dissent, the Afghan War, and a renewed arms race with the United States simply wore the Soviet state down.

The unprecedented prosperity of the United States and the West more generally allowed younger people to attend universities in record numbers, experiment with new ideas of living, and simply indulge their desires for fun and new experiences. The idealism of the era also played a role, as did the threat of the draft and the larger threat of nuclear war. For many, the materialism of the age repelled them and made them long for a simpler, more "authentic" existence. Thus, a popular motto from the time was "turn on, tune in, drop out."

▶ **Why did such radically different lifestyles emerge in the United States and the West during the 1960s and 1970s? What is their legacy today?**

▶ **Why did some nations that had emerged from colonialism and war make great strides in their development while others seemed to stagnate?**

By and large, the nations that prospered were the ones that had already achieved self-sufficiency in agriculture, had at least the basic of a transportation and communications infrastructure, and were resourceful in adopting policies that maximized their labor force. Taiwan, South Korea, and Singapore are good examples of countries that made great strides in their development during this period. China, under Deng Xiaoping, followed a modified version of this strategy and was already growing at record levels by 1991. In the following decades, nearly all Asian countries (an exception being North Korea) would follow suit, with India moving into the top ranks of development and growth. Many Latin American countries—in particular, Brazil—also make great strides, and the drive to follow the example of using cheap labor to create a successful export manufacturing base was also took hold in Africa.

In all cases, culture and ideology could and did play a powerful role in setting the psychological conditions for citizens to believe that progress was possible. Peace and stability also played, for obvious reasons, an important role. he many internal conflicts that pockmarked Latin America and Africa held back development during this period.

Chapter 31

1991-2011

A Fragile Capitalist-Democratic World Order

Population increase, 1950–2010
Country where population increased by:
☐ 0–100%   ☐ 200–300%
☐ 100–200%   ■ over 300%

It was a scene that had been repeated hundreds of times across North Africa and the Middle East during the winter of 2010 and the early spring of 2011. First in Tunisia in December, then with daily regularity in Egypt, Libya, Bahrain, Yemen, and Syria, growing crowds gathered to remonstrate with authoritarian governments over a wide range of issues that had marked the process of modernity for two centuries: the constitutional rights of life, liberty, security, economic opportunity, emancipation of minorities and women, and freedom of expression; the rights of ethnic and religious groups to nationhood, autonomy, or even mere existence.

Seeing Patterns

▶ How did the United States acquire its dominant economic position toward the end of the twentieth century? How did it accelerate the process of globalization?

▶ What made capitalist democracy so attractive toward the end of the twentieth century that it became a generic model for many countries around the world to strive for?

▶ Which policies did China and India pursue so that they became the fastest industrializing countries in the early twenty-first century?

▶ How have information technology and social networking altered cultural, political, and economic interactions around the world?

▶ What is global warming, and why is it a source of grave concern for the future?

The governments challenged by these movements had long been entrenched behind brutal and repressive security services. Unable or unwilling to broaden political participation, aging authoritarian rulers had groomed their sons or favorites to succeed them. The rulers pretended to have liberalized the economies of their countries, but instead "crony capitalism" benefited their relatives and followers and discouraged entrepreneurial innovation. Chronic unemployment and underemployment left both the poor and the middle class in despair over their future. For many years, the unemployed youth of the Middle East had found solace in an Islamism whose preachers promised it would be the solution for all ills. But the ability of these preachers to deliver had turned out not to be any better than that of the increasingly despised rulers. A general stagnation had set in throughout the region.

By mid-spring 2011 the relentlessly repeated, massive, and unarmed street protests had toppled the governments of Tunisia and Egypt. Crowds massed as well in Syria, Bahrain, Libya, and Yemen. Syria and Bahrain sought to suppress the democracy movements while in Libya and Yemen civil wars tore the populations apart. More remarkably, however, was that

The Arab Spring. Tawakkol Karman, a religiously conservative journalist and mother of three, received the 2011 Nobel Peace Prize for her nonviolent struggle for democracy and the safety of women. Throughout the year, she remained steadfastly devoted to a democratic future for Yemen even as the country descended into civil war. Here she leads a rally in Sana, the capital.

1101

here in this male-dominated bastion of conservative Islam, the movement was being led by that most "modern" of world personalities, a charismatic female journalist and grassroots organizer. Armed with computers, smart cell phones burgeoning with apps, Twitter, Facebook, and all the latest tools of social networking, Tawakkol Karman, 32, leader of "Women Journalists Without Chains" and mother of three, harangued mostly male crowds of thousands with calls for revolution. "We will make our revolution or we will die trying," she thundered, her words echoing those of so many insurgents of the recent past. "We are in need of heroes," said one Yemeni observer. "She manages to do what most men cannot do in a society that is highly prejudiced against women." But with her personal role models including Nelson Mandela of South Africa, Mohandas Gandhi of India, and Martin Luther King Jr. and Hillary Clinton of the United States, Karman as much as any woman of her time embodied the choices and challenges marking the patterns of world history in the rapidly globalizing early twenty-first century.

Many of the challenges faced by Yemen today are shared by many small, poor, largely traditional societies confronting the growing momentum of capitalist-democratic modernity. Its authoritarian government, for all its faults, has maintained a fragile balance among Yemen's many feuding tribes and religious groups; if and when it falls, what will take its place? Will its tribal groups unite or "balkanize?" As the war on terror continues, will the United States and the West risk chaos in the region as a magnet for such opponents of secular culture as al-Qaeda? What prospects are there for emancipation of women in such a traditional society, especially if economic development in this harsh land stays problematic? How will the continued progress of environmental degradation affect a new regime's approach to economic modernization? Little grows in many parts in the best of times; moreover, like many peoples in the region, Yemenis have traditionally enjoyed chewing *qat*, a mildly narcotic shrub leaf. But the plants themselves and the water needed to process them take up precious resources. Will a future government act to curtail the practice? At what cost? And perhaps the most immediate question: Will political empowerment along constitutional lines resulting from a revolution be sufficient to satisfy the aspirations of the Yemenis who took to the streets?

In the largest sense, then, achieving modernity through the surviving route of urbanization, science, industrialization, the accumulation of capital, and grassroots participation in political pluralism has become close to a universal goal in the world. Where it will lead is anyone's guess. But the story of how this pattern of modernity has grown to become nearly universal—and the old and new forces that oppose it—is the focus of this final chapter in our survey of world history.

Capitalist Democracy: The Dominant Pattern of Modernity

With the demise of communism, the struggle among the three ideologies of modernity that had characterized much of the twentieth century now was over. In the first flush of enthusiasm, some Western observers declared history to have ended, henceforth to be written merely as a series of footnotes to the triumph of capitalism and democracy in the world. Others prophesized soon after that culture would replace ideology as the basis for world competition. More sober observers expressed the hope that capitalist modernity in the coming decades would become an increasingly generic pattern, adoptable in non-Western cultures. But they also realized that democracy would not spread rapidly as long as countries remained poor and stuck in inherited forms of authoritarianism or even autocracy. History continued, the nation-state (as problematic as it was in many parts of Africa and Asia) became standard across the world, and its citizens strove for adaptation to the now dominant pattern of modernity: capitalism, democracy, and consumerism.

A Decade of Global Expansion: The United States and the World in the 1990s

In the aftermath of the oil crisis of 1985–1986, and with even greater vigor after the collapse of communism in 1991, the United States advocated free trade, fiscal discipline, and transnational economic integration as the proper course for world development. It did so as the most economically and politically powerful country. Two characteristics made the United States the sole superpower it currently is. First, the United States dominated the so-called dollar regime—that is, dollars functioned as the currency for all oil sales and purchases. In fact, despite the growth in popularity of the European Union's euro, and other major currencies like the English pound, Swiss franc, and Japanese yen, the dollar remained in a very real sense the world's currency. Second, with its giant consumer economy, the United States functioned as the world's favored destination for manufactured goods, particularly from East Asia. The leverage which the United States gained from these two economic functions was bolstered by overwhelming military force, which made the United States the principal enforcer of peace in the world.

A Hierarchy of Nations   During the 1990s, there were some 190 sovereign countries in the world, forming a three-tier hierarchy. At the top of the first tier, almost in a category of its own, was the United States. It was the richest, most evolved constitutional nation-state, based on a mature scientific–industrial society,

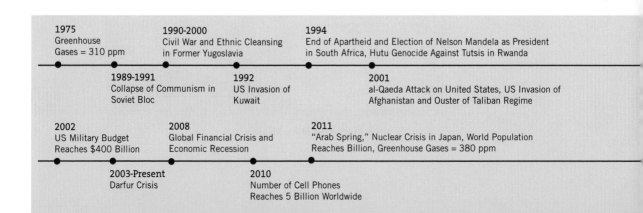

1975
Greenhouse
Gases = 310 ppm

1990-2000
Civil War and Ethnic Cleansing
in Former Yugoslavia

1994
End of Apartheid and Election of Nelson Mandela as President
in South Africa, Hutu Genocide Against Tutsis in Rwanda

1989-1991
Collapse of Communism in
Soviet Bloc

1992
US Invasion of
Kuwait

2001
al-Qaeda Attack on United States, US Invasion of
Afghanistan and Ouster of Taliban Regime

2002
US Military Budget
Reaches $400 Billion

2008
Global Financial Crisis and
Economic Recession

2011
"Arab Spring," Nuclear Crisis in Japan, World Population
Reaches Billion, Greenhouse Gases = 380 ppm

2003-Present
Darfur Crisis

2010
Number of Cell Phones
Reaches 5 Billion Worldwide

sophisticated financial institutions, and by far the most powerful military. In addition, it could boast the densest infrastructure of universities, colleges, public libraries, museums, theaters, and other cultural institutions. Below the United States, the fully industrialized democracies in Europe, North America, and Australia occupied the rest of the first tier. In the course of the 1990s, four "newly industrialized countries" joined this tier, the Asian "Tigers" or "Dragons:" Taiwan, South Korea, Hong Kong, and Singapore. Such was the economic power of the 30 fully industrialized and largely democratic countries in the top tier that they alone conducted nearly three-quarters of all world trade in goods and services.

In the second tier of the world hierarchy were 88 "middle-income countries," according to the United Nations' definition. These were developing countries in economic and democratic "transition." They were either industrializing states in the Middle East, South Asia, East Asia, and Latin America or reindustrializing states located in the former Communist Bloc. The reindustrializing states were replacing their obsolete communist-era manufacturing infrastructures with modern systems. In the broad bottom tier were 66 countries defined as "low-income" or "poor," located for the most part in sub-Saharan Africa and Southeast Asia. Many of these countries were in early stages of economic development, with little or no democratization (see Map 31.1).

In 2000, about one-fifth of the world's population of 6 billion lived in fully industrialized countries, two-thirds in middle-income countries, and 15 percent in poor countries. The world population was still expanding, but the pace of the expansion was slowing, largely as a result of improved female education and contraceptives. The dominance of scientific–industrial society was such that only two centuries after

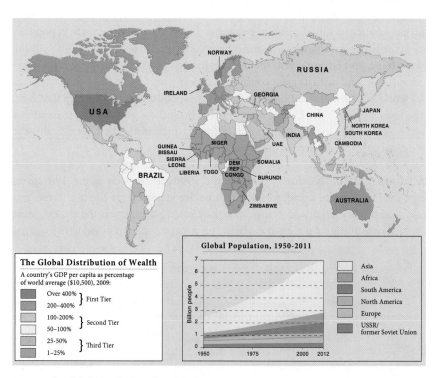

MAP **31.1** **The Global Distribution of Wealth, 2009.**

its beginnings 90 percent of the world population was more or less integrated into the pattern of capitalist modernity characterized by market exchange and consumerism and no longer by traditional agrarian–urban subsistence agriculture.

The Dollar Regime   The United States stood at the top of the world hierarchy thanks largely to the power of its financial system. The beginnings of this system date back to the years following 1971 when President Richard Nixon took the dollar off the gold standard. At that time, in a period of war expenditures in Vietnam and high inflation, the United States was running out of gold payable for dollars at the internationally agreed price of $35 an ounce. Two years later, Nixon persuaded the Middle East–dominated Organization of Oil-Producing Export Countries (OPEC) to accept only dollars as means of payment for oil. In support of Egypt and Syria against Israel in the October War of 1973, OPEC had just quadrupled oil prices. Despite American support for Israel, however, OPEC was anxious to remain in the good graces of the United States as its largest buyer. As a result of the Nixon–OPEC deal, the dollar took over from gold as the acknowledged international standard of exchange.

Under the **dollar regime**, all oil-importing countries, except for the United States, had to manage two currencies. One, denominated in dollars, was for energy purchases; the other, in domestic currencies, was for the internal market of oil consumption. Countries had to carefully look after the strength of their domestic currency as rising dollar prices could lead to severe crises in efforts to control inflationary domestic prices and pay back foreign, dollar-denominated loans. OPEC countries on their part invested their "petrodollars" in US Treasury bills ("T-bills"), as well as in American stocks and bonds. There were repeated grumblings among the non-oil producers of the world, both developed and developing, about being cheated by the dollar regime. But the US–OPEC deal did endure, backed up by a gigantic American financial system that emerged as a result of the dollar regime.

Dollar regime: A system maintained by the United States whereby dollars are the sole currency in which the price of oil and most other commodities and goods in the world are denominated; the regime forces most countries to maintain two currencies, with consequent financial constraints.

The United States as an Import Sinkhole   In a parallel development, the United States tied the industrial countries of the world to itself by becoming the country to which everyone wanted to export. Building these ties was particularly important in East Asia. During the Cold War, the United States had encouraged import substitution industrialization along the lines of Japan in Korea, Taiwan, Hong Kong, Thailand, and Southeast Asian countries. By becoming prosperous, so it was assumed, these countries would be less susceptible to the expansion of communism. Although uneven, the industrialization process advanced apace in most East Asian countries. In the 1990s, it reached levels where the United States began to pressure the Asia Tigers to reduce import substitution protectionism and replace it with free trade. In return for the United States buying their industrial goods, the countries of East Asia agreed to give free access to American financial institutions, such as banks and hedge funds.

In the meantime, communism collapsed and China, pushing its own import substitution industrialization, began to export cheap industrial goods as well to the United States. In the 1990s, aided by abundant cheap labor, these goods undercut those produced by the Asian Tigers and the United States became an even deeper "sinkhole," this time for textiles, toys, and simple electrical and electronic devices made in the People's Republic of China. The United States in effect underwrote China's industrialization, binding the country's economic interests closely to its own financial interests within the dollar regime (see Map 31.2).

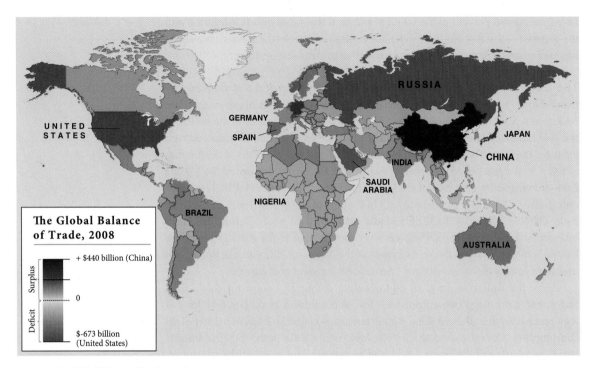

MAP **31.2** **The Global Blance of Trade, 2008.**

US Technological Renewal and Globalization Communism had collapsed in part because the Soviet Union had been unwilling or unable to leap into the new industrial age of consumer electronics. The United States, by contrast, transformed itself thoroughly in the 1990s. Electronics was one of those periodic new technologies with which capitalism, always threatened by falling profit rates in maturing industries, became more profitable again. By computerizing industrial processes, businesses saved on labor. Personal computers in offices made bureaucratic procedures more efficient. A fledgling Internet speeded up communication. An entirely new branch of industry, **information technology (IT)**, put cell phones, online delivery of music and entertainment, and a vast array of other services into the hands of consumers. In the phrase of the Nobel Prize Laureate in economics, Joseph Stiglitz, the United States had entered the "roaring nineties."

During this decade, the national budget was balanced; America became the leader in what was now called the "high-tech industry" of electronics, microbiology, and pharmacology; unemployment shrank; inflation remained low; and the foreign debt was moderate. Worldwide, the volume of trade goods doubled and the volume of capital flows quadrupled. The US Federal Reserve kept up with demand and printed more than half as many dollars in the course of the 1990s as were already in circulation. The domestic economy was humming, and the dollar was literally as good as gold even in remote corners of the world.

The only blemish in the **globalization** process, from an American perspective, was continued protectionism and low consumption in many Asian countries. President Bill Clinton's (in office 1993–2000) closest economic advisors were bankers and investors who had greatly expanded the size and influence of the financial services sector since the Nixon years. This sector handled the spectacularly enlarged

Information technology: The array of computers, information, electronic services, entertainment, and storage available to business and consumers; with information increasingly stored in "the cloud," that is, storage centers rather than individual computer hard drives.

volume of dollars floating around in the world. Alongside the traditional means of investment—stocks and bonds—new, more speculative instruments called "derivatives" gained in popularity. Derivatives were complex bets on higher or lower future prices of stocks, bonds, commodities, currencies, or anything else traded on the world market. The US globalization offensive in the 1990s was thus in large part an effort to open protected foreign markets to American financial institutions.

Globalization: The ongoing process of integrating the norms of market economies throughout the world and binding the economies of the world into a single uniform system.

Globalization and Its Critics   In many ways, the dollar and sinkhole regimes were so complex that they attracted critics from the entire political spectrum dissatisfied with one or another specific aspect of the evolving system. Conservative critics were appalled that the United States no longer adhered to the gold standard and sacrificed its sovereignty to oil sheikhs trading oil for dollars. They furthermore bemoaned the disappearance of the traditional manufacturing sector and its replacement by financial institutions and Internet start-ups that produced nothing tangible. In their judgment, the United States could be held hostage to policy dictates by the foreign holders of T-bills.

Progressive critics accused the United States of using its arrangements with OPEC and the East Asian countries to exclude the poorer countries in the world that had little to offer. In their opinion, the United States pursued the establishment of an imperialist capitalist system that limited wealth to a minority of industrialized and industrializing countries and refused to share it with the have-nots. Progressive criticisms were expressed in vociferous protests and occasionally even riots, accompanying meetings among the leaders of the industrial nations, usually in posh resorts around the world. Overall, however, both conservative and progressive criticisms remained marginal during the 1990s, given the general prosperity of the industrial countries.

US Military Dominance   Parallel to pursuing global economic integration, the United States emphasized a number of basic political principles in the 1990s. A first principle was that America was and must continue to be the unchallenged military power in all regions of the world. It defined itself as the guarantor of last resort for the maintenance of world peace. Accordingly, in the year 2002, the US military budget amounted to $400 billion. This astronomical sum was considerably smaller than during the Cold War but still larger than the defense budgets of the next eight countries combined. On the basis of this military machine, President Bill Clinton operated from a position of de facto world dominance. His successor, George W. Bush (in office 2001–2009), articulated this dominance in an official doctrine, the "national security strategy" of 2002. American might was highly visible in all parts of the world, generating considerable resentment among those for whom the combined economic–military power of the United States amounted to a new kind of world dominance (see Map 31.3)

Intervention in Iraq   The national security strategy elevated two policies already in practice into doctrine: prevent countries from establishing dominance in a region and destroy terror organizations bent on destruction in the United States. The first policy was enacted after Saddam Hussein (1937–2006) and his Baath regime occupied Kuwait (1990–1991). President George H. W. Bush (in office 1989–1993) intervened when it became clear that Saddam Hussein, by invading

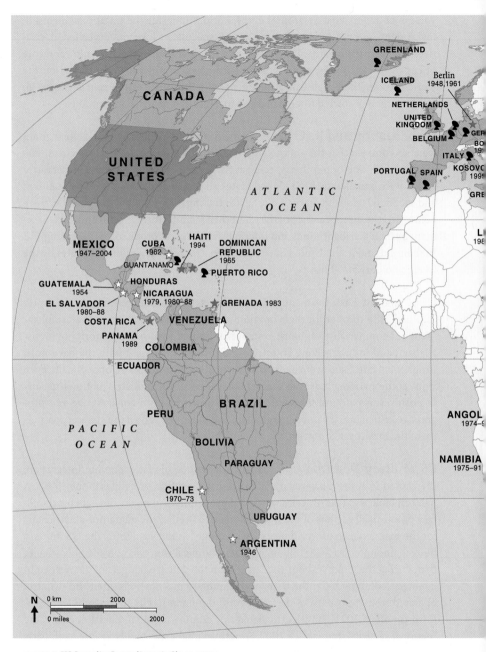

MAP **31.3** **US Security Commitments Since 1945.**

Kuwait, wanted dominance over Middle Eastern oil exports from Saudi Arabia and the region was unable or unwilling to prevent him from achieving it. At the head of a coalition force and with UN backing, in 1992 Bush ordered US troops to evict the Iraqis from Kuwait in Operation Desert Storm. In a devastating combined air and ground war of 6 weeks the coalition force drove the Iraqi occupiers from Kuwait.

In the following decade, the United States and United Nations subjected Iraq to a stringent military inspection regime to end Saddam Hussein's ambitions for acquiring nuclear and chemical weapons. The inspectors discovered large quantities

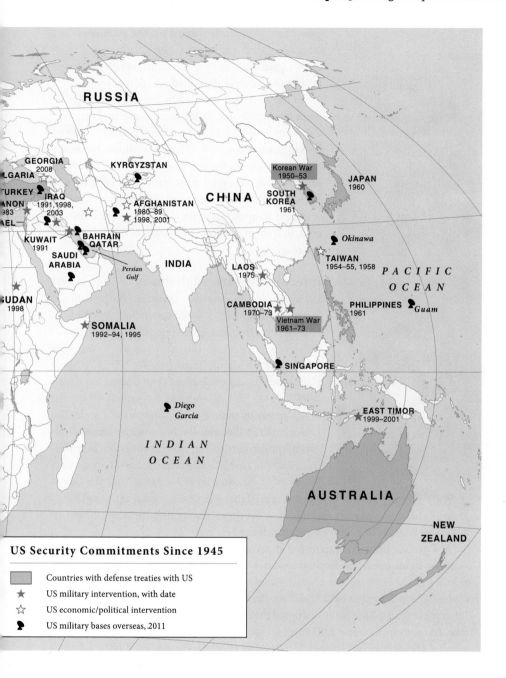

US Security Commitments Since 1945

▨ Countries with defense treaties with US
★ US military intervention, with date
☆ US economic/political intervention
♟ US military bases overseas, 2011

of weapons and supervised their destruction. But in the face of massive Iraqi efforts at obstruction, the inspectors eventually left. Their departure was followed by a retaliatory US bombardment of Baghdad in 1998. After the US invasion of Afghanistan in 2001, a chastened Saddam Hussein readmitted the inspectors. Their inability to find anything significant touched off an intense debate among the members of the UN Security Council. The United States and Great Britain considered further inspections worthless, while France, Russia, and China argued that these inspections should be given more time. A stalemate ensued, and in an extraordinarily

Day of Infamy. Smoke billowing from the north tower of the World Trade Center in New York on September 11, 2001. The south tower had already collapsed. Nearly 3,000 people died in the inferno, in which the heat of the exploding commercial airplanes in the interior of the high rises melted the steel girders supporting the buildings.

passionate worldwide discussion the multilateralists who advocated continued United Nations–led sanctions squared off against the unilateralists favoring a preemptive United States–led invasion of Iraq.

In the end, in March 2003, President George W. Bush espoused the unilateralist cause and ordered a preemptive invasion without Security Council backing, arguing that Iraq had once more become a regional threat. To the surprise of many, Saddam Hussein's regime put up little resistance and fell after just 3 weeks to the vastly superior US armed forces. Afterward, no weapons of mass destruction were discovered, in spite of an intense scouring of every corner of the country.

Intervention in Afghanistan   The second US principle announced in President Bush's national security strategy was swift retaliation, prevention, and even preemption against nonstate challengers of American supremacy. This doctrine was a response to the rise of Islamic terrorism. In 1992, al-Qaeda ("the base") under the leadership of Osama bin Laden (1957–2011) had emerged as the principal terrorist organization operating on an international scale. Bin Laden, multimillionaire son of a wealthy Yemen-born Saudi Arabian contractor, won his spurs as a holy warrior (*mujahid*) for Islam against the Soviet occupation forces in Afghanistan (1979–1989). After the Soviet retreat from Afghanistan, he turned against the United States. In his eyes, America was a godless country without moral principles, bent on a Western crusade to destroy Muslim independence.

Al-Qaeda's campaign of terrorism climaxed on September 11, 2001. Suicide commandos, in an operation beyond anyone's imagination, hijacked four commercial airliners in the northeastern United States and crashed them into the World Trade Center's Twin Towers in New York City, the Pentagon outside Washington, D.C., and (after passengers on the plane disrupted the attempted hijacking) a field near Shanksville, Pennsylvania. Nearly 3,000 people died in the disasters. In response, US troops invaded Afghanistan on October 7, 2001, in an effort to eliminate bin Laden, who was protected by the regime in power. They destroyed the pro-al-Qaeda government of the Taliban, receiving support from anti-Taliban Afghans, and drove the al-Qaeda terrorists to western Pakistan. It took another decade for the United States to track down and assassinate bin Laden (May 2011) and several of his close collaborators and to come to grips with the resurgent Taliban terrorists in its ongoing war in Afghanistan.

The United Nations and Regional Peace   Even though it was the United States and sometimes the North Atlantic Treaty Organization (NATO) that guaranteed peace in the 1990s and early 2000s and not the United Nations, the UN nevertheless fulfilled vital, if not always successful, peace missions in regional conflicts.

An important example of a failure in this regard was the Rwandan civil war of 1994, in which mostly French peacekeeping troops serving under UN auspices looked the other way as the Hutu ethnic majority massacred the Tutsi ethnic minority by the hundreds of thousands. On the other hand, despite the bloodshed on both sides, the crisis in the Sudan saw the United Nations fare somewhat better. Two vicious civil wars raged between Arab Muslim northern Sudan, on the one hand, and Christian and animist southern Sudan (1983–2005) and the African Muslim region of Darfur in western Sudan (2003–present), on the other. After lengthy efforts under UN mediation, the two sides in the first conflict agreed to the secession of South Sudan as an independent country in 2011. The second conflict continued to smolder, with the United Nations pursuing criminal charges against the president of Sudan and an African Union force seeking to protect the refugees from Arab-inspired attacks. First steps toward settling the ethnic–religious conflicts in Sudan were taken, but much more needed to follow.

American Finances Go Global: Crisis and Recovery

Under the umbrella of world peace maintained by the United States and United Nations, the world economy dominated by the dollar regime expanded during the early 2000s. In the so-called Washington Consensus, lasting a little more than a decade (1989–2002), Western economists and foreign aid officers preached "stabilize, privatize, and liberalize" to the governments of the emerging nations. To receive investments, foreign aid, or emergency loans to overcome recurrent economic crises, recipient countries had to submit to stringent rules concerning balanced budgets, the privatization of state firms, and the opening of protected branches of the economy. Submission to the Washington consensus, however, in many cases had unforeseen consequences.

Spurred by the consensus in the 1990s, private US investors had nearly tripled the value of their assets abroad, to a total of over $6.5 trillion. On the other hand, the now more accessible public and private financial systems in many newly industrialized and developing countries were often not sufficiently robust to respond adequately. In a first crisis, the Mexican government—pressured in 1994 by inflation, budget deficits, and political instability—could not avoid devaluing the peso. It promptly ran out of pesos to service its short-term, dollar-denominated debt. Fortunately, President Clinton was at that time anxious to complete the North American Free Trade Agreement (NAFTA) with Canada and Mexico. He had Congress and the International Monetary Fund (IMF) bail out Mexico with a massive infusion of loans. (The IMF is an international bank, with the US government as the largest shareholder, that provides emergency loans to countries in sudden financial distress.) With the help of this loan, the Mexican government paid off the foreign lenders and steadied its financial system.

The next crisis began in 1997 in Thailand. Here, the state finances were more solid than in Mexico. The liberalized private banking sector was still in its infancy however, with huge unpaid loans on its books. When many private banks could not pay back their American creditors, the latter began withdrawing what they could from Thailand. American funds for derivatives moved in to speculate on the distress. Derivative managers specializing in currency bets sensed an imminent devaluation of the Thai currency, the *baht*. Since they bet with hundreds of billions of dollars, their speculation became a self-fulfilling prophecy. Accordingly, when the devaluation of the baht finally happened, it stripped Thailand of its currency reserves.

Thailand—in good times one of the world's leading tourist destinations—scraped along the edge of bankruptcy, recovered in 1999, but was thrown again into turmoil in 2010–2011 in a near-civil war over allegations of corruption in the government.

From Thailand the crisis expanded in 1998 quickly to Malaysia, Indonesia, and finally even the newly industrialized Korea, Singapore, and Taiwan. These countries suffered from variations of the same problem of overcommitted banks with nonperforming portfolios. They thereby made themselves also vulnerable to American derivatives speculators invading their financial markets. The IMF had to move in with massive loans to the Southeast and East Asian countries. In return, these countries had to tighten credit, close unprofitable banks and factories, tolerate higher unemployment, and promote increased exporting.

Newly industrialized South Korea was relatively successful with its reforms and quickly cranked up its exports again. Less developed Indonesia, however, was singularly unsuccessful. Large-scale demonstrations forced President Mohammed Suharto (in office 1967–1998) from office. Under weak successors and a slow recovery beginning in 2000, enraged Indonesian Muslims turned to militant Islamism or even terrorism as their solution for the country's persistent poverty. Thanks to the majority of moderate Muslims firmly opposed to terrorism and supportive of the new democratic process, however, an Islamic war of secession in Aceh ended in 2005 and politics entered regular democratic channels.

Russia's Crisis and Recovery   Russia defaulted in 1998 on its internal bonds and from 1999 to 2001 on several of its external loans. These defaults were a culmination of the disastrous postcommunist economic free fall. In the decade after 1991, Russia's gross domestic product (GDP) dropped by nearly half, a decline far worse than that experienced by the United States during the Great Depression of the 1930s. Ordinary Russians had to reduce their already minimal consumption by half of what they had been used to under communism. Moreover, the government had yet to dismantle the system of unproductive former state enterprises financing themselves through local tax collection. Consequently, the state was periodically starved of funds needed for the repayment of its external loans. Fortunately, higher oil prices after 2001 eased the debt situation of Russia somewhat.

The oil and gas revenues from state firms available directly to the government, however, strengthened its autocratic tendencies. The former KGB officer Vladimir Putin, president of Russia 2000–2008, was the principal engineer of this autocracy. He eliminated independent television and had state prosecutors go after potential political rivals. Pervasive corruption and obedience to state directives undermined the rule of law so severely that it was no longer possible to speak of the rule of law in Russia. Politically motivated assassinations of journalists, carried out by secret operatives suspected of enjoying government protection, went unpunished. Rival political parties were intimidated and elections manipulated. An obedient parliament changed the federal constitution so that presidents in the republics of the Russian Union were no longer elected but appointed. Given the small size of the private sector in the early 2000s, the country was still years away from subjecting its state enterprises to market rules and creating a comprehensive market economy.

After the Mexican, Asian, and Russian debt crises, private investors began to lose interest in the emerging markets of developing countries. With funds drying up, debt-ridden Latin American states became vulnerable. Thanks to an emergency IMF loan in 1999, Brazil narrowly avoided a financial meltdown. Argentina, however, in 2002 was less fortunate. Here, the government imprudently prolonged a recession with a tax hike. A yawning budget deficit remained unbalanced, high foreign debts were unpaid, and the peso had to be devalued. This time, however, the IMF did not bail out the government with an emergency loan, arguing that Argentina had been reckless with its finances. Without a loan, the government fell, the middle class was virtually wiped out, and the country—like Russia—limped in the next few years from one loan default to another. Recovery set in only toward the end of the decade.

Globalization and Poor Countries   The mixed record of development in the middle-income countries was mirrored in the bottom tier of poor countries. Even the World Bank had to admit in a 2000 report that the 1990s expansion with its freewheeling financial sector had brought little improvement to many countries in the bottom tier. Since these countries still had weak manufacturing bases, their governments relied on the export of mineral or agricultural commodities to finance development. Apart from the oil-rich desert states of the Middle East, some 50 poor states depended on three or fewer commodities for over half of their export earnings. In about 20 of these states, these commodities even made up over 90 percent of export earnings. As a result of overproduction on the world market, commodity prices were depressed through most of the 1990s. The price depression imposed severe budget cutbacks on many poor countries, with consequent unemployment, middle-class shrinkage, reduction in education, and a rise in AIDS cases.

Sex and Violence in the New Russia. An often lurid mixture of sex and violence has been a defining feature of post-Soviet popular culture and a source of much public concern. The illustration above shows the cover of a popular detective novel by Alexandra Marinina, *Death and a Little Love,* in 1995. Note the provocative positioning of the automatic pistol jutting at the face of the women in a way both startling and demeaning.

In a global view, however, the developing world benefited from the globalization of the 1990s. Poverty declined up until the recession of 2007, although this decline was unevenly distributed among the regions of the world. The World Bank defines as "absolutely poor" a man or woman who has to live on less than $1.25 a day. According to statistics compiled during 1990–2000, the total number of the poor went down from 29 to 24 percent, even though the world population grew by nearly 1 billion. As encouraging as this figure was, the gains were concentrated almost exclusively in East and South Asia, particularly China, Vietnam, and India. The number of the absolute poor actually increased in sub-Saharan Africa, Southeast Asia (except Vietnam), Russia and central Asia, and Latin America. Thus, while globalization benefited an absolute majority of humans, its uneven geographical distribution made the benefits look substantially smaller in many regions.

Contrasting Worlds. A quiet street early in the morning in Havana, with an old American car parked on the curb. The American embargo, together with a still dominant command economy prohibiting imports, forces most car owners in Cuba to hold on to their clunkers, repairing them over and over (a). A Vietnamese woman in a traditional straw hat and with two baskets, balanced on a pole, passing by a French luxury goods store in Hanoi, the capital of Vietnam. The country enjoyed near double-digit growth rates in its economy during the first decade of the 2000s (b).

The Communist Holdouts: North Korea, Cuba, China, and Vietnam

Communism as an official ideology survived in North Korea, Cuba, China, and Vietnam. North Korea and Cuba stubbornly continued to cling to both the command system and party control. China and Vietnam opened their command economies to the market but maintained single-party control and some large state firms. In both cases, the parties remained communist in name but became in fact ordinary autocracies presiding over capitalist economies.

North Korea and Cuba   After the death of North Korea's founding leader, Kim Il-Sung (b. 1912), in 1994, his son Kim Jong-il (b. 1941) became the Communist Party secretary and, thereby, the head of North Korea's government. He inherited a command economy in free fall, with Soviet subsidies having ended and strained relations with China after that country's normalization of relations with South Korea. Several years of floods and drought in the 1990s had accelerated the economic breakdown, culminating with a colossal famine, which killed some 2.5 million people—nearly one-fifth of the population. A moderate turnaround finally began in 1998 with the inauguration of an industrial zone with foreign investments and a limited free market. Kim Jong-il, the army, and the party remained unified during the catastrophic 1990s and continued their iron grip even through 2008 when the leader allegedly suffered a stroke. Since North Korea was a highly armed nuclear country asserting itself regularly through military provocations against South Korea, the political situation on the Korean peninsula continued to be unstable.

Cuba, too, suffered a severe setback when Soviet communism collapsed. Without Soviet subsidies and the ability to continue its sugar exports, the Cuban GDP shrank by one-third, imposing severe hardship on the population. President Fidel Castro (b. 1926) and the Communist Party were forced to reduce their reliance on the command economy. They allowed farmers to exceed their state quotas and grow fruits and vegetables for the open market, and a limited number of urban workers were allowed to open their own shops. Tourism was opened up, catering mostly to Europeans and East Asians since the long-standing US embargo continued almost unchanged. Thanks to a highly developed health sector, Cuba also built export-oriented pharmaceutical and biotechnological industries. During the early 2000s, the government was able to turn the economy around and achieve high growth rates. The hope of discovering substantial offshore oil fields even injected excitement into the country. Castro's resignation from the presidency for health reasons in 2008, however, raised questions of transitional politics similar to those concerning North Korea. In both countries communism remained outwardly as unreconstructed as ever.

The Chinese New Middle Class After the crushing experience of Tiananmen Square, the new Chinese middle class benefiting from the economic reforms of the Open Door and Four Modernizations had to accommodate itself as best it could to a repressive top layer and a corrosively corrupt bottom layer of a monopoly party that was communist in name but autocratic in practice. The basic characteristics of the middle class were remarkably similar to those of India and Turkey, discussed later in this chapter. Socially conservative migrants from the provinces to the cities found unskilled jobs in the early 1980s. They acquired skills and earned enough to send their children to school. From around 2005, the children, now with college degrees, took jobs as managers, technicians, professionals, and entrepreneurs in state companies, private firms, and Chinese branches of foreign firms. They began to flex their muscles as consumers.

The social conservatism of the middle class was rooted in rural popular religious practices, such as ancestral offerings and funeral rituals, blessings, or birthday festivals of gods that involved processions and pilgrimages to and from temples under the leadership of local Daoist priests. During the Maoist period, many temples were destroyed and practices outlawed, disrupting for nearly a generation the transmission of traditional customs. Since the mid-1990s, however, the government authorized or tolerated the reconstruction of temples and resumption of practices, while at the same time regulating the training and accreditation of Daoist and Buddhist ritual specialists. In villages, retired folk who remembered the customs participated in the reconstitution of temple committees, the collection of funds, and the staging of operas, marionette and puppet shows, or movies. In cities, the merged rural and urban scriptural traditions expressed themselves in a standardized Confucianism–Daoism–Buddhism under government control.

To keep the middle class from demanding political participation outside the Communist Party, the government pursued accelerated annual GDP growth, which in some years went into double digits. Wages rose beyond those paid in Vietnam,

Two Views of China Today. Despite recent attempts to regulate its pace, China's economic acceleration continues at or near double digits. In 2010, its GDP surpassed that of Japan to become second only to that of the United States. The new prosperity has created startling contrasts and a growing diversity of lifestyles in the PRC. In the image above, young Chinese hipsters sport T-shirts harkening back with purposeful irony to revolutionary leaders Mao Zedong and Cuba's romantic figure of Che Guevara. In the lower panel, China's current leadership—smartly decked out in Western suits and "power ties"—strive to steer the country toward continued growth as the means to preserve the ascendancy of the Chinese Communist Party.

Disharmonious Society

"On the other hand . . . there now are so many acutely 'unharmonious' factors in Chinese society that the party policymakers have to spend their annual gathering to ponder possible solutions. For if society were quite harmonious, the party elite would devote their precious time to other more urgent issues.

"Indeed, social problems, such as the widening wealth gap and social injustices, have piled up to such an extent that if the CCP [Communist Party] were to fail to address them properly, its very legitimacy would be questioned and challenged . . .

"And there are good reasons for the CCP elite to be deeply concerned. The wealth gap has caused increasingly serious social differentiation, threatening social stability . . .

"One of the major causes for rapidly expanding wealth disparity is social injustice, which is also a major source of growing public discontent. Many people have gained their wealth not through their own enterprise but through their connections with officialdom . . ."

—Wu Zhong. "China Yearns for Hu's 'Harmonious Society.'" *Asia Times*, October 11, 2006, http://www.atimes.com/atimes/ China/HJ11Ad01.html.

Bangladesh, India, and Pakistan. Instead of spending its earnings, however, the middle class saved at rates double those in Japan or Europe prior to the recession of 2007. The only partially subsidized new health-care and education systems consumed much of those savings, even though the payments were bearable under the continued conditions of the one-child law. In addition, urban real estate and rental apartments became increasingly unaffordable in many Chinese cities during the early 2000s. Under the slogan of the "harmonious society"—in which all segments of the populace worked together with no toleration for "disruptive elements," or those advocating independence for Tibet or Uighur regions in Xinjiang—the government and party staked its continued legitimacy on ongoing economic progress.

The Chinese Countryside   This high-wire act was even more pronounced in the countryside. The government maintained the Maoist-era *hukou* registration system, which did not allow farmers to move to cities and find work without a permit, even though this system was largely ignored. The government reformed the system marginally but still refused to grant amnesty to some 100 million migrants working illegally in cities or allow their children access to urban schools. An equal number of farmers were pushed off their lands by authorities eager to make room for businesses, roads, and railroads. Since land continued to be state-owned and farmers were merely leaseholders, corrupt local authorities found it easy to cheat the farmers out of their land. The value of *guanxi* ("connections") thus continued more or less unabated. Tens of thousands of local protests annually in the early 2000s attested to a smoldering resentment in the villages, no matter how loudly the government touted its success in reducing the poverty rate.

The Transformation of Vietnam   As a country that looked to the Soviet Union for leadership, Vietnam was as surprised as Cuba when Soviet-style communism collapsed in 1991. Like the Soviet Union, Vietnam had begun economic liberalization reforms in 1986, especially in agriculture where farmers were permitted to sell above-quota harvests on the open market. Vietnam quickly became the world's third largest rice exporter, after the United States and Thailand, and reduced its poverty rate as drastically as China. But vehement ideological struggles over political liberalization did not end until a decade later with the decision to avoid a multiparty system, as did China a little later. Now the path to a full commitment to economic liberalization was open. In 1995–1996 Vietnam normalized relations with the United States, took out a large World Bank loan, revitalized foreign investment, and began reforming its unprofitable state firms by encouraging the participation of private domestic capital.

With stellar double-digit growth rates in the 1990s, Vietnam outpaced other poor Asian neighbors, such as Cambodia and Bangladesh, diversifying its manufacturing sector from textiles to footwear and electronics. Hong Kong, Taiwanese, and Korean companies, the principal foreign investors, showed a strong preference for Vietnam, on account of its advanced literacy rate and lower wages compared to China. A major new export sector from the later 1990s onward was *aquaculture*, the farming of shrimp, catfish, and tilapia. Vietnam was poised at the beginning of the second decade of the 2000s to move from the poor to the intermediate countries on the world list of nations moving to modernity.

A Decade of Global Shifts: Twenty-First Century Currents and Cross-Currents

In the first decade of the 2000s, there was a palpable swing toward pessimism in the West. Two recessions framed the decade, the Washington consensus fell apart over protests from borrower countries, and the problematic postwar settlement in Iraq demonstrated the limits of US power. The Middle East fared even worse, with terrorism, suicide bombings, no Arab–Israeli peace, and a potential Iranian nuclear bomb. By contrast, China and India, with strong economic growth rates, expanded their educated and entrepreneurial middle classes. Africa and Latin America, benefiting from the voracious demand for oil and minerals in China and India, experienced similarly strong growth. By the second decade of the 2000s, it was clear that, while there might be doubts about the course of modernity in the West, the commitment to it was growing everywhere else.

Unease in the West Two recessions in the first decade of the 2000s in the United States sapped much of the enthusiasm about the future of modernity that had begun so optimistically after the fall of communism. The first recession, of 2001–2003, was the so-called dot.com crisis, which had its origins in uncontrolled speculation about the expansion of the new medium of the Internet and the World Wide Web. The second recession, of 2007–2011, was rooted in private and public overspending (housing and credit). By 2011, US debts reached the astronomical sum of nearly $14.6 trillion (for comparison, the US GDP was $14.5 trillion).

The recession of 2001–2003 hit the African American and Hispanic working class particularly hard; in the following recession of 2007–2011 many white workers lost their jobs. An unraveling of the credit markets built on speculation on financial derivatives and "credit default swaps" in the mortgage sector spurred a cascade of financial failures in 2008. Only massive intervention by the federal government prevented a general financial panic. As anger over corporate greed, government bailouts, massive federal economic stimulus packages, and health-care reform grew among largely white, middle-class, older, and evangelical voters, a new "Tea Party" movement ("Taxed Enough Already") introduced radically populist antiestablishment and antiforeigner agendas into the political debate. The largely conservative middle classes of self-employed small businesspeople and professionals found themselves squeezed between unskilled and low-earning workers on the bottom and an expanding, increasingly rich upper middle class of corporate officers and Internet entrepreneurs on top, causing no small amount of unease.

The campaign and eventual election of Barack Obama (b. 1961, in office beginning 2009), a law professor and the first African American president of the nation, provided much optimism to a majority of Americans. At first, it appeared that the president's deficit-spending helped in steadying the recession of 2007–2011. But

> ### Edge People
>
> "Being 'Danish' or 'Italian,' 'American' or 'European' won't just be an identity; it will be a rebuff and a reproof to those whom it excludes. The state, far from disappearing, may be about to come into its own: the privileges of citizenship, the protections of card-holding residency rights, will be wielded as political trumps. Intolerant demagogues in established democracies will demand 'tests'—of knowledge, of language, of attitude—to determine whether desperate newcomers are deserving of British or Dutch or French 'identity.' They are already doing so. In this brave new century we shall miss the tolerant, the marginals: the edge people."
>
> —Tony Judt. "Edge People." *The New York Review of Books*, March 25, 2010. Judt, who died in 2010, was one of the leading critics of capitalist democracy.

soon this spending turned out to be insufficient, and the grind of the 2007–2011 recession soon dragged the ebullient mood down again. Meanwhile, conservatives and Tea Party activists relentlessly targeted government spending, health-care reform, illegal immigrants, and especially the slow economic recovery. In the 2010 elections, the Republicans regained the House and rejected tax increases to offset budget deficits out of hand.

A year later the Tea Party wing of the Republican Party held the nation hostage in the negotiations for an increase of the national debt ceiling. It nearly drove the country into default and the credit worthiness of the United States was damaged. Given the unwillingness of lawmakers to reform the tax code, the gap between the wealthy and poor—beginning with the electronic revolution and apparent opportunities for new wealth—continued to widen. This gap increasingly threatened the ability of middle-class Americans to consume and thereby sustain the capitalist system, given that 45–70 percent (depending on conservative or liberal calculations) of the GDP was consumer-generated.

Europe saw a similar trend of rising income disparities, although it was mitigated by a stronger manufacturing sector (around 20 percent of GDP vs. 11 percent in the United States in 2010) and a more generous social safety net. But the costs of this net weighed heavily on the budgets of many countries, seriously imperiling the future not only of, for example, Greece, Portugal, and Ireland (which fell into near bankruptcy in 2008–2011) but also of the European Union (1992) itself, as well as the euro, which was launched with great fanfare in 1999. Since the unemployed were entitled to long-term support in most European countries, the angry populist debate was more muted. Nevertheless, the rise of anti-Muslim immigrant political parties in Scandinavia and the Netherlands and the spectacle of unemployed youth in Portugal and Spain (up to 40 percent) setting up makeshift camps in major cities were stark reminders of the lack of confidence in the future of many young Europeans. As in the United States, optimism about the future of modernity was at a low ebb by the start of the new decade.

On the other hand, given the still comparatively strong, export-oriented manufacturing sector, Europe was years ahead of the United States in industrial innovation. In the first decade of the 2000s, European countries became the leading producers of renewable energy technologies, such as wind turbines, solar cells, and batteries. A study, carried out in Germany in 2010, suggested that it would be feasible for the country to shift entirely from fossil fuels to green energy by 2050. Europe also had an edge in the manufacture of fuel-efficient or electric cars and the exploration of hydrogen propulsion. Though nuclear energy was widely used, particularly in France, its future was open to question after the earthquake, tsunami, and partial nuclear power plant meltdown in Sendai, Japan, in the spring of 2011. The commitment to environmentalism in the early 2000s was much stronger in Europe than in the United States and in this sector at least, gloom is tempered with considerable hope.

A Bloody Civil War in Yugoslavia Eastern Europe and the Balkans went through an economic collapse and political restructuring similar to Russia, Ukraine, Belarus, and the other republics after the end of communism in 1991. This collapse and restructuring was mostly peaceful except for Yugoslavia, where a civil war raged from 1990 to 1995. Until the 1980s, communism was the main ideology in Yugoslavia through which the country's ethnic nationalisms of the Orthodox Christian Serbs (one-third of the population), Catholic Croats (20 percent), Muslim Bosnians (9 percent), Catholic Slovenes (8 percent), and mostly Muslim Kosovo Albanians (8 percent) were kept under the mantle of a federal constitution granting these ethnic groups a degree of autonomy. The main enforcer of communist unity, through carrot and stick, was President Josip Tito (1892–1980), a Croat whose authority—based on his legitimacy as an underground fighter against the Nazi occupation during World War II—was unimpeachable. After his death, however, the Serb president Slobodan Milošević (1941–2006) exploited the demographic superiority of his ethnic community for the establishment of political dominance while holding on to communism as the pro forma ideology.

Yugoslavia, like many Eastern European communist states, had borrowed heavily from Western countries to keep its industries from collapsing during the oil price slump of 1985–1986. At the end of the 1980s it was practically bankrupt, with hundreds of thousands of unemployed workers carrying their dashed hopes for the good life of consumerism in the city back to their native villages. This disappointment exploded in 1990 with extraordinary fury into deadly religious–nationalist hatred, led by the smaller ethnic groups against Serbs on their territories. The Serb supremacist-nationalist backlash, with an effort to "cleanse" minorities from their "greater Serbian" territory, was no less explosive. It took more than a decade for the European Union and the United States to stop the Serbs from murdering Bosnians and Albanians and enforce a semblance of peace in the Balkans.

Since then, the five successor states of Yugoslavia have struggled to adapt to capitalism and democracy. Slovenia did so quite successfully, while others like

Ethnic Cleansing. The upheavals in the wake of the breakup of the former Yugoslavia brought long simmering ethnic and religious tensions to the surface, particularly in the struggles between the Orthodox Serbs seeking to create a "greater Serbia" in Bosnia and Herzegovina and Bosnia's Muslims. In the accompanying photo, a woman, Hajra Eatiae--the president of the Association of Women of Srebenica--takes a poignant private moment in front of a wall of photographs of the 8,000 Bosnian victims of the massacre in the city of Srebenica at the hands of Serbs. Eatiae herself lost her husband and son in this largest European mass murder since World War II.

Bosnia-Herzegovina, Serb-controlled Bosnia, and Kosovo have not yet at all. Serb supremacist nationalism survived the longest and only gradually died down when the democratically elected pro-European government decided to arrest the main perpetrators of ethnic cleansing, Radovan Karadžić (b. 1945) and Ratko Mladić (b. 1943) in 2008 and 2011, respectively. The two had lived more or less openly in Serbia for years, protected by diehard followers. With these arrests and much relief, the Serbian government opened the way toward joining the European Union.

The Middle East: Paralysis, Islamism, and Liberation   As in the United States and Europe, the momentum that was generated after the collapse of communism had largely expired in the Middle East and North Africa by the early 2000s. In fact, with the exception of Turkey, a pall of economic and political paralysis hung over the region. The republics in the 1990s and early 2000s (e.g., Egypt, Syria, Algeria, Tunisia, and Yemen) inched intermittently toward privatization of state-run businesses but not at all toward democratization. Monarchies (Saudi Arabia, Jordan, Oman, and the Gulf sheikhdoms) actively encouraged private investment, especially in the oil sector, but were extremely cautious, if not altogether hostile, toward democratic reforms. Under the impact of the Arab Spring, in 2011 the kingdom of Morocco adopted constitutional reforms allowing for greater democracy. The "rejection front" of autocratic regimes in Iran and Syria, as well as the guerilla terrorist organizations Hezbollah in southern Lebanon and Hamas in the Gaza Strip, opposed Washington and globalization out of hand. Syria did, however, open state-controlled economy ever so cautiously to privatization in the early 2000s.

Islamism: Religious-nationalist ideology in which the reformed Sunni or Shiite Islam of the twentieth century is used to support the institutions of the state.

Islamism was a major factor accounting for the immobility of "republican autocrats" as well as monarchs. Western secular observers often expressed their surprise at the strength of the religious resurgence in the Middle East after watching its apparent demise with the rise of secular Arab nationalism and Arab socialism. In this case, however, while Islam was less visible in the region in the twentieth century when the political elites consisted of secular liberals and nationalists, it had not receded at all from the villages and poor city quarters, where it remained as vital as ever (see Map 31.4).

The key to understanding the rise of Islamism lay in the acceleration of rural–urban migration in the Middle East in the late 1990s and early 2000s. Ever since the 1960s, when Middle Eastern and North African governments built the first large state-run manufacturing plants in their cities, the workers were largely peasants arriving from villages with highly localized cultures of saintly Sufi or mystical Islam. They encountered militant preachers in the cities who—representing a unified, standard, urban Sunni Islam—were appalled by the "un-Islamic" saint cults among the workers. The children of these workers learned a similar standardized Islam in the schools, intended to buttress Arab nationalism, in which the Prophet Muhammad was the first nationalist. Standard Islam and militant urban Islamism gradually crowded out the rural saintly Islam and eventually produced small but potent offshoots of Islamist terrorism, such as al-Qaeda and the Taliban.

In the 1990s and early 2000s Middle Eastern governments essentially barricaded themselves behind their secret services and armies against the onslaughts of these Islamists. Terrorists attacked tourists, as happened periodically in Egypt, seeking to bring down a government that relied heavily on Western tourism. Sometimes they picked weak states such as Yemen, which, relying on dwindling oil revenues began

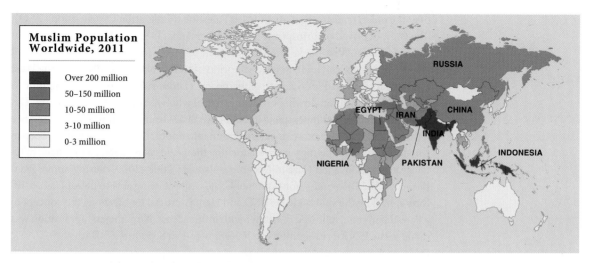

MAP **31.4** **Muslim Population Worldwide, 2011.**

to lose control of its nomadic tribes in the east, agricultural minorities in the north, and urban secessionists in the south, became a haven for al-Qaeda terrorists. Even a stronger state, Algeria, suffered a devastating civil war that claimed 150,000 victims from 1992 to 2002. Under the threat of Islamist terrorism, Middle Eastern and North African governments found it impossible to proclaim bold new initiatives of the kind that China or India advanced (see Map 31.4).

Islamic Terrorism and Israel   Two areas where Islamists achieved breakthroughs of sorts were Lebanon and the Gaza Strip. Hezbollah ("Party of God"), an Islamist guerilla organization with attendant social services and recruits from among the Shiite majority of Lebanese Muslims, waged an underground war against Israel and Westerners in Lebanon and abroad. Hezbollah was accused of bombing the US embassy in Beirut in 1983, hijacking an American airliner in 1985, and two bombings against Jews in Argentina in 1992 and 1994. Thereafter, the party changed its tactics, focusing its forces entirely on driving Israel out of southern Lebanon, which it achieved in 2000. Since then, it has steadily increased its role in the Lebanese government and in the Arab–Israeli conflict, regularly firing rockets into northern Israel. After a retaliatory Israeli invasion in 2006, Hezbollah and Israel, kept apart by a contingent of UN soldiers, returned to an uneasy standoff.

Israel successfully transformed itself during the globalization of the 1990s into an advanced economy specializing in high-tech software and microbiology. In 1994, it was officially at peace with two Arab neighbors, Egypt and Jordan. But it continued to face a hostile Arab Middle East and North Africa, in general, and restless Palestinians in the occupied territories on the West Bank and in Gaza, in particular. To protect its citizens from guerilla attacks, the Israeli government began building a border fence in 2002, supplemented in places by a wall of concrete slabs, inside the entire length of the occupied West Bank. In a parallel move it withdrew from the fenced-in Gaza Strip in 2005. Suicide attacks were fewer, but cross-border rocket attacks (from Gaza) increased, trapping Israel in a cat-and-mouse game of low-level cross-border warfare.

After 2006, Israel slid into an even worse trap. The first ever Palestinian elections gave the victory in Gaza to the Islamic guerilla organization Hamas, founded in 1988, over the older, secular, ethnic-nationalist Palestinian Liberation Organization (PLO). The PLO, deprived of its inspiring leader Yasser Arafat (1929–2004), was able to prevail only in the West Bank. The PLO refused to recognize the elections, and a civil war broke out, in which Hamas was victorious, forcing the PLO to retreat to the West Bank. Israel imposed a complete embargo on Hamas-ruled Gaza, in an attempt to bring the organization down. For those in Israel who wished to renew the Camp David peace process, left incomplete in 2000, the PLO–Hamas split was a disaster since it threw the entire idea of a two-state solution into doubt. Hamas was happy to deepen this doubt in the following years by launching thousands of rockets against Israel. In retaliation, Israel invaded Gaza in December–January 2008–2009, causing unmitigated misery for the Palestinian population of Gaza, without being able to defeat Hamas. Efforts at healing the split between PLO and Hamas, crucial for salvaging the concept of a Palestinian state, followed thereafter with little success. Nonetheless, application was made to the UN for recognition of a Palestine state in September 2011.

Israel's Predicament and the Iranian Bomb   Predictably, the failure of the invasion brought a conservative government into power in Israel. The government renewed the open pursuit of Israeli settlement construction on the West Bank while tightening the embargo on Gaza. But neither more Jewish settlements on the West Bank (making the two-state solution illusory) nor punishing Israel's neighbors Hezbollah and Hamas with invasions and/or embargoes brought the country closer to peace. Israel's long dominance over its neighbors, gradually acquired in the last half of the twentieth century, appeared to have reached its limits in the early years of the twenty-first.

Hezbollah and Hamas were able to assert themselves against Israel thanks to Iran, which supplied them with rockets. Iran, a leader of the rejection front against Israel, had experienced a "pragmatic" period after the death of its spiritual guide, Ruhollah Khomeini, in 1989. This pragmatism had raised the hope that the Shiite Islamist regime was lessening its policy of eradicating what it viewed as the "satanic" Western culture of secularism, liberalism, and pop culture. But the reformers were timid, and the still powerful clerics systematically undermined attempts at democratic and cultural reforms.

Any remaining hopes for reform were dashed when Mahmoud Ahmadinejad (b. 1956) [Ah-ma-DEE-nay-jahd], an engineer from a modest rural background, was elected president. He renewed the anti-Western crusade and adopted a policy of populism, with subsidies for food and gas as well as cash distributed by the suitcase on his cross-country trips. Most importantly, under his leadership, the Revolutionary Guard became not only the most effective military organization but, by investing in a wide variety of businesses, also a huge patronage machine. The precipitous decline of revenues from oil exports during the recession of 2008–2011, however, seriously reduced Ahmadinejad's populist largesse. Hence, he needed the Revolutionary Guard commanders to falsify the elections of 2009 to stay in power. Food and gasoline subsidies were cut substantially, but a nuclear program begun three decades earlier continued unabated. Suspected Iranian ambitions for acquiring a nuclear bomb, coupled with North Korea's already existing nuclear arsenal, created recurrent nightmares in the world about nuclear proliferation, "dirty" nuclear material in the hands of terrorists, and the possibility of nuclear war by "rogue" nations.

Guardians of the Revolution.
Female Iranian members
of parliament listening to
Iranian President Mahmoud
Ahmadinejad as he presents
his annual budget bill in
February 2011. Iran follows
strict gender segregation, with
women required to wear the
chador, a black cloak that covers
the full body, and the *hijab*,
a white headdress. Women
have, however, full access
to education and at present
number about 60 percent of all
university students.

The Ascent of Turkey   Turkey was the one Middle Eastern country to have
largely escaped Islamist militancy and become one of the most dynamic newly industrialized countries in the world. It became the top producer of TV sets in Europe and
began the construction of high-speed rail links as well as the world's deepest prefab-
ricated tunnel, under the Bosporus. In contrast to other regimes in the Middle East,
Turkish Muslims found access to the political process, thanks to a well established
and functioning multiparty system. After many false starts and interruptions by military coups d'état, an Islamic party in 1983 not only captured the premiership of the
country but simultaneously implemented bold new initiatives of economic privatization and industrial export orientation. Benefiting from these initiatives, an entire new
middle class of socially conservative but economically liberal entrepreneurial businesspeople arose. In an even more effective second wave of middle-class expansion
after 2003 under Prime Minister Recep Erdogan [RAY-jep Er-dow-AHN] (b. 1954),
Turkey's GDP climbed to become the world's fifteenth largest. Elections in June 2011
enabled Erdogan's party to garner slightly more than half of the vote and, on the basis of this vote, begin constitutional reforms which will rescind the military's role in
politics. Thus, Turkey largely completed its arrival in capitalist-democratic modernity.

The Arab Spring of 2011   Turkey was a model example for the compat-
ibility of Islam and democracy. But in spring 2011 Tunisia and Egypt each saw
constitutional-nationalist revolutions, which demonstrated that democracy can
sprout in Arab countries as well. On December 17, 2010, 26-year-old Mohamed
Bouazizi set himself ablaze in a last spectacular act of despair brought about by
the humiliations he had suffered at the hands of a Tunisian policewoman. For
months she had sought to drive him and his illegal produce cart from the streets of
Sidi Bouzid in central Tunisia. In a region plagued by 30 percent unemployment,
Bouazizi had become moderately successful selling his produce, which earned him
enough to support the university studies of one of his sisters. But on this day he had
finally had enough.

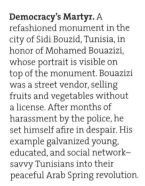

Democracy's Martyr. A refashioned monument in the city of Sidi Bouzid, Tunisia, in honor of Mohamed Bouazizi, whose portrait is visible on top of the monument. Bouazizi was a street vendor, selling fruits and vegetables without a license. After months of harassment by the police, he set himself afire in despair. His example galvanized young, educated, and social network–savvy Tunisians into their peaceful Arab Spring revolution.

Bouazizi's heartbreaking death touched off the mostly peaceful democratic revolutions dubbed the "Arab Spring," on which we centered this chapter's opening vignette. Beginning in Tunisia, they snowballed into Egypt, Libya, Bahrain, Yemen, and Syria in the course of early 2011. In Tunisia and Egypt they ousted longtime and aging autocrats, Tunisia's Zine El Abidine Ben Ali (r. 1987–2011) and Egypt's Hosni Mubarak (r. 1981–2011). After months of fighting, Libya's Muammar el-Qaddafi (r. 1969–Sep. 2011; killed October 20) was finally toppled. Autocratic rulers in countries seeing similar protests held on with iron nerves and unrestrained brutality. Central to the nonviolent daily rallies in Tunisia and Egypt, continuing for days and weeks, were demands for freedom, equality, fair elections, the end of corruption (especially crony capitalism), new democratic constitutions, the rule of law, and, last but not least, jobs.

The demonstrators, for the most part young, Internet-savvy, educated, and fully conversant with international youth culture, documented the events through pictures, videos, and blogs and revealed police violence for the world to instantly see. Social connectedness and the direct transmission of facts on the ground gave these constitutional revolutions a new character. Now a world public watching these events could declare solidarity with the demonstrators and demand action from its own politicians. As these democratic revolutions were beginning to be implemented, they raised the question of how closely the young demonstrators were integrated with the rest of the population—Islamists as well as the poor urban and rural traditional Muslims—to make constitutional and economic reforms meaningful for them as well (see Map 31.5).

The New Middle Class in India   The rise of a conservative Islamic middle class in Turkey had its parallel in India in the rise of a religiously conservative Hindu middle class of shopkeepers, traders, merchants, and small manufacturers who had chafed under the tyranny of the petty socialist bureaucrats from the Congress Party in the 1980s. The leading businesspeople in this middle class came from the relatively privileged commercial occupations within the Vaishya stratum of the caste system and were represented by the Indian People's Party (Bharatiya Janata Party, BJP). They demanded the dismantling of the Soviet-style state socialist system,

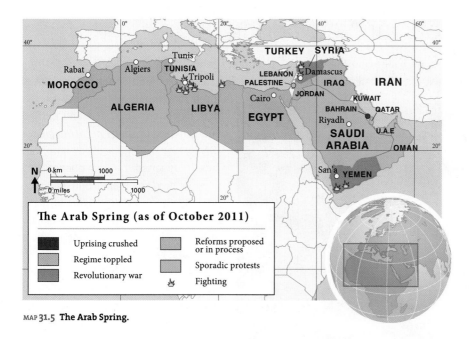

MAP 31.5 **The Arab Spring.**

which had dominated India since the 1950s and had run into the same financial difficulties as the Soviet Union in the 1970s. Not surprisingly, the BJP won the 1991 elections on a platform of economic reform and globalization.

The BJP government, however, did not accomplish much. Once in power, it succumbed to its traditional supremacist-nationalist ideology of "Hinduness" (*hindutva*), which the business leaders had sought to tone down. In 1992, the BJP protected radical local hindutva organizations that whipped up a crowd of 150,000 Hindus to raze the Babri Mosque (allegedly founded in the place of a Hindu temple) in the northern Indian state of Uttar Pradesh, home to 31 million Muslims. In the predictable Muslim backlash, some 2,000 Indians died. In the elections of 1998, the BJP played down its hindutva tradition and won again, but its involvement in renewed incidents of communal violence contribtued to an alienation of the voters in 2004. The Congress Party, now also enthusiastically in favor of economic liberalization, returned to power.

The new Indian middle class—defined by a cell phone, motorized transportation, and a color TV—included anywhere between 60 and 300 million Indians, in a population of 1.2 billion in 2010. The most dynamic members of this class lived and worked in the southern heavy industry and high-tech hub of Bangalore. Because the city is 12.5 hours ahead of California, it is perfect for effecting linkages to maintain around-the-clock computing with Silicon Valley. By the second decade of the 2000s, these two leading world centers of information technology on opposite sides of the globe had become closely integrated.

The rapid expansion of urban centers, such as Bangalore, greatly contributed to the decline of the traditional caste divisions in Hinduism within the urban and even, to some degree, rural context. Since descent could be hidden in the cities, even the untouchable caste (*dalit*) began to enter the new middle class. Widespread protests in 2006 against the complex affirmative action system introduced in the 1990s in favor of less privileged social groups indicated the beginning of a dissolution of the caste divisions in the urban environment.

Patterns Up Close | Social Networking

As we have seen, the Tunisian revolution sparked a wave of revolts across Africa and the Middle East in what has come to be called the "Arab Spring." What makes these movements unique, however, is that they were organized and carried out by means of *social networking sites* (SNSs) like Twitter, Facebook, and YouTube, supported by cell phones and other modern communication technologies. But what are the origins of these devices and how have they developed into such important tools of political and social revolution?

SNSs can ultimately be traced back to the origins of the Internet and the World Wide Web. The Internet is a product of the Cold War. Stunned by the Soviet launch of Sputnik the previous year, in 1958 President Eisenhower called for the creation of a national electronic communication network to help protect the United States from a nuclear attack launched from space. In 1969 the US government initiated the Advanced Research Projects Agency (ARPA), which created a system inking computers at major universities into a network that allowed them to share vital information. From this small, highly classified step the Internet expanded during the 1990s into a global computer network. The World Wide Web (or www) was conceived in 1989 and launched two years later as a part of the Internet. Simply put, the "web" uses the Internet to gain access to categories of data, documents, and other resources found within the larger network.

SNSs sprang up in the 1990s when it was recognized that the Internet and the World Wide Web provided social groups the means to easily communicate with each other and to share information. Among the earliest of these were Classmates.com (1995) and SixDegrees (1997), which enabled users to "network" with each other by means of shared e-mail addresses. The next step allowed users to develop personal sites from which to share information with like-minded readers. The first of these was Friendster in 2002, followed by Linked In and MySpace in 2003, YouTube in 2004, and Facebook and Twitter by 2006. Along with a welter of personal "blogs" (from "web-logs") these sites represented a global explosion of instantaneously distributed information that revolutionized the nature of communication.

Easily the most recognizable use of SNSs to effect change relates to the recent wave of uprisings in North Africa and the Middle East. An early example of this came in Iran in 2009. Called the "Twitter Revolution," anti-government activists used the full range of SNSs while engaged in an ultimately futile effort to overthrow the Iranian regime. Following the success of the Tunisian revolution, however, an even more spectacular display of the power of SNSs erupted in Egypt on January 25, 2011, when thousands of protesters took to the streets to demand the ouster of

The Face of Revolution. Perhaps the most novel aspect of the ongoing "Arab Spring" has been the widespread use of electronic media and Social Networking Sites (SNSs) in recruiting, organizing, and popularizing the efforts of activists in various countries. The inventiveness of the participants in avoiding government scrutiny and bypassing restrictions on SNSs by means of proxy servers and third-party connections to outside sites has become legendary. In Syria, the government lifted a ban on these sites in an attempt to stave off unrest in the wake of the successful uprisings in Tunisia and Egypt. Here a Syrian man logs into his Facebook account "legally" for perhaps the first time in February, 2011. Most observers agree, however, that such restrictions have had little effect in blocking access to the most popular SNSs.

authoritarian President Hosni Mubarak. This "Facebook Revolution," was launched by the April 6 Youth Movement, a Facebook group comprised of social and political activists. In 2011 the movement was propelled forward by Wael Ghonim, a young Google marketing executive, who set up a Facebook site to mobilize participants for a rally against harsh governmental policies. Ghonim hoped for a gathering of 50,000 protesters. When, however, over 100,000 showed up, he observed, awe-struck, that "I have never seen a revolution that was preannounced before" [NY Times, February 14, 2011]. Moreover, the Egyptian success was made possible in part by valuable lessons gleaned from SNS exchanges with anti-government coun-terparts in Tunisia. One message, for example, read: "Advice to the youth of Egypt: Put vinegar or onion under your scarf for tear gas" [Ibid.].

For all their success in facilitating uprisings against authoritarian governments, however, SNSs are used with equal effectiveness by extremist terrorist groups. Al Quaeda and the Taliban have learned to take advantage of Facebook and Twitter to broadcast their calls for global *jihad*. SNSs are also used to solicit financial sup-port and share information concerning plans for forthcoming attacks. Moreover, SNS—particularly Facebook—serve as effective recruitment tools. The recent death of Anwar al-Awlaki, known popularly as "the bin Laden of the Internet," especially brought into the open the effectiveness of YouTube to inspire *jihad*. The Taliban, too, has established an effective network of sites to get out its propaganda and re-cruitment messages to a global audience. As its "Voice of Jihad" proclaims, "Wars today cannot be won without media. Media aims at the heart rather than the body, [and]if the heart is defeated, the battle is won" [blog posted by Stephanie Maier, May 15, 2011]. There is even an American website, "Jihadology," which recently lamented the death of Al Quaeda leader Osama Bin Laden: "Goodbye, Oh Honor-able Shaykh," "You Lived Benevolent and Died a Martyr. . . " [Ibid.].

In the origin and evolution of social networking sites we are afforded yet another example of how the power of modern technologies has altered the course of world history. How ironic that Internet websites originally intended for exchanges among friends have been transformed into to tools to spread revolution, violence, and ter-rorism. Indeed, the wave of protests and revolutionary fervor initiated in Tunisia and Egypt represent only the beginning of uprisings in the modern Middle East; on-going revolts have spread to Libya—where strongman Muammar Gaddafi was overthrown and executed—as well Syria, Bahrain, Jordan, and Yemen. As one of the organizers of the Egyptian revolution so presciently predicted: "Tunis is the force that pushed Egypt, but what Egypt did will be the force that will push the world" [NY Times, February 14, 2011]. And the sinews binding this force are now electronic.

Questions

• How do SNSs show how an innovation can be adapted for purposes wholly differ-ent from the original purposes for which they were intended?

• Do you believe SNSs have allowed young people around the world to make their wishes and aspirations more powerfully felt? If so, what does this say about the connection between technology and youth?

Driving Toward Prosperity.
The Bajaj scooter was the early status symbol of the emerging Indian middle class. On account of their size, the Indian and Chinese middle classes, numbering perhaps in the hundreds of millions, are a powerful group, representing a huge reservoir of ever more demanding consumers. This picture is from 2010, when the Indian middle class had come of age.

The success of the middle class in India, impressive as it is, must also be measured against conditions in the countryside, much of which is still largely outside the market economy. Almost three-quarters of the population lived in villages with poor water, electricity, and roads during the beginning of the twenty-first century. An overwhelming majority of villagers lived in extreme poverty (less than $1.25 per day), existing completely outside the market circuit and depending on handouts. Although this majority in 2010 was somewhat smaller, perhaps by one-quarter, a birth rate that refused to decline below 2.8 percent did not help much in poverty reduction. A major factor in the persistence of poverty was incomplete land reform. Landlordism and tenancy continued to encompass nearly half of the rural population. Large landholdings had been abolished after independence, but medium and small landlordism persisted undiminished. As a major voting bloc in the Congress Party, the landlords were successful in resisting further land reform.

The unproductive landlord system, providing India with little more than wheat and rice, required enormous state subsidies in seed, fertilizer, and irrigation infrastructures to keep going. These subsidies discouraged investments in a much needed agricultural diversification. The e-Choupal system by the Indian conglomerate ITC was a remarkable exception. ITC developed the system in 2000, about a decade after India had opened its borders to the world market, and used it in its strategy to counter the invading American, European, and Japanese multinationals with competitive Indian exports. Through e-Choupal, Indian soybean farmers were equipped with computers (hooked up to solar panels), through which they could follow soybean prices on the Chicago futures market as well as their nearby ITC station, selling their harvests at the latter instead of in the traditional markets, where brokers collected high fees. A decade later, e-Choupal was a highly successful venture and attracted other private firms. Collectively, its impact was still slight, but every initiative that empowers local farmers to link up with larger markets signifies a gradual improvement.

African Transformations   The half-decade between the oil price slump, debt crisis, and disappearance of communism (1985–1991) was as challenging for sub-Saharan Africa as for India. The continent's GDP in the early 1990s was down by almost half from what it was in 1975 when all main social and economic indicators were at their peak. The decline of living conditions was particularly devastating in the health services, cut back by half in almost all countries, in spite of a steady increase in HIV/AIDS. Many countries expended more hard currency on their debt services than on education. With a doubling of the population at the absolute poverty level ($1.25 per day), sub-Saharan Africa became by far the poorest region in the world.

During this time, the urban population of sub-Saharan Africa increased to almost one-third of the total population, making it more numerous than in India but still smaller than in China, where nearly half of the population was urban. This urbanization process was an important factor in the political consequences of the crisis: Students, civil servants, and journalists became restless and demanded political reforms. Up until the early 1990s, almost everywhere state structures were patronage hierarchies: the civilian or military rulers in power provided cushy government jobs for the ethnic groups from which they hailed. Although all 54 African countries were officially "nations" with seats in the United Nations, none (except South Africa) was either a functionally constitutional or ethnically uniform nation. Urban dwellers, however, were less tied to ethnicity and more committed to constitutionalism. They felt little sympathy for autocratic rulers and their kin running the states into financial ruin and pushed for democratic reforms in the late 1990s and early 2000s.

Freedom, Justice, and Dignity. The end of apartheid in 1994 and the election of Nelson Mandela, seen here visiting his former prison cell, was an inspiring event in Africa and the world. South Africa is the richest and most industrialized country of Africa, with large mineral and agricultural resources. Nearly 80 percent of the population is black, speaking its own languages isiZulu and isiKhosa, but Afrikaans (a Dutch-originated language) remained the dominant media language, with English being only the fifth most spoken language. In spite of South Africa's relative wealth, years of apartheid have resulted in vast income disparities.

Unfortunately, the push for reforms had mixed results. On the one hand, while a majority of rulers in power prior to 1991 had exited office as a result of coups or assassinations, after 1991 they either resigned voluntarily or stepped down after losing elections. On the other hand, incumbents still won more often than not and honest elections were rare. Some regime changes were truly thrilling, notably the end of apartheid and the election of Nelson Mandela (b. 1918, president 1994–1999) in the Republic of South Africa; two cycles (2004 and 2008) of clean multiparty elections in Ghana; the first election of a female president, the Harvard-trained economist Ellen Johnson Sirleaf (b. 1938, in office beginning 2006) in Liberia; and the relatively clean Nigerian presidential elections of 2007 and 2011. African adherence to constitutional politics so painfully fraught in the past was now definitely coming of age.

Ethnic and Constitutional Nationalism   Unfortunately, the beginning of movement away from ethnic nationalism to broader constitutional nationalism was offset by plenty of violence and state instability. The Rwandan Tutsi genocide of 1994 continued on a lower but equally vicious scale in the neighboring Democratic Republic of Congo. This country suffered not only a new military revolution in 1997 but unending military challenges and lootings of mineral resources ever since. Successful coups d'état occurred in no less than eight African countries during the two decades between 1991 and 2010.

A particularly sad case was the political and economic implosion of Zimbabwe, following the expropriation of white farmers in 2000. Here, President Robert Mugabe (b. 1924), in power since overthrowing the white minority regime of Rhodesia (1980), became impatient with the slow process of legal land reform. Mugabe inherited a state whose tiny minority of white farmers controlled 70 percent of all farmland and whose highly productive, modern farms grew most of Zimbabwe's agricultural exports of coffee, tea, and tobacco. In 2000 Mugabe encouraged

A Black American Confronts Africa

"How can anyone talk about democracy and constitutions and the rule of law in places where paramilitary security forces firebomb the offices of opposition newspapers? Where entire villages get burned down and thousands of people are made homeless by competing political loyalties? Where whole chunks of countries are under the sway of armed guerrillas? And where traditional belief runs so deep that a politician can be arrested and charged with casting magic spells over poor villagers to force them to vote for him?"

—Keith B. Richburg. *Out of America: A Black Man Confronts Africa*, pp. 226–227. New York: Basic Books, 1997.

his followers to seize the vast majority of white farms in a violent occupation movement, with the effect that commercial agriculture broke down, the economy collapsed, and hyperinflation ravaged the country. The overall situation in Zimbabwe became so desperate that Mugabe was forced to accept his despised rival Morgan Tsvangirai (b. 1952) as prime minister in 2009 and return to a semblance of constitutionalism. Since then, the economy has begun to improve, with small-plot farmers producing beyond self-sufficiency again, even if overall production was still only one-third of what it was in 2000.

Another example was the corrupt election of 2007 in Kenya, resulting in 1,000 deaths during riots among ethnic groups. When order was reestablished, the two top opponents, incumbent President Mwai Kibaki (b. 1931) and challenger Raila Odinga (b. 1945), came together in a grudging compromise of shared power between them, the former filling the position as president and the latter in the newly created but constitutionally unsanctioned position of prime minister. Odinga, successful in transcending ethnic affiliation for a constitutionalist-nationalist presidential bid, had been widely seen as the winner; and the unrest after the fraud-ridden elections was a regrettable relapse into ethnic nationalism. To repair constitutionalism, it was necessary to make the prime-ministerial arrangement legal, a necessity which was incorporated into a wider constitutional reform. Accordingly, Kenyans adopted a new constitution in 2010, which created a senate in addition to the existing parliament and devolved power from the center to the counties while reverting to a pure presidential system. Endemic corruption, however, continued to accompany the efforts to return to stability (see Map 31.6).

In Ivory Coast, elections in 2010 similarly ended initially in an impasse. President-elect Alassane Ouattara (b. 1942) was able to take office only after a 5-month hiatus (November 2010–April 2011), during which his supporters attempted to depose his defeated predecessor, Laurent Gbagbo (b. 1945) [BAG-bow]. Gbagbo had refused to step down even though the electoral commission had declared Ouattara the winner. The one encouraging note in this continuing cycle of power grabs in the first decade of the 2000s was that there were "only" half as many illegal office seizures in Africa as in 1970–1991. Still, authoritarianism and military rule continued to endure.

Economic Recovery   Similarly spotty was the economic recovery, although it picked up in the early 2000s, mostly because of rising commodity prices. The main oil exporters (Nigeria, Angola, Chad, Sudan, Gabon, Cameroon, Equatorial New Guinea, and the two Republics of Congo) benefited from higher oil prices, as did the mining countries of South Africa, Zambia, both Congos, and Malawi with their diamonds, gold, copper, silver, zinc, lead, and rare metals. In a United Nations–sponsored scheme in 1998, "blood diamonds" mined to finance civil wars, as in Angola, Sierra Leone, Liberia, Ivory Coast, and both Congos, were subjected to certification so as to prevent future wars. (Diamonds mined in Zimbabwe were exempted since Zimbabwe's disintegration into a failed state was not considered to be the effect of a civil

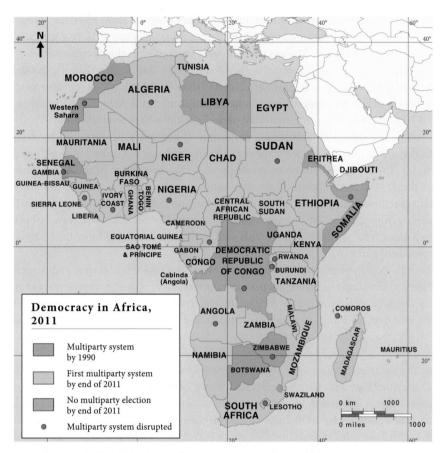

MAP 31.6 **Democracy in Africa, 2011.**

war.) Apart from minerals, agricultural products, such as coffee, cotton, and fresh flowers for the European market, also regained significance in the early 2000s. The recession of 1990–2011 did not have a major impact, largely because of the arrival of China on the scene as a major buyer and investor. Optimism about a sustained recovery and modernity within reach was clearly visible on the continent.

Latin American Expansion   Elections after the scare of the financial meltdowns in the freewheeling 1990s produced more fiscally restrained, socially engaged governments in the large Latin American countries during the early 2000s. Orderly democratic transitions in Mexico, Brazil, Argentina, and Chile (the latter three with socially oriented governments) demonstrated that the unhappy years of military dictatorships in the 1980s had been left behind. In Mexico the long rule of the Institutional Revolutionary Party came to an end in 2000, with an orderly transition to less socially engaged Christian Democratic presidents in the following two elections. Either way, however, the continent enjoyed a sustained economic recovery.

Two extraconstitutional events in smaller Latin American countries, however, demonstrated that authoritarian temptations still survived. The first was an abortive uprising in 2002 of army units in Paraguay, allegedly instigated by a former commander outside the country and wanted for an earlier coup attempt. The second, in Honduras in 2009, was the forcible removal of the president, who intended to hold a referendum on his unconstitutional plan for reelection, even though forbidden by the Honduran constitutional court. More disruptive were continued efforts by revolutionary Marxists in Colombia to overthrow the government, even though their liberation movement, founded in 1964, declined in the early 2000s. In neighboring Venezuela, President Hugo Chávez (b. 1954), a former officer from a working-class background, was alone in mainland Latin America in his adherence to state socialism, encountering periodic middle-class resistance. Mexico, by contrast, deepened its democratic commitment but was severely tested by drug traffickers, organized as cartels for the shipping of drugs to markets in the United States. These cartels became increasingly violent in the course of the first decade of the 2000s, to the point where they infiltrated the police as well as the army and even interfered with elections. Central and South American governments, still reeling from the population explosion of the second half of the 1900s, were not yet rich enough to pay their civil servants well so that the latter could resist the narco-traffickers' bribes.

Although the business of drugs was a blight in Colombia, Mexico, and several Central American countries, the mainstream economy recovered impressively after the financial meltdowns of the 1990s. The countries continued to rely on exports of oil, minerals, and tropical agricultural goods. But industrialization, until the 1990s largely through foreign investments, stimulated state-run firms to become competitive and even private. In some cases, as with Brazilian Embraer commercial airplanes or the electronics and information technology industry of Guadalajara in Mexico, Latin American countries have become world competitors. All four large economies—Brazil, Mexico, Argentina, and Chile—exported more manufactured goods than commodities by 2008. Brazil, in fact, is a member of the "BRIC"—which also includes Russia, India, and China—countries that have attained advanced economic development since the 1990s. As increasingly important trade partners with China and India, these countries clearly demonstrated the features of scientific–industrial modernity by the second decade of the 2000s.

The Environmental Limits of Modernity

What we have defined in the last two parts of this book as *modernity*—the political systems marked by constitutional nationalism and ethnic nationalism and the economic systems propelled by science and industrialism—has now become not simply a regional or "Western" phenomenon but a global one. In the absence of the competing subpatterns of modernity—communism and supremacist nationalism—the systems of capitalism, consumerism, and democracy characterized by the United States, Canada, and Western Europe have increasingly become the ones to emulate. All new nations in the world either are industrializing or want to do so if they have the financial means. The principal obstacle for these nations is the debilitating poverty of the great majority of their inhabitants, who are still mired in either subsistence farming or marginal work in the shantytowns of sprawling cities. The poorest are unskilled and uneducated and, because of high infant mortality rates and the need for farm labor, still view large families as a necessity. Improved public health care is helping to raise life spans for the poorest people, but the combination of modern medicine and the desire for large families has caused a startling increase in the world population since the middle of the twentieth century (see Map 31.7).

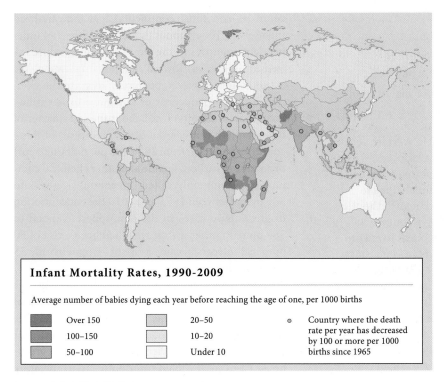

Infant Mortality Rates, 1990-2009

Average number of babies dying each year before reaching the age of one, per 1000 births

	Over 150		20–50	⊙	Country where the death rate per year has decreased by 100 or more per 1000 births since 1965
	100–150		10–20		
	50–100		Under 10		

MAP **31.7** Infant Mortality Rates, 1990–2009.

Demography and Job Creation   Even though the demographic increase is beginning to slow, there is no question that for the foreseeable future the manufacturing and service sectors of modern industry will not be able to offer enough employment to increase the affluence of the poor and significantly raise their rates of consumption. **Consumerism**, however, is what drives the economics of scientific–industrial modernity; thus, we are dealing with a vicious circle: Without consumers, industry cannot offer sufficient numbers of jobs and the poor cannot become consumers because they are jobless.

As with all vicious circles, this can be overcome only through gradual transformation on both sides of the equation: Scientists, industrialists, and businesspeople have to be innovative and offer new consumer products requiring new jobs; and the poor, through enhanced access to education, need to acquire the resources to motivate them to find their way into modernity. So far, this gradualism appears to be working, albeit slowly. Perhaps the most striking example is the victorious march of the cell phone across the world. In 2010 the world population reached 6.9 billion, the number of cell phones was 5 billion, and the number of computers was close to 1 billion. The e-Choupal example in India is still a drop in the bucket, but it demonstrates how electronics, the most recent industrial innovation, are beginning to make a difference.

Sustainability and Global Warming   The critical factor in this gradualism is modernity's long-term environmental sustainability. In 1800, there was only one country (Great Britain) embarking on industrialization; by 1918, there were about a dozen countries (Europe and Japan); and by 1945, about three dozen

Consumerism: The acquired habit to shop for goods and gadgets (often with built-in obsolescence) beyond the basic needs of food and shelter.

Pope John Paul II on Consumerism

"The historical experience of the West, for its part, shows that even if the Marxist analysis and its foundation of alienation are false, nevertheless alienation—and the loss of the authentic meaning of life—is a reality in Western societies too. This happens in consumerism, when people are ensnared in a web of false and superficial gratifications rather than being helped to experience their personhood in an authentic and concrete way. Alienation is found also in work, when it is organized so as to ensure maximum returns and profits with no concern whether the worker, through his own labor, grows or diminishes as a person, either through increased sharing in a genuinely supportive community or through increased isolation in a maze of relationships marked by destructive competitiveness and estrangement, in which he is considered only a means and not an end."

—Pope John Paul II. "On the Hundredth Anniversary of Rerum Novarum: Centesimus Annus." Encyclical letter of May 1, 1991. Washington, DC: Office for Publishing and Promotion Services, United States Catholic Conference, 1991.

countries (on three continents) had industrialized themselves. Today, about two-thirds of the 194 independent countries of the world are either industrialized or on the way toward full industrialization. We are only now, however, beginning to grasp the environmental consequences of this move to scientific–industrial modernity. Until about the last quarter of the twentieth century the carbon footprint of these countries had risen from 280 parts per million (ppm) of volume of carbon dioxide and other chemical compounds—commonly called "greenhouse gases"—to 330 ppm. Between 1975 and 2010 the concentration of greenhouse gases in the atmosphere climbed to 380 ppm. In other words, what had been a rise of 50 ppm in 175 years became a rise of 70 ppm in only 35 years (see Figure 31.1).

While there has been considerable debate over the last several decades on the nature and degree of global warming—whether it is a natural cyclical phenomenon or human-produced or even if it exists at all—there is a general scientific consensus that greenhouse gases are the main contributors to temperature increases on earth. Scientists generally assume that at current rates of greenhouse gas production the earth will reach a "tipping point" of 450 ppm that will have catastrophic consequences for the planet's climate before the middle of this century.

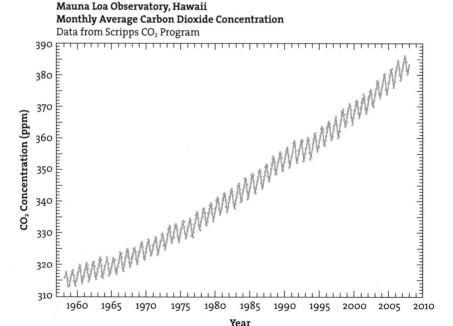

Figure 31.1 Greenhouse Gas Emissions Since 1950.

What will happen when this tipping point is reached? If projections hold true, the polar ice caps and high mountain glaciers will have melted. Ocean levels, rising from the melted ice, will have submerged many islands and made inroads on the coasts of all continents. Widespread droughts and violent storms will regularly pound various parts of the earth, eroding by wind and flood what in many places had shortly before been fertile land. The world's tropical forests, already considerably reduced from timber harvesting and agricultural expansion, may well be wiped out, removing the most important agents for cleaning the atmosphere of greenhouse gases. Pollution and overfishing threaten the world's oceans and marine life. The consequence of these grim developments will likely be a severe reduction of the earth's arable land and fisheries needed for the production of food. In addition, biodiversity will be dramatically reduced, further decreasing food supplies (see Map 31.8).

The ultimate outcome of this prospective climate transformation will be much worse for the new countries with less wealth to cushion them than for the older ones that industrialized early and have the resources to adjust. The crushing irony of such projections, therefore, is that the nations which viewed their adaptation to modernity as their salvation may well find themselves among the condemned.

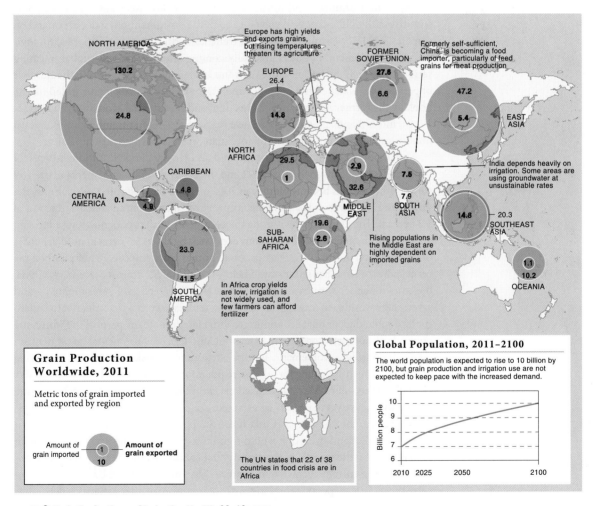

MAP 31.8 **Grain Production and Irrigation Use Worldwide, 2011.**

A Smoggy Future. China, the world's worst emitter of greenhouse gases, has large numbers of coal-fed power plants and factories which continue to belch carbon dioxide as well as toxic substances into the air, with little scrubbing or other devices to clean the emissions before they reach the atmosphere. Here, a power plant on the outskirts of Linfen in Shanxi Province southwest of Beijing fouls the environment in 2009.

Scientific and Political Debate   There is a general consensus among scientists that the warming trend in the world from greenhouse gases is real. Very few scientists still hold a skeptical view—though the prominent physicist Freeman Dyson (b. 1923), for example, remains a trenchant critic and advocate of technological fixes. The general public is gradually coming around to taking global warming seriously, though in Europe more than the United States. To judge by the number of people who watched the 2006 documentary *An Inconvenient Truth*, based on the book by the former American vice president and presidential candidate Al Gore (b. 1948), interest and agreement may have reached their own tipping point. But vocal minorities still vociferously denounce climate warming as a hoax or conspiracy.

So far, political response has been tepid and largely divided. Although two UN conferences have convened since 1992 and the environmental agreements of the 169 participating nations became binding in 2005 in the so-called Kyoto Protocol, only the European Union was on track to meet its provision mandating an annual reduction of 5.2 percent. The United States, during the George W. Bush presidency, refused to sign on to Kyoto and increased its emissions every year by about 1.5 percent until the onset of the recession in late 2007. Sweden, on the other hand, imposed a hefty carbon tax on its industries and has so far stayed below the critical 5.2 annual percentage. China, the worst offender with over half of all the world's greenhouse gases emitted—and seven of the world's ten most polluted cities—refuses to comply in order not to endanger its double-digit annual economic growth. Here, as in many parts of the world, the political risks of curtailing growth in favor of long-term environmental investment are seen as increasingly problematic. But the environmental risks associated with staying the course—such as drilling for oil—were put into stark relief in 2010 when a massive oil spill in the Gulf of Mexico wreaked catastrophic environmental damage, the full effects which have yet to be fully ascertained.

At present, the consensus is that if the 5.2 percent reduction rate were to continue after 2012 and everyone would sign on to reduction, the eventual decline in temperature by the middle of the twenty-first century would be 0.2 degree Fahrenheit below the current average temperature. Whether this would be sufficient to reverse the melting of polar ice and the onset of irregular weather patterns is debatable.

But if present trends continue, the projected temperature increase in 2050 will be more likely in the range of 3–4 degrees Fahrenheit—enough for the projections to indicate the catastrophic consequences we have mentioned, which are widely agreed to be irreversible.

Thus, global warming and its relationship to greenhouse gas emissions remains at present a problem in which some agreement has been achieved as to ends but very little as to means. Its relative imperceptibility makes it difficult to stir people to decisive action on a mass scale. Recessions and economic vitality, the demands of growth, and, at the most basic level, whether one has a job or not—these are all much more immediate problems than small temperature increases or even a few more droughts, storms, and floods, which always seem to hit others and not ourselves. It does seem safe to say, however, that the relationship of all aspects of the patterns of modernity to the environment will be a central problem of the coming decades.

Putting It All Together

The first decade of the twenty-first century witnessed the final transformation of the world from a centuries-old agrarian–urban pattern of life to a new scientific–industrial pattern. All of this was accomplished in the breathtakingly short span of 200 years. What had begun as a culturally specific, western European–pioneered transition, first from descriptive to mathematical science and then from agriculture to industry, had become ubiquitous. Everywhere in the world people have been adapting to a new role as individuals with well-defined "human rights," who aspire to be educated, find fulfilling jobs, become consumers, and achieve a materially secure life—in short, they are becoming *modern*.

The twentieth century also saw the original pattern of modernity split into three. World War I was a cataclysm that produced proponents of a first modernity, who sought to create competitive, capitalist, democratic societies; a second modernity, which sought to collapse power hierarchies and differences of wealth through equality in socialist-communist societies; and a third modernity, in which supremacist-nationalist societies sought to impose the will of allegedly superior races or ethnic groups through conquest (if not complete elimination) of inferior ones. Tremendous suffering and destruction accompanied the struggle among the proponents of these visions of modernity, and in a gradual process of elimination, it was the messiest and most unruly of the three forms of modernity—capitalist democracy—that survived.

Today, the faith in democracy that marked the exuberant beginnings of modernity at the end of the eighteenth century appears to be just as vigorous and unbounded in places far outside its birthplace. People—young, poor, educated, ambitious—continued to be its martyrs (Tiananmen Square, 1989; Tehran, 2009; Arab, Spring 2011) as well as its proud and triumphant flag bearers (Tunisia and Egypt, 2011).

Faith in the future of the environment at this point is a good deal more subdued, however. Here, the devil's bargain of materialism that accompanied the evolution of

---

Rooted in the Earth

"Yes, the only real hope of people today is probably a renewal of our certainty that we are rooted in the earth and, at the same time, the cosmos. This awareness endows us with the capacity for self-transcendence. Politicians at international forums may reiterate a thousand times that the basis of the new world order must be universal respect for human rights, but it will mean nothing as long as this imperative does not derive from the respect of the miracle of Being, the miracle of the universe, the miracle of nature, the miracle of our own existence. Only someone who submits to the authority of the universal order and of creation, who values the right to be a part of it and a participant in it, can genuinely value himself and his neighbors, and thus honor their rights as well."

—Vaclav Havel. "The Need for Transcendence in the Postmodern World." *The Futurist*, July–August 1995.

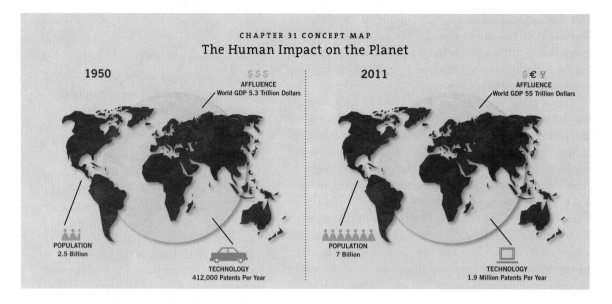

CHAPTER 31 CONCEPT MAP
The Human Impact on the Planet

1950

$$$
AFFLUENCE
World GDP 5.3 Trillion Dollars

POPULATION
2.5 Billion

TECHNOLOGY
412,000 Patents Per Year

2011

$ € ¥
AFFLUENCE
World GDP 55 Trillion Dollars

POPULATION
7 Billion

TECHNOLOGY
1.9 Million Patents Per Year

modernity continues to haunt us: On the one hand, it gave us the human right to a decent existence in material security; on the other hand, the means of achieving that security through exploitation of the earth's material resources has given us the nightmare prospect of an irreversibly changed nature that may allow for fewer and fewer of the comforts we currently enjoy (see Concept Map). The pattern of modernity and the scientific–industrial society that supports it will no doubt continue, but its future shape will be just as unknowable to us as the patterns of society in the past were to those living through them.

Review and Respond

1. What is the dollar regime? Explain its function in the world.

2. Discuss the two basic principles of the American military posture in the world since 1992.

3. What is IT? How has it transformed cultural interactions? Economic activity?

4. Which countries remained communist after 1991 and in which form?

5. What is globalization? Do the benefits of globalization outweigh its drawbacks? Are the effects of globalization the same throughout the world?

6. Explain the connection in the pattern of modernity between industrialization and consumerism.

7. Is the future of the world environment a grave problem, and if yes, why? Can a balance between the desire to preserve the environment and the need to save jobs be achieved?

> For additional resources, including maps, primary sources, visuals, and quizzes, please go to www.oup.com/us/vonsivers. Please see the Further Resources section at the back of the book for additional readings and suggested websites.

Thinking Through Patterns

▶ **How did the United States acquire its dominant economic position toward the end of the twentieth century? How did it accelerate the process of globalization?**

The United States acquired its dominant economic position through the dollar regime and by becoming the sinkhole for industrial exports from developing countries. In compensation for the latter, it expanded the reach of its financial system worldwide. The result was the globalization of the world economy.

Capitalist democracy became the universal model of modernity in part because growing middle classes in cities demanded liberalized markets where they could develop personal initiative and accumulate capital for business ventures. Socially conservative new middle classes became the engines that powered more than half a dozen successful industrialization processes throughout Asia, Latin America, and Africa.

▶ **What made capitalist democracy so attractive toward the end of the twentieth century that it became a generic model for many governments around the world to strive for?**

▶ **Which policies did China and India pursue so that they became the fastest industrializing countries in the early twenty-first century?**

China and India accelerated their industrialization by systematically encouraging the expansion of their middle classes as the engines of investment and innovation. China, however, did not allow the development of a multiparty system, fearing the chaos of popular agitation. India, by contrast, possessed constitutional-nationalist traditions reaching back to the nineteenth century that contained constraints against populism and allowed for peaceful democratic competition.

Perhaps more than any other innovation in the last 20 years, or even the last 200 years, the communications revolution has reshaped the way humans interact with each other. The exponential growth of networking boggles the mind. In 2006, 50 billion e-mails were sent. Just 4 years later, that number had risen to 300 billion. Because of this connectedness, politics, culture, and economic activity now mutate more rapidly--and with more volatility--than ever before.

▶ **How have information technology and social networking altered cultural, political, and economic interactions around the world?**

▶ **What is global warming, and why is it a source of grave concern for the future?**

Global warming is caused by the increase of carbon dioxide and other gases that accumulate in the upper atmosphere and trap the sun's heat in the lower atmosphere. Warming and cooling trends have occurred periodically since the end of the last Ice Age, and for a long time scientists labored to distinguish clearly between a temporary trend toward warmer temperatures and a permanent, greenhouse gas–caused trend toward a catastrophic tipping point that will permanently alter nature as we know it. Today, there is an overwhelming scientific consensus concerning the reality of global warming. But politicians and the general public are not yet entirely convinced that the efforts begun with the Kyoto Protocol of 2005 should be decisively intensified.

Further Resources

Chapter 22

Israel, Jonathan I. *A Revolution of the Mind: Radical Enlightenment and the Origins of Modern Democracy.* Princeton, NJ: Princeton University Press, 2010. Israel is a pioneer of the contemporary renewal of intellectual history, and his investigations of the Enlightenment tradition are pathbreaking.

Kaiser, Thomas E., and Dale K. Van Kley, eds. *From Deficit to Deluge: The Origins of the French Revolution.* Stanford, CA: Stanford University Press, 2011. Thoughtful reevaluation of the scholarly field that takes into account the latest interpretations.

Kitchen, Martin. *A History of Modern Germany: 1800 to the Present.* Hoboken, NJ: Wiley-Blackwell, 2011. A broadly conceived historical overview, ranging from politics and economics to culture.

Rakove, Jack. *Revolutionaries: A New History of the Invention of America.* Boston: Houghton Mifflin, 2010. A new narrative history focusing on the principal figures in the revolution.

Riall, Lucy. *Risorgimento: The History of Italy from Napoleon to Nation-State.* New York: Palgrave Macmillan, 2009. Historical summary, incorporating the research of the past half-century, presented in a clear overview.

Wood, Gordon S. *The American Revolution: A History.* New York: Modern Library, 2002. A short, readable summary reflective of many decades of revisionism in the discussion of the American Revolution.

WEBSITES

http://www.nationalismproject.org/what.htm. Nationalism Project. A large Website with links to bibliographies, essays, new books, and book reviews.

http://chnm.gmu.edu/revolution/. This website boasts 250 images, 350 text documents, 13 songs, 13 maps and a timeline all focused on the French Revolution.

Chapter 23

Allen, Robert C. *The British Industrial Revolution in Global Perspective.* Cambridge: Cambridge University Press, 2009. An in-depth analysis, well supported by economic data, of not only why the Industrial Revolution occurred first in Britain but also how new British technologies carried industrialism around the world.

Dublin, Thomas, ed. *Farm to Factory: Women's Letters, 1830–1860.* New York: Columbia University Press, 1981. A fascinating collection of correspondence written by women who describe their experiences in moving from rural areas of New England to urban centers in search of work in textile factories.

Headrick, Daniel R. *The Tools of Empire: Technology and European Imperialism in the Nineteenth Century.* Oxford: Oxford University Press, 1981. A fascinating and clearly written analysis of the connections between the development of new technologies and their role in European imperialism.

Hobsbawm, Eric. *The Age of Revolution: 1789–1848.* London: Vintage Books, 1996. A sophisticated analysis of the Industrial Revolution (one element of the "dual revolution," the other being the French Revolution) that examines the effects of industrialism on social and cultural developments from a Marxist perspective.

Mokyr, Joel. "Accounting for the Industrial Revolution." In *The Cambridge Economic History of Modern Britain,* vol. 1. Edited by Roderick Floud and Paul Johnson. Cambridge: Cambridge University Press, 2004. An analysis of the industrial movement that emphasizes its intellectual sources, embraced in the term "Industrial Enlightenment."

More, Charles. *Understanding the Industrial Revolution.* London: Routledge, 2000. A comprehensive explanation of how theories of economic growth account for the development of the industrial movement in Britain.

Stearns, Peter N. *The Industrial Revolution in World History.* Boulder: University of Colorado Press, 1993. A comprehensive study of the origin, spread, and influence of the European industrial revolution and its impact on globalization.

WEBSITES

http://www.thomasedison.org/. Remarkable website that explores Thomas Edison's impact on modernity through his innovations and inventions. This site also reproduces all of Edison's scientific sketches which are available to download as PDF files.

http://www.monetpainting.net/. A visually beautiful website which reproduces many of Monet's masterpieces, this site also includes an extensive biographical account of the famous painter's life and works. It also includes information about his wife Camille, his gardens at Giverny, and a chronology.

http://darwin-online.org.uk/. This website has reproduced, in full, the works of Charles Darwin. In addition to providing digitized facsimiles of his works, private papers and manuscripts it has also added a concise biographical account and numerous images of Darwin throughout his life.

http://www.alberteinstein.info/. Fantastic and informative website that houses digitized manuscripts of Einstein's work. Also includes a gallery of images.

Chapter 24

China

Cohen, Paul. *Discovering History in China.* New York: Columbia University Press, 1984.

Fairbank, John K., and Su-yu Teng. *China's Response to the West.* Cambridge, MA: Harvard University Press, 1954.

Kang, David C. *East Asia Before the West: Five Centuries of Trade and Tribute.* New York: Columbia University Press, 2010.

Spence, Jonathan D. *The Search for Modern China.* New York: Norton, 1990.

Spence, Jonathan D. *God's Chinese Son.* New York: Norton, 1996.

Japan

Beasley, W. G. *The Meiji Restoration.* Stanford, CA: Stanford University Press, 1972.

Reischauer, Edwin O., and Albert M. Craig. *Japan: Tradition and Transformation.* Boston: Houghton Mifflin, 1989.

Totman, Conrad. *Japan Before Perry.* Berkeley: University of California Press, 1981.

Totman, Conrad. *A History of Japan.* Oxford: Blackwell, 2000.

WEBSITES

http://www.asian-studies.org/eaa/. Education About Asia. This site provides the best online sources for modern Chinese and Japanese history.

http://www.asian-studies.org/ This is the site of the Association for Asian Studies, the home page of which has links to sources more suited to advanced term papers and seminar projects.

http://sinojapanesewar.com/. Packed with maps, photographs and movies depicting the conflict between Japan and China at the end of the 19th century, students can learn more about causes and consequences of the Sino-Japanese war.

Chapter 25

Gaudin, Corinne. *Ruling Peasants: Village and State in Later Imperial Russia.* DeKalb: Northern Illinois University Press, 2007. A close and sympathetic analysis of rural Russia.

Inalcik, Halil, and Donald Quataert, eds. *An Economic and Social History of the Ottoman Empire.* Vol. 2, *1600–1914.* Cambridge: Cambridge

University Press, 1994. A pioneering work with contributions by leading Ottoman historians on rural structures, monetary developments, and industrialization efforts.

Kasaba, Resat, ed. *The Cambridge History of Turkey*. Vol. 5, *Turkey in the Modern World*. Cambridge: Cambridge University Press, 2008. An ambitious effort to assemble the leading authorities on the Ottoman Empire and provide a comprehensive overview.

Lieven, Dominic. *Empire: The Russian Empire and Its Rivals*. New Haven, CT: Yale University Press, 2002. Broad, comparative history of the Russian Empire, in the context of the Habsburg, Ottoman, and British Empires.

Nikitenko, Aleksandr. *Up from Serfdom: My Childhood and Youth in Russia, 1804–1824*. Translated by Helen Saltz Jacobson. New Haven, CT: Yale University Press, 2001. Touching autobiography summarized at the beginning of the chapter.

Poe, Marshall T. *Russia's Moment in World History*. Princeton, NJ: Princeton University Press, 2003. A superb scholarly overview of Russian history, written from a broad perspective and taking into account a good number of Western stereotypes about Russia, especially in the nineteenth century.

Quataert, Donald. *Manufacturing in the Ottoman Empire and Turkey, 1500–1950*. Albany: State University of New York Press, 1994. The author is still the leading American historian on workers and the early industrialization of the Ottoman Empire.

Riasanovsky, Nicholas, and Mark Steinberg. *A History of Russia*, 8th ed., 2 vols. New York: Oxford University Press, 2011. A comprehensive, fully revised history, ranging from politics and economics to literature and the arts.

Uyar, Mesut, and Edward J. Erickson. *A Military History of the Ottomans: From Osman to Atatürk*. Santa Barbara, CA: Praeger Security International, 2009. A detailed, well-documented history of the Ottoman Empire from the perspective of its imperial designs and military forces, by two military officers in academic positions.

WEBSITES

http://www.paradoxplace.com/Insights/Topkapi/Suleiman%20Topkapi%20Ottomans.htm. A basic web site on the Ottoman Empire at its height, with numerous illustrations.

http://www.russianlegacy.com/en/go_to/history/russian_empire.htm. Russian Legacy, a website devoted to the Russian Empire, organized as a timeline with links.

Chapter 26

Belich, James. *Replenishing the Earth: The Settler Revolution and the Rise of the Anglo-World, 1783–1939*. Oxford: Oxford University Press, 2009. Important study by an Australian historian, focusing on the British settler colonies.

Burbank, Jane, and Frederick Cooper. *Empires in World History: Power and Politics of Difference*. Princeton, NJ: Princeton University Press, 2010. Well-written and remarkably comprehensive comparative work.

Ferguson, Niall. *Empire: The Rise and Demise of the British World Order and the Lessons for Global Power*. New York: Perseus, 2002. Controversial but widely acknowledged analysis of the question of whether imperialism deserves its negative reputation.

Fieldhouse, David K. *Economics and Empire, 1830–1914*. New York: Macmillan, 1984. A classic, profoundly influential study of the economic costs of imperialism, coming to the conclusion that it was not cost-effective.

Hobsbawm, Eric. *The Age of Empire, 1875–1914*. New York: Vintage, 1989. Immensely well-informed investigation of the climactic period of the new imperialism at the end of the nineteenth century.

Jefferies, Matthew. *Contesting the German Empire, 1871–1918*. Malden, MA: Blackwell, 2008. Up-to-date summary of the German historical debate on the colonial period.

Ricklefs, Merle Calvin. *A History of Modern Indonesia Since c. 1200*, 3rd ed. Stanford, CA: Stanford University Press, 2001. Standard history with relevant chapters on Dutch imperialism and colonialism.

Singer, Barnett, John Langdon, and John W. Langdon. *Cultured Force: Makers and Defenders of the French Empire*. Madison: University of Wisconsin Press, 2004. Study of the principal (military) figures who helped create the French nineteenth-century empire.

WEBSITES

http://www.allempires.com/. All Empires Online History Community. Website dedicated to assembling materials on all historical empires, including those of the nineteenth century.

http://www.bbc.co.uk/history/british/empire_seapower/east_india_01.shtml. The BBC looks back at its colonial past and its presence in India. Topics include the East India Company, regional politics, company government and territorial expansion.

Chapter 27

Bulmer-Thomas, Victor. *The Economic History of Latin America Since Independence*, 2nd ed. Cambridge: Cambridge University Press, 2003. A highly analytical and sympathetic investigation of the Latin American export and self-sufficiency economies, calling into question the long dominant dependency theories of Latin America.

Burkholder, Mark, and Lyman Johnson. *Colonial Latin America*, 6th ed. New York: Oxford University Press, 2008. Overview, with focus on social and cultural history.

Dawson, Alexander. *Latin America Since Independence: A History with Primary Sources*. New York: Routledge, 2011. Selection of topics with documentary base; for the nineteenth century on the topics of the nation-state, caudillo politics, race, and the policy of growth through commodity exports.

Drake, Paul W. *Between Tyranny and Anarchy: A History of Democracy in Latin America*. Palo Alto, CA: Stanford University Press, 2009. The author traces the concepts of constitutionalism, autocracy, and voting rights since independence in clear and persuasive strokes.

Eakin, Marshall Craig. *The History of Latin America: Collision of Cultures*. New York: Palgrave Macmillan, 2007. A Brazilianist with a special eye on the ethnic and social class system of Latin America.

Meade, Teresa A. *A History of Modern Latin America: 1800 to the Present*. Chichester, UK: Wiley-Blackwell, 2010. The nineteenth-century portion of this study presents a comprehensive political, social, and economic survey, going more deeply into the details of many aspects discussed in this chapter.

Prados de la Escosura, Leandro. "The Economic Consequences of Independence in Latin America." In: *The Cambridge Economic History of Latin America*. Vol. 1, *The Colonial Era and the Short Nineteenth Century*. Edited by Victor Bulmer-Thomas, John H. Coatsworth, and Roberto Cortés Conde, pp. 463–504. Cambridge: Cambridge University Press, 2006. Superb analysis of the main factors characteristic for Latin America's special path toward economic development without industrialization.

Thurner, Mark, and Andrés Guerrero, eds. *After Spanish Rule: Postcolonial Predicaments of the Americas*. Durham, NC: Duke University Press, 2003. Collection of articles by different authors on the multiple cultural and social challenges which Latin Americans faced after independence.

Wasserman, Mark, and Cheryl English Martin. *Latin America and Its People*, 2nd ed. New York: Pearson Longman, 2007. Thematic approach, drawing general conclusions by comparing and contrasting the individual countries of Latin America.

WEBSITES

http://www.casahistoria.net/latin_american_history19.html. Casahistori.net. Website on nineteenth-century Latin America, for students.

http://www.suite101.com/latinamericanhistory. Suite101.com. A website featuring a long list of short essays on Latin American topics.

http://blpc.bl.uk/onlinegallery/features/spanishamericanind/homepage.html. The British Library looks back at the Spanish-American Independence from the movements origins and key figures to Bolívar's triumphant march. The site has also reproduced extracts from contemporary texts.

Chapter 28

Berend, Ivan T. *An Economic History of Twentieth-Century Europe: Economic Regimes from Laissez-Faire to Globalization*. Cambridge: Cambridge University Press, 2006. Includes Europe-wide, comparative chapters on laissez-faire and state-directed economies, including deficit spending.

Bose-Sugata, and Ayesha Jalal. *Modern South Asia: History, Culture, Political Economy*. New York: Routledge, 2004. Well-informed analyses by two of the foremost South Asia specialists.

Fritzsche, Peter. *Life and Death in the Third Reich*. Cambridge, MA: Harvard University Press, 2008. Book that seeks to understand the German nation's choice of arranging itself to Nazi rule.

Gelvin, James L. *The Modern Middle East: A History*, 3rd ed. Oxford: Oxford University Press, 2011. Contains chapters on Arab nationalism, British and French colonialism, as well as Turkey and Iran in the interwar period.

Gordon, Andrew. *A Modern History of Japan: From Tokugawa Times to the Present*, 2nd ed. Oxford: Oxford University Press, 2009. Detailed overview of Japan's interwar period in the middle chapters.

Grasso, June M., J. P. Corrin, and Michael Kort. *Modernization and Revolution in Modern China: From the Opium Wars to the Olympics*, 4th ed. Armonk, NY: M. E. Sharpe, 2009. General overview with a focus on modernization, in relation to the strong survival of tradition.

Lombardo, Paul A., ed. *A Century of Eugenics in America: From the Indiana Experiment to the Human Genome Era*. Bloomington: Indiana University Press, 2011. Study of a dark chapter in U.S. history.

Martel, Gordon, ed. *A Companion to Europe 1900–1945*. Malden, MA: Wiley-Blackwell, 2010. Collective work covering a large variety of cultural, social, and political European topics in the interwar period.

Meade, Teresa A. *A History of Modern Latin America: 1800 to the Present*. Malden, MA: Wiley-Routledge, 2010. Topical discussion of the major issues in Latin American history, with chapters on the first half of the twentieth century.

Snyder, Timothy. *Bloodlands: Europe Between Hitler and Stalin*. New York: Basic Books, 2010. Book that chronicles the horrific destruction left behind by these two dictators.

WEBSITES

http://www.ushistory.org/us/. Maintained by Independence Hall Association in Philadelphia, it contains many links to topics discussed in this chapter.

http://www.bbc.co.uk/history/worldwars/wwone/ and http://www.bbc.co.uk/history/worldwars/wwtwo/. The BBC's treatment of the causes, course and consequences for both WWI and WWII from an Allied position.

http://www.marxists.org/subject/bolsheviks/index.htm. A complete review of the Bolshevik party members including biographies and links to archives which contain their works.

http://www.ushmm.org/wlc/en/article.php?ModuleId=10005151. The U.S. Holocaust Memorial Museum looks back on one of the darkest times in western history. http://www.nanking-massacre.com/Home.html. A disturbing collection of pictures and articles tell the gruesome history of the Raping of Nanking.

Chapter 29

Baret, Roby Carol. *The Greater Middle East and the Cold War: US Foreign Policy Under Eisenhower and Kennedy*. London: Tauris, 2007. Thoroughly researched analysis of American policies in the Middle East, North Africa, and south Asia.

Birmingham, David. *Kwame Nkrumah: Father of African Nationalism*. Athens: University of Ohio Press, 1998. Short biography by a leading modern African historian.

Conniff, Michael L. *Populism in Latin America*. Tuscaloosa: University of Alabama Press, 1999. The author is a well-published scholar on modern Latin America.

Damrosch, David, David Lawrence Pike, Djelal Kadir, and Ursula K. Heise, eds. *The Longman Anthology of World Literature*. Vol. F, *The Twentieth Century*. New York: Longman/Pearson, 2008. A rich, diverse selection of texts. Alternatively, Norton published a similar, somewhat larger anthology of world literature in 2003.

De Witte, Ludo. *The Assassination of Lumumba*. Translated by Ann Wright and Renée Fenby. London: Verso, 2002. An admirably researched study of the machinations of the Belgian government in protecting its mining interests, with the connivance of CIA director Allen Dulles and President Dwight D. Eisenhower.

Goscha, Christopher E., and Christian F. Ostermann. *Connecting Histories: Decolonization and the Cold War in Southeast Asia, 1945–1962*. Stanford, CA: Stanford University Press, 2009.

Guha, Ramachandra. *India After Gandhi. A History of the World's Largest Democracy*. New York: Harper Collins, 2007. Highly readable, popular history with well-sketched biographical treatments of leading individuals, more obscure cultural figures, and ordinary people. Accessible to even beginning students.

Hasegawa, Tsuyoshi. *The Cold War in East Asia, 1945–1991*. Stanford, CA: Stanford University Press, 2011. A new summary, based on archival research by a leading Japanese historian teaching in the United States. New insights on the Soviet entry into WWII against Japan.

WEBSITES

http://www.economist.com/node/7218678. The Economist Magazine looks back on 'An Affair to Remember, the Suez Crisis and its implications.

http://www.nasa.gov/mission_pages/shuttle/sts1/gagarin_anniversary.html. In addition to providing information and video footage regarding Yuri Gagarin's orbit of the earth, students will also find information on America's space history.

http://www.newseum.org/berlinwall/. The Newseum's interactive website looks at what life was like on both sides of the Berlin Wall.

Chapter 30

Duara, Prasenjit. *Decolonization: Perspectives from Now and Then*. London: Routledge, 2004. A leading scholar of China and postcolonial studies edits essays in this offering in the Rewriting Histories series on the fall of the colonial empires by scholars such as Michael Adas and John Voll and activists and leaders such as Frantz Fanon and Kwame Nkrumah.

Fanon, Frantz. *The Wretched of the Earth*. New York: Grove Press, 1961. One of the most provocative and influential treatments of theoretical and practical issues surrounding decolonization. Fanon champions violence as an essential part of the decolonization process and advocates a modified Marxist approach that takes into consideration the nuances of race and the legacies of colonialism.

Frieden, Jeffrey. *Global Capitalism: Its Fall and Rise in the Twentieth Century*. New York: W. W. Norton, 2006. Despite the title, a comprehensive history of global networks from the days of mercantilism to the twenty-first century. Predominant emphasis on twentieth century; highly readable, though the material is best suited for the nonbeginning student.

Gaddis, John Lewis. *The Cold War: A New History*. New York: Penguin, 2005. Though criticized by some scholars for his pro-American positions, America's foremost historian of the Cold War produces a vivid, at times counterintuitive, view of the Cold War and its global impact. Readable even for beginning students.

Gitlin, Todd. *The Sixties: Years of Hope, Days of Rage*, rev. ed. New York: Bantam, 1993. Lively, provocative account of this pivotal decade by the former radical, now sociologist. Especially effective at depicting the personalities of the pivotal period 1967–1969.

Liang Heng and Judith Shapiro. *After the Nightmare: A Survivor of the Cultural Revolution Reports on China Today*. New York: Knopf, 1986.

Highly readable, poignant, first-person accounts of people's experiences during the trauma of China's Cultural Revolution by a former husband and wife team. Especially interesting because China was at the beginning of its Four Modernizations and the wounds of the Cultural Revolution were still fresh.

Smith, Bonnie. *Global Feminisms Since 1945*. London: Routledge, 2000. Part of the Rewriting Histories series, this work brings together under the editorship of Smith a host of essays by writers such as Sara Evans, Mary Ann Tetreault, and Miriam Ching Yoon Louie on feminism in Asia, Africa, Latin America, as well as Europe and the United States. Sections are thematically arranged under such topics as "Nation-building," "Sources of activism," "Women's liberation," and "New waves in the 1980s and 1990s." Comprehensive and readable, though some background in women's history is recommended.

WEBSITES

www.wilsoncenter.org/program/cold-war-international-history-project. Cold War International History Project of the Woodrow Wilson International Center for Scholars. Rich archival materials including collections on the end of the Cold War, Soviet invasion of Afghanistan, Cuban Missile Crisis, and Chinese foreign policy documents.

Codlibrary.org. College of DuPage Library. Typing in the "search" box "Research guide to 1960s websites" yields a wide-ranging set of relevant topics.

http://news.bbc.co.uk/onthisday/hi/dates/stories/june/4/newsid_2496000/2496277.stm. BBC's archive ON THIS DAY shows video footage from the Tiananmen Square massacre in 1989.

Chapter 31

Béja, Jean-Philippe, ed. *The Impact of China's 1989 Tiananmen Massacre*. New York: Routledge, 2011. Highly diverse contributions on this watershed event and the devastating effect it had on middle-class self-evaluation.

Chau, Adam Yuet, ed. *Religion in Contemporary China*. New York: Routledge, 2011. Collection of fascinating chapters on the revival of Daoist, Confucian, and Buddhist traditions and their adaption to middle-class modernity, with their proponents operating often in a gray zone between official recognition and suppression.

Daniels, Robert V. *The Rise and Fall of Communism in the Soviet Union*. New Haven, CT: Yale University Press, 2010. A magisterial summary of the communist period by a specialist.

Dillon, Michael. *Contemporary China: An Introduction*. New York: Routledge, 2009. Concise yet quite specific overview of the economy, society, and politics of the country.

Eichengreen, Barry. *Exorbitant Privilege: The Rise and Fall of the Dollar and the Future of the Monetary System*. New York: Oxford University Press, 2011. The author is an academic specialist on US monetary policies, writing in an accessible style and presenting a fascinating picture of the role of something as prosaic as greenbacks.

Meade, Teresa A. *A History of Modern Latin America: 1800 to the Present*. Malden, MA: Wiley-Blackwell, 2010. The book is an excellent, comprehensive analysis and has a strong final chapter on recent Latin America.

Saxonberg, Steven. *The Fall: A Comparative Study of the End of Communism in Czechoslovakia, East Germany, Hungary, and Poland*. Amsterdam: Harwood Academic, 2001. A well-informed overview of the different trajectories by an academic teaching in Prague.

Speth, James Gustav. *The Bridge at the Edge of the World: Capitalism, the Environment, and Crossing from Crisis to Sustainability*. New Haven, CT: Yale University Press, 2008. A strong plea to change our capitalist system.

Swanimathan, Jayshankar M. *Indian Economic Superpower: Fact or Fiction?* Singapore: World Scientific Publishing, 2009. A thoughtful evaluation of the pros and cons, in concise overviews.

Wapner, Kevin. *Living through the End of Nature: The Future of American Environmentalism*. Cambridge, MA: MIT Press, 2010. A specialist's look at the vast transformation of nature which is taking place according to the best evidence science can marshal.

WEBSITES

http://sierraclub.org/. Balanced and informative environmental websites.

http://www.bbc.co.uk/history/worldwars/wwone/yugoslavia_01.shtml#four. Tim Judah traces the destruction and violence which led to mass genocide in the conflict known as the Yugoslav Wars.

http://www.epa.gov/climatechange/. The U.S. Environmental Protection Agency's website reviews the threat to the world's climate and the implications of consistent abuse. The site also looks at various initiatives to help reverse some of the damage already done.

http://www.bbc.co.uk/news/world-africa-12305154. The BBC News looks back at the life and career of Nelson Mandela.

Credits and Notes

Credits

Chapter 22: pg. 746–747 © Trustees of the British Museum; pg. 752 Stock Sales WGBH / Scala / Art Resource, NY; pg. 754 Courtesy of the Library of Congress; pg. 756 (top left) © Bettmann / CORBIS; pg. 756 (bottom left) © Gianni Dagli Orti / CORBIS; pg 756 (right) © Gianni Dagli Orti / CORBIS; pg. 758 © Gianni Dagli Orti / CORBIS; pg. 759 Courtesy of the Library of Congress; pg. 760 Musée de l'Armée / Dist. Réunion des Musées Nationaux / Art Resource, NY; pg. 763 SSPL / Science Museum / Art Resource, NY; pg. 767 (top) Courtesy of the Library of Congress; pg. 767 (bottom) Courtesy of the Library of Congress; pg. 768 bpk, Berlin / Art Resource, N; pg. 771 © Lebrecht Music & Arts / Corbis; pg. 773 © The Print Collector / Corbis; pg. 774 © Hulton-Deutsch Collection / CORBIS; pg. 778 National Folklore Collection, University College Dublin; pg. 781 (top left) National Gallery, London / Art Resource, NY; pg 781 (bottom left) Erich Lessing / Art Resource, NY; pg 781 (right) Saturn Devouring one of his Children, 1821–23 (oil on canvas), Goya y Lucientes, Francisco Jose de (1746–1828) / Prado, Madrid, Spain / The Bridgeman Art Library International; pg. 782 © Hulton-Deutsch Collection / CORBIS.

Chapter 23: pg. 786–787 Courtesy of the Library of Congress; pg. 792 SSPL via Getty Images; pg. 793 The 'Ma Roberts' and an Elephant in the Shallows, Lower Zambezi, 1859, Baines, Thomas (1820–75) / © Royal Geographical Society, London, UK / The Bridgeman Art Library International; pg. 800 Peter Newark Military Pictures; pg. 804 © Bettmann / CORBIS; pg. 806 The Stapleton Collection; pg. 807 © Bettmann / CORBIS; pg. 809 (top) Archives Charmet; pg. 809 (bottom) © Everett Collection Inc / Alamy; pg. 810 Photo: IAM / akg-images; pg. 811 Archives Charmet; pg. 812 Peter Newark Pictures; pg. 814 Professor Darwin, 'This is the ape of form' Love's Labour's Lost, Act V, scene II, Charles Darwin (1809–72) as an ape, 1861 (colour litho), English School, (19th century) / Natural History Museum, London, UK / The Bridgeman Art Library International; pg. 816 akg-images / ullstein bild; pg. 818 (left) The Scream, 1893 (oil, tempera & pastel on cardboard), Munch, Edvard (1863–1944) / Nasjonalgalleriet, Oslo, Norway / © DACS / The Bridgeman Art Library International; pg. 818 (right) Giraudon.

Chapter 24: pg. 822–823 © Philadelphia Museum of Art / CORBIS; pg. 827 (left) The Art Archive; pg. 827 (right) Courtesy of the Library of Congress; pg. 829 The Art Archive / Eileen Tweedy; pg. 833 (top) National Palace Museum; pg. 833 (bottom) © The Print Collector / Heritage / The Image Works; pg. 834 (left) akg-images / British Library; pg. 834 (right) Peter Newark Pictures; pg. 837 (top left) © Philadelphia Museum of Art / CORBIS; pg 837 (top right) © Philadelphia Museum of Art / CORBIS; pg 837 (bottom) © Mary Evans Picture Library / The Image Works; pg. 838 Tz'U-Hsi (1835–1908) Empress Dowager of China with ladies of the court, 1903 (b / w photo), Chinese School, (20th century) / Private Collection / The Bridgeman Art Library International; pg. 841 (top) Courtesy of the Library of Congress; pg. 841 (bottom) Courtesy of the Library of Congress; pg. 842 IAM / akg / NA; pg. 851 Courtesy of the Library of Congress; pg. 853 © Mary Evans Picture Library / The Image Works; pg. 854 Courtesy of the Library of Congress.

Chapter 25: pg. 858–859 Auction of Serfs, 1910 (w/c on paper), Lebedev, Klavdiy Vasilievich (1852–1916) / Arkhangelsk Museum, Russia / The Bridgeman Art Library International; pg. 865 (top) Bibliothèque nationale de France or BnF; pg. 865 (middle) Réunion des Musées Nationaux / Art Resource, NY; pg. 865 (bottom) akg-images / British Library; pg. 867 © Bettmann / CORBIS; pg. 869 © Bettmann

/ CORBIS; pg. 870 (top) Courtesy of the Library of Congress; pg. 870 (bottom) Portrait of George Gordon (1788–1824) 6th Baron Byron of Rochdale in Albanian Dress, 1813 (oil on canvas), Phillips, Thomas (1770–1845) / National Portrait Gallery, London, UK / The Bridgeman Art Library International; pg. 875 © Roger-Viollet / The Image Works; pg. 876 (left) © Diego Lezama Orezzoli / CORBIS; pg. 876 (top right) © Tibor Bognar / Corbis; pg. 876 (bottom right) © Paule Seux / Hemis / Corbis; pg. 877 Courtesy of the New York Public Library; pg. 879 Courtesy of the Library of Congress; pg. 883 © Heritage Images / Corbis; pg.887 © Reproduced by permission of The State Hermitage Museum, St. Petersburg, Russia / CORBIS; pg. 893 RIA Novosti.

Chapter 26: pg. 896–897 Kharbine Tapabor; pg. 900 (top) © National Portrait Gallery, London; pg. 900 (bottom) (c) The British Library Board, Add.Or.3079; pg. 903 (top) The Art Archive / United Society for Propagation of Gospel / Eileen Tweedy; pg. 903 (bottom) © CORBIS; pg. 906 / akg-images / British Library; pg. 908 (top) Réunion des Musées Nationaux / Art Resource, NY; pg. 908 (bottom) Archives Charmet; pg. 910 Dorling Kindersley; pg. 912 National Library of Australia; pg. 913 Werner Forman / Art Resource, NY; pg. 915 Snark / Art Resource, NY; pg. 917 © Hulton-Deutsch Collection / CORBIS; pg. 921 Getty Images; pg. 922 © Bojan Brecelj / CORBIS; pg. 923 ullstein bild / The Granger Collection , New York; pg. 926 (left) Werner Forman / Art Resource, NY; pg. 926 (top right) HIP / Art Resource, NY; pg. 926 (bottom right) © Stapleton Collection / Corbis; pg. 929 Courtesy of the Library of Congress; pg. 930 Courtesy of the Library of Congress.

Chapter 27: pg. 934–935 The Jacob and Gwendolyn Lawrence Foundation / Art Resource, NY; pg. 939 Battle on Santo Domingo, a painting by January Suchodolski; pg. 940 Schalkwijk / Art Resource, NY; pg. 945 Erich Lessing / Art Resource, NY; pg. 946 (left) Published by permission of the Archival Center, Archdiocese of Los Angeles; pg. 946 (right) Ralph Arnold Collection, Huntington Library, San Marino, California; pg. 947 © CORBIS; pg. 949 (top) Rebecca Emery / Getty Images; pg 949 (bottom) Win Initiative (Getty Images); pg. 954 The Granger Collection, New York; pg. 955 Schomburg Center for Research in Black Culture / Manuscripts, Archives and Rare Books Division / New York Public Library; pg. 957 Courtesy of the Library of Congress; pg. 962 © Bettmann / CORBIS; pg. 965 Courtesy of the Library of Congress; pg. 966 © akg-images / The Image Works.

Chapter 28: pg. 974–975 Courtesy of the Library of Congress; pg. 977 © Hulton-Deutsch Collection / CORBIS; pg. 980 Popperfoto / Getty Images; pg. 984 Courtesy of the Library of Congress; pg. 986 Getty Images; pg. 990 The Granger Collection, NYC—All rights reserved; pg. 991 (left) © The Museum of Modern Art / Licensed by SCALA / Art Resource, NY; pg. 991 (top right) © The Museum of Modern Art / Licensed by SCALA / Art Resource, NY; pg. 991 (bottom left) © 2007 Artists Rights Society (ARS), New York / VEGAP, Madrid; pg. 994 © Instructional Resources Corporation; pg. 995 Getty Images; pg. 996 Getty Images; pg. 1000 © Bettmann / CORBIS; pg. 1002 © K.J. Historical / CORBIS; pg. 1006 © Hulton-Deutsch Collection / CORBIS; pg. 1007 © Arcaid / Corbis; pg. 1010 Courtesy of the Library of Congress; pg. 1014 Getty Images; pg. 1016 © Bettmann / CORBIS.

Chapter 29: pg. 1020–1021 Getty Images; pg. 1023 Time & Life Pictures / Getty Images; pg. 1027 Associated Press; pg. 1029 © Bettmann / CORBIS; pg. 1030 © Rykoff Collection / CORBIS; pg. 1032 © CORBIS; pg. 1033 SSPL via Getty Images; pg. 1034 ABC via Getty Images; pg. 1035 Chris Brown; pg. 1038 (left) © The Museum of Modern

Art / Licensed by SCALA / Art Resource, NY; pg. 1038 (right) © 2009 Museum Associates / LACMA / Art Resource, NY; pg. 1044 Courtesy of the Library of Congress; pg. 1045 AFP / Getty Images; pg. 1049 Courtesy of the Library of Congress; pg. 1051 © Volkmar K. Wentzel / National Geographic Society / Corbis; pg. 1052 Courtesy of the Library of Congress.

Chapter 30: pg. 1060–1061 © Alain DeJean / Sygma / CORBIS; pg. 1064 Courtesy of Spacephotos.ru; pg. 1065 © CORBIS; pg. 1067 © Robert Maass / CORBIS; pg. 1069 AP Photo / Yuri Romanov; pg. 1074 (top left) © Bettmann / CORBIS; pg 1074 (top right) © Jack Moebes / CORBIS; pg. 1074 (bottom) © Bettmann / CORBIS; pg. 1077 (top) © Bettmann / CORBIS; pg. 1077 (bottom) India Today Group / Getty Images; pg. 1078 (left) © Henry Diltz / CORBIS; pg. 1078 (right) © Bettmann / CORBIS; pg. 1083 © Bettmann / CORBIS;

pg. 1086 (left) © Jacques Langevin / Sygma / Corbis; pg. 1086 (right) © Reuters / CORBIS; pg. 1088 (top) © Tim Page / CORBIS; pg. 1088 (bottom) © Bettmann / CORBIS; pg. 1091 © Bettmann / CORBIS; pg. 1092 Courtesy of the Library of Congress; pg. 1095 © Bernard Bisson / Sygma / Corbis.

Chapter 31: pg. 1100–1001 Getty Images Europe; pg. 1110 © Hubert Boesl / dpa / Corbis; pg. 1113 Courtesy of Eliot Borenstein; pg. 1114 (left) © Lee Frost / Robert Harding World Imagery / Corbis; pg. 1114 (right) Getty Images; pg. 1115 (top) ASSOCIATED PRESS; pg. 1115 (bottom) AP Images; pg. 1120 © Manca Juvan / In Pictures / Corbis; pg. 1123 AFP / Getty Images; pg. 1124 © Samuel Aranda / Corbis; pg. 1126 Associated Press; pg. 1128 Associated Press; pg. 1129 © Louise Gubb / CORBIS SABA; pg. 1136 AFP / Getty Images.

Notes

Chapter 23: p 747 Mary Paul to Bela Paul, September 13, November 20, December 21, 1845, November 27, 1853, in Thomas Dublin, *Farm to Factory: Women's Letters, 1830–1860*, (New York: Columbia University Press, 1993), pp. 124–125, 128, 135; p. 808 Karl Marx, Friedrich Engels, *The Communist Manifesto. A Modern Edition*. With an introduction by Eric Hobsbawm, (London: Verso, 2001) p. 77.

Chapter 24: p. 822–824 All quotes in the vignette are from John K., and Su-yu Teng. *China's Response to the West*. Cambridge, MA: Harvard

University Press, 1954. p. 126; p. 832 Prince Gong to Rutherford Alcock, 1869, quoted in Robert Hart, *These From the Land of Sinim* (London: Chapman and Hall,1901), p. 68

Chapter 31: p. 1102 Dexter Filkins, "After the Uprising," *The New Yorker* (online edition) (April, 11, 2011), pp. 5; Sudarsan Raghavan, "In Yemen, Female Activist Struggles for an Egypt-like Revolution," *The Washington Post*, February 15, 2011, Section A, p, 1; p. 1127 NY Times, February 14, 2011. Ibid. "explosives" quote from IPT News, December 10, 2010; p. 1130–1131 NY Times, February 14, 2011.

Index